# Western Civilization

## Beyond Boundaries

# Western Civilization

## Beyond Boundaries

**Volume I: To 1715**

**Seventh Edition**

Thomas F. X. Noble
*University of Notre Dame*

Barry Strauss
*Cornell University*

Duane J. Osheim
*University of Virginia*

Kristen B. Neuschel
*Duke University*

Elinor A. Accampo
*University of Southern California*

David D. Roberts
*University of Georgia*

William B. Cohen
*Late of Indiana University*

**WADSWORTH**
CENGAGE Learning·

Australia · Brazil · Japan · Korea · Mexico · Singapore · Spain · United Kingdom · United States

## WADSWORTH
### CENGAGE Learning

*Western Civilization: Beyond Boundaries, Volume I: To 1715*, **Seventh Edition**

Thomas F. X. Noble, Barry Strauss, Duane J. Osheim, Kristen B. Neuschel, Elinor A. Accampo, David D. Roberts, and William B. Cohen

Senior Publisher: Suzanne Jeans

Acquiring Sponsoring Editor: Brooke Barbier

Development Editor: Lauren Floyd

Assistant Editor: Jamie Bushell

Editorial Assistant: Katie Coaster

Managing Media Editor: Lisa Ciccolo

Executive Brand Manager: Melissa Larmon

Marketing Coordinator: Jack Ward

Senior Marketing Communications Manager: Linda Yip Beckstrom

Senior Content Project Manager: Jane Lee

Senior Art Director: Cate Rickard Barr

Manufacturing Planner: Sandee Milewski

Senior Rights Acquisition Specialist: Jennifer Meyer Dare

Production Service: Lachina Publishing Services

Text Designer: Greg Johnson

Cover Designer: Susan Shapiro Design

Cover Image: "March: Felling Trees," from *A Book of Hours*, c.1540 (vellum), by Bening, Simon (c.1483–1561), Flemish. Credit: British Library, London, UK/The Bridgeman Art Library.

Compositor: Lachina Publishing Services

For product information and technology assistance, contact us at **Cengage Learning Customer & Sales Support, 1-800-354-9706.**

For permission to use material from this text or product, submit all requests online at **www.cengage.com/permissions.** Further permissions questions can be emailed to **permissionrequest@cengage.com.**

Library of Congress Control Number: 2012943416

Student Edition:

ISBN-13: 978-1-133-60272-9

ISBN-10: 1-133-60272-X

**Wadsworth**
20 Channel Center Street
Boston, MA 02210
USA

Cengage Learning is a leading provider of customized learning solutions with office locations around the globe, including Singapore, the United Kingdom, Australia, Mexico, Brazil, and Japan. Locate your local office at: **international.cengage.com/region**

Cengage Learning products are represented in Canada by Nelson Education, Ltd.

For your course and learning solutions, visit **www.cengage.com**

Purchase any of our products at your local college store or at our preferred online store **www.cengagebrain.com**

**Instructors:** Please visit **login.cengage.com** and log in to access instructor-specific resources.

Printed in the United States of America
2 3 4 5 6 7    19 18 17 16 15

# Brief Contents

# Contents

# Maps

# The Global Record

# The Visual Record

# The Written Record

# Preface

A spate of recent books bearing such titles as *What Makes Civilization? The Ancient Near East and the Future of the West*; *Why the West Rules—For Now: The Patterns of History, and What They Reveal About the Future*; *Civilization: The West and the Rest*; and *No One's World: The West, the Rising Rest, and the Coming Global Turn* attests to the continuing fascination with Western civilization. Everyone agrees that for the last five hundred years the West has ruled the globe. Some agree that Western dominance has been not only effective but also beneficial. Others argue that Western rule has been predatory and harmful. Some believe that Western rule will persist while others think it is coming to an end with various new possibilities in prospect. No one believes that the West appeared fully formed in, say, 1500. Thus an understanding of the long foundational period running from ancient Mesopotamia and Egypt down to the dawn of the modern era remains crucial to any discussion of the modern West. This book tells that story from the beginnings of Western civilization to the present day.

As we launch the seventh edition of this book, we are once again acutely aware of the need to address big questions in ways that make sense to teachers and students right now, in the world we live in today. As these words are being written, the news is full of reports from Afghanistan, Iraq, Iran, Syria, Libya, Nigeria, Brazil, and North Korea. The world's economy is in a perilous state. The United States is locked in a contentious presidential campaign. In such circumstances we might well ask, "What is the West? What is Western?" Some believe that we are engaged in a "Clash of Civilizations." Is one of these Western civilization? If so, who or what is its adversary? The West is sometimes understood geographically and sometimes culturally. For most people, the West means western Europe. And yet western Europe itself is the heir of the peoples and cultures of antiquity, including the Sumerians, Egyptians, Persians, Greeks, Romans, Jews, Christians, and Muslims. In fact, Europe is the heir of even earlier civilizations in Asia and Africa. As a cultural phenomenon, "Western" implies many things: freedom and free, participatory political institutions; economic initiative and opportunity; monotheistic religious faiths (Judaism, Christianity, and Islam); rationalism and ordered thought in the social, political, and philosophical realms; science and technology; an aesthetic sensibility that aspires to a universal sense of beauty. But the West has felt free to evoke tradition as its guiding light and also to innovate brilliantly, to accommodate slavery and freedom simultaneously, and to esteem original thought and persecute people who deviate from the norm. "Western" indeed has meant many things in various places at different times. This book constantly and explicitly attempts to situate its readers in place, time, and tradition.

Another big question is this: What exactly is civilization? No definition can win universal acceptance, but certain elements of a definition are widely accepted. Civilization is the largest unit within which any person might feel comfortable. It is an organizing principle that implies common institutions, economic systems, social structures, and values that extend over both space and time. Cities are crucial; with cities emerge complex social organizations that involve at least a minimal division of labor. Some people work in the fields, some in the home. Soldiers defend the city, and artisans provide its daily goods. Governing institutions have a wide measure of acceptance and have the ability to enforce their will. Civilizations also develop religious ideas and authorities; literatures and laws that may be oral or written; monumental architecture, especially fortifications, palaces, and temples; and arts such as music, painting, and sculpture. Every civilization enfolds many cultures, a term that may be applied to the full range of expressions of a people in a given place and time. So, for example, the cultures of Egypt, Greece, and Rome were distinctive but all fit under the broad umbrella of Western civilization.

Western civilization has had an influence on almost every person alive today. The West deserves to be studied because its tale is compelling, but it demands to be studied because its story has been so central to the development of the world in which we live. Many of the world's dominant institutions are Western in their origin and in their contemporary manifestations—most notably parliamentary democracy. Commercial capitalism, a Western construct, is the world's dominant form of economic organization. The Internet, fast food, and hip-hop music are all western in origin but worldwide in reach today.

Until a generation or so ago, Western civilization was a staple of college and university curricula and was generally studied in isolation. Although it was, and is, important for us to know who we are, it is also important for us to see that we have changed in dramatic ways and that we can no longer understand ourselves in isolation from the world around us. Accordingly, this book repeatedly sets the experience of the West into its global context. This is not a world history book. But it is a book that sees Western civilization as one significant segment of the world's history.

## Basic Approach

More than two decades ago the six original authors of *Western Civilization: Beyond Boundaries* set out to create a textbook for a course that would, as a total effort, inform students about essential developments within a tradition that has powerfully, though not always positively, affected everyone in the contemporary world. Although each of us found something to admire in all of the existing textbooks, none of us was fully happy with any of them. We were disappointed with books that claimed balance but actually stressed a single kind of history. We regretted that so many texts were uneven in their command of recent scholarship. Although we were convinced of both the inherent interest of Western civilization and the importance of teaching the subject, we were disconcerted by the celebratory tone of some books, which portrayed the West as resting on its laurels instead of creatively facing its future.

We decided to produce a book that is balanced and coherent; that addresses the full range of subjects that a Western Civilization book needs to address; that provides the student reader with interesting, timely material; that is up-to-date in terms of scholarship and approach; and that is handsome to look at—in short, a book that helps the instructor to teach and the student to learn. We have kept our common vision fresh through frequent meetings, correspondence, critical mutual readings, and expert editorial guidance. The misfortune of the untimely death of one member of our team has brought us the fortune of a new colleague who has inspired and challenged the rest of us in new ways. Because each of us has focused on his or her area of specialization, we believe that we have attained a rare blend of competence, confidence, and enthusiasm. Moreover, in moving from plans for a first edition to the preparation of a seventh, we have been able to profit from the experience of using the book, the advice and criticism of dozens of colleagues, and the reactions of thousands of students.

Western civilization is a story. Therefore, we aimed at a strong chronological narrative line. Our experience as teachers tells us that students appreciate this clear but gentle orientation. Our experience tells us, too, that an approach that is broadly chronological will leave instructors plenty of room to adapt our narrative to their preferred organization or to supplement our narrative with one of their own.

Although we maintain the familiar, large-scale divisions of a Western Civilization book, we also present some innovative adjustments in arrangement. For instance, we incorporate a single chapter on Late Antiquity, the tumultuous and fascinating period from about A.D 300 to 600 that witnessed the transformation of the Roman Empire into three successors: Byzantine, Islamic, and European. One chapter studies those three successors, thereby permitting careful comparisons. But we also assign chapters to some of the greatest issues in Western civilization, such as the Renaissance, the age of European exploration and conquest, the Scientific Revolution, and the industrial transformation. Our twentieth-century chapters reflect an understanding of the last century formed in its closing years rather than in its middle decades. What is new in our organization represents adjustments grounded in the best scholarship, and what is old represents time-tested approaches.

In fashioning our picture of the West, we took two unusual steps. First, our West is itself bigger than the one found in most textbooks. We treat the Celtic world, Scandinavia, and the Slavic world as integral parts of the story. We look often at the lands that border the West—Anatolia/Turkey, western Asia, North Africa, the Eurasian steppes—in order to show the to-and-fro of peoples, ideas, technologies, and products. Second, we continually situate the West in its global context. Just as we recognize that the West has influenced the rest of the world, we also carefully acknowledge how the rest of the world has influenced the West. We begin this story of mutual interaction with the Greeks and Romans, carry it through the European Middle Ages, focus on it in the age of European exploration and conquest, and analyze it closely in the modern world of industry, diplomacy, empire, immigration, and questions of citizenship and identity.

Another approach that runs like a ribbon throughout this textbook involves balance and integration. Teachers and students, just like the authors of this book, have their particular interests and emphases. In the large and diverse American academy, that is as it should be. But a textbook, if it is to be helpful and useful, should incorporate as many interests and emphases as possible. For a long time, some said, Western Civilization books devoted excessive coverage to high politics—"the public deeds of great men," as an ancient Greek writer defined the historian's subject. Others felt that high culture—all the Aristotles and Mozarts—was included to the exclusion of supposedly lesser figures and ordinary men and women. In the 1970s, books began to emphasize social history. Many applauded this new emphasis even as they debated fiercely over what to include under this heading.

In this book, we attempt to capture the Western tradition in its full contours, to hear the voices of all those who have made durable contributions. But because we cannot say everything about everybody at every moment, we have had to make choices about how and where to array key topics within our narrative. Above all, we have tried to be integrative. For example, when we talk about government and politics, we present the institutional structures through which power was exercised, the people who possessed power as well as the people who did not, the ideological foundations for the use of power, and the material conditions that fostered or hindered the real or the would-be powerful. In other words, instead of treating old-fashioned "high politics" in abstract and descriptive ways, we take an approach that is organic and analytical: How did things work? Our approach to the history of women is another example. A glance at this book's table of contents and then at its index is revealing. The former reveals very few sections devoted explicitly and exclusively to women. The latter shows that women appear constantly in every section of this book. Is there a contradiction here? Not at all. Women and men have not been historical actors in isolation from one another. Yet gender, which is relational, reciprocal, and mutual, is an important variable that has shaped individual and collective experience. Hence we seek to explain why certain political, economic, or social circumstances had differing impacts on men and women, and how such conditions led them to make different choices.

Similarly, when we talk of great ideas, we describe the antecedent ideas from which seemingly new ones were built up, and we ask about the consequences of those ideas. We explore the social positions of the authors of those ideas to see if this helps us explain the ideas themselves or gauge their influence. We try to understand how ideas in one field of human endeavor prove to be influential in other fields. For instance, gender is viewed as connected to and part of the larger fabric of ideas including power, culture, and piety.

We invite the reader to look at our narrative as if it were a mosaic. Taken as a whole, our narrative contains a coherent picture. Viewed more closely, it is made up of countless tiny bits that may have their individual interest but do not even hint at the larger picture of which they are parts. Finally, just as the viewer of a mosaic may find his or her eye drawn especially to one area, feature, color, or style, so too the reader of this book will find some parts more engaging or compelling than others. But it is only because there is, in this book as in a mosaic, a complete picture that the individual sections make sense, command our attention, excite our interest.

One word sums up our approach in this book: "balance." We tell a good story, but we pause often to reflect on that story, to analyze it. We devote substantial coverage to the typical areas of Greece, Rome, Italy, France, Great Britain, and so forth, but we say more about western Europe's frontiers than any other book. We do not try to disguise our Western Civilization book as a World History book, but we take great pains to locate the West within its global context. And we always assume that context means mutuality and reciprocity. We have high politics and big ideas alongside household management and popular culture. We think that part of the fascination of the past lies in its capacity to suggest understandings of the present and possibilities for the future.

Our subtitle, "Beyond Boundaries," is intended to suggest growth, challenge, and opportunity. The West began in Mesopotamia but soon spread to all of western Asia. Gradually the Greeks entered the scene and disseminated their ideas throughout the Mediterranean world. The Romans, always heirs of the Greeks, carried ideas and institutions from Britain to Mesopotamia. As the Roman order collapsed, Rome's imprint was left on a small segment of Europe lying west of the Rhine and south of the Danube. Europeans then crashed through those boundaries to create a culture that extended from Iceland to the Russian steppes. At the dawn of the modern age Europe entered into a complex set of commercial, colonial, military, and political relations with the rest of the globe. Our contemporary world sees Western influences everywhere. No western "boundary" has ever been more than temporary, provisional.

## Distinctive Features

To make this book as accessible as possible to students, we have constantly been aware of its place in a program of teaching and learning. In the preceding paragraphs something has been said about this book's distinctive substantive features and how, we believe, they will contribute to the attainment of a deeper understanding of Western civilization, as well as of its importance and place in the wider history of the earth's peoples. Teaching and learning also involve pedagogical techniques and innovations. We have attended conscientiously to pedagogical issues from the start.

Our chapters have always begun with a vignette that is directly tied to an accompanying picture. These vignettes alert the reader to one or more of the key aspects of the chapter. Thus the readers have encountered a thematic introduction that evokes interest while pointing clearly and in some detail to what follows.

To make our chapter introductions more effective, which means to give students greater confidence as they proceed through the book, we have taken numerous steps. First, as in past editions, we reviewed and revised our opening vignettes to connect text and picture more closely and to use both to invite the reader into the chapter.

Second, the second page of each chapter contains a succinct Overview that immediately and dramatically tells the reader what he or she is going to encounter in the following pages. Third, the Chapter Overview includes Focus Questions that both echo the introduction and set the reader off on the right path into the following pages. Fourth, as the student begins to read the chapter proper, a Chronology serves as yet another orientation to the material contained in the chapter. Subject-specific chronologies still appear in various parts of the book, but we felt readers would benefit from a chronological guide at the beginning of each chapter.

We have repeated each Focus Question at the head of the section to which it pertains. At the end of each major section, we provide a succinct Section Summary. Each chapter concludes with a Chapter Summary that reiterates the Focus Questions and briefly answers them once again.

As a complement to text coverage, a ready reference, and a potential study guide, all of the Key Terms have been gathered into a Glossary included in the website that accompanies the book. We have also placed definitions in the margins of the pages where the Key Terms first appear.

In addition to this fundamental attention to chapter themes and contents, we have sought to improve the book's teachability by including a pronunciation guide. Whenever we use an unfamiliar name or term, we show the reader how to pronounce it. Instead of using the intricate rules of phonetics, we provide commonsense guides to pronunciation in parentheses directly following the word.

Having always been conscious of this book's physical appearance, we have adopted a dynamic, single-column design to enhance the reader's experience of the book. Attractively laid-out pages, a handsome full-color design, engaging maps, and beautifully reproduced pictures enhance the book's appearance. In keeping with our desire to integrate the components of the book into a coherent whole, we carefully anchor the maps and pictures into the volume. Our maps, always chosen and conceptualized by the authors, have for the seventh edition been reviewed to make them fresher, more attractive, and more informative. Map captions have been carefully written, and revised, to make them effective elements of the book's teaching program. The same is true of the pictures: the authors selected them, worked with the book's designers to place them advantageously (and not just decoratively), and wrote all the captions. For this edition, we paid particular attention to reviewing all the captions and to revising some of them. All of the maps are cross-referenced in the text, some of them several times, and the text often refers directly to the pictures.

From the start, every chapter in this book has had boxed documents, one of which treated a "global" theme, as well as a two-page feature entitled "Weighing the Evidence." Beginning with the sixth edition, we reviewed our features and decided to take some decisive steps to make them work better for teachers and students. First, we reduced the number of features to three per chapter. Second, we introduced a uniform structure and format. One feature, entitled "The Global Record," presents a significant document that sets some aspect of Western civilization within the global perspective. These documents are substantial, are carefully introduced, and conclude with study questions. This edition contains eleven new Global Record features. Another feature is called "The Written Record." This feature contains a significant document relevant to the text materials then under discussion with a careful introduction and study questions. For this edition we have introduced nineteen new Written Record features. The third feature is called "The Visual Record." This feature represents a reconceptualization of our former "Weighing the Evidence" feature. Most of those features did focus on visual evidence, but now the Visual Record features all do so. As with the Global Record and Written Record features, the Visual Records have helpful questions. Whereas the Weighing the Evidence features always concluded our chapters, now the Visual Records are placed into the chapters at the most appropriate position. For the fifth edition, we cast a careful eye over all the Visual Record features and prepared eight new ones, and for the sixth edition, we prepared two new ones. This edition has one new Visual Record. Finally, we took two last steps. We deleted the "Looking Ahead" sections because reviewers suggested that this "telegraphing" of what was to come might confuse the student reader as to what he or she has just read. And we moved the "Suggested Readings" to the book's website.

## Organization and Content Changes

Throughout the book, the authors have made changes to improve the narrative, to incorporate new ways of talking about particular topics, and to respond to reviewers. Revisions to Chapters 1 through 7 focused on the features. New features now include "Crossing Borders, for Better and Worse" (Global Record in Chapter 1), "Rebellion, Religion, and Royal Authority in an Empire" (Global Record in Chapter 2), "A Woman Wins at the Olympics" (Written Record in Chapter 3), "Alexander in Battle" (Written Record in Chapter 4), "Luxury Goods and Gender Wars" (Visual Record in Chapter 5), and "Two Views of Augustus" (Written Record in Chapter 6). Chapter 7 includes two new features, "Divorce Roman Style" (Written Record), as well as "Cosmas Indicopleustes Finds Christians in Asia," a new Global Record. Chapter 8 has new and expanded material on the Vikings. Chapter 9 has expanded its discussion of the Crusades and includes a new Global Record titled "Ahmad ibn Fadlan Describes the Rus."

Chapter 10 has a new Written Record on "The Rules of Love." Chapter 11 has new material on the plague based on recent discoveries in medical archaeology; enhanced treatment of the Great Schisms and conciliarism; a fuller treatment of the Ottomans; and a new Global Record on "The Origins of the Janissaries." Chapter 12 opens with new material setting the Renaissance into historical perspective and has expanded coverage of the Ottomans, emphasizing their interest in Western art and culture. Chapter 12 also features a new Written Record on "The Education of Women," as does Chapter 13 on "Vasco da Gama Arrives in India." Chapter 14 contains a new Global Record, "The Sultan Suleiman"; a new Written Record, "The Twelve Articles"; expanded treatment of women; and, once again, talks more fully about the Ottomans.

The political narrative in Chapter 15 has been clarified, while the material on the Glorious Revolution has been updated in Chapter 16. Chapter 16 also features a new Global Record, "Dutch Colonies in the Americas: The Challenges of a Trading Empire," and a new Written Record, "The Putney Debates." In Chapter 17 the material on Galileo has been clarified and the Summary has been revised, and a new Global Record, "Voyages for Scientific Observation," has been added. Chapter 18 now contains a more detailed discussion of Immanuel Kant's contribution to the Enlightenment, a revised Summary, and a new Written Record, on "Condorcet's Optimism About Human Progress."

Chapter 20 offers two new features. The first, a Global Record entitled "A Persian Discovers the British Rail System," includes a foreigner's 1836 graphic description of railroad technology and the sentient experience of riding in a railcar that conveys the revolutionary aspects of this new form of travel. The second new feature, a Written Record titled "A British Working-Class Family," is an 1833 testimony of a working-class mother to the British Parliamentary Commission on child labor. This excerpt lends itself to a nuanced interpretation and graphically illustrates quite how families depended on child labor and how difficult their moral choices were. The revisions in Chapter 21 place greater emphasis on slavery, reflecting recent scholarly concentration on the Atlantic history of the slave trade. A new Written Record, "Alexis de Tocqueville's Argument Against Slavery in the Colonies," documents how sentiments about abolition were becoming central to national identities of France and Great Britain. A new image depicting the abolition of slavery compliments this feature. This chapter also has a new image depicting the Irish Famine and its impact. Changes in Chapter 22 benefit from recent scholarship on the Crimean War and its significance for the modernizing world. It contains a new Written Record, "A New Breed of 'War Correspondent,'" which captures the ravages of this war, medical responses, and the importance of new technologies such as the telegraph and photography in influencing public opinion about the war. Chapter 23 has a new Written Record, "'Survival of the Fittest' and Social Darwinism." It features an excerpt from the writings of Herbert Spencer showing how he applied Darwin's theory of evolution to human social behavior, particularly with regard to warfare. This excerpt poignantly foregrounds attitudes toward warfare among Fascists and Nazis in the twentieth century. This chapter also includes a new image that lends further dimension to the analysis of gender roles: Honoré Daumier's cartoon "An Excusable Error (1857)" satirizes crinolines, or hoop skirts, that became fashionable in the 1850s. The caricature invites students to analyze middle-class opulence of the era, the significance of fashion, and the impracticality of female clothing. Chapter 24 offers a riveting new Global Record, "Atrocities in the Congo," featuring Robert Casement's famous 1904 report on outrages in King Leopold II's Congo Free State. This document not only graphically reveals inhumane practices of imperialism but also gives students a rare glimpse of native African voices, albeit mediated by Casement's translation; it thus invites students to analyze the nature of recorded history on several levels.

Chapter 25 features a new Written Record, "Domestic Mobilization and the Role of Women," as well as new material on the Bolsheviks. Chapter 26 also includes a new Written Record, titled "Doubts About Mass Society." Chapter 28 includes new material on Mussolini, as well as a new Written Record, "Churchill's 'Iron Curtain' Speech," and Chapter 29 includes a new Written Record on "Female Freedom and the Future of Gender Relations." As always, Chapter 30 received considerable attention to bring its coverage up to date. In particular, this chapter has new material on the Greek, or Eurozone, financial crisis; on globalization; on uncertainties about the welfare state; on the rise of China and its implications for the West; and on the "Arab Spring." This chapter also features a new Written Record, "Questioning the State of Western Civilization," in which British historian Niall Ferguson discusses the future of the West.

## Ancillaries

### Instructor Resources

***PowerLecture DVD with ExamView® and JoinIn®*** This dual platform, all-in-one multimedia resource includes the Instructor's Resource Manual; the Test Bank, prepared by Donald Prudlo of Jacksonville State University, which includes multiple choice questions, essay questions, identification, and true/false questions; *JoinIn*® PowerPoint® slides with clicker content, prepared by Timothy Fehler of Furman University; and Microsoft® PowerPoint® slides of both lecture outlines and images and maps from the text that can be used as offered or customized by importing personal lecture slides or other material. Also included is ExamView, an easy-to-use assessment and tutorial system that allows instructors to create, deliver, and customize tests in minutes. Instructors can build tests with as many as 250 questions using up to 12 question types, and using ExamView's complete word-processing capabilities, they can enter an unlimited number of new questions or edit existing ones.

***eInstructor's Resource Manual*** Prepared by John Warne Monroe of Iowa State University. This manual has many features, including learning objectives, chapter outlines, lecture topics, suggested readings, and research/classroom debate/discussion topics. Available on the instructor's companion website.

***WebTutor***™ on Blackboard With WebTutor's text-specific, preformatted content and total flexibility, instructors can easily create and manage customized course websites. WebTutor's course management tool gives instructors the ability to provide virtual office hours, post syllabi, set up threaded discussions, track student progress with the quizzing material, and much more. For students, WebTutor offers real-time access to a full array of study tools, including animations and videos that bring the book's topics to life, plus chapter outlines, summaries, learning objectives, glossary flashcards (with audio), practice quizzes, and weblinks.

***WebTutor***™ ***on WebCT***® With WebTutor's text-specific, preformatted content and total flexibility, instructors can easily create and manage customized course websites. WebTutor's course management tool gives instructors the ability to provide virtual office hours, post syllabi, set up threaded discussions, track student progress with the quizzing material, and much more. For students, WebTutor offers real-time access to a full array of study tools, including animations and videos that bring the book's topics to life, plus chapter outlines, summaries, learning objectives, glossary flashcards (with audio), practice quizzes, and weblinks.

***CourseMate*** Cengage Learning's History CourseMate brings course concepts to life with interactive learning, study, and exam preparation tools that support the printed textbook. Watch student comprehension soar as your class works with the printed textbook and the textbook-specific website. History CourseMate goes beyond the book to deliver what you need! History CourseMate includes an integrated eBook, interactive teaching and learning tools including quizzes, flashcards, videos, and more, and EngagementTracker, a first-of-its-kind tool that monitors student engagement in the course. Learn more at www.cengagebrain.com.

***Aplia*** Aplia™ is an online interactive learning solution that improves comprehension and outcomes by increasing student effort and engagement. Founded by a professor to enhance his own courses, Aplia provides automatically graded assignments with detailed, immediate explanations on every question and innovative teaching materials. Our easy-to-use system has been used by more than 1,000,000 students at over 1,800 institutions. Features include "flipbook" navigation that allows students to easily scan the contents; chapter assignments, developed specifically for your textbook and customizable for your course, that are automatically graded and provide detailed responses to students; a course management system so you can post announcements, upload course materials, host student discussions, e-mail students, and manage your gradebook; and personalized support from a knowledgeable and friendly team. Our support team also offers assistance in customizing our assignments to your course schedule. To learn more, visit www.aplia.com.

## Student Resources

***Book Companion Site*** A website for students that features a wide assortment of resources to help students master the subject matter. The website, prepared by Peter Moloney of Boston College, includes a glossary, flashcards, chapter outlines, learning objectives, focus questions, interactive quizzing, essay questions, primary source exercises, and suggested readings.

**CL eBook** This interactive multimedia eBook links out to rich media assets such as video and MP3 chapter summaries. Through this eBook, students can also access the glossary, flashcards, chapter outlines, learning objectives, focus questions, interactive quizzing, essay questions, primary source exercises, suggested readings, primary source documents with critical thinking questions, and interactive (zoomable) maps. Available at www.cengagebrain.com.

**Cengagebrain.com** Save your students time and money. Direct them to www .cengagebrain.com for choice in formats and savings and a better chance to succeed in your class. Cengagebrain.com, Cengage Learning's online store, is a single destination for more than 10,000 new textbooks, eTextbooks, eChapters, study tools, and audio supplements. Students have the freedom to purchase à la carte exactly what they need when they need it. Students can save 50% on the electronic textbook and can pay as little as $1.99 for an individual eChapter.

**Writing for College History, 1e Prepared by Robert M. Frakes, Clarion University.** This brief handbook for survey courses in American history, Western civilization/European history, and world civilization guides students through the various types of writing assignments they encounter in a history class. Providing examples of student writing and candid assessments of student work, this text focuses on the rules and conventions of writing for the college history course.

**The History Handbook, 2e Prepared by Carol Berkin of Baruch College, City University of New York, and Betty Anderson of Boston University.** This book teaches students both basic and history-specific study skills such as how to take notes, get the most out of lectures and readings, read primary sources, research historical topics, and correctly cite sources. Substantially less expensive than comparable skill-building texts, *The History Handbook* also offers tips for Internet research and evaluating online sources. Additionally, students on the go can purchase and download the *eAudio* version of *The History Handbook* or any of its eighteen individual units at www.cengagebrain.com to listen to wherever they are.

**Doing History: Research and Writing in the Digital Age, 2e Prepared by Michael J. Galgano, J. Chris Arndt, and Raymond M. Hyser of James Madison University.** Whether students are starting down the path as history majors or simply looking for a straightforward and systematic guide to writing a successful paper, they'll find this text to be an indispensable handbook to historical research. This text's soup-to-nuts approach to researching and writing about history addresses every step of the process, from locating sources and gathering information to writing clearly and making proper use of various citation styles to avoid plagiarism. Students will also learn how to make the most of every tool available—especially the technology that helps conduct the research process efficiently and effectively. The second edition includes a special appendix linked to CourseReader (see below), where students can examine and interpret primary sources online.

**The Modern Researcher, 6e Prepared by Jacques Barzun and Henry F. Graff of Columbia University.** This classic introduction to the techniques of research and the art of expression is used widely in history courses but is also appropriate for writing and research methods courses in other departments. Barzun and Graff thoroughly cover every aspect of research from the selection of a topic through the gathering, analysis, writing, revision, and publication of findings, presenting the process not as a set of rules but through actual cases that put the subtleties of research in a useful context. Part One covers the principles and methods of research; Part Two covers writing, speaking, and getting one's work published.

**CourseReader** Our new CourseReader lets you create a customized electronic reader in minutes! With our easy-to-use interface and assessment tool, you can choose exactly what your students will be assigned—simply search or browse Cengage Learning's extensive document database to preview and select your customized collection of readings. Once you've made your choice, students will always receive the pedagogical support they need to succeed with the materials you've chosen: each source document includes a descriptive headnote that puts the reading into context, and every selection is further supported by both critical thinking and multiple-choice questions designed to reinforce key points.

***Reader Program*** Cengage Learning publishes a number of readers, some containing exclusively primary sources, others a combination of primary and secondary sources, and some designed to guide students through the process of historical inquiry. Visit Cengage .com/history for a complete list of readers.

***Custom Options*** Nobody knows your students like you, so why not give them a text that is tailor-fit to their needs? Cengage Learning offers custom solutions for your course—whether it's making a small modification to *Western Civilization: Beyond Boundaries* to match your syllabus or combining multiple sources to create something truly unique. You can pick and choose chapters, include your own material, and add additional map exercises along with the Rand McNally Atlas to create a text that fits the way you teach. Ensure that your students get the most out of their textbook dollar by giving them exactly what they need. Contact your Cengage Learning representative to explore custom solutions for your course.

***Rand McNally Historical Atlas of Western Civilization, 2e*** This valuable resource features more than 45 maps, including maps that highlight classical Greece and Rome; document European civilization during the Renaissance; follow events in Germany, Russia, and Italy as they lead up to World Wars I and II; show the dissolution of Communism in 1989; document language and religion in the western world; and describe the unification and industrialization of Europe.

***Document Exercise Workbook Prepared by Donna Van Raaphorst, Cuya-hoga Community College.*** A collection of exercises based around primary sources. Available in two volumes.

***Music of Western Civilization*** Available free to adopters, and for a small fee to students, this CD contains a broad sampling of many important musical pieces of Western Civilization.

***Exploring the European Past*** A web-based collection of documents and readings that give students first-hand insight into the period. Each module also includes rich visual sources that help put the documents into context, helping the students to understand the work of the historian.

## Acknowledgments

The authors have benefited throughout the process of revision from the acute and helpful criticisms of numerous colleagues. We thank in particular: **Stephen Andrews**, Central New Mexico Community College; **Sascha Auerbach**, Virginia Commonwealth University; **Jonathan Bone**, William Paterson University; **David Burns**, Moraine Valley Community College; **Kathleen Carter**, High Point University; **Steven Catania**, Loyola University Chicago; **Edmund Clingan**, Queensborough Community College/CUNY; **Gary Cox**, Gordon College; **Janusz Duzinkiewicz**, Purdue University North Central; **Derrick Griffey**, Gadsden State Community College; **Padhraig Higgins**, Mercer County Community College; **Andrew Kelley**, Bradley University; **John Kemp**, Meadows Community College; **Michael Khodarkovsky**, Loyola University; **William Paquette**, Tidewater Community College; **David Paradis**, University of Colorado, Boulder; **Sandra Pryor**, Old Dominion University; **Ty Reese**, University of North Dakota; **Michael Saler**, University of California, Davis; **Monique Vallance**, Modesto Junior College; **Janette VanBorsch**, Midlands Technical College; **Steve White**, Mount St. Mary's University; **Steven J. Williams**, New Mexico Highlands University; and **Matthew Zembo**, Hudson Valley Community College.

Each of us has benefited from the close readings and careful criticisms of our coauthors, although we all assume responsibility for our own chapters. Barry Strauss has written

Chapters 1–6; Thomas Noble, 7–10; Duane Osheim, 11–14; Kristen Neuschel, 15–19; and David Roberts, 25–30. Originally written by William Cohen, Chapters 20–24 have been substantially revised and updated by Elinor Accampo.

Many colleagues, friends, and family members have helped us develop this work as well. Thomas Noble continues to be grateful for Linda Noble's patience and good humor. Noble's coauthors and many colleagues have over the years been sources of inspiration and information. He also thanks several dozen teaching assistants and more than 4,000 students who have helped him to think through the Western civilization experience.

Barry Strauss is grateful to colleagues at Cornell and at other universities who offered advice and encouragement and responded to scholarly questions. He would also like to thank the people at Cornell who provided technical assistance and support. Most important have been the support and forbearance of his family. His daughter, Sylvie; his son, Michael; and, above all, his wife, Marcia, have truly been sources of inspiration.

Duane Osheim thanks family and friends who continue to support and comment on the text. He would especially like to thank colleagues at the University of Virginia who have engaged him in a long and fruitful discussion of Western civilization and its relationship to other cultures. They make clear the interdependence of the cultures of the wider world. He particularly wishes to thank H. C. Erik Midelfort, Arthur Field, Brian Owensby, Joseph C. Miller, Chris Carlsmith, Beth Plummer, and David D'Andrea for information and clarification on a host of topics.

Kristen Neuschel thanks her colleagues at Duke University for sharing their expertise. She is especially grateful to Sy Mauskopf, Bill Reddy, Tom Robisheaux, Phil Stern, Tricia Ross, and Peter Wood. She also thanks her husband and fellow historian, Alan Williams, for his wisdom about Western civilization and his support throughout the project, and her children, Jesse and Rachel, for their patience and interest over many years.

Elinor Accampo remains indebted to the late Bill Cohen whose chapters in the first four editions offered a model of expertise. She owes special thanks to all her coauthors for support and advice, particularly Kristen Neuschel, whose friendship has been a sustaining source of inspiration and good humor. She also thanks colleagues and students at USC for their insights and suggestions; her daughter, Erin Hern, for her expert input; and, as always, her husband, Robert Hern, for his encouragement and enduring support.

David Roberts wishes to thank Sheila Barnett for her able assistance and Walter Adamson, Timothy Cleaveland, Karl Friday, Michael Kwass, John Morrow, Miranda Pollard, Judith Rohrer, John Short, William Stuek, and Kirk Willis for sharing their expertise in response to questions. He also thanks Beth Roberts for her constant support and interest and her exceedingly critical eye.

The first plans for this book were laid in 1988, and over the course of twenty-four years there has been remarkable stability in the core group of people responsible for its development. The author team lost a member, Bill Cohen, but Elinor Accampo stepped into Bill's place with such skill and grace that it seemed as though she had been with us from the start. Our original sponsoring editor, Jean Woy, moved up the corporate ladder but never missed an author meeting with us. Through five editions we had the pleasure of working with production editor Christina Horn and photo researcher Carole Frohlich. For the sixth edition Jane Lee and Catherine Schnurr filled those roles, and we are grateful for their efforts, and honored to be working with Jane and Carole (assisted by Elisa Gallagher) again on this edition. Our sponsoring editor for more than a decade, Nancy Blaine, was a tower of strength. Brooke Barbier has now become our sponsoring editor. We have been fortunate in our editors, Elizabeth Welch, Jennifer Sutherland, Julie Swasey, Adrienne Zicht, and Lauren Floyd. All these kind and skillful people have elicited from us authors a level of achievement that fills us at once with pride and humility.

Thomas F. X. Noble

# About the Authors

**Thomas F. X. Noble**   After receiving his Ph.D. from Michigan State University, Thomas Noble taught at Albion College, Michigan State University, Texas Tech University, and the University of Virginia. In 1999 he received the University of Virginia's highest award for teaching excellence and in 2008 Notre Dame's Edmund P. Joyce, C.S.C., Award for Excellence in Undergraduate Teaching. In 2011 he received the Charles Sheedy, C.S.C., award for excellence in teaching and scholarship from Notre Dame's College of Arts and Letters. In 2001 he became Robert M. Conway Director of the Medieval Institute at the University of Notre Dame and in 2008 chairperson of Notre Dame's history department. He is the author of *Images, Iconoclasm, and the Carolingians*, which won the 2011 Otto Gründler Prize, and *The Republic of St. Peter: The Birth of the Papal State, 680–825*. He has edited six books. He was a member of the Institute for Advanced Study in 1994 and the Netherlands Institute for Advanced Study in 1999–2000. He has been awarded fellowships by the National Endowment for the Humanities (three times) and the American Philosophical Society (twice). He was elected a Fellow of the Medieval Academy of America in 2004. In 2012 he served as president of the American Catholic Historical Association.

**Barry Strauss**   Professor of history and classics at Cornell University, Barry Strauss holds a Ph.D. from Yale. He has been awarded fellowships by the National Endowment for the Humanities, the American Academy in Rome, the American School of Classical Studies at Athens, The MacDowell Colony for the Arts, the Korea Foundation, and the Killam Foundation of Canada. He is the recipient of the Clark Award for excellence in teaching from Cornell. He is Chair of Cornell's Department of History, Director of Cornell's Program on Freedom and Free Societies, and Past Director of Cornell's Peace Studies Program. His many publications include *Athens After the Peloponnesian War: Class, Faction, and Policy, 403–386 B.C.*; *Fathers and Sons in Athens: Ideology and Society in the Era of the Peloponnesian War*; *The Anatomy of Error: Ancient Military Disasters and Their Lessons for Modern Strategists* (with Josiah Ober); *Hegemonic Rivalry from Thucydides to the Nuclear Age* (coedited with R. New Lebow); *War and Democracy: A Comparative Study of the Korean War and the Peloponnesian War* (coedited with David R. McCann); *Rowing Against the Current: On Learning to Scull at Forty*; *The Battle of Salamis, the Naval Encounter That Saved Greece—and Western Civilization*; *The Trojan War: A New History*; *The Spartacus War*; and *Masters of Command: Alexander, Hannibal, Caesar and the Genius of War*. His books have been translated into seven languages. His book *The Battle of Salamis* was named one of the best books of 2004 by the *Washington Post*.

**Duane J. Osheim**   A Fellow of the American Academy in Rome with a Ph.D. in History from the University of California at Davis, Duane Osheim is professor of history at the University of Virginia. He has held fellowships from the American Council of Learned Societies, the American Philosophical Society, the National Endowment for the Humanities, and the Fulbright Program. He is author and editor of *A Tuscan Monastery and Its Social World*; *An Italian Lordship: The Bishopric of Lucca in the Late Middle Ages*; *Beyond Florence: The Contours of Medieval and Early Modern Italy*; and *Chronicling History: Chroniclers and Historians in Medieval and Renaissance Italy*.

**Kristen B. Neuschel**   After receiving her Ph.D. from Brown University, Kristen Neuschel taught at Denison University and Duke University, where she is currently associate professor of history and Director of the Thompson Writing Program. She is a specialist in early modern French history and is the author of *Word of Honor: Interpreting Noble Culture in Sixteenth-Century France* and articles on French social history and European women's history. She has received grants from the Josiah Charles Trent Memorial Foundation, the National Endowment for the Humanities, and the American Council of Learned Societies. She has also received the Alumni Distinguished Undergraduate Teaching Award, which is awarded annually on the basis of student nominations for excellence in teaching at Duke.

**Elinor A. Accampo**   Professor of history and gender studies at the University of Southern California, Elinor Accampo completed her Ph.D. at the University of California, Berkeley. Prior to her career at USC, she taught at Colorado College and Denison University. She specializes in modern France and is the author of *Blessed Motherhood; Bitter Fruit: Nelly Roussel and the Politics of Female Pain in Third Republic France*; and *Industrialization, Family, and Class Relations: Saint Chamond, 1815–1914*. She has coedited (with Christopher Forth) *Confronting Modernity in Fin-de-Siècle France* and (with Rachel Fuchs and Mary Lynn Stewart) *Gender and the Politics of Social Reform in France*. She has received fellowships and travel grants from the German Marshall Fund, the Haynes Foundation, the American Council of Learned Societies, and the National Endowment for the Humanities, as well as an award for Innovative Undergraduate Teaching at USC.

**David D. Roberts**   After receiving his Ph.D. in modern European history at the University of California, Berkeley, David Roberts taught at the Universities of Virginia and Rochester before becoming professor of history at the University of Georgia in 1988. At Rochester he chaired the Humanities Department of the Eastman School of Music, and he chaired the History Department at Georgia from 1993 to 1998. A recipient of Woodrow Wilson and Rockefeller Foundation fellowships, he is the author of *The Syndicalist Tradition and Italian Fascism; Benedetto Croce and the Uses of Historicism; Nothing but History: Reconstruction and Extremity After Metaphysics; The Totalitarian Experiment in Twentieth-Century Europe: Rethinking the Poverty of Great Politics*; and *Historicism and Fascism in Modern Italy*, as well as two books in Italian and numerous articles and reviews. He is currently Albert Berry Saye Professor of History Emeritus at the University of Georgia.

**Male and Female Statuettes** Early Dynastic Period, Mesopotamia Iraq Museum, Baghdad/Scala/Art
Resource, NY

# The Ancestors of the West

1

Their huge staring eyes peer out across the centuries. He has long hair, a flowing beard, and a pleated skirt. She has short, black hair and wears a simple dress and cloak that go down to her ankles. The man is taller and broader and grabs our attention with his big hair and his hands clasped in prayer. The woman seems modest and may originally have had a child beside her. They represent one of history's oldest couples, dating back to about 2500 B.C.

The powerful gaze of their inlaid alabaster eyes is a way of looking toward heaven. In fact, the couple may have represented gods. Certainly, they did not lack for company, to judge from the dozen other figurines and busts found with them; most of them are smaller than the couple and are probably priests and worshipers. One is inscribed with a name, no doubt of an important person. They all come from a temple in the ancient Mesopotamian city of Eshnunna (modern Tell Asmar in Iraq), where they had been placed as an offering to the gods. The statuettes show us that early civilization was religious, artistic, literate, structured by rank and status, and fascinated by the relationship between men and women.

The world of 2500 B.C. had already seen the most momentous inventions in human history. They began approximately 100,000 years ago, when the first modern humans evolved from humanlike ancestors. Human beings wrestled with an often-hostile environment, engaging in a continuing series of experiments, until beginning about 10,000 B.C., they learned how to plant crops and tame animals. The shift from a food-collecting to a food-producing economy dramatically increased the amount of human life that the earth could support. Then between 3500 and 3000 B.C., in parts of what is today the Middle East, human society reached a new stage. These complex societies were marked by inequality among people and governed by states whose administrators used the first written records. In short, these societies had achieved civilization.

What we call Western civilization, however, was still more than two thousand years away. As a term, *Western civilization* is imprecise, inviting disagreement about its definition and about the lands, peoples, and cultures that it embraces at any given time. In the strictest sense, Western civilization means the "West," and that, in turn, has traditionally meant the lands and peoples of western Europe.

## Chapter Overview

### Origins, to ca. 3000 B.C.

◆ *How did the earliest human beings adapt to their environments and create the first civilizations?*

### Mesopotamia, to ca. 1600 B.C.

◆ *What were the Mesopotamians' major contributions to government, religion, and art and culture?*

### Egypt, to ca. 1100 B.C.

◆ *How did the king's power affect various aspects of Egyptian society?*

Initially, however, the West embraced the Greek and Roman peoples, plus the foundational monotheistic religions of Judaism and Christianity. These first Westerners, in turn, borrowed many ideas and institutions from the earlier civilizations of western Asia and Egypt. (These civilizations are sometimes referred to as the ancient Near East.) Indeed, civilization began in those lands and came only relatively late to Europe.

Western Asia and Egypt contributed greatly to the cultures of Greece and Rome and to the religious visions of the Jews and Christians. Yet, those earlier civilizations are sufficiently different from the West and its society, politics, and religion that they are better considered as ancestors or forerunners of the West rather than as its founders. (For a longer discussion of the definition of Western civilization, see the preface.)

So, after briefly surveying the origins of the human species, the historian of the West must begin with the emergence of civilizations, after 3500 B.C., in two great river valleys: the valley of the Tigris (TY-gris) and Euphrates (yoo-FRAY-tees) in Mesopotamia (today, Iraq and Syria) and the valley of the Nile in Egypt. Impressive in their own right, Mesopotamia and Egypt influenced a wide range of other early civilizations in western Asia and northern Africa, including the Hittites and the Canaanite city-states.

# Origins, to ca. 3000 B.C.

*How did the earliest human beings adapt to their environments and create the first civilizations?*

The earth is old; modern human beings are young; and civilization is a recent innovation. Scientists have made great strides in explaining human origins, but great disagreement still reigns. We can be more certain about the series of processes, beginning around 10,000 B.C., that led to the emergence of civilization by 3500 to 3000 B.C. The period studied in this chapter includes both prehistory—the term often used for time before the invention of writing—and recorded history. Writing appeared last among the complex of characteristics that marks the emergence of civilization.

Over a period of several thousand years, humans abandoned a mobile existence for a sedentary one. They learned to domesticate animals and to cultivate plants. They shifted from a food-collecting economy to a predominantly food-producing economy. They developed the first towns, from which, over several millennia, the first urban societies slowly evolved. The result—the first civilizations, found in western Asia and Egypt—laid the groundwork on which would be built the founding civilizations of the West: the Greeks, the Romans, and Hebrews.

## The First Human Beings

Anatomically modern human beings, *Homo sapiens sapiens*—genus *Homo*, species *sapiens*, subspecies *sapiens*—first appeared about 100,000 years ago, but the human family is much older. Also known as **hominids**, the human family includes many ancient and extinct species.

Africa is the cradle of humanity. The first hominids appeared in Africa's tropics and subtropics over 4 million years ago. By 2.5 million years ago, they had evolved into creatures who invented the first technology, simple stone tools. Prehistory is traditionally referred to as the Stone Age because stone was the primary medium from which hominids made tools. The hominids were migratory: not less than 1.6 million years ago and perhaps much earlier, they appeared in East Asia and the eastern edge of Europe. The next important stage in human evolution is *Homo erectus* ("upright person"), a hominid with a large brain who used more complex stone tools and may have acquired language. The appearance of *Homo erectus*

**hominids** The primate family *Hominidae*, which includes humans. The modern human being, *Homo sapiens sapiens*, is the only species of this family still in existence.

is usually dated to 1.8 million years ago, but a recent discovery in China may date *Homo erectus* as early as 2.25 million years ago.

About 800,000 years ago, another species of early humans lived in Europe. They are sometimes known as *Homo heidelbergensis* ("Heidelberg person") from the discovery spot of a jawbone near Heidelberg, Germany. Beginning about 400,000 years ago, Europe was home to the ancestors of the best-known archaic people, the Neandertals. Neandertals lived in Europe and western Asia until about 30,000 years ago. They had strong and stocky physiques, perhaps an adaptation to the rugged climate of the Ice Age, the period of fluctuating cycles of warm and cold, beginning about 730,000 years ago and ending only about 10,000 years ago, an era when glaciers ebbed and flowed. Yet, the Neandertals were no brutes, as they are usually imagined to be. They were, for example, among the first people to bury their dead, often with grave offerings—for example, flint, animal bones, or flowers—which suggests they were sensitive enough to mourn their losses. Recent research shows that Neandertals were both clever enough to use tools to attack one another and caring enough to nurse their wounded back to health.

Neandertals, however, were not modern humans. The most recent research suggests that all anatomically modern humans are descended from a single African ancestor. About 89,000 years ago, the *Homo sapiens sapiens*, from whom we are all descended, was born in Africa. About 70,000 years ago, descendants of that person left Africa for the other continents.

Modern humans entered Europe about 35,000 years ago. Within 5,000 years, Neandertals had disappeared—whether through war, disease, or an inability to compete with modern humans, we do not know. The first modern humans tended to be taller and less muscular than Neandertals. They also used their hands more precisely and walked more efficiently, and they lived longer. The modern human skull, with its high forehead and tucked-in face, is distinctive, but differences between the modern and archaic human brains are a matter of scholarly debate. What no one debates, however, is that, with the disappearance of Neandertals, modern humans put into effect a revolution in culture.

## The Revolution in Human Culture, ca. 70,000–10,000 B.C.

Before the emergence of modern humans, people had relatively little ability to change the natural environment. Modern humans changed that. They exploited natural resources, largely by means of technology and organization. Thus, they began the process of human manipulation of the environment that—sometimes brilliantly, sometimes disastrously—has remained a leading theme of the human experience ever since. The key to this change was a dramatic increase in the amount and complexity of information being communicated—what might be called the first information revolution. The twin symbols of the revolution are cave paintings and notations made on bone, signs that humans were thinking about their environment and their experiences.

It was long thought that these dramatic changes began in Europe about 40,000 B.C.* Recently, however, they have been traced to southern Africa, probably more than 70,000 years ago. The discovery there of carefully worked bone tools and stone spearheads pinpoints

| CHRONOLOGY | |
|---|---|
| ca. 4.4 million years ago | Earliest hominids |
| 800,000 years ago | First humans in Europe |
| ca. 100,000 years ago | *Homo sapiens sapiens* |
| 40,000–10,000 B.C. | Upper Paleolithic era |
| 10,000–2500 B.C. | Neolithic era |
| 3500–3000 B.C. | First civilizations |
| 3500–3100 B.C. | First writing in Mesopotamia |
| 3300–3200 B.C. | First writing in Egypt |
| ca. 3200 B.C. | Unification of Nile Valley |
| 2800–2350 B.C. | Early Dynastic Period |
| 2695–2160 B.C. | Egyptian Old Kingdom |
| 2500–2350 B.C. | Cuneiform texts from Ebla |
| 2025–1786 B.C. | Egyptian Middle Kingdom |
| 1650–1180 B.C. | Hittite Old, Middle, and New Kingdoms |
| 1550–1075 B.C. | Egyptian New Kingdom |
| 1450–1300 B.C. | First international system |
| 1250–1150 B.C. | Sea Peoples invade |

(All dates in this chapter are approximate.)

---

*We follow the traditional practice in the West of expressing historical dates in relation to the birth of Jesus Christ (actually, to a now discredited calculation of his birth date, because in fact Jesus was not born in A.D. 1; see page 167). Dates before his birth are labeled B.C. (which stands for "before Christ"), and dates after his birth are labeled A.D. (*anno Domini*, Latin for "in the year of the Lord"). A widely used alternative refers to these dates as B.C.E. ("before the common era") and C.E. ("of the common era").

**Chauvet Cave Art** This black-painted panel shows horses, rhinoceroses, and wild oxen. The purpose of cave paintings is unknown, but perhaps they served as illustrations of myths or as attempts to control the environment through magic.

hunter-gatherer Refers to food-collecting society in which people live by hunting, fishing, and gathering fruits and nuts, with no crops or livestock being raised for food.

the dawn of modern human technology. Still, it is not in Africa, but elsewhere, that we can best trace the early evolution of the modern human mind. Europe from about 40,000 to about 10,000 B.C. provides reliable evidence of the life and the culture of early human hunter-gatherer societies, which survived by a food-collecting economy of hunting, fishing, and gathering fruits and nuts. This period is sometimes called the Upper Paleolithic (Greek for "Old Stone") era. Then, around 10,000 B.C., a second revolution began in western Asia: the invention of a food-producing economy through the domestication of animals and the cultivation of crops. The period from about 10,000 to 3000 B.C. is sometimes called the Neolithic (Greek for "New Stone") era.

Archaeology tells us something about early people's way of life. So do analogies from contemporary anthropology, for even today a few people still live in hunter-gatherer societies in isolated corners of the globe. An educated guess is that early humans lived in small groups, of maybe twenty-five to fifty persons, related by kinship or marriage. Early **hunter-gatherers** moved from place to place, following the seasonal migration of game, but by the eve of the invention of agriculture, some hunter-gatherers had settled down in villages. Modern cases suggest that work was usually, but not always, divided by sex. Usually, women gathered plants and cared for children and elders and men went hunting. In some modern cases, however, women hunt as well as or better than men, and that might have been the case in Paleolithic times too.

It was probably common for men and women to pair off, have children, and establish a family, much as marriage is a near-universal practice among humans today. Compared with other animals, humans produce extremely dependent infants who require years of attention. To ensure the survival of the young to adulthood, men as well as women may have needed to play a role in child rearing.

Early people found shelter by building huts or, frequently, by living in caves or rock shelters—hence, our notion of the "caveman." Caves offered shelter, could be heated, and made a naturally good vantage point for observing prey and hostile humans. In the Upper Paleolithic era, about 30,000 years ago, caves were the site of the earliest representational art. The most spectacular Upper Paleolithic paintings discovered so far have been found in caves in southern France (for example, at Lascaux [lass-CO] and at Chauvet [show-VAY] Cave) and in Spain (at Altamira). European cave paintings of animals, such as the bison, horse, reindeer, and woolly mammoth (a huge, extinct member of the elephant family with hairy skin and long, upward-curving tusks), attest to early human artistic skill.

Other early art includes engravings on stone of animals, birds, and stylized human females, as well as female figurines carved from ivory or bone. Usually represented with exaggerated breasts or buttocks, the carvings are called Venus figurines, after Venus, the Roman goddess of love. They may represent an attempt to control fertility through magic.

Upper Paleolithic craftsmanship is as impressive as the art. The early human tool kit included the first utensils in such easily worked materials as antler and ivory. Stone tools became longer and more varied. The first stone and bone spear points, the first bows and arrows, and the first bone needles and awls (probably for sewing animal skins) all appeared.

Hunting was a communal enterprise. Related families probably joined together in clans, which in turn may have formed tribes. Many scholars think of these groups as patriarchal (literally, "ruled by the father"), that is, with the family governed by the father, and the tribe by a male headman or chief. Yet, some later myths (for example, among the ancient Greeks) envision women as the rulers of prehistoric society. Today, some historians see the possibility of matriarchy (literally, "rule by the mother") in the Venus figurines but that is not firm evidence of matriarchy. If chiefs were generally male, as in later periods, some tribes may have had no chief at all, following the decision of the community rather than an individual leader.

## The Coming of Agriculture, ca. 10,000–5000 B.C.

The human invention of agriculture was dramatic, meriting the name **Neolithic Revolution** that scholars sometimes give it. Yet if dramatic, the invention spread slowly and unevenly. In most areas, hunting and fishing continued to be a major source of food, even though agriculture fed more people. Agriculture was first invented sometime after 10,000 B.C. in western Asia, then discovered again independently in other parts of the world. By 5000 B.C., information about the new practices had spread so widely that farming could be found in many places around the world.

The story begins about 13,000 B.C., when humans began to specialize in the wild plants they collected and the animals they hunted. They had good reason to do so because hunter-gatherer society had become increasingly complex, and in some places permanent settlements had appeared. There were now probably more mouths to feed, requiring more food. The next step is not surprising: learning how to domesticate plants and animals.

The first animals to be domesticated were probably dogs because they were useful in hunting. Then came sheep, goats, and cattle. Wheat and barley were the first plants that humans learned to grow, followed by legumes (beans). With males occupied in hunting, it may well have been females who first unraveled the secrets of agriculture.

Domestication began in a crescent-shaped zone of land with dependable annual rainfall. The region stretches west to east from what is today southern Jordan to southern Iran: scholars call it the Fertile Crescent (see **Map 1.1**). With domestication came small agricultural settlements, which were increasingly common after 7000 B.C. Thus was born the farming village, probably the place that most people have called home since the spread of agriculture around the world.

Scholars once thought of Neolithic villages as simple places devoted to subsistence agriculture, with no craft specialization, and as egalitarian societies lacking social hierarchies. In recent years, new evidence and a rethinking of older information have altered this picture considerably. A Neolithic village site in eastern Anatolia (modern Turkey), for example, provides evidence of metalworking (of copper) and specialization of labor (in beadmaking) from approximately 7000 to 6000 B.C. The site also contains the world's earliest known example of cloth, probably linen, woven around 7000 B.C. Artwork shows men wearing loincloths and headdresses, women wearing pants and halter tops, and both sexes wearing jewelry.

The Neolithic town of Çatal Hüyük (CHAH-tal Her-yerk) in south-central Anatolia (see **Map 1.1**) had six thousand people in 6000 B.C., making it by far the largest settlement in its time. It was probably a trading center and perhaps a religious shrine. Carbonization from fire has preserved many objects showing Çatal Hüyük's sophistication, including woven fabrics, obsidian (a sharp volcanic glass used in tools), mirrors, wooden vessels, and makeup applicators.

Agriculture made human populations richer and more numerous, but it also bred disease and probably increased the scale of war. More men than ever before were available to fight because agriculture proved to be so efficient a source of food that it freed people for specialized labor—including war.

Evidence of war comes from Jericho (JEH-rih-co). Located in Palestine near the Dead Sea (see **Map 1.1**), Jericho may be the oldest continuously settled community on earth. Around 7000 B.C., Jericho was a town surrounded by massive walls 10 feet thick and 13 or more feet high, about 765 yards long, and probably enclosing an area of about 10 acres. The most prominent feature of the walls was a great tower 33 feet in diameter and 28 feet high with an interior stairway. Inside the walls lived a densely packed population of about two thousand people.

**Neolithic Revolution** Human discovery and spread of agriculture, between about 10,000 and 5000 B.C. People first domesticated dogs and other animals and then learned to cultivate crops.

🌐 **Map 1.1 Western Asia** The Neolithic Revolution began after 10,000 B.C. in the Fertile Crescent, an arc-shaped region of dependable annual rainfall. In this area between the Tigris and Euphrates Rivers known as Mesopotamia, the world's first urban civilization took root about 3500 to 3000 B.C. © Cengage Learning 2014

This is not to say that war in Neolithic times was sophisticated. Indeed, it was probably more a matter of group skirmishes and sporadic raids than of systematic warfare. Spanish rock art shows a confrontation between two groups of archers, one following what seems to be a leader. The scene may be a ritual rather than a violent conflict, but we have evidence, too, of actual bloodshed. The earliest known evidence of what may have been organized warfare comes from a cemetery in Sudan dating from 12,000 to 4500 B.C. Of fifty-nine human skeletons there, nearly half died violently, including women and children.

## Neolithic and Copper Age Europe, ca. 7000–2500 B.C.

**Europe** The westernmost peninsula of Eurasia, Europe is one of the world's seven continents. Civilization came late to Europe, although the continent was destined to become the center of the West.

Europe was one day to become the center of Western civilization, but the region lagged behind its neighbors at first. Innovations from the east reached Europe after 7000 B.C. and slowly transformed it. At the same time, Europeans developed their unique culture.

Today, "Europe" has a political meaning, referring to specific countries or to the European Union, but its most basic meaning is geographical. The term **Europe** refers to a vast peninsula of the Eurasian continent with several distinct regions. Southern Europe is made up of a rugged and hilly Mediterranean coastal strip, linked to northern Africa and western Asia by the sea and by similarities in climate and landscape. High mountains are found in the Alps of south-central Europe, from which chains of lower mountains radiate toward the southwest and southeast. Northern Europe, by contrast, consists in large part of a forested plain, indented here and there by great rivers. In the southeast, the plain, or steppe, becomes open and mostly treeless. The eastern boundaries of Europe are, in the north, the Ural Mountains and, in the south, the Caucasus Mountains. Georgia, Armenia, and Azerbaijan are all considered parts of Europe.

Before 7000 B.C., Europeans lived a traditional hunter-gatherer existence. Then came farming, which was introduced in southeastern Europe around 7000 B.C. by migrants from western Asia. Agriculture expanded across Europe between about 6000 and 4500 B.C., but not until 2500 B.C. did the majority of Europeans adopt a food-producing way of life. Yet, Europe was hardly static in the meantime. The era of European prehistory from 4500 to 2500 B.C. is known as the Late Neolithic Age, or the Copper Age, because copper came into use on the Continent during this time, as did gold.

Between about 3500 and 2500 B.C., Copper Age Europe grew in sophistication. The urbanization of Mesopotamia (in modern-day Iraq; see **Map 1.1**) had an impact on southeastern Europe, which supplied raw materials for western Asia. Greece underwent the greatest transformation, to the extent that it developed its own urban civilization by about 2000 B.C. (see Chapter 2). The recent discovery of a Copper Age corpse, preserved in the ice of the Italian Alps, opens a window into northern Italian society of about 3200 B.C. (See the feature, "The Visual Record: The Iceman and His World.")

On Europe's northern and western edges, people began to set up megaliths—stone tombs and monuments—often of huge blocks. Such monuments may illustrate an awareness of time created by the spread of agriculture, with its seasonal rhythms. In Britain, megalithic architecture reached its peak with Stonehenge, built in stages from about 2800 to 1500 B.C. This famous monument consists of a circle of stones oriented precisely on the rising sun of midsummer—a sign both of early Europeans' interest in the calendar and of their skill in technology.

## The Emergence of Civilization, ca. 3500–3000 B.C.

Civilization comes from the Latin word *civitas*, meaning "commonwealth" or "city." Yet, it is not the city—an urban space—but the state—government—that marks the first civilizations, which began in Mesopotamia and Egypt between 3500 and 3000 B.C. Cities played a major role in Mesopotamia but were less important in Egypt. Civilization allowed human beings to think big. A large and specialized labor force, organized by a strong government, made it possible to expand control over nature, improve technology, and trade and compete over ever widening areas. An elite class emerged that was able to pursue ever more ambitious projects in art and thought and to invent systems of writing. In short, the advent of civilization in the fourth millennium B.C. marked a major turning point. Thereafter, the human horizon expanded forever.

Civilization arose in Iraq, in the valley between the Tigris and Euphrates Rivers (see **Map 1.1**), a region that the Greeks named Mesopotamia (literally, "between the rivers"). At around the same time or shortly afterward, civilization also began in the valley of the Nile River in Egypt. Both Mesopotamia and Egypt are home to valleys containing alluvial land—that is, a relatively flat area where fertile soil is deposited by a river. Although these civilizations developed largely independently, some borrowing between the two took place.

The first states emerged through a process of action and reaction. In order to feed rulers, priests, and warriors, farmers worked harder, used better techniques, and increased the amount of land under cultivation. Meanwhile, both the number and variety of settlements increased.

## The Development of Writing

Along with states came writing, which developed between about 3500 and 3100 B.C. in Egypt and Mesopotamia. The growth of writing from simple recordkeeping can be traced step by step. Before writing, Mesopotamian people used tiny clay or stone tokens to represent

## The Iceman and His World

*On September 19, 1991, a German couple went hiking in the Italian Alps. At 10,530 feet above sea level, in a mountain pass, they thought they had left civilization and its problems behind until they stumbled on an unexpected sight: the body of a dead man lying in the melting ice. Nor was that their only surprise. At first they thought the corpse was the victim of a recent accident. When the authorities arrived, however, the body was discovered to be very old. A helicopter was ordered, and the body was brought to a research institute in Innsbruck, Austria. When the investigators were through, it was clear that the hikers had chanced upon one of the most remarkable archaeological discoveries of the century.*

He was 5,300 years old. The Iceman—as the corpse has become known—is a natural mummy, preserved under the snow: the oldest known remains of human flesh. If that weren't striking enough, consider the clothes and extensive gear that survived with him—they are a window into the European world of about 3200 B.C. The most difficult and most fascinating question is this: Who was the Iceman?

His body offers an introduction. The Iceman stood 5 feet 2 inches tall. He was in his mid-40s and probably had a beard. Genetic testing shows that he was a European, a close relative of modern northern and alpine Europeans. His sinewy frame points to a life of hard work, and scientific tests indicate other difficulties. His growth was arrested by periods of illness, grave hunger, or metal poisoning. His teeth are badly worn, the result perhaps of chewing dried meat or, alternatively, of working leather. He may have undergone a kind of acupuncture; at any rate, he is tattooed, which in some cultures is a medical treatment rather than a form of decoration. He has several broken ribs, which indicates either damage under the ice, mishandling when the body was discovered, or an ancient accident or fight.

The Iceman died violently. The story began in a valley south of the mountains one spring day—pollen analysis specifies the season. There the Iceman ate goat meat and vegetables. Then he decided to climb into the mountains, perhaps to escape after a fight. At least several days before he died, the Iceman received a severe cut on his right hand from a rough blade, which should indicate trouble.

In the mountains the Iceman enjoyed his last meal, consisting of red deer and some cereals. Soon afterwards he encountered someone who shot him in the shoulder with an arrow. The arrow struck a major artery, which caused the Iceman to bleed to death within minutes. Who killed the Iceman and why? We don't know. Some evidence suggests that as many as four people attacked him, possibly in two attacks.

© South Tyrol Museum of Archaeology · www.iceman.it

**Mummy of Iceman**

**Artist's Rendition of the Iceman**

© Michael Rothman

"polypores" threaded on a leather thong, probably used as a natural antibiotic; and fourteen arrows, all, oddly, broken. In short, it appears that the Iceman was equipped with a state-of-the-art mountain survival kit of his day. It is not clear why he carried broken arrows, but he would not have had time to change his gear before he fled.

Scholars differ about the Iceman's occupation. The evidence tends to make him a herdsman but he might have been a hunter, trader, warrior, outlaw, or shaman (a priest who uses magic). The Iceman's complex weapons and well-made clothing point to a sophisticated culture. The copper ax is the key to that culture and its relationship with the wider world. Similar axes have been found in northern Italian tombs in Remedello, about 240 miles south of the Alps. Before the discovery of the Iceman, archaeologists believed that Italians learned the metalwork technology needed for such an ax from Anatolia, where similar pieces of metalwork are dated to approximately 2700 to 2400 B.C. Hence, the Remedello culture was usually also dated to that period. The discovery of the Iceman means that Remedello must be backdated by about five hundred years. It is clear, then, that by about 3200 B.C., northern Italians not only borrowed from the more advanced eastern Mediterranean areas but also created an original technology and culture. Thus, a small object (a copper ax) placed within a larger body of evidence (Italian and Anatolian metalwork) permits broad generalization about the interaction and independence of ancient cultures.

Whoever killed the Iceman pulled out the shaft and left the arrowhead in his victim. Nor did the killer take any of the Iceman's valuable gear, which may suggest that he didn't want to be caught with any of the dead man's property. Today that gear provides tantalizing clues to the Iceman's social status. Look at the artist's drawing. A woven grass or reed cape lies over the Iceman's deerskin coat, which in turn covers a leather loincloth and garter, held in place by a leather belt. A bearskin hat, skin leggings, and calfskin shoes, stuffed with grass for insulation, complete his wardrobe. The Iceman and his contemporaries knew how to dress for the cold weather of the mountains.

The Iceman carries a rich tool kit. Notice his copper ax and 6-foot-long bow made of yew, the best wood then available for making bows. A quiver (arrow case), two birch-bark containers, a waist pouch, and a frame—probably part of a backpack—hang from his body. Among his items of equipment are flint tools (including a dagger, a retouching tool, and a scraper); a piece of net; two birch-fungus-like

## Questions

1. *What do the Iceman's clothing, tools, and weapons tell us about his society?*

2. *How do modern, scientific tests add to our knowledge of the Iceman?*

3. *How does the discovery of the Iceman change our understanding of the relationship between Europe and Anatolia about five thousand years ago?*

4. *How skilled at technology was Copper Age Europe?*

5. *What role did violence play in prehistoric human relations?*

---

*For an introduction to the Iceman, see Brenda Fowler, *Iceman: Uncovering the Life and Times of a Prehistoric Man Found in an Alpine Glacier* (Chicago: University of Chicago Press, 2001); Stephen S. Hall, "Last Hours of the Iceman," *National Geographic* (July 2007), http://ngm.nationalgeographic.com/2007/07/iceman/hall-text/1; James H. Dickson, Klaus Oeggl, and Linda L. Handley, "The Iceman Reconsidered," *Scientific American* (May 2003); and <http://www.mummytombs.com/mummylocator/featured/otzi.htm>.

**The Maltese Female**
The "Sleeping Lady," a terra-cotta statuette of the late fourth millennium B.C. from Malta, shows a reclining woman, perhaps a goddess or priestess. Her double-egg–shaped buttocks are thought to symbolize fertility or regeneration. Erich Lessing/Art Resource, NY

objects being counted or traded. By 3500 B.C., with 250 types of token in use, the system had grown unwieldy enough for people to start using signs to indicate tokens. It was a short step to dropping the tokens and placing the signs on a clay tablet by making indentations in the clay with a reed stylus: writing. New words were soon added through pictographs (pictures that stand for particular objects). The pictographs evolved into ideograms—that is, abstract symbols that are no longer recognizable as specific objects and thus can be used to denote ideas as well as things.

In the centuries following its introduction, Mesopotamian writing became standardized. Scholars call the signs **cuneiform**, from the Latin for "wedge-shaped," a good description of what early writing looks like (see **Figure 1.1**). In its first centuries, cuneiform was used almost entirely for economic records or commercial transactions. Then it was used to record offerings to the gods. By 2350 B.C., cuneiform had evolved into a mixed system of about six hundred signs, most of them phonetic (syllabic), with relatively few ideograms.

Egyptian writing developed independently, beginning around 3300 to 3200 B.C.: It was not derived from or related to cuneiform. Whether writing began in Egypt or Mesopotamia, therefore, is an open question. What is clear, however, is that writing was invented to meet economic rather than creative needs. In Egypt, the earliest writing includes records of the delivery of linen and oil as taxes to King Scorpion I (ca. 3250 B.C.). The writing consists of

| Uruk IV<br>ca. 3100 B.C. | Sumerian<br>ca. 2500 B.C. | Old Babylonian<br>ca. 1800 B.C. | Neo-Babylonian<br>ca. 600 B.C. | SUMERIAN<br>Babylonian |
|---|---|---|---|---|
| | | | | **APIN**<br>epinnu<br>plow |
| | | | | **ŠE**<br>še'u<br>grain |
| | | | | **ŠAR**<br>kirû<br>orchard |
| | | | | **KUR**<br>šadû<br>mountain |
| | | | | **GUD**<br>alpu<br>ox |
| | | | | **KU(A)**<br>nunu<br>fish |
| | | | | **DUG**<br>karpatu<br>jar |

From *Babylon*, by Joan Oates. Published by Thames and Hudson Ltd., 1978. Reprinted by permission of the publisher.

**Figure 1.1 Early Mesopotamian Writing** The pictographs of early writing evolved into a system of phonetic syllables and abstract symbols. Simplified and standardized, this writing was *cuneiform*, or "wedge-shaped." Over time, it was adapted from Sumerian to Babylonian and other languages throughout western Asia.

early *hieroglyphs* (literally, "sacred carvings"), a system of pictures and abstract signs that represent sounds or ideas, later to become more formal and standardized.

Either Egyptian or a Mesopotamian language called Sumerian was the first written language. They are the earliest known of the many thousands of human languages that have existed in history. Most belong to large groupings of related languages called language families. Egyptian, for instance, is part of the Afro-Asiatic family of languages. Sumerian, in contrast, stands on its own; it cannot be reliably classified into any language family.

Incising cuneiform on clay was much clumsier than writing with pen and ink on **papyrus**, as became possible in Egypt. The papyrus plant grew in the Nile marshes and it was the source of the ancient world's favorite writing material. (Our word *paper* comes from *papyrus*, although modern paper comes from a different source, trees or recycled fibers or other materials.) Nonetheless, cuneiform was flexible enough to be used for poetry as well as for bookkeeping. Moreover, cuneiform became the standard script in western Asia for several thousand years. Clumsy it may have been, but cuneiform was writing, and writing is both a catalyst for change and the historian's best friend. Mesopotamia after 3000 B.C. was dynamic, sophisticated, and, best of all, intelligible to us.

# Mesopotamia, to ca. 1600 B.C.

*What were the Mesopotamians' major contributions to government, religion, and art and culture?*

After 3000 B.C., the people of Mesopotamia flourished. They experimented in government, in cooperation and conflict among ethnic groups, in law, and in the working-out of class and gender relations. Keenly aware of human limitations and vanity, they sought divine justice, as their literary and religious texts show. Their engineering skill, mathematics, and astronomy set ancient science on an upward path. In later centuries, Western civilization would build on these foundations and then take off in new directions.

The fertile Tigris-Euphrates plain had to be tamed by would-be farmers. Most of the soil was either so dry or so marshy that agriculture required considerable irrigation and drainage—that is, the use of channels, dikes, or dams to control floodwaters and improve the fertility of the land. Making matters worse, Mesopotamia was also given to extreme heat and scorching winds. Some scholars argue that the very hostility of Mesopotamia's environment generated the cooperation and control that civilization requires.

Archaeologists sometimes refer to the third and second millennia in the eastern Mediterranean and western Asia as the Bronze Age. In this period, people mastered the technology of making bronze, an alloy of copper and tin, and bronze frequently replaced stone as a primary material for everyday use.

## The City-States of Sumer

Though their culture is long dead, the Sumerians live on. Whenever someone today counts the minutes, debates politics, or quotes the law, the Sumerians live, for these are all legacies of that ingenious society.

The dominant inhabitants of Mesopotamian civilization in its first flowering are named **Sumerians**. Present in southern Mesopotamia by 3200 B.C., and probably earlier, the

**SECTION SUMMARY**

- Anatomically modern human beings are called *Homo sapiens sapiens* and first appeared about 100,000 years ago.
- Humans lived by hunting animals and gathering nuts and berries until agriculture was invented shortly after 10,000 B.C. in western Asia.
- Early Europeans were skilled metalworkers and architects, but they lagged behind the more advanced regions, Egypt and Mesopotamia.
- The first civilizations in Mesopotamia and Egypt emerged between 3500 and 3000 B.C. and probably contained the first cities.
- Civilization meant bigger and more complex societies, with specialized labor forces, strong governments, and well-structured armies.
- Along with cities came writing, which developed independently in Egypt and Mesopotamia between about 3500 and about 3100 B.C.

**cuneiform** First writing system in Mesopotamia, consisting of wedge-shaped impressions in soft clay. Named from the Latin word for "wedge-shaped," it was developed about 3500–3100 B.C.

**papyrus** Paperlike writing material used by the ancient Egyptians, Greeks, and Romans. Made primarily in Egypt from the papyrus plant, it was durable, flexible, and easy to write on.

**Sumerians** Dominant inhabitants of Mesopotamia in the third millennium B.C. They established the world's first civilization, thirty flourishing city-states with a common culture, commerce, and tendency to make war on one another.

**city-state** State consisting of an independent city and the surrounding territory under its control. Early examples were the Sumerian city-states in the third millennium B.C.

Sumerians entered their great age in the third millennium B.C., when their **city-states** enjoyed a proud independence (see **Map 1.1**).

The formative era of Mesopotamian civilization is known as the Uruk Period (ca. 3800–3200 B.C.), after one of its major archaeological sites. During the Uruk Period, the Sumerians invented the wheel and the plow, planted the first orchards—of dates, figs, or olives—and developed the first sophisticated metal-casting processes. They built some of the first cities, for example, Uruk. They expanded the size of territories and populations, the scale of war, the complexity of society, and the power of government. Finally, as if to cap a period of remarkable change, at the end of the Uruk Period, the Sumerians invented cuneiform writing.

By the period that scholars have named the Early Dynastic Period (2800–2350 B.C.), named for the first royal dynasties (ruling families), large Mesopotamian cities had grown to the point where they might cover 1,000 acres surrounded by more than 5 miles of walls, within which lived about fifty thousand people. Such cities were part of a network of thirty such city-states. It was a web of culture, commerce, and competition, sometimes leading to war. The system was bigger, more complex, and more technologically advanced than any predecessor. Hence, the city-states of Mesopotamia may be called the first civilization.

It was a land of cooperation and conflict. The Sumerian cities had much in common: language, literature, arts and sciences, and religion. Yet, the cities often quarreled, often over farmland boundaries or water rights. Each city had its own urbanized area and surrounding agricultural land irrigated by canals. Cities traded with one another and with the outside world. The primary political units of southern Mesopotamia for most of the third millennium B.C., Sumerian city-states were an incubator of civilization.

A history of Sumerian government begins in the Early Dynastic Period because good evidence for earlier times is lacking. Historians once labeled these cities as temple-states, governed by priests, but there is no proof of that. Certainly, the first Sumerian temples were wealthy and powerful. Each city had at least one temple, the house of its patron god and the common symbol of the community.

By the Early Dynastic Period, around 2800 B.C., political power in a Sumerian city rested largely with its Council of Elders, whose members were probably wealthy landowners. Some scholars argue that the council shared power with a popular assembly, creating, in effect, a bicameral legislature and perhaps even a primitive democracy. But this is just a theory.

Ordinary people enjoyed only limited freedom. Even if they owned their own land, farmers often had to provide forced labor for the state—maintaining the vast Mesopotamian irrigation system, for example—as a kind of taxation. There was also apparently a large group of semi-free people who owned no land of their own but worked others' land. Finally, there were slaves—that is, people who could be bought and sold. Slaves were not numerous because there was no policing system to catch runaways. Slaves were usually foreign prisoners of war, but some were local people who had been sold into slavery to pay off a debt; often, poor parents sold their own children (especially daughters).

By about 2700 B.C., political power shifted. War between cities became chronic and many felt the times demanded a strong hand. The new ruler was not a council of elders but rather a "big man" (*legal*) or, less often, a "governor" (*ensi*)—that is, a king or, occasionally, a queen. Kings and queens sponsored irrigation works, raised fortification walls, restored temples, and built palaces, but the monarch was first and foremost a warrior.

One of the earliest Sumerian kings, dating from about 2700 to about 2600 B.C., was Gilgamesh (GIL-ga-mesh) of Uruk, a hero of epic poetry whom many scholars consider a genuine historical personage. In the cities of Ur and Lagash, the king's wife was often a power in her own right. Kish was ruled by Ku-baba (r. ca. 2450 B.C.), history's first recorded reigning queen.

Though warriors, Sumerian monarchs also recognized a responsibility for promoting justice. History's earliest known reformer of law and society was Uru-inim-gina, king of Lagash around 2400 B.C. Surviving documents describe Lagash as a city in which wealthy landowners interfered with the temples and oppressed the poor and in which royal administrators mistreated ordinary people. Uru-inim-gina attempted to manage the bureaucracy, protect the property of humble people, and guard the temples. He also put into effect the first known wage and price controls. Uru-inim-gina's proclaimed intention was to promote impartial justice, a goal that he expressed in the formula "[the king] will protect the mother that is in distress, the mighty man shall not oppress the naked and the widow."* No doubt he also wanted to weaken independent sources of power threatening royal authority. As it turned out, Lagash was conquered only a few years after Uru-inim-gina's reign. His reforms nonetheless survived as the precedent for a long Mesopotamian tradition of royal lawgiving.

## Conquest and Assimilation, ca. 2350–1900 B.C.

The poor and hardy peoples of the desert and the mountains coveted Mesopotamia's wealth. They attacked—some from without, by raising armies and assaulting cities, while others immigrated and climbed to power from within the Sumerian city-states. The attackers were sufficiently impressed by Sumerian culture to adopt a great many Sumerian customs and ideas. The most successful attacker was Sargon (r. 2371–2316 B.C.), who rose from nowhere to a high position under the king of the city of Kish before founding his own capital city, Agade (ah-GAH-day). Notice that Sargon was a native speaker not of Sumerian but of Akkadian.

*"The exaltation of Inana (Inana B)," Electronic Text Corpus of Sumerian Literature, ETCSL translation, t.4.07.2, http://etcsl.orinst.ox.ac .uk/cgi-bin/etcsl.cgi?text=t.4.07.2#

**The Standard of Ur, Peace Panel**    This scene from a Sumerian mosaic from about 2650 B.C. is part of a larger work of art depicting scenes of war and peace. Here we see a king banqueting on agricultural produce brought by servants. Werner Forman/Art Resource, NY

The Akkadians were originally a seminomadic people who lived as shepherds on the edge of the desert. They had begun settling in the northern cities of southern Mesopotamia by the end of the Uruk Period, in a part of southern Mesopotamia known as Akkad. Their language, Akkadian, belongs to the Semitic group of languages, a subfamily of the Afro-Asiatic language family. Semitic languages include Arabic and Hebrew.

As commander of one of history's first professional armies, Sargon conquered all of Mesopotamia, and his power extended westward along the Euphrates and eastward into Iran. Rather than rule conquered peoples directly, the Akkadians generally were satisfied with loose control, as long as they could monopolize trade. They adopted Sumerian religion and wrote Akkadian in cuneiform.

Sargon's dynasty boasted that it reigned over "the peoples of all lands" or "the four quarters of the earth." Sargon proved to be one of western Asia's most influential figures because his ideal of universal rule would continue to inspire future conquerors. Sargon's son inherited his throne.

Assimilation was another lasting Akkadian legacy. Although Sargon made Akkadian the language of administration, he made many concessions to Sumerian practices. For instance, his daughter Enkheduanna (en-khe-du-AN-na), whom he appointed high priestess at Ur and Uruk, wrote poetry in Sumerian and is still quoted in Sumerian texts hundreds of years after her death.

Enkheduanna may be the earliest known poet in the history of literature. Although Akkadian, she celebrated the Sumerian goddess of Ur, Inanna. She described Inanna as a symbol of authority: "When humanity comes before you in awed silence at the terrifying radiance and tempest, you grasp the most terrible of all the divine powers."

As a political reality, Akkadian rule proved short-lived, but assimilation survived as a cultural ideal. Around 2200 B.C., the Akkadian kingdom broke up into a series of smaller successor states. Then, after a century of rule by invaders from the east, the Sumerians returned to power under the Third Dynasty of Ur (2112–2004 B.C.). Far from stripping away Akkadian influence, the new Sumerian rulers spoke of themselves as "kings of Sumer and Akkad." The title would have a long and potent history: For the next fifteen hundred years, many of the great kings of western Asia would use it in recognition of a common Mesopotamian society.

After renewed turmoil in Mesopotamia around 2000 B.C., a new kingdom emerged in the south under the rule of the Amorites around 1900 B.C. The Amorites were Semitic speakers and shared Mesopotamian culture and traditions. Babylon, northwest of Ur in the central part of Mesopotamia, became the Amorite capital. From Babylon, Amorite kings issued cuneiform decrees that, although written in a Semitic language, drew heavily on Sumerian material.

## Hammurabi's Code

The most famous Amorite king, Hammurabi (r. 1792–1750 B.C.) ruled in Babylon about six hundred years after Sargon. Much of his forty-two-year reign was devoted to creating a Mesopotamian empire. He was a careful administrator who ushered in an era of prosperity and cultural flowering. He is most famous for the text known as **Hammurabi's Code**. Although the work was less a "code" than a collection listing various crimes and their punishments—a kind of treatise on justice glorifying Hammurabi's qualities as a judge—we shall use the familiar name. Hammurabi's Code became both a legal and a literary classic, much copied in later times.

**Hammurabi's Code** An influential collection of various crimes and punishments, this work was named for the famous Amorite King Hammurabi (r. 1792–1750 B.C.).

Hammurabi's Code offers a portrait of Mesopotamian society. The document contains nearly three hundred rulings in cases ranging from family to commercial law, from wage rates to murder. The administration of justice in Mesopotamia was entirely practical: we find no notion of abstract absolutes or universal principles, not even a word for "law."

Though occasionally less harsh than earlier law codes, which date as far back as around 2100 B.C., Hammurabi's Code was by no means lenient. Whereas earlier codes were satisfied with payment in silver as recompense for crime, Hammurabi's Code was the first to stipulate such ruthless penalties as mutilation, drowning, and impaling. It also introduced the law of retaliation for wounds: "If a man has destroyed the eye of a member of the aristocracy: they shall destroy his eye. If he has broken his limb: they shall break the (same) limb." Moreover, children could be punished for the crimes of their parents.

The code was inscribed in forty-nine vertical columns on a stone stele about 7 1/2 feet high and displayed in a prominent public place. Thus, Hammurabi's Code symbolized the notion that the law belonged to everyone. Although ordinary people could not read, it was possible for them to find a patron who could. Yet, the societies of western Asia and Egypt were anything but egalitarian, and Hammurabi's society was no exception. Punishments were class-based: Crimes against a free person, for example, received harsher treatment than crimes against a slave or a semi-free person. Debt seems to have been a serious and widespread problem, frequently leading to debt slavery. While women could own and inherit property and testify in court, the code tended to enshrine the power of the male head of the family.

## Divine Masters

The Sumerians were polytheists—that is, they had many gods—and their gods (like the later gods of Greece) were anthropomorphic, or human in form. Indeed, Sumerian gods were thought to be much like humans, by turns wise and foolish, except that they were immortal and super powerful. Many Sumerian gods represented the forces of nature: An, the sky-god; Enki, the earth-god and freshwater-god; Enlil, the air-god; Nanna, the moon-god; and Utu (Semitic, Shamash), the sun-god. Other Sumerian gods embodied human passions or notions about the afterlife: Inanna (Semitic, Ishtar), goddess of love and war; and Ereshkigal, goddess of the underworld.

The Sumerians sometimes envisioned their gods holding an assembly, much like a boisterous Sumerian assembly. The Sumerians and Akkadians considered Enlil, city-god of Nippur, to be the chief god. The Babylonians replaced him with Marduk, city-god of Babylon.

Every Mesopotamian city had its main temple complex, the most striking feature of which was a *ziggurat*, or stepped tower. Constructed originally as simple raised terraces, ziggurats eventually became seven-stage structures. Unlike the pyramids of Egypt, ziggurats were not tombs but "stairways" connecting humans and the gods.

The keynote of Mesopotamian religion was pessimism. It is not surprising that the Mesopotamians, living in a difficult natural environment, regarded the gods with fear and awe. Although the gods communicated with humans, their language was mysterious. To understand the divine will, the Mesopotamians engaged in various kinds of divination: They interpreted dreams, examined the entrails of slaughtered animals, and studied the stars (which stimulated great advances in astronomy, as we will see).

Most people expected nothing glorious in the afterlife, merely a shadowy existence. It was thought that with a person's last breath, his or her spirit embarked on a long journey to the Netherworld, a place under the earth. More than one Mesopotamian text describes the Netherworld as the "Land-of-no-return" and "the house wherein the dwellers are bereft of light, / Where dust is their fare and clay their food, / Where they see no light, residing in darkness."* The dead resided there permanently, though in some texts their spirits return to earth, often with hostile intent toward the living.

Archaeological evidence indicates a possible shift in such attitudes toward death, at least on the part of the Mesopotamian upper classes, by the late third millennium B.C. The kings and nobles of the Third Dynasty of Ur were buried with a rich set of material objects and with their servants, who were apparently the victims of human sacrifice following the master's death. Perhaps the rulers now expected to have the opportunity to use their wealth again in a comfortable immortality, possibly influenced by Egyptian ideas (see pages 20–22).

## Arts and Sciences

The people of Mesopotamia were deeply inquisitive. They focused on the beginning and the end of things. "How did the world come into being?" and "What happens to us when we die?" are perhaps the two basic questions of their literature. Consider, for example, the Babylonian

---

*James B. Pritchard, ed., *Ancient Near Eastern Texts Relating to the Old Testament*, 3d ed., with Supplement, p. 107. Copyright © 1969 by Princeton University Press. Reprinted with permission.

creation epic, known from its first line as *Enuma Elish* ("When on high"). An epic poem is the story of heroic deeds, in this case, the deeds of the gods of order, who triumphed over the forces of chaos. Another important Babylonian literary form, known as wisdom literature, responded to life's ups and downs with teachings that are sometimes simple, sometimes sophisticated. It proved eventually to influence the wisdom literature of the Hebrew Bible.

The best-known example of Mesopotamian literature is the *Epic of Gilgamesh*. Frequently translated and adapted by various western Asian peoples, *Gilgamesh* might originally have been a Sumerian work dating to about 2500 B.C. King Gilgamesh of Uruk was probably a real historical person, but the poem concerns his fictionalized personal life. The main themes are friendship, loss, and the inevitability of death. As king, Gilgamesh is a tyrant; Enkidu arrives and puts him in his place, and then the two become close friends and comrades in arms. Enkidu's untimely death makes Gilgamesh aware of his own mortality. Distraught by his friend's passing, Gilgamesh goes on a vain quest for immortality. The *Epic of Gilgamesh* contains stories that presage the later biblical Eden and Flood narratives; there is little doubt but that those narratives found their way from Mesopotamia to the Hebrew Bible. (See the feature, "The Written Record: Heroism and Death in Mesopotamia.")

Cuneiform spread beyond Mesopotamia to Anatolia and the Levant (le-VANT)—the geographic region consisting today of such countries as Syria, Lebanon, Israel, Palestine, and Jordan. One cultural advance took place at Ebla (EH-bla) (modern Tell Mardikh), in northern Syria, where the world's earliest known dictionaries were written down between 2500 and 2300 B.C. A prosperous city, Ebla was known for commerce and artisanry as well as scholarship.

The Mesopotamians, meanwhile, made advances in mathematics, astronomy, medicine, and engineering. The Sumerians had two systems of numbers: a decimal system (powers of ten) for administration and business and a sexagesimal system (powers of sixty) for weights and mathematical or astronomical calculations. Like the Babylonians, we still divide hours by sixty today. Furthermore, our modern system of numerical place-value notation—for example, the difference between 42 and 24—is derived, through Hindu-Arabic intermediaries, from the Babylonian system. The Babylonians were adept at arithmetic and could solve problems for which we would use algebra. A millennium before the Greek mathematician Pythagoras (who claimed to have studied the Mesopotamian tradition) proved the validity of the theorem that bears his name, they were familiar with the proposition that in a right triangle the square of the longest side is equal to the sum of the squares of the other two sides. In the first millennium B.C., the Babylonians developed a sophisticated mathematical astronomy (see page 35). As early as the seventeenth century B.C., they made systematic, if not always accurate, recordings of the movements of the planet Venus.

In medical matters, they demonstrated considerable critical ability. Physicians made advances in the use of plant products for medicines and in very rudimentary surgery. The Babylonians had a simple pregnancy test of moderate accuracy, for example, and their surgeons were experienced at setting broken bones. When they became ill, however, most people in Mesopotamia set more store by magic and incantations than by surgery or herbal medicine.

**Epic of Gilgamesh** The best-known example of Mesopotamian literature, the *Epic of Gilgamesh* is one of the earliest known poems and, in its original form, may date back to the Sumerians circa 2500 B.C.

## SECTION SUMMARY

- Approximately thirty city-states of southern Mesopotamia spoke Sumerian and flourished in the third millennium B.C.
- Sargon, an Akkadian, conquered the Sumerian cities of Mesopotamia and united them in one kingdom.
- Hammurabi's Code (1792–1750 B.C.), one of the earliest collections of laws, reveals the inequality and harshness of Mesopotamian society.
- Mesopotamians were religious, believed in many gods, and expected only a grim and shadowy Netherworld after death.
- Mesopotamia's rich culture excelled in mathematics, astronomy, and epic poetry.

# Egypt, to ca. 1100 B.C.

*How did the king's power affect various aspects of Egyptian society?*

From Babylon to the valley of the Nile River was about 750 miles by way of the caravan routes through Syria southward—close enough to exchange goods and customs but far enough for a distinct Egyptian civilization to emerge. As in Sumer, civilization in Egypt arose in a river

## Heroism and Death in Mesopotamia

*The Epic of Gilgamesh sheds light on notions of gender and power in Mesopotamia. Men such as King Gilgamesh and his friend Enkidu have heroic adventures and risk death. Women lead quieter lives but are wiser and more realistic, as the following excerpts show. Here Gilgamesh, who wanders in his grief over the death of Enkidu, comes to the cottage of the tavern keeper Siduri.*

Who are you? You are no one that I know. / I am Gilgamesh, who killed Humbaba / And the bull of heaven with my friend.

If you are Gilgamesh and did those things, why / Are you so emaciated and your face half-crazed?

I have grieved! Is it so impossible / To believe? He pleaded. / My friend who went through everything with me / Is dead!

No one grieves that much, she said. / Your friend is gone. Forget him. / No one remembers him. He is dead Enkidu. Enkidu. Gilgamesh called out:

Help me. They do not know you as I know you?

Then she took pity on him / And let him enter and lie down and rest. / She gave him her bed to fall into and sleep / And rubbed his back and neck and legs and arms / When he was coming out of sleep, still muttering / About the one "who went with me through everything." / Like those old people who forget their listeners / Have not lived through their past with them, / Mentioning names that no one knows. / Enkidu, whom I loved so much, / Who went through everything with me / He died—like any ordinary man. / I have cried both day and night. / I did not want to put him in a grave. / He will rise, I know, one day. / But then I saw that he *was* dead. / His face collapsed within / After several days, / Like cobwebs I have touched / With my finger.

She wiped his face with a moist cloth / Saying: Yes yes yes yes, / As she made him cooler / Trying to help him forget / By the steady softness of her flesh. / She moved her lips across his chest / And caressed the length of his tired body / And lay over him at night until he slept.

You will never find an end to grief by going on, / She said to the one half sleeping at her side, / Leaning forward to wipe the perspiration from his face. / His eyes were open though his whole self felt asleep / Far off alone in some deep forest / Planted in his flesh / Through which he felt his way in pain / Without the help / Of friends. / She spoke as to a child who could not understand / All the futility that lay ahead / Yet who she knew would go on to repeat / Repeat repeat the things men had to learn. The gods gave death to man and kept life for / Themselves. That is the only way it is. / Cherish your rests; the children you might have; / You are a thing that carries so much tiredness.

### Questions

1. *What differences between men and women appear in this excerpt?*
2. *Why is it so hard for Gilgamesh to accept Enkidu's death?*
3. *Is Siduri's view of the gods pessimistic or realistic?*

valley, but Egypt was much earlier than Mesopotamia in becoming a unified kingdom under one ruler. Moreover, ancient Egypt survived as a united and independent kingdom for over two thousand years (to be sure, with some periods of civil war and foreign rule). Egypt made great strides in a variety of areas of human achievement, from the arts to warfare. Western civilization borrowed much from Egypt, especially in technology and religion.

Ancient Egypt is a product of the unique characteristics of the Nile River (see **Map 1.2**). Yet, most of Egypt is desert. Today, only about 5 percent is habitable by humans, including a few oases, the Nile Delta, and the Nile Valley itself, which extends about 760 miles from Cairo to Egypt's modern southern border: Upper Egypt, a long and narrow valley never more than about 14 miles wide. North of Cairo, in "Lower Egypt," the Nile branches out into the wide, low-lying delta before flowing into the Mediterranean Sea.

## Divine Kingship

The fertility of the Nile River gave ancient Egypt a prosperous economy and optimistic culture. The river's annual floods, which took place during late summer and autumn, were generally mild and predictable. With less human effort than was required in Mesopotamia, the Nile's floodwaters could be used to irrigate most of the farmland in the Nile Valley. As a result, Egyptian agriculture was one of the wealthiest in the ancient world.

No wonder many Egyptians considered change undesirable. Even death appeared to be a minor event compared with the eternal regularity of the Nile, which may help explain the

**Map 1.2 Ancient Egypt and the Levant**

The unique geography of the Nile Valley and its fertile soil left a stamp on ancient Egypt. Egypt enjoyed trade and cultural contact—and sometimes went to war—with nearby lands such as Nubia and the Levant. © Cengage Learning 2014

prominence in Egyptian religion of belief in the afterlife. In addition, the static outlook helped promote the idea of an absolute, all-powerful, and all-providing king—namely, **pharaoh**. Although the name "pharaoh" did not emerge until ca. 1400 B.C., it is commonly used today to refer to ancient Egypt's kings, following the Hebrew Bible.

Agriculture and settled village life emerged in Egypt around 5000 B.C. By 4000 B.C., villages had grown into towns, each controlling a strip of territory. By about 3100 B.C., Egyptian communities up and down the Nile Valley had cleared marshes and expanded the amount of land under cultivation, which in turn could support a larger population. The Nile Valley became one unified kingdom of Egypt, with a capital city perhaps at Memphis.

The new kingdom had monumental architecture, writing, and a king. For several centuries, Egyptians consolidated their institutions. Although few specifics are known about this Archaic period (3200–2695 B.C.), it clearly laid the groundwork for the next era. Around 2700 B.C., a remarkable, distinctive, and relatively well-documented period of creativity began.

The history of third- and second-millennium B.C. Egypt is usually divided into three distinct eras of great prosperity: the Old Kingdom (2695–2160 B.C.), the Middle Kingdom (2025–1786 B.C.), and the New Kingdom (1550–1075 B.C.). Each kingdom is subdivided into dynasties, that is, ruling families. Between the kingdoms, central authority broke down in the Intermediate Periods. Broadly speaking, the Old Kingdom was an era of spectacular creativity and originality, symbolized by the building of the great pyramids; the Middle Kingdom, an era of introspection and literary production; and the New Kingdom, an era in which Egypt's traditional isolation gave way to international diplomacy and expansion.

Egypt's was the first government in recorded history to govern a large territory. Indeed, a chart of Egypt's power structure would look like a pyramid, with a broad base of laborers and artisans supporting a small commanding elite. The holder of the highest point of power was considered so important that, for centuries, Egyptians referred to the office rather than to the person, calling it "the Great House"—in Egyptian, *per-aa*, as the ruler himself (or occasionally herself) was eventually called.

Egyptian kingship was sacred monarchy. In Mesopotamia, the king generally claimed to have been appointed by the gods. In Egypt, pharaoh was deemed to *be* a god. The most dramatic symbol of the king's divinity was a building—or, rather, a series of buildings—the pyramids. The ancients built thirty-five major and many smaller pyramids, of which the best known are the three gigantic, perfectly symmetrical limestone tombs in Giza. Now, nearly five thousand years later, the Great Pyramid of King Khufu (r. 2589–2566 B.C., better known by his Greek name, Cheops) is still the largest all-stone building in human history. Near this pyramid stands the Great Sphinx, a human-headed lion carved out of a rock outcropping, perhaps representing Khufu's son, King Khafre (r. 2558–2532 B.C.; Greek name, Chephren), for whom the second pyramid at Giza was built.

The pyramids were not just monuments to an ego, but also temples where the king would continue to be worshiped and served in the afterlife. The structures served a political purpose as well. When the pyramids were constructed, the kingdom of Egypt was still young and

**pharaoh** Ancient Egyptians' title for their king, an absolute, all-powerful, and all-providing ruler.

**Pyramids of Giza**   Royal funerary monuments of three Egyptian kings of the twenty-sixth century B.C., the pyramids symbolize the power and ambition of the Old Kingdom. The Great Pyramid of King Khufu (or Cheops, rearmost in the photo) is still the largest all-stone building in human history.

fragile. By building a pyramid, the king made a statement of his power—an eloquent, simple, and irrefutable statement. The sheer size of the Great Pyramid demonstrated the king's ability to organize a vast labor force. Indeed, the encampment of workers at Giza may have been the largest gathering of human beings to that date.

In theory, the king owned all the land, but in practice, Egypt's economy was a mixture of private enterprise and centralized control. The king delegated authority to a large group of officials, including governors, mayors, military commanders, judges, treasurers, engineers, agricultural overseers, scribes, and others. The highest official was the vizier, a sort of prime minister who had more day-to-day power than pharaoh himself.

The essence of good government was what the Egyptians called *ma'at*, whose basic meaning is "order"—in government, society, or the universe; *ma'at* can also mean "truth" or "justice." Egypt had a well-functioning system of judges who heard lawsuits, and it probably also had a detailed law code, although few written laws survive.

## Life and Afterlife

Egyptian life was full of religious practices, from daily rituals and seasonal festivals to ethical teachings and magic. Egyptian religion tended toward *syncretism*—that is, the blending of mutually opposed beliefs, principles, or practices. For example, Egyptian mythology taught variously that the sky was a cow, was held up by a god or by a post, or was a goddess stretched over the earth. No one was troubled by such inconsistencies, as a modern worshiper might be, because Egyptians believed that a fundamental unity underlay the varieties of nature.

Egypt's religion had many greater and lesser deities, including human, animal, and composite gods. Various animals, from cats and dogs to crocodiles and serpents, were thought to represent the divine. Important deities included Thoth, the moon-god and god of wisdom; Nut, goddess of the sky; Ptah, a creator-god; Osiris, who invented agriculture and became lord of the dead; Horus, son of Osiris, a sky-god imagined as a giant falcon; and Isis, wife of Osiris and mother of Horus, a mother-goddess. Temples were numerous and lavish.

**Egyptian Book of the Dead** This scene from a lavishly illustrated papyrus shows a dead person's appearance before a divine court of judgment. His heart is being weighed in the balance to determine his fate in the afterlife. Courtesy of the Trustees of the British Museum

Egyptian religion focused on the afterlife. Unlike the Mesopotamians, the Egyptians believed that death could be a pleasant continuation of life on earth. Hence, they actively sought immortality. The wealthy built tombs that were decorated with paintings and inscriptions and stocked with cherished possessions for use after death. The most cherished possession of all was the body, and the Egyptians provided for its preservation through their mastery of the science of embalming—thus, the Egyptian mummies.

Reserved for the king and his officials in the Old Kingdom, the afterlife became, as it were, democratized by the Middle Kingdom. "Now you are a king's son, a prince/as long as your soul exists, so long will your heart be with you,"* says a text inscribed inside coffins in the Middle Kingdom. Funerary texts contained the relevant prayers. The texts emphasize ritual—incantations, magic spells, prayers—as the key to eternal life. Yet, from time to time, we find other texts, especially from the Middle Kingdom, that say that ritual is not enough; ethical behavior also is required. New Kingdom texts describe the details of a dead person's appearance before a divine court for judgment. The sinless are admitted into eternal life in the kingdom of the blessed. The guilty, their heavy hearts devoured by a beast, suffer a second, final death.

Egyptian women did not enjoy equal status with men, but they had more freedom than women in other ancient societies, particularly in legal matters. As in Mesopotamia, so in Egypt, a woman could buy or sell, bequeath or inherit, sue or testify in court, but a married Egyptian woman, unlike her eastern sisters, could do so without a male guardian's approval. A married woman in Egypt remained legally independent. She could own property without her husband's involvement. But how often did women exercise such privileges? Egyptian women worked in agriculture and trade, in the textile and perfume industries, in dining halls, and in entertainment, but they were rarely managers. Women also served as priestesses of various kinds. Yet, in Egypt, as elsewhere, women were expected to make the home the focus of their activities.

## War Abroad, 1786–ca. 1150 B.C.

The humane attitudes of the Middle Kingdom were swept away after about 1700 B.C., when Semitic-speaking immigrants from Canaan**—the Hyksos (HICK-sos)—conquered much of Egypt. In many ways gentle conquerors, the Hyksos worshiped Egyptian gods, built

---

*From *Myth and Symbol in Ancient Egypt* by R. T. Rundle Clark. © 1959, reprinted by Thames & Hudson Ltd., London.
**Canaan is an ancient name for the lands currently called Israel, Palestine, and coastal Syria and Lebanon.

and restored Egyptian temples, and intermarried with natives. As foreigners, however, the Hyksos were unpopular. Eventually, a war launched from Upper Egypt, which had retained a loose independence, drove the Hyksos out.

The first restored Egyptian ruler of the New Kingdom was Ahmose I (r. 1550–1525 B.C.). His Egypt proved to be a new Egypt indeed. The Hyksos had brought advanced military technology to Egypt, including the horse-drawn war chariot, new kinds of daggers and swords, and the composite bow. Made of laminated materials, including wood, leather, and horn, the composite bow could hit a target at 600 yards.

Warlike, expansionist, and marked by a daring attempt at religious reform, the New Kingdom's Eighteenth Dynasty (1540–1293 B.C.) has long held a special fascination for historians. One of the dynasty's memorable names is that of Queen Hatshepsut (HAT-shep-soot). Widow of Thutmose II (r. 1491–1479 B.C.), Hatshepsut first served as regent for her young stepson and then assumed the kingship herself (r. 1479–1457 B.C.). Other Egyptian queens had exercised royal power before, but Hatshepsut was the first to call herself king. Although Hatshepsut dispatched Egyptian armies to fight, her reign is best known for peaceful activities: at home, public works and temple rebuilding; abroad, a commercial expedition over the Red Sea to the "Land of Punt" (perhaps modern Somalia, in eastern Africa).

After her death, Hatshepsut was succeeded by the stepson for whom she had earlier served as regent, now called Thutmose III (r. 1479–1425 B.C.). Late in his reign, he tried to erase his stepmother's memory by having Hatshepsut's statues destroyed and her name expunged from records. A warrior pharaoh, Thutmose III led his dynasty's armed expansion in western Asia and northern Africa. Thutmose won his greatest victory during his first campaign, at the Battle of Megiddo in Canaan in 1457 B.C. (see **Map 1.2**), where Egypt's triumph prevented the kingdom of Mitanni from expanding southward. Egypt now ruled an empire with territory in Nubia and Canaan.

The years from about 1450 to about 1300 B.C. marked a period of peace among the great powers from Egypt to Anatolia and Mesopotamia—what historians call the first international system. The arts of peace are illustrated in surviving treaties and letters among monarchs, many of which come from Amarna.

The Amarna Archives (mid-fourteenth century B.C.), written in Akkadian cuneiform, illustrate formal communication among states. Rulers of great powers addressed each other as "brother," while Canaanite princes called pharaoh "my lord and my Sun-god" and assured him that they were "thy servant and the dirt on which thou dost tread."[*] The texts reveal a system of gift exchange and commerce, politeness and formality, alliance and dynastic marriage, subjects and governors, rebels and garrisons. Because of a rough equality of power, no king was likely to defeat the others, so the parties avoided all-out war. They preferred instead to compete by jockeying for allies among the small Canaanite border states.

Sometimes, the competition turned into war. By the late fourteenth century B.C., Egypt had a new rival abroad, the **Hittites**, who had built a great empire in Anatolia. The Hittites were masters of the horse and rank among the leading charioteers of what was the golden age of chariot battle. They made full use of Anatolia's mineral wealth and made a limited number of iron weapons as well as the more usual bronze.

The Hittite state was vibrant if often divided. Hittite kings were powerful, but they had to deal with a strong nobility. Hittite queens and queen mothers often had considerable power. Puduhepa (pu-du-HE-pa), wife of King Hattusilis (hat-tu-SIL-is) III (r. 1267–1237 B.C.), played a memorable role in state affairs. Some of her prayers were written down and survive to this day.

Hittite is the oldest recorded Indo-European language, the language group to which English belongs. Thousands of Hittite texts have survived. They paint a picture of a sophisticated society with rich traditions in law, scholarship, poetry, and religion. One thing that stands out in their texts is the Hittites' vivid sense of history.

**Hittites** Builders of a great empire in Anatolia in the Late Bronze Age, the Hittites fought Egypt to a standstill and made history's first peace treaty between equals. Hittite is the oldest recorded Indo-European language, the language group to which English belongs.

**Egyptian Queen** This elegant, red granite statue of the pharaoh Hatshepsut (r. 1479–1457 B.C.) is one of the few to depict her as a woman. She is usually shown as a man, complete with beard, to symbolize her royal power. Centuries later the proportions and carving techniques of Egyptian stone sculpture would influence the Greeks, although Greek artists chose less to copy the Egyptians than to try to outdo them (see the photo on page 66).

Brian Brake/Photo Researchers, Inc.

---

[*]"Peace and Brotherhood," from Gary Beckman, *Hittite Diplomatic Texts*, 2/e (Society of Biblical Literature, 1999), p. 97.

🌐 **Map 1.3 The International System, ca. 1500–1250 B.C.** This era of competing kingdoms and city-states witnessed considerable war, especially between Egypt and the Hittites for control of the Canaanite states. Yet it was also a period of international trade, diplomacy, and, from 1450 to 1300 B.C., peace.

During the Hittite New Kingdom (ca. 1360–1178 B.C.), the Hittites' power extended into Syria and northern Mesopotamia (see **Map 1.3**), which became the arena of conflict with Egypt. (See the feature, "The Global Record: Crossing Borders, for Better and Worse.")

The most dramatic episode was the Battle of Qadesh in northern Syria in 1274 B.C., where twenty thousand Egyptian troops faced seventeen thousand Hittites. Qadesh is the first well-documented battle in history. Since neither of the two evenly matched powers managed to conquer the other, they made peace. The treaty between them still survives, promising to establish "good brotherhood and good peace between us forever." It is the oldest surviving peace treaty between equals.

However, peace was temporary. Between about 1200 and 1150 B.C., the international system came to a crashing end. From Mesopotamia to Greece, from Anatolia to Egypt, one state after another collapsed. Surviving evidence is fragmentary, but it suggests that both foreign and domestic problems were devastating. Raiders and invaders beset the eastern Mediterranean in this period. Called "Sea Peoples" by the Egyptians, they attacked both on land and at sea. We do not know precisely who they were. In addition, some evidence of regional famine and climatic change indicates that natural causes may have led to disruption and rebellion.

Whatever the cause, what followed would prove to be a different world. Yet the end of the international system did not result in the disappearance of ancient cultures. Although new peoples appeared and old peoples changed, both continued to borrow from the cultures that had flowered before 1200 B.C.

## Reform at Home and Its Aftermath, 1352–ca. 1075 B.C.

Empire brings power, and power often causes conflict. In imperial Egypt during the fourteenth century B.C., kings and priests struggled over authority. Consider the Amarna (a-MAR-na) reform, named for a major archaeological site at the modern town of Tell el-Amarna.

## Crossing Borders, for Better and Worse

*These two documents of Hittite King Mursilis II (r.1321–1295 B.C.) illustrate relations between the Hittites (referred to below as Hatti) and Egypt during the reign of his father, King Suppiluliumas I (r. 1344–1322 B.C.). They demonstrate a great variety of exchange between Late-Bronze-Age states: soldiers, diplomats, captured livestock, prisoners, royal marriage partners—and disease, too.*

### (a) Suppiluliumas and the Egyptian Queen

While my father was down in the country of Karkamis [in Syria], he dispatched Lupakkis and Tessub-zalmas to the country of Amqa [in Lebanon]. They proceeded to attack the country of Amqa and brought deportees, cattle (and) sheep home before my father. When the people of the land of Egypt heard about the attack on Amqa, they became frightened. Because, to make matters worse, their lord Bibhururiyas [probably Tutankhamun] had just died, the Egyptian queen [probably Ankhesenamun] who had become a widow, sent an envoy to my father and wrote him as follows: "My husband died and I have no son. People say that you have many sons. If you were to send me one of your sons, he might become my husband. I am loath to take a servant of mine and make him my husband." . . .When my father heard that, he called the great into council (saying): "Since of old such a thing has never happened before me" He proceeded to dispatch Hattu-zitis, the chamberlain, (saying): "Go! Bring you reliable information back to me. They may try to deceive me: As to whether perhaps they have a prince bring reliable information back to me!"

During Hattu-zitis's absence in the land of Egypt my father vanquished the city of Karkamis. . . .

The Egyptian envoy, the Honorable Hanis, came to him. Because my father had instructed Hattu-zitis while sending him to the land of Egypt as follows: "Perhaps they have a prince; they may try to deceive me and do not really want one of my sons to (take over) the kingship," the Egyptian queen answered my father in a letter as follows: "Why do you say: 'They may try to deceive me'? If I had a son, would I write to a foreign country in a manner which is humiliating to myself and to my country? You do not trust me and tell me even such a thing. He who was my husband died and I have no sons. Shall I perhaps take one of my servants and make him my husband? I have not written to any other country, I have written (only) to you. People say that you have many sons. Give me one of your sons and he is my husband and king in the land of Egypt." Because my father was generous, he complied with the lady's wishes and decided for (sending) the son.

### (b) Plague Prayers of Mursilis

**4..** . . . My father sent foot soldiers and charioteers who attacked the country of Amka, Egyptian territory. Again he sent troops, and again they attacked it. When the Egyptians became frightened, they asked outright for one of his sons to (take over) the kingship. But when my father gave them one of his sons, they killed him as they led him there. My father let his anger run away with him, he went to war against Egypt and attacked Egypt. The Hattian storm-god, my lord, by his decision even then let my father prevail; he vanquished and smote the foot soldiers and the charioteers of the country of Egypt. But when they brought back to the Hatti land the prisoners which they had taken, a plague broke out among the prisoners and they began to die.

**5.** When they moved the prisoners to the Hatti land, these prisoners carried the plague into the Hatti land. From that day on, people have been dying in the Hatti land.

### Questions

1. *To what extent did trust or distrust characterize Hittite-Egyptian relations?*

2. *Based on the text, does the Egyptian queen seem powerful or powerless?*

3. *What role did royal marriage play in Late-Bronze-Age international relations?*

The **Amarna reform** was carried out by Thutmose III's great-great-grandson, King Amenhotep IV (r. 1352–1336 B.C.). Earlier, the god Amun-Re had become the chief deity of the New Kingdom. As supporters of imperialism, his temple priests had been rewarded with so much land and wealth that their power now rivaled pharaoh's own. Amenhotep IV responded by forbidding the worship of Amun-Re and replacing him with the god Aten, the solar disk. The king changed his own name to Akhenaten ("pleasing to Aten"). He also created a new capital city: Akhetaten (modern Amarna). Akhenaten's wife, Nefertiti, figures prominently in Amarna art, and she too may have played an important role in the reform.

The reformers gained power, but we need not doubt their sincerity. Contemporary literature suggests intense religious conviction in Aten as a benevolent god and one who nurtured not only Egypt but all countries. Although the Aten cult focuses on one god, only Akhenaten

**Amarna reform** Term for the ancient Egyptian King Amenhotep IV's seizure of power from temple priests by replacing the god Amun-Re with Aten and renaming himself Akhenaten.

**Hittite God** This figurine in gold, standing only 1.5 inches high, represents Hittite art of the Old Kingdom (ca. 1650–1450 B.C.). The clothes, shoes, and conical hat are typical of Hittite depictions of gods.

Réunion des Musées Nationaux/Art Resource, NY

and his family were permitted to worship Aten directly; the rest of the Egyptian population was expected to worship the god through pharaoh.

Bold as the reform was, it was too radical to last. After Akhenaten's death, his son-in-law and successor, Tutankhaten (r. 1336–1327 B.C.) restored good relations with the priests of Amun-Re, which he signaled by changing his name to Tutankhamun. The Amun-Re cult was revived, the Aten cult was abolished, and the city of Akhetaten was abandoned.

## Arts and Sciences in the New Kingdom

The Egyptians were superb builders, architects, and engineers. In addition to pyramids and irrigation works, they constructed monumental royal tombs, palaces, forts, and temples, and they erected looming obelisks. At their best, Egyptian architects designed buildings in harmony with the unique landscape—one of the reasons for the structures' lasting appeal. Their most original and enduring work was done in stone. Stone temples, for example, culminated in the imposing pillared structures of the New Kingdom. That period also saw the construction of rock-cut temples, the most famous of which is Ramesses II's (r. 1279–1213 B.C.) project at Abu Simbel (see **Map 1.2**). In front of the temples sit four colossal statues of Ramesses, also carved out of rock. Obelisks were slender, tapering pillars carved of a single piece of stone. Inscribed with figures and hieroglyphs, and usually erected in pairs in front of a temple, obelisks were meant to glorify the sun-god.

Throughout history, royal courts have excelled as patrons of the arts; the Egyptian court was one of the first and greatest. Egyptian craftspeople were master goldsmiths, glassmakers, and woodworkers. The major arts are well represented in tombs, which were decorated with rich, multicolored wall paintings, the first narrative depictions.

Sculpture was another art form in which Egyptians excelled. Carved in stone, wood, or metal, Egyptian sculpture is a study in contrasts. The body posture is usually rigid and stiff, the musculature only sketchy; the face, in contrast, is often individualistic, the expression full of character and drawn from life. Statues represent kings and queens, gods and goddesses, husbands and wives, adults and children, officials, priests, scribes, and animals.

Ancient Egyptian literature is notable for its variety. Religious subjects, historical and commemorative records, technical treatises in mathematics and medicine, and secular stories survive alongside business contracts and royal proclamations. Egyptian writing is best known for hieroglyphs. Elaborate and formal, hieroglyphs were generally used after the Archaic period only for monuments and ornamentation. Two simplified scripts served for everyday use.

The people who built the pyramids had to be skilled at arithmetic and geometry. Egyptians were able to approximate pi ($\pi$, the ratio of the circumference of a circle to its diameter) and to solve equations containing one or two unknowns. The Egyptian calendar was also a remarkable achievement. Based on observation of the star Sirius, the Egyptian calendar, with its 365-day year, approximates the solar calendar. Corrected to 365 1/4 days, it survives to this day as the calendar of Europe, the Americas, and much of the rest of the world.

Egyptian medical doctors were admired in antiquity and in demand abroad. They knew how to set a dislocated shoulder and used a full battery of splints, sutures, adhesive plasters, elementary disinfectants (from tree leaves), and burn treatments (fatty substances). One Egyptian treatise offers something like modern triage, dividing diseases into three categories: treatable, possibly treatable, and untreatable. Egyptian doctors may have done postmortem dissection in order to understand the human body better.

## SECTION SUMMARY

- The Nile River, with its dependable annual flooding, gave ancient Egypt fertile soil, economic prosperity, and an optimistic worldview.

- Egypt invented the idea of worshiping the king as a god; eventually, the king became known as pharaoh.

- Egyptians believed in a happy life after death, as long as the gods judged that the dead person had led a life without sin.

- Egypt's New Kingdom was a great military power that expanded into southwest Asia.

- The earliest known Indo-European civilization is that of the Hittites, who established a great kingdom in today's Turkey and left thousands of documents.

- The conflicts between Hittites and Egyptians led to history's first great system of diplomacy, its first well-documented battle (Qadesh), and its first peace treaty between equals.

- The Amarna reform of the 1300s was history's first great struggle between church and state.

- The Egyptians excelled at architecture, such as the pyramids, as well as at sculpture and medicine, and they invented the solar calendar that we still use (in revised form) today.

- We are not sure why, but the great ancient civilizations of Egypt and western Asia all declined, split apart, or collapsed not long after 1200 B.C.

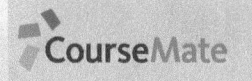

# Chapter Summary

◆ *How did the earliest human beings adapt to their environments and create the first civilizations?*

The earliest human beings, probably beginning before 70,000 B.C., invented human culture—that is, they developed communications well enough that people could cooperate and exploit their natural environment by means of technology. Next came the move from a food-collecting to a food-producing economy. After beginning in the Fertile Crescent region of western Asia shortly after 10,000 B.C., food production spread to Europe beginning around 7000 B.C. Over the thousands of years following the invention of agriculture, human society became more complex and won increasing control of the natural environment. The result was the emergence of civilization in Egypt and Mesopotamia after 3500 B.C.

◆ *What were the Mesopotamians' major contributions to government, religion, and art and culture?*

The first cities appeared in Mesopotamia about 3500 B.C. and maybe even earlier. Writing was invented independently in Mesopotamia and Egypt between 3500 and 3000 B.C. In Mesopotamia, the Sumerians and Akkadians flourished in city-states, which were eventually conquered and united into a kingdom. The Mesopotamians wrote the first law codes, including the famous Hammurabi's Code (1792–1750 B.C.). Mesopotamians were religious, believed in many gods, and expected only a grim and shadowy Netherworld after death. Mesopotamia's rich culture excelled in mathematics, astronomy, and epic poetry.

◆ *How did the king's power affect various aspects of Egyptian society?*

Egyptian society and culture was focused on the king. Egypt invented the idea of worshipping the king as a god; eventually, the king became known as pharaoh. Early Egypt was relatively peaceful and inward-looking, but after a period of foreign rule, the newly liberated Egypt of the New Kingdom was a great military power that expanded into southwest Asia. The Egyptians excelled at architecture, such as the pyramids, as well as at sculpture and medicine, and they invented the solar calendar that we use (in revised form) today.

Our language, English, belongs to the Indo-European language group; the first known Indo-European civilization is that of the Hittites, the dominant power in Anatolia from 1650 to 1180 B.C. The conflicts between Hittites and Egyptians led to history's first great system of diplomacy, its first well-documented battle (Qadesh), and its first peace treaty between equals. The great ancient civilizations of western Asia all either declined, split apart, or collapsed not long after 1200 B.C. Although this destruction is often attributed to the Sea Peoples, the cause is still uncertain.

# Key Terms

**hominids** (p. 4)
**hunter-gatherers** (p. 6)
**Neolithic Revolution** (p. 7)
**Europe** (p. 8)
**cuneiform** (p. 13)
**papyrus** (p. 13)
**Sumerians** (p. 13)

**city-states** (p. 14)
**Hammurabi's Code** (p. 16)
*Epic of Gilgamesh* (p. 18)
**pharaoh** (p. 21)
**Hittites** (p. 23)
**Amarna reform** (p. 25)

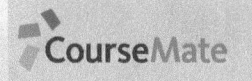
**CourseMate**

Go to the CourseMate website at **www.cengagebrain.com** for additional study tools and review materials—including audio and video clips—for this chapter.

**Bull from Ishtar Gate, Babylon** bpk, Berlin/Vorderasiatisches Museum, Staatliche Museen, Berlin/Art Resource, NY

# The Ship, the Sword, and the Book: Western Asia, ca. 1500–400 B.C.

The bull in brick relief shown on the left symbolizes power even today, twenty-six hundred years after it was molded and glazed. About 4 feet high, this bull was one of several dozen figures of bulls and dragons that decorated the massive Ishtar Gate, which led through the inner town wall of Babylon (BAB-eh-lon) into the palace. The gate represents only a small part of a magnificent reconstruction of the city by the Neo-Babylonian kings who ruled western Asia from around 600 to 539 B.C.

Imagine the king's surprise had he known that under his nose an obscure prophet—we know him only as "Second Isaiah" (eye-ZAY-ah)—was preaching a bold message to his compatriots, a conquered people living in exile in Babylon. Isaiah reminded them that Yahweh (YAH-way), their god, was a god of justice and mercy—the one and only true god of the entire world—and that Yahweh had chosen the king of mountainous, backward Persia to conquer western Asia and redeem Yahweh's people. The Neo-Babylonian king might have laughed at the idea. Yet the Persians, under Cyrus the Great, conquered Babylon in 539 B.C. and proclaimed the freedom of Yahweh's people—the Jews—to return to Palestine and re-establish the Temple to their god in the city of Jerusalem (juh-ROO-suh-lem). They did so, and around this time, they wrote down their religious and historical traditions in large sections of what would become the Hebrew Bible, or Old Testament.

It was a momentous development because the Hebrew Bible founded the West's religious tradition. Along with Greece and Rome, ancient Israel may be considered one of the three founders of the West. Greece began the western tradition of philosophy and politics; Rome began Western law and administration; Israel gave the West ethical monotheism, the idea that God is one and that everything he does is good.

In contrast to ancient Israel, the other peoples studied in this chapter are all ancestors of the West: the Phoenicians and other Canaanites, the Neo-Babylonians and the other great empires of the era, the Assyrians and Persians. Traders or conquerors, they came to power through merchant ships or by the sword, but once in power they spread civilization, serving as conduits through which the achievements of earlier civilizations were transmitted. They spread trading networks that brought the alphabet to the Greeks, which would prove essential to preserving the brilliant culture that later

## Chapter Overview

### Traders Invent the Alphabet: Canaanites and Phoenicians, ca. 1400–450 B.C.

◆ *Who were the Phoenicians and what did they contribute to Western civilization?*

### Assyrians, Neo-Babylonians, and Persians, ca. 1200–330 B.C.

◆ *What made the first-millennium B.C. empires of the Assyrians, Neo-Babylonians, and Persians so much more effective than earlier empires?*

### Israel, ca. 1500–400 B.C.

◆ *What was the religious experience of ancient Israel, and what is its legacy today?*

developed in Greece. They built great empires whose institutions were eventually transformed into notions of mass citizenship under law and justice in a universal empire by the third founder of the West, Rome.

The first half of the first millennium B.C., therefore, left a divergent legacy to the West. On the one hand, new empires arose that were more systematically organized, farther-flung, and more diverse ethnically than those created before. On the other hand, prophets and poets looked in new and deeper ways into the human soul.

In this chapter we look at the deeply influential developments in empire, religion, and thought forged in the first half of the first millennium B.C. At the same time, we consider the peaceful expansion in this era, through trade and colonization, particularly under the Phoenicians. Finally, we examine the material innovation that has earned the period the title "Iron Age."

# Traders Invent the Alphabet: Canaanites and Phoenicians, ca. 1400–450 B.C.

*Who were the Phoenicians and what did they contribute to Western civilization?*

Canaan (CAY-nan) is an ancient name for the lands currently called Israel, Palestine, Lebanon, and Syria. Often eclipsed by Egypt, Mesopotamia, and the Anatolian kingdoms, the Canaanite (CAY-nan-ite) city-states made important contributions to the West. Not only did they take part in the first international system of states, the era documented by the Amarna Archives (ca. 1450–1300 B.C.), but they also served as the cradle of Western writing systems. After surviving the invasions of the Sea Peoples, the Canaanite city-states on the coast prospered in the first millennium B.C. Now known as Phoenicians, these people were great sailors who planted colonies throughout the Mediterranean and spread the alphabet.

## The Canaanite City-States, ca. 1400–1200 B.C.

**Ugarit** A thriving, cosmopolitan Mediterranean port in what is today Syria, whose scribes developed an alphabet in the 1300s B.C.

Canaanite centers thrived both inland and on the Mediterranean coast. The first flowering of Canaanite civilization came in the third millennium B.C. at such sites as Ebla, but Ebla's greatest days were behind it after being conquered around 2000 B.C. To find a much more vibrant city in Syria after 2000 B.C., we need only look at the coast and the city of **Ugarit** (see **Map 1.3**). Ugarit (OO-ga-rit) was a thriving Mediterranean port, especially around 1400 to 1180 B.C. It was located in what is today Syria, at the modern Ra's Shamrah, near today's port of Latakia. We can almost hear the pride of Ugarit's inhabitants in their city in the prayer of one of its kings: "Well-being for Ugarit, well-being for her gates!"*

A multiethnic city, Ugarit's cosmopolitanism made it distinctive among western Asian city-states. As a trading center, it linked ships coming from the eastern Mediterranean island of Cyprus and the Anatolian ports with land caravans heading to Babylonia. The native inhabitants of Ugarit spoke a Semitic language. The merchants of Ugarit, however, were often foreigners, and the bazaars echoed with a multitude of languages. In its heyday, Ugarit housed documents written in at least four languages.

**alphabet** A set of letters (written symbols), each of which represents roughly one sound in a spoken language.

Ugarit played an important role in the spread of one of history's most important writing systems: the **alphabet**. Unlike the pictographic or syllabic systems of Mesopotamia, Egypt, and China, in an alphabet each letter—that is, written symbol—stands for one sound in a spoken language or for several closely related sounds such as the "s" in "say" and the "s" in "was." In the 1300s B.C., scribes in Ugarit developed an alphabet. It was not the first alphabet, however. In Egypt, in the desert west of the Nile, limestone inscriptions have recently been

---

*Dennis Pardee, "Ugarit Ritual Texts," *The Oriental Institute News and Notes 172* (Winter 2002) as made available electronically at http://oi.uchicago.edu/research/pubs/nn/win02_pardee.html.

found in a Semitic script with Egyptian influences. Dated to about 1900 to 1800 B.C., during the Middle Kingdom, the writing is now recognized as the earliest known example of an alphabet.

We do not know whether that alphabet was invented by Egyptians or by speakers of a Semitic language who were visiting Egypt, nor do we know if that alphabet influenced Ugarit. What is clear is that Ugaritic scribes invented thirty cuneiform signs as an alphabet to write their Semitic language. Later adapted by the Phoenicians and, through them, the Greeks, the Ugaritic alphabet is the source of the Roman alphabet, used today by English and many other languages around the world.

## The Phoenicians, ca. 1050–450 B.C.

Ugarit was destroyed by the Sea Peoples around 1180 B.C. Most Canaanite cities survived, however. After the invasions of the Sea Peoples and others, the Canaanites' once-large territory was reduced to a narrow strip along the Mediterranean in the area of modern Lebanon and northern Israel (see **Map 2.2** on page 42). Between 1050 and 750 B.C., the inhabitants of the area flourished; historians call them, as did the ancient Greeks, "Phoenicians." Their purple-dyed textiles gave the Greeks their word for the color purple: *phoenician*. Besides textiles, the Phoenicians exported the famous cedars of Lebanon for shipbuilding.

In the Hebrew Bible, the **Phoenicians** (fuh-NEESH-anz) loom large as merchants and seamen, as "traders the world honored" (Isaiah 23:8). Phoenicians were Canaanites, speakers of a Semitic language and heirs to the civilization that had prospered in Ugarit around 1400 B.C. (see page 30). Few Phoenician texts survive, and they emphasize religion, like this inscription of the king of Byblos (in today's Lebanon) to the goddess Astarte: "May the Lady of Byblos bless and preserve Yehawmilk, king of Byblos, and prolong his days and years in Byblos, for he is a righteous king."*

The Phoenicians were master shipbuilders and sailors. Around 600 B.C., their ships accomplished the first known circumnavigation of Africa. Around 450 B.C., they made the first known commercial sailing trip to the British Isles. Some scholars think they even reached Brazil.

Phoenician colonies were located in Cyprus, North Africa, Sicily, Malta, Sardinia, Italy, southern France, and Spain and Portugal. Many of their colonies eventually became independent states. The greatest Phoenician colony was Carthage (CAR-thidge), founded by the city of Tyre around 750 B.C. It was the major port city of the western Mediterranean for much of the next thousand years. There was also a Phoenician colony at the western gateway to the Mediterranean, at Gibraltar.

Phoenician culture was open to outside influences. Phoenician religious art is full of Egyptian sphinxes, coffins that look like mummy cases, and women wearing wigs in the style of Egypt's New Kingdom. But Phoenician art also contains Near Eastern seals and figures out of Greek myths.

Phoenician traders introduced advanced material goods, slaves, and possibly law codes to the Greeks. It was probably from the Phoenicians, whose alphabet derived from Ugarit, that the Greeks adapted their alphabet, probably shortly after 800 B.C.

One aspect of Phoenician culture is less attractive than any yet mentioned: child sacrifice. The Hebrew Bible, as well as Greek and Roman writers, state that Phoenician and other

## CHRONOLOGY

| | |
|---|---|
| ca. 1900–1800 B.C. | Earliest known alphabet |
| ca. 1400–1180 B.C. | Height of Ugarit |
| 1250–1150 B.C. | Sea Peoples invade the eastern Mediterranean |
| 1180 B.C. | Ugarit destroyed |
| 1075–656 B.C. | Third Intermediate Period in Egypt |
| ca. 1050–750 B.C. | Height of Phoenician city-states |
| 1004–928 B.C. | Reigns of David and Solomon |
| 722 B.C. | Assyrians conquer kingdom of Israel |
| 612 B.C. | Conquest of Nineveh ends Assyrian power |
| 598 B.C. | Neo-Babylonians conquer kingdom of Judah |
| 559–530 B.C. | Reign of Cyrus the Great |
| 550–330 B.C. | Achaemenid Persian Empire |
| 539 B.C. | Cyrus conquers Babylon; permits Jews to return to Palestine |
| ca. 425 B.C. | Judean assembly accepts the Torah |
| 701 B.C. | Siege and destruction of Lachish |

**Phoenicians** Canaanites whose civilization flourished about 1050–750 B.C. in present-day coastal Syria, where they established major trading ports. Master sailors, they planted colonies around the Mediterranean, many of which, including Carthage, became independent states.

---

*From J.B. Pritchard, *Ancient Near Eastern Texts Related to the Old Testament*, 3rd ed., with Supplement, p. 656. Copyright © 1969 by Princeton University Press. Reprinted with permission.

Canaanite parents sacrificed a child, especially their first-born child, to a god in return for divine favor. Many Phoenician archaeological sites contain an area with large numbers of infant burials. While skeptics consider that evidence only of infant mortality, most scholars hold it as confirmation of the literary record.

Around 750 B.C., the Phoenician city-states lost their independence to the Assyrians, and in later years Neo-Babylonians, Persians, and other foreign conquerors followed. But Phoenician culture survived—at home, in the colonies, and among the many Mediterranean peoples influenced by it. The result, though unintended, was that Phoenician colonists exported the civilization of western Asia to the western Mediterranean.

# Assyrians, Neo-Babylonians, and Persians, ca. 1200–330 B.C.

*What made the first-millennium B.C. empires of the Assyrians, Neo-Babylonians, and Persians so much more effective than earlier empires?*

Ancestors of the West, three great multiethnic empires emerged between the eighth and fifth centuries B.C. Ruthless soldiers, brutal conquerors, and innovative administrators, the Assyrians established an empire in western Asia and Egypt during the ninth through seventh centuries B.C. They were followed in turn by a Neo-Babylonian empire in the late seventh and sixth centuries. However, neither of these was as successful or as durable as the empire of the Persians (ca. 550–330 B.C.). At its height, the Persian Empire stretched from central Asia and northwest India in the east to Macedonia and Libya in the west (see **Map 2.1**). Persia's

🌐 **Map 2.1 The Assyrian and Persian Empires** In the 660s B.C., the Assyrians ruled the largest empire the ancient world had seen, extending from the Tigris to the Nile. The Persian Empire was even greater. Around 500 B.C., it reached from its heartland in southwestern Iran westward to Macedonia and eastward to India. © Cengage Learning 2014 vast empire was loosely governed by a Persian ruling elite and its native helpers. Unlike the ironfisted Assyrians, the Persians were relatively tolerant and respectful of their subjects' customs. Many of Persia's kings were followers of Zoroastrianism, an ethical and forceful religion. A period of relative peace in most of Persia's domains from the 530s to the 330s B.C. fostered widespread economic prosperity.

The Persians borrowed the administrative methods of the Assyrians and Medes (meedz) and the long-established officialdom of Babylon and built a new and durable imperial government. Their official art stressed the unity of the peoples of the empire under Persian leadership. Persian rule represented the greatest success yet in implementing the notions of universal kingship that dated back to Sargon of Agade (r. 2371–2316 B.C.) (see page 16). In turn, Persia transmitted the idea of absolute kingship to later ambitious rulers, from Alexander the Great to the caesars of Rome and from the Byzantine emperors to the Muslim caliphs.

## Assyrians and Neo-Babylonians

The **Assyrians** already had a long history as a military and commercial power in the Bronze Age. They lived in what is today northern Iraq and spoke a Semitic language. Around 1200 B.C., their state collapsed during that era of international crisis (see page 24), but they held on to a small homeland of about 5,000 square miles, roughly the size of Connecticut. The toughened survivors emerged with an aggressive, expansionist ideology.

Assyria's greatest successes came in the eighth and seventh centuries. One by one, states large and small fell— Babylonia, Syria, the kingdom of Israel, Cilicia in southern Anatolia, even Egypt (though Assyrian rule there lasted only a generation). Assyria became the first state to rule the two great river valleys of the ancient Near East, the Nile and the Tigris-Euphrates (see **Map 2.1**).

The Assyrians were warriors. Ashur, their main deity, was a war-god. Theirs was an ideology of power, conquest, and control. The key to Assyria's success was its army— 100,000 to 200,000 men strong—which made an unforgettable impression on observers and foes. The Israelite prophet Isaiah of Jerusalem ("First Isaiah") said of Assyrian soldiers: "[Their] arrows are sharpened, and all their bows bent, their horses' hoofs are like flint, their chariot wheels like the whirlwind. Their growling is like that of a lion" (Isaiah 5:28–29). He might have added that Assyrian spearmen, archers, and cavalrymen were equipped with weapons and armor of iron.

Thanks to new heating and cooling techniques, metal smiths in the ancient world produced an alloy of carbon and iron that was harder and more durable than bronze. It was also easier to obtain since iron ore is widespread—unlike tin, an essential element of bronze. Iron tools and weapons were often stronger and cheaper than their bronze predecessors, which opened up new technical and military possibilities.

Adding to its might, Assyria was the first major state to employ regular cavalry units (rather than charioteers) as the main strike force. The Assyrians were also excellent engineers, adept at taking walled cities by siege.

In addition, the Assyrians displayed superb organizational skills. The central standing army was supplemented with draftees conscripted from around the empire. Provinces were kept small to prevent the emergence of separate power bases, and independent-minded nobles were regularly checked by the kings.

**Assyrians** Warlike people who ruled the ancient Near East during the first millennium B.C. Their innovations included using cavalry as their main striking force and having weapons and armor made of iron.

**Assyrian Winged Genie**   This alabaster relief comes from a temple of the Assyrian king Ashurnasirpal II (r. 883–859 B.C.) at his capital of Calah (Nimrud). The figure holds an incense pouch in one hand and a pinecone in the other, perhaps symbols of the tree of life. Image © The Metropolitan Museum of Art/Art Resource, NY

**Phoenician Ivory**   This delicately carved plaque of a cow and calf, just 3 inches high, illustrates the wealth of artistic talent at the disposal of the Phoenicians, whose civilization reached its peak between 1050 and 750 B.C. National Museum, Baghdad, Iraq/Scala/Art Resource, NY

To control the restive subjects of their far-flung empire, the Assyrians met rebellion with ferocious reprisals. Disloyal cities were attacked and, if need be, destroyed. Sculptured reliefs and inscriptions were set up to show, often in gruesome detail, the fate awaiting Assyria's enemies. We see or read of cities burned to the ground; of men flayed alive, even though they had surrendered, and walls covered with their skin; and of piles of human skulls. (See the feature, "The Visual Record: The Siege of Lachish" on pages 44–45.)

The Assyrians also engaged in mass deportations. They uprooted the people of a conquered country, resettled them far away—often in Assyria itself—and colonized their land with Assyrian loyalists. The so-called Ten Lost Tribes of Israel—the people of the northern Israelite kingdom (see pages 40–41)—were conquered by Assyria in 722 B.C., and many of them were transported to Mesopotamia, where they disappeared from history. (Those who remained in Israel mixed with colonists, and the new group became known, and scorned, as Samaritans.)

Assyrian policy was the result of careful calculation. The political goal was to punish rebellion; the economic goal was to create a varied labor force. For example, although it is estimated that the Assyrians deported several million people, they deported not whole populations but a carefully chosen cross section of professions. They also deported entire families together, to weaken deportees' emotional ties to their former homes.

Assyria's success also was due in part to the relative weakness of other powers. After a period of great warrior-pharaohs and builder-pharaohs during the Nineteenth Dynasty (ca. 1291–1185 B.C.), Egypt suffered a series of weak kings who lost power to the priests of Amun during the Twentieth Dynasty (ca. 1185–1075 B.C.). When the Twentieth Dynasty ended in 1075 B.C., the New Kingdom ended with it, and regional conflict between the Nile Delta and Upper Egypt broke out.

Egypt was at the mercy of factions and invaders for much of the Third Intermediate Period (1075–656 B.C.). Around 950, for example, the kingship came into the hands of Libyan mercenaries. From the eighth century on, their rule was challenged, in turn, by invaders from the south, rulers of a new Nubian kingdom called Kush (see **Map 1.2** on page 20). Kushite pharaohs governed Egypt from around 719 until 656, when they withdrew back south. It was they who faced the Assyrian attacks in 671 and 667.

The conquest of Egypt marked imperial Assyria's greatest extent—and its overextension (see **Map 2.1**). A coalition army consisting of soldiers from a new Babylonian kingdom and from the Medes (who had formed a powerful state in Iran) conquered Nineveh (NIN-eh-veh), the Assyrian capital, in 612 B.C. and defeated the remnants of the Assyrian army in battles in 609 and 605. Few of its subjects mourned the empire's passing.

The destruction of Assyria led to revival for Babylon, whose rulers attempted to recapture the glories of Hammurabi's day (see pages 16–17). For a short period, until the Persian conquest in 539 B.C, the Neo-Babylonian dynasty (founded in 626 B.C), as it is known today, and the Medes of Iran were the dominant military forces in western Asia. The Neo-Babylonian king Nebuchadrezzar II (neh-boo-khad-REZ-zar) conquered the kingdom of Judah (in southern Palestine) in 598 and destroyed Jerusalem, its capital, in 586. He deported many thousands of Judeans to Babylon, an event remembered by Christians and Jews as the Babylonian Captivity. Most of the rest of western Asia also fell to Nebuchadrezzar's troops. His most enduring achievement was rebuilding Babylon on a grand scale. In addition to the city's numerous temples, shrines, and altars, he created the so-called Hanging Gardens

**Neo-Babylonians** Rulers of western Asia between 612 and 539 B.C., who elaborately rebuilt Babylon, creating the famous Hanging Gardens. They destroyed Jerusalem, deporting many Judeans in what is known as the Babylonian Captivity.

celebrated by later Greek writers. They describe the structure as a large terraced complex that Nebuchadrezzar built for his queen, although it may have been a plant-covered ziggurat.

The Neo-Babylonians and Assyrians both made great strides in astronomy. Their primary motive was not scientific but religious—that is, a belief in astrology (the study of the movements of heavenly bodies in the belief that they influence human affairs). Astrology led to advances in the scientific observation of the heavens. Assyrian priests had produced relatively accurate circular diagrams (astrolabes) that showed the positions of the major constellations, stars, and planets over the course of the year. By 600 B.C., Assyrian and Neo-Babylonian astronomers could predict solstices, equinoxes, and lunar eclipses.

Astronomy in Mesopotamia reached its heights in the centuries after 500 B.C. The zodiac, a diagram showing the movement of the sun and planets relative to the constellations, was invented in Persian-ruled Babylon in the fourth century B.C. In the third and second centuries B.C., when Babylonia was under Hellenistic Greek rule, native scientists made impressive advances in mathematical astronomy, composing tables that could be used to calculate movements of the moon and planets. More sophisticated mathematical astronomy would not be produced in the West until the Scientific Revolution of the sixteenth century A.D.

## Building the Persian Empire

A thousand miles east of Phoenicia, a great empire took root. Indo-European–speaking peoples, the Medes and Persians arrived in what is now western Iran, probably around 1500 B.C. but perhaps not until 900 B.C. The two peoples were closely related in language and customs. Both peoples lived in the rugged Zagros Mountains (today in western Iran). The Medes lived in what is now central western Iran, while the Persians made their homeland farther south in today's southwestern Iran. At first, the Medes ruled the Persians, but in 550 B.C. the tables were turned when the Medes were suddenly conquered by the young Persian king Cyrus the Great (r. 559–530 B.C.).

It took Cyrus only twenty years to conquer most of western Asia and much of central Asia. Within five years of his death in 530 B.C., his son and successor, Cambyses (kam-BYE-seez) (r. 530–522 B.C.), added Egypt and Libya. Cambyses' successor, Darius (dah-RYE-us) (r. 522–486 B.C.), corralled northwestern India and Thrace. The frontier regions, especially Egypt, were often in revolt, and the attempt of Darius and his successor, Xerxes (ZURK-seez) (r. 486–465 B.C.), to extend Persian rule to Greece ended in failure (see page 71). But the Achaemenid (ah-KEE-men-id) **Persian Empire** (named after a legendary founder, Achaemenes) survived for two hundred years, until a Greco-Macedonian army under Alexander the Great, king of Macedon (r. 336–323 B.C.), destroyed it.

**Persian Empire** Vast, prosperous, and law-abiding West Asian empire, from about 550 to 330 B.C., it represented the greatest success yet of a universal kingship. The Persians also built the first great navy.

Achaemenid Persia had three reasons for success: military, political, and administrative. Persia was ruled by a warrior-aristocracy whose traditional values, according to the Greek historian Herodotus, were "riding, hunting, and telling the truth." The state was able to field a huge army of about 300,000 men, conscripted from the various subject peoples. The Persians excelled as bowmen and cavalrymen. Following the Assyrians, they made cavalry into the decisive strike force of the battlefield, assigning a more minor role to chariotry. Persia was even more innovative at sea, where it had its subjects build the first great navy.

Politically, Persia preferred generosity and tolerance to the terrorism and brutality of the Assyrians. After conquering Babylon, for example, Cyrus said he had entered the city "as a friend." He said: "My numerous troops walked around in Babylon in peace, I did not allow anyone to terrorize (any) place of [the country of Sumer] and Akkad."* Cyrus did not hesitate to break with Assyrian and Neo-Babylonian population transfers, as witnessed in his edict permitting the Jewish exiles in Babylon to return to Judea.

Persia showed skill at administration and organization. Darius played a crucial role in reorganizing the imperial administration and finances. Like the Assyrian Empire, the Persian domain was divided into provinces, called *satrapies* (SAY-truh-peez). Each of the twenty satrapies was a unit of administration and tax collection. For the first time, taxes could be paid with a stable, official coinage: the gold daric (named after Darius) and the silver shekel.

*From J.B. Pritchard. *Ancient Near Eastern Texts Relating to the Old Testament*, 3d ed., with Supplement, p. 316. Copyright © 1969 by Princeton University Press. Reprinted with permission.

**Achaemenid Persian Silver** This silver rhyton (drinking vessel) is in the shape of a griffin, a mythological animal that is part lion and part eagle. Persian rulers commanded the talents of western Asia's best artists and craftsmen, silversmiths among them. Courtesy of the Trustees of the British Museum

The provincial governors, or *satraps*, were powerful, often quasi-independent figures, but the king tried to keep a firm hand on them. Each province had a royal secretary and was visited regularly by traveling inspectors called "the king's eyes." A network of good roads radiated from the capital cities of Susa and Persepolis. The most famous road, the so-called Royal Road, stretched 1,600 miles from western Iran to western Anatolia (see **Map 2.1**). Covering the whole distance took most travelers three months, but the king's relay messenger corps could make the trip in a week, thanks to a series of staging posts furnished with fresh horses.

Another unifying element was a society that was law-abiding and prosperous. Darius proclaimed in an inscription that he had fostered the rule of law: "These countries [of the empire] showed respect toward my law; as was commanded to them by me, thus it was done."* Darius and other Persian kings helped create the conditions for compliance and security by taking an interest in the economy. For example, they opened to commercial traffic Persian roads and a canal connecting the Red Sea and the Nile.

Language, too, built unity. Not Persian, which relatively few people spoke, but Aramaic, the most widespread language of western Asia, became the empire's basic language of commerce and administration. A Semitic language related to Hebrew, Aramaic was first used by the Aramaeans (air-uh-MAY-unz), a nomadic people who settled in northern Syria about 1100 B.C. and ruled an area extending into Mesopotamia before succumbing to Assyrian conquest about 725 B.C. The Aramaeans dominated the overland trade routes, which, combined with the simple and easily learned Aramaic alphabet, contributed to the spread of their language. Aramaic facilitated the development of literacy and recordkeeping. Aramaic would become the common language of western Asia for over a thousand years, until Arabic replaced it; Jesus of Nazareth was to be its most famous native speaker.

## The King of Kings

Persia's empire had several weaknesses. First, Cyrus had bequeathed a legacy as a charismatic war leader. Feeling the need to live up to his example, his successors sometimes undertook ambitious and expensive expeditions that failed, such as wars with the Scythians (a tough nomadic people in Ukraine) and the Greeks. Second, however mild Persian rule, however peaceful and prosperous, it was still ruled by foreigners and it still involved taxation. Persian officials, military garrisons, and colonists were found—and were resented—in every corner of the empire. Native resentment, particularly in Egypt, and the independence of certain satraps led to intermittent provincial revolts.

The exaltation of the Persian king served as a counterweight to rebellious tendencies. From Darius on, the Persian monarch tried to overawe his officials with his majesty and might. The "King of Kings," as the monarch called himself, sat on a high, gold and blue throne, dressed in purple, decked out in gold jewelry, wearing fragrant oils and cosmetics, and attended by corps of slaves and eunuchs (castrated men employed in high positions). Although he was not considered a god, he had to be treated with reverence. Persians spoke of the king's *khvarna*, his "kingly glory," a mysterious aura of power. Anyone who came into the royal presence had to approach him with a bow to the ground, face-down.

Impressive as the court ceremonial was, Persian kings were not all-powerful. They were bound by the rule of law and by the considerable power of Persia's proud nobility, on whom they relied to fill the top administrative positions. Competing factions of ministers, wives,

---

*Full Translation of the Behistun Inscription, http://en.wikipedia.org/wiki/Full_translation_of_the_Behistun_Inscription, in turn slightly adapted from L.W. King and R.C. Thompson, *The Sculpture and Inscriptions on the Rock of Behistun in Persia* (British Museum: London, 1907).

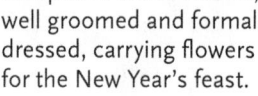

**Frieze at Persepolis**
This sculptured relief lines the stairway to the audience hall of King Darius (r. 521–486 B.C.). It depicts Persian nobles, well groomed and formally dressed, carrying flowers for the New Year's feast.
Ronny Jaques/Photo Researchers, Inc.

concubines, eunuchs, and sons often brought intrigue and discord to court, especially in the fourth century B.C., a time of frequent rebellion.

Royal authority was symbolized in the decoration of the great palaces at Susa and Persepolis, a project begun by Darius I and completed by his son and successor, Xerxes. Craftsmen from as far east as today's Uzbekistan and as far west as today's Turkey took part in the construction of the Susa palace. As Darius proclaims in an inscription, "This palace which I built at Susa, its materials were brought from afar."* The Persepolis palace, too, displayed the heterogeneity of the empire in its architecture. The palace was placed on a terrace, as in Mesopotamia, but contained columned halls as in Egypt, with Assyrian-style column capitals or tops. In Persepolis, a frieze of sculpted relief panels lining a monumental stairway leading to the palace emphasized the king's vast power.

## Zoroastrianism

Like ancient Israel, Persia developed a highly ethical religion in the first millennium B.C. From obscure beginnings, **Zoroastrianism** (zoh-roh-AS-tree-un-izm) became the religion of Persia that persisted until the Muslim conquest in the seventh century A.D. Although largely extinct in today's Iran, an Islamic country, Zoroastrianism survives in small communities elsewhere, primarily in India. Some scholars argue that Zoroastrian beliefs eventually influenced Judaism and Christianity, as well as Roman paganism and Indian Buddhism.

It is easier to describe ancient Zoroastrianism in broad strokes than in detail, partly because the religion changed radically over the course of its ancient history, and partly because relatively little information survives before A.D. 300. This much is clear: The religion was founded by a great reformer and prophet named Zarathustra (*Zoroaster* in Greek). Zarathustra (zah-ruh-THOOS-truh) lived in eastern Iran. His teachings survive in the *Gathas* ("Songs"), a portion of the Zoroastrian holy book called the *Avesta*. Some scholars date Zarathustra as late as 550 B.C.; others prefer an earlier date, 750 or even 1000 B.C.

Zarathustra's society was dominated by warriors whose religion consisted of blood cults, violent gods, animal sacrifice, and ecstatic rituals in which hallucinogens were eaten. Zarathustra rejected such violent practices in favor of an inward-looking, intellectual, and ethical religion. He favored ceremonies involving fire, considered a symbol of purity. Zarathustra was not a strict monotheist like the Jews, but he did emphasize the power of one god over all

**Zoroastrianism**
Religion founded about 1000–550 B.C. by the Persian prophet Zarathustra (*Zoroaster* in Greek). Zoroastrians believe in a supreme deity and a cosmic contest between good and evil within each individual.

*From *The Persian Empire from Cyrus II to Artaxerxes*, translated and edited by Maria Brosius, copyright 2000 London Association of Classical Teachers. Reprinted by permission of L.A.C.T.

people, the supremely good and wise creator of the universe, whom he called Ahura Mazda ("Wise Lord"). Unlike the Jews, Zarathustra considered the problem of evil to be the central question of religion. If god was one, good, and omnipotent, how could evil exist?

Zarathustra's answer might be called *ethical dualism* (dualism is the notion of a grand conflict between good and evil). Ahura Mazda had twin children: the Beneficent Spirit and the Hostile Spirit. Each spirit had made a free choice: one for the "truth" and the other for the "lie"—that is, one for good and the other for evil. Every human being faces a similar choice between good and evil. "Reflect with a clear mind—man by man for himself—upon the two choices of decision, being aware to declare yourselves to Him before the great retribution," says Zarathustra.* Indeed, humanity is caught in a great cosmic struggle in which individuals are free to make a momentous choice. Zarathustra distinguished between two states of being: the spiritual and the material. The more a person pursued spiritual purity, the greater was the person's ability to choose good rather than evil.

Zarathustra held a linear conception of history, similar to that in the Hebrew Bible. His religion is marked by a strong *eschatology* (interest in the end of the world) as well as *soteri-ology* (belief in a savior). He believed that one day, through an ordeal by fire, Ahura Mazda would judge all the people who had ever lived. Those who had chosen good would be rewarded, and those who had chosen evil would be punished. Then would follow a Last Judgment in which the dead would be transfigured and restored to a glorious bodily existence. There would be, Zarathustra promised, "long destruction for the deceitful but salvation for the truthful." The notion of a savior who would initiate the Last Judgment is an early Zoroastrian belief, if perhaps not a doctrine of Zarathustra himself.

It is tempting to attribute Cyrus's policy of toleration to the ethical teachings of Zarathustra, but it is uncertain whether Cyrus was Zoroastrian. We are on firmer ground with later Persian kings, particularly Darius I, who had an image of himself alongside Ahura Mazda carved on the face of an Iranian cliff. In an accompanying inscription, Darius claims the support of Ahura Mazda. (See the feature, "The Global Record: Rebellion, Religion, and Royal Authority in an Empire.")

## SECTION SUMMARY

- Iron arms and armor, engineering skill, organizing ability, and brutality all helped build Assyria's empire, at its height in the 660s B.C.
- The Neo-Babylonian kingdom (626–539 B.C.) was famous for its Hanging Gardens and astronomers.
- Phoenicia's outstanding sailors spread the alphabet and established the great city of Carthage.
- From their homeland in Iran, the Persians built the ancient world's largest empire yet, the Achaemenid Empire (ca. 550–330 B.C.).
- Rather than try to "Persianize" the empire, the Persian kings emphasized the variety of peoples under their rule.
- Zoroastrianism, an ethical religion emphasizing the struggle between good and evil, flourished in Achaemenid Persia.

# Israel, ca. 1500–400 B.C.

*What was the religious experience of ancient Israel, and what is its legacy today?*

In the first millennium B.C., a small, often-conquered people turned imperialism on its head. Human achievement is meaningless, they argued; only the power of divinity matters. There is only one god, they said; all other gods are false. The one true god had revealed himself not to the awesome, imperialistic Assyrians, but to the less powerful Hebrews—ancient Jews. They founded the Western tradition of religion. The God of ancient Israel eventually gave rise to the God of Christianity and of Islam, as well as of modern Judaism.

The Hebrews, also known as Israelites, had existed as a people since about 1200 B.C. and perhaps for centuries earlier. They spoke a Semitic language.

## The Hebrew Bible as a Historical Record

As literature and as religious teaching, the Bible is the most influential single text in the history of Western civilization. As a source of history, however, it presents difficulties. Many

---

*S. Insler, *The Gathas of Zarathustra: Acta Iranica*, 8 (Leiden: E.J. Brill, 1975), p. 33.

## Rebellion, Religion, and Royal Authority in an Empire

*In the famous Behistun Inscription, carved on a cliff side in western Iran ca. 500 B.C., King Darius proclaims his power and piety. It was inscribed in three languages—Old Persian, Elamite, and Babylonian—to reach the diverse audience of a multicultural empire.*

**(1)** I am Darius, the great king, king of kings, the king of Persia, the king of the provinces, the son of Hystaspes, the grandson of Arsames, the Achaemenid.

**(6)** King Darius says: These are the provinces which are subject unto me, and by the grace of Ahura Mazda I became king of them: Persia, Susiana, Babylonia, Assyria, Arabia, Egypt, the countries by the Sea, Lydia, the Greeks, Media, Armenia, Cappadocia, Parthia, Drangiana, Aria, Chorasmia, Bactria, Sogdiana, Gandara, Scythia, Sattagydia, Arachosia and Maka; twenty-three lands in all.

**(7)** King Darius says: These are the provinces which are subject to me; by the grace of Ahura Mazda they became subject to me; they brought tribute unto me. Whatsoever commands have been laid on them by me, by night or by day, have been performed by them.

**(8)** King Darius says: Within these lands, whosoever was a friend, him have I surely protected; whosoever was hostile, him have I utterly destroyed. By the grace of Ahura Mazda these lands have conformed to my decrees; as it was commanded unto them by me, so was it done.

**(9)** King Darius says: Ahura Mazda has granted unto me this empire. Ahura Mazda brought me help, until I gained this empire; by the grace of Ahura Mazda do I hold this empire.

**(16)** King Darius says: . . . . And a certain Babylonian named Nidintu-Bêl, the son of Aniri, raised a rebellion in Babylon: he lied to the people, saying: "I am Nebuchadnezzar, the son of Nabonidus." Then did all the province of Babylonia go over to Nidintu-Bêl, and Babylonia rose in rebellion. He seized on the kingdom of Babylonia.

**(18)** King Darius says: Then I marched against that Nidintu-Bêl, who was Nebuchadnezzar. The army of Nidintu-Bêl held the Tigris; there they were posted, and they also had ships. Then I divided the army; some I made riders of camels, for the rest I led forward horses. Ahura Mazda brought me help; by the grace of Ahura Mazda we crossed the Tigris. Then did I utterly overthrow that host of Nidintu-Bêl.

**(19)** [Darius describes victory in battle.]

**(20)** King Darius says: Then did Nidintu-Bêl flee with a few horsemen into Babylon. Thereupon I marched to Babylon. By the grace of Ahura Mazda I took Babylon, and captured Nidintu-Bêl. Then I slew that Nidintu-Bêl in Babylon.

**(52)** King Darius says: This is what I have done. By the grace of Ahura Mazda have I always acted. After I became king, I fought nineteen battles and by the grace of Ahura Mazda I overthrew nine kings and I made them captive.

**(63)** King Darius says: On this account Ahura Mazda brought me help, and all the other gods, all that there are, because I was not wicked, nor was I a liar, nor was I a tyranny, neither I nor any of my family. I have ruled according to righteousness. Whosoever helped my house, him I favored; he who was hostile, him I destroyed.

**(64)** King Darius says: You who may be king hereafter, whosoever shall be a liar or a rebel, or shall not be friendly, destroy him!

### Questions

1. *What does Darius consider to be special signs that heaven favored him? Why does he say he deserves that favor?*

2. *What signs of his prowess does Darius offer? Of his virtue?*

3. *Why does Darius emphasize lies and lying?*

---

Slightly adapted from L.W. King and R.C. Thompson, eds., *The Sculpture and Inscriptions on the Rock of Behistun in Persia* (London: British Museum, 1907).

---

Jews and Christians today believe that God gave the Hebrew Bible (called the Old Testament by Christians) in its entirety to the Jewish people at Mt. Sinai. In addition, Jews believe that unwritten laws were handed down at Sinai as well, and that these laws were preserved via oral tradition across the generations. Some scholars argue differently. They consider the Hebrew Bible man-made and based on written sources probably dating back at least as far as the early Israelite monarchy of about 1000 B.C. Archaeological evidence from the area of ancient Israel; a small number of inscriptions, that is, writings on stone or other durable material (almost all after 800 B.C.); and some information in Greek and Roman literary sources provide an alternative source of information, but it is limited and imperfect.

The Hebrew Bible reached something close to its current form a century or two before the birth of Christ. It consists of three main sections: (1) the **Torah** (TOE-rah), also known as the Pentateuch, or five books of Moses (that is, the first five books of the Bible); (2) the Prophets,

**Torah** First five books of the Bible. Accepted as sacred by the Hebrews around 425 B.C., it relates the working out of God's pact, or covenant, with the Hebrews, his chosen people.

**Israelite Seal** This seal stone, which shows a roaring lion, was used by a man named Shema, an official of King Jeroboam II of Israel (r. 784–748 B.C.). The stone was used to make an impression in hot wax, creating a seal on a document. Reuben and Edith Hecht Collection, University of Haifa, Israel/Erich Lessing/Art Resource, NY

**covenant** As told in the Hebrew Bible, the pact God made with Abraham, the first patriarch of Israel. In return for the land of Canaan and the promise of becoming a great nation, the Israelites agreed to worship no other gods.

**Israelites** People who settled on the eastern shore of the Mediterranean around 1200 B.C., or perhaps earlier. Their belief in one God directly influenced the faith of Christians, Muslims, and modern Jews.

that is, the "historical" books of the early prophets (Joshua, Judges, Kings, and Chronicles) and the books of the later prophets (Isaiah, Jeremiah, Ezekiel, and the twelve "minor prophets"); and (3) the Writings, various books of poetry, proverbs, and wisdom literature.

The books of the Hebrew (and Christian) Bible are canonical: one by one, each was accepted by established authority as sacred. The introduction of the Torah (literally, "teaching") made its followers into what they have been ever since: "a people of the Book," as the Muslims would put it centuries later. The written tradition and literacy became central to the Hebrews.

The Hebrews are the first people we know of to have a single national history book. That book was written not as secular history but as sacred history. It is the story of the working-out of God's pact, or **covenant**, with the Hebrews, his chosen people. All ancient peoples told stories of their semidivine foundation. Only the Hebrews imagined the nation created by an actual treaty between the people and their God.

The central fact of human existence in the Hebrew Bible is God's covenant with the Hebrews. Because of the covenant, history has meaning. History is the story of the success or failure of the Hebrew people in carrying out God's commandments. The focus is on the individual: on individual people taking actions that have not just moral but also military and political consequences that unfold over time.

Many of the themes, narrative details, and styles of writing in the Hebrew Bible derive from earlier cultures. The biblical Flood story, for example, seems to have been modeled on a similar flood in the *Epic of Gilgamesh* (see page 18). Biblical poems in praise of God are often similar to Egyptian poems in praise of pagan gods, and biblical wisdom literature (that is, works containing proverbs and rules of conduct) often recalls Egyptian or Babylonian parallels. In spite of such borrowings, the Hebrew Bible is dramatically different from its predecessors because it subordinates everything to one central theme: God's plan for humanity and, in particular, for his chosen people—the Hebrews.

## The Emergence of Hebrew Monotheism, ca. 1500–600 B.C.

We first hear of the Hebrews, outside of the Bible, in an inscribed monument of the New Kingdom Egyptian pharaoh Merneptah (r. 1224–1214 B.C.). After a military expedition into Canaan (CAY-nan), pharaoh declared triumphantly that "Israel is laid waste." Most scholars accept this as evidence of an Israelite presence in Canaan, but the question is, how did they get there? The Bible says that the **Israelites** settled Palestine by conquering its earlier inhabitants. Most scholars now reject that account. Archaeological evidence suggests, rather, a more complex process. The Israelites, it seems, were a combination of three groups: armed conquerors, shepherds who gradually entered the country and later settled down to farming, and dispossessed and oppressed Canaanites who rebelled against their masters.

From such sources, the Israelites may have emerged. The Bible, however, tells a different story of Israelite origins. Although much of it is credible, none of it is confirmed by nonbiblical sources. Still, the biblical story of Israelite origins has been so influential in later Western culture that we must examine it. If one follows the Bible, Hebrew history began sometime during the period 2000 to 1500 B.C., with the patriarchs, or founding fathers. Abraham, the first patriarch, migrated to Canaan from the city of Haran in northern Mesopotamia. A seminomadic chieftain, Abraham settled on territory north and west of the Dead Sea, where he grazed his herds. Seminomadic clans in the region frequently made long migrations in antiquity, so the biblical account of Abraham and his descendants, Isaac and Jacob, is plausible.

The Bible, however, emphasizes the implausible: Abraham's extraordinary decision to give up Mesopotamian polytheism for belief in one god. This god commanded Abraham to leave Haran; indeed, he made a treaty, or covenant, with Abraham. In return for Abraham's faith, said the god, "As a possession for all time I shall give you and your descendants after you the land in which you are now aliens, the whole of Canaan, and I shall be their God" (Genesis 17:8). Abraham was not a strict monotheist: Although he worshiped only one god, he did not deny the existence of other gods. (See, for a comparison, the discussion of Akhenaten on pages 25–26.) Nevertheless, he took a giant step on the road to pure monotheism by coming to believe that only one god rules *all* peoples.

According to the Bible, the next important step took place several hundred years later. In a time of famine in Canaan, many of Abraham's descendants left for prosperous Egypt. At first, they thrived there, but in time, they were enslaved and forced to build cities in the Nile Delta. Eventually, Moses, a divinely appointed leader, released the Hebrews from bondage in Egypt and led them back toward Canaan and freedom. Again, this is the Biblical version.

The Exodus ("journey out," in Greek), as this movement has been called, is a rare example of a successful national liberation movement in antiquity. Among those who accept its historicity, a date in the thirteenth century B.C. is frequently assigned to the Exodus. According to the Bible, the Exodus marked the key moment of another covenant, this time between the god of Abraham and the entire Israelite people. At Mount Sinai (SYE-nye), traditionally located on the rugged Sinai Peninsula between Egypt and Palestine, the Israelites are said to have first accepted as their one god a deity whose name is represented in Hebrew by the letters corresponding to YHWH. YHWH is traditionally rendered in English as "Jehovah," but "Yahweh" is more likely to be accurate. The Israelites accepted Yahweh's laws, summarized by the Ten Commandments. In return for obedience to Yahweh's commandments, they would be God's chosen people, his "special possession; . . . a kingdom of priests, . . . [his] holy nation."*

The Ten Commandments are both more general and more personal than the laws of Hammurabi's Code. They are addressed to the individual, whom they commit to a universal standard. They emphasize prohibitions, saying more about what one should *not* do than about what one should do. The first three commandments establish Yahweh as the sole god of Israel, prohibit any sculpture or image of God, and forbid misuse of the divine name. The next two commandments are injunctions to observe the seventh day of the week (the Sabbath) as a day free of work and to honor one's parents. The sixth and seventh prohibit destructive or violent acts against neighbors, in particular adultery and killing. The final three commandments regulate community life by prohibiting stealing, testifying falsely, and coveting another man's wife or goods. In contrast to the starkness of the Ten Commandments, an enormous amount of detailed legal material is also found in the Hebrew Bible.

Many scholars doubt whether Hebrew monotheism emerged as early as the thirteenth century. In any case, the Bible makes clear that many ordinary Hebrews remained unconvinced. For centuries afterward, many Israelite worshipers deemed Yahweh their greatest god but not their only god. Unready for the radical innovation that monotheism represented, they carried out the rituals of various Canaanite deities, whom they worshiped on hilltop altars. Forging a national consensus for monotheism took centuries.

From the thirteenth to the late eleventh century B.C., the Hebrews were governed by a series of tribal leaders, referred to as "judges" in the Bible, but eventually the military threat posed by the Philistines (FILL-uh-steenz) persuaded the tribes to accept a centralized monarchy. The Philistines were one of the Sea Peoples, those raiders and invaders who beset the eastern Mediterranean in the Late Bronze Age. The Philistines had settled on the Palestinian coast, where they prospered and eventually, seriously endangered Israel. The first Israelite king, Saul (r. ca. 1020–1004 B.C.), had some success against them but eventually fell in battle along with his son, Jonathan. The next king, David (r. 1004–965 B.C.), a former mercenary captain for the Philistines, defeated them decisively.

A recent discovery may provide archaeological evidence of the early Israelite monarchy. A fortress near Jerusalem provides the earliest example of Hebrew script yet discovered, dating from about 1050–970 B.C. The text contains the words "judge," "slave," and "king." It was written in ink on a piece of pottery. The work of a trained scribe, it might be a legal text, although further study is needed to be sure.

David was Israel's greatest king. He extended the kingdom into parts of modern Jordan, Lebanon, and Syria and conquered the Canaanite city of Jerusalem, which he made Israel's capital. David's son and successor, Solomon (r. 965–928 B.C.), was also a great king. His most famous accomplishment was the construction of the magnificent Temple in Jerusalem. The Temple priesthood and sacrifices became the focus of the national cult of Yahweh.

**monotheism** Belief that there is only one God. The Hebrew Bible places this belief as originating about 2000–1500 B.C., when God commanded Abraham to give up Mesopotamian polytheism for belief in one God.

**Ten Commandments** According to the Hebrew Bible, these ten basic ethical and religious rules were given by God to Moses and the Israelites at Mt. Sinai. They have played an immensely influential role in Judaism and Christianity.

---

*From *The Oxford Study Bible: Revised English Bible with the Apocrypha* (New York: Oxford University Press, 1992), p. 474.

🌐 **Map 2.2  Ancient Israel**  The Israelites settled in the Canaanite hill country west of the Jordan River and the Dead Sea after 1200 B.C. (*top map*). Control of Israelite territory after 928 B.C. was shared by two monarchies (*bottom map*): the kingdoms of Israel (conquered by the Assyrians in 722 B.C.) and Judah (conquered by the Babylonians in 598 B.C.). © Cengage Learning 2014

Previously, that focus had been a humble, movable wooden chest, encased in gold, known as the Ark of the Covenant, and containing the stone tablets of the ten commandments.

Solomon's reign represented the high-water mark of the power of the Israelite monarchy. Under his successors, the monarchy was split into a large northern kingdom of Israel with a capital at Samaria and a smaller southern kingdom of Judah (JOO-duh) centered on Jerusalem (see **Map 2.2**). In 722 B.C., the Assyrians conquered the kingdom of Israel and deported its inhabitants. Judah survived, first as a state controlled by Assyria, and then as an independent power.

The religious history of the period of the two kingdoms (928–722 B.C.) and the Judean survivor-state (722–587 B.C.) is marked by an intense drive toward monotheism. The kings of Judah in the seventh century B.C. aggressively attacked the worship of all gods other than Yahweh and all centers of Yahweh worship other than the Temple in Jerusalem. The kings also began the process of canonizing the Hebrew Bible.

The Judean kings could not have succeeded without the help of the prophets, who were prominent from approximately 900 to 500 B.C. Seers, uttering divinely inspired predictions, were universal figures in ancient religion. No other culture of antiquity, however, has anything like the Hebrew prophets: charismatic, uncompromising, terrible figures who announced God's anger and ultimate forgiveness. The prophets remind us of the most radical spiritual teachings of Israel: absolute monotheism, an insistence on righteousness, contempt for materialism and worldly power, love of the powerless. They often supported the kings but did not shrink from confronting authority and insisting on uncompromising justice. Among them were Amos, a humble shepherd who preached the superiority of righteousness to ritual; Jeremiah, who prophesied the destruction of Jerusalem as punishment for the people's idolatry; and Isaiah, who predicted the coming of a savior who would inaugurate a new day of universal peace and justice.

A characteristic story of the prophets is the confrontation between Elijah, perhaps the most famous prophet, and Ahab, king of Israel (r. 871–852 B.C.). Ahab coveted the vineyard of one Naboth, but Naboth refused Ahab's offer to buy it. Spurred on by his wife, Jezebel, Ahab trumped up charges against Naboth, who was unjustly stoned to death. Ahab then confiscated the vineyard. God sent Elijah to declare to Ahab that, as punishment for committing murder, "dogs will lick [Ahab's] blood" and that of his family (1 Kings 21:19). In a remarkable scene, we witness not only Elijah's courage in confronting the king but also the king's surrender and repentance before Elijah's spiritual authority. The Western tradition of civil disobedience owes much to the courage of the Hebrew prophets.

## Exile and Return, 598–ca. 400 B.C.

The prophets taught the people of Judah how to survive. They correctly predicted ruin and exile and the promise that divine providence would guarantee return. The Judeans clung to this message with remarkable tenacity. Indeed, they had to, for between 598 and 586 B.C., the Neo-Babylonians conquered Judah, destroying Jerusalem and the Temple. The cultural, political, and economic elite were deported eastward to Babylon. Those who could do so fled for safety in the opposite direction, westward to Egypt. The dispirited remnant in Palestine shared their land with colonists from neighboring regions, with whom they intermarried and among whom their religion all but disappeared.

And that, given the usual fate of exiled and uprooted peoples in antiquity, should have been that. Yet, not only did the Judeans in the Babylonian Captivity persevere in their religious loyalty; they actually returned to Palestine in large numbers.

The Neo-Babylonian rulers allowed Judean deportees to continue to practice their religion. Judeans in Babylon were not slaves; rather they rented land on royal estates, and some became prosperous. Although some Babylonian Judeans assimilated to local ways, many continued a Judean religious life. Communal worship was observed in open places, perhaps with associated buildings. Some scholars argue that synagogues ("gatherings" in Greek), modest centers of prayer and study that have been the focus of Jewish worship ever since, first emerged in Babylon. It is also possible that the exiles put together the Torah in something like its current form. Elders led the community, while prophets continued to speak out: Two examples are Ezekiel, who preached the restoration of the Temple, and the man known to us only as "Second Isaiah" (Isaiah 40–66). Second Isaiah emphasized the universal aspect of the god of Israel, who made empires rise and fall and would bring the exiles home from far-off Babylon.

The Temple in Jerusalem was rebuilt around 515 B.C., only seventy years after its destruction. This remarkable turn of events was possible partly because of the Persians, who conquered Babylon in 539 B.C. According to the Hebrew Bible, Cyrus proclaimed the freedom of the Jews to "go up to Jerusalem in Judah, and build the house of the Lord the God of Israel, the God who is in Jerusalem."

Second Isaiah's message points to a second important development among the exiles of Judah. As striking as the return to Palestine was the survival of large numbers of Judeans as an unassimilated people outside of Judah—in other words, as Jews. The terms *Jew* and *Jewish* began to be used in the fifth century B.C. For the first time, membership in a community of worship was divorced from residence. Jewish communities flourished in Babylon, Persia, and Egypt, but the members often chose not to become Babylonians, Persians, or Egyptians. From the sixth century B.C. on, a majority of Jews were living outside Palestine, and the Jewish Exile, or Diaspora ("dispersion"), became a permanent fact of history.

## The People of the Covenant

Equality, limited government, and the rule of law under God were basic Israelite political principles. Eventually, they would become fundamental political ideals for many in the West, and they would be applied not only to Israelites but also to all people.

According to Israelite belief, God made humans in his own image. Thus, all individuals were equal in a fundamental sense; all were bound by God's law. A king who disobeyed this law was illegitimate. Indeed, Israel was ambivalent at best about the institution of kingship, which was tolerated as an evil made necessary only by the country's many armed enemies. God's covenant with the Hebrews was a religious contract with political consequences, rendering God the only true king of Israel. Far from being gods themselves, or even God's representatives, Israel's kings were merely God's humble servants.

Israelite egalitarianism was restricted to men. Israelite women usually could not own or inherit property, as women could in Hammurabi's Babylon; or sue in court, as women could in pharaonic Egypt; or initiate a divorce, as women could in Classical Athens (see page 70). The powerful goddesses of other ancient cultures were absent in Israel. Women participated in the rituals of early Israelite religion and the original Temple (ca. 940–586 B.C.) but were segregated in a separate women's courtyard in the rebuilt Temple (ca. 515 B.C.–A.D. 79) and kept out of Temple ritual. Indeed, the perspective of the Hebrew Bible is predominantly male. Consider just two examples. First, of the 1,426 names in the Hebrew Bible, 1,315 are

## The Siege of Lachish

From the distance, it looks like one of the foothills that surround it. Up close, though, it can be clearly seen for what it is: Tel Lachish (LAH-kish), the mound of the biblical city of Lachish. It is a link in the chain of evidence that tells one of the most remarkable stories in biblical history.*

Lachish was a great city, a royal fortress, and second only to Jerusalem in its importance to the kingdom of Judah (928–587 B.C.). In 701 B.C., the Assyrians under King Sennacherib (r. 704–681 B.C.) besieged Lachish and took it by force. A wealth of independent sources documents the siege. In addition to reports in the Hebrew Bible are many Assyrian written documents. Furthermore, Sennacherib (seh-NAH-keh-rib) commemorated his victory with carved reliefs erected in his royal palace at Nineveh. Finally, the mound itself has been excavated.

Originally a Canaanite town, Lachish was fortified by the Israelite kings because of its strategic location between the Judean hills and the Philistine coast (see **Map 2.2**). By the reign of King Hezekiah of Judah (r. 715–686 B.C.), Lachish was a large garrison city constructed on a monumental scale.

Hezekiah joined Egypt and the Philistine cities in a revolt soon after Sennacherib came to the throne in 704 B.C. Sennacherib responded by attacking in 701. The Hebrew Bible states: "In the fourteenth year of the reign of Hezekiah, Sennacherib king of Assyria attacked and took all the fortified cities of Judah" (2 Kings 18:13). We can read the results of the campaign in one of Sennacherib's inscriptions:

*Discussion in David Ussishkin, *The Conquest of Lachish by Sennacherib* (Tel-Aviv: Tel-Aviv University, Institute of Archaeology), 1982.

© Institute of Archaeology of Tel Aviv University

**Artist's Reconstruction of an Assyrian Assault on Lachish**

"As to Hezekiah, the Jew, he did not submit to my yoke. I laid siege to 46 of his strong cities, walled forts and to the countless small villages in their vicinity, and conquered (them) by means of well-stamped (earth-) ramps, and battering-rams brought (thus) near (to the walls) (combined with) the attack by foot-soldiers, (using) mines, breeches as well as sapper work [that is, digging away foundations]." Bowing to Assyrian power, Hezekiah gave up territory (though not Jerusalem) and agreed to an increase in tribute.

The Lachish reliefs (in Sennacherib's palace) offer a vivid picture of the attack on the city. Lachish was well fortified and well defended, but the Assyrians were experts in taking cities by storm. The reliefs show the camp of the

male; only 111 women's names appear, about 9 percent of the total.* Second, only men and boys can bear the sign of the Lord's covenant with Israel—that is, circumcision.

Nevertheless, Israelite women claimed honor as mothers and partners in running the household. The Hebrew Bible states that woman (as exemplified by Eve, the first woman) was created as "a suitable partner" for man (Genesis 2:18, 20). Reproduction and hence motherhood assume great importance in the Hebrew Bible; the Lord enjoins humans to "be fruitful and multiply" (Genesis 1:28). The Bible also commands that children honor both their father and their mother: The two parents are equal in parental authority (Exodus 20:12).

The Hebrew Bible sometimes displays sympathy for and insights into the strategies that women used to counter the abuses of male power. Rebecca, for instance, thwarts her husband Isaac's plan to give his blessing to their son Esau. As the eldest, Esau was entitled to this honor, but Rebecca preferred her younger son Jacob, and she saw to it that he and not Esau obtained her husband's blessing.

Only about a half dozen women in the Hebrew Bible served as leaders of Israel, but that is more than in the literature of most other ancient cultures. Deborah (ca. 1125 B.C.),

*Carol L. Meyers, "Everyday Life: Women in the Period of the Hebrew Bible," in *The Women's Bible* Commentary, ed. Carol A. Newsom and Sharon H. Ringe (Louisville, KY.: Westminster/John Knox Press, 1992), p. 245.

British Museum/Erich Lessing/Art Resource, NY

**Detail of the Assyrian Conquest of Lachish, a Relief from the Palace of Sennacherib**

evidently civilians killed during the attack and then buried in mass graves.

The Lachish reliefs also depict rows of captives and deportees marching toward Sennacherib on his throne. Look at this detail of the relief, showing a large Judean family leaving Lachish for exile. They are allowed to bring cattle with them, and a woman and child are permitted to ride on a wagon. The Assyrians claimed to have deported 200,150 people from Judah, of whom many men ended up as slave laborers working on Sennacherib's palace.

As for Lachish, it was burned to the ground, as the excavations confirm. Sometime in the seventh century the city was restored, but it was destroyed again in 598 B.C., during the first of two military campaigns in Judah by Nebuchadrezzar, the Neo-Babylonian king. The city's misfortune has proved illuminating to students of the past.

## Questions

1. What makes the evidence for the siege of Lachish unique in biblical history?

2. What are the various sources of evidence for the siege of Lachish?

3. Why was the city of Lachish so important to the kingdom of Judah?

4. What do we learn about the siege of Lachish from the Assyrian Lachish Reliefs?

5. What information about the siege of Lachish does archaeology at Tel Lachish reveal?

attackers, Assyrian archers and slingers advancing on the city, battering rams and siege engines in action against the walls, flaming chariots thrown down by the defenders, and, after the city was taken, captives impaled on sharp stakes.

Look at the artist's reconstruction of an Assyrian assault on the city, based on the archaeological evidence. The soldiers are climbing a massive siege ramp that the Assyrians built against a "vulnerable" point in the city walls. The excavators of Lachish found the ramp, the oldest siege ramp so far discovered in the ancient world. In and around the city was other evidence of the battle: hundreds of arrowheads, many sling stones, a number of pieces of bronze sheet mail used in armor, and what may be the crest of a helmet worn by one of the Assyrian spearmen shown attacking the city walls in the Lachish reliefs. Most dramatic, the excavators discovered about seven hundred skeletons,

for example, a charismatic Israelite prophet, organizes an army that destroys the forces of a Canaanite commander. In a later book, Esther, a Hebrew woman, becomes the wife of a Persian king whom the Bible calls Ahasuerus (probably Xerxes, r. 485–465 B.C.). Esther works ferociously at the Persian court to defeat a conspiracy to wipe out her people, and she saves them. The Book of Ruth (date uncertain) tells the story of a selfless and loyal woman, Ruth, who rescues her mother-in-law, Naomi, from ruin and poverty. The Bible celebrates Ruth as Naomi's "devoted daughter-in-law, who has proved better to you [Naomi] than seven sons." (See the feature, "The Written Record: Ruth" on page 46.)

Israelite culture prized women for their cunning, courage, and perseverance—qualities that allowed the people to survive. Military prowess was highly valued in men, but their inner qualities were appreciated as well. Schooled in defeat and exile, many Israelites came to the conclusion that "wisdom is better than weapons of war" (Ecclesiastes 9:18). Thus, the Hebrew Bible stresses God's primary interest in goodness of soul: "The Lord does not see as man sees; men judge by appearances, but the Lord judges by the heart" (1 Samuel 16:7). The God of Israel prized righteousness above wealth, might, sacrifice, and ritual.

One might say that Israelite law reflected a similar tension between power and righteousness. On the one hand, just as the God of Israel was omnipotent and jealous, so the law

45

## Ruth

*Some parts of the Hebrew Bible prohibit intermarriage. The Book of Ruth, however, praises marriage between modern Judean men and women from neighboring Moab (modern Jordan; see Map 2.2). This excerpt illustrates such unions, as it does the problem of food shortages, which were a special burden for widows.*

Once, in the time of the Judges when there was a famine in the land, a man [Elimelech] from Bethlehem in Judah went with his wife [Naomi] to live in Moabite territory....

Elimelech died, and Naomi was left a widow with her two sons. The sons married Moabite women, one of whom was called Orpah and the other Ruth. [After ten years the sons died.] ... Then Naomi, bereaved of her two sons as well as of her husband, got ready to return to her own country with her daughters-in-law, because she had heard in Moab that the Lord had shown his care for his people by giving them food. Accompanied by her two daughters-in-law she left the place where she had been living and they took the road leading back to Judah.

Naomi said to her daughters-in-law, "Go back, both of you, home to your own mothers. May the Lord keep faith with you, as you have kept faith with the dead and with me; and may he grant each of you the security of a home with a new husband." And she kissed them goodbye. They wept aloud and said, "No, we shall return with you to your people." But Naomi insisted, "Go back, my daughters, go; for I am too old to marry again. But if I could say that I had hope of a child, even if I were to be married tonight and were to bear sons, would you, then, wait until they grew up? Would you on their account remain unmarried? No, my daughters! For your sakes I feel bitter that the Lord has inflicted such misfortune on me." At this they wept still more. Then Orpah kissed her mother-in-law and took her leave, but Ruth clung to her.

"Look," said Naomi, "your sister-in-law has gone back to her people and her God. Go, follow her." Ruth answered, "Do not urge me to go back and desert you. Where you go, I shall go, and where you stay, I shall stay. Your people will be my people, and your God my God. Where you die, I shall die, and there be buried. I solemnly declare before the Lord that nothing but death will part me from you." When Naomi saw that Ruth was determined to go with her, she said no more.

[They returned to Naomi's hometown, Bethlehem, in Judah.]

Naomi had a relative on her husband's side, a prominent and well-to-do ... [man named] Boaz. One day Ruth the Moabite asked Naomi, "May I go to the harvest fields and glean [collect excess grain] behind anyone who will allow me?" "Yes, go my daughter," she replied. So Ruth went gleaning in the fields behind the reapers. [She met Boaz in his fields.] ...

Boaz said to Ruth, "Listen, my daughter: do not go to glean in any other field. Do not look any farther, but stay close to my servant-girls. Watch where the men reap, and follow the gleaners; I have told the men not to molest you. Any time you are thirsty, go and drink from the jars they have filled." She bowed to the ground and said, "Why are you so kind as to take notice of me, when I am just a foreigner?" Boaz answered, "I have been told the whole story of what you have done for your mother-in-law since the death of your husband, how you left father and mother and homeland and came among a people you didn't know before. The Lord reward you for what you have done. ..."

[Eventually, Boaz marries Ruth; their great grandson would be Israel's greatest king, David.]

### Questions

1. *In this excerpt, what are the various ways in which people cope with hunger and famine?*

2. *Why does Ruth, a foreign widow, stay with her mother-in-law and go to Judah?*

3. *Why does Boaz admire and eventually marry Ruth?*

Revised English Bible © 1989 by Oxford University Press and Cambridge University Press. Reprinted by permission of Oxford University Press.

## SECTION SUMMARY

- The Bible, including the Hebrew Bible (called Old Testament by Christians) and the Christian New Testament, is the single most influential text in Western civilization.
- The central theme of the Hebrew Bible is God's covenant with his chosen people—the Hebrews.
- Hebrew monotheism evolved between the 1200s and 600 B.C. with tribal leaders, kings, and prophets each playing a major role.
- Jews, deported to Babylon after 598 B.C., maintained their religion and some returned home after the Persians conquered Babylon in 539 B.C.
- Equality, limited government, and the rule of law under God were Israelite political notions that have greatly influenced the later West.

of Israel was meant to be comprehensive and forceful. Capital punishment existed for murder, rape, incorrigible rebelliousness of a son against his parents, adultery by a married woman (both she and her lover were to be executed), a woman's loss of her virginity before marriage, and other offenses. Harsh punishment was mandated for Canaanite towns taken by siege: The entire population was to be killed so as not to corrupt Israel with their religious practices.

On the other hand, by taking intention into account, Israelite law echoed a note already present in Mesopotamia. The so-called Law of the Goring Ox, for instance, allowed a person to go unpunished for owning an ox that gores a person to death, unless the owner knew beforehand that the animal was dangerous. If the owner did know, however, the owner had to be put to death. Israelite law, moreover, demonstrated a belief in the sanctity of human life by prohibiting human sacrifice. An Israelite had to be ready in his or her heart (but *only* in his or her heart) to sacrifice his or her child to Yahweh, as Abraham was willing to sacrifice Isaac when Yahweh so commanded. After ascertaining Abraham's willingness to obey, even to the point of sacrificing his son, Yahweh freed Isaac from the altar and supplied a ram as a substitute offering. Israelite monotheism thus broke with its Canaanite neighbors and rejected human sacrifice, as did the religions later derived from it.

## Chapter Summary

◆ *Who were the Phoenicians and what did they contribute to Western civilization?*

The first half of the first millennium B.C. witnessed dramatic developments among both the ancestors of the West and its founders. The Phoenicians in the Canaanite city-states created trading networks and spread colonies across the entire length of the Mediterranean Sea. The ships of these great sailors circled Africa and reached faraway Britain. Closer to home, they influenced the culture of Greece, to which they introduced the alphabet, borrowed from an earlier Canaanite city, Ugarit. The Greek alphabet, derived from the Phoenician alphabet, in turn, led to the Roman alphabet, the basis of the English alphabet today.

◆ *What made the first-millennium B.C. empires of the Assyrians, Neo-Babylonians, and Persians so much more effective than earlier empires?*

A new form of empire appeared. New military technology, the frank adoption of brutal and inhumane methods, and improvements in administration led to the creation of the Assyrian Empire, stretching from western Iran to Palestine and briefly even to Egypt. After short-lived hegemonies by Neo-Babylonians and Medes, the Persians established an empire that was larger, better organized, and more tolerant than the empire of the Assyrians. Multi-ethnic, far-flung, and claiming to be universal, such an empire would one day be brought into the Western tradition of Rome.

◆ *What was the religious experience of ancient Israel, and what is its legacy today?*

The most important developments of the era, however, were not in commerce, weaponry, or imperialism, but in new conceptions of the nature and meaning of human life. Persia developed the highly ethical religion of Zoroastrianism. More important for the West were the Israelites. They conquered Palestine and, even after losing it, held on to their identity by means of a tenacious belief in one god. They broke with tradition by insisting that their god was merciful and just. Omnipotent, God gave history meaning and direction. The purpose of life, in the Israelite view, was to serve God by acting righteously. The new religion laid the foundation for Judaism as well as Christianity and Islam. The Jews wrote down their religious and historical traditions in a book that, along with the Christian New Testament, proved to be the most influential single text in the history of the West: the Hebrew Bible.

## Key Terms

Ugarit (p. 30)

alphabet (p. 30)

**Phoenicians** (p. 31)

**Assyrians** (p. 33)

**Neo-Babylonians** (p. 34)

**Persian Empire** (p. 35)

**Zoroastrianism** (p. 37)

**Torah** (p. 39)

**covenant** (p. 40)

**Israelites** (p. 40)

**monotheism** (p. 41)

**Ten Commandments** (p. 41)

CourseMate

Go to the CourseMate website at www.cengagebrain.com for additional study tools and review materials—including audio and video clips—for this chapter.

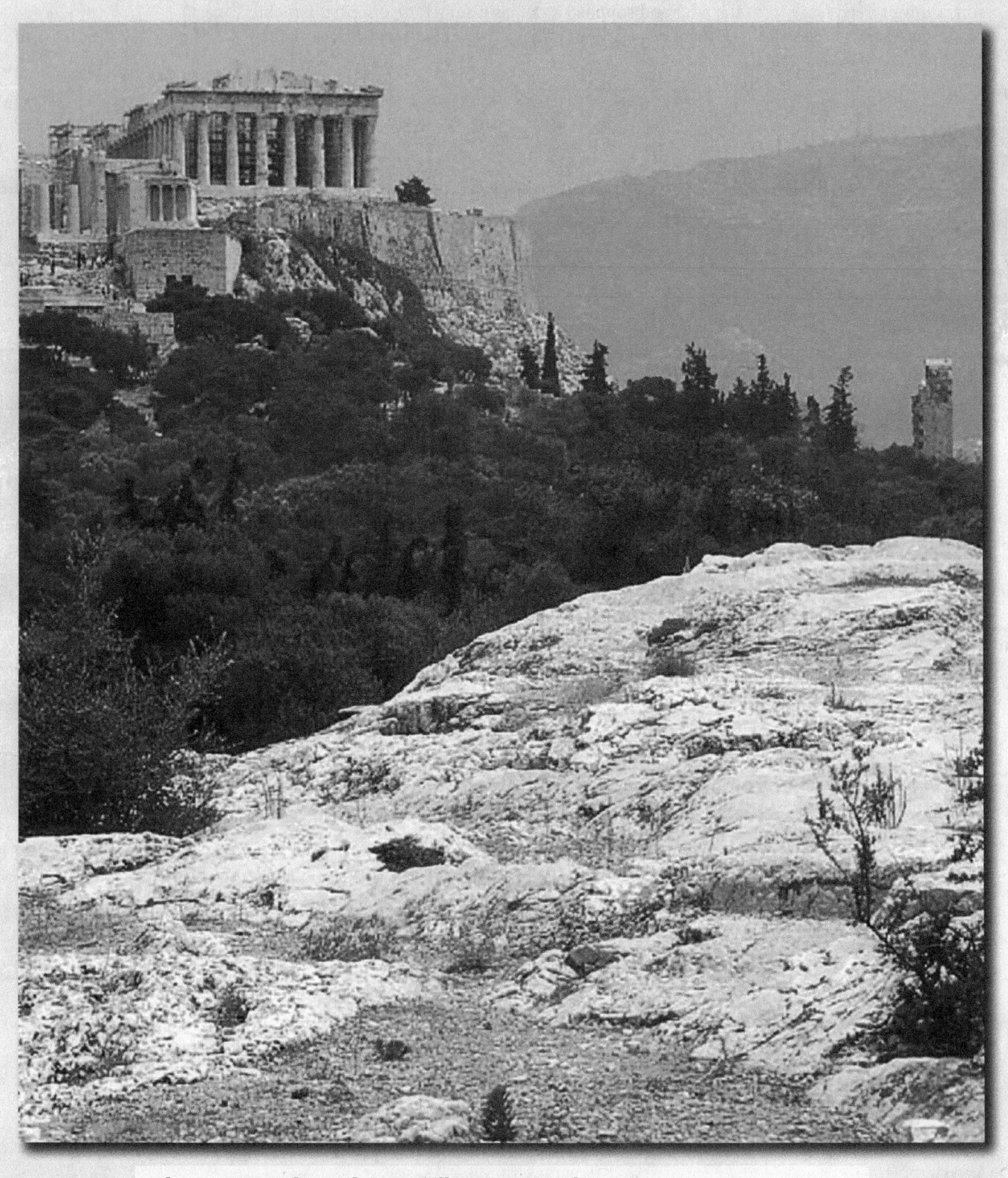

**Athenian Acropolis, with Pnyx Hill in Foreground** Julia M. Fair

# The Greeks in the Polis to ca. 350 B.C.

It is dawn. The light reveals a hillside in the city of Athens, a natural auditorium. Its rocky slopes, visible in the photograph opposite, would have been covered, beginning about 500 B.C., with wooden benches facing a platform cut into the rock. The six thousand men gathered there constitute a diverse group, ranging from farmers to philosophers, from dockyard workers to aristocrats. As they take their seats, these, the citizens of Athens, watch priests conducting prayers and offering a sacrifice. Then all eyes turn to the individual who mounts the platform—a herald. His booming voice asks the question that marks the start of business: "Who wishes to speak?" Someone rises to address the assembly. It is the first democracy in history—and the central laboratory in this great experiment in participation.

The assembly meeting recalls the defining features of what was, in its era, the characteristic political institution in much of Greece: the **polis** (PO-liss) (plural, *poleis*). The polis dominated Greek life from around 750 to around 350 B.C., an era that is sometimes called the Hellenic Period. By the time the polis emerged, Greece was old. Two great civilizations had already risen and fallen in Greek lands, the Minoans and Mycenaeans. Now, several centuries after their fall, the polis appeared, and its dawn was marked by a great cultural achievement. Around 725 B.C., Homer composed his two great epic poems, the *Iliad* and the *Odyssey*. These poems preserved many of the religious and historical traditions of Greece's earlier period. Yet, in their focus on the individual, they also heralded a new era, one that would differ greatly from the palace economies and warrior kingdoms of Bronze Age Greece.

Usually translated as "city-state," the polis is better understood as "citizen-state." The polis was the product of communal activities—whether in the assembly, the military, or the theater—undertaken by its members: its citizens. Not every polis was a democracy, but every polis emphasized cooperative activities whose participants enjoyed at least a measure of equality. Every polis also sought a balance between the group and the individual, be that person the speaker, a military hero, or a freethinker.

## Chapter Overview

### Before the Polis: Early Greece, to ca. 725 B.C.

◆ How did early Greece develop before the polis and what light do the Homeric poems shed on its history?

### Society and Politics in Archaic Greece, ca. 750–500 B.C.

◆ What was the Greek polis, and how did it develop in Sparta, Athens, and Corinth in Archaic Greece?

### The Culture of Archaic Greece

◆ How did Western individualism and rationalism take root in Archaic Greece?

### Classical Greece

◆ What was Athenian democracy and how did it clash with Sparta in the Peloponnesian War?

### The Public Culture of Classical Greece

◆ How did tragedy, comedy, philosophy, and history all begin and develop in the culture of Classical Greece?

**polis** Term for an ancient Greek city-state, a system that reached its height around 700–300 B.C.

Balance is a difficult state to achieve, however, and the equilibrium of the polis was frequently disturbed by tension and exclusion. Greek democracy failed to grant equal rights to women or immigrants, and it depended on slave labor. Relations among poleis were less often a matter of cooperation than of war. Although the Greeks created magnificent religious architecture, a portion of their intellectual elite came to the conclusion that the gods were of little importance in explaining the universe. Whereas one leading polis, Sparta, was a paragon of militarism, obedience, and austerity, scorning the life of the mind, another, Athens, prided itself on freedom and cultural attainments. Yet, the Greeks made the most even of such tensions, exploring them in literary genres—tragedy, comedy, history, and philosophy—that focused on the polis as a central theme. Creative tensions also marked Greek achievements in sculpture, painting, and architecture.

The era of the polis proved to be a defining moment in Western history. Although the Greeks of this era borrowed much from neighboring cultures, they were remarkably original. In the mid-first millennium B.C., the monotheistic religious heritage of the West first emerged among the Jews. During that era, the Greeks founded the Western tradition in a broad range of culture, including politics; philosophy; literary genres, such as comedy, tragedy, and history; and the visual and plastic arts of painting, sculpture, and architecture. The Jews and the Greeks represent two poles of Western culture: the sacred and the worldly, revelation and reason.

**"La Parisienne"** This masterpiece of Minoan art shows a priestess in a long robe, with her hair tied in a special knot. A fresco from Knossos, it was dubbed "the Parisian lady" because of its elegance. Erich Lessing/Art Resource, NY

# Before the Polis: Early Greece, to ca. 725 B.C.

*How did early Greece develop before the polis and what light do the Homeric poems shed on its history?*

The ancient Greek genius reached its height in the Classical period (480–323 B.C.), but it is already visible in the *Iliad* (IL-ee-ud) and the *Odyssey* (ODD-uh-see), the epic poems of Homer. Homer's poems shaped Greece's national identity and provided the basis of Greek education. Homer probably lived around 725 B.C., but his works have roots in the civilization that had flourished in Greece a thousand years earlier. Along with the discoveries of archaeologists, Homer's poems provide evidence for the rise and fall of two great civilizations: the Minoans on the island of Crete and the Mycenaeans on the Greek mainland (see **Map 3.1**).

## Minoans and Mycenaeans, 3000–1180 B.C.

Europe's first civilization appeared in what is today Greece, on the Aegean island of Crete (KREET) around 2000 B.C., and soon spread to the Greek mainland. Civilization came relatively late to Greece, but in comparison with Egypt or western Asia, Greece is not a hospitable land. It is mountainous and dry, and it contains little cultivable farmland. Yet, it was destined for greatness.

Cretan civilization would influence early Greece considerably, but in 2000 B.C., Crete was not yet a Greek-speaking island. The Cretans of that era were literate and used a syllabary, or a writing system of syllables that form words, known as "Linear A." Although we know its language is not Greek, we do not know what it is. Most of the evidence of Cretan civilization comes from the excavations of the island's palaces—monumental structures that first appeared at various locations on Crete around 2000 B.C. and reached their height between 1800 and 1490 B.C. Scholars call the palace builders and their civilization "Minoan" (mih-NO-un), after King Minos of later Greek myth. He was supposed to have ruled a great sea empire from his palace at Knossos (see **Map 3.1**).

The Minoan palaces were not merely royal residences but centers of administration, religion, and economics. The largest palace, Knossos (NOS-us), sprawled across 3 acres. It was built around a large central court, probably used for public ceremonies, and surrounded by a mazelike structure of staterooms, residence quarters, storage rooms, workshops, and bathrooms, interconnected by corridors, ramps, and stairways. The Minoans exploited Crete's natural wealth in agriculture and timber and set up a trading network from the Levant to Sicily. A Minoan settlement flourished on the Aegean island of Thera, 70 miles north of Crete (see **Map 3.1**). This settlement was destroyed sometime in the late 1600s B.C. by one of the most violent volcanic eruptions ever. It might have given rise to the legend of Atlantis, the city that sank beneath the sea.

Peace and prosperity are themes of Minoan culture, yet Minoan civilization came to a violent and relatively sudden end. All of the palaces except Knossos were destroyed around 1490 B.C.; Knossos fell around 1375 B.C.

## CHRONOLOGY

| | |
|---|---|
| ca. 1800–1490 B.C. | Minoan civilization at its height |
| ca. 1400–1180 B.C. | Mycenaean civilization at its height |
| ca. 750 B.C. | Greek colonization of Magna Graecia begins |
| ca. 725 B.C. | Sparta conquers Messenia |
| ca. 675 B.C. | Pheidon becomes tyrant of Argos |
| ca. 625 B.C. | Sappho active as poet |
| 594 B.C. | Solon is archon in Athens |
| ca. 560 B.C. | Pisistratus becomes tyrant of Athens |
| 508 B.C. | Cleisthenes begins reforms in Athens |
| 499 B.C. | Ionians revolt against Persia |
| 490 B.C. | Battle of Marathon |
| 480–479 B.C. | Persia invades Greece |
| 477 B.C. | Delian League founded |
| 460–429 B.C. | Pericles at peak of power |
| 458 B.C. | Aeschylus's *Oresteia* first performed in Athens |
| 431–404 B.C. | Peloponnesian War |
| 399 B.C. | Trial of Socrates |
| 395–386 B.C. | Corinthian War |
| 371 B.C. | Battle of Leuctra |

The archaeological evidence strongly supports the notion of an invasion, but by whom? To find the answer, let us look to the Greek mainland.

Around 1700 B.C., the sleepy Greek mainland suddenly appears to have burst into power and prosperity. The evidence is a series of burial sites, especially those found at Mycenae (see **Map 3.1**), where the tombs of kings and queens contain a treasure house of objects in gold and other precious metals. The inhabitants of Mycenae (my-SEE-ne) were Greek-speakers. They and the wider civilization they represent are called Mycenaean (my-suh-NEE-un). The **Mycenaeans** had arrived in Greece sometime between 2300 and 1700 B.C., either through migration or invasion.

Warriors at heart, the Mycenaeans went on raids, around the Aegean, aimed at acquiring loot and prestige. Around 1490 B.C., they achieved their greatest feat: the conquest of Crete. The Mycenaeans adopted the Minoans' palace economy and wide trading network.

Mycenaean civilization was at its height between about 1400 and 1180 B.C. A Mycenaean royal household was organized to produce textiles, arms, and armor, with raw materials provided by the common people. Our knowledge of the palace economy comes primarily from thousands of clay tablets inscribed by palace scribes around 1200 B.C. They are written in a script scholars call "Linear B," an early form of Greek consisting of a combination of syllabary and ideograms (a system of symbols that stand for words or ideas).

It appears likely that Mycenaean Greece suffered from a combination of internal weakness and foreign invasion similar to that experienced by most of the eastern Mediterranean around 1250 to 1150 B.C., the era of the Sea Peoples (see page 24). By 1180 B.C., most of the fortified sites had been destroyed. Afterward, only a few people continued to live in the old towns.

**Minoan** Society that flourished between 2000 and 1490 B.C. on the Aegean island of Crete, where Greece's first civilization appeared. Their sophisticated culture and economy were administered from their magnificent palaces.

**Mycenaeans** Militaristic people from the Greek mainland who conquered the Minoans around 1490–1375 B.C. Mycenaean civilization was a center of Bronze Age culture until its destruction around 1100 B.C.

## Homer and History

The era from the fall of Mycenae to the rise of the Greek city-states is often referred to as the Greek Dark Ages. New archaeological evidence renders the period less dark but no less gloomy: The evidence shows depopulation, poverty, and invasion. Northern Greeks, probably Dorians, came south, driving out or dominating the Mycenaean Greeks. Many Mycenaean refugees migrated eastward around 1000 B.C. to the Aegean coast of Anatolia, which was destined to become an important center of Greek culture.

In spite of its material poverty, Dark Age Greece produced notable painted pottery and preserved an oral tradition of poetry handed down from the Mycenaean era. After 800 B.C., more settled and more prosperous times led to dramatic changes in politics, warfare, and culture. Around 725 B.C., Greece reached a milestone in literary artistry that heralded a new age: the epic poetry of Homer.

Had ancient Greece produced a bible, the *Iliad* and the *Odyssey* of Homer would have been its two testaments. Only Hesiod (HEE-see-ud), a poet who lived around 700 B.C., had as much influence on later generations, but his poems (*Theogony* and *Works and Days*), though composed in the epic tradition, were shorter than Homer's and less dramatic. Homer's and Hesiod's poems inspired and educated the Greeks—a large part of a Greek boy's education consisted of learning to recite Homer from memory. Homer's poems shaped Greece's national identity by praising its heroes and by looking back toward the glory days of the Mycenaeans.

**Homer** Greatest ancient Greek poet, credited as the author of the epics the *Iliad* and the *Odyssey*, both written during the eighth century B.C. His dramatic stories inspired, moved, and educated the Greeks.

🌐 **Map 3.1 Aegean Greece** The Minoan civilization (height: ca. 1800–1490 B.C.) and Mycenaean civilization (height: ca. 1400–1180 B.C.) flourished in turn in the Aegean region during the second millennium B.C. The center of Minoan civilization was the island of Crete. A mainland people, the Mycenaeans conquered Minoan Crete around 1490 B.C.

© Cengage Learning 2014

The *Iliad* and the *Odyssey* focus on the Trojan War and its aftermath. The *Iliad* is set in the tenth year of the conflict. The long war leads to a quarrel between Greek chieftains: Agamemnon, king of Mycenae and the leader of the expedition, and Achilles (uh-KIL-eez), the greatest Greek warrior. The most prominent Trojans, King Priam and his eldest son, Hector, are less petty but suffer the greater ruin. The *Odyssey* is the story of the Greek hero Odysseus (oh-DIS-ee-us) and his struggle to return home to his kingdom after a twenty-year absence, ten years at Troy and ten years wandering homeward. It also focuses on the loyalty and ingenuity of Odysseus's wife, Penelope, who saves the household in his absence, and the maturation of their son, Telemachus (te-LEH-muh-kus), who helps his father regain his kingdom.

Homer's poems look back, but did the Trojan War really happen? That is a controversial subject, but both archaeology and the evidence of inscriptions suggest that the answer is probably yes. Troy really existed: It was a big, wealthy city, strategically located near the entrance to the Hellespont (or Dardanelles), the straits that lead toward the Black Sea. The king of Troy was attached politically to the Hittite empire, and his city had strong trading relations with the Mycenaean Greeks. But Mycenaeans turned quickly from trade to war. Troy was destroyed violently in the period 1210–1180 B.C., possibly by Mycenaean warriors.

Homer lived in a Greek city in Ionia (eye-OH-nee-uh), a region of the western coast of Anatolia (see **Map 3.2**). Although Homer lived centuries after the end of Troy, he could have drawn some of his material from native populations and traditions. Besides, Homer worked in a continuous, Greek, poetic tradition going back to the Mycenaean Age, which gave him knowledge of a bygone day. His poems combine accurate details of Mycenaean palace life with historical fiction and details of his own, much later society.

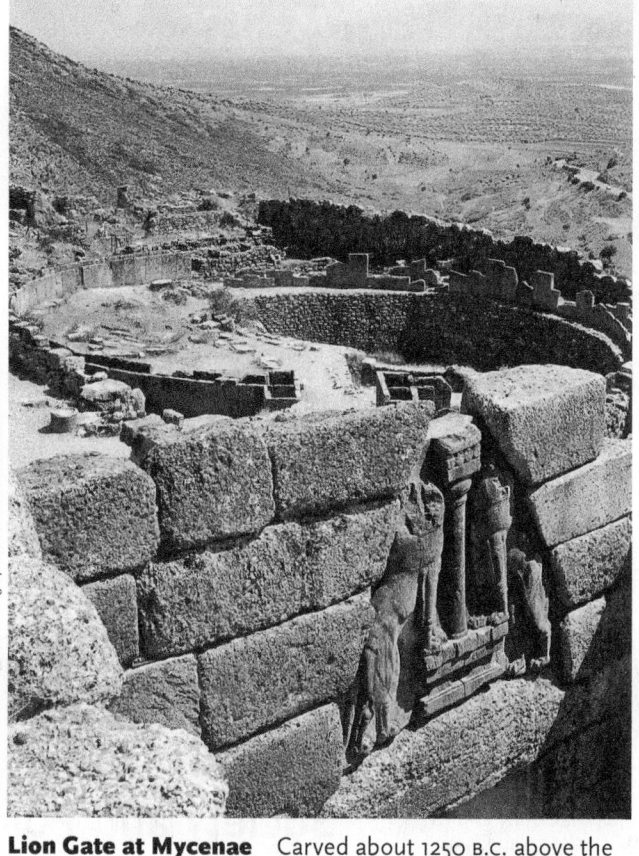

**Lion Gate at Mycenae** Carved about 1250 B.C. above the main gate of the citadel's massive walls, the lions—flanking a column, their front paws resting on altars—probably represent royal authority. Inside the walls is Grave Circle B, a royal burial site.

Dmitrios Harissiadis. From the Photographic Archives of the Benaki Museum

Homer focuses on the elite. Homeric men and women hold aristocratic values and tend to look down on ordinary people. But society in Homer's day was more level and egalitarian. Except for a small number of traders and craft specialists who lived in towns, most Greeks lived in villages and hamlets. Most farmed or herded pigs, goats, or sheep, and most were free. The people of each community were called the *demos* (DEE-mus); the leading men, *basileis* (bah-see-LACE). *Basileis* means "kings," but it is more accurate to understand them as chiefs.

The main activity of Homer's basileis is warfare. The *Iliad* consists largely of a series of battlefield contests. Since women did not take part in battle, they are not presented as men's equals, but Homer's women are neither timid nor helpless. Penelope, for example, personifies female resourcefulness: By refusing to marry until she has finished weaving a shroud for Odysseus's elderly father, and then by unraveling every night what she has woven during the day, she puts the noble suitors off for years. She is as concerned with honor as any Homeric man. By refusing to accept an offer of marriage while Odysseus might still be alive, Penelope does honor to her own good name and to her husband's.

Both in Mycenaean times and in Homer's day, the Greeks were polytheists. The gods figure prominently in early Greek poetry, but they are less powerful than the Hebrew God, less immediate, and less interested in the inner life of men and women. Already emerging at the beginning of the Greek cultural tradition was the belief that became the hallmark of ancient Greece: that "man is the measure of all things," as the thinker Protagoras would declare in the fifth century B.C.

## SECTION SUMMARY

- The Minoans built Greece's first civilization, centered on the island of Crete around 2000–1375 B.C.
- Greek-speakers arrived in Greece about 2300–1700 B.C. and established the wealthy and warlike Mycenaean civilization on the mainland, at its height about 1400–1180 B.C.
- From 1100 to 800 B.C., between the fall of Mycenaean civilization and the rise of the city-states, Greece was largely poor and illiterate.
- Homer did not live until 725 B.C. or later, but an oral tradition of poetry, going back to Mycenaean times, means that the *Iliad* and *Odyssey* are based on a kernel of historical truth.
- Homer expresses the heroic and aristocratic values of elite men and women that would influence Greek antiquity for centuries.

*arête* Originally meaning "warrior prowess" or "excellence," *arête* was a key term of ancient Greek culture. It evolved over the centuries to apply to politics and philosophy and to women as well as men.

The gods embody the values of a warrior society that put a premium on *arête* (ah-reh-TAY), meaning warrior prowess or excellence. Because they were thought to live on Mount Olympus, a 9,500-foot-high peak in northern Greece (see **Map 3.1**), the Greek gods were called the Olympians. The "household" of the Olympians—modeled on a noble's household—included Zeus (ZOOS), a sky-god and the "father of gods and men," and his sister and consort, Hera; Zeus's brother, Poseidon, god of the sea, earthquakes, and horses; Ares, god of war; and Aphrodite, goddess of love. Also in the "household" were Zeus's children: Athena, goddess of wisdom and cunning; Hephaestus, god of craftsmen; Hermes, god of travelers and thieves; Apollo, god of disease and healing; and Artemis, goddess of the hunt, of maidens, and of childbirth.

Loyalty to the family played an important role in social relations. A person's obligations to kin included the duty to avenge crime or murder. Friendship, cemented by an exchange of gifts, was another important social institution. Even humble peasants prided themselves on hospitality.

Such values served Homeric society well. Although they would survive in later centuries, they would be challenged after 700 B.C. by the increasing emphasis on public life as the Greek city-state evolved.

# Society and Politics in Archaic Greece, ca. 750–500 B.C.

*What was the Greek polis, and how did it develop in Sparta, Athens, and Corinth in Archaic Greece?*

**Archaic Greece** Period of ancient Greek history from around 700 to 500 B.C.

Historians usually call the era in Greek history from roughly 750 to 500 B.C. the "Archaic period." **Archaic Greece** was a patchwork of hundreds of separate city-states, tribal leagues, and monarchies (see **Map 3.2**). Nevertheless, it displayed a distinctive style and outlook, not only in art, but also in politics, military arrangements, technology, economics, literature, and religion.

The Archaic era laid the groundwork for much of lasting importance in Western civilization. Archaic Greece witnessed the simultaneous growth of individualism and a tight community spirit, the emergence of social cohesion despite a continual state of war, and the coexistence of deep religious piety and the West's first nontheistic philosophy. The Archaic period also saw the origin of characteristic Western types of governmental regimes—tyranny, oligarchy, and the first steps toward democracy—and of fundamental Western notions of citizenship and the rule of law.

## Agriculture, Trade, Colonization, and Warfare

An observer of ninth-century B.C. Greece would hardly have predicted greatness of that poor, illiterate society of small settlements and low-level trade. Yet, everything began to change in Greece in the eighth century B.C. It was out of these changes that a new communal institution emerged: the polis.

Change was a product of peace, which stimulated a sharp population rise. In response, the economy shifted from herding to farming, a more efficient source of food. Seeking new agricultural land in the rocky Greek peninsula, farmers terraced hillsides and drained marshes. The typical agricultural unit was the family farm. Most farms were small and roughly equal in size and so served to stimulate social and political equality.

🌑 **Map 3.2  Archaic and Classical Greece**   The region of the Aegean Sea was the heartland of Greek civilization around 750 to 350 B.C. The mountainous terrain, rugged coastline, and numerous islands encouraged political fragmentation. © Cengage Learning 2014

Greek commerce, too, was expanding. Shortly before 800 B.C., Greeks from the island of Euboea (you-BEE-uh), perhaps following the example of Phoenician merchants and seafarers, who had been casual traders in Greece for a century (see pages 31–32), established a trading post in Syria at Al-Mina, at the end of the chief caravan route from Mesopotamia (see **Map 3.3**). Shortly afterward, Euboeans established another trading post in the west, on an island in the Bay of Naples in Italy. In both east and west, Greek merchants sought iron and luxury goods. What they offered in return was probably silver, of which ancient Greece had rich deposits, and slaves.

From commerce, it was but a short step to colonization. Colonies provided new opportunities for a growing population. In colonization as in trade, the Greeks may have followed the Phoenicians, who had begun establishing colonies probably in the ninth century B.C. Between about 750 and 500 B.C., the Greeks founded colonies throughout the Mediterranean and the Black Sea regions, planting nearly as many cities as already existed in Greece (see **Map 3.3**). Colonization in Italy and Sicily began in earnest around 750 B.C.; in the lands of the northeast Aegean perhaps a generation later; in the territory around the Sea of Marmara (in modern Turkey) about 680 B.C.; in North Africa around 630 B.C.; and in region of the Black Sea about 610 B.C. In the far west, Massalia (modern Marseilles, France) was established about 600 B.C.

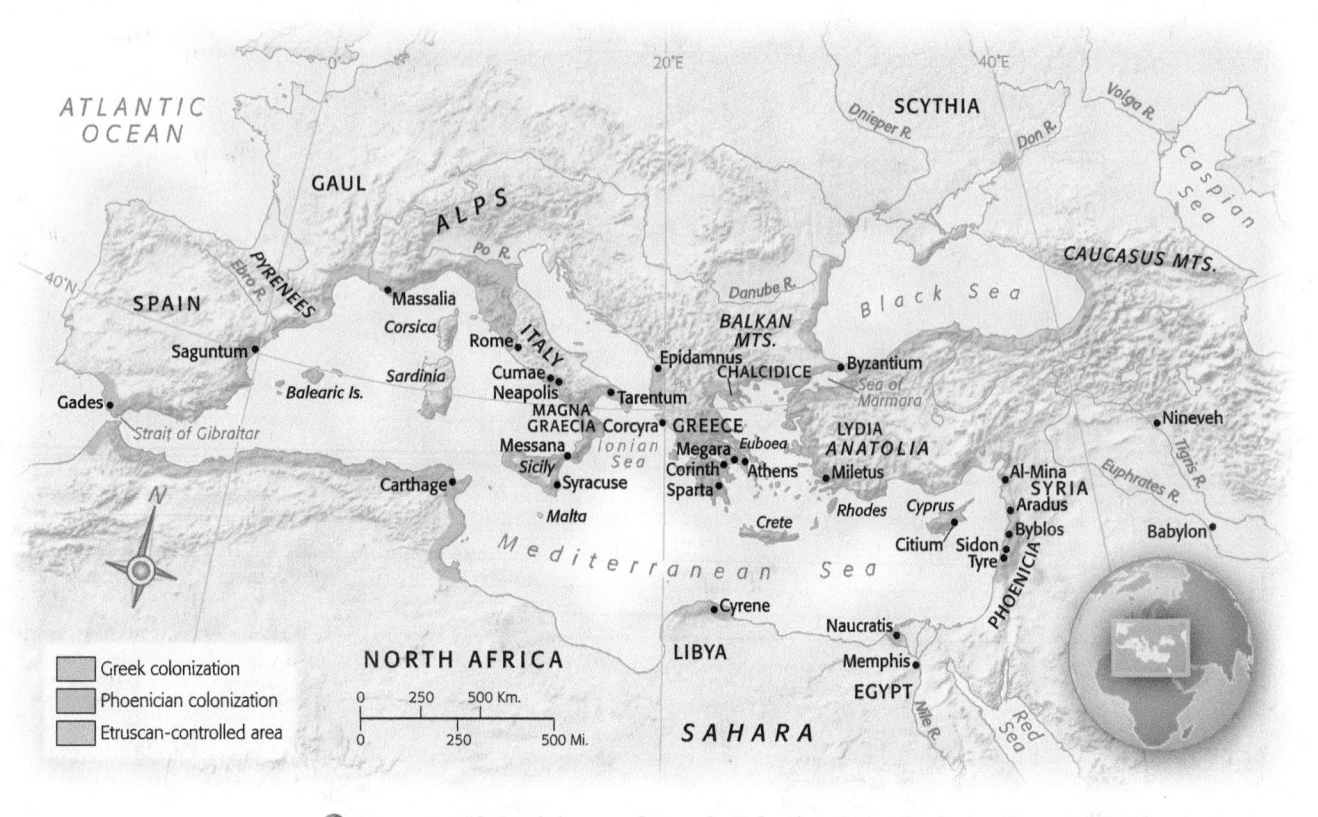

**Map 3.3 Phoenician and Greek Colonization** Both the Phoenicians (beginning perhaps after 900 B.C.) and the Greeks (beginning around 750 B.C.) established numerous colonies on the coasts of the Mediterranean and Black Seas. © Cengage Learning 2014

Southern Italy and Sicily, whose climate and landscape recalled the Aegean, were especially intense areas of Greek settlement, so much so that the Romans later called the region *Magna Graecia* ("Great Greece"). Greek colonization spread urban civilization westward, especially into Italy.

One important consequence of foreign contact was the introduction to Greece of the alphabet, borrowed from the Phoenicians shortly after 800 B.C. The Greeks made one significant addition to the Phoenician alphabet by adding vowels. Vowels are not essential to reading a Semitic language, but an Indo-European language like Greek would be almost indecipherable without them. The alphabet spread rapidly and widely after 750 B.C. Literacy underlay the achievements in poetry, philosophy, and the law that Archaic Greece has left behind. However, so few people could read and write well that ancient Greece remained primarily an oral culture.

Another consequence of foreign contact was the introduction of new military technology, which the increase in wealth allowed the Greeks to adopt. Social changes, furthermore, fostered new tactics on the battlefield. The result was the **hoplite phalanx** (HOP-lite FAY-lanks), a tightly ordered unit of heavily armed, pike-bearing infantrymen. The phalanx not only became the dominant military force in Archaic Greece, but, with relatively few changes in equipment and tactics, it remained supreme on land in Greece, western Asia, and other Mediterranean regions for centuries, until its defeat by a Roman army in 197 B.C.

The phalanx emerged through a process of evolution rather than in a revolutionary leap. Before 800 B.C., single combat among the basileis appears to have decided battles. Around 800 to 750 B.C., armies began to include more men, fighting in close formation. Around 700 B.C. came new armaments. The result was the phalanx. The heavily armed infantryman (hoplite) of the fighting unit (phalanx) wore bronze armor on his shins and chest and a bronze helmet with a narrow opening for eyes and mouth. He carried a heavy wooden shield in his left hand. His weapons were a pike—a heavy, wooden, iron-tipped thrusting spear at least 9 feet long—and a short, iron stabbing sword.

**hoplite phalanx**
Battlefield tactic of Archaic Greece that relied on a tightly ordered unit of heavily armed, pike-bearing infantrymen (hoplites).

The men of the phalanx were arranged in close ranks, normally four to eight deep. Soldiers stood together in line, each man's shield overlapping his neighbor's. Hoplite combat involved set battles—head-to-head, army-against-army, all-or-nothing affairs—rather than individual skirmishes or guerrilla raids. Battle usually consisted of a charge followed by a grueling contest, like the one described by the poet Tyrtaeus (ca. 650 B.C.) in these words of advice to young soldiers: "Let each man close the foe, and with his own long spear, or else with his sword, wound and take an enemy, and setting foot beside foot, resting shield against shield, crest beside crest, helm beside helm, fight his man breast to breast with sword or long spear in hand."* Finally, one side would give way and run. The victors stayed and erected a trophy.

Greek hoplite warfare rested on deep societal roots. Only independent men of means could afford hoplite armor. Thanks to the spread of the family farm, such men were common in Greece by around 700 B.C. Hoplites were amateur soldiers. Most were full-time farmers outside the fighting season, which lasted only for the summer months. The notion of the farmer-soldier, independent and free, would have a lasting impact on Western political thought. So would the warrior values of what became a way of life in Greece.

Unlike in Homer, whose warriors sought aretê mainly for personal and familial honor, hoplites fought for the community. According to Tyrtaeus, a good soldier's death brought glory not only to his father but also to his city and his countrymen. Although the battlefield remained the favored arena for displays of aretê, the assembly or the council house became increasingly acceptable as an alternative.

## Characteristics of the Polis

The polis was both a product of the changes of the eighth century B.C. and a stimulus for change. As an urban settlement, the polis existed as early as the ninth or even the tenth century B.C., but its intense communal spirit did not emerge until around 750–700 B.C.

*Tyrataeus in Elegy and Iambus with an English Translation by J. M. Edmonds. Cambridge, MA. Copyright © 1931 by the President and Fellows of Harvard University, Cambridge, Mass; Reprinted with permission.

Réunion des Musées Nationaux/Art Resource, NY

**Hoplites**    A detail from a Corinthian vase of 625 to 600 B.C. shows pike-wielding hoplites closed in battle over a fallen comrade. In this image as elsewhere, Greek artists rendered warriors seminude and fighting in small groups, but in reality hoplites went into battle wearing heavy armor and fought in large units.

*Polis* came to denote not just a city but the community as a whole, corresponding roughly to a country or nation. One crude gauge of the centrality of the polis is the number, not to mention the significance, of words the Greeks derived from it: among them, *polites* (citizen), *politeia* (constitution), *politeô* (to govern), *ta politika* (politics), and *politikos* (politician).

Most poleis (PO-lays) were small, many less than 100 square miles. Athens was one of the largest. Its territory, known as Attica (see **Map 3.4**), covered 1,000 square miles (approximately the size of Rhode Island). At its height (ca. 430 B.C.), the population of Athens was about 400,000, but a typical polis contained only between 5,000 and 10,000 people. The philosopher Aristotle (AR-is-tot-il) (384–322 B.C.) wrote that an ideal polis should be small enough that the citizens know one another personally.

The polis consisted of two parts: the urban area, which usually was tiny, and the surrounding countryside, where most people lived. From the earliest times, the urban public space included both a defensible hill (preferably with a water supply), called a "high city" (*acropolis* [uh-CROP-uh-liss]), and a "gathering place" (*agora* [AH-go-rah]) used as a marketplace and meeting area. There was at least one temple. After 500 B.C., stone buildings, including council houses, theaters, covered porticoes, gymnasia, and baths, became increasingly common.

What distinguished the early polis, however, was not its buildings but its spirit. As the poet Alcaeus (b. ca. 630 B.C.) puts it, "Not houses finely roofed or the stones of walls well-built, nay nor canals and dockyards, make the polis, but men able to use their opportunity."

The Greeks came to call the polis a "common thing" (*koinon*). It belonged to its people, not to a few nobles or to a king or a god. As early as about 700 B.C., important public documents were inscribed in stone. Acts of state were attributed not to a personified polis but to the community—for example, not to Thera but to "the Thereans," not to Sybaris but to "the Sybarites." The emphasis is on the plurality.

The emphasis was on equality as well. The polis developed an ethos of moderation. The ideal citizen was thought to be neither rich nor poor but of moderate means. Women were not considered citizens and were excluded from taking part in politics. Yet, women's behavior was considered important to the polis. For example, some poleis passed laws against extravagant jewelry or unrestrained mourning (mourning the dead was considered women's work).

In theory, all citizens were supposed to be roughly similar, but this was not always true in practice, as the politics of the early polis makes clear.

## Corinth and Tyranny

Trade and colonization inspired change at home, for one thing, making increasing numbers of Greeks into seafarers and so generating wealth. Centrally located Corinth became a great seaport and the wealthiest city in mainland Greece. And Corinth was in the forefront of political change.

Political change followed economic trends. Although some Greeks shot to the top of the economic ladder, many of these newly rich lacked the status of the elite basileis. In order to claim a share, the newly rich seem to have made common cause with the independent farmers who staffed the hoplite phalanx. The result was tyranny.

*Tyrant* originally referred not to an arbitrary and oppressive ruler but rather to a champion of the people. Having overthrown a narrow and entrenched aristocracy, tyrants were popular at first. *Tyrant* did not become a negative word until roughly 550 B.C., when the people soured on the second and third generation of tyrants.

Greek tyranny began in Argos, a polis in the northeastern Peloponnesus (pel-uh-puh-NEE-suss), around 675 B.C. (see **Map 3.2**). The first tyrant was an Argive named Pheidon. By 660 B.C., tyranny had spread to nearby Corinth. During the seventh and sixth centuries B.C., all the major Greek poleis except Sparta became tyrannies.

Much of what the tyrants did, especially in the first generation, was popular and progressive. It appears that they had the support of the prosperous farmers who fought in the phalanx. Tyrants stimulated the economy by founding colonies on trade routes, standardizing weights and measures, and encouraging the immigration of skilled craftsmen from

🌐 **Map 3.4 Attica** Mountains and plains alternate in the 1,000-square-mile area of ancient Attica. The Long Walls connecting Athens with the port city of Piraeus were built around 450 B.C. © Cengage Learning 2014

other poleis. They built temples and instituted festivals, providing both jobs and leisure-time activities.

When tyrants passed power on to their sons, however, the second generation tended to rule oppressively. Buoyed by the discontent of the people, the basileis regrouped and tried to take back power. One second-generation tyrant advised accordingly: To maintain power, a tyrant should "lop off the tallest ears of grain"—that is, execute or exile aristocrats in order to deny leaders to the opposition. However, the tide of discontent was not to be stopped. Few tyrannies lasted beyond the third generation, when they were overthrown and replaced by oligarchy (literally, "rule by the few") or, less often, by democracy (literally, "power of the people"). By 500 B.C., tyranny had disappeared from most of Greece.

## Sparta

Sparta was located in Laconia, an isolated valley in the south-central Peloponnesus, in the southern part of mainland Greece, and seemed destined by geography for no special glory (see **Map 3.2**). Yet Sparta proved to be a powerful model of citizenship and constitutionalism, virtue and community, austerity and militarism.

Sparta was closed and secretive, which makes its history difficult to write. Scholarship has lifted the veil a little, however. For example, Spartans believed that their unique way of life was created all at once by the legendary lawgiver Lycurgus in the 700s B.C. Archaeological evidence, however, suggests gradual innovations in Sparta rather than revolutionary change, beginning around 650 B.C., and it is by no means clear that there ever was a Lycurgus.

## Government

The foundations of the Spartan regime were laid around 650 B.C., when a three-part class system emerged. Helots (HEL-uts), unfree laborers who worked the land, were at the lowest level. In the middle ranks were *perioikoi* (roughly, "neighbors"), who were free but under the thumb of the highest class. At the top stood Similars, who were the only full citizens. We do not know the number of helots, but we do know that they vastly outnumbered the other two classes.

Compared with individuals of the other classes, a Similar had a good life. If male and over age 30, he had the right to attend the assembly and to hold public office. Each male Similar, moreover, was given a basic allotment of land worked by helots, which freed him to fight. As the name implies, Similars were alike but not equal. Wealthy Similars owned more land than the basic allotment.

Although Sparta is remembered as a conservative society, the idea of a large group of men sharing power was radical in its day. When the system began around 650 B.C., Similars numbered about nine thousand. What gave them their clout and prestige? The Similars were probably hoplites, the backbone of Sparta's army.

In the mid-seventh century B.C., Sparta depended on its army to keep the helots down. Most helots were Messenians, whose very fertile land had been conquered by Sparta in about 725 B.C. Although fellow Greeks, Messenians were forced to work for the conquerors. Sparta profited, but it now faced a security problem. The restive helots had to be policed, and a revolt sometime between 675 and 650 B.C. almost succeeded. To keep Messenia, Sparta needed a crack army; to get that, Sparta made all its hoplites into Similars, thus giving hoplites an investment in Sparta because they could now own land and have a say in politics.

Sparta was no democracy, however. The ancients classified the Spartan government as "mixed" because it combined monarchy, oligarchy (that is, rule by an elite few), and popular government. The assembly of Similars was the popular element, but its powers were limited. Real power was shared among those Similars who were kings, elders, and *ephors* (overseers), men generally belonging to a few wealthy families.

## Society

The elite did not lead lives of luxury, however, at least not after around 550 B.C., when austerity became the order of the day. Society was reordered to promote military discipline. For example, the Spartans' diet was famous for its simplicity. The preferred food was a black broth of pork cooked in its own blood and spiced with salt and vinegar. To discourage consumption, Sparta issued no coins; the official "currency" consisted of heavy and clumsy iron skewers. Since the outside world was considered corrupt, Sparta engaged in little trade and admitted few foreigners to its territory—and those who were admitted were subject to periodic expulsion.

Whereas other poleis offered little or no formal public education, Sparta schooled its sons from childhood to be soldiers—a system known as the *agoge* (ahgo-GAY) ("upbringing"). Limited to male Similars, the agoge created a life cycle unique in Greece. At birth, babies were examined by public inspectors. Those who were considered deformed or unfit were "exposed"—that is, they were abandoned without food or shelter. The victims might die, but they might also be sold into slavery or even secretly adopted. (Other Greeks also practiced exposure of infants, but the choice was a family matter, not public policy.) Surviving children were raised at home up to the age of 7, at which point, boys left the family to be boarded with a "herd" of their age-mates. For the eleven years from age 7 to age 18, a boy went through rigorous training. On the theory that good soldiers should be strong and silent, boys learned only enough reading and writing for practical ends—for example, to transmit messages to and from military headquarters.

Many boys between the ages of 18 and 20 served in the *krypteia* (secret service), living secretly in the hills of Messenia, where they survived by hunting, foraging, and stealing. They spied on the ever rebellious Messenian helots, whom they could kill freely because every year Sparta declared war on helots. By age 20, all Similars became hoplites, and they continued to serve in the army until age 60. Supported by helot labor, they devoted all their time to fighting and training the next generation.

Sparta offered more opportunities to elite women than did other Greek states. For example, unlike most Greek girls, Spartan girls received a public education—limited, however, to physical training, which was thought to strengthen females for childbearing. The sight of girls running, wrestling, and throwing the discus and javelin, which was common in Sparta, was unthinkable elsewhere in Greece. So was Sparta's unique recognition of the risks of maternity. Like Spartan men who died in battle, Spartan women who died in childbirth were allowed to have their names inscribed on their tombstones. All other Spartan burials were anonymous. (See the feature, "The Written Record: A Woman Wins at the Olympics.")

Spartan women were relatively more independent than women elsewhere in Greece. With the men consumed by military training or warfare, women ran the day-to-day operations of life, controlling the helot farmworkers and servants and raising the girls and the very small boys. Spartan women also had the advantage of being able to inherit property, unlike Athenian women.

Beginning around 550 B.C., Sparta used its military might to build up a network of alliances (dubbed the "Peloponnesian League" by scholars) in the Peloponnesus and central Greece. It may seem paradoxical that a society that feared foreigners, as Sparta did, became the *hegemon* (HEJ-uh-mahn) (literally, "leader") of an extensive alliance system, but Sparta's fear made its leadership slow and careful. Sparta intervened in the wider world only to prevent threats from arising on the horizon and usually only after a great deal of debate and with the utmost caution.

By around 500 B.C., every Peloponnesian polis except Argos was an ally of Sparta, and in central Greece, Thebes came aboard shortly thereafter. Until its breakup after the Peloponnesian War (431–404 B.C.; see page 72), the Peloponnesian League was the dominant land power in Greece and, after the defeat of Persia in 480 B.C., in the entire eastern Mediterranean.

Sparta exemplified community spirit and respect for law. The people of Sparta, as the historian Herodotus (he-ROD-uh-tus) (ca. 485–425 B.C.) quotes a Spartan king, "are free . . . , but not entirely free; for they have a master, and that master is Law, which they fear." Sparta was also an exemplar of equality—limited equality, to be sure, but equality extended to a wider group than ever before in Greece. The notion of the Similars, moreover, contains the germ of the idea of the citizen: a free member of the political community who, unlike a subject, has rights as well as duties. Few other poleis could match the stability and sense of civic duty fostered by Sparta. In the realms of equality and citizenship, however, Sparta was eventually outstripped by Athens. In the realm of liberty, Athens wrote a new chapter in Western history.

**Spartan Woman**   This bronze statuette (4 3/4 inches tall) from Laconia (ca. 530 B.C.) shows a woman running. Unlike other Greek women, elite Spartan women underwent physical education. Although their personal freedom was limited, women in Sparta suffered fewer restrictions than their counterparts in democratic Athens.
C.M. Dixon/Ancient Art & Architecture Collection Ltd

## Early Athens

Around 650 B.C., the basileis of the Attic Plain, who proudly called themselves the Eupatrids ("well-fathered men"), ruled Athens (see **Map 3.4**). They served in one-year magistracies and afterward became life members of the Areopagus (ar-ee-OP-uh-gus), a council of elders named for its meeting place on the "hill of Ares." This aristocratic council dominated both politics and justice, for it also served as a court. The demos (DEE-mus) (the people) met in an assembly. Probably from early times on, the assembly had, in theory, supreme lawmaking power as well as authority over war and peace, but voting was by shouting, and few people challenged Eupatrid wishes.

## A Woman Wins at the Olympics

*Cynisca, a Spartan royal princess, was the first woman to win at the ancient Olympic games. That is, her horses won the chariot race (in 396 and 392 B.C.) but Cynisca wasn't there, since women weren't allowed at the games. Was Cynisca an early feminist or was she used by her brother, King Agesilaus (r. 400–360 B.C.)? Consider these ancient texts.*

### (a) Inscription at Olympia (ca. 390 B.C.)

Cynisca set up a statue of herself at Olympia with this proud inscription:

> Kings of Sparta are my fathers and brothers,
> Cynisca, victorious with a chariot of swift-footed horses,
> Put up this statute. I declare that I am
> Alone among the women of all Greece to take the crown.
> Apelles the son of Callicles made it [the statue]."

### (b) Plutarch (ca. A.D. 50–120) on Spartan Women

Perhaps Cynisca exemplified the physical fitness of Spartan women that Plutarch celebrated:

> [Lycurgus] toughened the girls physically by making them run and wrestle and throw the discus and javelin. Thereby their children in embryo would make a strong start in strong bodies and would develop better, while the women themselves would also bear their pregnancies with vigor and would meet the challenge of childbirth in a successful, relaxed way. He did away with prudery, sheltered upbringing and effeminacy of any kind.

### (c) Athenaeus (ca. A.D. 200) on a Spartan Festival

Cynisca might have raced chariots in the annual Hyacinthia Festival:

> As for the girls, some are carried in wicker carts which are sumptuously ornamented, others parade in chariots yoked to two horses, which they race, and the entire city is given over to the bustle and joy of the festival.

### (d) Xenophon (ca. 430–354 B.C.) on Cynisca

But perhaps Cynisca was placed in a not very flattering role by her brother, the king:

> Surely, too, he [Agesilaus] did what was seemly and dignified when he adorned his own estate with works and possessions worthy of a man, keeping many hounds and war horses, but persuaded his sister Cynisca to breed chariot horses, and showed by her victory that such a stud marks the owner as a person of wealth, but not necessarily of merit.

### Questions

1. Does the inscription show Cynisca's independence or her reliance on men?
2. What do Plutarch, Athenaeus, and Xenophon each say about the status of Spartan women?
3. Which text is most convincing? Least convincing? Why?

*Based on Donald Kyle, "The Only Woman in All Greece: Kyniska, Agesilaus, Alcibiades, and Olympia," *Journal of Sport History* 30, no. 2 (Summer 2003): 183–203; Text (a), Dittenberger, Wilhelm, and Karl Purgold. Die Inschriften von Olympia. «Olympia», 5. Berlin 1896, trans. Barry Strauss, http://epigraphy.packhum.org/inscriptions/main?url=oi%3Fikey%3D213965%26bookid%3D224%26region%3D2%26subregion%3D5, © Cengage Learning; Richard J. A. Talbert, trans., *Plutarch on Sparta.* Copyright © 1988 by Penguin Books Ltd. Reprinted with permission; Charles Burton Gulick, trans., Athenaeus, Deipnosophistae, vol. 2. Copyright © 1928 by the President and Fellows of Harvard University, Cambridge, Mass.; Reprinted with permission from Harvard University Press; Xenophon. *Xenophon in Seven Volumes*, 7. E. C. Marchant, G. W. Bowersock, tr. Constitution of the Athenians. Copyright © 1925 by the President and Fellows of Harvard University, Cambridge, Mass.; Reprinted with permission from Harvard University Press.

By 632 B.C., the aristocrats faced trouble in Athens as elsewhere because of corruption, economic change, and assertive hoplites. A failed attempt that year to establish a tyranny left the forces for change eager. In 621 B.C., a loose coalition opposed to Eupatrid rule forced a codification of the laws, which were then issued in writing. This Code of Draco (DRAY-co), named for its main drafter, was infamous for its harsh provisions (hence, our adjective *draconian*); it was written, a later commentator suggested, "not in ink but blood." Yet, Draco's Code seems only to have whetted an appetite for change. A wealthy non-Eupatrid elite of hoplites was emerging, grown rich exporting olive oil. Some were merchants; most were prosperous farmers. They now wanted political power. As for ordinary Athenians, they typically worked small family farms. Over the years, bad harvests and soil exhaustion had sent many into debt. Those who had pledged their land as collateral became known as *hektemoroi* ("sixth-parters"), probably because they owed one-sixth of their crops to their creditors. Other farmers sank even further into debt and had only themselves or their children as collateral. Some ended up as slaves, sometimes sold abroad. Because both rich and poor Athenians had grievances against the Eupatrids, revolution was in the air.

Enter **Solon** (ca. 630–560 B.C.), who was appointed to the emergency position of sole *archon* (chief officer) for one year, probably 594 B.C. A Eupatrid who had become a merchant, Solon (SO-lun) understood both the old and the new elite, and he was sympathetic to ordinary Athenians as well. As his surviving writings show, Solon was a moderate. He could have become tyrant, but he preferred to be a mediator.

Solon reformed both economics and politics. Many of his measures were aimed at encouraging Athenian trade, and they led to a commercial boom. More important, Solon helped ordinary people by the "shaking off of burdens," measures that abolished the institution of *hektemorage* and probably canceled some debts. He also abolished the practice of making loans on personal surety and set up a fund to redeem Athenians who had been sold into slavery abroad. By freeing the hektemoroi, Solon ensured Athens a large class of independent small farmers.

Solon made fundamental changes in Athenian government, too. He changed qualifications for office from birth to wealth, a boon to the non-Eupatrid elite. He established four census classes based on agricultural production. Most offices were reserved for men of property, but the poorest class, known as *thetes*, could participate in the assembly and courts. Solon probably established the Council of 400, which prepared the assembly's agenda. He is probably also responsible for setting a regular schedule of council and assembly meetings and for replacing the assembly's voice votes with the counting of hands.

Solon's moderation, respect for law, and liberation of the poor and downtrodden are milestones in Greek history. Without his reforms, it is doubtful that democracy could have later taken root in Athens. Yet Solon's work also had an unexpected byproduct: the growth of slavery in Athens. Though booming, the Athenian economy lost its cheap labor when Solon freed debt slaves and hektemoroi. The solution was to buy slaves abroad and import them to Athens. After Solon, Athenian society grew to depend on slave labor. Unlike helots, slaves could be bought and sold and were often uprooted, and the system was better policed than in earlier societies.

In the centuries after Solon, slavery became widespread in Athens. Some slaves served in agriculture, some labored under miserable conditions in Athenian silver mines, and some were engaged in commerce or the military (where some rowers were slaves). Most, however, worked as domestics or in small workshops as, for example, metalworkers or furniture makers. The vast majority of slaves were non-Greek. Most were prisoners of war; some were victims of pirates or debtors from states where, unlike Athens, citizens might end up in debt slavery. Thrace (roughly, modern Bulgaria) and Anatolia were the main sources of slaves, but some slaves came from North Africa and other Mediterranean regions.

Living conditions for slaves were usually poor and those in the silver mines were abysmal. Some slaves were, however, allowed to save money and buy their freedom. Emancipation was more common in Athens than in the American South before 1865. A few ex-slaves even rose to positions of wealth and power in Athens.

If free Athenians had any moral doubts about slavery, they went unrecorded. Yet, there was much dissatisfaction with Solon's reforms, since his middle way satisfied neither Eupatrids nor champions of the free poor. After years of conflict, around 560 B.C., advocates of radical reform established a tyranny under Pisistratus (pie-SIS-trah-tus) (ca. 600–528 B.C.). He and his sons held power for forty of the next fifty years.

Supported by the common people, the Pisistratids exiled many Eupatrids and confiscated and redistributed their land. Pisistratus kept the façade of Solon's reforms while ensuring that loyal supporters held all key offices.

The tyranny was a stable regime that witnessed prosperity at home and the expansion of Athenian influence abroad. Yet, Pisistratus's dynasty lasted only two generations and was deposed in 510 B.C. Athens's elites by birth and wealth were ready to establish an oligarchy, but the way was open for an unexpected development: the emergence of popular government.

**Solon** Statesman of early Athens, he transformed Greek society through mediation, moderation, respect for law, and measures that liberated the poor and downtrodden.

## SECTION SUMMARY

- Trade, colonization, and the invention of the Greek alphabet and of the hoplite phalanx all contributed to the emergence of the polis around 750–700 B.C.

- The polis was a community of citizens that emphasized participation and equality.

- Corinth is the best example of a polis where new wealth led to the emergence of the first tyrants—originally, popular champions.

- Sparta's austere and militaristic society turned boys into soldiers and trained girls to be tough and assertive wives and mothers.

- Solon's reforms freed the poor, but unintentionally laid the foundations for the growth of slavery.

# The Culture of Archaic Greece

*How did Western individualism and rationalism take root in Archaic Greece?*

While one trend in Archaic culture was communal solidarity, as reflected in the hoplite phalanx, another was the opposite: a growing elevation of individualism. Increased prosperity and mobility (social, geographic, and political) during the Archaic period encouraged the breakdown of old ties and left some people with a sense of their uniqueness. Archaic poetry and sculpture both demonstrate this new consciousness of the self.

Meanwhile, although most Archaic Greeks celebrated religion, a small group of thinkers expressed religious doubts. While monumental stone temples and international centers for divination were being erected to honor the pantheon of gods, Greek thinkers began to move away from divine and toward abstract and mechanistic explanations of the universe. Their defection marked the start of the Western philosophical tradition.

**Sappho** Ancient Greek poet from the island of Lesbos, she wrote odes, wedding songs, and hymns expressing intimate feelings, including love for other women.

**Classical Greece** Period of ancient Greek history from about 480 to 323 B.C.

## Revealing the Self: Lyric Poetry and Sculpture

Between approximately 675 and 500 B.C., the dominant Greek literary form was lyric poetry. This genre consisted of short poems written in a variety of styles but sharing a willingness to experiment, sometimes by revealing private feelings, sometimes by commenting on politics. Epic poetry, by contrast, was longer, grander in theme and tone, and less personal.

Homer never speaks directly about himself, and Hesiod reveals only a few personal details. In contrast, Archilochus (ar-KIL-uh-kus) of Paros (ca. 700–650 B.C.), the earliest known of the lyric poets, flaunts the self. Born on the Cycladic island of Paros, Archilochus was the son, perhaps the illegitimate son, of a noble. He was a mercenary soldier (that is, he fought for pay for a foreign city) and a colonist before returning home and dying in a hoplite battle against a neighboring island. The varied subjects of Archilochus's poetry include love, travel, and war. Much of his poetry is satire, sometimes mocking and ironic, sometimes vicious and abusive. Archilochus takes a cynical and detached view of hoplite ideals, freely admitting that he once tossed away his shield to escape the battlefield: "And that shield, to hell with it! Tomorrow I'll get me another one no worse."[*]

**Sappho** of Lesbos (ca. 625 B.C.) is also famous as a private poet, one who composed unmatched descriptions of intimate feelings, among them love for other women. Sappho (SAF-foh) is one of the few women poets of antiquity whose work has survived—very little, unfortunately, but enough to show that she was educated, worldly, and versed in politics. Like a modern experimental poet, she uses language self-consciously. Sappho's sensuality comes through in a description of her feelings at seeing a woman whose company she desires talking with a man: her heart shakes, her tongue is stuck, her eyes cannot see, her skin is on fire. "I am greener than grass," Sappho writes. "I feel nearly as if I could die."[**]

Sappho discusses female sexuality, a subject that Greek elite culture, dominated by males, tended to ignore. We know little about the sexuality of Greek women or of non-elite males. Among the male elite, romantic love in Archaic and **Classical Greece** was homosexual love or, to be precise, *pederasty* ("boy love"). The ideal relationship was supposed to involve a man in his twenties and a boy in his teens. The male elite was, strictly speaking, bisexual. By age 30, a man was expected to marry and raise a family. Perhaps bisexuality prevailed among elite females as well; Sappho, for example, eventually married and had a child.

**Athenian Kore** This statue of a young woman (*kore*) exemplifies Archaic Greek sculpture's interest in the idealized human form. Note the slight smile, the carefully coifed hair, and the elaborate clothes. Influenced by contemporary Egyptian statues, Greek sculptors nonetheless created a new and original style. Nimatallah/Art Resource, NY

---

*Charles Rowan Beye, *Ancient Greek Literature and Society*, 2d ed. (Ithaca, N.Y.: Cornell University Press, 1987), p. 78.
**Ibid., p. 79.

Another sign of the interest in the personal in Archaic Greece is the growing attention paid to the depiction of the human body, both in painting (most of the surviving examples are painted pottery) and in sculpture. Archaic artists displayed increasing skill and sensitivity in depicting the human form. The rich marble deposits in Greek soil gave sculptors promising material; baked clay (terra cotta) and bronze were other common sculptural media.

Early Archaic marble sculpture (seventh century B.C.) was strongly influenced by the way Egyptian sculpture represented the human body. Like Egyptian statuary, early Greek sculpture tended to be formal and frontal. Over the course of the seventh and sixth centuries B.C., Greek sculptors experimented with a greater variety of poses and with increasing realism in showing musculature and motion. This realism, however, was expressed within limits, for the favorite subject of Archaic sculptors was not ordinary people but idealized, beautiful youth. The goal was to show people not as they were but as they might be.

## Religious Faith and Practice

The Olympian gods who had been worshiped in the Mycenaean era survived in later ages, adapted to fit new political and social conditions. In the Archaic period, accordingly, the Olympian gods became gods of the polis.

Although the Olympians were revered throughout Greece, each polis had its patron deity, as well as its favorite heroes or demigods. Devotees considered it important to build a "house"—that is, a temple—for the local patron god or at least for his or her statue. The first temples were built of wood; the earliest stone temple, a temple of Apollo at Corinth, was built around 550 B.C.

As in other ancient cultures, so in Greece, divination was an important element of religion. Divination was institutionalized in *oracles*, places where a god or hero might be consulted for advice. The most famous Greek oracle was that of Apollo at Delphi (DEL-fye) in central Greece. At Delphi, Apollo spoke through the Pythia, a priestess who went into a trance. The utterances of Apollo at Delphi were known for being ambiguous. Because different people might interpret them in different ways, Apollo could not be blamed after the fact if things did not turn out as the listener expected. Politicians and poleis regularly consulted Delphi about public policy.

Archaic thinkers pondered the theme of divine justice. In Archaic literature, we see less of the petty squabbling among the gods than in Homer and more of Zeus's majesty and justice. Although the wicked might seem to prosper, Zeus eventually punishes them or their descendants.

Archaic writers delighted in portraying human emotions, but they had no confidence about the human ability to master emotions. In Archaic literature, people are weak and insignificant; their fortune is uncertain and mutable. Further, the gods are jealous of human success. People who aim too high are guilty of *hubris*—arrogance with overtones of violence and transgression. Hubris inevitably brings *nemesis*, "punishment" or "allotment." The safest course is for a person to be pious and humble.

So, Archaic religion taught a humbling, even pessimistic, lesson. Yet, its teachings were not always heeded. The pages of Archaic history are full of people who aimed high and sought success with seemingly little worry or dire consequences. In Ionia (see **Map 3.2**), one group of Greek thinkers made a radical break with Archaic religion and invented speculative philosophy.

## The Origins of Western Philosophy

Abstract, rationalistic, speculative thinking emerged in Greece during the sixth century B.C. The first developments took place in Miletus (my-LEE-tus), an Ionian city. It is often said that the thinkers of Miletus (the Milesians) and their followers in other parts of Ionia invented philosophy and science. So they did, but we must be precise about what this means.

The Ionians were not the first to ask questions or tell stories about the nature and origins of the universe; virtually every ancient people did so. By 600 B.C., moreover, mathematics, astronomy, medicine, and engineering had been thriving for over two thousand years in

Egypt and Mesopotamia, a heritage with which the Ionians were familiar and from which they borrowed.

The real importance of the Ionians is as pioneers of rationalism. They began the movement away from anthropomorphic or divine explanations and toward an abstract and mechanistic explanation of the universe. Later Greek philosophers were rarely (if ever) atheists, but they took for granted what the Ionians labored to establish: the primacy of human reason.

The Ionians saw themselves as students of nature—*physis* (from which the word *physics* is derived). Although they also commented on morality and politics, their interest in natural phenomena is what makes the Ionians significant. In their own day, the Ionians were called "wise men" (*sophoi*); to a later generation, they were "lovers of wisdom," *philosophoi* (from which *philosopher* comes).

Thales (THAY-leez), the first Milesian thinker, made a name for himself by successfully predicting a solar eclipse in 585 B.C. He is credited with founding Greek geometry and astronomy. Little survives of his writings or those of the other Milesians, but it is clear that he created the first general and systematic theory about the nature of the universe. According to Thales, the primary substance, the element from which all of nature was created, was water. He emphasized the mobility of water and its ability to nourish life.

A reply followed soon. Around 550 B.C., Anaximander of Miletus wrote the first known book of prose in Greek, expounding his own philosophy of nature. He attacked Thales for oversimplifying the dynamism of nature. Anaximander accepted Thales' monist assumption—that all matter originated from one primary substance—but he called the substance "the unlimited" or "the undefined" rather than water. A third Milesian, Anaximenes, replied that the primary substance might be unlimited but it was not undefined. It was air, whose properties of condensation and rarefaction symbolized the dynamic and changing nature of things.

Humble as these theories might seem today, they represent a dramatic development: an open and critical debate among thinkers, each of whom was proposing an abstract and rational model of the universe. Why Miletus? Why the sixth century B.C.? There are no sure answers, although certain influences have been suggested. Among them are Miletus's contacts on the trade routes with sophisticated Babylon, the proximity of Ionia to non-Greek peoples and the resulting Milesian appreciation of variety and complexity, and the search for law and order in contemporary Greek political life and its extension to the philosophical plane.

In its second generation, early Greek philosophy moved to other Ionian cities and then migrated westward across the Mediterranean. Heracleitus (her-uh-CLY-tus) of Ephesus (ca. 500 B.C.) proposed fire as the primary substance. Although fire was ever changing, it had an underlying coherence. According to Heracleitus, this paradox nicely symbolized the nature of the universe. He summed up the importance of change by the aphorisms "All things flow" and "You cannot step into the same river twice." The universe witnessed a constant struggle of opposites, yet an essential unity and order prevailed. To describe this order, Heracleitus used the term *logos* (LOH-gos). This key concept of Greek philosophy is difficult to translate; among other definitions, *logos* can mean "word," "thought," "reason," "story," or "calculation." The term *logos* embodies the importance of reason in ancient Greek civilization.

Heracleitus's contemporary, Pythagoras (py-THAG-uh-russ) of Samos, was both a rationalist and a religious thinker. On the one hand, Pythagoras was a mathematician who discovered the numerical ratios determining the major intervals of the musical scale—that is, the range of sound between high and low. It is less certain if, as tradition has it, he discovered the so-called Pythagorean theorem—that in a right triangle the hypotenuse squared is equal to the sum of the squares of the other two sides.

On the other hand, Pythagoras believed that the purity of mathematics would improve the human soul. Just as he had imposed numerical order on the musical scale, so could philosophers understand the entire universe through number and proportion. The resulting knowledge was no mere academic exercise, but a way of life. Pythagoras devoted himself to "observation" or "contemplation"—to *theoria* (from which *theory* comes).

In Magna Graecia (southern Italy), Pythagoras founded a religious community. Its members observed strict secrecy, but it appears that they abstained from meat because they believed in the kinship of all living things. They also believed in the reincarnation of the human soul, though not necessarily into a human body.

The early Greek philosopher whose work is most fully preserved is Parmenides (par-MEN-uh-deez) of Elea in Magna Graecia. Parmenides (b. ca. 515 B.C.) completely distrusted the senses. He believed that reality was a world of pure being: eternal, unchanging, and indivisible, comparable to a sphere. To Parmenides, change was a mere illusion. Parmenides, therefore, is the first Western philosopher to propose a radical difference between the world of the senses and reality. This fundamental strain of Western thought would be taken up by Plato and his followers and then passed to Christianity.

To sum up, in philosophy, as in so many other endeavors, the Archaic Greeks were great borrowers and even greater innovators who left a profound mark on later ages. By the late sixth century B.C., Archaic Greece was poised on the brink of a revolution that would give birth to the Classical period of Greek civilization.

## SECTION SUMMARY

- Lyric poetry and Archaic sculpture display a groundbreaking interest in individual feelings and the human body.
- Archaic Greek religion was pessimistic. It feared human arrogance (*hubris*) and divine punishment (*nemesis*).
- Western philosophy began in Ionia in the 500s B.C.
- The first philosophers were rationalists who offered abstract and mechanistic explanations of nature.

# Classical Greece

*What was Athenian democracy and how did it clash with Sparta in the Peloponnesian War?*

The word democracy comes from the Greek *demokratia* (deh-mo-kra-TEE-uh), coined in Athens early in the fifth century B.C. *Demokratia* literally means "the power (*kratos*) of the people (*demos*)." Modern democracy is characterized by mass citizenship, elections, and representative government. Athenian demokratia, in contrast, was a direct democracy in which elections mattered less than direct participation, citizenship was restricted, women were excluded from politics, immigrants could rarely become citizens, and citizens owned slaves and ruled an empire. Modern democracies are big, but Athens encompassed only 1,000 square miles. Modern democracies emphasize individual rights, but Athens placed the community first. Yet Athenian demokratia established principles enshrined in democracy today: freedom, equality, citizenship without property qualifications, the right of most citizens to hold office, and the rule of law.

*demokratia* Term coined in Athens in the fifth century B.C. to describe the city's system of direct government.

The young democracy's greatest achievement was to spearhead Greece's victory over the Persian invaders in 480 B.C. After that victory, Athens became Greece's leading sea power. Yet Sparta remained the superior land power, and the two poleis were soon locked in a cycle of competition and war. The result nearly destroyed Athenian democracy. Even more serious, it undermined Greece's very independence.

## The Development of Demokratia, 508–322 B.C.

In Athens after Pisistratid rule, conditions were ripe for revolution. Solon had left a society of independent small farmers, while the Pisistratids had strengthened the ranks of immigrants and weakened the Eupatrids. Elite leaders nonetheless tried to establish an Athenian oligarchy. We may imagine strong popular opposition.

Ironically, a Eupatrid, Cleisthenes (KLICE-the-neez) (d. ca. 500 B.C.), led the revolution. Originally, Cleisthenes aimed to head the oligarchy, but his rivals shut him out of power. He turned then to the demos, whose leader he became. The watchwords of the day were *equality* and *mixing* (that is, mixing people from different regions of Attica in order to break down local, aristocratic power bases).

Frightened by the assertive populace, the oligarchs called for Spartan military assistance, but to no avail: Cleisthenes rallied the people to victory. The Athenian triumph proved, in Herodotus's opinion, "that equality is an excellent thing, not in one way only but in many.

For while they were under a tyranny, [Athenians] were no better at fighting than any of their neighbors, but once they were rid of tyrants they became by far the best."*

Cleisthenes extinguished Eupatrid power once and for all by attacking its local bases of support. For example, he abolished the four traditional tribes and apportioned the people among ten new tribes. The tribes formed the basis of a new Council of 500 to replace Solon's Council of 400. The council was divided into ten tribal units, each serving as a kind of executive committee for one of the ten months of the civic year.

The centerpiece of the government was the assembly, some of whose members, emboldened by the new spirit of equality, now spoke up for the first time. The new Council of 500, like its predecessor, prepared the assembly's agenda, but assemblymen felt free to amend it. Only the Areopagus council remained a privileged preserve.

The last and most unusual part of the Cleisthenic system was ostracism, a sort of annual *un*popularity contest that received its name from the pieces of broken pottery (*ostraka*) on which the names of victims—prominent Athenian citizens—were chiseled. The "winner" was forced into ten years of exile, although his property would not be confiscated. Ostracism was meant to protect the regime by defusing factionalism and discouraging tyrants. Judging by Athens's political stability, it worked.

In 508 B.C., the poorest Athenians had relatively little power in Cleisthenic government, but changes by the 450s made Athens even more democratic. During that period, the oldest principle of Greek politics came to the fore: Whoever fights for the state governs it. To counter the Persian threat against Greece in the 480s (see page 71), Athens built a great navy. The standard ship was a trireme (TRY-reem), an oared warship rowed by 170 men on three decks. The core of the rowers consisted of thetes, the poorest free men in Athens. Just as hoplites supported new regimes in Greece after 700 B.C., so rowers supported new regimes in Greece after 500 B.C.

A second revolution occurred around 461 B.C., when Ephialtes (d. ca. 460 B.C.) and his young associate **Pericles** (ca. 495–429 B.C.) targeted the last bulwark of privilege, the Areopagus. They stripped away the council's long-standing supervisory powers over the regime and redistributed those powers to the Council of 500 and the people's court. The decade of the 450s B.C. saw another innovation: payment for public service, specifically for jurors, who received a half-drachma (perhaps half a day's wages) for a day of jury duty. Eventually, other public servants also received pay. Conservatives complained bitterly because they perceived, rightly, that state pay made political activity by poor people possible. State pay was, an Athenian said, "the glue of demokratia."

Demokratia became closely connected with Pericles (PAIR-ih-kleez), who inherited the constituency of Ephialtes after his assassination around 460 B.C. For much of the next thirty years, Pericles dominated Athenian politics. An aristocrat who respected the common

**Pericles** Leader of fifth century B.C. Athens, he established Athens as a great center of art and literature as well as a great empire.

*Herodotus, *The Histories*, trans. Barry S. Strauss. © Cengage Learning.

**Greek Trireme**
*Olympias* is a hypothetical reconstruction of an Athenian war galley of about 400 B.C. Rowed by 170 oarsmen arranged on three decks, the trireme fought by ramming an enemy ship with the bronze ram attached to its bow. John Coates/Trireme Trust Foundation

people, an excellent orator who benefited from an education in philosophy, an honest and tireless worker, and a general who led in peace as well as war, Pericles was a political giant. Under his leadership, demokratia became firmly entrenched as the government and way of life in Athens.

Pericles was much influenced by a woman, Aspasia (uh-SPAY-see-uh). She belonged to the small group of noncitizen women called *hetairai*, or courtesans (that is, prostitutes patronized by men of wealth and status). An educated woman from Miletus, Aspasia was Pericles' mistress and bore him a son. Aspasia and Pericles gathered around them a glittering circle of thinkers and artists. Some say that Aspasia even influenced Pericles' political decisions.

Athenian democracy survived, with occasional oligarchic intrusions, for 150 years after Pericles' death. During those years, it became more institutionalized and cautious, but it also became more thoroughly egalitarian.

## How Demokratia Worked

Unlike most modern democracies, Athenian demokratia was direct and participatory. Pericles once claimed that in Athens, "people pay attention both to their own household and to politics. Even those occupied with other activities are no less knowledgeable about politics."* This is part boast, but only part. Large numbers of ordinary citizens attended the assembly from time to time and held public office or served on the Council of 500 for a year or two.

## Government

The central institution was the assembly. Open to all male citizens over age 20, assembly meetings were held in the open air, on a hillside seating several thousand on benches (see the photograph on page 48). In the fourth century B.C., the assembly gathered a minimum of forty times per year, about once every ten days.

The assembly heard the great debates of the day. It made decisions about war and peace, alliance and friendship; it conferred honors and issued condemnations; it passed decrees relating to current issues and set up commissions to revise fundamental laws. In the assembly, top orators addressed the people, but everyone, however humble, was theoretically entitled to speak.

The judicial branch consisted of courts, which, with a few exceptions, were open to all citizens, no matter how poor. Aristotle or a member of his school comments that "when the people have the right to vote in the courts, they control the constitution." Juries were large, commonly consisting of several hundred men chosen by lottery; small juries, it was felt, were easily bribed. After a preliminary hearing, cases were decided in a single day.

The executive consisted of the Council of 500 and some seven hundred public officials (also, under Athens's empire in the fifth century B.C., several hundred others living abroad). All male citizens over age 30 were eligible to serve. Most public officials were chosen by lottery, which put rich and poor, talented and untalented, on an equal footing. To guard against installing incompetents or criminals, all officials had to undergo a scrutiny by the council before taking office and an audit after the term. Most magistracies, moreover, were boards, usually of ten men, so even if a bad man managed to pass this scrutiny, he would be counterbalanced by his colleagues. Only generals and treasurers were chosen by election.

Athens had a weak executive and no president or prime minister. Generals and orators led debates and sometimes exercised great influence, but ordinary people set the agenda and made the decisions by taking votes at each assembly meeting. On the local level, every deme (county) had an annually chosen executive and a deme assembly of all citizens.

So novel and populist a system of government has not been without critics, either in antiquity or today. Some have charged that the Athenian people were uneducated, emotional, and easily swayed by oratorical tricks. Others say that demokratia degenerated into mob rule after the death of Pericles. Still others complain about the lack of a system of formal public education, which denied many citizens equality of opportunity.

---

*From Thucydides, *The Peloponnesian War*, trans. Barry S. Strauss.

## Women and Resident Aliens

Another serious charge against Athenian demokratia is that it was democracy for an elite only. Adult male citizens never amounted to more than one-tenth of the population, approximately 40,000 out of a total population—men, women and children, resident aliens, and slaves—of about 400,000. To become a citizen, a boy at age 18 had to prove that he was the legitimate son of a citizen father and a citizen maternal grandfather. Girls were never officially registered as citizens. Although the term *citizeness* existed, Athenian citizen women were usually referred to as "city women." Resident aliens rarely attained citizenship.

In the fifth and fourth centuries B.C., Athens had a large population of foreigners. Some were transient. Others were officially registered resident aliens, or *metics* (MEH-tiks). Metics came by the thousands from all over the Greek world and beyond. Some, like Aristotle (a native of a Greek colony in Macedonia [mah-suh-DOE-nee-uh]), were attracted by the city's schools of philosophy, but most came because of its unparalleled economic opportunities. Metics could not own land in Athens, and they had to pay extra taxes and serve in the Athenian military. Nevertheless, they prospered in Athenian commerce and crafts.

Athenian women were excluded from politics and played only a modest role in commerce as small retailers. In legal matters, women usually had to be represented by a male guardian. Demokratia also promoted an ideal of the male as master of his household, with women obedient and reserved. As Pericles put it: "To a woman not to show more weakness than is natural to her sex is a great glory, and not to be talked about for good or for evil among men."*

Practice, however, was another matter. As Aristotle asks rhetorically, "How is it possible to prevent the wives of the poor from going out?" *Poor* is a synonym for *ordinary* in ancient Greek. Ordinary women could not stay at home because they had work to do in the city or fields. Ordinary houses, moreover, were small and cramped, and in the Mediterranean heat, women could not stay inside all the time.

We occasionally get glimpses, sometimes more, of Athenian women resisting or working behind the scenes to correct male mistakes. An inheritance case reveals a woman go-between interceding among her quarreling male relations. Greek comedy shows women mocking male pretensions and establishing sisterly friendships. A woman who brought a large dowry into a marriage could use it and the threat of divorce to influence her husband (the dowry had to be returned to the woman's father or guardian if there was a divorce). In short, Athenian women had some access to the world outside the household and some influence within the household. There existed, nonetheless, a real disparity in power between men and women.

Athenian demokratia lacked many features of modern democracy, including a notion of human rights, the mass naturalization of immigrants, gender equality, the abolition of slavery, and public education. To its small citizen body, however, Athenian demokratia offered freedom, equality, and responsibility, as well as a degree of participation in public life seldom equaled. Demokratia was a model of what democracy could be, but not of who could take part.

## The Persian Wars, 499–479 B.C.

In 500 B.C., Sparta, hegemon of the Peloponnesian League, was the most prominent power of the Greek mainland. Across the Aegean Sea in Anatolia, the Greek city-states had been under Persian rule for two generations, since Cyrus the Great's conquest in the 540s B.C. In 499 B.C., however, events began to unfold that not only would revolutionize that balance of power but also would throw the entire eastern Mediterranean into two hundred years of turmoil.

Led by Miletus, the Ionian Greek city-states rose in revolt against Persia in 499 B.C. Athens sent troops to help, but despite initial successes, Athens reconsidered the alliance and withdrew its forces. The Ionian coalition broke down thereafter and was crushed by Persia. Miletus was besieged and destroyed, but otherwise Persia was relatively lenient in Ionia.

---

*Quote from Thucydides translated into English; with introduction, marginal analysis, notes, and indices. Volume 1. Thucydides. Benjamin Jowett. translator. Oxford. Clarendon Press. 1881.

Upstart Athens, however, could not go unpunished. In 490 B.C., Darius I sent a large naval expedition against Athens. About 25,000 infantrymen and 1,200 cavalrymen (with horses) landed at Marathon, some 24 miles from the city of Athens (see **Map 3.4**). Athens sent 10,000 men (including 1,000 allies) to defend Marathon, and a great battle ensued.

Persian overconfidence and the superiority of the Greek phalanx over Persia's loosely organized infantrymen won Athens a smashing victory. Persia suffered 6,400 casualties, Athens only 192. (The story, unconfirmed, that a messenger ran from the battlefield to the city of Athens with the news, "Rejoice, we conquer!" is the inspiration for the modern marathon race, a slightly longer distance of about 26 miles.) After the battle, Athens experienced a burst of confidence that propelled it to power and glory.

Meanwhile, Persia sought a rematch. After Darius's death in 486, his son and successor, Xerxes, amassed a huge force of about a thousand ships and several hundred thousand soldiers and rowers. Athens, under the leadership of Themistocles (ca. 525–460 B.C.), prepared by building a fleet of two hundred ships. Athens joined Sparta and twenty-nine other poleis in the Hellenic League of defense, with Sparta in overall command. Most poleis either stayed neutral or, like Thebes and Argos, collaborated with Persia. The Greeks had only three-hundred-plus ships and about fifty thousand infantrymen.

Persia invaded Greece in 480 B.C. and won the opening moves. At the narrow pass of Thermopylae in central Greece (see **Map 3.2**), the Persians outflanked and crushed an army of three hundred Spartans, who died fighting to the last man, including their king, Leonidas. This sacrifice added to the Spartan reputation for courage but left the road south open. Abandoned by its defenders, Athens was sacked.

The tide then turned. The Greeks lured the Persian fleet into the narrow straits between Athens and Salamis. The Persians could not use their numerical superiority in this confined space, and the Greeks had the home advantage. The result was a crushing Persian defeat under the eyes of Xerxes himself, who watched the battle from a throne on a hillside near the shore.

Because their sea links to the Levant had been cut, Xerxes and the remainder of the Persian fleet left for home. Soon afterward, the united Greek army, under Spartan leadership, defeated Persian forces on land at Plataea (just north of Attica; see **Map 3.2**) in 479 B.C. At about the same time, the Greek fleet defeated a reorganized Persian fleet off the Anatolian coast. The victorious Greeks sailed the coast and liberated the Ionians. Not only did Persia fail to conquer the Greek mainland, but it also lost its eastern Aegean empire.

Greeks did not remember the invader fondly. After 480, they thought of Persians not merely as enemies but as barbarians—that is, cultural inferiors. (See the feature, "The Global Record: The Enemy as Barbarian.") At the same time, Greeks became more conscious of their own common culture.

**Amazon Queen** This red-figure Athenian cup (ca. 440 B.C.) shows the Greek warrior Achilles about to slay the Amazon queen Penthesilea during the Trojan War, in which she fought on Troy's side. She was a symbol of feminine courage and beauty.

bpk, Berlin/Staatliche Antikensammlungen und Glyptothek, Munich/Art Resource, NY

## Struggles to Dominate Greece, 478–362 B.C.

The Greek unity forged by the struggle against Persia was fragile and short-lived. What followed was a constant struggle in diplomacy and war among city-states, usually arranged in leagues under hegemons.

Following the Greek victory over Persia, Athens expanded its power as hegemon of a new security organization. Founded on the island of Delos in the Aegean Sea, the so-called Delian League aimed both at protecting Greek lands and at plundering Persian territory. The number of allies grew from about 150 in 477 B.C. to about 250 in 431 B.C., at the height of the league.

Because they feared entanglement outside the Peloponnesus, most Spartans preferred to leave the Aegean to Athens. Some Spartans, nonetheless, watched with unease and jealousy as Athenian power boomed.

## The Enemy as Barbarian

*Classical Greeks no longer regarded the enemy as honored rivals, as Homer's heroes had regarded Trojans. Rather, they looked down on the enemy as barbarians. Greece's archenemies, the Persians, were portrayed as indulgent, effeminate, emotional, slavish, cruel, and dangerous. Consider the contrasting portraits of Persians and Greeks in these excerpts from the historian Herodotus's account of Persia's invasion of Greece in 480 B.C.*

### The Persians

He [King Xerxes of Persia] then prepared to move forward to Abydos, where a bridge had already been constructed across the Hellespont from Europe to Asia.... It was here not long afterwards that the Greeks under Xanthippus the son of Ariphron took Artayctes the Persian governor of Sestos, and nailed him alive to a plank—he was the man who collected women in the temple of Protesilaus at Elaeus and committed various acts of sacrilege. This headland was the point to which Xerxes' engineers carried their two bridges from Abydos—a distance of seven furlongs.... The work was successfully completed, but a subsequent storm of great violence smashed it up and carried everything away. Xerxes was very angry when he learned of the disaster, and gave orders that the Hellespont should receive three hundred lashes and have a pair of fetters thrown into it. And I have heard before now that he also sent people to brand it with hot irons. He certainly instructed the men with the whips to utter, as they wielded them, the following words: "You salt and bitter stream, your master lays this punishment upon you for injuring him, who never injured you. But Xerxes the King will cross you, with or without your permission. No man sacrifices to you, and you deserve the neglect by your acrid and muddy waters"—a highly presumptuous way of addressing the Hellespont, and typical of a barbarous nation. In addition to punishing the Hellespont Xerxes gave orders that the men responsible for building the bridge should have their heads cut off. This unseemly order was duly carried out . . .

### The Greeks

To the Spartan envoys . . . [the Athenians] said: "No doubt it was natural that the Lacedaemonians [Spartans] should dread the possibility of our making terms with Persia; nonetheless it shows a poor estimate of the spirit of Athens. Were we offered all the gold in the world, and the fairest and richest country the earth contains, we should never consent to join the common enemy and bring Greece into submission. There are many compelling reasons to prevent our taking such a course, even if we wish to do so: the first and greatest is the burning of the temples and images of our gods—now mere heaps of rubble. It is our bounden duty to avenge this desecration with all the power we possess—not to clasp in friendship the hand that wrought it. Again, there is the Greek nation—the common blood, the common language; the temples and religious ritual; the whole way of life we understand and share together—indeed, if Athens were to betray all this it would not be well done. We would have you know, therefore, if you did not already know it, that we will never make peace with Xerxes so long as a single Athenian remains alive."

### Questions

1. *Find at least three examples in these passages of Persian barbarism.*

2. *By deciding to make war instead of negotiating peace, are the Athenians barbarians or civilized people?*

3. *Does Herodotus offer convincing proof that the Persians are more barbarous than the Greeks? Is he fair?*

From THE HISTORIES by Herodotus, translated by Aubrey de Selincourt, revised with introductory matter and notes by John Marincola (Penguin Classics 1954, Second revised edition 1996). Translation copyright 1954 by Aubrey de Selincourt. This revised edition copyright © John Marincola, 1996. Reproduced by permission of Penguin Books Ltd.

Afraid of the new titan, the major allied states rebelled, beginning with Thasos in 465 B.C., but Athens crushed each rebellion. Sometimes after surrender, rebels were executed and their wives and children sold into slavery. Allied complaints began to stir Sparta, who moved against Athens in a series of clashes known as the First Peloponnesian War, between about 460 and 445 B.C. A larger conflict, however, loomed between Greece's greatest land power, Sparta, and Greece's greatest sea power, Athens.

The Peloponnesian War, as this conflict is known today, came in 431 B.C. and lasted intermittently until 404 B.C. The war proved bloody and bitter. Battles between huge fleets, economic warfare, protracted sieges, epidemic disease, and ideological struggle produced a devastating war. It was clear that the Greeks could not maintain their unity against Persia; indeed, they appeared to be destroying themselves.

In this era, both democratic Athens and oligarchic Sparta sought to promote their respective ideologies. Some unfortunate states became ideological battlegrounds, often at great cost of life. In Corcyra (modern Corfu; see **Map 3.5**), for example, bloody civil war marked a series of coups and countercoups in the 420s B.C.

Given Spartan supremacy on land and Athenian mastery of the sea, it is not surprising that the Peloponnesian War remained undecided for a decade and a half. The balance of power shifted only after an Athenian blunder, an expedition to conquer Sicily (415–413 B.C.) that became a quagmire and then a disaster, leading to total defeat and thousands of Athenian casualties. In the aftermath, most of the Athenian empire rose in revolt. Persia re-emerged and intervened on Sparta's side—in return for Sparta's restoration of Ionia to Persia, an ironic counterpoint to Sparta's role in driving Persia from Greece in 479. Athens, nevertheless, was sufficiently wealthy and plucky to hold out until 404 B.C.

Sparta won the Peloponnesian War, but establishing a new Greek order proved beyond its grasp. Spartans were soldiers, not diplomats; infantrymen, not sailors; and commanders, not public speakers. They made poor leaders. Sparta took over Athens's former empire and quickly had a falling-out with its allies: Persia, Corinth, and Thebes.

In addition, Sparta suffered a vast decline in the number of citizens. The original nine thousand Similars of the seventh century B.C. had dropped to only about fifteen hundred in 371 B.C. The main problem seems to have been greed. Rich Spartans preferred to get richer by concentrating wealth in fewer hands rather than open the elite to new blood. Thousands of men could no longer afford to live as elite soldiers.

The result was military disaster. In 371 B.C., the Boeotian army crushed the Spartans at the Battle of Leuctra, killing a thousand men (including four hundred Similars) and a Spartan king. In the next few years, Boeotia invaded the Peloponnesus, freed the Messenian helots, and restored Messenia to independence, after some 350 years of bondage. It was a fatal blow to Spartan power, but Boeotia, too, was exhausted and its main leaders were dead. None of the Greek city-states had been able to maintain hegemony.

🌐 **Map 3.5 Greece in the Peloponnesian War**  During the long and bloody Peloponnesian War (431–404 B.C.), much of the Greek world was divided into two camps: one led by Sparta, the other by Athens.

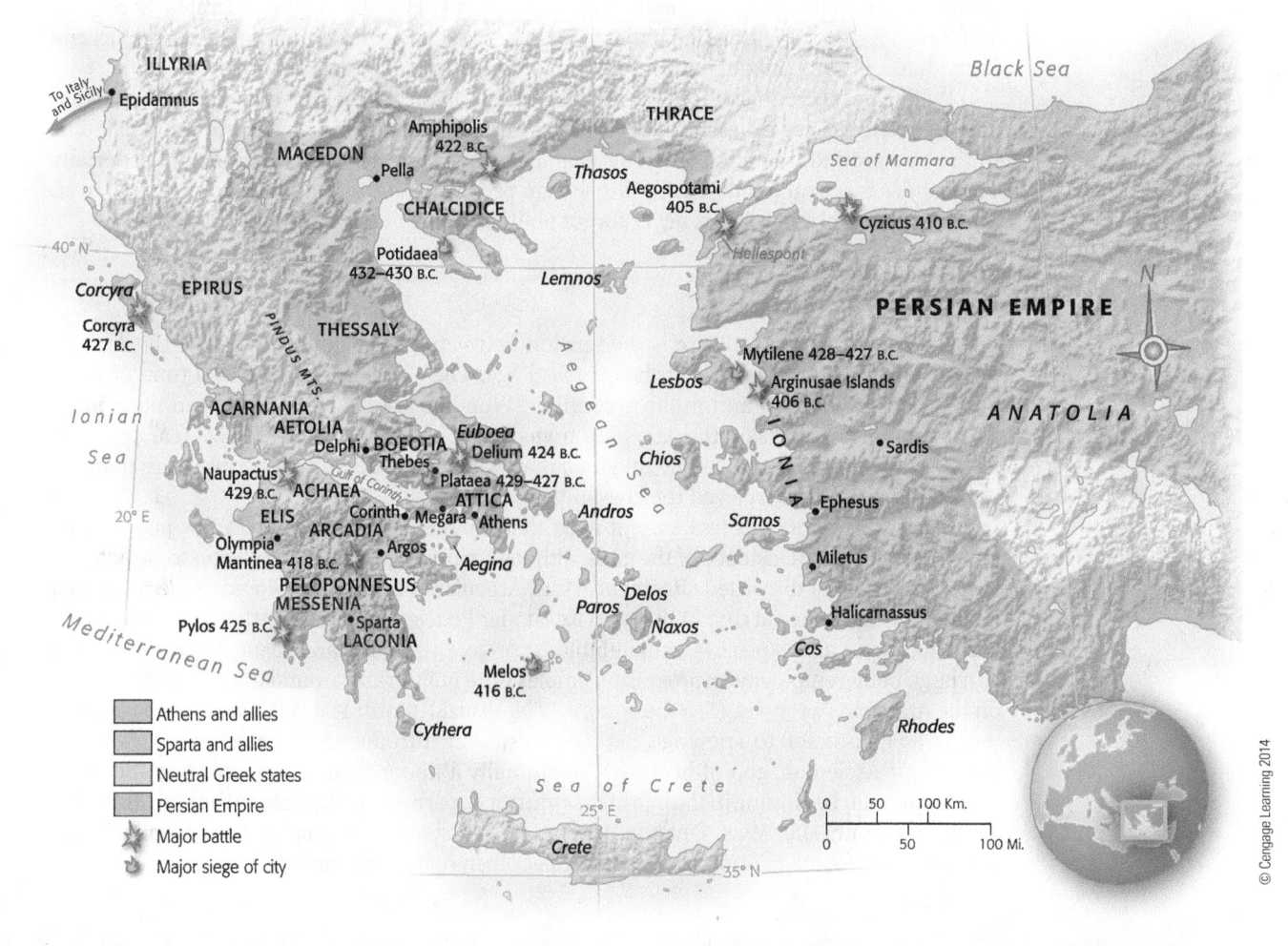

Athens and allies
Sparta and allies
Neutral Greek states
Persian Empire
⭐ Major battle
🔥 Major siege of city

© Cengage Learning 2014

## SECTION SUMMARY

- Democracy or "people power" (*demokratia*) began in ancient Greece, and Athens was the most influential Greek democracy.
- Athenian democracy was direct and participatory for adult male citizens, but women, resident aliens, and slaves were all denied citizen rights.
- Persia's massive invasion of mainland Greece in 480–479 B.C. was defeated by a coalition led by Sparta and Athens.
- The Greek *poleis* then turned on each other in a series of wars that lasted about a century.
- Sparta defeated Athens in the most intense phase of these conflicts, known today as the Peloponnesian War (431–404 B.C.).

# The Public Culture of Classical Greece

*How did tragedy, comedy, philosophy, and history all begin and develop in the culture of Classical Greece?*

The word *classical* means "to set a standard." The culture of Greece between 480 and 322 B.C. proved so influential in the later West that it may justly be called classical. Classical Greek culture was public culture. Poets were not inward-looking or alienated figures. Rather, to quote the Athenian playwright Aristophanes (air-ih-STOF-uh-neez) (ca. 455–385 B.C.), they were "the teachers of men," who commented on contemporary public debate. (As the quotation might also suggest, men, especially citizens, dominated public life.) Dramas were performed in a state theater at state religious festivals. The philosopher Socrates (sock-ruh-TEEZ) (469–399 B.C.) discussed philosophy in marketplaces and gymnasia. It was not private individuals, but the public, that was the major patron of sculpture and architecture.

Public life, accordingly, is the central theme of Classical Greek art and literature. In tragedy, for example, regardless of the particular hero or plot, the same character always looms in the background: the polis. The Classical historians Herodotus, Xenophon, and especially Thucydides focus on public affairs rather than private life. Classical philosophy ranged from biology to metaphysics, but it never forgot politics.

## Religion and Art

A hallmark of Classical culture is the tension between the religious heritage of the Archaic period and the worldly spirit of the Classical age. The Classical period was a time of prosperity, political debate, and military conflict. "Wonders are many on earth, and none more wondrous than man," said the Athenian tragedian Sophocles (sof-uh-KLEEZ) (ca. 495–406 B.C.). Yet Sophocles was a deeply religious man who also believed that people were doomed to disaster unless they obeyed the laws of the gods.

Classical religion was less sure of itself than its Archaic predecessor. A few people even questioned the very existence of the gods, although most Greeks wanted religion to be adapted to the new age, not discarded altogether. Thus, Athenian religion was tailored to the needs of a democratic and imperial city. In the 440s B.C., under Pericles' leadership, Athens embarked on a vast, ambitious, and expensive temple-building project, using Delian League funds and serving as a large public employment program. Temples were built in and around the city, most notably on the Athenian Acropolis. (See the feature, "The Visual Record: The Parthenon" on page 76.)

To adapt religion to a new age, new cults also were introduced. The most popular was the worship of Asclepius, god of healing. Traditionally a minor figure, Asclepius became enormously popular beginning in the late fifth century B.C., perhaps in response to the high mortality of the Peloponnesian War. Outside Athens, large shrines to Asclepius became pilgrimage centers in the fourth century B.C. for ailing people in search of a cure.

**The Parthenon**
The temple of Athena Parthenos ("the Maiden") on the Athenian Acropolis, the Parthenon was dedicated in 438 B.C. One of the largest and most complex Greek temples, it was built of fine marble. The partially restored ruins symbolize the wealth, power, and greatness of Classical Greece.

William Katz/Photo Researchers, Inc.

Women played a major role in Classical Athenian religion. They were priestesses in more than forty major cults. They participated each year in many festivals, including several reserved only for women. One such festival, the Thesmophoria, a celebration of fertility held each autumn, featured a three-day encampment of women on a hillside in the city, right beside the Athenian assembly amphitheater. Women also attended public funeral orations in honor of soldiers who had died in battle. They probably attended plays as well.

In art, Classical sculptors completed the process begun by their Archaic forebears of mastering the accurate representation of the human body. In anatomical precision, Classical Greek sculpture was the most technically proficient sculpture the world had seen. Like Archaic sculpture, it was not, however, an attempt to portray humans "warts and all" but rather an idealization of the human form.

## The Sophists and Socrates

Success in democratic politics required knowledge of oratory. This demand was met in the late fifth century B.C. by the arrival in Athens of professional teachers of *rhetoric*, the art of speaking. They were known as **Sophists** (SOF-ists) (from a word meaning "to instruct" or "to make wise"). Sicilian Greeks invented rhetoric around 465 B.C. by drawing up the rules of argument. For a fee—rarely small and sometimes astronomical—Sophists taught young Athenians the art of speaking. Their curriculum consisted not only of rhetoric but also of the rudiments of linguistics, ethics, psychology, history, and anthropology—in other words, any aspect of "human nature" that might help an aspiring politician. Within a few years, most ambitious young Athenians of prosperous families were studying with Sophists.

At their best, Sophists sharpened young minds. Athenian tragedians, historians, and philosophers all benefited from sophistic teaching. Protagoras (b. ca. 485 B.C.), perhaps the best-known Sophist, summed up the spirit of the age in his famous dictum, "Man is the measure of all things"—an appropriate credo for the interest in all things human that is apparent in Classical literature and art. There is, however, a more troubling side to the Sophists. As teachers of rhetoric, they taught respect for success, not for truth. Thus, they acquired a reputation as word-twisters who taught men how to make "the weaker argument defeat the stronger."

Much to the distress of conservatives, Sophists drew a distinction between *nomos*, a word that means "law" or "convention," and *physis*, which means "nature." The distinction had revolutionary potential. In general, Sophists had little respect for the established order,

**Sophists** Professional teachers of rhetoric and other subjects in the mid-fifth century B.C., whose training of ambitious young Athenians challenged the stability of standard values and established institutions. Today, "sophist" has come to mean "twister of words."

## The Parthenon

The Parthenon, completed in 432 B.C., dominates both the skyline of Athens and the historical imagination of the West. The building's fine marble and Classical proportions symbolize the free, confident, and united society that one might expect of Periclean Athens, the world's first democracy (see the photograph on page 75). A close look, however, suggests a more complex story. The Parthenon's sculpture offers glimpses of the tensions behind the Classical façade.

The temple of Athena Parthenos ("the Maiden"), as the Parthenon is formally known, was a public project of Greece's wealthiest city-state, leading naval power, and premier democracy. Athenians spared no expense on its construction. Sculpture included a gold and ivory statue of the goddess Athena inside the temple and, on the outside, statuary in each pediment (the triangular space under the eaves) and sculptured reliefs running around the building above the exterior and interior colonnades.

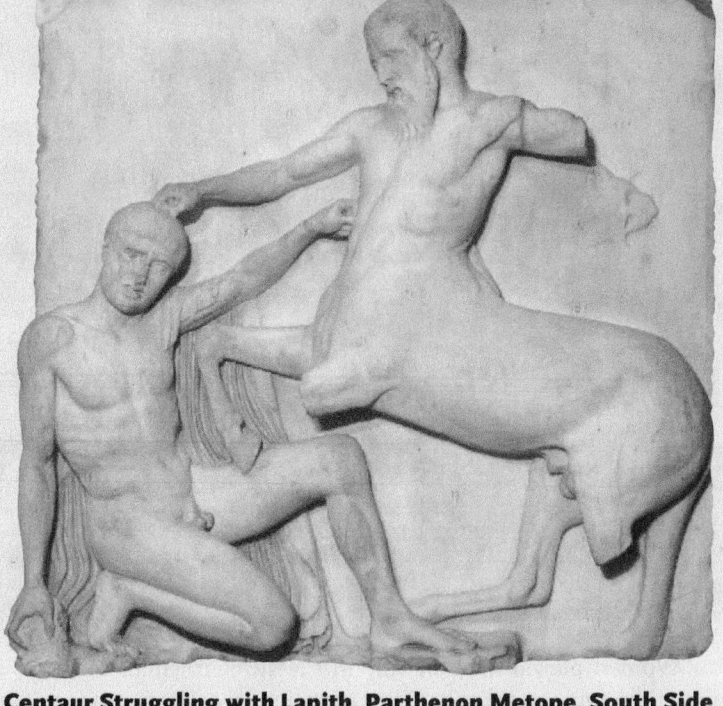

**Centaur Struggling with Lapith, Parthenon Metope, South Side**

So lavish a program of art demonstrated Athenian wealth but also served an educational purpose: to illustrate basic Athenian values. Because every Athenian male was expected to fight for the city when called on, militant competition is a central theme. Above the exterior colonnade, for example, ninety-two panels of relief sculpture depict gods and heroes fighting foes, such as giants and centaurs.

See the detail from the south wall. It shows a fight between a human male and a centaur, a mythological creature who was half-man, half-beast. Both the man and the centaur are powerful, but the centaur is old and ugly, while the man is young and handsome. The man fights fairly, while the centaur makes a savage attack with arm and forelegs. The man belongs to a Greek people known as the Lapiths. According to myth, the centaurs attacked the Lapiths during a wedding celebration, but they were driven off by the Lapith men, led by the bridegroom and his Athenian friend, the hero Theseus.

To a real-life Athenian observer, the triumph of the Lapiths might have symbolized Athens's victory over the Persians. It was easy to make the connection because the Parthenon was in effect a war memorial as well as a temple. When the Persians invaded Athens in 480 B.C., they destroyed the temples on the Acropolis. For forty years after Greece's victory, Athens left the Acropolis empty as a reminder of Persian barbarism. Then Pericles sponsored a building program of new temples, of which the Parthenon was the grandest.

Delian League funds were diverted to pay for the new buildings, which raised controversy. Ironically, democratic Athens used allied money, earmarked for defense, to glorify itself. Some people considered that oppressive.

or nomos. They considered it mere convention. A great man trained by a Sophist might rise above convention to realize the limitless potential of his nature, or physis. If he used his skill to overturn democracy and establish a tyranny, so much the worse for democracy. Indeed, the Sophists trained both unscrupulous democratic politicians and many of the oligarchs who launched coups d'état against Athenian democracy at the end of the fifth century B.C. As a result, *sophist* became a term of abuse in Athens and remains so to this day.

Classical Greek advances in rhetoric, therefore, were as problematic as they were brilliant. The Sophists influenced many branches of thought. Consider, for example, the work of the philosopher Democritus (dee-MOCK-ruh-tus) (b. ca. 460 B.C.). Democritus was not a Sophist, but he shared the common Sophistic notion that the reality of nature was far more radical than conventionally thought. He concluded that all things consisted of tiny,

**Four Women in Procession, Parthenon Frieze, East Wall**

Art Resource, NY

The sculpture above the interior colonnade is a continuous band, or frieze, around the four sides of the building, and it illustrates a procession. Warriors aplenty, primarily cavalrymen but also hoplites and charioteers, compose the lineup. Like the Lapith, the cavalrymen are depicted without clothes, and so they embody the ideal of strong bodies in the service of the polis.

Not all of the men in the interior frieze are warriors, though. Women, too, are depicted. See the detail from the east wall. Look at the four women shown here. The women are on foot, clothed and in solemn procession. The heavy folds of their robes, the hands held at their sides, and the expression on the one visible face all suggest calm and decorum.

From both of these pieces, we may detect Athenian commonplaces about gender. Young women were expected to be maidenly, reserved, and modest. Their bodies were to be kept private. Young men were expected to be outgoing and assertive. Although men wore clothes in public, they exercised naked in gymnasia, wrestling grounds, and stadiums, competing in a healthy activity considered to be effective preparation for war.

The historian finds subtler messages in the two scenes. For example, however constrained the role of women, their very presence in the frieze is significant. Women were not permitted to attend the Athenian assembly, but they participated in the rituals and festivals that played so large a role in Athenian public life. Notice, for instance, the two girls shown in the back who are carrying ritual vessels.

Scholars disagree about the subject of the procession in the frieze. Most scholars argue that the subject is the Pan-Athenaic procession, held once every four years to honor Athena. The people depicted are said to be the people of Athens—a daring novelty, considering that all previous Greek temple sculpture was restricted to gods, heroes, and mythological figures. Some scholars view the scene as an illustration of a legend from the early history of Athens. In either case, one thing is clear: The Parthenon sculptures depict the Athenians the way they wanted to see themselves—as courageous, pious, and public-spirited.

## Questions

1. *In what sense is the Parthenon an example of public education in democratic Athens?*

2. *What does the Parthenon have to say about gender in Athens?*

3. *What does the Parthenon have to say about Greek-Persian relations?*

indivisible particles, which could be arranged and rearranged in an infinite variety of configurations. He called these particles *atoma,* "uncuttable" (from which the word *atom* is derived).

The physicians of the Aegean island of Cos are known as Hippocratics, from Hippocrates (hih-POKruh-teez) (b. ca. 460 B.C.), the first great thinker of their school. If they were not directly influenced by the Sophists, they shared similar habits of thought. Like the Sophists, the Hippocratics were religious skeptics. They considered disease to be strictly a natural phenomenon in which the gods played no part. Hippocratic medicine was noteworthy for its methodology, which emphasized observation and prognosis (the reasoned prediction of future developments). The Hippocratics were the most rigorously naturalistic physicians to date, although no more successful in healing illness than earlier practitioners.

© The Trustees of the British Museum/Art Resource, NY

**Socrates** This figure emphasizes the colorful character of one of ancient Greece's greatest philosophers. Note his advanced age, unrefined face, and simple clothing.

In the fifth century B.C., not all thinkers welcomed the Sophists. Their most notable critic, and the greatest of all fifth century B.C. philosophers, was **Socrates** (469–399 B.C.). Unlike the Sophists, he charged no fees, had no formal students, and did not claim to teach any positive body of knowledge. His main virtue, he believed, was his awareness of his ignorance. Unlike the Sophists, most of whom were metics, Socrates was an Athenian citizen.

Socrates, however, resembled the Sophists in his attention to political theory. Like any good Athenian citizen, Socrates served in the military—as a hoplite during the Peloponnesian War. He had his doubts about democracy, which he considered inefficient and uneducated. He preferred rule by a wise elite. Nonetheless, Socrates was too loyal an Athenian to advocate revolution.

Yet Socrates made many enemies because of his role as a self-styled "gadfly." He stung the pride of Athens's leaders by demonstrating their ignorance. Mistakenly considered a Sophist by the public because of his unconventional opinions, Socrates was tried, convicted, and executed in 399 B.C. by an Athenian court for alleged atheism and "corrupting the young." The Athenian public soon had second thoughts, and the trial of Socrates is usually considered one of history's great miscarriages of justice, as well as one of Athenian democracy's greatest blunders.

Socrates was trained in the Ionian natural philosophy tradition. He went beyond it, as the Roman thinker Cicero later said, by bringing philosophy "down from the heavens into the streets"; he changed the emphasis from the natural world to human ethics. Like most Greeks, Socrates believed that the purpose of life was the pursuit of aretê. Unlike his contemporaries, however, he did not consider aretê to be primarily excellence in battle or in public life but rather excellence in philosophy. One became good by studying the truth, which is part of what Socrates meant by his saying "Virtue (aretê) is knowledge." He also meant that no one who truly understood goodness would ever choose to do evil.

Teach people well, Socrates says, and they will behave morally. Socrates has gone down in history as an inspiring teacher, despite his protestations of not teaching anything. His emphasis was not on research or writing, and in fact, he refused to write anything down. He believed that truth can be found only in persons, not through books—that philosophy requires a thoughtful verbal exchange. His favorite technique was to ask people difficult questions. Teaching that relies on inquiry is still called the "Socratic method."

## Plato and Aristotle

Because Socrates never wrote anything down, we are dependent on others for our knowledge of him. Fortunately for us, he inspired students who committed his words and ideas to paper. Socrates' most distinguished student, and our most important source for his thought, was Plato (427–348 B.C.), who in turn was the teacher of Aristotle (384–322 B.C.). Together, these three men laid the foundations of the Western philosophical tradition. They were thinkers for the ages, but each was also a man of his times.

Socrates grew up in confident Periclean days. **Plato** (PLAY-toe) came of age during the Peloponnesian War, a period culminating in the execution of Socrates. Shocked and disillusioned, Plato turned his back on public life, although he was an Athenian citizen. Instead of discussing philosophy in public, Plato founded a private school in an Athenian suburb, the Academy. Plato held a low opinion of democracy, and when he did intervene in politics, it was not in Athens but in far-off Syracuse (in Sicily). Syracuse was governed by a tyranny, and Plato hoped to educate the tyrant's heir in philosophy—a vain hope, as it turned out.

A voluminous writer, Plato is not easily summarized. The word that best characterizes his legacy, though, is *idealism*, of which Plato is one of Western philosophy's greatest exponents. Like Parmenides, Plato distrusted the senses. Truth exists but comes only by training the mind to overcome commonsense evidence. The model for Plato's philosophical method is geometry. Just as geometry deals not with this or that triangle or rectangle but with ideal forms—with a pure triangle, a pure rectangle—so the philosopher could learn to recognize purity. A philosopher would not, say, compare aretê in Athens, Sparta, and Persia; a philosopher would understand the meaning of pure, ideal aretê. No relativist, Plato believed in absolute good and evil.

Philosophy is not for everyone, according to Plato. Only a few people have the necessary intelligence and discipline. In the *Republic*, perhaps his best-known work, Plato displays his idealism and its political consequences. He envisions a society whose elite would study philosophy and attain enlightenment. They would understand the vanity of political ambition but would accept the responsibility of governing the masses. Plato never makes clear precisely why they should assume this burden. Perhaps he was enough of a traditionalist, in spite of himself, to consider a citizen's responsibility to the polis to be obvious. In any case, Plato's ideal state was one in which philosophers would rule as kings, benevolently and unselfishly.

The ideal state would be like a small polis: self-sufficient and closed to outside corruption like Sparta but committed to the pursuit of things intellectual like Athens. Society would be divided into three classes—philosophers, soldiers, and farmers—with admission to each class based on merit rather than heredity. Poetry and drama would be censored. Plato advocated public education and toyed with more radical notions: not only gender equality but also the abolition of the family and private property, which he felt led to disunity and dissension.

Plato's ideas have always been controversial but rarely ignored. The writings of his great student Aristotle better suited contemporary tastes. Originally from Macedonia, **Aristotle** spent most of his life in Athens, first as a student at the Academy, then as founder of his own school, the Lyceum (lie-SEE-um). Like Plato, Aristotle wrote dialogues, but none survive. His main surviving works are treatises, largely compilations by students of his lecture notes. One of the most wide-ranging intellectuals, Aristotle thirsted for knowledge. His writings embrace politics, ethics, poetry, botany, physics, metaphysics, astronomy, rhetoric, zoology, logic, and psychology.

> **Aristotle** Ancient Greek philosopher, student of Plato and tutor of Alexander the Great. In later centuries, his writings had a major impact on Byzantine, Islamic, and Latin Christian thinkers.

Though influenced by Plato's idealism, Aristotle was a far more practical, down-to-earth thinker. His father had been a doctor, which may account for Aristotle's interest in applied science and in biology and the biological method. Unlike Plato, Aristotle placed great emphasis on observation and fieldwork and on classification and systemization.

Aristotle agreed with Plato about the existence of absolute standards of good and evil, but he emphasized the relevance of such standards to everyday life. Unlike Plato, Aristotle considered the senses important guides. Change, he believed, was not an illusion but rather an important phenomenon. Aristotle's view of change was teleological—that is, he emphasized the goal (*telos* in Greek) of change. According to Aristotle, every organism changes and grows toward a particular end and is an integral and harmonious part of a larger whole. The entire cosmos is teleological, and each and every one of its parts has a purpose. Behind the cosmos was a principle that Aristotle called "the unmoved mover," the supreme cause of existence.

Aristotle defined an object's aretê as the fulfillment of its inherent function in the cosmos. The aretê of a horse, for example, was to be strong, fast, and obedient; the aretê of a rose was to look beautiful and smell sweet. As for the aretê of a human being, Aristotle agreed with Plato: Only the philosopher achieved true aretê. As a pragmatist, however, Aristotle did not imagine philosophers becoming kings. He advocated a blend of oligarchy and democracy, sometimes called "polity." The poor could vote in the assembly, but high office would be dominated by wealthy gentlemen who had been trained by philosophers—not the best regime imaginable but, in Aristotle's opinion, the best one possible.

Aristotle believed that men had stronger capacities to make judgments than women and so should rule over them. He condemned states like Sparta that accorded power to women. Hence, Aristotle would be cited in later centuries to justify male dominance. Ironically, however, Aristotle was more enlightened on gender issues than most of his contemporaries. For example, he believed that since women played a crucial role in the family, they should receive education in morality.

Aristotle may be the most influential thinker in Western history. Byzantine and Islamic thinkers studied and admired him. In the High Middle Ages, the rediscovery of Aristotle in western Europe had a major impact on Latin Christian thought.

## Athenian Drama

Perhaps the greatest art form that emerged in the polis was drama. Modern comedy and tragedy find distant ancestors in Athens's theater of Dionysus, named for the god of unrestraint, liberation, and wine. Comedy and tragedy began in religious festivals honoring Dionysus (also known as Bacchus) but quickly became an independent forum for comment on public life. Ancient drama was poetry, not prose. Because it highlighted the relation of the individual to the community, drama proved to be the most suitable poetic medium for the ideology of the polis.

According to ancient tradition, **tragedy** was first presented at the Dionysian festival in Athens by Thespis in the 530s B.C. (hence, the word *thespian* for "actor"). The first surviving tragedy dates from the 470s B.C., the first surviving comedy from the 420s B.C. A play in the fifth century B.C. consisted of a chorus (a group of performers working in unison) and three individual actors, who played all the various individual speaking parts. Plays were performed in an open-air theater on the south hillside of the Acropolis. Enormously popular, drama spread all over Greece, and eventually most poleis had a theater.

Classical Athenian tragedy was performed at the annual Dionysia in March. Each playwright would submit a trilogy of plays on a central theme, plus a raucous farce to break the tension afterward. Comedies, which were independent plays rather than trilogies, were performed both at the Dionysia and at a separate festival held in winter. Wealthy producers competed to outfit the most lavish and impressive productions. Judges would award prizes for the best plays—a typical reflection of Greek competitiveness.

*Tragedy* is not easy to define, except generally: a serious play with an unhappy ending. Perhaps a short tag from the playwright Aeschylus (ESS-kih-luhs) can be said to sum up tragedy: *pathos mathei*, "suffering teaches." The essence of tragedy is what has been called the tragic sense of life: the nobility in the spectacle of a great man or woman failing but learning from failure. In *Oedipus the Tyrant* (ca. 428 B.C.) by Sophocles, for example, the hero unknowingly kills his father and unknowingly marries his mother. Oedipus cannot escape the consequences of his deeds, but he can react to his fate with dignity and heroism. Oedipus loses his power as tyrant and goes into exile, but he retains a degree of honor. He carries out his own punishment by blinding himself. As Aristotle observed, tragedy derives its emotional power from the fear and pity that it evokes and from the purification of the senses (*katharsis*) that it leaves in its aftermath.

The great period of Attic tragedy began and ended in the fifth century B.C. Aeschylus (525–456 B.C.), Sophocles (ca. 495–406 B.C.), and Euripides (ca. 485–406 B.C.) were and are considered the three giant playwrights. Although other tragedians wrote plays, only the works of these three men have survived. Aeschylus was perhaps the most pious of the three. His plays—notably the trilogy of the *Oresteia* (the *Agamemnon*, the *Libation Bearers*, and the *Eumenides*), the only surviving tragic trilogy, dating from 458 B.C.—take as their central question the justice of Zeus. The subject is the myth of the House of Atreus—in particular, the murder of King Agamemnon by his much-wronged wife, Clytemnestra, and her murder in turn by their son, Orestes, avenging his father. Aeschylus casts this primitive saga into an epic of the discovery of justice.

Sophocles, too, was interested in divine justice. His tragedies focus on the relationship between the individual and the community. Heroic individuals have a spark of the divine in them, but their towering virtues are threats to ordinary people. In *Antigone* (ca. 442 B.C.), for example, the heroine refuses to compromise with injustice. Her late brother had committed treason, for which his corpse is denied burial—the standard Greek punishment. Antigone, however, insists on following a higher law, which she calls "the unwritten and unfailing statutes given us by the gods,"* and which demands that all bodies be buried. Turmoil, disorder, and death ensue, but Antigone stays true to principle.

Of the three tragedians, Euripides (yoo-RIP-uh-deez) is the least traditional and the most influenced by the Sophists. His plays reflect the disillusionment of the Peloponnesian War era. Euripides was more impressed by divine power than by divine justice. The central gods of Aeschylean drama are Zeus the father and Apollo the lawgiver, while Sophocles focuses on semidivine heroes, but Euripides' major deities are Dionysus and Aphrodite, goddess of erotic passion. In the *Bacchae* (406 B.C.), for example, an arrogant young king named Pentheus is punished for refusing to recognize the power of Dionysus (Bacchus). When he goes to the

---

**tragedy** Serious play with an unhappy ending. Greek tragedy emerged and reached its height in the fifth century B.C. in the works of Aeschylus, Sophocles, and Euripides.

---

*Quote from Sophocles, *Antigone*, lines 454-55, in Sophocles. *The Antigone of Sophocles*. Edited with introduction and notes by Sir Richard Jebb. Sir Richard Jebb. Cambridge. Cambridge University Press. 1891.

**Theater at Delphi**  Open to the air, an ancient Greek theater contained tiers of stone benches above a circular area where the action took place, behind which backdrops could be erected. The audience often had a view of stirring scenery that, at Delphi, included the temple of Apollo and the valley below. Vanni/Art Resource, NY

hills to spy on drunken women, called "Bacchae," who are worshiping the god, he ends up as their prisoner. Driven to frenzy by Dionysus, the women do not recognize the king. Indeed, Pentheus's own mother, one of the Bacchae, mistakes him for an animal and kills him.

The changes in tragedy from Aeschylus to Euripides reflect the changes in Athens as first imperial arrogance and then the Peloponnesian War took their moral toll. Aeschylus's trust in the community's goodness gives way, first to a focus on the individual struggling to be good and then to a fundamental doubt about the possibility of goodness. The civic order, celebrated so confidently at the end of the *Oresteia* (458 B.C.), looks less certain in Sophocles' *Oedipus* (ca. 428 B.C.), and by the time of Euripides' *Bacchae* (406 B.C.), seems feeble.

Comedy, too, was invented in Athens in the Classical period. Like tragedy, comedy offers a moral commentary on contemporary Athenian life. Unlike tragedy, which is usually set in the past and takes its characters from mythology, Athenian comedy (the so-called Old Comedy) is set in the present and pokes fun at politicians and public figures.

The greatest writer of comedy in the fifth century B.C. was Aristophanes (ca. 455–385 B.C.). His extant plays are lively, ribald, even scatological, and full of allusions to contemporary politics. Aristophanes loved to show the "little guy" getting the better of the powerful and women deflating the pretensions of men. In *Lysistrata* (411 B.C.), his best-known play, he imagines the women of Greece stopping the Peloponnesian War by going on a sex strike, which forces the men to make peace.

**comedy** Play with a happy ending. Greek comedy emerged and reached its first height in the fifth century B.C. in the works of Aristophanes.

## Historical Thought and Writing

Like drama, history flourished in the exciting intellectual atmosphere of classical Athens. Indeed, its two greatest historians, Herodotus (ca. 485–425 B.C.) and Thucydides (ca. 455–397 B.C.), are among the founders of history-writing in the West. This judgment is not meant to discount the contributions of, for example, the Hittites or Hebrews, or the chronicles, inventories, and genealogies of early Greece. Herodotus and Thucydides, however, are more rationalistic than their predecessors, and their subject matter is war, politics, peoples, and customs—what we think of as the stuff of history-writing today. Indeed, the word *history* comes from a word used by Herodotus, *historiai*, meaning "inquiries" or "research."

The works of Herodotus (*The Histories*) and Thucydides (*The Peloponnesian War*) have unifying themes. The thread through *The Histories* is the cyclical rise and fall of empires. Herodotus sees the Persian Wars as merely one episode in a vast historical drama. Again and again, hardy, disciplined peoples conquered their neighbors, grew wealthy, were corrupted by a life of luxury, and were eventually conquered in turn. Success made people arrogant, driving them to commit injustices, which were eventually punished by Zeus. The breadth of

**Herodotus** Credited, along with Thucydides, of founding history-writing in the West. The word *history* comes from the word *historiai* used by Herodotus.

**Thucydides** Ancient Greek historian; with Herodotus, a founder of history-writing in the West.

## SECTION SUMMARY

- The culture of Greece during 480–322 B.C. is called classical because it has proved influential throughout the history of the West.

- Classical Greek sculpture was the most technically proficient sculpture seen yet, and it set a standard for all future work.

- The Athenian Socrates changed the emphasis of Greek philosophy from nature to human ethics.

- The idealist philosopher Plato and his more practical student, Aristotle, are the most influential philosophers of the West.

- Comedy and tragedy were invented in Athens, flourished in public festivals, and offered a moral commentary on contemporary life.

- Herodotus and Thucydides are among the founders of history-writing in the West.

Herodotus's vision is noteworthy. A native of Halicarnassus (a polis on the southwestern coast of Anatolia; see **Map 3.5**), Herodotus traveled widely, eventually settling in Athens. He wrote not only about Greeks but also about Persians, Egyptians, and a host of other peoples in Europe, Asia, and Africa. (See the feature, "The Global Record: The Enemy as Barbarian," on page 72.)

Only a child at the time of the Persian Wars, Herodotus gathered information by interviewing older people in various countries, as well as by checking what limited written public records existed. Herodotus also wrote about previous centuries and places he had not visited, but with uneven accuracy. He could rarely resist a good story, and alongside solid research are tall tales, unconfirmed accounts, and myths.

Thucydides, by contrast, prided himself on accuracy. He confined himself mainly to writing about an event that he had lived through and participated in: the Peloponnesian War. A failed Athenian general, Thucydides spent most of the Peloponnesian War in exile, carefully observing, taking notes, and writing.

Like Herodotus, Thucydides was influenced by the grandeur of Classical tragedy. He also shows the signs of the Sophist movement, especially in the finely crafted speeches he includes in his writing. Thucydides' great theme is the disastrous effect of war on the human soul. In Thucydides' opinion, Periclean Athens was a high point in the history of civilization. The strain of prolonged war, however, destroyed Athens's moral fiber as well as its empire.

## Chapter Summary

◆ *How did early Greece develop before the polis and what light do the Homeric poems shed on its history?*

The focus of ancient Greek life between around 750 and around 350 B.C. was the polis. Trade, colonization, and the invention of the Greek alphabet and of the hoplite phalanx all contributed to the emergence of the polis around 750–700 B.C. Earlier, in the Bronze Age, Minoan and Mycenaean kingdoms had ruled Greek lands. Homer evoked their memory brilliantly in the *Iliad* and the *Odyssey* around 725 B.C. but, by then, the spirit of Greek civilization had changed radically. The Bronze Age kingdoms were palace economies, dominated by a noble elite.

◆ *What was the Greek polis, and how did it develop in Sparta, Athens, and Corinth in Archaic Greece?*

The polis was a city-state that emphasized participation and equality and invented the idea of the citizen. Archaic Sparta developed Greece's best citizen-army whose job was to prevent helot uprisings or attacks from abroad. Sparta's stable government and austere culture fostered the idea that public duty is more important than private advantage. Archaic Corinth is the prime example of tyranny, a widespread form of government in Greece in which new wealth led to the emergence of popular champions. Archaic Athens developed, thanks to

Solon's reforms, a large class of independent small farmers. They later turned out to be the backbone of democracy. Solon unintentionally created conditions for the growth of slavery.

◆ *How did Western individualism and rationalism take root in Archaic Greece?*

Western philosophy, science, politics, sculpture, painting, and literary genres, such as comedy, tragedy, and history, all emerged in Archaic and Classical Greece. The culture of Archaic Greece was the seedbed of Western individualism and rationalism. Lyric poetry emphasized individual emotion, and Archaic sculpture focused on the human body. Although Archaic Greece was a religious society, it also gave rise to the first philosophers. They lived in Ionia in the 500s B.C. and offered a rationalistic and nontheistic explanation of nature.

◆ *What was Athenian democracy and how did it clash with Sparta in the Peloponnesian War?*

Democracy or "people power" (*demokratia*) began in ancient Greece, and the Athenian version is best known. Athenian democracy was direct and participatory but limited to adult males. Classical Greece was a period of intense war. Athens and Sparta united to lead a Greek coalition that defeated Persia's invasion in 480–479 B.C. Afterward, the two poleis turned on each other, most violently in the Peloponnesian War (431–404 B.C.). With its democracy, freedom, and high culture, Athens stands for one aspect of the achievement of the polis; with its hierarchy, militarism, and citizen virtue, Sparta stands for another.

◆ *How did tragedy, comedy, philosophy, and history all begin and develop in the culture of Classical Greece?*

Classical Greek culture has proved influential again and again in the history of the West. Athens became Greece's cultural center. Here, comedy and tragedy were invented, history-writing was founded, sculpture reached a peak of proficiency in showing the human body, and philosophy changed its emphasis from nature to human ethics. The philosophers Socrates, Plato, and Aristotle are among the West's greatest thinkers.

## Key Terms

**polis** (p. 49)
**Minoan** (p. 51)
**Mycenaeans** (p. 51)
**Homer** (p. 52)
*aretê* (p. 54)
**Archaic Greece** (p. 54)
**hoplite phalanx** (p. 56)
**Solon** (p. 63)
**Sappho** (p. 64)
**Classical Greece** (p. 64)

*demokratia* (p. 67)
**Pericles** (p. 68)
**Sophists** (p. 75)
**Socrates** (p. 78)
**Plato** (p. 78)
**Aristotle** (p. 79)
**tragedy** (p. 80)
**comedy** (p. 81)
**Herodotus** (p. 81)
**Thucydides** (p. 81)

**CourseMate**

Go to the CourseMate website at **www.cengagebrain.com** for additional study tools and review materials—including audio and video clips—for this chapter.

**Stag Hunt Pebble Mosaic from Pella** HIP/Art Resource, NY

# Alexander the Great and the Spread of Greek Civilization, ca. 350–30 B.C.

The young men in the pebble mosaic shown opposite wield ax and sword against the stag whom they are hunting. The artist, named Gnosis, was a master at rendering perspective and drama. Clearly, no expense was spared on the work, dated around 325 B.C. Both the vigor of the scene and the quality of the craftsmanship symbolize the spirit of a young man who was born in Pella, the Macedonian (mah-seh-DOE-nee-un) capital where the mosaic was displayed: That man was Alexander the Great. Alexander was a fearless warrior and one of the most brilliant generals in the history of the world. In just twelve years, he conquered all the territory between Greece and India, as well as Egypt.

Alexander created new realities of power as king of Macedon (r. 336–323 B.C.). A northeastern Greek kingdom that had previously been only a fringe power, Macedon rose meteorically under Alexander's father, Philip II (r. 359–336 B.C.), to become the leading military power in Greece. Philip was a brilliant and ambitious general, but Alexander outstripped him.

Alexander laid the foundations of a new Greek world: the world of the Hellenistic (hel-len-IS-tik) period (323–30 B.C.), in which Hellenic, or Greek, language and civilization spread and were transformed. This era was distinct in many ways from the preceding Hellenic period (ca. 750–323 B.C.). In Hellenistic times, Macedonians and Greeks replaced Persians as the ruling people of Egypt and western Asia. Large numbers of Greek-speaking colonists moved south and east. Governed by Macedonian dynasties, Egypt and the Levant became integral parts of the Greek world and remained so until the Arab conquest in the seventh century A.D. Greek-speaking kingdoms thrived briefly as far east as modern Afghanistan and Pakistan.

Conquest put huge amounts of wealth into Greek hands. Alexander and his successors built great new cities: Antioch (AN-tee-ock) in Syria, Pergamum in Anatolia, Seleucia (seh-LOO-she-uh) in Mesopotamia, and, greatest of all, Alexandria in Egypt. Trade increased and expanded southward and eastward. In political life, individual cities continued to be important, but federal leagues (that is, unions of city-states) and monarchies ruled most of the Greek-speaking world.

## Chapter Overview

### Philip and Alexander

- *How did Macedon under Philip and Alexander conquer both the Greek city-states and the Persian Empire?*

### The Hellenistic Kingdoms, 323–30 B.C.

- *What new states emerged as a result of Alexander's conquests and how did they integrate Greek settlers with native peoples?*

### Hellenistic Culture

- *How did Greek civilization spread during the Hellenistic era, and what were the main trends in literature, science, and art?*

### The Turn Inward: New Philosophies, New Faiths

- *What new philosophies and religions emerged in the Hellenistic period?*

Material and political expansion led to unanticipated cultural changes, which may be summarized as a turn inward. Frequently finding themselves among strange peoples, the Greeks sought comfort in the inner life: new philosophies, religions, and modes of literary and artistic expression. Many of these new cultural forms emphasized people's emotions and intentions, not simply their actions. Science, meanwhile, flourished under royal patronage, as did the emerging discipline of literary criticism. The prestige of royal women tended to promote improvements in the overall status of Greek women.

Hellenistic Greeks boasted of having created one world—a common, or ecumenical (from the Greek *oikoumene* [oy-koo-men-AY], "inhabited"), region. In truth, that world was complex. Native cultures flourished, while Greeks adapted and Hellenized a number of Egyptian and Asian deities.

Hellenistic Greek contact with one native culture in particular—Judaism—proved to have a lasting impact on the West. Under the impact of the Greeks, Judaism became more self-conscious and placed a greater emphasis on salvation, martyrdom, and individual study and prayer. Some Jews resisted Greek culture, others adopted it, and still others resolved to convert Greeks to Judaism. Reshaped by its contacts with the Greeks, Hellenistic Judaism was poised to transform Western religion.

# Philip and Alexander

*How did Macedon under Philip and Alexander conquer both the Greek city-states and the Persian Empire?*

The Hellenistic world was founded by two conquerors: Philip II of Macedon (382–336 B.C.) and his son, Alexander III, known as Alexander the Great (356–323 B.C.). After a century of indecisive warfare among the Greek city-states, Philip swept south and conquered them in twenty years. In even less time, Alexander conquered Egypt and all of western Asia as far east as modern India. The legacy of these impressive conquests was to spread Greek civilization and to change it, both of which consequences were revolutionary developments.

## *The Rise of Macedon*

**Macedon** Weaker, less culturally advanced state on Greece's northern border that was unified and led to power by Philip II and Alexander the Great.

**Macedon** was a border state, long weaker than its more advanced neighbors but capable of learning from them and ultimately of conquering them. Though rich in resources and manpower, Macedon lacked the relatively efficient organization of the polis. Several dialects of Greek were spoken, some unintelligible to southern Greeks, who considered Macedonians "barbarians" (from the Greek *barbaros*, meaning "a person who does not speak Greek"). Ordinary Macedonians lived hardy lives, while the king and the royal court inhabited a sophisticated capital city, Pella, where they sponsored visits by leading Greek artists and writers. **Philip II** confounded Greek stereotypes of Macedonian barbarism by turning out to be a brilliant soldier and statesman. He was tough and seemingly unstoppable. As the Athenian Demosthenes (de-MOSS-thuh-neez) (ca. 385–322 B.C.) complained, Philip "was ready to sacrifice to the fortune of war any and every part of his body, if only the life of the shattered remnant should be a life of honor and renown."* Although vain, lustful, and a hard drinker, he was also an excellent orator and general. Philip's goals were to make himself dominant in Macedon and then, after neutralizing opposition in Greece, to conquer the Persian Empire, or at least its western part. He accomplished all but the last.

**Philip II** King of Macedon and father of Alexander the Great, he was a brilliant soldier and statesman who conquered the Greek world.

---

*Quote from *Demosthenes II De Corona and De Falsa Legatione XVIII, XIX*, trans. by C.A. and J. H. Vince, Loeb Classical Library (Cambridge, Mass.: Harvard University Press, 1963), p. 61.

Philip owed success to his army, a well-trained, professional, year-round force. Macedon, with its plains and horses, was cavalry country, and Philip raised cavalry to a new level of importance. In battle, the Macedonian phalanx would first hold the enemy phalanx until the cavalry could find a weak spot and break the enemy line. Then, the phalanx would attack and finish the job. Macedonian hoplites carried extra-long pikes to keep the enemy at a distance. Philip also mastered the technology of siegecraft, raising it to a level unseen since Assyrian days (see pages 32–33).

Philip used his army effectively. After capturing a gold mine in Thrace (modern Bulgaria), he turned to the Greek city-states nearby. Olynthus, the most important, fell in 348 B.C. Led by Demosthenes, the central and southern Greek city-states prepared to make a stand, but it was too late. By 338 B.C., when an Atheno-Theban army met the Macedonians, Philip had already won over much of the Greek world through diplomacy, bribes, and threats. His complete military victory at Chaeronea, in central Greece, was followed up with a lenient settlement. In a new League of Corinth, all the Greeks except Sparta acknowledged Philip's hegemony (see **Map 4.1**). The polis would no longer decide the fate of the eastern Mediterranean.

In 336 B.C. Philip was murdered by a disgruntled courier, and the invasion of the Persian Empire fell to his 20-year-old son, Alexander, the new king.

## Alexander the Conqueror

Alexander III of Macedon (r. 336–323 B.C.), better known as **Alexander the Great**, is as famous in art as in literature, in romance as in history, in Iran and India as in Europe and America. Yet, the evidence for the historical Alexander is frustrating. After his untimely death shortly before his thirty-third birthday, contemporaries wrote histories and memoirs, but none has survived. Several good historical accounts, based on earlier texts, are extant, but none was written less than three hundred years after Alexander's day. Alexander, moreover, was not only a legend in his own time but also a master propagandist. Many of the incidents of his life took place in remote regions or among a few individuals, and they tended to grow with the telling.

Still, Alexander's virtues are clear. He was charismatic, handsome, intelligent, and well educated; as a teenager he had Aristotle himself as a private tutor. Alexander was ruthless as well as cultured. He brought a team of Greek scientists along with him on his expedition through the Persian Empire. He founded ten cities. One of those cities, born in 331 B.C. at the site of a fishing village in the northwestern part of Egypt's delta, later grew into the largest city in the Mediterranean: Alexandria.

Alexander certainly had vices as well. He began his reign with a massacre of his male relatives. He destroyed the great cities of Thebes and Tyre and had their inhabitants killed or sold into slavery. He burned Persepolis, Persia's capital, to the ground. He massacred large numbers of civilians during his campaigns in central Asia.

For all his varied interests, Alexander was first and foremost a warrior. Battlefield commander of the Macedonian cavalry at age 18, he devoted most of the rest of his life to warfare. His military operations displayed audacity. As one historian put it, "When risks had to

## CHRONOLOGY

| | |
|---|---|
| 359–336 B.C. | Reign of Philip II of Macedon |
| ca. 342–292 B.C. | Life of playwright Menander |
| 338 B.C. | Greece falls to Philip at Battle of Chaeronea |
| 336–323 B.C. | Reign of Alexander the Great |
| 331 B.C. | Battle of Gaugamela completes Persian defeat |
| 323–275 B.C. | Wars of the Successors |
| 313 B.C. | Zeno founds Stoic philosophy in Athens |
| 312 B.C. | Seleucus I conquers Babylon |
| 304 B.C. | Ptolemy I king of Egypt |
| 294 B.C. | Museum founded in Alexandria |
| 276 B.C. | Antigonus Gonatas king of Macedon |
| 263 B.C. | Kingdom of Pergamum founded |
| ca. 246 B.C. | Parthia revolts from Seleucids |
| ca. 245 B.C. | Bactria gains independence |
| 244–222 B.C. | Reforms of Agis and Cleomenes in Sparta |
| ca. 225 B.C. | Eratosthenes of Cyrene calculates the earth's circumference |
| 217 B.C. | Battle of Raphia brings Palestine under Ptolemies |
| 167–142 B.C. | Maccabean revolt in Judea |
| 146 B.C. | Antigonid Macedonia becomes a Roman province |
| 64 B.C. | Seleucid Syria becomes a Roman province |
| 30 B.C. | Ptolemaic Egypt becomes a Roman province |

**Alexander the Great** King of Macedon and conqueror of the Persian Empire, he spread Greek civilization to western Asia, Egypt, and India.

🌐 **Map 4.1 Conquests of Philip and Alexander**   Between 359 and 323 B.C., the armies of Macedon conquered first the Greek city-states and then the Persian Empire. Macedonian power extended from Greece and Egypt eastward to modern India. © Cengage Learning 2014

be taken, he took them with the utmost boldness, and his ability to seize the moment for a swift blow, before the enemy had any suspicion of what was coming, was beyond praise."* As a leader of men, Alexander was popular and inspiring, and he shared hardships with his troops. Knowing the value of propaganda, he told the Greeks that he was fighting a war of revenge for Persia's invasion of Greece in 480 B.C. (See the feature, "The Written Record: Alexander in Battle" on page 91.)

On the eve of invasion, Persia vastly outnumbered Macedon on both land and sea. Darius III of Persia was rich; Alexander's treasury was virtually empty. The Macedonian expeditionary force was short on supplies. The peoples in Persia's multiethnic empire were restive, but so too were Alexander's Greek allies, the mainstay of his fleet. One of Darius's advisers proposed a naval campaign to raise a revolt in Greece and force the Macedonians home. How, then, did Alexander propose to conquer Persia?

The answer was the Macedonian army. Although Alexander invaded Anatolia with only about fifty thousand men, they were the fastest-marching, most experienced, and most skilled army in the eastern Mediterranean. If Persia would fight the Macedonians in a set battle, Alexander might be confident of victory—and proud Persia insisted on fighting. As expected, Macedon won the war in three great battles (see **Map 4.1**): at the Granicus River in Anatolia (334 B.C.), at Issus in Syria (333 B.C.), and at Gaugamela in Mesopotamia (331 B.C.). By 328 B.C., Alexander's claim to be king of Persia was sealed with blood and iron.

---

*Quote from *The Campaigns of Alexander* by Arrian, translated Aubrey de Selincourt, revised with an introduction and notes by J.R. Hamilton (Penguin Classics, 1958, revised edition, 1971).

🌐 **Map 4.2  Hellenistic Kingdoms, Leagues, and City-States, ca. 240 B.C.**   After Alexander's death, his empire lost its political unity. Great new cities and kingdoms arose in the lands he had conquered. © Cengage Learning 2014

Having conquered the Persian heartland, Alexander turned eastward and fought for seven more years. Alexander pushed his army not only into the eastern parts of the Persian Empire but beyond, into India, which had not been controlled by Persia since the early fifth century B.C. The Macedonians won a big victory there in 326 B.C., near the Hydaspes River (modern Jhelum River), over the army of King Porus, which had as many as two hundred elephants (see **Map 4.1**). Alexander's infantry suffered heavy casualties before inflicting enough wounds on the elephants to make them uncontrollable. Alexander wanted to continue eastward, perhaps as far as the Bay of Bengal, but his exhausted and homesick men mutinied and forced Alexander to turn back.

Meanwhile, Alexander tightened the screws of power. He turned on the proud and independent Macedonian nobility via a series of conspiracy trials, purges, and assassinations. Alexander offended Macedonians by adopting some customs of the Persian royal court. He offended Greek city-states by insisting that they deify him. "If Alexander wishes to be a god, let him be"* was the concise reply of the Spartans, but Alexander had set a precedent for both Hellenistic monarchs and Roman emperors.

Another theme of Alexander's later career is his policy of fusion. In 325 B.C., Alexander began training an army of thirty thousand Persians and dismissed a large number of Macedonian troops. He forced his commanders to marry Persian women, just as he himself did. He publicly prayed that Macedonians, Persians, and others enjoy "harmony as partners in the government." Many Macedonians would have preferred to keep their former enemy at arm's length, but Alexander sought a new power base independent of the Macedonian nobility.

*Quote from Arrian, *Anabasis of Alexander*, Books V-VII, Indica, with an English translation by P. A. Brunt, Loeb Classical Library (Cambridge, Mass: Harvard University Press, 1983), p. 241.

## SECTION SUMMARY

- Macedon rose to power under King Philip II and conquered the Greek city-states.
- Alexander was a brilliant soldier and leader of the most skilled army in the eastern Mediterranean, created by his father Philip.
- Alexander and the Macedonians won battles with the seemingly more powerful Persian army thanks to Persia's proud but foolish decision to fight the enemy in pitched battles.
- A march into India, increasing despotism, and a policy of fusion of Greeks and Macedonians all marked Alexander's last years.
- By conquering the Persian Empire, Alexander ushered in a new age in Greek history: the Hellenistic era.

Alexander died in Babylon in June 323 B.C., a month before he turned 33, probably of malarial fever, although some contemporaries suspected poison and some historians have suggested drunkenness. Alexander did not name a successor. The Macedonian generals fought a long and bloody round of wars over the spoils of empire. Not until some fifty years later, in 275 B.C., was it clear that three large kingdoms—Macedon (under the Antigonid dynasty), Ptolemaic (tol-eh-MAY-ik) Egypt, and the Seleucid (seh-LOO-sid) realm—would inherit most of Alexander's empire. The rest was divided among small kingdoms, federal leagues, and independent city-states (see **Map 4.2**).

In the long run, Alexander's life was far more influential than his death. His conquests did nothing less than lay the foundations of the Hellenistic world. Whether it was exalting a savior or debunking a hero, much of Hellenistic culture centered on the myth of heroism that Alexander had engendered. Historians who insist that the individual is insignificant will rarely have a more challenging refutation than Alexander.

# The Hellenistic Kingdoms, 323–30 B.C.

*What new states emerged as a result of Alexander's conquests and how did they integrate Greek settlers with native peoples?*

Variety, flexibility, and the creation of a new elite to transmit Greek culture compose the Hellenistic political legacy. Hellenistic political units ranged from multiethnic kingdoms to small, ethnically homogeneous city-states (see **Map 4.2**). The Greek peninsula saw both a monarchy, with republican leanings, as well as experiments in federalism and social revolution. In Asia and Egypt, a new ruling elite emerged, consisting both of Greeks and Macedonians and of natives. Although the first group tended to dominate high office, natives were by no means excluded. The immigrants wanted land, wealth, or adventure. Their paths were smoothed by a new ideology that identified being Greek less with loyalty to an individual city than with participation in a common Greek civilization.

Although the Hellenistic world became relatively peaceful after 275 B.C., conflict among the kingdoms continued. Generally waged at a low level of intensity, with bribes and diplomacy as weapons, the conflict nonetheless sometimes broke out into major battles. A number of small states emerged in Anatolia, notably Pergamum, whose wealthy rulers were patrons of literature and art, and Galatia (guh-LAY-shuh), carved out by Celtic invaders from Europe.

## Colonialism, Greek Style

Many Greeks and Macedonians emigrated during the fourth and third centuries B.C. in search of prosperity or adventure. Agriculture was the main economic pursuit, but trade, industry, finance, administration, and military service also offered opportunities. The few available statistics indicate a significant migration but not a mass exodus. In the second century B.C., a large number of Jews left war-torn Judea, particularly for Egypt. Ptolemaic Egypt and the Seleucid realm were also the most common destinations for Greek and Macedonian migrants.

Greek migrants could take advantage of a new definition of being Greek that had begun to emerge even before Alexander's conquests. Isocrates (eye-SOCK-rah-teez) (428–338 B.C.), an Athenian thinker, redefined Greek identity by promoting the idea that Greece was not a collection of city-states but a civilization. "The people we call Hellenes"—that is, Greeks—he wrote, "are those who have the same culture as us, not the same blood."[*]

---

*Isocrates, "Panegyricus," trans. H.I. Marrou, in *A History of Education in Antiquity*, trans. George Lamb (New York: Mentor Books/New American Library, 1956), p. 130.

## Alexander in Battle

*In this account of the Battle of the Granicus River in 334 B.C. in what is now western Turkey, the historian Arrian (ca. A.D. 86–160) shows how Alexander shared the risks with his men. It was inspiring—and dangerous.*

For some time the two forces on the river's brink, dreading to precipitate the event, remained still and in deep silence on either side. For the Persians were waiting for the Macedonians, so as to fall on them emerging from the river, whenever they attempted the crossing; but Alexander leapt on his horse, and calling on his suite to follow and show themselves brave men and true, ordered the *prodromoi* [Macedonian mounted skirmishers] and the Paeonians [allied unit of light horsemen] to plunge first into the stream. . .; then he himself, leading the right wing, with bugles sounding, and the battle cry going up the God of Battles, went into the stream, continually extending his troops obliquely in the direction in which the current was pulling them, so that the Persians should not fall on him in column as he emerged, but that he himself might attack them, as far as might be, in deep formation.

. . .The first Macedonians who came to grips with the Persians were cut down, despite their valor, save those of them who fell back on Alexander as he approached. For he was already near, with the right wing which he was leading, and he charged the Persians at the head of his men just where cavalry were massed and the Persian commanders were posted. A fierce fight raged round him; and meanwhile the Macedonians, battalion after battalion, kept crossing, a task now not so difficult. Though the fighting was on horseback, it was more like an infantry battle, horse entangled with horse, man with man in the struggle, the Macedonians trying to push the Persians once and for all from the bank and force them on to the level ground, the Persians trying to bar their landing and thrust them back into the river.

. . . . Seeing [the Persian] Mithridates, son-in-law of Darius, riding far ahead of the line and leading on a wedge shaped body of horse, [Alexander] charged out alone in advance of his own men, thrust his lance into Mithridates' face and hurled him to the ground. Then Rhoesaces [a Persian] rode at Alexander, and struck him on the head with his scimitar; though he sheared off part of the helmet, still the helmet parried the blow. Alexander hurled him too to the ground, piercing with his lance through the cuirass into his chest. Sphithridates [a Persian] had already raised his scimitar against Alexander from behind when Clitus son of Dropides [a Macedonian], slipping in first, struck Sphithridates' shoulder with his scimitar and cut it off. Meanwhile cavalry who made good their way down stream kept coming up and joining the band round Alexander.

### Questions

1. *What risks did Alexander take in this battle and why?*
2. *Was Alexander's behavior wise or foolish?*
3. *Who saved Alexander? How?*

---

"Alexander in Battle," from Arrian, vol. I, with an English translation by P. A. Brunt, Loeb Classical Library. Copyright © 1983 by the President and Fellows of Harvard University Press. Reprinted with permission.

**Alexander Mosaic**
This detail of a Roman-era mosaic from Pompeii shows Alexander the Great in battle, probably at Issus. Shining in his battle armor, Alexander is bareheaded, with a wide-eyed, intense gaze betokening his power. The larger scene includes the Persian king Darius, fleeing in his chariot.

Scala/Art Resource, NY

The ideal of Greek culture made it easier for the migrants to maintain a Greek identity. For that matter, it was now possible for foreigners to become Greek by learning the Greek language and literature. A new, simplified form of Greek, known as Koine (that is, "common") Greek, replaced various regional Greek dialects. The number of Hellenized foreigners was relatively small, yet their very existence marked a break from the Classical polis, where even a resident genius, such as Aristotle, could not obtain Athenian citizenship because he was not of Athenian descent.

The Greek language also served as a common denominator, along with Aramaic, both of which became the languages of trade in the eastern Mediterranean. To get a sense of the importance of Isocrates' redefinition of **Hellenism**, consider that one of the most famous Greek-speakers of all antiquity was Paul, the Christian apostle who was born a Jew in Tarsus, a city in southern Anatolia.

In the Ptolemaic and Seleucid realms, administration was a joint effort of immigrants and natives. The upper ranks of government were dominated by Greeks and Macedonians, while native elites usually held low- or mid-level government positions. Especially after about 200 B.C., some natives even reached high office. Others worked in the traditional native administrative structures that survived largely intact in the new kingdoms—for example, as judges or village headmen or priests.

To create a hereditary military group in the countryside, Ptolemy (TOL-eh-mee) I settled his soldiers on land grants there. Native Egyptians were excluded from the army at first, although they served as policemen, but by the second century B.C., the dynasty needed native Egyptians too as soldiers. In return, natives now received land, tax breaks, and the right to call themselves Hellenes. Their Hellenism sometimes just scratched the surface, but other times it went deeper.

Temples, which often administered large estates, represented important sources of local power. Because priests shaped local opinion, they demanded royal patronage. Both **Ptolemies** and **Seleucids** complied: from Babylon to Edfu, money poured into temple-building and renovation.

The Seleucids addressed the security needs of their far-flung realms by establishing over seventy colonies extending to central Asia. Some colonies were civilian, but most were military, composed of retired or reserve soldiers, mostly Greeks or Macedonians but also Jews and other non-Greek peoples. Colonists received land allotments. Greek-style public buildings were erected, and some cities were laid out according to a rectilinear grid reminiscent of the Classical polis. The gymnasium attained a great practical and symbolic importance as both the center of Greek culture and the preparatory school for entry into the elite. The Hellenistic gymnasium offered education in literature, philosophy, and oratory as well as athletics.

Some Seleucid colonies developed into flourishing Greek cities, particularly in Anatolia and on the coast of Syria. Greek urbanization should not create the false impression, however, that the Seleucids were motivated by some civilizing mission. They were not. They established colonies to increase their power.

## Economic Expansion

Immigration and colonization were not the only sources of new economic opportunities. At the beginning of the Hellenistic era, Alexander turned the huge gold and silver reserves of Persia into coinage and released it onto the market virtually all at once. The result was about seventy-five years of inflation but also a commercial boom. In particular, money largely replaced barter in Egypt, which increased production and trade, helping to render Egypt an economic powerhouse. Another stimulus to trade was the creation of thriving new Hellenistic cities, especially Alexandria with its great harbors, canals, marketplaces, and infrastructure of banks, inns, courts, and shipbuilding facilities.

During Hellenistic times, commerce tended to shift from Greece proper to Anatolia and Egypt (see **Map 4.3**). The island of Rhodes, located off the southwest tip of Anatolia, grew into a major trading center, especially for grain. Egypt, too, had many products to trade. Grain was the most important, but textiles, glass, papyrus, and luxury goods were also significant.

**Hellenism**  Term used to designate ancient Greece's language, culture, and civilization.

**Ptolemies**  Dynasty founded by Ptolemy I and ruled by Egyptian kings; it was the wealthiest, most sophisticated, and longest lasting of the Hellenistic kingdoms.

**Seleucids**  Dynasty founded by Seleucus and governed by rulers of Anatolia from 312 to 64 B.C., it established seventy colonies throughout the Near East.

🌐 **Map 4.3 The Eastern Mediterranean, ca. 200 B.C.** The great Hellenistic powers contended for control of this vibrant, turbulent, and prosperous region. Conflict centered on Palestine and the Aegean islands, the rulership of which frequently changed hands. © Cengage Learning 2014

A network of canals connecting Alexandria to the Nile and the Red Sea beyond made trading possible with Sudan, Arabia, and India.

The Seleucid kingdoms controlled trade routes to the east. Commerce benefited from good roads, safe sea travel between the Persian Gulf and India, and a unified royal coinage. The Seleucids traded agricultural goods and manufactured products for spices from India and Arabia. In the first century B.C., they even imported silk from China. The kingdom of Pergamum, which stretched inland from Anatolia's northwest coast, exported its rich agricultural products, as well as the local gray-blue building stone and, as an alternative to Egyptian papyrus, parchment.

Slavery was an important part of the Hellenistic social and economic scene. Although war and piracy were the main sources of enslavement, some people were born into slavery. In Sicily and southern Italy, slaves worked huge plantations, but eastern Mediterranean slaves were commonly found in the household or in administration and in cities rather than in the countryside. Many unfree laborers worked on farms in Egypt and western Asia. Following the pre-Greek traditions of those regions, they were generally tenant farmers tied to kings or potentates rather than outright slaves.

On some plantations, conditions for slaves were harsh enough to lead to mass uprisings. It was not unusual, however, for domestic or administrative slaves to buy their freedom, sometimes using savings they were allowed to keep, sometimes borrowing money from the

**Antigonids** Dynasty founded by Antigonus Gonatas in 276 B.C. and governed by Macedonian rulers for about 140 years, until the Roman conquest.

master or from friends. Greeks enslaved fellow Greeks, but often, it seems, with guilty consciences; they frequently made special efforts to help Greek slaves win their freedom. Even in bondage, therefore, Greeks had special privileges.

## Macedon and Greece

Macedon was the last of the three great Hellenistic kingdoms to emerge from civil war after Alexander's death. Not until 276 B.C. was Antigonus Gonatas, grandson of Alexander's general Antigonus the One-Eyed, established on the throne. His Antigonid (an-TIG-on-id) dynasty lasted about a century, until the Romans conquered Macedon.

The **Antigonids** projected an image of simplicity and toughness. Antigonus expressed interest in the doctrines of the new Stoic philosophy taught in Athens. As king, he devoted himself to the Stoic dictates of duty, describing his office as "noble servitude" and his diadem as a mere "rag." Antigonus shared the traditional Macedonian ambition to dominate the Greek city-states, but he faced rival powers. Besides Ptolemaic Egypt, there was the kingdom of Epirus in northwestern Greece and two new federal leagues in the south, the Aetolians (ay-TOL-ee-unz) (north of the Corinthian Gulf) and the Achaeans (uh-KEE-unz) (in the Peloponnesus; see **Map 4.3**).

The leagues were dominated by the wealthy; they were not democracies. Yet, the leagues were models of federalism that would one day influence the founders of the United States. The Achaeans, for example, successfully balanced local and federal authorities.

Extremes of wealth and poverty, problems of debt, and class conflict challenged Hellenistic Greece. Athens remained a vibrant democracy until the late third century B.C., when the oligarchic upper classes finally won the upper hand for good. The wealthy now contributed less to the public good in taxes and amassed private fortunes instead. Still, they usually made just enough concessions to avoid full-scale revolution.

Sparta was an exception. In the late third century B.C., two Spartan kings, Agis and Cleomenes, launched a social revolution from above. They aimed to reestablish Sparta's past greatness through a program of debt relief, redistribution of land, and restoration of Classical Spartan austerity and equality. Popular in Sparta, the revolution threatened to spread elsewhere. Peloponnesian oligarchs called in Macedonian forces, which crushed Sparta in 222 B.C. and ended the revolution.

## Ptolemaic Egypt

The wealthiest, most sophisticated, and longest-lasting Hellenistic kingdom was Ptolemaic Egypt. One of Alexander's great generals, Ptolemy (d. 283 B.C.), founded a dynasty that lasted until Rome annexed Egypt in 30 B.C., after the suicide of the last ruler of the line, Queen Cleopatra (see pages 136–137). By then, Rome had already conquered or annexed all the other Hellenistic kingdoms.

Unlike the Antigonids, the Ptolemies gloried in wealth and grandeur. Ptolemy I showed the way to his successors when he had Alexander's funeral procession hijacked on its way to Macedonia and established a tomb and

**Tanagra Figurine** A terra-cotta (baked clay) statuette of around 320 B.C. shows a modestly dressed woman wearing a hat and carrying a fan. Named for its place of manufacture in Greece, this popular style of figure demonstrates the Hellenistic taste for ordinary, household themes.

## Egyptians Versus Greeks in a Temple

*This second-century B.C. papyrus, a petition to the authorities from a Greek worshiper of Serapis, provides insight into relations between Greeks and Egyptians in Hellenistic Egypt. It shows how Greeks lived in the temple at Memphis in order to worship Serapis, a Hellenized Egyptian god (see pages 106–107). It also depicts violence and hostility across ethnic lines.*

To Dionysius, general and one of the "friends" [of the king], from Ptolemy son of Glaucias, a Macedonian, one of those "held in detention" [that is, on a voluntary, religious retreat] for twelve years in the great temple of Serapis in Memphis. As I have suffered grave injustice and my life has been frequently endangered by the temple cleaners whose names are listed below, I am taking refuge with you in the belief that in this way I would best secure justice. For on . . . [November 9, 161 B.C.] They came to the temple of Astarte, which is in the sanctuary, and in which I have been living "in detention" for the number of years mentioned above; some of them had stones in their hand and others sticks, and they tried to force their way in, in order to seize the opportunity to plunder the temple and to put me to death because I am a Greek, like men laying a plot against my life. But when I anticipated them and shut the door of the temple, and shouted to them to withdraw in peace, they did not go away even so.

When Diphilus, one of the worshipers held "in detention" by Serapis besides me, expressed indignation at their conduct in such a temple, they pushed him back, handled him very roughly and beat him up, so that their lawless brutality was clear for all to see. When these same men treated me in the same way in. . . .[November 163 B.C.], I immediately addressed a petition to you, but as I had no one to look after the matter further, they were let off scot-free and became even more arrogant. I therefore ask you, if you please, to order them to be brought before you, so that they may receive the punishment they deserve for all these misdeeds. Farewell.

### Questions

1. What is the complaint of Ptolemy, son of Glaucias, about? Is this the first time he has made such a complaint?

2. Why was Ptolemy unable to get justice before? What does this tell us about the way petitions were handled by the government?

3. Why were Ptolemy and Diphilus attacked? What does the attack indicate about Greek-Egyptian relations in second century B.C. Egypt?

Adapted from M.M. Austin, *The Hellenistic World from Alexander to the Roman Conquest: A Selection of Ancient Sources in Translation*, Second Edition. Copyright © 2006 by Cambridge University Press. Reprinted with the permission of Cambridge University Press.

then a cult in the capital city, **Alexandria**—a Greek hero-shrine in the land of the pyramids. Ptolemy I made arrangements to have himself proclaimed "savior god" after his death; his successors, less reticent, took divine honors while still alive.

**Alexandria** Thriving Hellenistic city in northern Egypt founded by Alexander the Great in 332 B.C.

Like the pharaohs, the Ptolemies intervened in the Egyptian economy on a massive scale. Putting to use the science of the Museum, the great institute in Alexandria (see page 98), the Ptolemies sponsored irrigation and land reclamation projects, the introduction of new crops (for example, new varieties of wheat), and the greatly expanded cultivation of old ones (such as grapes for wine).

Most Egyptians made their living in agriculture, either as independent small farmers or as tenants on large estates. Government enriched itself through taxes, rents, demands for compulsory labor, state monopolies (on such diverse items as oils, textiles, and beer), and various internal tolls and customs duties. The result was boom times under strong kings and queens in the third century B.C. Egypt became the most prosperous part of the Hellenistic world, and Alexandria became the wealthiest, most populous city in the Mediterranean, as well as its literary capital (see **Map 4.3**). In the second century B.C., however, economic decline set in, which created conditions for revolt.

To defeat the Seleucids at the Battle of Raphia in Gaza in 217 B.C., the Ptolemies had to enroll thousands of Egyptians in the Macedonian phalanx because of a shortage of Greek mercenaries. Emboldened by their new military power, people in Upper Egypt soon broke into armed revolt against the government in far-off Alexandria. Unrest continued for about a century.

The rebels tried to stoke anti-Greek sentiment. Yet, although friction between immigrants and natives sparked from time to time, most Egyptians accepted the Ptolemies as long as they brought peace and prosperity. (See the feature, "The Global Record: Egyptians Versus Greeks in a Temple.")

And the Ptolemies reasserted their power. In 196 B.C., for example, Ptolemy V Epiphanes celebrated his coronation in full pharaonic ceremonial in Memphis. Egyptian priests

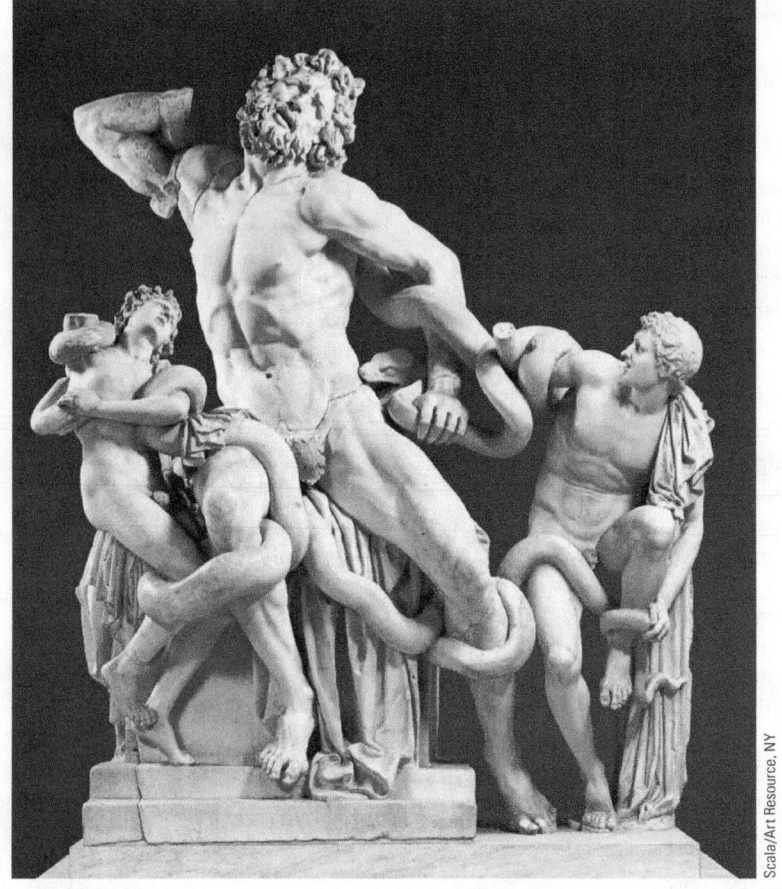

**Laocoön** This famous statue group of the second or first century B.C. shows the Trojan priest Laocoön and his sons being strangled by snakes sent by the gods. The scene's emphasis on extreme emotion is typical of Hellenistic art.

Scala/Art Resource, NY

commemorated the occasion in a decree written in Egypt's traditional language of kingship in a trilingual inscription (Greek, hieroglyphic, and demotic—ordinary—Egyptian). This inscription, discovered by French soldiers in 1799 and dubbed the Rosetta stone (named for the place where it was found), led to the modern European deciphering of hieroglyphics.

Despite the frictions, evidence points to native settler cooperation, especially in the countryside, where intermarriage and bilingualism became common. By 98 B.C., assimilation was evident in the cultural hybrid of a group of 18- and 19-year-old male youths who received traditional Greek military and literary training but prayed to Egypt's crocodile-god.

## Western Asia

The kingdom founded by Alexander's general Seleucus (suh-LOO-kus) (ca. 358–281 B.C.) experienced shifting borders and inhabitants between its founding in 312 B.C. and its end in 64 B.C. when Syria became a Roman province. The first three kings ruled a domain stretching from the Aegean to Bactria (BACK-tree-uh) (modern Afghanistan), but by the early second century B.C., most of Iran and the lands eastward had been lost. At its height, in the third century B.C., the Seleucid kingdom had three nerve centers: Ionia (in western Anatolia), with a capital at Sardis; Syria, with a capital at Antioch; and Babylonia, whose capital was Seleucia-on-the-Tigris (near modern Baghdad; see **Map 4.2**).

To administer their far-flung and multiethnic lands, the Seleucid kings took over the Persian system of satraps (provincial governors), taxes, and royal roads and post (see page 36). They added a Macedonian-style army, a common coinage, a Hellenistic ruler cult, and colonies. Greek and Macedonian soldiers and administrators dominated, but natives also filled bureaucratic slots.

**Antioch** Located near the present-day Turkish-Syrian border, it was the greatest of the cities founded by Seleucus, a general of Alexander the Great.

The greatest Seleucid city was **Antioch**, which became one of the wealthiest and most luxurious of all eastern Mediterranean cities; only Ptolemaic Alexandria outstripped it. The intellectual and artistic capital of Greek Asia in Hellenistic times, however, was not Antioch but Pergamum, in northwestern Anatolia (see **Map 4.3**).

The rulers of Pergamum, the Attalid dynasty of kings, carved out a small kingdom that became independent of the Seleucids in 263 B.C. and fell into Roman hands in 133 B.C. The Attalids made Pergamum into a showplace of Greek civilization, a would-be second Athens.

Pergamum was famous for its sculptors and for a library second only to Alexandria's. Pergamene writers focused on scholarship, to the exclusion of poetry, perhaps as a result of the influence of Stoic philosophers, who disapproved of poetry's emotionalism.

**Bactria** Bactria flourished as an independent Greek-ruled state in what is today Afghanistan, beginning in the mid-third century B.C., and expanded into what is today India and Pakistan.

## The Greco-Indian Interaction

The Seleucids' hold on Alexander's vast eastern domains turned out to be temporary. A new Persian dynasty, the Parthians (PAR-thee-unz), achieved independence in the mid-third century B.C. and over the next century, extended westward into Mesopotamia. But to the east, Bactria remained Greek, if not Seleucid. From the mid-third century B.C., an independent Greek **Bactria** prospered (see **Map 4.2**).

**A Greek-Influenced Indian Statue**　This figure of a *bodhisattva* ("enlightened one") belongs to the Gandharan school, which was heavily influenced by Hellenistic sculpture. The statue's proportions, facial features, and draped clothing particularly recall Hellenistic motifs, suggesting that it may be the work of a Greek sculptor. Photograph courtesy of the Royal Ontario Museum, © ROM

Vivid evidence of Greek colonization in Bactria comes from the site of Aï Khanum (its ancient name is unknown) in northern Afghanistan. This prosperous and populous city contained many reminders of Greece, among them a gymnasium, theater, and library. A pillar in the gymnasium was inscribed in the mid-third century B.C., with 140 moral maxims from Delphi in Greece, over 3,000 miles away.

In the second century B.C., Bactrian kings extended their rule into the Indus River valley and the Punjab, a region with a modest Greek presence since the fifth century B.C., when the Persians settled Greek mercenaries there. Virtually no literary evidence survives, but monuments and, particularly, coins demonstrate Greco-Indian cultural interaction. For example, some coins from the second century B.C. show bilingual inscriptions in Greek and Indian languages. Their designs include a variety of Indian religious motifs, such as the lotus plant, symbol of Lakshmi, goddess of wealth and good fortune. Indians admired Hellenistic astronomy; one text goes so far as to say that Greek scientists should be "reverenced like gods."

The Hellenistic world seems to have intrigued King Asoka (uh-SO-kuh) (r. ca. 270–230 B.C.), who ruled almost the entire Indian subcontinent. Asoka is best remembered as a religious reformer. A convert to Buddhism, he played a major role in its spread, which proceeded under the slogan of *dhamma*—that is, "morality" or "righteousness." One of his inscriptions apparently records embassies, aimed at spreading Buddhism, to the Hellenistic kingdoms.*

The envoys apparently found few converts, for it is difficult to find any trace of Buddhism in Hellenistic Greek culture, at least outside the Greco-Indian kingdoms. There, one of the most powerful Greek rulers, Menander Soter Dikaios (r. ca. 155–130 B.C.), may have converted to Buddhism in the mid-second century B.C. But certain aspects of Indian religion—especially India's powerful currents of asceticism, mysticism, and monasticism—interested Greek intellectuals around the Mediterranean in Hellenistic and Roman times. Observers on Alexander's expedition, Hellenistic envoys, merchants, and philosophers in search of Eastern wisdom all served as conduits between East and West. One of the most influential was Megasthenes, a Seleucid ambassador to the court of Asoka's grandfather, who published his *Indika*, a description of India, around 300 B.C.

Yet, the degree to which this interest influenced Greek and Roman culture is debatable. Although ancient writers mention Greek or Roman philosophers who were attracted by Indian culture, modern scholars tend to be cautious. The ancients had a weakness for tall tales and exotic stories. For example, the great Neo-Platonic philosopher Plotinus (A.D. 235–270) is reported to have traveled with the Roman emperor Gordian's army eastward, hoping in vain to reach India. Some scholars see Indian influence in Plotinus's mysticism and pantheism, but others dismiss the idea.

Central Asian nomads overran Bactria in the late second century B.C. The Hellenistic kingdoms of India and Pakistan, however, survived until about the time of Christ, and some Greek communities lasted until the fifth century A.D. The Gandharan sculptors who flourished in a formerly Greek-ruled region in about A.D. 200 used Greek artistic techniques to depict Buddhist subjects, which might suggest the impact of Indian culture on the remaining Greek population.

---

*Romila Thapar, *As'oka and the Decline of the Mauryas* (Oxford: Oxford University Press, 1961), p. 256.

## SECTION SUMMARY

- Greek and Macedonian colonists and their descendants dominated the army and administration in the Ptolemaic and Seleucid kingdoms, but natives played a role as well.
- Greek culture made only a small impact in the multiethnic kingdoms of the Ptolemies and Seleucids; native cultures flourished.
- The Antigonid dynasty of Macedon and federal leagues joined city-states as prominent features of Hellenistic Greek political life.
- Ptolemaic Egypt, with its capital of Alexandria, was the wealthiest, most sophisticated, and longest lasting Hellenistic kingdom.
- Seleucid Antioch and Attalid Pergamum were new and thriving cities of Hellenistic southwest Asia.
- Hellenistic Greek kingdoms prospered for centuries in parts of Afghanistan, India, and Pakistan.

# Hellenistic Culture

How did Greek civilization spread during the Hellenistic era, and what were the main trends in literature, science, and art?

The capital of Egypt, Alexandria, was also the main laboratory for transforming Hellenistic Greek culture and so facilitating its spread. By the first century B.C., Alexandria was a city of half a million or more inhabitants. It was one of the largest and wealthiest cities in the world. The bulk of the people were Egyptian, but Greeks and Jews made up large minorities, and no one would have been surprised, in this cosmopolitan center, to see an Indian or a Celt, an Italian or a Persian.

Archaeologists today, looking for submerged parts of the city in Alexandria harbor, have found Egyptian sphinxes and obelisks, as well as Greek statues. Written sources portray a picture of social change in the elite, an increase in leisure time, a growth in educational opportunities for both sexes, royal patronage of culture, and the value of even a limited knowledge of Greek literature as the ticket to advancement.

## Athens and Alexandria

In 294 B.C., King Ptolemy I invited the deposed tyrant of Athens, Demetrius of Phalerum, to found an institution of culture in Alexandria. Demetrius had studied with Aristotle's successor at the Lyceum, Theophrastus (the-uh-FRAS-tus) (ca. 370–288 B.C.), a practical man interested in compiling and cataloging knowledge.

**Museum** Literally "House of the Muses," the Museum was Alexandria's most important scholarly and scientific center. It included the Library, which housed the world's largest collection of Greek writing.

The new institution was called the **Museum** (literally, "House of the Muses," or the home of the female deities who inspired creativity). The Museum was a residence, study, and lecture hall for scholars, scientists, and poets. It was also a research center to keep the king's engineers up to date on new technology for warfare and agriculture. One of the Museum's key components was the Library, in its day, the largest collection of Greek writing in the world. In the third century B.C.—at the height of the Ptolemaic kingdom—the Library contained 700,000 papyrus rolls, the equivalent of roughly 50,000 modern books. Its nearest competitor, at Pergamum, contained less than a third as many rolls. The Library reflects the growth of the Hellenistic reading and writing public. The names of over a thousand writers of the Hellenistic era survive, and after 300 B.C., anthologies, abridgments, and school texts multiplied.

Though modeled on Athens's Lyceum, the Museum represented a break from the public culture of the Classical period. The residents of the Museum were an elite, dependent on royal patronage and self-consciously Greek and not Egyptian. One wit dismissed them as pedants and "fatted fowls that quarrel without end in the hen coop of the Muses."

The background to Alexandrian literature is Hellenistic Athenian literature, which broke from its Classical roots. The greatest Hellenistic Athenian writer, a man famous throughout the ancient world, was Menander (ca. 342–292 B.C.). He wrote a style of comedy called "New Comedy," as distinguished from the "Old Comedy" of Aristophanes a century earlier (see page 81). Where Old Comedy was raucous and ribald, New Comedy was restrained; where Old Comedy focused on public affairs, New Comedy was domestic and private. New Comedy illustrates the turn away from public life in Hellenistic times.

Menander wrote over seventy plays, but only one complete work has survived, *Dyskolos* (*The Grouch*). There are also large excerpts from several other comedies, as well as Roman imitations. Menander favored stock plots and stock characters: the boastful soldier, the clever slave, the dashing but inept young man, the sweet maiden, and the old miser. Within those limitations, Menander created realistic and idiosyncratic characters. As a Hellenistic critic asked rhetorically: "O Menander and Life, which of you imitated the other?"

Like Menander, Alexandrian writers spurned public themes, but in Alexandria, the characteristic literary figure was not the playwright but the critic: a professional man of letters. Adopted by the Romans, Alexandrian critical standards have influenced the West to this day.

Of the three greatest Alexandrian writers, two—Callimachus (305–240 B.C.) and Apollonius of Rhodes (b. ca. 295 B.C.)—worked at the Library; the third, Theocritus (ca.

300–260 B.C.), probably lived on a stipend from the Ptolemies. Popular for centuries, Callimachus was probably the most influential, the complete Hellenistic poet. A native of Cyrene (see **Map 4.2**) who came to Alexandria as a schoolteacher, Callimachus worked in the Library to compose a virtually universal history of all recorded Greek (and much non-Greek) knowledge.

Callimachus was a prolific writer, but he aimed at brevity: "Big book, big evil" was his maxim. While earlier Greek poets were usually austere and public-minded, Callimachus preferred the private, the light, and the exotic. "Don't expect from me a big-sounding poem," he writes. "Zeus thunders, not I."* Callimachus was an expert at the pithy statement in verse—the epigram.

Another major Alexandrian writer was Callimachus's student Apollonius of Rhodes, who wrote the epic poem *Argonautica* (ar-go-NAW-tih-kuh) (*Voyage of the Argo*). The subject is Jason and the heroes who travel on the ship *Argo* to the Black Sea, in pursuit of the Golden Fleece (the skin of a winged ram). With the help of the princess Medea, who falls in love with Jason, they succeed and return home safely after many adventures.

Apollonius's Jason is no hero of old. Whereas Homer describes Odysseus as "never at a loss," Apollonius describes Jason as "helpless." Men move the action in the *Iliad* and the *Odyssey*; Jason depends on a woman, Medea, for his success. Indeed, much of the *Argonautica* focuses on Medea and her love for Jason. All in all, the *Argonautica* is less a traditional epic than a romance.

Theocritus, a native of Syracuse, composed thirty-one subtle and refined poems, conventionally known as idylls. The best known poems focus on country life. They are the first known pastoral poems; indeed, Theocritus probably invented the genre. Through his Roman admirers, Theocritus's love of nature has exerted a powerful hold on the Western literary imagination.

Outside the Museum, Alexandria had a lively popular culture, much of it Egyptian or influenced by Egyptian models. A glimpse of this culture is offered in the seven surviving mimes, or farces, of an obscure writer named Herondas or Herodas. Though written in literary Greek, they discuss commonplace subjects—shopping for shoes, tourism, lawsuits, and beatings at school—and titillating themes, such as adultery and prostitution.

## Advances in Science and Medicine

The Ptolemies not only reaped practical benefits in military and agricultural technology from their Museum but also became the patrons of a flourishing period in the history of pure scientific inquiry. Antigonid patronage of ethical and political philosophy helped keep Athens preeminent in those fields. In contrast, the study of science tended to shift to Alexandria and to Pergamum in Anatolia and, far to the west, Syracuse, a flourishing Hellenistic city in Sicily. Hellenistic science benefited from several factors, including the era's wealth, improved communications and literacy, continued warfare, and cross-fertilization between Greek and non-Greek traditions.

## Mathematics

Some of the best-known figures of Hellenistic science were mathematicians. In his *Elements*, the Alexandrian Euclid (active ca. 300 B.C.) produced a systematic study of geometry that was hugely influential in both Western and Islamic civilizations.

But the greatest mathematician of Greek antiquity was a Sicilian Greek, **Archimedes** (ar-kuh-MEE-deez) of Syracuse (287–212 B.C.). Among other things, Archimedes calculated the approximate value of pi (the ratio of a circle's circumference to its diameter) and made important discoveries in astronomy, engineering, optics, and other fields. Although Archimedes looked down on practical things as "ignoble and vulgar," he was a notable inventor. His most important invention was the water snail, also known as Archimedes' screw—a device to raise water for irrigation. Created by Archimedes during a stay in Egypt, the screw

**Archimedes** The greatest ancient Greek mathematician, Archimedes of Syracuse (287–212 B.C.) calculated the approximate value of pi (the ratio of a circle's circumference to its diameter) and invented the water snail (also known as Archimedes' screw).

---

*Charles Rowan Beye, *Ancient Greek Literature and Society*, 2d ed. (Ithaca, N.Y.: Cornell University Press, 1987), p. 265.

**Street Musicians** The lively scene of a mixed group of young and old, male and female, recalls the jaunty mimes popular with the Hellenistic public. A mosaic from about 100 B.C., the artwork comes from a private villa in the Greco-Italian city of Pompeii. Erich Lessing/Art Resource, NY

made it possible to irrigate previously barren land, as did the ox-driven water wheel, another innovation of this period.

Advances in mathematics promoted advances in astronomy. Aristarchus of Samos (active ca. 275 B.C.) is known for his heliocentric hypothesis, which confounded tradition by having the earth revolve around the sun, instead of the sun around the earth. He was right, but Hellenistic astronomy lacked the data to prove his theory, so its rejection was not unreasonable at the time. Eratosthenes (er-uh-TOSS-the-neez) of Cyrene (active ca. 225 B.C.) was saddled with the frustrating nickname of "Beta" (the second letter of the Greek alphabet) because he was considered second best in every branch of study. This "second best" nonetheless calculated through simple geometry an extraordinarily accurate measurement of the earth's circumference.

## Medicine

Hellenistic medicine thrived in Alexandria. Both Greece and Egypt had long-established medical traditions, but the key to medical advance was the dissection of human cadavers in Alexandria, a first in the history of science. In Greece, as in many ancient societies, religious tradition demanded that dead bodies not be mutilated. But in the frontier atmosphere of early Alexandria, this traditional taboo lost much of its force. Although Egyptians did not practice dissection, they did practice embalming, which may have helped Alexandrian Greeks overcome the prohibition against cutting open the human body.

The leading scientific beneficiary was Herophilus (her-AH-fih-lus) of Chalcedon (ca. 320–250 B.C.), a practicing physician in Alexandria. Among his achievements was the recognition (against Aristotle) that the brain is the center of the nervous system, a careful dissection of the eye, the discovery of the ovaries, and the description of the duodenum, which he named (*duodenum* is a Latin translation of a Greek word meaning "twelve fingers," describing the organ's length). In addition, Herophilus developed a detailed theory of the diagnostic value of measuring pulse rates.

## Engineering

Hellenistic technology has long fascinated and frustrated scholars. The great engineers invented both numerous engines of war and various "wonderworks" to amuse the royal court. Among the latter were mechanical puppets and steam-run toys. Given these advances, why did the Greeks achieve neither a scientific revolution, along the lines of the one begun in the early modern era by thinkers such as Copernicus and Galileo, nor an industrial transformation, such as was ushered in by the steam engine around A.D. 1800? Historians are not entirely sure but can venture a guess. Greek machine-making technology was not as sophisticated as that of eighteenth-century Europe. The prevalence of slavery in antiquity discouraged labor-saving machines; steam was used only for playthings and gadgets.

Perhaps the most important point is the Greek attitude toward nature. Whereas Jews and Christians learned from the Bible that human beings have dominion over nature, thereby making possible the conclusion that it is appropriate to conquer nature, the Greeks thought in more restricted terms. They believed that nature set limits, that a virtuous person tried to follow nature, not subdue it. Thus, Greek engineers were not inclined to make the revolutionary changes that their modern counterparts have promoted.

## Men and Women in Art and Society

Like Hellenistic literature, Hellenistic art attests to changing male attitudes toward women and toward gender issues. The portrait of Jason and Medea in Apollonius's *Argonautica* makes fun of masculine pretensions and celebrates the triumph of female intelligence. It also presents a sympathetic portrait of a woman's romantic desire for a man, as does Theocritus's work. In the Classical period, depictions of romantic love were generally restricted to relationships between males. Accordingly, statues of naked males were common, but women were almost always depicted clothed. Hellenistic sculpture, by contrast, affords many erotic examples of the female nude.

There are indications that the Hellenistic Greek male of the elite was much more willing than his Classical predecessor to see lovemaking as a matter of mutuality and respect. Classical vase-painting often depicts heterosexual lovemaking with a lusty and explicit mood. In contrast, in Hellenistic vase-painting, the emphasis is more often on tenderness and domesticity. Hellenistic men wrote with sensitivity about satisfying a woman's needs and desires. The vogue for representations of Hermaphrodite (her-MAF-ro-dyte), the mythical creature who was half-female and half-male, may suggest a belief that the feminine was as important a part of human nature as the masculine.

Many a Hellenistic artist or writer seems to be as interested in emotion as in action and to focus on the inner as much as on the outer life. Hellenistic art often depicts women, children, and domestic scenes. Representations of warriors are as likely to focus on their unrestrained emotions as on their soldierly self-control.

Hellenistic women enjoyed small improvements in political and legal status and bigger improvements in economic and ideological status. Greek women, particularly in the elite, benefited from the spread of monarchy. Queens and princesses had more power than female commoners in city-states. Also, in the new cities, as in many a frontier society, women were permitted to inherit and use property more often than in old Greece.

It was an era of powerful queens: Olympias, Alexander the Great's mother, played kingmaker after her son's death. Arsinoe II Philadelphus was coruler of Egypt with her husband (who was also her brother) for five years at the height of Ptolemaic prosperity around 275 B.C. Laodike III, wife of the great Seleucid king Antiochus III (r. 223–187 B.C.) had the authority to give a city grain for ten years, specifying that "the money realized from

## Images of Cleopatra

*"Cleopatra's nose: if it had been shorter, the whole face of the earth would have changed,"* wrote the French Blaise Pascal (1623-1662). He does Cleopatra an injustice. It was not a pretty face and classical features that enabled her to win the throne of Egypt (r. 51-30 B.C.), to obtain first Julius Caesar and then Mark Antony as ally and lover, and finally to come close to gaining control of the Roman Empire. Intelligence, daring, charm, and extraordinary diplomatic skill account for Cleopatra's success.

Let us consider the queen's manipulation of her public image—no mean task, given the fragility of Ptolemaic power in the first century B.C. Within Egypt, the monarch had to satisfy several ethnic groups. Most important were the Greeks and Macedonians—who dominated government, the military, and the economy—and the native Egyptian majority. Daughter of Ptolemy XII (r. 80-51 B.C.), Cleopatra was supposed to rule jointly with her brother, but they had a falling-out. She grabbed the throne from him and then from another brother and thus had to assert her legitimacy. Also, Ptolemaic Egypt had to project an image of unity to the Romans, who were threatening to annex it, as they had the other Hellenistic monarchies.

Cleopatra, like earlier Ptolemaic monarchs, met these challenges by presenting two faces to the world. To the Greeks and Romans, she was a Hellenistic monarch; to the Egyptians, she was an ancient pharaonic queen. Look first at the bronze coin of Cleopatra issued at Alexandria probably in the 30s B.C. The queen is shown as a young woman. Her hair, tied in a bun at the nape of her neck, is in the so-called melon style often seen in Hellenistic female portraits. She wears a diadem (royal headband), its ends hanging behind her neck. More commonly worn by Hellenistic kings than by queens, the diadem signifies Cleopatra's claim to authority.

So does the queen's profile. She is portrayed with a prominent chin, a large mouth, and a rugged nose. These features may not be the standard attributes of beauty, but they are precisely the features that mark coin portraits of Cleopatra's father. By emphasizing Cleopatra's physical similarity to her father, the portrait artist perhaps subtly suggests her right to sit on his throne.

**Bronze Coin of Cleopatra**

The side of the coin not shown here is far from subtle: Its legend states clearly in Greek, "Queen Cleopatra." The illustration is of an eagle and thunderbolt and a double cornucopia (horn of plenty) entwined with a diadem. The eagle and thunderbolt recall the Greek god Zeus, and the two cornucopias suggest fertility and prosperity. All are recurrent symbols of Ptolemaic royalty. The coin thus portrays Cleopatra as a Greek monarch, the worthy heir of her father. It would have been an effective image in Alexandria, a city dominated by Greeks and visited by Romans, but not in the countryside, especially south of the Nile Delta, in Upper Egypt, an area that was primarily Egyptian. Following dynastic custom, Cleopatra changed her image there.

In Upper Egypt, earlier Ptolemies frequently had been represented in stone in traditional pharaonic style, and they were great restorers of ancient Egyptian temples and builders of new ones. Look at the sculptural relief from the temple of the Egyptian cow-goddess Hathor at Dendera in Upper Egypt. The temple was a monumental structure initiated and underwritten by Ptolemy XII. Cleopatra, his daughter, added an enormous relief on the outside of the rear wall. Carved into the stone are two persons carrying offerings for Egyptian deities. The persons are Cleopatra (*left*) and her son Ptolemy XV Caesar, who ruled with his mother from 44

these [sales of a portion of the grain] be assigned to dowries for the daughters of the poorer citizens."*

The most famous Hellenistic woman, Cleopatra VII, was queen of Egypt from 51 to 30 B.C. Although she was the lover of two of the most powerful men in the world, the Romans Julius Caesar and Mark Antony, Cleopatra was no exotic plaything. Rather, she was a brilliant and ambitious strategist who nearly succeeded in winning a world empire for her family. (See the feature, "The Visual Record: Images of Cleopatra" above.)

---

*Quote from Stanely M. Burstein, ed. and trans. *The Hellenistic Age from the Battle of Ipsos to the Death of Kleopatra VII* (Cambridge, England: Cambridge University Press, 1985), p. 48.

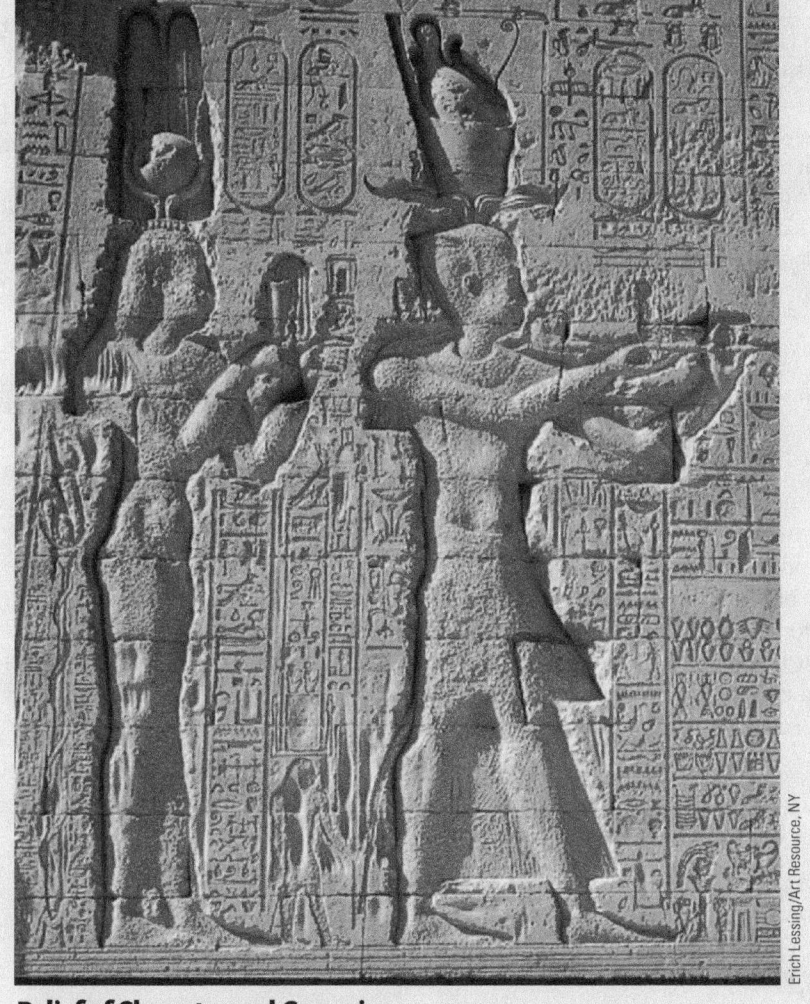

**Relief of Cleopatra and Caesarion**

sun-disk of Hathor, the tall plumes of Isis, and the ram's horn of Amon. Caesarion is shown as a pharaoh, wearing the double crown of Upper and Lower Egypt. Mother and son offer incense to the local deities. The small figure between Caesarion and Cleopatra is his *ka*, or soul.

Cleopatra's face is in profile but otherwise has very little in common with her portrait on the Alexandrian coin. Although the features are stylized pharaonic commonplaces, the shape of her head perhaps echoes the elegant and graceful relief portraits of Hatshepsut (r. 1479–1457 B.C.), the most famous female pharaoh before Cleopatra. Cleopatra commissioned other artworks and monuments in the native style in the Nile Valley. This was the custom of her dynasty, and Cleopatra had absorbed its traditions, but she stands second to none of the Ptolemies in shrewdness and subtlety. She was the only Ptolemaic monarch to learn to speak Egyptian, and she was the only one to come even close to gaining the upper hand over Rome. As the artifacts shown here indicate, she was able to put on an Egyptian face as easily as a Greek one, but she never lost sight of her true interests.

### Questions

1. *Why did Cleopatra need to show two faces to the world?*

2. *Does Cleopatra's coin emphasize her good looks? Why or why not?*

3. *What image of herself does Cleopatra present at the Temple of Hathor at Dendera? Why?*

to 30 B.C. Alleged to be the illegitimate son of Julius Caesar, Ptolemy XV was commonly known as Caesarion, or "little Caesar." At Dendera, however, he and his mother are shown neither as Romans nor as Greeks but as Egyptians.

Look closely at Cleopatra. She wears a long body-hugging robe. On her head is a royal headdress with symbols of the Egyptian gods: the lyre-shaped cow horns and

Writers in the new Hellenistic cities often described freedom of movement for women. Theocritus and Herondas, for example, show women visiting a temple or a show. In Hellenistic Athens, aristocratic fathers put up inscriptions in honor of their daughters who had participated in the cult of Athena. Although women generally continued to need a male guardian to represent them in public, in some situations, at least in Egypt (where the evidence is most plentiful), a woman could represent herself. A woman could petition the government on her own behalf. Widows and mothers of illegitimate children could give their daughters in marriage or apprentice their sons. A few cities granted women citizenship and even permitted them to hold public office.

Some Hellenistic cities admitted women to the gymnasium, previously a male preserve. Previously, only Sparta had promoted physical education for women, but by the first century

## SECTION SUMMARY

- Alexandria's Museum (a research institute) and Library were the focal point of much of Hellenistic literature and science.
- The playwright Menander and the poets Callimachus, Apollonius of Rhodes, and Theocritus represent the Hellenistic era's turn away from civic and heroic themes.
- Mathematics, astronomy, and medicine are all fields in which notable advances were made in the Hellenistic era, thanks in part to royal patronage.
- Philosophy and science first became separate disciplines, as they are today.
- Hellenistic women experienced real, though limited, improvements in status and power.

A.D., women were even competing in the great Pan-Hellenic games. Gymnasia were also centers of education in music and reading. One consequence of growing literacy was the re-emergence of women poets and the first appearance of women philosophers in the West. Before dying at age 19, Erinna, who lived on the Aegean island of Telos during the late fourth century B.C., wrote the *Distaff*, a poem in memory of her childhood friend Baucis. This three-hundred line poem, famous in antiquity, describes the shared experiences of girlhood. Hipparchia (hih-PAR-kee-uh) of Maroneia (b. ca. 350 B.C.), like her husband, Crates of Thebes, studied Cynic philosophy. The Cynics, like another philosophical school, the Epicureans, supported a measure of equality between women and men. Hipparchia and Crates led an itinerant life as popular teachers and the Hellenistic equivalent of counselors or psychologists.

Much of the explanation for the relative freedom of elite women lies in the new economic power of this group. The new cities generally imposed fewer restrictions on women's economic roles than had Classical poleis such as Athens. In many cities, women could sell land, borrow money, and decide whether their husbands could make loans or contracts on the strength of their dowries. Free women could manumit slaves as well.

Hellenistic women never attained the equality that sometimes exists between men and women today, but they did enjoy genuine improvements in status. Men and women played new roles in a changed, complex world. The new Hellenistic philosophies and religions attempted to address that complexity.

# The Turn Inward: New Philosophies, New Faiths

*What new philosophies and religions emerged in the Hellenistic period?*

The events of the Hellenistic era—emigration, a trend from independent city-states to monarchies and federal leagues, new extremes of wealth and poverty, and contact with foreign peoples and customs—all generated uncertainty. In response, Greek culture was spread and transformed. As literacy expanded, more Greeks than ever before could participate in cultural debate. New philosophies and religions arose to meet new spiritual concerns, generating ideas that would be influential for centuries.

The meeting of Jews and Greeks proved to be just as significant. Challenged by Greek conquest, Greek colonization, and their own migration to Greek lands, Jews alternately embraced Hellenism and engaged in resistance, both cultural and armed. In the process, first Judaism and then Hellenism were changed forever.

## Hellenistic Philosophy

Although the polis lost its military and political preeminence in the fourth century B.C., philosophy continued to thrive. It was, however, much changed. With the city-state losing significance as a focus of

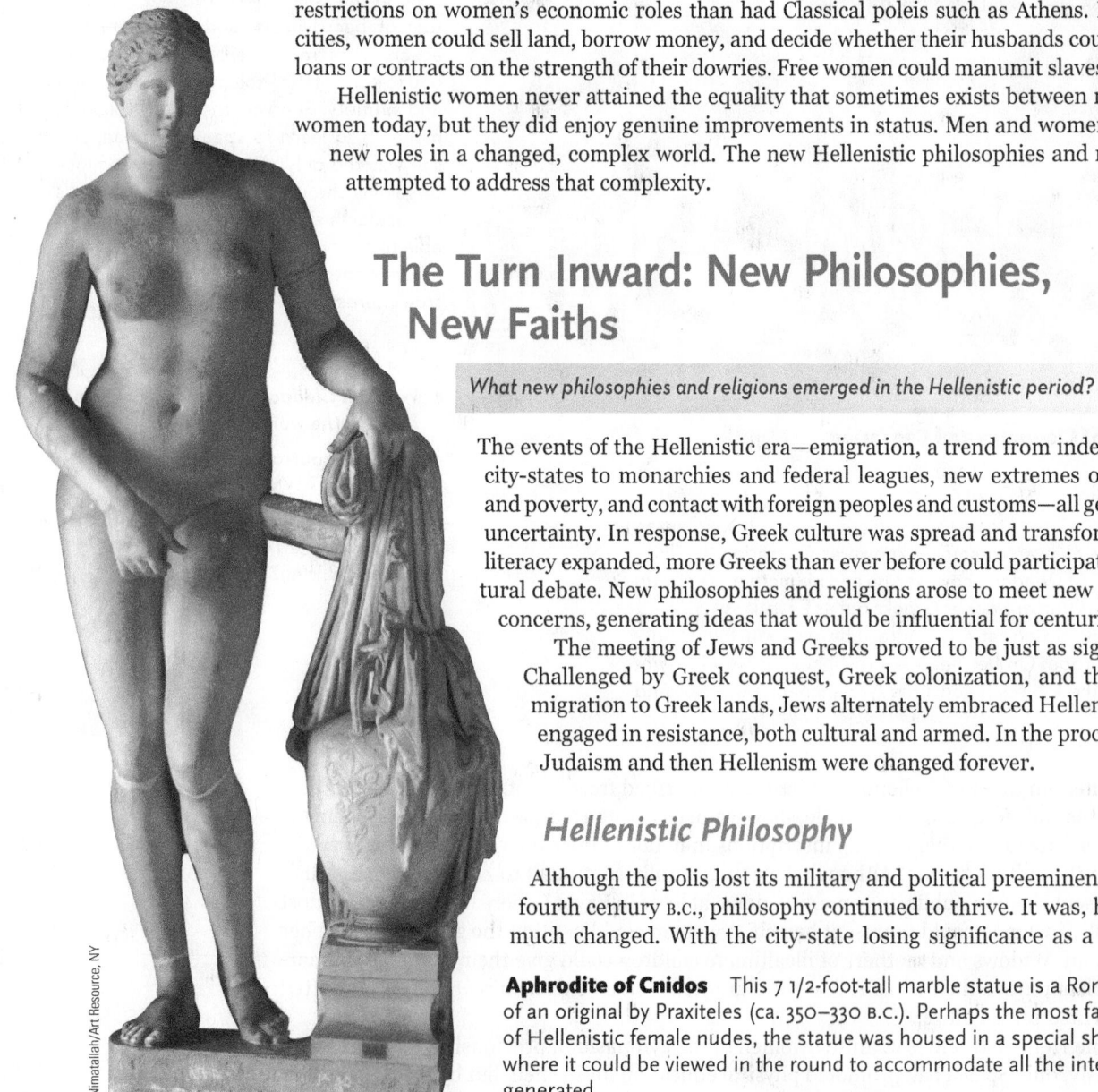

**Aphrodite of Cnidos** This 7 1/2-foot-tall marble statue is a Roman copy of an original by Praxiteles (ca. 350–330 B.C.). Perhaps the most famous of Hellenistic female nudes, the statue was housed in a special shrine where it could be viewed in the round to accommodate all the interest it generated.

Nimatallah/Art Resource, NY

loyalty, and with the Greek-reading public growing in size and geographic extent, Hellenistic philosophy paid less and less attention to politics. Since Hellenistic science tended to become a separate discipline from philosophy, philosophers focused on ethics, the discovery of the best way to live. The essence of the good life, most philosophers agreed, was peace of mind, or freedom from troubles. Hellenistic philosophy won a wide following; indeed, for many people, primarily in the elite, philosophy became a way of life, even a religion.

## Cynicism

Several competing philosophical schools emerged, beginning with Cynicism (SIN-uh-sizm). Never a widespread philosophy, Cynicism is nonetheless important as a precursor of the two most popular doctrines, Stoicism and Epicureanism. Skepticism rejected the main philosophies and proposed instead a commonsense attitude toward ethics.

The first Cynic was Diogenes (dye-AH-juh-neez) of Sinope (ca. 400–325 B.C.). An exile in Athens, Diogenes developed a philosophy that rejected all conventions. People find happiness, he decided, by satisfying their natural needs with simplicity. Accordingly, Diogenes chose a life of poverty. A beggar in rags, he delighted in shocking conventional morality. Famous for wit and shamelessness, he was nicknamed "Dog" (*kuon*) because the Greeks considered dogs to be shameless animals; his followers were called "Doglike" (*kunikoi*, whence the name *Cynic*).

## Stoicism

Although he founded no school, Diogenes cast a wide shadow. Among those whom he indirectly influenced was Zeno (ZEE-no) (335–263 B.C.), who began one of the most important philosophical systems of antiquity: Stoicism (STO-ih-sizm). Zeno came to Athens in 313 B.C. from Citium in Cyprus, a multiethnic city; he was possibly of Phoenician origin. Influenced by both Cynicism and Socratic philosophy, Zeno developed his own doctrines, which he taught in the *Stoa Poikile* ("Painted Porch," hence the name *Stoic*), a public building.

Like Plato and Aristotle, Zeno sought an absolute standard of good on which to base philosophical decisions. He found it in the divine reason (*logos*), which he considered the principle of the universe and the guide to human behavior. The best life was spent in pursuit of wisdom—that is, a life of philosophy. Only that rare and forbidding figure, the Sage, could truly attain wisdom; ordinary people could merely progress toward it through study and the attempt to be free from all passion.

Stoicism may seem harsh. It is not surprising that *stoical* has come to describe austere indifference to pain. In some ways, however, Stoicism was comforting. The **Stoics** were empiricists—that is, they trusted the evidence of the senses, an attitude that they thought would inspire confidence and security. They believed in human brotherhood—led, to be sure, by a Greek-speaking elite. Since brothers have a duty to one another, the Stoics argued that a good person should play an active role in public life.

The Stoics emphasized the inner life. They believed that intentions matter. This was an important departure from Greek tradition, which tended to emphasize the outcome of an action, not its motivation. Stoicism also departed from traditional Greek localism, embracing a more cosmopolitan outlook. "This world is a great city, [and] has one constitution and one law," wrote Philo of Alexandria (30 B.C.–A.D. 45), a Stoic and a Jew. Many Stoics believed in a natural law or law of nations—that is, that overarching and common principles governed international relations.

With its emphasis on duty and order, Stoicism became popular with Greek ruling elites, and eventually with the Romans, who used its concept of a universal state to justify their empire. Many Stoic principles were later embraced by early Christian writers.

**Stoics** Believers in a philosophical system begun in Athens by Zeno, which emphasized the pursuit of wisdom, the reliability of sensory experience, and freedom from all passion.

## Epicureanism

Epicurus (341–270 B.C.), an Athenian citizen, founded his philosophical school at around the same time as Zeno founded Stoicism. There were other similarities: Both schools were empiricist and materialist (that is, they tended to trust the evidence of the senses), both sought peace of mind, and both inspired widespread followings. Epicurus, however, taught not in a public place but in a private garden. Whereas the Stoics encouraged political participation, the **Epicureans** counseled withdrawal from the rough-and-tumble of public life. "Calm" and "Live in hiding" are famous Epicurean (eh-pi-kyuh-REE-un) maxims.

Epicurus's materialism is based on the atomic theory of Democritus (see pages 76–77). It envisions a thoroughly mechanistic universe in which the gods exist but play no active role in events. Individuals need fear neither fickle deities nor an unhappy afterlife because the soul is merely a combination of atoms that ceases to exist after death. The purpose of life was the avoidance of pain and the pursuit of pleasure. The latter was called hedonism (from *hedone*, Greek for "pleasure"), but not, as the word has come to mean today, indulgence in food, drink, or sex. Instead, Epicureans meant intellectual pleasure. Friendship and fraternity were Epicurean ideals—the private analogs, as it were, of Stoic brotherhood.

The Epicureans raised eyebrows and sometimes ire, occasionally suffering persecution by the state. They were accused of atheism and sensuality. Classical Greek philosophy defined virtue as the highest good. The Epicurean emphasis on pleasure, even spiritual pleasure, seemed perverse to some. Yet, Epicureanism was simple, sure of itself, and practical, and it offered both friendship and a sense of community. It became a popular philosophy, especially among the wealthy.

## Skepticism

Skepticism (SKEP-tih-sizm) was founded by Pyrrho of Elis (ca. 360–270 B.C.), a Greek who traveled with Alexander to India. Like Stoics and Epicureans, Skeptics sought peace of mind. They rejected those thinkers' conclusions, however, on the grounds that they were dogmatic—that is, based not on positive proof but merely on opinion (*doxa*). Considering the senses unreliable, Skeptics rejected the commonsense approach of Stoics and Epicureans. They preferred to suspend judgment on the great philosophical questions (hence, our term *skepticism* for a doubting state of mind). Whoever was able to do so could accept the customs of the community, avoid politics, and thereby obtain peace of mind.

## The Mystery Religions

The name "mystery religion" comes from the Greek word for "secret." A mystery religion initiated worshipers into secret teachings via secret ceremonies. Long a feature of Greek religion, the **mystery religions**—there were several—grew very popular in Hellenistic times. Like the philosophical schools, they offered hope and guidance but to a broader public. As the mystery religions rose, the traditional Greek religion of the Olympian gods declined.

The old Greek gods came under attack on every front in the Hellenistic era. Philosophers called them immoral and divine kings stole their spotlight. Around 300 B.C., one Euhemerus of Messene wrote that Zeus and others were not gods but merely great kings of the past who were deified.

Three new religious movements were prominent: the divinization of kings, the cult of Tyche (Fortune), and the mystery religions.

Under the Ptolemies and Seleucids, ruler-worship became standard procedure. For some it was just a patriotic formality, while others prayed sincerely to the god-king or god-queen. Meanwhile, the old Greek city-states, especially democracies, bristled. "To transfer to men the honor due to the gods," said one Athenian playwright, "is to dissolve the democracy."

He might have said as much about the Hellenistic cult of Tyche (TOO-kay) (Fortune or Luck), often worshiped as a goddess, sometimes as the protector of the city. The most famous example was the Tyche of Antioch, personified as a statue of a woman wearing the battlements of the city on her head like a crown—a very popular statue, to judge by the many copies found around the Hellenistic world.

Various mystery religions flourished. In the Athenian suburb of Eleusis, the long-standing cult of Demeter, goddess of fertility, grew in popularity. Participants received promises of life after death.

New mystery religions from Egypt grew even more popular, particularly the cults of Serapis and of Isis. Created under Ptolemy I, Serapis (SEH-ruh-pis) combined Osiris, the

Egyptian god of the afterlife, with Apis, the god of the Nile flood, with a hint of Pluto, the Greek god of the underworld. Hence, Serapis represents the common Hellenistic practice of religious syncretism, or fusion. Serapis became popular in the Greek world as the patron of healing and sailing.

An Egyptian deity, Osiris's wife, Isis (EYE-sis), also became a popular Greek and, later, Roman goddess. Called the Goddess of Ten Thousand Names, Isis was said to symbolize all female deities. As a suffering but tender and loving mother, Isis was popular among women.

Thus, under Ptolemaic sponsorship, ancient Egyptian cults were reworked and spread throughout the Greek-speaking world, circulating such notions as the suffering mother, the Last Judgment, and blessed eternal life after death. Early Christianity was much influenced by such Greco-Egyptian religious notions, but it was more directly the product of debate and ferment within Hellenistic Judaism.

## Hellenistic Judaism

Few consequences of Alexander's conquests had so lasting an impact as the mixing of Greeks and Jews. When Alexander conquered it in 332 B.C., Judea had been a Persian province for 200 years. Now, the fates of Greeks and Jews grew intertwined.

Jewish responses to Greek culture varied. At one extreme stood the Hellenizers, who admired Greek culture and wanted to assimilate to it. At the other extreme were traditionalists, who defended Jewish law as interpreted by scholars and rabbis. Their disagreement led to war, which broke out as follows.

After Alexander's death, Hellenistic Judea was governed first by the Ptolemies until 200 B.C., then by the Seleucids, until the establishment of an independent Jewish state in 142 B.C., which came in turn under Roman control in 63 B.C. The Greeks were not absentee rulers. Rather, they established a large number of Greek colonies in and around Judea, especially under the Seleucids. Many Jews, especially wealthy ones, adopted some degree of Greek culture. Some Hellenizers gave up Jewish customs altogether for the Greek gymnasium, theater, and political institutions. With the help of the Seleucid king Antiochus IV Epiphanes (r. 175–163 B.C.), Jewish Hellenizers in 175 B.C. had Jerusalem proclaimed a Greek polis; they built a gymnasium at the foot of the Temple Mount. They looted the Temple's treasury. In 167 B.C., they attacked the essence of Judaism by outlawing Sabbath observance, prohibiting circumcision, and rededicating the Temple to Olympian Zeus, to whom they sacrificed pigs.

The traditionalists, however, rallied the Jewish masses into opposition. Soon a guerrilla revolt began in the countryside, led by the Hasmonean family, also known as the **Maccabees**, whose successes are celebrated today by Jews during the holiday of Hanukkah. The guerrilla movement developed into a disciplined armed uprising, which restored all Jewish religious practices and rededicated the Temple. The revolt also forced the Seleucids to tolerate an independent state under the Hasmonean dynasty. Jewish independence lasted from 142 B.C., until the Roman conquest in 63 B.C.

During the struggle over Hellenism, new elements of lasting significance became part of Judaism. First, the Jews developed a literature of spiritual resistance to the foreigner. This literature was apocalyptic—that is, it claimed to reveal dramatic, heretofore secret truths. Drawing on both biblical and Mesopotamian traditions, Jewish apocalyptic writing predicted

Scala/Art Resource, NY

**Tyche of Antioch**    This Roman-era copy is based on a Greek original of around 300 B.C. It depicts the goddess Tyche (Fortune) of the city of Antioch, shown wearing the city's battlements as a crown.

**Maccabees** Traditionalist Jews led by the Hasmonean family, who, in 167 B.C., revolted against Hellenizing laws and influences.

**Bronze Coin with Menorah** This issue of Mattathias Antigone (r. 40–37 B.C.), the last Hasmonean king, is an early example of the use of the seven-branched candelabrum as the symbol of the Jewish people. A similar candelabrum was used in the Temple of Jerusalem. Erich Lessing/Art Resource, NY

a future cataclysm, when a royal redeemer would evict the foreigner and establish a new kingdom of Israel. The redeemer was often identified with another notion that first became popular in this era: the Messiah (literally, "anointed one"), someone anointed with oil signifying his election as king, a descendant of King David, who would save Israel. Another new aspect of Hellenistic Judaism was martyrdom, the notion of the holy sacrifice of one's life for a religious cause. There was also a growing belief in a final Judgment Day and resurrection, when God would raise the meritorious dead to live again on earth in their own bodies.

Hellenistic Judaism was diverse. Various sects each proposed its own version of Judaism. Among these sects were the Sadducees (SAJ-oo-seez) (the disciples of one Tzadok), a wealthy establishment group for whom the rituals of the Temple in Jerusalem were the heart of Judaism. Their opponents were the Pharisees (FAIR-ih-seez) (from the Hebrew *perushim*, "those who separate themselves," that is, in order to observe the laws of ritual purity). The Pharisees believed that the written law of the Hebrew Bible needed to be supplemented by an oral tradition that they traced back to Moses and Mt. Sinai. They saw themselves as the only true interpreters of that tradition. They proposed a kind of guided democratization of Judaism, emphasizing study and prayer in small groups under their leadership. Eventually, after several centuries, the Pharisees prevailed: they are the ancestors of modern Judaism. A third group was the Essenes (EH-seenz), generally identified with the Qumran (koom-RAHN) community in the Judean desert (see page 159).

Most Jews of the Hellenistic era lived outside Judea. Some had left voluntarily in search of wealth or adventure, while others had been taken captive in various wars. The Diaspora had spread into (among other places) Syria, Anatolia, the Greek mainland, Babylon, and Egypt, where a strong Jewish presence during the Persian period grew even stronger, particularly in Alexandria. Jews served the Ptolemies as soldiers, generals, bureaucrats, and tax collectors. They also prospered in private enterprise. Hostility to Jews by some Greeks and Egyptians spawned the first anti-Semitic literature. Sporadic violence at times broke into riots and persecution. Yet, there was also considerable admiration among Greek intellectuals for what they saw as Jewish virtue and antiquity.

Greek was the common tongue of Diaspora Jews. Between around 300 and 100 B.C. in Alexandria, the Hebrew Bible was translated into Greek. Known as the Septuagint, or Seventy, from the number of translators who, legend has it, labored on the project, this text made the Bible accessible to a Jewish community increasingly unable to understand Hebrew or Aramaic. In later centuries, the Septuagint became the Old Testament of Greek-speaking Christians.

Foreign conversions and immigration into the Diaspora began to change the meaning of the word *Jew*. The word came to mean less "inhabitant of Judea" than "practitioner of Judaism."

## SECTION SUMMARY

- Philosophy changed its emphasis from politics to ethics and won a wide following in the Greek-speaking elite.
- Stoicism, austere and public-spirited, and Epicureanism, which called for withdrawal into private life, were the most popular Hellenistic philosophies.
- The traditional Olympian religion of Greece declined, while so-called mystery religions, which offered secret teachings, grew popular.
- While some Jews adopted the Greek customs of their Seleucid rulers, traditionalists revolted and reestablished an independent Jewish state in Palestine.
- Most Jews in the Hellenistic era lived outside Palestine, in the Diaspora, where they had frequent contacts with other peoples.

# Chapter Summary

◆ *How did Macedon under Philip and Alexander conquer both the Greek city-states and the Persian empire?*

As king, Philip built a state and an army that allowed Macedon to conquer the Greek city-states and prepared to invade the Persian Empire. Upon Philip's assassination, his son Alexander replaced him and led an army of invasion. Although outnumbered and outspent by Persia, the Macedonians won because of their army. As Alexander's empire stretched into India, he became despotic and he planned a fusion of Greeks and Persians. His conquests laid the foundation of the Hellenistic age.

◆ *What new states emerged as a result of Alexander's conquests and how did they integrate Greek settlers with native peoples?*

After fifty years of war following Alexander's death, several new states emerged: The most important were Macedonia under the Antigonid dynasty, Egypt under the Ptolemies, and western Asia under the Seleucids. Hellenistic Greek kingdoms were founded in lands as far away as Afghanistan, Pakistan, and India, and they lasted for centuries. Greek and Macedonian colonists to the Ptolemaic and Seleucid kingdoms dominated the army and administration, but there was some room for natives. But few natives adopted Greek ways, and native culture thrived in these multiethnic empires. New cities, such as Alexandria, Antioch, and Pergamum, were flourishing centers of commerce and culture.

◆ *How did Greek civilization spread during the Hellenistic era, and what were the main trends in literature, science, and art?*

Under royal patronage, the Museum (a research institute) and Library were founded in Alexandria and became a focus of Hellenistic literature and science. Hellenistic writers turned away from civic life and heroic themes toward private life and ordinary events. Hellenistic science flourished and there were great achievements in mathematics, astronomy, and medicine. Hellenistic women made small gains in status and power, compared to earlier Greek women.

◆ *What new philosophies and religions emerged in the Hellenistic period?*

New beliefs emerged as faith in the Olympian gods declined. Ethics replaced politics as the focus of philosophy. The two most popular new philosophical schools were Stoicism and Epicureanism, the first austere and public-spirited, the second emphasizing withdrawal into private life. So-called mystery religions, which offered secret teachings, drew a wide public. Greeks and Jews came into increasing contact, both in the Diaspora and in Palestine, where Ptolemaic and Seleucid kings ruled in turn. Jews were divided into various schools of thought, with Hellenizers and traditionalists representing the two poles of opinion.

# Key Terms

**Macedon** (p. 86)

**Philip II** (p. 86)

**Alexander the Great** (p. 87)

**Hellenism** (p. 92)

**Ptolemies** (p. 92)

**Seleucids** (p. 92)

**Antigonids** (p. 94)

**Alexandria** (p. 95)

**Antioch** (p. 96)

**Bactria** (p. 96)

**Museum** (p. 98)

**Archimedes** (p. 99)

**Stoics** (p. 105)

**Epicureans** (p. 106)

**mystery religions** (p. 106)

**Maccabees** (p. 107)

Go to the CourseMate website at **www.cengagebrain.com** for additional study tools and review materials—including audio and video clips—for this chapter.

**The Forum, Rome** Alinari/Art Resource, NY

# Rome, From Republic to Empire

Here is the Roman Forum. We are standing in the heart of the ancient city, near the arch of the emperor Septimius Severus, looking south toward two columns that once held statues of great citizens. Beyond them are the Sacred Way, Rome's oldest street, and the three elegant columns of the Temple of Castor and Pollux. In the background, beyond a market and vaulted warehouse, is the Palatine Hill. The photograph takes us from an arch celebrating military triumph to ruins evoking citizenship and piety, to a reminder of the everyday needs of the masses of Rome, and finally, to a historic hill. On this hill, shepherds founded the city of Rome, and on this hill, centuries later, emperors lived. We see, in short, the civic center of the city destined to give the Western world many of its fundamental ideas about government and empire. It may well be the most important public space in the history of the world.

The ancient Romans were a practical people. Virgil (70-19 B.C.), for example, the greatest Roman poet (see page 146), celebrates not his countrymen's artistry or cultivation, but rather their pragmatic accomplishments:

> For other peoples will, I do not doubt,
> still cast their bronze to breathe with softer features,
> or draw out of the marble living lines,
> plead causes better, trace the ways of heaven
> with wands and tell the rising constellations;
> but yours will be the rulership of nations,
> remember, Romans, these will be your arts:
> to teach the ways of peace to those you conquer,
> to spare defeated peoples, tame the proud.*

The Romans turned an Italian city-state into one of the largest empires in history, including all the countries of the Mediterranean, as well as large parts of western Asia and of northern and central Europe. By holding this empire for centuries and

---

\* From *The Aeneid of Virgil*, trans. Allen Mandelbaum. Copyright © 1971 by Allen Mandelbaum. Reprinted by permission of Bantam Books, a division of Bantam Doubleday, Dell Publishing Group, Inc.

## Chapter Overview

**Before the Republic, 753–509 B.C.**

◆ *What was early Rome like and how was it shaped by relations with its neighbors?*

**The Early and Middle Republic at Home, ca. 509–133 B.C.**

◆ *How was the Roman Republic governed, and how did that government shape the Western political tradition?*

**The Early and Middle Republic Abroad, ca. 509–133 B.C.**

◆ *How did Rome conquer an empire?*

**The Late Republic and Its Collapse, 133–31 B.C.**

◆ *How did the unintended consequences of conquest on Rome lead to a revolution that destroyed the Republic?*

by promoting prosperity in every corner, Rome planted in what would become Britain, France, Germany, and Spain (among other places) the seeds of the advanced civilizations of the Mediterranean.

Rome is no less important for its influence on the Western civic tradition. Much of the modern vocabulary of politics, from *president* to *inauguration* to *forum*, can be traced back to Rome. After an early period of monarchy, Rome was for centuries a republic (Latin, *res publica*, literally "public thing") before becoming essentially a monarchy again under the Caesars. The Roman Republic mixed popular power with government controlled by wealthy landowners. The government was divided into three branches, which created a system of checks and balances that tended toward consensus. The result was efficiency and, for centuries, stability.

Roman politicians sought to control ordinary citizens but in some ways were more flexible than Greek democrats. Unlike Greece, Rome extended its citizenship to a large population, first throughout Italy and then across its entire empire. The modern nation-state with its mass citizenship owes much to Rome. Indeed, although Rome was not democratic, modern democracy—that is, popular government with a large population, whose officials are elected by the people—has roots in the Roman Republic as well as in the Greek city-state.

Fueled by fear, ambition, and greed, Roman expansion generated its own momentum. Rome's arrogance matched its success: In consolidating power over huge territories, the Romans committed atrocities, enslaved whole peoples, and destroyed cities with little provocation. Ironically, military success slowly undermined both Rome's political stability at home and the socioeconomic basis of its army. Meanwhile, the Romans showed great open-mindedness in borrowing from other societies, in particular, from the Greeks, to whom the Republic owed great cultural debts. Also fascinating is the shrewdness and generosity with which the Romans shared their citizenship with the elites whom they had conquered, thereby winning their loyalty and strengthening Rome's grip on their territories.

Historians conventionally divide the Republic into three periods: Early (509-287 B.C.), Middle (287-133 B.C.), and Late (133-31 B.C.). This chapter begins with the origins of the city of Rome in the early first millennium B.C. and then traces the Republic from its foundation to its imperial conquests to its collapse under their weight. Success spoiled Rome. The unintended consequences of conquest on Rome's society, politics, and culture led to a revolution that, in the century beginning in 133 B.C., saw the Republic's downfall.

## Before the Republic, 753–509 B.C.

*What was early Rome like and how was it shaped by relations with its neighbors?*

**Romulus** Legendary founder of Rome in 753 B.C., whose name supplies a convenient etymology for the city; he may have really existed, as archaeology suggests.

The ancient Romans believed that their city was founded on April 21, 753 B.C., by **Romulus**, a descendant of refugees from the Trojan War. Although the name "Romulus" supplies a convenient origin for "Rome," we cannot take the story at face value. Nevertheless, archaeology shows that by the eighth century B.C. Rome was already on its way to being a city and it had a king. Archaeologists have recently discovered a palace in the Forum from this era. They have also found traces of sanctuaries and a defensive wall. Nearby stands the Palatine Hill, one of the seven hills on which Rome would cluster and the place where tradition puts the settlement of 753 (see inset, **Map 5.2**, on page 123). Archaeologists have recently found fortification walls on the Palatine from around 750 B.C., which lends support to tradition. They have also found an underground chamber there that some would identify with the cave where, according to legend, Romulus was nursed by a she-wolf. In any case, the first settlers on the hills of Rome came even earlier, around 1000 B.C., as pottery and graves show.

Archaeological evidence raises some basic questions: What were Rome's origins, and how did it grow? Are seeds of Roman greatness visible in its early history? By examining the data of archaeology and of those elements in ancient historiography that seem to be based on accurate tradition, we can answer these questions, at least in outline.

## The First Romans and Their Neighbors

Italy is a long peninsula, shaped roughly like a boot, extending about 750 miles from the Alps into the Mediterranean (see **Map 5.1**). In the far north, the high Alps provide a barrier to the rest of Europe. To the east, the Adriatic Sea separates Italy from modern Slovenia and Croatia; to the west, the Tyrrhenian Sea faces the large islands of Sardinia and Corsica (and the smaller but iron-rich island of Elba) and, beyond, the coasts of France and Spain. Off the "toe" of the Italian boot and separated from the mainland by a narrow, 3-mile strait of water is the large island of Sicily, rich farm country in ancient times. Sicily is only 90 miles from North Africa. In short, Italy is centrally located in the Mediterranean. It was both a target for conquerors and a springboard for conquest.

Italy contained some of the ancient Mediterranean's most fertile and metal-rich land. From the watershed of the Po and Adige Rivers in the north, the agriculturally rich plains of Etruria (modern Tuscany), Latium (the region of Rome), and Campania (the region of Naples) unfold southward down Italy's west coast. Although the Apennine (AP-puh-nine) mountains run north-south along most of the Italian peninsula, they are low compared with the Alps and contain many passes, permitting the movement of armies.

In the first millennium B.C., Italy was a hodgepodge of peoples and languages. They included the Etruscans in the north, Greek colonists in southern Italy and in Sicily, and such mountain peoples as the Sabines and the Samnites. The Samnites spoke Oscan, an Indo-European language, as did the Campanians, who lived around Naples, and the Lucanians, who lived in south-central Italy. Both the Samnites and the Lucanians were warlike peoples who conquered their neighbors before finally being conquered by Rome.

Latium (LAY-shum) was home to a number of small Latin-speaking towns, one of them Rome. In the fifth century B.C., another important people arrived on the Italian scene: Celts (called Gauls by the Romans), large numbers of whom crossed the Alps and settled in northern Italy after roughly 500 B.C. Most of these various peoples spoke Indo-European languages, of which **Latin**, the language of the Romans (as well as other peoples of Latium), was one.

Rome's location in Italy was central and protected. Located 15 miles inland on the Tiber (TY-ber), the largest river on Italy's west coast, Rome had access to the sea. A midstream island makes Rome the first crossing place upstream from the Tiber's mouth, which offered the Romans freedom of movement north and south. Yet strategically, Rome was protected. It was far enough from the sea to be safe from raiders and pirates. And its seven hills offered a natural defense—from nature as well as humans—because the Tiber often flooded its banks.

In the eighth century B.C., Archaic Rome (as the pre-Republican period is called) began to change from a large village into a city. By the sixth century B.C., Rome had streets, walls,

## CHRONOLOGY

| | |
|---|---|
| 753–509 B.C. | Monarchy (traditional dates) |
| 509–287 B.C. | Early Republic |
| 449 B.C. | Law of the Twelve Tables |
| 338 B.C. | Latin League dissolved; Roman citizenship extended |
| 289 B.C. | First Roman coinage (traditional date) |
| 287–133 B.C. | Middle Republic |
| 264–146 B.C. | Punic Wars |
| 240 B.C. | First play produced at Rome |
| 197 B.C. | Rome defeats Macedonian phalanx |
| 146 B.C. | Rome destroys Carthage and Corinth |
| 133–31 B.C. | Late Republic |
| 133–121 B.C. | The Gracchi |
| 107–78 B.C. | Marius and Sulla |
| 73–71 B.C. | Spartacus's revolt |
| 66–62 B.C. | Pompey's eastern campaigns |
| 63 B.C. | Consulship of Cicero |
| 58–51 B.C. | Caesar conquers Gaul |
| 44 B.C. | Caesar assassinated |
| 31 B.C. | Antony defeated at Actium; Octavian in power |

**Latin** Indo-European language of ancient Rome and its empire, from which today's Romance languages developed.

🌐 **Map 5.1 Early Italy and Region of City of Rome** Early Italy comprised a variety of terrain and peoples. Rome is located in the central Italian region of Latium. The Alps separate Italy from northern Europe. The Apennine mountain range runs almost the entire length of the Italian peninsula. Much of the rest of Italy is fertile plain. © Cengage Learning 2014

drains, temples, and a racetrack. What caused the transformation? Perhaps the key factor was contact with Magna Graecia (MAG-nuh GREE-shuh), the Greek colonies to the south (see **Map 5.1**). Established in the eighth and seventh centuries B.C., the colonies transported westward the sophisticated urban civilization of the eastern Mediterranean (see pages 55–56).

Less well understood is the impact on early Rome of its neighbors to the north, the **Etruscans** (ee-TRUS-kunz). The twelve Etruscan city-states were organized in a loose confederation centered in Etruria (ee-TROO-ree-uh). They grew rich from the mining of iron, copper, and silver, from piracy, from trade, and from a network of influential Etruscan emigrants throughout central Italy, probably including Rome's last three kings (traditionally dated 616–509 B.C.).

The Etruscans were brilliant, wealthy, and warlike. We know less about them than we would like, from their language, which is only partly understood, to their origins, which

**Etruscans** Inhabitants of twelve loosely confederated city-states north of Rome; they were conquered by the Romans by the early third century B.C.

probably lay in Italy but possibly in Anatolia. Etruscan power extended to many places in central, northern, and even southern Italy. Many scholars argue that the Etruscans conquered pre-Republican Rome, but the evidence does not support that theory. Rather, an Etruscan nobleman, Lucius Tarquinius Priscus, migrated to Rome and was eventually elected king. Under him and his son (or perhaps grandson), Lucius Tarquinius Superbus, who was Rome's last king, Etruscan culture left an impact on Rome. For example, the Tarquins sponsored several building projects in Rome, including the great Temple of Jupiter on the Capitoline Hill in the center of Rome. But scholars disagree as to whether the Etruscan impact on Roman culture was superficial or deep.

At least we can be sure that the Etruscans were great artists and architects and very religious. They believed that it was possible to learn the will of the gods by interpreting the sight and sound of lightning and thunder and by carefully examining the internal organs, especially the liver, of sacrificial animals. Etruscan elite women had high status compared with their Greek or Roman counterparts. Etruscan women kept their own names, and Etruscan children bore the names of both parents. In addition, Etruscan elite women were permitted to attend athletic contests in spite of the presence of naked male athletes.

**Etruscan Tomb Painting**   This wall painting from Tarquinia shows a married aristocratic couple at a banquet. The style of the figures is derived from Greek art, but the depiction of husband and wife dining on the same couch is characteristically Etruscan. Scala/Art Resource, NY

## The Roman Monarchy

Tradition says that Rome was ruled by seven kings before the foundation of the Republic. Although the number of kings may be a later invention, their existence is undoubted. In addition to traces of the monarchy in Republican institutions, there is archaeological proof: A form of the Latin word *rex* ("king"), for example, has been found inscribed on a Roman monument from the early sixth century B.C. The king's power, called *imperium* (from *imperare*, "to command"), was very great, embracing religious, military, and judicial affairs.

The king was advised by a council of elders, called the "fathers" (*patres* in Latin) or the "senate" (*senatus*, from *senex*, "old man"). In theory, the senate was primarily an advisory body, but in practice, it was very powerful. Senators were the heads of the most important families in Rome, so the king rejected their advice at his peril. Romans spoke of the senate's *auctoritas* (from which our word *authority* comes), a quasi-religious prestige.

Most senators were patricians (puh-TRIH-shunz), as early Rome's hereditary aristocracy was known. The rest of the people, the bulk of Roman society, were called plebeians (pleh-BEE-unz). Plebeians were free; most were ordinary people, though some were wealthy. Patricians monopolized the senate and priesthoods, and they did not intermarry with plebeians. The Romans called these two social classes **orders**. Both in the monarchy and, later, in the Republic, most wealthy Romans were landowners.

**orders** An order is a social class whose members share a common rank.

The whole people, probably both patricians and plebeians, met in an assembly organized in thirty local units, or *curiae*, hence, the name *curiate assembly*. Although the assembly's numbers were large, its powers were limited. Before becoming law, resolutions of the assembly required approval by the senate.

## SECTION SUMMARY

- Rome was first settled as a village around 1000 B.C. and added a palace and sanctuaries in the 700s B.C.

- Rome borrowed much from the more advanced culture of the Greek colonies in southern Italy and Sicily.

- The twelve Etruscan city-states, north of Rome, were rich, powerful, and sophisticated. Rome's last three kings were probably Etruscan immigrants who added Etruscan elements to Roman culture.

- Early Rome was a class-based society with a monarchy and a sharp division between patricians (aristocrats) and plebeians (commoners).

Early Rome was a class-based society, but it was open to foreigners. Among others, Etruscans, Sabines, and Latins—as the inhabitants of other Latin-speaking towns are called—came to settle in Rome. Foreigners, at first, had low status, but they gained equality around 550 B.C., for pragmatic purposes. Rome needed soldiers to fight its wars; in order to expand the body of loyal infantrymen, the immigrants were granted citizenship—a reform traditionally associated with King Servius Tullius (578–535 B.C.).

Servius probably introduced to Rome the hoplite phalanx (see page 56), with immigrants included in its ranks. The changes in the army contributed to the process that, within several generations of Servius's reform, took Rome from monarchy to republic.

# The Early and Middle Republic at Home, ca. 509–133 B.C.

*How was the Roman Republic governed, and how did that government shape the Western political tradition?*

Tradition says that the Roman Republic was established in 509 B.C., when the kings were overthrown. Nowadays, scholars envision a long process rather than a single, dramatic upheaval. In either case, the Republic differed from the monarchy in two basic ways. First, the Republic stood for liberty, which for the Romans meant both freedom from the arbitrary power of a king and freedom to participate in public affairs. Second, the Republic was a commonwealth, in Latin, *res publica* (rays POO-blee-kuh), literally "public thing," as opposed to *res privata*, "private thing," as the Romans characterized monarchy. As a kingdom, Rome belonged to the royal family, but as a republic, it belonged to the Roman people. In theory, the Roman people were sovereign—that is, the people ruled the state.

*res publica* Latin for "public thing," it was the Romans' concept of their republic, which uniquely influenced Western political institutions.

But which people? This is a key question because the Romans did *not* embrace another principle that might seem to follow from liberty: equality. Rather, they believed in order, balance, and competition, all of which are central themes of Roman Republican history. Roman society and culture, moreover, were conservative. Once the young Republic had its new values in place, it tried to maintain those values over the centuries, with little change.

We know relatively little about the Early Republic (509–287 B.C.) but enough to know that it witnessed centuries of social and political conflict. The Middle Republic (287–133 B.C.) was a shorter and better documented period of relative consensus at home and massive expansion abroad. Social and political conflict broke out again with a vengeance in the Late Republic (133–31 B.C.), ultimately rendering the Republic a deathblow.

## Political Institutions

The best and most even-handed ancient analyst of Roman politics is the historian Polybius (po-LIH-bee-us) (ca. 200–118 B.C.). A Greek and former hostage who lived in Rome, Polybius observed his adopted city with an outsider's careful eye. Polybius argued that in the Middle Republic of his day, Rome was a "mixed constitution," balancing the power of the masses with the authority of the elite. The result was a strong and stable state.

Polybius divides Roman political institutions into three branches: executive, deliberative, and legislative. The American founders adopted a similar division, but they combined the legislative and deliberative functions and added a judicial branch. In Rome the executive branch also administered justice. Rome's executive branch was made up of magistrates—that is, public officials; the deliberative branch consisted of the Roman senate; and the legislative branch was composed of four different assemblies of the people.

Executive power lay in the hands of Rome's powerful magistrates. They were elected and not chosen by lottery, as in Greek democracy. Election required campaigning, which in turn took money and connections. Magistracies were time-consuming jobs but offered no salary, unlike in Greek democracy. Thus, only a wealthy few could afford to hold public office in Rome.

Eager for strong magistrates but afraid that power corrupts, Romans imposed the principles of *collegiality* and *annuality* on their officials. Every magistrate had one or more colleagues and held office for only one year. The chief magistrates were eventually called consuls, of which there were two. Each consul had the power to veto the other's actions. Like the former king, each consul had *imperium*, the power to issue commands and order punishments, including execution.

From about 500 B.C. to about 300 B.C., other public offices were created to help the consuls as administration grew more complex. In addition, the Romans elected two censors, older men chosen once every few years for eighteen-month terms. At first, their job was to supervise the census, the military register of citizens that recorded each man's property class. Later, the censors became, as it were, supervisors of public morals, since they could punish "bad" citizens.

The Republic's government adapted flexibly to trying circumstances. In times of emergency, for example, the Republic turned power over to a single magistrate. The dictator, as he was called, made binding decisions, but he held office for only six months.

The Roman senate guided and advised the magistrates. During most of the Republic, the senate consisted of three hundred men, all former magistrates and each of whom served for life. Senators possessed great authority. They supervised public expenditures and were, for all practical purposes, in charge of foreign policy.

Only the assemblies of the people could make laws. There were four assemblies: the curiate assembly, the centuriate assembly, the council of the plebs, and the tribal assembly. Roman assemblies combined democratic and nondemocratic features. On the one hand, all decisions were made by majority vote, and only after speeches or campaigning. Assembly meetings were often preceded by public meetings, typically in the Forum, which featured lively debate. Women, free noncitizens, and even slaves could attend. On the other hand, voting took place by groups, and those groups were unrepresentative. Furthermore, in contrast to Greece, assembly participants stood rather than sat down and received no salary for attendance.

Although the curiate assembly of the monarchy survived in the Republic, it had a largely ceremonial role. The centuriate assembly held real power: It elected magistrates, voted on laws and treaties, accepted declarations of war and peace, and acted as a court in cases of treason, homicide, and appeals of the magistrates' decisions. But this assembly was dominated by wealthy men, especially the equestrians, or cavalrymen. The poorest men, known as *proletarii* ("breeders"), often did not have even the chance to vote.

The two other assemblies were the council of the plebs and the tribal assembly. The tribal assembly eventually replaced the plebs and, in fact, became Rome's main legislative body in the third century B.C., outstripping the centuriate assembly in making laws. To understand the evolution and workings of the tribal assembly, we turn now to the class conflicts in Rome during the fifth through third centuries B.C.

**senate** In the ancient Roman Republic and Empire, the influential and powerful council of elders.

## Struggle of the Orders, 494–287 B.C.

Social and political conflict between the patricians and plebeians severely tested the Roman state in the fifth century. There were only 136 patrician families in 509 B.C., but they dominated the Early Republic. The plebs, in contrast, comprised masses of peasants and a tiny number of artisans, traders, and shopkeepers. For a century and a half, the various groups of plebeians worked together against patrician power, writing an important chapter in the history of political resistance.

Wealthy plebeians wanted access to high office, from which they had been largely excluded. Debt and hunger loomed large as concerns of ordinary plebeians. If a free man could not repay a loan, he had to work off what he owed, often for the rest of his life.

Plebeians wanted this harsh system abolished. The average plebeian-owned farm was too small to feed a family, so most peasants depended on public land for farming and grazing. Time and again throughout Republican history, however, public land was taken by the wealthy, who denied access to the poor. The only plebeian hope was to change the system.

The plebeians organized themselves as a kind of state within the state, complete with their own assembly (the council of the plebs) and officials (the tribunes of the plebs). The decisions of the council of the plebs, called *plebiscita* (from which *plebiscite* comes), were binding only on the plebs; they did not receive the full force of law for over two hundred years. Yet, the plebs did not retreat. On several occasions during the Early Republic, they resorted to secession: The plebs, as a whole, left the city, often for the Aventine Hill, where they stayed until their grievances were addressed (see inset, **Map 5.2**).

The ten tribunes (TRIB-yoonz), elected annually by the plebs, were the people's champions. Inside the city of Rome, a tribune had the right to veto any act of the magistrates, assembly, or senate that harmed plebeians. In return, the plebs swore to treat the tribunes as sacrosanct and to lynch anyone who harmed them.

But the patricians struck back. They controlled important priesthoods and had many supporters in the military. Furthermore, patricians dominated the new tribal assembly, created around the same time as the council of the plebs. The tribal assembly elected lower magistrates and, like the centuriate assembly, voted on laws and acted as a court of appeals.

Still, the plebeians forced concessions from the patricians. A key moment came in 449 B.C., with publication of the law code known as the "Twelve Tables," eventually, if not at first, on twelve bronze tablets in the Forum. By modern standards, the code was tough and primitive. For example, one law states, "A person who had been found guilty of giving false witness shall be hurled down from the Tarpeian Rock [cliff and execution site overlooking the Roman Forum]."* Yet, the code's very existence was a plebeian victory because published law was accessible and dependable. Unfortunately, the complex legal procedure remained a secret of the priests for another 150 years, which meant that no poor man could go to court without the help of a rich patron.

Continued plebeian pressure slowly yielded other gains through the fourth century B.C. Around 445 B.C., the patricians accepted patrician-plebeian intermarriage, but it took nearly another eighty years, until 367 B.C., when they agreed to plebeian consuls. That same year saw a debt-relief law, and further debt relief came in 326 B.C.

Finally, in 287 B.C., the patrician and plebeian orders were formally merged, and a law called the "lex Hortensia" made decisions of the council of the plebs and the tribal assembly binding on the whole community, including patricians. Rome's new, combined patrician-plebeian elite was based on wealth, not heredity. Most Romans were non-elite, but at least they had won something: debt relief, access to the published laws, increased power for their assembly, and, most important, protection from arbitrary power.

Courtesy of the Trustees of the British Museum

**A Clear Sign of Power**   The lictor, or official, depicted in this bronze statuette (ca. first century A.D.) accompanied Roman magistrates, who had *imperium*, the power to issue punishments resulting in execution. That power is visible in the fasces—an ax in a bundle of wooden rods bound with straps—that he holds.

## Families and Patronage

The family was the basic unit of Roman society and a model of political authority, both foreign and domestic. Elite Roman families stuck together and wielded great power.

---

*Oliver J. Thatcher, ed., *The Library of Original Sources* (Milwaukee: University Research Extension Co., 1901), Vol. III: *The Roman World*, pp. 9-11, as cited at The Internet Ancient History Sourcebook, http://www.fordham.edu/halsall/ancient/12tables.asp.

The Latin word *familia* is broader in meaning than the English word *family*. Better translated as "household," it connotes slaves, animals, and property, as well as the members of a nuclear family and their ancestors or descendants. In theory, though not always in practice, the Roman household was an authoritarian institution governed by a male; thus, the familia is an example of patriarchy.

The legal head of the familia was the *paterfamilias* (PAH-ter-fah-MIL-ee-us)—the oldest living male, usually the father. Roman respect for the paterfamilias stemmed from Roman esteem for ancestors, who were more important than in Greek culture. All patricians and some plebeians belonged to a *gens* (plural, *gentes*), a kinship group that traced its ancestry back to a purported common ancestor. All Roman males had a personal and a family name, and patricians and elite plebeians also had a third (middle) name, indicating their gens—for example, Gaius Julius Caesar, whose personal name "Gaius" was followed by the gens name "Julius" and the familia name "Caesar."

According to Roman law, the paterfamilias had supreme power within the household. He had the right to sell family members into slavery. A son, no matter how old, was always legally subject to the authority of a living paterfamilias. However, practice was more complex than theory. Roman fathers rarely used their power to kill an errant wife or child. The sources are full of fathers who showed affection, love, and even indulgence toward their children. Moreover, Roman women usually married in their late teens and men in their late twenties. Given the low life expectancies, it was common for a man of 25 to have already buried his father. Many, perhaps even most, adult males were independent of a paterfamilias.

Unlike men, Roman women never became legally independent, even on the death of a paterfamilias. Instead of receiving a personal name, a daughter was called by the name of her father's gens. For example, Gaius Julius Caesar's daughter was called Julia; if Caesar had had a second daughter, she would have been Julia Secunda ("Julia the Second"). Although fathers were expected to support all male children, they had to support only the first of their daughters. In other words, they were free to "expose" additional daughters—that is, leave them in the open to die or, as was perhaps more likely, to be adopted or raised as a slave. A father also arranged a daughter's marriage and provided her with a dowry. In theory, again, the customs suggest a most severe relationship, but the evidence shows considerable father-daughter affection, including married daughters who sought advice or aid from their fathers.

Most women in early Rome married *cum manu* (kum MAN-oo) (literally, "with hand"); that is, they were "handed over" to their husbands, who became their new paterfamilias. Even so, Roman wives and mothers had more prestige and freedom than their counterparts in Classical Greece. Legends of early Rome mention some elite women of influence who were peacemakers, negotiators, and catalysts of quarrels among men. Roman women regularly shared meals and social activities with their parents and were expected to take an interest in their husbands' political lives.

Roman society was modeled on the hierarchy of the Roman family. At the center of things stood patrons and clients. *Patron* (derived from *pater*, "father") means "defender" or "protector." *Client* means "dependent." Roman society consisted of pyramidal and hereditary patron-client networks. Most patrons were in turn clients of someone more powerful; only a few men stood at the top of the pyramid. Various paths led to the status of client. A peasant in need of help on his farm might ask a wealthy neighbor to become his patron. A freed slave became the client of his former owner. A conquered foe became the client of the victorious general.

Patron and client helped each other in various ways. A patron might provide a client with food, with property for a dowry, or with legal assistance. In return, a client owed his patron his vote and his presence in public on important occasions—possession of a large clientele signified prestige and power.

Cloaked in an elaborate language of goodwill, the patron-client relationship was considered a matter of *fides* (FEE-days) ("good faith" or "trustworthiness"). Romans spoke not of a client submitting to a patron's power, but rather of a client "commending himself" to the patron's fides. A patron spoke not of his clients, but of his "friends," especially if they were men of standing or substance.

*paterfamilias* Oldest living male in an ancient Roman family, who had supreme legal power within the household.

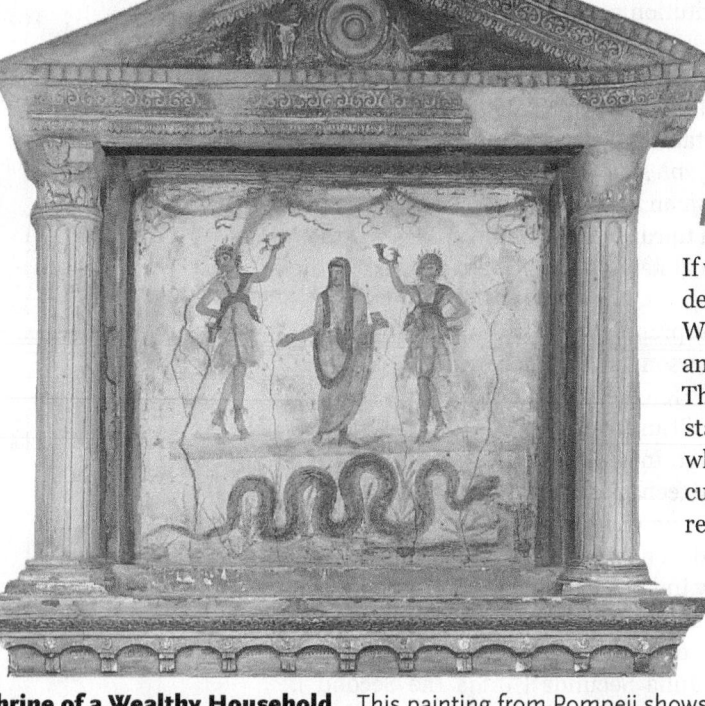

**Shrine of a Wealthy Household**   This painting from Pompeii shows the spirit of the paterfamilias in a toga, which is wrapped around his head in keeping with the Roman procedures of sacrifice. He is flanked by the spirits of departed ancestors. A snake symbolizes fertility.
Alinari/Art Resource, NY

Patronage played an important role in domestic politics and in foreign affairs. Experience as patrons schooled Roman leaders in treating the peoples they conquered as clients, often as personal clients. Moreover, the Roman state sometimes took foreign countries into its collective "fides"—much as a patron did a client—thus, allowing Rome to extend its influence without the constraints of a formal alliance.

## Religion and Worldview

If we knew nothing about early Roman religion, we could deduce much about it from the familia and patronage. We could expect to find an emphasis on powerful fathers and binding agreements, and both are indeed present. The task of a Roman priest, whether an official of the state or an individual paterfamilias, was to establish what the Romans called the "peace of the gods." Roman cults aimed at obtaining the gods' agreement to human requests, at "binding" the gods—the Latin term for which is *religio*.

The earliest Roman religion was animistic—that is, it centered on the spirits that, the Romans believed, haunted the household and the fields and forests and determined the weather. The spirit of the hearth was Vesta; of the door, Janus; of the rain and sun, Jupiter (later identified with the Greek sky-god and the father-god Zeus), and of the crops and vegetation Mars (later identified with the Greek war-god Ares). The Romans believed that these spirits needed to be appeased—hence, the contractual nature of their prayers and offerings. Over the years, as a result of Greek influence, anthropomorphism (that is, the worship of humanlike gods and goddesses) replaced Roman animism.

Roman state religion grew out of house religion. Vesta, the hearth-goddess, became goddess of the civic hearth; Janus, the door-god, became god of the city's gates; Jupiter became the general overseer of the gods; and Mars became the god of war. When trade and conquest brought the Romans into contact with foreign religions, the Romans tended to absorb them. The senate screened and sometimes rejected new gods, but by and large, Roman religion was tolerant and inclusive.

The Republic sponsored numerous priestly committees, or colleges, to secure the peace of the gods. Originally restricted to patricians, most of the highest priesthoods were opened to plebeians by law in 300 B.C. Although some priesthoods were full-time jobs, most left the officeholder free to pursue a parallel career as a magistrate or a senator. The two most important priestly colleges were the augurs (AW-gers), who were in charge of foretelling the future from omens and other signs, and the pontiffs, who exercised a general supervision of Roman religion. The chief pontiff, the *pontifex maximus* (PON-tih-fex MAX-ih-mus), was the head of the state clergy. He was chosen by election. The pontiffs alone controlled the interpretation of the law until the fourth century B.C. The Romans allowed priests to interpret the law on the theory that an offense against humans was also an offense against the gods.

There were also two colleges of priestesses: those of Ceres, goddess of fertility and death, and those of the Vestal Virgins. The six Vestals tended the civic hearth and made sure that its fire never went out. They served, as it were, as wives of the whole community, as guardians of the civil household. The Vestals were the only Roman women not under the authority of a paterfamilias. Chosen between the ages of 6 and 10 by the pontifex maximus, they had to remain virgins while they served or face death, but enjoyed honorable retirement after thirty years.

Roman ideology promoted simple and austere farmers' virtues—discipline, hard work, frugality, temperance, and the avoidance of public displays of affection, even between spouses. Such virtues underlined the difference between the Republic and the kings, with their luxury and sophistication. At the same time, these virtues papered over class distinctions between rich and poor and so promoted stability.

Other Roman ideals included the supreme virtue of the household, *pietas*—devotion and loyalty to the familia, the gods, and the state. Household duties and gender obligations were defined clearly. Women were to be modest, upright, and practical. Men were to project *gravitas* ("weight" or "seriousness"), never lightness or levity. A serious man would display self-control and constancy, the ability to persevere against difficult odds. The masculine ideal was *virtus* (literally, "manliness"), which indicated excellence in war and government.

Roman men who attained virtus considered themselves entitled to the reward of *dignitas*, meaning not only public esteem but also the tangible possession of a dignified position and official rank—in short, public office. The ultimate test of virtus, however, was in battle. Rome's wars supplied ample occasion to display it.

## SECTION SUMMARY

- Republican government consisted of three branches: executive, deliberative, and legislative.
- The magistrates, the senate, and the assemblies were Rome's three main political institutions.
- The Struggle of the Orders led to debt relief for the poor and a combined patrician-plebeian nobility for the rich.
- The Roman household, headed by the *paterfamilias*, was a model of political authority.
- Roman society was made up of networks of patrons and clients.
- Romans idealized *pietas*, that is, loyalty to household, the gods, and the Republic.

# The Early and Middle Republic Abroad, ca. 509–133 B.C.

*How did Rome conquer an empire?*

At the beginning of the Republic (ca. 509 B.C.), Roman territory comprised about 500 square miles. By 338 B.C., Rome controlled the 2,000 square miles of Latium and was moving north into Etruria and south into Samnite country. Three-quarters of a century later, in 265 B.C., Rome controlled all of the Italian peninsula south of an imaginary line from Pisae (modern Pisa) to Ariminum (modern Rimini), an area of about 50,000 square miles (see **Map 5.2**). By 146 B.C., Roman provinces included Sicily, Cisalpine Gaul (northernmost Italy), Sardinia, Corsica, and Spain (divided into two provinces). Once-great Carthage was the Roman province of Africa (roughly, modern Tunisia), and once-mighty Macedon was the province of Macedonia, whose governor was also effectively in charge of Greece. The Seleucid kingdom was free but fatally weakened. Rome was the supreme power between Gibraltar and the Levant. It was the greatest empire of the ancient West. How and why had Rome, from its humble beginnings as a local power, reached this breathtaking height?

## Republican Expansion: The Conquest of Italy, ca. 509–265 B.C.

Romans maintain that they conquered an empire without ever committing an act of aggression. When war was declared, a special college of priests informed the gods that Rome was merely retaliating for foreign injury. True, the Romans were frequently attacked by others but often only after provocative behavior by Rome had left its rivals little choice.

### Why Rome Fought

Rome's early conquests reveal many of its lasting motives for expansion. Greed, particularly land-hunger, was a perennial theme. Sometimes a domestic political motive was at work, for foreign adventure was a convenient way of deflecting plebeian energies. Perhaps the most significant factors, however, were the personal ambitions of a warrior elite and the presence of conflict in early Italy.

**Greek Tomb Painting**
This wall painting from the Tomb of the Diver in Paestum, dated 480/70 B.C., shows a man of leisure reclining at a drinking party. It demonstrates the values of the upper classes of the Greek colonies of southern Italy.

Scala/Art Resource, NY

Victory in battle promised both prestige and booty and the political success that might follow. Military achievement brought unique acclaim. For example, certain victorious generals were allowed to celebrate a **triumph**; no such ceremony rewarded the feats of peacemakers or distinguished judges or other public benefactors. The triumphant general rode a chariot through the city to the Temple of Jupiter on the Capitoline Hill. He was accompanied by his troops, by the spoils of victory, including famous captives, and by the magistrates and senators. One feature served to keep the general from getting a swollen head, as the sources report: "A public slave . . . rode with the victor in the chariot itself, holding over him the crown of precious stones set in gold, and kept saying to him, 'Look behind!'"*

**triumph** Elaborate procession through the streets of ancient Rome to salute a general's victory over a foreign army.

In the harsh environment of Italian states, Rome could not have survived without the willingness to fight. Yet, what began as a pragmatic response to present dangers hardened into a habit of meeting even remote threats with force.

## How Rome Fought

Rome organized its military resources well. The Roman military camp was a more regular and systematic place than anything seen since Assyrian days. Beginning in the fourth century B.C., Rome began to give its soldiers regular pay; this and the distribution of conquered land improved morale. Even more significant for Rome's military success was the willingness to utilize foreign military technology.

Borrowed from the Greeks in the sixth century B.C., the hoplite phalanx suited Rome on the relatively level ground of Latium but fared poorly in the rugged Apennines against the Samnites. Following a major defeat in 321 B.C., the Romans adopted with great success the Samnites' equipment and tactics.

**legion** Ancient Roman battle formation in which many semi-independent groups broke their enemies' order with javelins at long range, then charged with sword and shield.

Unlike the phalanx, which overpowered the enemy by fighting as one thickly massed unit, a Roman **legion** was flexible and adaptable. Legions were divided into units of thirty maniples ("handfuls"), which were subdivided into sixty centuries (literally, "hundreds," although the number of men per century varied); each century was commanded by a centurion. The semi-independence of the maniples, each with its own commander and banner, created a more maneuverable army than that of the phalanx and one better suited for mountain fighting. When it went into battle, it drew up into three lines. If one line failed,

*Naphtali Lewis and Meyer Reinhold, eds., *Roman Civilization: Selected Readings, vol. 1: The Republic and the Augustan Age*, 3d ed. (New York: Columbia University Press, 1990), p. 231.

🌐 **Map 5.2　Roman Italy, ca. 265 B.C.**　Rome controlled a patchwork of conquered territory, colonies, and allied states in Italy, held together by a network of treaties and of roads. The city of Rome (*inset*) was built on seven hills beside the Tiber River. © Cengage Learning 2014

there were two more lines to turn to. Unlike hoplites, who engaged the enemy at short range, legionnaires first threw their javelins at long range. Then, having broken the enemy's order, they charged and fought with sword and shield.

## Keeping the Peace

Rome used victory wisely. It treated its allies with a combination of generosity and firmness, beginning with its fellow Latin states. Rome was the leading power in Latium, where it led in an alliance known as the Latin League. Under Roman leadership, the Latin League successfully defended Latium's borders against a series of enemies during the fourth and fifth centuries B.C. But eventually, Rome had to confront a bitter two-year-long Latin revolt (340–338 B.C.).

The year 338 B.C. marked a turning point. Defeated peoples in the ancient world were often executed or enslaved, but not now. The Latin League was dissolved. Some of its member

**The Appian Way**
Named for the censor Appius Claudius Caecus, who proposed its construction, Rome's first great road was built in 312 B.C. during the Samnite Wars. It originally ran 132 miles from Rome to Capua and was extended an additional 234 miles, probably by 244 B.C., to Brundisium, on Italy's southern Adriatic coast.

F. H. C. Birch/Sonia Halliday Photographs

states were annexed, but their inhabitants became Roman citizens, not slaves; others retained independence and alliance with Rome though no longer with one another. The non-Latin allies of the former rebels were also annexed, but they received the unique halfway status of "citizenship without suffrage." They had all the rights of Roman citizenship except the vote; they also maintained local self-government. The settlement of 338 B.C. broke new ground by making it possible for Rome and its former enemies to live together on the basis of relative equality.

The settlement also set a precedent. As Rome conquered Italy, some privileged cities (called *municipia*) received the status of citizenship without suffrage. Others remained independent but were tied to Rome by alliance. Romans often annexed a portion of the land of these states.

If municipia were the carrots of Roman imperialism, the stick was a network of military roads and colonies in Italy, which kept Rome's eye on potential rebels. Roman roads allowed the swift movement of troops and linked a network of colonies in strategic areas. The inhabitants, Roman and Latin, owed military service to Rome.

In later years, Italians would complain about treatment by Rome, but compared with Roman provinces outside Italy, they had a privileged status. Romans too would complain about allied demands for equality, but Rome received, from its allies, a huge pool of military manpower. They staffed the armies that conquered the Samnites, Etruscans, and Gauls, all of whom came into Rome's orbit by the early third century B.C. Manpower abundance won Rome's war (280–276 B.C.) against the Greek general Pyrrhus (PIR-us) of Epirus (319–272 B.C.), who invaded southern Italy. Although Pyrrhus won battle after battle, he was unable to match Roman willingness to sustain casualties. Pyrrhus's seeming victories, therefore, turned out to be defeats, which sent him home to Greece disappointed and left us with the expression "Pyrrhic victory."

As for Rome, by 265 B.C., it emerged as the ruler of all of Italy south of the Pisae-Ariminum line (see **Map 5.2**). One might say that Rome unified Italy, although Italy was less a unity than a patchwork of Roman territory and colonies and of diverse cities, states, and peoples each allied to Rome by a separate treaty.

## Punic Wars and Conquest of the Greek East

The conquest of Italy made Rome one of two great powers in the central Mediterranean. The other was Carthage (CAR-thidge). Founded around 750 B.C. by Phoenicians from Tyre, Carthage controlled an empire in North Africa, Sicily, Corsica, Sardinia, Malta, the Balearic

Islands, and southern Spain. (The adjective *Phoenician* is *Punicus* in Latin, hence, the term *Punic* [PYOO-nik] for *Carthaginian*.) Like Rome, Carthage was guided by a wealthy elite, but it was mercantile in character rather than agrarian. Rome was a land power, Carthage a sea power. Rome had virtually no navy. Carthage commanded a great war fleet, and its merchant ships dominated the western Mediterranean and played a major role in the east.

Carthage had many strengths. It was an economic powerhouse. The Carthaginians exploited the mineral-rich mines of Spain. They were the first Mediterranean people to organize large-scale plantations of slaves for the production of single crops. Carthage also boasted brilliant generals, especially in the Barca family, whose most famous member was Hannibal (HAN-uh-bull) (247–183 B.C.). Carthage might have seemed the favorite at the outbreak of its long wars with Rome in 264 B.C., yet Carthage was weaker and Rome was stronger than it seemed.

Unlike Rome, Carthage did not have a citizen army. The commanders were Carthaginian, but most of the soldiers were mercenaries and of questionable loyalty. Unlike Rome, which treated its Italian allies well, Carthage showed contempt for its troops, who repaid the favor by revolting often. Carthage fielded large armies, but not as large as Rome's.

At the start of the **Punic Wars**, Rome had no navy or commanders to match the Barca family, but it proved adaptable, tenacious, and ruthless. To win the First Punic War (264–241 B.C.), for example, Rome not only built a navy but also outlasted the enemy in a long and bloody conflict. After initially granting a mild peace treaty, Rome took advantage of later Carthaginian weakness to seize Sardinia and Corsica and to demand an additional indemnity.

Forced to give in to Rome's demands, Carthage decided to build a new and bigger empire in Spain, beginning in 237 B.C., under Barca family leadership. With Spain's rich silver and copper mines in its hands, Carthage once again posed a threat so, in the mid-220s B.C., Rome challenged Carthaginian power in Spain. The new Carthaginian commander, 27-year-old Hannibal, was not to be cowed, however, and the Second Punic War broke out (218–201 B.C.).

Carthage was willing to fight because Hannibal promised a quick and decisive victory. Because Carthage no longer had a fleet, the Romans felt secure in Italy; Hannibal surprised them by marching overland to Italy, making a dangerous passage across the Alps. He even took war elephants with him, although most of them died along the way. A tactical genius, Hannibal reckoned that with his superior generalship, he could defeat the Romans in battle and cause them enormous casualties, and he was right. Hannibal's forces dominated the battlefield. Among his victories was the Battle of Cannae in Apulia (southeastern Italy), where, in 216 B.C., Carthage gave Rome the bloodiest defeat in its history, killing perhaps fifty thousand Romans.

But huge casualties alone could not bring Rome to its knees. Nor did many of Rome's allies revolt, as Hannibal had hoped. Most stood by Rome, which had treated them relatively well in the past. After Cannae, Rome's leadership followed a cautious strategy of harassment, delay, refusal to fight, and attrition. Hannibal was stymied by an enemy who lost battles but refused to surrender. In addition, Hannibal did not have the power to take the city of Rome.

A new Roman military star now emerged: Publius Cornelius Scipio (SIP-ee-o) (236–183 B.C.), a Roman who finally understood Hannibal's tactics and matched them. First, Scipio conquered Carthage's Spanish dominions, and then he forced Hannibal back to North Africa for a final battle in 202 B.C. near Zama (in modern Tunisia). Scipio won the battle and gained the surname Africanus ("the African"). Hannibal ended his days in exile from Carthage, fighting for the Seleucids in their unsuccessful war against Rome.

The peace settlement of 201 B.C. stripped Carthage of its empire. Yet, soon its economy rebounded, reviving old Roman fears of Carthage's political ambitions. In the Third Punic War (149–146 B.C.), Rome mounted a three-year siege under the leadership of Scipio Aemilianus (185–129 B.C.) and destroyed the city of Carthage in 146 B.C. Approximately a century later, Carthage was resurrected as a Roman colony and became one of the empire's greatest cities. In the meantime, it was left desolate, its people killed or enslaved.

Rome emerged from the Punic Wars as the greatest power in the Mediterranean. It had acquired new provinces in Sicily, Sardinia, Corsica, Spain, and North Africa (where Carthage's former territory was annexed as the province of Africa). Exhausted as it was,

**Punic Wars** Three wars during which the Roman Empire eventually destroyed Carthage.

**Carthaginian Craftsmanship** These pendants of male heads are made of colored glass and come from Carthage. The Phoenicians and their colonists excelled in glasswork as a medium for the production of luxury goods.

Erich Lessing/Art Resource, NY

Rome immediately leaped into a long conflict in Greece and Anatolia. The king of Macedon, Philip V (r. 221–179 B.C.), had made an alliance with Hannibal after Cannae, which left Rome with a score to settle. Rome won a relatively quick and easy victory when, in 197 B.C., the legions crushed the Macedonian phalanx at Cynoscephalae in central Greece (see **Map 5.3**). The age of the phalanx was over; the legion had defeated it decisively.

Rome had hoped to impose a patron-client relationship on Greece and Macedon, thereby avoiding having to sustain a permanent military presence, but the independent-minded Greeks refused to submit to Roman domination. Several years of tension followed, only to lead to renewed wars. First the Seleucids, under the ambitious king Antiochus III (r. 223–187 B.C.), moved into the Greek peninsula and challenged Rome for hegemony. It was in this war that Hannibal took a small, doomed part. Roman forces made short work of the enemy. Driven out not only from Greece but from Anatolia as well, the Seleucids in effect recognized Roman supremacy in the Mediterranean (188 B.C.).

Then came another two rounds of war that pitted Rome against a resurgent Macedon and various Greek states (171–167 and 150–146 B.C.). Victorious in both wars, Rome deprived the Greeks and Macedonians of their independence. Wherever democracy had survived in Greece, it was replaced with oligarchy. In 146 B.C., Rome destroyed Corinth, one of Greece's wealthiest cities, as a warning against further rebellion. For the next two centuries, Rome would pay little attention to its Greek province except to tax it.

By annexing Carthage, Macedon, and Greece in the mid-second century B.C., Rome created a dynamic for expansion around the entire Mediterranean. Before the century was over, southern Gaul was annexed, and Rome had gained a foothold in Asia. The kingdom of Pergamum (northwestern Anatolia) had supported Rome throughout Rome's wars in the east. When Attalus III of Pergamum died without an heir in 133 B.C., he surrendered his kingdom to the Roman people, who made it into a province of Asia.

Two great Hellenistic states remained independent: the Seleucid kingdom, that is, Syria, and Ptolemaic Egypt. Rome frequently interfered in their affairs, however, and no one was surprised when, in the first century B.C., they too were annexed.

## The Socioeconomic Consequences of Expansion

Expansion led to big and unintended changes in Rome's society, economy, and culture. Already wealthy, the Roman elite now came into fabulous riches. Huge profits awaited the generals, patrons, diplomats, magistrates, tax collectors, and businessmen who followed Rome's armies. In Italy, most profits were in the form of land; the provinces offered not

🌐 **Map 5.3 Roman Expansion, 264–44 B.C.**   Wars against Carthage, the major Greco-Macedonian powers, Gauls, Germans, North Africans, and other peoples brought Rome an empire on three continents. © Cengage Learning 2014

only land but also slaves, booty, and graft. One of the worst grafters, Gaius Verres, governor of Sicily from 73 to 71 B.C., was prosecuted by Cicero (see page 138) for allegedly extorting tens of thousands of pounds of silver from his province. However, even Cicero skimmed off several thousand pounds of silver as governor of the province of Cilicia (southern Anatolia) from 51 to 50 B.C.

The first Roman coinage, traditionally dated to 289 B.C., facilitated commercial transactions. Previously, the Romans had made do with barter, uncoined bronze, and cast bronze bars, but now they imitated the workmanship and style of Greek coins. Equally prominent in the homes of wealthy Romans were Greek metalwork, jewelry, art objects, and other luxury goods. Conservatives bemoaned the decline of Roman austerity, but they fought a rear-guard action. (See the feature, "The Visual Record: Luxury Goods and Gender Wars" on pages 130–131.)

Ordinary Romans needed no reminder of the virtues of austerity, for they did not share in the elite's profit from Roman expansion. Indeed, a century of warfare—from the outbreak of the Punic Wars in 264 B.C. to the destruction of Carthage and Corinth in 146 B.C.—pushed the Roman people to the breaking point. Hannibal's invasion ruined much of the farmland of southern Italy and reduced Italian manpower considerably. Yet, most people would have soon rebounded from these problems if they had not faced other serious troubles.

Conscription had become the norm. The average term of military service, between ages 17 and 46, was six years; the maximum term was twenty years. Because experienced legionnaires were at a premium, commanders did not want to release them from service. But the longer a man served, the harder it was for his wife and children to keep the family farm running. A patron might have helped, but most patrons, in fact, added to the problem through the introduction to Italy of large-scale agricultural entrepreneurship.

A revolution in the Italian countryside brought ruin on the free peasantry of Italy. Wealthy Romans wanted to invest in large landed estates, or *latifundia* (lat-uh-FUN-dee-uh), worked by slaves. These estates were either mixed farms (most often devoted to cultivating vines, olives, and grain) or ranches (establishments where animals were raised for meat, milk, and wool). One devotee of the latter was the prominent conservative Marcus Porcius Cato (KAY-toe) (234–149 B.C.), known as **Cato the Censor**. Cato argued that there were only three ways to get rich: "pasturage, pasturage, and pasturage." All a would-be entrepreneur needed was land, which Rome had conquered a huge amount of in Italy. Called public land, Rome's new territory belonged to the Roman people, but an individual was legally entitled to claim about 320 acres as his own. Many entrepreneurs flouted the law, however, and grabbed much more than their fair share of public land. In addition, they often forced families of absent soldiers off private land, either by debt foreclosure or by outright violence. Sometimes, families would leave the land for the city, but usually they stayed as tenants.

> **Cato the Censor** Name given to Marcus Porcius Cato, a Roman general and statesman. He was the first Roman historian to write in Latin.

The last two centuries B.C. witnessed the transformation of Roman rural society from one of independent farmers to one in which slave labor played a major role. By the end of the first century B.C., Italy's slave population was estimated at two million, about a third of the peninsula's total. Prisoners of war and conquered civilians provided a ready supply of slaves. Most worked in agriculture or mining, and their treatment was often abominable; the fewer house slaves were usually better off.

There were few escape routes from poverty. Before about 170 B.C., poor Romans were sometimes able to find land in colonies, but by 170 B.C., Rome had established all the colonies in Italy that its security demanded. A displaced farmer who wanted to compete in the labor market would have found it difficult to underbid cheap slave labor. In any case, Roman ideology frowned on wage labor by citizens. Nor was it practical for a poor farmer to sue a wealthy patron who seized his land because a plaintiff himself had to bring the accused into court.

The situation of the Italian peasantry was becoming increasingly miserable by the mid-second century B.C. As one modern scholar has put it, "In conquering what they were pleased to call the world, the Romans ruined a great part of the Italian people."[*]

## The Impact of Greece on Rome and Its Empire

Rome learned much from its new encounters with foreign peoples—and from none more than the Greeks. Wealthy Romans cultivated interests in Greek art, literature, rhetoric, and speculative thought; poor and rich alike enjoyed Greek drama. Before the mid-third century B.C., Roman literature was virtually nonexistent. An oral tradition of songs, ballads, and funeral oratory kept alive the deeds of the famous, for writing was generally restricted to commercial and government records and inscriptions. In short, the Romans conquered Italy without writing about it.

Contact with the Greek cities brought changes. Large numbers of Roman soldiers in Magna Graecia (southern Italy and Sicily) were introduced to comedy, tragedy, mimes, and sophisticated song lyrics, and many developed a permanent taste for them. It is no accident that the first production of a drama at Rome took place in 240 B.C., the year after the end of the First Punic War. Afterward, the annual production of such dramas became standard procedure.

No one could accuse the Romans of rushing headlong into a new age, however. The authorities continued to look down on theater as emotional and corrupt. They did not allow the building of a permanent theater in Rome until 55 B.C., nor did the Roman elite readily become playwrights or poets. The first gentleman poet in Rome, Lucilius (180–102 B.C.), did not arrive until the second century B.C., and he was a Latin, not a Roman. His predecessors, the founders of Latin literature, were all of low social status; little of their work survives.

The two great early Latin playwrights are Titus Maccius Plautus (ca. 254–184 B.C.) and Publius Terentius Afer, today known as Terence (ca. 195–159 B.C.). Both of them wrote comedies on the model of the great Greek playwright Menander (see page 98). Plautus was a poor man from northern Italy who learned his Latin in Rome; Terence was a North African slave, educated and freed in Rome. Twenty-one plays by Plautus and six by Terence survive. Plautus's plays are generally slapstick farces. They are set in Greece, not Rome, in part, out of escapism (many were written during the Second Punic War), in part, out of the censorial demands of the Roman authorities. They nonetheless reveal much about Roman society. Terence's plays are more subtle than Plautus's, indicating the growing sophistication of Roman theatergoers.

---

[*]P. A. Brunt, *Social Conflicts in the Roman Republic* (New York: Norton, 1971), p. 17.

Latin prose developed more slowly than did poetry and drama. The first histories by Romans, composed after the Second Punic War, were written in Greek, for Latin lacked the vocabulary or the audience for history. Cato the Censor was the first historian of Rome to write in Latin. His *Origines*, of which we have only remnants, recounted Roman history from the origin of the city to about 150 B.C. The earliest surviving Latin prose work is Cato's *On Agriculture*.

In the traditional education of a Roman aristocrat, parents and close family friends played the primary role. Although this practice continued, wealthy Romans in the second century B.C. began acquiring Greek slaves to educate their sons in the Greek language and Greek literature. Soon Greek freedmen began setting up schools offering the same subjects. Before long, similar Latin grammar schools also opened.

One of the forms of Greek literature that appealed most to the practical-minded Romans was rhetoric. Roman orators studied Greek models, and many would say that they eventually outdid the Greeks. Cato was the first Roman to publish his speeches, and he also wrote a book on rhetoric. Both gave impetus to the spread of sophisticated rhetoric in Rome.

Scipio Aemilianus, conqueror of Carthage in 146 B.C., not only had a distinguished political and military career; he also served as patron of a group of prominent statesmen and soldiers who shared his love of Hellenism. Among the writers whom they supported were the playwright Terence, the poet Lucilius, the historian Polybius, and the Stoic philosopher Panaetius (ca. 185–109 B.C.). The Stoic emphases on duty, wisdom, and world brotherhood appealed both to Rome's traditional ideology and to its more recent acquisition of empire. Yet, not all Romans shared Scipio's admiration of Greek culture; Cato, for example, was famously ambivalent.

**Cornelia**, Scipio Aemilianus's mother-in-law, is an example of the political importance of elite women. She was an educated lover of Hellenism who wrote letters that existed several hundred years later as examples of elegant Latin prose. Her villa in the resort of Misenum on the Bay of Naples was well known for the distinguished guests whom she received there. When her husband, an outstanding statesman and general, died, Cornelia chose to remain a widow. One of the men who tried to change her mind was no less a figure than the king of Egypt. The widow spent her time managing her own estate and supervising the education of her two sons, the future tribunes Tiberius and Gaius Gracchus.

Although Cornelia's privileges were extraordinary, she is nonetheless a reminder of the opportunities that imperial expansion offered to wealthy Roman women. Marriage practices are one example of change. Few women were married *cum manu* anymore—that is, handed over by their fathers to their husbands. A woman's father or nearest male relative, not her husband, was most likely to be her paterfamilias, which meant that a husband's control over his wife's dowry was limited. The result was more freedom, at least for wealthy women.

**Cornelia** Mother of the Gracchi, Cornelia was an influential elite woman whose letters served as models of Latin prose style.

### SECTION SUMMARY

- The flexible infantry formation, known as the legion, was the key to Roman success in battle.
- Rome consolidated its control of Italy by wisely treating its allies with a mixture of firmness and generosity, including the extension of Roman citizenship.
- The strength of Rome's alliance led to success in the Punic Wars with Carthage and then drew Rome into conquering all the Hellenistic Greek states.
- Military expansion brought fabulous riches to the Roman elite, brought misery to the peasants of Italy, and established a slave system of two million people.
- Conquest of and contact with Greek civilization led to the rise of Latin literature.

# The Late Republic and Its Collapse, 133–31 B.C.

*How did the unintended consequences of conquest on Rome lead to a revolution that destroyed the Republic?*

A citizen of the Roman Republic in the mid-second century B.C. might have looked forward to a long and happy future for his country, unaware that the Republic—after 350 years of expansion—was about to begin a century of domestic and foreign unrest that would bring down the whole system. Why and how did the Republic collapse? More than a century of warfare weighed heavily on the ordinary people of Italy—the Romans and allied peasants whose farms were ruined while they were off fighting. The Roman elite was bitterly divided

## Luxury Goods and Gender Wars

The carefully wrought gold earrings shown here represent the height of fashion in the central Mediterranean around 200 B.C. Hellenistic taste favored such gold hoop earrings embellished with inlaid colored glass. This set, moreover, displays one of the favorite decorative motifs of the goldsmiths of Magna Graecia in southern Italy during this period: the dove. The artist has crafted the doves as pendants: note how each dove hangs from the earring and stands on a small base trimmed with a garland. Two inches tall, the earrings are miniature sculptures. A Roman woman might wear such jewelry proudly, certain that it bespoke not only good taste and wealth but also the power of her city to command the best artistry of the Greek world.

Not all Romans, however, looked with favor on such finery. Some said it represented not Roman success but decadence. While some observers saw, reflected in the gold, the sight of Greek craftsmen dancing to Roman tunes, others perceived a scene of corruption and wastefulness. Both men and women in the Roman elite began to indulge a taste for luxury in the third century B.C., but women came in for special criticism.

Conservatives considered women's luxuries a special threat because they represented not only foreign influence but also a challenge to right order in the household. A debate on women's luxuries raged in Rome around 200 B.C. Let us examine both its historical background and the position of its most famous participant, the conservative champion Marcus Porcius Cato (234–149 B.C.), known as Cato the Censor.

From their first conquest in Magna Graecia in the third century B.C., Romans began to bring home Greek artists and craftsmen and their works. The trickle of art flowing toward Rome became a flood when Roman armies entered Greece and Anatolia.

The new wealth and new tastes created a luxury goods industry in Rome. Traditionalist opinion was shocked as it became common for elite men to wear rings and their wives and daughters to don jewelry as well as fine clothes and cosmetics and—a particular sign of wealth and honor—to ride in carriages. Hannibal's invasion of Italy put the brakes on luxury, however, because it forced Romans to adopt austerity for the duration of the war. In 215 B.C. the Oppian Law put limits on the gold and fine clothing women could own and on their privilege of riding in carriages.

Twenty years later, in 195 B.C., when the emergency had passed, a proposal was made to repeal the law. Elite women demonstrated in favor of repeal. According to the historian Livy, Valerius (one of the consuls for 195) supported their position:

> Women cannot claim magistracies or priesthoods or triumphs or military decorations or awards or the spoils of war. Cosmetics and adornments are women's decorations. They delight and boast of them and this is what our ancestors called women's estate.

Enter Cato, the other consul for 195 and an advocate of traditional Roman values of austerity. Look at the Roman bust of him here, which emphasizes his stern character.

Pair of earrings with pendant doves, Greek, Hellenistic period, 150–100 B.C.; gold, garnet, and glass paste; L 5.2 cm. Photograph © Museum of Fine Arts, Boston

**Hellenistic Earrings, Gold and Inlaid Glass**

over what to do about the problems of the peasants. One group wanted to redistribute land on behalf of the poor; another group had no sympathy for them.

By the Late Republic, the city of Rome was crowded: Scholars estimate the number of inhabitants to have reached one million by the end of the first century B.C. The government had to take charge of the grain supply. But elite politicians exploited the issue for partisan purposes. Once before, during the struggle between the patrician and plebeian orders in the Early Republic, the elite had been similarly divided and had resolved its differences through compromise (see pages 117–118). In the Late Republic, however, ambitious nobles were no longer willing to subordinate themselves to the community. It was not long before competing armies of land-hungry peasants, thwarted from above, were marching across Italy.

Livy reports that Cato denounced luxury goods as signs of Greek corruption and women's license, even perhaps of women's eventual equality. Although some scholars doubt whether Cato ever so criticized the Greeks, there is no doubt about his hostility to luxury. As censor in 184 B.C., he assessed taxes on luxury goods and slaves at ten times their market value in order to discourage their use.

Nor is there any doubt about the degree of male worry about women's wealth in Cato's Rome—even though the repeal of the Oppian Law eventually passed in 195 B.C., over Cato's opposition. For example, a character in the play *Pot of Gold*, by Cato's contemporary Plautus, condemns wealthy wives with their "fine clothes and jewelry . . . and maids and mules and coachmen and footmen and pages and private carriages."* Twenty-one years later, in 169 B.C., a law was passed forbidding the wealthiest Roman men from leaving more than half of their property to a daughter, in order to prevent the loss through marriage of most of a family's wealth.

How can we explain such attention by the government to the behavior of elite women? The answer in large part is that war and empire had brought such women new power, power that elite men feared. While those men had often spent years abroad fighting Rome's wars, their wives had learned how to run households. The enormous wealth brought home from those wars often ended up as dowries. Women had the right to retain control of part of their dowries, which sometimes made them wealthier than their husbands. Cato complained that some wives went so far as to lend money to their husbands and then send slaves to reclaim the interest.

All this talk of luxury, however, should not blind us to the imbalance of wealth in Rome. As the carriages of wealthy women rolled by, the vast majority of Roman women could only stand and watch, hoping to catch a glimpse of gold.

### Questions

1. *Why did conservatives consider earrings like these to be a threat to Rome?*

2. *What was the Oppian Law and why was its repeal controversial?*

3. *Why and how did Cato intervene in the debate on luxury?*

---

*Translation by E. Fantham in Elaine Fantham, Helene Peet Foley, Natalie Boymel Kampen, Sarah B. Pomeroy, and H. A. Shapiro, *Women in the Classical World: Image and Text* (New York: Oxford University Press, 1994), p. 261.

**Bust of Cato the Censor**

Alinari/Art Resource, NY

## Reformers and Revolutionaries

Many Romans fretted over the military dimension of the agrarian crisis. In modern societies, draftees are often the poorest people. In Rome, military service was a prestigious activity, so a property qualification was imposed and the poor were not drafted. As fewer and fewer potential soldiers could afford to own property, however, during the second century, it became necessary to reduce the property qualification several times. If the free peasantry continued its decline, Rome would either have to drop the property qualification for the military altogether or stop fielding armies. Clearly, something had to be done.

Into the breach stepped Tiberius Sempronius Gracchus (GRAK-us) (d. 133 B.C.), one of the ten tribunes for the year 133 B.C. The son of Cornelia, and a distinguished general and ambassador (also named Tiberius), Tiberius belonged to the eminent **Gracchi** (GRAK-eye) family. He seemed an excellent spokesperson for a group of prominent senators who backed land reform to restore Rome's peasant soldiers.

In a stirring public speech, Tiberius made the case for reform. "The wild beasts that roam over Italy," he said, "have their dens, each has a place of repose and refuge. But the men who fight and die for Italy enjoy nothing but the air and light; without house or home they wander about with their wives and children."[*]

Tiberius's proposed law restored the roughly 320-acre limit to the amount of public land a person could own (plus an exception for a man with two sons, who was allowed to hold about 667 acres). A commission was to be set up to redistribute land to the poor, in small lots that were to be inalienable—that is, the wealthy could not buy them back. The former landowners would be reimbursed for improvements they had made, such as buildings or plantings.

The proposal was moderate, but wealthy landowners repudiated it outright. Many senators suspected that Tiberius wanted to set himself up as a kind of superpatron, buoyed by peasant supporters. Senators also disliked his pushy and heavy-handed legislative tactics. Finally, Tiberius broke with custom by running for a second consecutive term as tribune. While the tribal assembly prepared to vote on the new tribunes, some senators led a mob to the Forum and had Tiberius and three hundred of his followers clubbed to death.

This shocking event marked the first time in the Republic that a political debate was settled by bloodshed in Rome itself. Tiberius's killers had not merely committed murder but had attacked the traditional inviolability of the tribunes. The ancient sources agree that it was the beginning of a century of revolution. Over the next hundred years, violence grew as a weapon of politics in the Republic.

The land commission went ahead with its work, even without Tiberius. His younger brother, Gaius (GUY-us) (d. 121 B.C.) became tribune himself in 123 B.C. Gaius expanded Tiberius's coalition, adding to it supporters from the equestrian order and the urban populace, mainly composed of slaves and freedmen. He gave the plebs cheap grain at subsidized prices. The equestrians were wealthy landowners, similar to senators in most respects except for their failure to have reached the senate; they yearned for political power. A small but important group of equestrians was engaged in commerce and tax collection in the provinces. The senate regulated their activities through the so-called extortion courts, which tried corruption cases. Gaius staffed those courts with equestrians. Alluding to the new equestrian power, Gaius remarked, "I have left a sword in the ribs of the senate."

Gaius sponsored an extension of his brother's agrarian law, new colonies, public works, and relief for poor soldiers. Eventually, he ran aground on a plan to include the Italian allies as beneficiaries of reform—a farsighted notion, but one unpopular with the Roman people, who were jealous of their privileges. A riot by his supporters led the senate to pass a declaration of public emergency, empowering officials to use any means necessary to protect the state.

One of the consuls had Gaius and 250 of his followers killed. Another 3,000 Gracchans were executed soon thereafter. The Gracchan land commission gave land to approximately 75,000 citizens. The law, however, was amended to permit the resale of redistributed land, and the commission itself was abolished. With the wealthy poised to buy land back, the settlers' future was uncertain. The senatorial oligarchy was back in control.

Or so it seemed. In fact, Roman politics had become an unstable brew. In time, it became clear that the Gracchi had divided the political community into two loose groupings. On one side were the *optimates* (op-tee-MAH-tayz) ("the best people"; singular, *optimas*), conservatives who asserted the rule of the senate against popular tribunes and the maintenance of the estates of the wealthy in spite of the agrarian crisis. On the other side were the *populares* (pah-poo-LAH-rayz) ("men of the people"; singular, *popularis*), who challenged the rule of the senate in the name of relief of the poor. The populares were not democrats. Like the optimates, they were Roman nobles who believed in hierarchy, but, like the Gracchi, they

---

[*]Plutarch, "Life of Tiberius Gracchus," in Naphtali Lewis and Meyer Reinhold, eds., Roman Civilization: Selected Readings, vol. 1: The Republic and the Augustan Age, 3d ed. (New York: Columbia University Press, 1990), p. 252.

advocated the redistribution of wealth and power as a way of restoring stability and strengthening the military.

By 100 B.C., Rome's agrarian crisis had become a full-scale military crisis, too. Roman armies under senatorial commanders fared poorly, both in Numidia (modern North Africa) and in southern Gaul against Germanic invaders (see **Map 5.3**). The situation was saved by an outsider to established privilege, an equestrian named Gaius Marius (157–86 B.C.), the first member of his family to be elected consul, for 107 B.C. This "new man" proved to be a military reformer and a popularis. Marius made several moves to streamline and strengthen the Roman army: Camp followers were reduced in number, and individual soldiers were made to carry their own equipment. To meet the Germans, who attacked in overwhelming waves, maniples—the tactical subunits of a legion—were reorganized and combined into larger units called cohorts, rendering the army firmer and more cohesive. Most important, Marius abandoned altogether the property qualification for the military. As a result, Roman soldiers were no longer peasants doing part-time military service, but rather landless men making a profession of the military.

Politically, they became a force to be reckoned with. As an indispensable general, Marius demanded and won an unprecedented seven elections to the consulship, most of them in violation of the law requiring ten years between each consulship. Furthermore, after gaining victories in North Africa and Gaul, Marius championed his soldiers. In 100 B.C., he asked that land be distributed to them. The senate refused, but its triumph was temporary. The poor recognized that only military leaders, such as Marius, would give them land. As a result, ordinary Romans, who were all now eligible for the army, transferred their loyalty from the senate to their commanders.

Two new wars weakened the Republic further. First, its Italian allies rose against Rome in a bloody and bitter struggle from 91 to 89 B.C., known as the "Social War," that is, war with the *socii* ("allies"). The allies fought hard, and Rome, in order to prevail, had to concede to them what they had demanded at the outset: full Roman citizenship. The other conflict of this period pitted Rome against Mithridates (120–63 B.C.), a rebellious king in northern Anatolia with great ambitions. Mithridates conquered Roman territory in western Anatolia and slaughtered the numerous Italian businessmen and tax collectors there. He invaded Thrace and Greece, where he found great support. Once again a military man rose to save the day for Rome: Marius's former lieutenant, Lucius Cornelius Sulla Felix (ca. 138–78 B.C.), consul for the year 88 B.C.

Sulla was as ambitious as Marius, but he came from the opposite political camp: He was a patrician and an optimas. The two became deadly rivals. The two men's troops fought over the issue of the command against Mithridates. Sulla's forces won the first round by marching on Rome, but after they left for the east, Marius's men retook the city and settled scores. Victorious over Mithridates, Sulla returned to Italy in 83 B.C. and engaged in all-out civil war. Sulla defeated Marius's men in battle (minus Marius himself, who had died in 86), then sealed his victory by executing his political opponents, as many as two thousand men. Their land was confiscated and sold to Sulla's friends. Sulla also confiscated the land of any Italian community that had opposed him and gave it to his veterans, about eighty thousand men.

Having assumed the long-dormant office of dictator—but without a time limit on his tenure—Sulla attempted to restore the senatorial rule of pre-Gracchan days. To do this, he greatly weakened the tribunate and strengthened the senate, whose size he doubled, from about three hundred to about six hundred members.

Sulla retired in 79 B.C. and died a year later. His hope of restoring law and order under the senate died with him. The populares soon regained enough strength to restore the old powers of the tribunes. Discontent smoldered among the men whose land Sulla had confiscated. Equally serious, many senators, aspiring to what Sulla had done and not to what he had said, pursued personal power, not the collective interests of the senate.

## Caesar

At first, the dominant leader after Sulla was the optimas Pompey the Great (106–48 B.C.), a brilliant general and a supporter of Sulla. Young Pompey (POM-pee) went from command to command: He put down an agrarian rebellion in Italy and a rebellion in Spain, cleared the Mediterranean of pirates, defeated Mithridates again after that able king started another war, and added rich conquests to the empire in Anatolia, Syria, Phoenicia, and Palestine. In the fifties B.C., however, the tide began turning in favor of Gaius Julius **Caesar** (100–44 B.C.), an even more gifted general and politician—indeed, perhaps one of history's greatest. A popularis, Caesar (SEE-zer) had family connections to Marius. Caesar's career depended on his oratory, his boldness, and his sheer talent at war and politics. Caesar conquered Gaul, gained a foothold in Britain, and laid the foundations of Roman rule in Egypt (see **Map 5.3**).

**Caesar** Roman general gifted at war and politics, he was named dictator in 49 B.C. and was assassinated by the members of the senate in 44 B.C.

While the elite of the Late Republic struggled to maintain order and secure power, ordinary people struggled for survival. Violence had become a way of life in rural Italy. Many once-prosperous farmers, dispossessed peasants, and runaway slaves ended up as robbers or bandits. It was also an era of slave revolts, the most serious of which lasted from 73 to 71 B.C., under the leadership of Spartacus, a Thracian gladiator who had once served as a Roman allied soldier. An able commander, Spartacus beat nine separate Roman armies in two years before finally suffering defeat. (See the feature, "The Written Record: Spartacus's Slave Revolt" on page 135.) At the same time, Rome also faced major wars in its provinces.

Pompey and Caesar sought alliances with other families by marrying influential women or by becoming their lovers. In 80 B.C., for example, Pompey divorced his first wife to advance his career by marrying Aemilia, Sulla's stepdaughter. Aemilia was not only married at the time, but also pregnant by her first husband. Soon after her divorce and remarriage, she died in childbirth. Caesar had many lovers, among them the queen of Egypt, Cleopatra (see pages 102–103). Caesar had a penchant for certain Egyptian institutions, such as the Egyptian calendar, and he toyed with becoming a monarch himself, an inclination that Cleopatra perhaps encouraged.

Another of Caesar's lovers was Servilia, stepsister of Marcus Porcius Cato (Cato the Younger, 95–46 B.C.), great-grandson of the famous censor (see page 130). She was also the mother of Brutus, the man who would eventually help murder Caesar.

Pompey was an optimas, Caesar a popularis, but the two of them agreed that they, not the senate or the assemblies, should dominate Rome. Each man's ambition was more important to him than any political principles. In 60 B.C., they entered into a pact with a third ambitious noble, Marcus Licinius Crassus (d. 53 B.C.). Known today as the "First Triumvirate," this coalition amounted to a conspiracy to run the state. Their individual ambitions rebuffed by the senate, each man had an agenda that could be achieved by pooling resources in the triumvirate: for Pompey, ratification of his acts in the east and land for his veterans; for Caesar, who became consul for 59 B.C., a long period of command in Gaul and a free hand in his behavior there; for Crassus, a rebate for the tax collectors of Roman Asia, whom he championed, and eventually, a command in Syria to make war on Parthia (the new Persian Empire). To solidify the bond between the two men, Pompey married Caesar's daughter Julia.

Having achieved its goal, the triumvirate did not long survive, but its very existence shows how little the Republic now meant. Crassus died in an inglorious defeat against the Parthians at Carrhae in Syria in 53 B.C. (see **Map 5.3**). Frightened by Caesar's stunning victories in Gaul, Pompey returned to the senatorial fold, now led by Cato the Younger. The death (in childbirth) of Julia in 54 B.C. made it easier for Pompey to abandon Caesar. Cato and his supporters stood for the traditional rule of the senatorial oligarchy. In 49 B.C., they ordered Caesar to give up his command in Gaul, but instead Caesar marched on Italy with his army. Italy's northern boundary was marked by a tiny stream called the Rubicon; when Caesar defiantly crossed it, he declared, "The die is cast." Indeed it was, for civil war. Caesar swept to victory against the senate's army, led by Pompey, at Pharsalus in Greece in 48 B.C. Pompey fled but was assassinated. The complete destruction of the senate's forces took until 45 B.C.

The years of civil war took Caesar from Spain to Anatolia. During the fighting, he showed the qualities that made him great: He was fast, tough,

**Bust of Julius Caesar** This marble sculpture accurately conveys the conqueror's firmness of expression and perhaps his intelligence—but not his looks, since Caesar was bald. Scala/Art Resource, NY

## Spartacus's Slave Revolt

*Spartacus's revolt was the third and most famous of three great slave rebellions that rocked Italy and Sicily between 135 and 71 B.C. The revolt itself was not a success; all of the slaves were either imprisoned or killed. But Spartacus terrified the Roman elite and became a powerful symbol of the struggle for freedom to all who were oppressed. This account, by the ancient writer Appian, illustrates his fight.*

At about this same time, at the city of Capua in Italy, gladiators were being trained to fight in spectacles. Spartacus, a Thracian whom the Romans had imprisoned and then sold to be trained as a gladiator, had once fought as a soldier for the Roman army. He persuaded about seventy of the enslaved men to risk a break for freedom rather than to allow themselves to be put on display for the entertainment of others. Using force to overcome their guards, the men made their escape. The fugitives armed themselves with wooden clubs and daggers that they seized from travelers on the roads nearby, and then rushed to take refuge on Mount Vesuvius. Many fugitive slaves and even some free men from the surrounding countryside came to this place to join Spartacus. They began to stage bandit raids on nearby settlements. Spartacus had his fellow gladiators Oenomaus and Crixus as his two subordinate commanders. Since Spartacus divided the profits of his raiding into equal shares, he soon attracted a very large number of followers . . .

[Spartacus wins victories in southern and northern Italy.] With the 120,000 men under his command, he began a march on Rome. So that traveling would be as light as possible, he torched all unnecessary supplies, killed all prisoners of war, and slaughtered all pack animals. Many deserters from the Roman army came to him, but he accepted none of them. The consuls made a stand against him in a place in the land of Picenum. Another great armed struggle took place here and the Romans were defeated again. Spartacus changed his mind about an attack on Rome. He decided that he was not ready for an all-out battle and that his whole army was not yet properly armed for regular warfare. Moreover, so far no city had come over to his side, but only slaves, deserters, and the flotsam and jetsam of humanity . . .

[After many successes and some defeats, Spartacus is forced into a final battle with a Roman army led by Crassus.] Since so many tens of thousands of desperate men were involved, the result was a protracted battle of epic proportions. Spartacus took a spear wound in his thigh. Collapsing on one knee, he held his shield up in front of him and fought off those who were attacking him, until he and the large number of men around him were finally surrounded and cut down. The rest of his army was thrown into disarray and confusion and was slaughtered in large numbers. The killing was on such a scale that it was not possible to count the dead. The Romans lost about a thousand men. The body of Spartacus was never found. When the survivors among Spartacus's men, who were still a large number, fled from the battle, they went up into the mountains, where they were pursued by Crassus's forces. Splitting themselves into four groups, they continued to fight until all of them had perished—all, that is, except six thousand of them, who were taken prisoner and crucified along the whole length of the highway that ran from Capua to Rome.

### Questions

1. Why do you think Spartacus attracted so many followers?

2. Why do you think Spartacus was able to defeat the Romans time and again? Why do you think he finally failed?

3. What evidence does the passage offer to show that Spartacus and his men were brave and determined?

"Spartacus' Slave Revolt" from *Spartacus and the Slave Wars: A Brief History with Documents*. Translated, edited and with an Introduction by Brent D. Shaw. Copyright © 2001 by Bedford/St. Martin's. Used with permission of Bedford/St. Martin's.

smart, adaptable, and a risk-taker. He was a diplomat, too, offering mercy to any of his enemies who joined him. A talented writer, Caesar published two books about his military campaigns—*On the Gallic War* and *On the Civil War*—the latter appearing after his death. These works glorified Caesar's conquests and defended his decision to wage civil war. (See the feature, "The Global Record: Caesar on the Gauls" on page 136.)

Back in Rome, Caesar sponsored a huge number of reforms. His political goal was to elevate Italians and others at the expense of old Roman families. To achieve this, Caesar conferred Roman citizenship liberally, on all of Cisalpine Gaul (northernmost Italy), as well as on certain provincial towns. He enlarged the senate from six hundred to nine hundred, adding his supporters, including some Gauls, to the membership. Caesar sponsored social and economic reforms, too, including reducing debt and founding the first colonies outside Italy, where veterans and poor citizens were settled. He undertook a grand public building program in the city of Rome. Caesar's most long-lasting act was to introduce the calendar of 365 1/4 days, on January 1, 45 B.C. Derived from the calendar of Egypt, it is known as the Julian calendar.

## Caesar on the Gauls

*Julius Caesar (ca. 100–44 B.C.) advertised his achievements in conquering Gaul (58–51 B.C.) in his Commentaries on the Gallic War. The book focuses on battles and negotiations, but here Caesar discusses the society of the Gauls (also known as Celts). He depicts the inhabitants as superstitious and warlike.*

In the whole of Gaul two types of men are counted as being of worth and distinction. The ordinary people are considered almost as slaves: they dare do nothing on their own account and are not called to counsels. When the majority are oppressed by debt or heavy tribute, or harmed by powerful men, they swear themselves away into slavery to the aristocracy, who then have the same rights over them as masters do over their slaves. Of the two types of men of distinction, however, the first is made up of the druids (priests), and the other of the knights.

The druids are involved in matters of religion. They manage public and private sacrifices and interpret religious customs and ceremonies. Young men flock to them in large numbers to gain instruction, and they hold the druids in great esteem. For they decide almost all disputes, both public and private: if some crime has been committed, if there has been murder done, if there is a dispute over an inheritance or over territory, they decide the issue and settle the rewards and penalties. If any individual or group of people does not abide by their decision, the druids ban them from sacrifices. This is their most severe punishment. Those who are banned in this way are counted among the wicked and criminal: everyone shuns them and avoids approaching or talking to them, so as not to suffer any harm from contact with them. . . .

Druids are not accustomed to take part in war, nor do they pay taxes like the rest of the people. . . . The principal doctrine they attempt to impart is that souls do not die but after death cross from one person to another. Because the fear of death is thereby set aside, they consider this a strong inducement to physical courage. Besides this, they debate many subjects and teach them to their young men—for example, the stars and their movements, the size of the universe and the earth, the nature of things, and the strength and power of the immortal gods.

The second class is that composed of the knights. When necessity arises and some war flares up—which before Caesar's arrival used to happen almost every year, so that they were either on the offensive themselves or fending off attacks—they are all involved in the campaign. Each man has as many retainers and dependents about him as is appropriate to his status in terms of his birth and resources. This is the sole form of power and influence they know.

The whole of the gallic nation is much given to religious practices. For this reason those who are afflicted with serious illnesses and those who are involved in battles and danger either offer human sacrifice or vow that they will do so, and employ the druids to manage these sacrifices. For they believe that unless one human life is offered for another, the power and presence of the immortal gods cannot be propitiated.

### Questions

1. *According to Caesar, who were the druids, and what did they do? How did they help the Gauls succeed as warriors? How did the druids differ from the knights?*

2. *What was the status of ordinary people in Gaul?*

3. *What do you think Caesar and his readers thought of the Gauls' practice of human sacrifice?*

"Caesar on the Gauls" from Julius Caesar, *Seven Commentaries on the Gallic War with an Eighth Commentary by Aulus Hirtius*, translated by Carolyn Hammond. Copyright © 1996 Oxford University Press. By permission of Oxford University Press.

Caesar did not hide his contempt for Republican constitutional formalities. By accepting a dictatorship for life, he offended conservatives; by flirting with the title of king, he infuriated them. His career ended abruptly on March 15, 44 B.C. (the Ides of March by the Roman calendar), when sixty senators stabbed him to death. The assassination took place in the portico attached to the Theater of Pompey, in front of a statue of Pompey himself, where the senate was meeting that day. It had been eighty-nine years since the murder of Tiberius Gracchus.

The assassins called themselves Liberators, believing that they were freeing themselves from tyranny just as the founders of the Republic had done centuries before. Indeed, one of the chief conspirators, Marcus Junius Brutus (ca. 85–42 B.C.), claimed descent from Lucius Junius Brutus, traditional leader of the revolt against the Tarquins that was thought to have established the Republic. Like his co-conspirator, Gaius Longinus Cassius (d. 42 B.C.), Brutus had been a magistrate, military officer, and provincial administrator.

The assassination of Caesar threw Rome back into turmoil. Civil war followed for the next thirteen years. The Liberators and Caesar's partisans fought to settle whether the Senate or a dictator would rule Rome. Then, after they defeated the Senate, the two leading Caesarians struggled over power. The final conflict pitted Mark Antony (Marcus Antonius, ca. 83–30 B.C.), Caesar's chief lieutenant and the man who inherited his love affair with Cleopatra, against Octavian (Gaius Julius Caesar Octavianus, 63 B.C.–A.D. 14), Caesar's grand-nephew and adopted son and heir to Caesar's name and his huge fortune. At first, it looked as if Antony had the upper hand because Octavian was young and inexperienced, was not a general, and was cursed with poor health. Octavian was, however, a man of unusual cunning and prudence. His forces defeated Antony and Cleopatra at the naval battle of Actium (off northwestern Greece) in 31 B.C.; their suicides followed shortly. The Roman world held its breath to see how Octavian would govern it.

## The World of Cicero

Marcus Tullius **Cicero** (106–43 B.C.) is one of the best known figures of all antiquity. His enormous body of writings provides a vivid, detailed, and sometimes damning picture of Roman life at the end of the Republic. They demonstrate both Rome's genius for flexibility and its limits.

**Cicero** Philosopher, writer, and statesman who was Rome's greatest orator.

Like Marius, Cicero (SIS-er-o) was a wealthy equestrian from the central Italian town of Arpinum who, as consul (in 63 B.C.), became a "new man." Unlike Marius, Cicero was an optimas and defender of the senate. He was, however, ready for compromise with the equestrians, from whose ranks he himself had arisen. He made his name by successfully leading the opposition to Lucius Sergius Catilina, a down-and-out patrician who organized a debtors' revolt in Etruria; the army smashed the rebellion.

Young Cicero studied philosophy and oratory in Greece. As an adult, he produced writings that made the Latin language a vessel for the heritage of Greek thought, even if he never equaled the originality of Plato or Aristotle. Cicero produced over a hundred speeches, of which about sixty survive; several works on speech writing; philosophical works; poetry, of which little survives; and numerous letters. After his death in 43 B.C., his immense correspondence was published, with little censored.

Cicero was famous as an attorney. He once tried to justify a political thug who had murdered a rival like this: "The incident, gentlemen, took place exactly as I have described it. The attacker was defeated. Force was frustrated by force; or, to put the matter more accurately, evil was overcome by good. Of the gain to our country and yourselves and all loyal citizens, I say nothing."* Although he lost the case, Cicero demonstrated his rhetorical elegance.

## Politics, Society, and Law

Politics in the Late Republic was loud and boisterous. The elite prided itself on free speech and open debate. In senate deliberations, court cases, and public meetings in the Forum that preceded assembly votes, oratory—sometimes great oratory—was common.

Elite women benefited from increased freedom and greater educational opportunities in the Late Republic, which made it possible for women, as well as men, to study oratory. Private tutors were common among the aristocracy, and girls often received lessons alongside their brothers. Girls sometimes also profited from a father's expertise. A particularly dramatic case is that of Hortensia, daughter of Quintus Hortensius Hortalus (114–50 B.C.), a famous orator and rival of Cicero. An excellent speaker herself, Hortensia defied tradition by arguing successfully in the Roman Forum, in 42 B.C., against a proposed war tax on wealthy women.

Ordinary people lacked the education and freedom to express themselves in the manner of a woman like Hortensia, but a less civilized means of expression was open to them: the political gang. Brawls and violence between the rival groups of Clodius, a supporter of Caesar, and Milo, a supporter of the senate, became increasingly common in the fifties B.C. As dictator, Caesar abolished the gangs.

Cicero's works demonstrate the origin of the Western tradition of legal science. The era gave rise to the legal expert, a person devoted to explaining and interpreting the law. Roman law needed interpretation because it was largely an unsystematic and sometimes contradictory collection of annual statements by magistrates. Enter the jurisconsults, legal interpreters

---

*Cicero, "In Defense of Titus Annius Milo," in *Selected Political Speeches of Cicero*, trans. Michael Grant (Harmondsworth, England: Penguin, 1969), p. 234.

who emerged in the third and second centuries B.C. By the first century B.C., they became true jurists; their interpretations began to be considered authoritative. No earlier Mediterranean society had a professional class of legal experts, but no earlier society had faced issues as complicated and turbulent, or had grown to three million citizens, as the Roman Republic did in the mid-first century B.C.

### A New Elite?

Rome's political system, unlike its legal system, did not adapt flexibly to changing circumstances. The disenfranchised of the Late Republic had reasonable goals: land for those who had fought for their country and admission to the senate of a wider group. Yet the old elite resisted both. Cicero's solution was to build on Sulla's reforms by uniting the senatorial and equestrian orders and by widening the Roman ruling class to include the elite of all Italy. The expanded ruling class could close ranks and establish *otium cum dignitate*, "peace with respect for rank." Cicero's proposed new order was distinctly hierarchical.

In the turbulent times of the Late Republic, the Roman elite often turned to the Hellenistic philosophers. Under the influence of Stoicism (see page 105), Cicero put forth a generous view of human brotherhood. He argued that all people share a spark of divinity and are protected by natural law. Consequently, all persons have value and importance and should treat others generously. For Cicero, however, these ideas existed more as theory than as practice.

Cicero did not hide his lack of sympathy for his fellow citizens who were poor. In one speech, he castigated "artisans and shopkeepers and all that kind of scum"; in a letter, he complained about "the wretched half-starved populace, which attends mass meetings and sucks the blood of the treasury." Cicero also made his disdain for democracy clear: "The greatest number," he said, "should not have the greatest power."

Elitist as Cicero's views were, they were by no means extremist. Cassius, Brutus, and the other Liberators had little interest in even Cicero's limited compromises. Their stubbornness proved to be their downfall, for dispossessed peasants and ambitious equestrians transferred their loyalties to Julius Caesar and, later, to Augustus. One of Caesar's supporters, Sallust (86–ca. 34 B.C.), wrote biting and bitter works of history that indicted the greed and corruption of the optimates, whom he blamed for the decline of the Republic. In any case, peace was not restored, for the generation of Liberators was wiped out in renewed civil war, and a new generation emerged, weary for peace.

## SECTION SUMMARY

- After the Gracchi brothers' failed attempts at reform, the Roman poor threw their support to new patrons, military leaders who raised private armies to win land for their followers and glory for themselves.
- The general Marius turned Rome's citizen soldiers into professionals, and then fought a civil war against another general, Sulla.
- The next generation of Roman politics was divided into factions led by Pompey and Caesar, leading to another civil war.
- Caesar reformed Rome as dictator for life before being assassinated.
- The great orator Cicero symbolizes the rough-and-tumble of civilian politics in the Late Republic.

## Chapter Summary

◆ *What was early Rome like and how was it shaped by relations with its neighbors?*

Rome was destined to provide Western civilization with many basic notions about government and empire, but Rome sprang from humble origins. A central Italian village at first, Rome was urbanized after contact with more sophisticated neighbors, especially Greeks and Etruscans. Rome became a monarchy and then a republic.

♦ *How was the Roman Republic governed, and how did that government shape the Western political tradition?*

In the Early and Middle Republic, Rome was a mixed constitution. It combined popular power with control by an oligarchy. Government was shared by the magistrates, the senate, and the assemblies. The so-called Struggle of the Orders brought debt relief for the poor and a combined patrician-plebeian nobility for the rich. Roman society was composed of a network of households tied in patron-client relationships. The ingrained hierarchy of the Roman social and cultural system helped keep politics stable.

♦ *How did Rome conquer an empire?*

The elite channeled popular energies into protecting the young Republic from its numerous rivals in central Italy. Greed and ambition, as well as fear, were powerful motives of Rome's military expansion. Rome conquered most of Italy by 265 B.C., then fought the bloody Punic Wars against Carthage (264–201, 148–146 B.C.) and conquered all the Hellenistic Greek states (201–30 B.C.).

♦ *How did the unintended consequences of conquest on Rome lead to a revolution that destroyed the Republic?*

Rome consolidated its control of Italy by wisely treating its allies with a mixture of firmness and generosity. By extending Roman citizenship, Rome gave them a stake in continued Roman hegemony. Having defeated all opponents near and far, Rome seemed to have won absolute security by the mid-second century B.C. Yet, its strength was deceptive. Contact with Greek culture liberated the Romans from ruder, peasant ways but also loosened previous restraints. A huge influx of slaves made acquisition of large estates profitable, at the expense of Italy's peasant farmers. The result was a growing and dangerous social instability with military and political ramifications. After the Gracchis' failed reform attempts, the poor threw their support to new patrons, military leaders who raised private armies to win land for their followers and glory for themselves. First Marius and Sulla, then Caesar and Pompey, led Roman armies against each other in civil war. The great orator Cicero symbolizes the energy of civilian politics in the Late Republic, but the military leaders had the last word.

## Key Terms

**Romulus** (p. 112)
**Latin** (p. 113)
**Etruscans** (p. 114)
**orders** (p. 115)
*res publica* (p. 116)
**senate** (p. 117)
*paterfamilias* (p. 119)
**triumph** (p. 122)

**legion** (p. 122)
**Punic Wars** (p. 125)
**Cato the Censor** (p. 128)
**Cornelia** (p. 129)
**Gracchi** (p. 132)
**Caesar** (p. 134)
**Cicero** (p. 137)

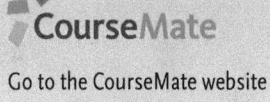
CourseMate

Go to the CourseMate website at **www.cengagebrain.com** for additional study tools and review materials—including audio and video clips—for this chapter.

**Ara Pacis (detail), Rome** Scala/Art Resource, NY

# Imperial Rome, 31 B.C.–A.D. 284

T he imperial family of Rome walks in stately procession to a sacrifice: Livia, wife of Augustus, first of the emperors; his daughter, Julia; Julia's husband, Agrippa; and various cousins and in-laws and their children. They are formally dressed in togas and gowns, heads wreathed. The men and women gaze seriously; the boys and girls have impish looks, betraying thoughts of mischief as they hold their parents' hands. They are all carved in stone, one of several sculptured reliefs decorating the walls of a public monument in Rome. Dedicated on Livia's birthday in 9 B.C., the monument shown here illustrates the propaganda themes of the new regime, among them, the happy family as a symbol of peace after generations of civil war. The senate, which had commissioned the monument, called it the *Ara Pacis Augustae*, or "Altar of Augustan Peace."

Having made peace was no idle boast on Augustus's part. Not only did he end the Roman revolution, but he also began a period of two hundred years of prosperity and stability in the Roman Empire. Augustus took advantage of Rome's war-weariness to create a new government out of the ruins of the Republic. Like the Early Republic's leaders, Augustus displayed a genius for compromise. Although he retained the final say, he shared a degree of power with the senate. He made financial sacrifices to feed the urban poor and distribute farms to landless peasants. He ended Rome's seemingly limitless expansion and stabilized the borders of the empire. He began to raise the provinces to a status of equality with Italy.

The *pax Romana* (PAHKS ro-MAHN-uh) ("Roman peace"), at its height between A.D. 96 and 180, was an era of enlightened emperors, thriving cities, intellectual vitality, and artistic and architectural achievement in an empire of 50 million to 100 million people. Yet, it was also an era of slavery. More positively, the Roman peace was a period of heightened spirituality. In the peaceful and diverse empire, ideas traveled from people to people, and the religious beliefs of an obscure sect from western Asia began to spread around the Mediterranean and into northern Europe. The new religion was Christianity.

After 180, Rome slowly passed into a period marked in turn by bad emperors, civil war, inflation, plague, invasion, and defeat. After reaching a low point around 235 to 253, Rome's fortunes began to improve under reformers who would forge a stronger and different empire.

## Chapter Overview

### Augustus and the Principate, 31 B.C.–A.D. 68

◆ *How did Augustus establish a new imperial government to replace the Roman Republic? Why was he so successful?*

### The Roman Peace and Its Collapse, A.D. 69–284

◆ *What was life like in the era of the Roman peace? Why did peace end during the third century A.D.?*

### Early Christianity

◆ *What were the origins of Christianity, and how did it fare among the other religions of the Roman world?*

# Augustus and the Principate, 31 B.C.–A.D. 68

*How did Augustus establish a new imperial government to replace the Roman Republic? Why was he so successful?*

**Augustus** Honorific title of Gaius Julius Caesar Octavianus, whose forty-five-year rule laid the foundations of two hundred years of prosperous Roman peace.

In 31 B.C., Gaius Julius Caesar Octavianus (63 B.C.–A.D. 14), or Octavian, as **Augustus** was then known, stood at the top of the Roman world. His forces had defeated those of Mark Antony and Cleopatra at the Battle of Actium in northwestern Greece, whereupon his two chief enemies committed suicide. Few could have predicted the vision and statesmanship that Octavian now displayed. He spent the next forty-five years healing the wounds of a century of revolution. He did nothing less than lay the foundations of the prosperous two centuries enjoyed by the empire under the Roman peace (see **Map 6.1**).

## The Political Settlement

Octavian was both astute and lucky. That is, if the length and violence of the civil wars can be called luck. After Actium, most of Octavian's enemies were dead, so establishing the one-man rule that he claimed was necessary to restore stability was relatively easy. He was also fortunate to live to be nearly 80—he had plenty of time to consolidate his rule. He was a cagey man and a sharp judge of others. Octavian learned the lesson of Caesar's greatest mistake. He understood that the Roman elite, however weakened, was still strong enough to oppose a ruler who flaunted monarchical power. To avoid a second Ides of March, therefore, Octavian was infinitely diplomatic.

Historians accurately call Octavian Rome's first emperor, but he avoided terms like emperor or dictator. Instead, Octavian took the title of *princeps* (PRIN-keps) ("first citizen"), an old title of respect in the senate. From *princeps* comes **Principate** (PRIN-sih-pate), a

**Principate** The constitutional monarchy of the Early Roman Empire, from 31 B.C. to A.D. 192.

🌐 **Map 6.1 The Roman World in the Early Empire** Many modern cities are built on the sites of Roman foundations, evidence of the immense extent of the Roman Empire at its height. © Cengage Learning 2014 term often used to describe the constitutional monarchy of the "Early Empire," the name that historians have given to the period from 31 B.C. to A.D. 192. Four years after Actium, in 27 B.C., the senate granted Octavian the honorific title *augustus*, symbolizing the augmentation, or increase, of his authority. He was also known as *Caesar* and *divi filius* ("son of a god"), which tied him to Julius Caesar. Another name, *imperator* ("commander" and, later, "emperor"), recalled the military might that Augustus (as we shall henceforth call him) could call on, if needed.

In 27 B.C., Augustus proclaimed "the transfer of the state to the free disposal of the senate and the people"—that is, the restoration of the Republic. Remembering similar claims by Sulla and Julius Caesar, few Romans were likely to believe this, and few would have wanted the Republic restored in any case. They, no doubt, appreciated their ruler's tact, however.

Two strokes of genius marked the new regime. First, Augustus held power without monopolizing public office. He held the civil authority of the tribunate without being a tribune and the military authority of provincial generals without holding a specific command. Generalships remained open to ambitious men as long as they accepted Augustus's power. Second, the new government divided the provinces between Augustus and the senate. To check any new would-be Caesar, Augustus kept for himself the frontier provinces, with the main concentration of armies, as well as grain-rich Egypt (which Rome had annexed after Actium). The local commanders were loyal equestrians who owed their success to Augustus. Most of the other provinces continued to be ruled as before, by senators serving as governors.

Augustus wanted advice without dissent. He used the senate, or rather a committee of senators and magistrates, as a sounding board; the group evolved into a permanent advisory body. Ordinary senate meetings, however, lost their old freedom of speech because of informers and the emperor's secret agents. The popular assemblies fared even worse, as their powers were limited and eventually transferred to the senate. Nor would unruly crowds be tolerated. Augustus established the city of Rome's first police force and also stationed there his own personal guard. Called the praetorians (pre-TOR-ee-unz), or Praetorian Guard, the name used for a Roman general's bodyguard, the guard would play a crucial role in future imperial politics.

More important for the public good, Augustus established the first civil service, consisting of a series of prefectures—or departments—supervising, for example, the city watch, the grain supply, the water supply, the building of roads and bridges, tax collection, and the provisioning of the armies. Equestrians and freedmen were prominent in these prefectures and in provincial government, so they enthusiastically supported the Principate.

Although one may speak loosely of "imperial bureaucracy," neither Augustus nor his successors ever established a tight administrative grip on their far-flung empire. As in all ancient empires, Roman government tended to be decentralized and limited. In an age in which few public officials received a salary, bribes were winked at.

## The Economic and Social Settlement

The old Roman ruling class made its peace with Augustus, but some never forgave him for ending their ancient privileges. The conservative historian Tacitus (TASS-ih-tus) (ca. A.D. 55–117) looked back wistfully to the Late Republic as a golden era of freedom, eloquence, and "the old sound morality." Even Tacitus, however, was forced to admit that most people in the Roman world welcomed and admired the Principate. The reason is simple: Augustus and his successors brought peace and prosperity after a century of disasters under

| CHRONOLOGY | |
|---|---|
| 31 B.C. | Octavian defeats Antony and Cleopatra at Actium |
| 27 B.C. | Augustus establishes Principate |
| 14 B.C.–A.D. 68 | Julio-Claudian dynasty |
| 19 B.C. | Death of Virgil |
| ca. A.D. 27–30 | Ministry of Jesus |
| ca. 67 | Death of Paul of Tarsus |
| 69–96 | Flavian dynasty |
| 70 | Temple in Jerusalem destroyed |
| 79 | Eruption of Vesuvius |
| 96–180 | The "Five Good Emperors" |
| ca. 117 | Death of Tacitus |
| 193–235 | Severan dynasty |
| ca. 200 | Mishnah and New Testament each completed |
| 212 | Almost all free inhabitants of empire awarded Roman citizenship |
| 235–284 | Period of military anarchy |

the Late Republic. The Augustan period enjoyed affluence, especially in Italy; the other provinces caught up with Italy by the second century A.D. Agriculture flourished with the end of civil war. Italian industries became leaders in exports. Italian glass bowls and windowpanes, iron arms and tools, fancy silver eating utensils and candlesticks, and bronze statues and pots circulated from Britain to central Asia.

The city of Rome's urban poor, many of them freedmen, enjoyed a more efficient system of free grain distribution under Augustus and a large increase in games and public entertainment—the imperial policy of "bread and circuses" designed to content the masses. Augustus also set up a major public works program, which provided jobs for the poor. He prided himself on having found Rome "a city of brick" and having left it "a city of marble."

The perennial problem of the Late Republic had been land-hunger, which drove peasants into the arms of ambitious generals. Augustus kept his troops happy by compensating 300,000 veterans with land, money, or both, often in new overseas colonies. At first, he paid from his own private sources; after A.D. 6, he made the rich pay via new taxes. The result kept the peace, but many nonsoldiers in Italy remained poor, as of course, did the huge number of slaves.

As for the renegade commanders who had bedeviled the Late Republic, Augustus cut their potential power base by reducing the size of the army, gradually cutting the number of legions from over sixty to twenty-eight. The total size of the army, including light infantry and cavalry, was about 300,000. This reduction lightened Rome's tax burden but left Augustus with little room to expand the empire. In A.D. 9, Rome lost three legions to a native revolt against Rome's plan to extend its rule in Germany as far east as the Elbe River. Short of manpower, Augustus had to accept the Rhine River as Rome's new German frontier (see **Map 6.1**).

Imperial defense remained a major issue. Strong Roman armies were a necessity along the hostile European frontier. On the friendlier border in western Asia and northern Africa, Augustus and his immediate successors set up client kingdoms, such as Judea and Armenia, to protect Roman territory.

To promote his ideology of renewal, Augustus sponsored social legislation embodying the old Republican virtues. He passed a series of laws encouraging marriage and childbearing and discouraging promiscuity and adultery. Such legislation was so flagrantly disobeyed that in 2 B.C., Augustus made an example of his own daughter, Julia (39 B.C.–A.D. 14), his only child, whose adulteries were the talk of Rome. As punishment, she was banished to a barren islet.

Augustus's era marks the beginning of the classical period of Roman jurisprudence, during which the professionalism that had begun to mark Roman law in the Late Republic became a permanent fact. It was probably Augustus who established the practice, followed by later emperors, of granting a few distinguished jurists the exclusive right to issue legal opinions "on behalf of the princeps." He ensured, therefore, that experts guided the administration of justice. The first law school was opened in Rome under Augustus. Roman jurists adapted Roman law to the practices of the provinces. Although various local legal systems remained in use, the international system of Roman law was also used widely in the provinces.

In religion, too, Augustus was a legislator and reformer. He restored once-neglected cults and temples in order to appear as Rome's savior. He would probably have approved when, after his death, he was deified, just as Julius Caesar had been. Even while he was still alive, Augustus was worshiped in the provinces as a god—in both the East, where the cult of Roma and Augustus grew in popularity, and the West, where centers of emperor-worship were established at the sites of Lyon and Cologne (see **Map 6.1**). The imperial cult, an important part of state propaganda until the empire became Christian in the fourth century A.D., was well underway.

Deification, whether formal or informal, was a heady brew, but Augustus deserved it more than most. He not only ended the Late Republican era of civil wars but also established the Roman Empire on a completely new footing. Republican freedom was gone, much to the distress of the elite, but the emperor and bureaucrats brought stability. The peace of the Augustan Principate would last, with few interruptions, for two hundred years. Few people in history have created order so successfully. (See the feature, "The Written Record: Two Views of Augustus.")

## Two Views of Augustus

*Shortly before dying in A.D. 14, the emperor Augustus arranged for the display of an official record, "the achievements of the Divine Augustus, by which he brought the world under the empire of the Roman people, and of the expenses which he bore for the state and people of Rome." Copies were exhibited around the empire. Writing nearly a century later, the historian Tacitus (ca. A.D. 56–after 117) offered a scathing view.*

### The Achievements of the Divine Augustus

**1.** At the age of nineteen on my own responsibility and at my own expense I raised an army, with which I successfully championed the liberty of the republic when it was oppressed by the tyranny of a faction. . . .

**3.** I undertook many civil and foreign wars by land and sea throughout the world, and as victor I spared the lives of all citizens who asked for mercy. 3. [sic] The Roman citizens who took the soldier's oath of obedience to me numbered about 500,000. I settled rather more than 300,000 of these in colonies or sent them back to their home towns after a period of service; to all these I assigned lands or gave money as rewards for their military service. . . .

**20.4.** In my sixth consulship I restored eighty-two temples of the gods in the city on the authority of the senate, neglecting none that required restoration at the time. . . .

**26.** I extended the territory of all those provinces of the Roman people on whose borders lay peoples not subject to our government. . . .

**27.** I added Egypt to the empire of the Roman people. . . .

**28.** . . . I compelled the Parthians to restore to me the spoils and standards of three Roman armies and to ask as suppliants for the friendship of the Roman people. Those standards I deposited in the innermost shrine of the temple of Mars the Avenger. . . .

**35.** In my thirteenth consulship the senate, the equestrian order and the whole people of Rome gave me the title of Father of my Country, and resolved that this should be inscribed in the porch of my house and in the Curia Julia and in the Forum Augustum below the chariot which had been set there in my honor by decree of the senate. 2. At the time of writing I am in my seventy-sixth year.

## Tacitus

Famous writers have recorded Rome's early glories and disasters. The Augustan Age, too, had its distinguished historians. But then the rising tide of flattery exercised a deterrent effect. . . . So I have decided to say a little about Augustus, with special attention to his last period, and then go on to the reign of Tiberius and what followed. I shall write without indignation or partisanship: in my case the customary incentives to these are lacking.

The violent deaths of Brutus and Cassius left no Republican forces in the field. Defeat came to Sextus Pompeius in Sicily, Lepidus was dropped, Antony killed. So even the Caesarian party had no leader left except the "Caesar" himself, Octavian. He gave up the title of Triumvir emphasizing instead his position as consul; and the powers of a tribune, he proclaimed, were good enough for him—powers for the protection of ordinary people.

He seduced the army with bonuses, and his cheap food policy was successful bait for civilians. Indeed, he attracted everybody's goodwill by the enjoyable gift of peace. Then he gradually pushed ahead and absorbed the functions of the senate, the officials, and even the law. Opposition did not exist. War or judicial murder had disposed of all men of spirit. Upper-class survivors found that slavish obedience was the way to succeed, both politically and financially. They had profited from revolution, and so now they liked the security of the existing arrangement better than the dangerous uncertainties of the old regime. Besides, the new order was popular in the provinces. There, government by Senate and People was looked upon skeptically as a matter of sparring dignitaries and extortionate officials. The legal system had provided no remedy against these, since it was wholly incapacitated by violence, favoritism, and—most of all—bribery.

### Questions

1. *According to Augustus, what were his greatest achievements?*

2. *How does Tacitus undercut Augustus's praise of himself?*

3. *Which account do you find more convincing and why?*

Sources: P. A. Brunt and J. M. Moore, eds., *Res Gestae Divi Augusti: The Achievements of the Divine Augustus*, pp. 19–37. Copyright © 1967 Oxford University Press. By permission of Oxford University Press. *Tacitus, The Annals of Imperial Rome*, rev. ed., trans. Michael Grant (Harmondsworth, England: Penguin, 1988), p. 32.

## The Culture of the Augustan Age

Like *Periclean*, the adjective *Augustan* (aw-GUS-tin) has come to signify an era of literary and artistic flowering. In both periods, strong elements of classicism shaped the arts—that is, an attempt to project heroic and idealized values, the values that the rulers of each epoch wished to promote. Both prose and poetry flourished under Augustus. The emperor and his

**Mosaic of the Doves**
This exquisite mosaic shows a number of doves drinking from or positioned around a gilded bronze basin on a marble pedestal. Derived from a Hellenistic work from Pergamum, this mosaic comes from a wealthy house in Pompeii.
Scala/Art Resource, NY

**Virgil** Roman poet whose works, including the *Aeneid*, contributed to the Augustan renewal.

friends were patrons of a number of important poets, chief among them Virgil (70–19 B.C.) and Horace (65–8 B.C.). The historian Livy (59 B.C.–A.D. 17), who wrote his history of Rome from the founding of the city to 9 B.C. under Augustus, also elicited the princeps's interest. All three writers contributed to the Augustan renewal and rededication of Rome.

In many ways, **Virgil** (VER-jill) speaks for his contemporaries. In the *Eclogues*—poems that, following an Alexandrian model (see pages 98–99), have rustic settings—Virgil describes the miseries of the civil wars and the blessings of peace under Augustus. "A god created this peace for us; for he will always be a god to me," one character says. In the Fourth Eclogue, Virgil speaks of the birth of a child to usher in a restored Golden Age. At the Council of Nicaea in A.D. 325 (see page 174) and later, this poem was given a Christian interpretation. In the *Georgics*, Virgil describes the glories of Italian agriculture, which, thanks to Augustus, could be practiced peacefully again.

Virgil's masterpiece is an epic poem, the *Aeneid* (ee-NEE-id), "the story of Aeneas," the legendary Trojan founder of Rome, or at least of the Latin town from which Rome's founders eventually came. Legend also makes Aeneas the ancestor of Augustus. Thus, the *Aeneid* indirectly celebrates Augustus, often considered Rome's second founder. The poem explores the pain and burden, as well as the glory, of empire.

If Virgil's work has the grandeur of marble, Horace's poems—*Odes*, *Epodes*, *Satires*, *Epistles*, and *Ars Poetica* (*Art of Poetry*)—are more like finely cut gems. They tend to be polished, complex, and detached. Like Virgil, Horace explores the themes of war and peace and praises Augustus. "With Caesar [Augustus] holding the lands, I shall fear neither turmoil nor violent death," declares one of the *Odes*. Both Horace and Virgil successfully adapted Greek models and, in the process, created something new. Few writers have had a greater influence on the later Western literary tradition.

Only 35 of the original 142 books of Livy's ambitious history have survived. Livy (LIV-ee) is both a master storyteller and a superb ironist. His anecdotes of Roman history are vivid and told in a grand rhetorical style. Livy is our major source for the Roman monarchy and Early Republic, although his account of early Rome is long on myth and short on fact. Nevertheless, Livy is not merely an entertaining stylist; he engages in frank, subjective judgments intended to inspire both patriotism and reflection on the ironies of history.

Augustus's circle also supported the poets Ovid, best known for works on love and mythology; Tibullus, an elegist; and his ward, Sulpicia. Although little survives of Sulpicia's work, more of her work exists than of any other Roman woman. She describes her passion for one Cerinthus: "a worthy man . . . at last a love . . . of such a kind that my shame, Gossip, would be greater if I kept it covered than if I laid it bare."*

Augustus and his entourage were also great patrons of the arts and of architecture, which they considered propaganda tools. They sponsored many major building projects throughout the empire, especially in Rome, which gained temples, a new Forum of Augustus, the Theater of Marcellus, the Baths of Agrippa, the Pantheon, and the Mausoleum of Augustus.

## The Julio-Claudians

**Livia** Wife of Augustus, she was suspected of poisoning several family members, including Augustus himself.

Under Augustus and his successors, most Romans enjoyed the benefits of stable, effective, and peaceful government. The emperors presented their household to the world as the ideal family, the very model of social order. Behind the walls of the palace, however, dwelt a troubled reality.

*Mary R. Lefkowitz and Maureen B. Fant, trans., *Women's Life in Greece & Rome: A Source Book in Translation*, 2d ed. (Baltimore: Johns Hopkins University Press, 1992), p. 9.

Augustus had only one child, Julia, from his first marriage, which ended in divorce. In 38 B.C., Augustus took as his second wife **Livia** (58 B.C.–A.D. 29), who divorced her husband to marry Augustus, even though she was pregnant with their second son. Livia (LI-vee-uh) did not bear Augustus children. Seeking a male successor, Augustus used Julia as a pawn in a game of dynastic marriage, divorce, and remarriage, but to no avail. Julia's first two husbands both predeceased her, as did two sons, each of whom Augustus had adopted. (In Rome, it was common for a man without a birth son to adopt a son.) In the end, Augustus was forced to choose as successor, and adopt, a man he disliked, Tiberius (ty-BEER-ee-us) (42 B.C.–A.D. 37), Livia's elder son.

Livia was among the most powerful women in Roman history. One of Augustus's main advisers, she pursued her own agenda brutally but deftly in order to secure the succession for Tiberius. Livia's enemies accused her of poisoning many people, including Julia's husbands and sons; her own grandson, Germanicus (a brilliant general whose popularity threatened Tiberius's); and even Augustus himself, who died in bed after a short illness in A.D. 14.

From A.D. 14 to 68, Rome was ruled by other emperors from Augustus's family. The dynasty, known as the **Julio-Claudians**, consisted of Augustus's step-son Tiberius, great-grandson Caligula, grandnephew Claudius, and great-great-grandson Nero. For many elite Romans, this era was one of decadence, scandal, and oppression of the old nobility, but ordinary people continued to enjoy good government.

The reign of Tiberius (r. 14–37) was later remembered by the elite for its treason trials and murders. The senate complained as it steadily lost power to the princeps. The Roman masses grumbled because Tiberius cut back on games and building projects. But despite his shortcomings, Tiberius was a skilled and prudent administrator. He wisely drew back from war on the borders, reduced taxes and spending, and promoted honesty among provincial governors.

His successor, his nephew Gaius (r. 37–41), nicknamed Caligula (ca-LIG-yoo-luh) ("Baby Boots," after the boots he had worn as a little boy in his father's army camp), humiliated the senate. It was bad enough that he tried to have himself declared a living god. On top of that, he appointed his favorite horse not only high priest of a new cult in his honor but also a member of the senate. Caligula raised taxes and accused people of treason in order to confiscate property. He wanted to have his statue erected in the Temple at Jerusalem, and he would have done so, but he was assassinated first, the victim of a high-level conspiracy. After his death, the senate debated restoring the Republic, but it was not to be.

Caligula's uncle, Claudius, was named emperor by the Praetorian Guard, which forced the senate to support him. Physically handicapped, Claudius (r. 41–54) was often the butt of jokes, but he was a man of substance: a historian, politician, and priest and someone fully versed in the cunning ways of his family. An activist emperor, he expanded the imperial offices with their powerful freedmen; oversaw the construction of an artificial harbor at Rome's silt-clogged port of Ostia; and conquered Britain, where Roman arms had not intervened since Julius Caesar's forays in 55 to 54 B.C.

Claudius's death may have been the result of poisoning by his wife, who was also his niece, Agrippina (a-grip-PIE-nuh) the Younger (15–59); in any case, her son by a previous marriage, Nero, became emperor (r. 54–68). Nero's scandalous behavior rivaled Caligula's, and his treason trials outdid Tiberius's. After a great fire destroyed half of Rome in 64, Nero mounted a big rebuilding program, including a 300-room villa for himself, and was accused of having started the fire. He found a scapegoat for the fire in the members of a small religious sect, the Christians,

**Julio-Claudians** Dynasty of Roman emperors founded by Augustus and ruling from A.D. 14 to 68.

Courtesy, Mondadori Electa S.P.A.

**Agrippina the Younger** This statue shows the mother of the emperor Nero praying. It is carved in basanite, a stone whose use is typical of the imperial Roman taste for art objects in exotic materials.

## SECTION SUMMARY

- Augustus, Rome's first emperor, shared a degree of power with the senate, while keeping the armies firmly under his control.
- Augustus gave Rome its first civil service and first police force; he gave Italy prosperity; he began to raise the status of the provinces.
- Augustus reduced military spending and compromised with Rome's enemies in order to stabilize the frontiers.
- The poets Virgil and Horace and the historian Livy are among the great writers of the flourishing culture of Augustan Rome.
- Although they included such scandalous figures as Nero, the Julio-Claudian emperors (A.D. 14–68) delivered peaceful and effective government.

whom he persecuted. Ordinary Romans supported Nero because he gave them good government. He was unpopular with the senators and, more serious, with the army, because he failed to pay all his troops promptly. Confronted with a major revolt in 68, Nero committed suicide.

The next year, 69, witnessed Rome's first civil war in about a century. Three men claimed the imperial purple after Nero. A fourth, Vespasian (ves-PAY-zhun) (Titus Flavius Vespasianus, r. 69–79), commander of the army quelling a revolt in the province of Judea, was able to make his claim stick. Peace was restored, but not the rule of Augustus's family. Vespasian founded a new dynasty, the Flavians (r. 69–96), which was followed in turn by the Nervo-Trajanic (r. 96–138) and Antonine (r. 138–192) dynasties. The ultimate tribute to Augustus may be that his regime was stable enough to survive the extinction of his family.

# The Roman Peace and Its Collapse, A.D. 69–284

*What was life like in the era of the Roman peace? Why did peace end during the third century A.D.?*

Much about Rome in the second century A.D. appears attractive today. Within the multiethnic empire, opportunities for inhabitants to become part of the elite were increasing. The central government was on its way to granting Roman citizenship to nearly every free person in the empire, a process completed in the year 212. The emperors emphasized sharing prosperity and spreading it through the provinces. Italy was no longer the tyrant of the Mediterranean, but merely first among equals. To be sure, rebellions were crushed, but few people rebelled. This period, known as the **pax Romana**, or "Roman peace," seems particularly golden in contrast with what followed: the disastrous and disordered third century A.D., in which the empire came close to collapse but survived because of a radical and rigid transformation.

## The Flavians and the "Good Emperors"

**pax Romana** Latin for "Roman peace," the term refers to the period of peace and prosperity in the Roman Empire from A.D. 69 to 180.

**Flavian** Dynasty of the Roman emperors Vespasian, Titus, and Domitian, whose rule was a time of relative peace and good government.

The **Flavian** dynasty of Vespasian (r. 69–79) and his sons Titus (r. 79–81) and Domitian (r. 81–96) provided good government, and their successors built on their achievements. Unlike the Julio-Claudians, Vespasian hailed not from the old Roman nobility but from an equestrian family from an Italian town. A man of rough-and-ready character, Vespasian is supposed to have replied when Titus complained that a new latrine tax was beneath the dignity of the Roman government, "Son, money has no smell." Unlike his father and brother, Domitian reverted to frequent treason trials and persecution of the aristocracy, which earned him assassination in 96, although the empire as a whole enjoyed peace and sound administration under his reign.

The so-called Five Good Emperors are Nerva (r. 96–98), Trajan (r. 98–117), Hadrian (r. 117–138), and the first two Antonines, Antoninus Pius (r. 138–161) and Marcus Aurelius (r. 161–180). They exemplify the principle of merit. Trajan, a Roman citizen born in Spain, was Rome's first emperor from outside Italy. Hadrian and Marcus Aurelius also came from Spain, and Antoninus Pius from Gaul. Each of the Five Good Emperors, except Marcus Aurelius, adopted the most competent person, rather than the closest relative, as his son and successor, thus elevating duty over sentiment. Marcus Aurelius, a deeply committed Stoic, gave full vent to his sense of duty in his *Meditations*, which he wrote in Greek while living in a tent on the Danube frontier, where he fought long and hard against German raids. Antoninus was surnamed "Pius" (Dutiful) because he was devoted to his country, the gods, and his adoptive father, Hadrian.

The Five Good Emperors made humaneness and generosity the themes of their reigns. Trajan, for example, founded a program of financial aid for the poor children of Italy. They also went to great lengths to care for the provinces. These emperors not only commonly received petitions from cities, associations, and individuals in far-off provinces, but also answered them. Yet, humaneness does not mean softness. Hadrian, for instance, ordered a revolt in Judea (132–135) to be suppressed with great brutality.

Like the Julio-Claudians, the Five Good Emperors advertised their wives to the world as exemplars of traditional modesty, self-effacement, and domesticity. In fact, they were often worldly, educated, and influential. Trajan's wife, Plotina, for example (d. 121 or 123), acted as patron of the Epicurean school at Athens, whose philosophy she claimed to follow. She advised her husband on provincial administration as well as dynastic matchmaking. Hadrian's wife, Sabina, traveled in her husband's entourage to Egypt (130), where her aristocratic Greek friend, Julia Balbilla, commemorated the trip by writing Greek poetry, which she had inscribed alongside other tourists' writings on the leg of one of two statues of Amenhotep III at Thebes.

A darker side of the second-century empire was the problem of border defense. Augustus and the Julio-Claudians had established client kingdoms, where possible, to avoid the expense and political dangers of raising armies. The emperors of the day tended to be more aggressive on the borders than their predecessors. They moved from client kingdoms to a new border policy of stationary frontier defense. Expensive fortification systems of walls, watchtowers, and trenches were built along the perimeter of the empire's border and manned with guards. A prominent example is Hadrian's Wall, which separated Roman Britain from the enemy tribes to the north. Stretching 80 miles, the wall required fifteen thousand defense troops.

The most ambitious frontier policy was that of Trajan, who crossed the Danube to carve out the new province of Dacia (modern Romania) and who used an excuse to invade Parthian Mesopotamia. He won battles as far away as the Persian Gulf, but he lost the war. As soon as his army left, Mesopotamia rose in revolt, followed by Germany. Trajan's reign marked the empire's greatest geographic extent, but Trajan had overextended Rome's resources. When he died, his successor, Hadrian, had to abandon Trajan's province of Mesopotamia (see **Map 6.1**).

## Prosperity and Romanization in the Provinces

Compared with a modern economy, the Roman economy was underdeveloped. Most people worked in agriculture, employed primitive technology, and lived at a subsistence level. Even so, the Roman Empire experienced modest economic growth during the first two centuries A.D. The chief beneficiaries were the wealthy few, but ordinary people shared in the economic expansion. In addition to stability and peace, several other factors encouraged economic development. The western provinces witnessed the opening of new lands to agriculture, where improved techniques were applied, thereby meeting increased agricultural demand from the growing cities of the region. Changes in Roman law aided commerce by making

Scala/Art Resource, NY

**Double Portrait, Pompeii**  This wall painting from a house joined to a bakery depicts a married couple, possibly the wealthy baker P. Paquius Proculus and his wife. The portraiture is realistic. The couple carries symbols of education: She holds wax tablets and a stylus (pen), while he grasps a sealed scroll.

it easier to employ middlemen in business transactions. Travel and communications were relatively easy and inexpensive.

## Prosperity

Trade boomed, as an archaeological discovery in the Italian city of Pisa (PEE-zuh) recalls. Nineteen Hellenistic and Roman ships were found at the site of the ancient harbor, beginning in 1999. Several are merchant ships, both coastal freighters and small harbor craft. One of the ships was filled with amphoras (storage jars), still stacked in neat rows and filled with wine and sand. Both of those goods came from the region of the Bay of Naples, whose sand was used for concrete that could set underwater. The finds, which seem to date from the mid-second century A.D., offer a vivid picture of trade along the coast of Italy. When the cargo was unloaded at Pisa, the ships probably picked up the local grain and marble, which was shipped in turn to Rome.

Rome was an economic magnet, but so, to a lesser extent, were all cities, and the second century A.D. was a great age of city life. New cities were founded far from the Mediterranean. They began as veterans' colonies, market towns, and even army camps, and some grew into cities of permanent importance in European history: Cologne (Colonia Claudia Agrippinensis), Paris (Lutetia Parisiorum), Lyon (Lugdunum), London (Londinium), Mérida (Emerita Augusta), Vienna (Vindobona), and Budapest (Aquincum).

Whether old or new, cities attracted large elite populations. In the Principate, ambitious people wanted to live in great cities, in emulation of the greatest city of the empire, Rome, which was by Augustus's day a city of perhaps a million people. In cities, men competed for positions as magistrates, in imitation of the two consuls, or for seats on the local town council, often called a *curia* (KYOO-ree-uh), like the senate in Rome. Town councilors were called *decurions* (day-KYOO-ree-uns) and known collectively as the *curial order*. Decurions played one-upmanship in sponsoring public buildings in the Roman style—one man endowing a new forum, another a triumphal arch, a third a library, a fourth an amphitheater, and so on. From Ephesus in Anatolia to Colchester in Britain, from Mainz in Germany to Leptis Magna in Libya, a Roman could find familiar government institutions, architecture, and street plans.

Unlike men, women did not usually hold magistracies, but wealthy women of the empire could and did lavish money on public projects. Women endowed temples and synagogues, amphitheaters and monumental gateways, games and ceremonies. They were rewarded with wreaths, front-row seats, statues, priesthoods, and inscriptions honoring them as "most distinguished lady," "patron," and even "father of the city."

## Romanization

The buildings were visible examples of Romanization, although the Romans did not use the term. If they had, it would have had a limited meaning because the emperors neither would nor could impose a cultural uniformity on their subjects. The empire was too big and ancient technology too primitive for that. The total population of the empire consisted of between 50 million and 100 million people, most of whom lived in the countryside. The small and largely urbanized Roman administration had little direct contact with most people. So, for example, only a minority of the inhabitants of the empire spoke Latin; in the East, Greek was the more common language of administration. Millions of people spoke neither Greek nor Latin. Celtic, Germanic, Punic, Tamazight (Berber), Coptic, Aramaic, and Syriac were other common languages in Roman domains. In short, the empire lacked the unity of a modern nation-state.

What, then, besides buildings and language might "Romanization" entail? One index has already been suggested: the participation of provincials in the central government, even as emperor. By around A.D. 200, for example, about 15 percent of the known Roman equestrians and senators came from North Africa. By this time, the senate was no longer dominated by Italians but was representative of the empire as a whole.

Participation in government implies another index of Romanization—the extension of Roman citizenship outside Italy to magistrates, decurions, or even whole cities. Citizens took Roman names reflecting the emperor or Roman official who had enfranchised them. Thus, the provinces were full of Julii, Claudii, and Flavii, among others.

The spread of Roman customs is another measure of Romanization. For example, the gladiatorial shows that Romans loved became popular from Antioch to England. Combats between gladiators advertised both Roman culture and Roman brutality. (See the feature, "The Visual Record: Gladiators" on pages 154–155.)

By the same token, native customs might be adopted by Romans. Consider the case of Egypt, where, in the late 1990s, archaeologists discovered a vast Roman-era cemetery about 230 miles southwest of Cairo, in the Bahriya Oasis. The population was Romanized here. Yet, the cemetery, with its dozens of gilded mummies from the first and second centuries A.D., shows the persistence of the mummification processes of the pharaohs.

Another ambiguous symbol of Romanization is found in A.D. 212. In a law known as the *Constitutio Antoniana*, the emperor Caracalla (r. 211–217) rendered nearly all of the free inhabitants of the empire Roman citizens. On the one hand, the law is a historical landmark. Near-universal Roman citizenship was a kind of halfway point between ancient empire and modern mass democracy. On the other hand, the *Constitutio Antoniana* was something of a gimmick. It was probably less an instrument of unification than of taxation, for citizens had a heavier tax burden than noncitizens.

The Roman army, by contrast, did promote Romanization. In antiquity, as today, military service offered education and social mobility. Only citizens could join the legions; non-Romans served as auxiliaries. They received Roman citizenship after completing their regular term of service, twenty-five years. Non-Italians had, and took, the opportunity to rise high in the army or government. This was all to Rome's credit. Yet, as Italians became a minority in the Roman army, and as ever larger numbers of frontier peoples were recruited, it became conceivable that someday the army might abandon its loyalty to Rome.

## Roman Law on Class and Marriage

Roman law is one of the ancient world's most influential and enduring legacies. Logical, practical, orderly, and—within the limits of a society of patriarchal fathers and of slaves and masters—relatively fair, Roman law has influenced the legal systems of most Western countries and many non-Western countries. The law governing Roman citizens was called *ius civile*, or "civil law." Originally, this term covered a very broad range of legal matters, but in the empire its meaning was narrowed to private matters. Criminal law became a separate category.

The law helped Rome administer its empire. Roman law was not universal, and noncitizens continued to use their own laws for local matters, but the governors used Roman law to run their provinces, so local elites became familiar with it. Like so many Roman customs, the law was both hierarchical and flexible. Let us consider two areas in which the law affected daily life: class and marriage.

The law reflected Roman society's ingrained social inequality. Traditional classes, such as senators and equestrians, survived to be joined by the new distinction between citizens and noncitizens. Even when all free people became Roman citizens, another important division maintained class distinctions: the division between *honestiores* (in general, the curial order) and *humiliores* (everyone else). Previously, Roman citizens enjoyed certain privileges, such as exemption from flogging by officials, but now citizens who were *humiliores* tended to lose those privileges.

The most basic legal distinction was that between free and slave—and the empire contained millions of slaves. A third category, ex-slaves or freedmen, also became increasingly important.

A slave's lot depended largely on circumstance. It was generally easier being a city slave than a country slave. A good master could make all the difference in a slave's life. Unlike slaves in the American South, quite a few Roman slaves could save money to buy their freedom. And yet, the cruelty of Roman slavery must not be forgotten, as these words of advice to masters from a first-century A.D. manual remind us: "It should be an established custom for the landowner to inspect the slaves chained in the prison, to examine whether they are securely chained, whether their quarters are safe and well guarded, whether the foreman has put anyone in chains or released anyone from chains without his master's knowledge. . . ."*

---

*Jo Ann Shelton, *As the Romans Did: A Sourcebook in Social History*, 2d ed. (New York: Oxford University Press, 1998), p. 169.

**Roman Slaves**
This first-century A.D. wall painting from Herculaneum, Italy, shows Roman ladies with their slave hairdressers. Note the elaborate hairstyle of the seated woman.

Scala/Art Resource, NY

Freedmen owed service to their former masters, who became their patrons. A few freedmen grew rich in commerce or wielded enough power in imperial administration to lord it over even Roman aristocrats. The result was strong elite hostility toward freedmen, which is often reflected in Roman literature. Witness the stereotype of the vulgar freedman, embodied in Trimalchio in the *Satyricon* (suh-TEER-uh-con), a novel by Petronius (first century A.D.). Trimalchio had more estates than he could remember and so much money that his wife counted it by the bushel-load.

As regards marriage, Roman family law was strict and severe in principle. In practice, however, it often proved pragmatic and even humane. Most Roman women married without legally becoming members of their husbands' families—or their children's. Yet, society recognized a woman's wish to leave her property to her children, and imperial law increasingly made it possible for her to do so. Roman law gave slaves no right to marry, and it made slave children the property of the owner of the slave mother. Yet, during the Early Empire, the law conceded that slave children owed devotion and loyalty (*pietas*) to their slave parents.

Career soldiers, from at least the time of Augustus on, could not marry, probably on the grounds of military discipline. Yet, many soldiers cohabited anyhow, often with noncitizen women in the areas where they served, and frequently, children were the result. Not until the reign of Septimius Severus (SEH-ver-us) (r. 193–211) were soldiers permitted to marry formally, and then, only after twenty-five years of service. Yet, commanders had permitted cohabitation for two centuries, and the law too made concessions now and then.

## The Culture of the Roman Peace

In Latin poetry, the century or so after the death of Augustus (roughly A.D. 18–133) is often referred to as the "Silver Age," a term sometimes applied to prose as well. The implication is that this period, though productive, fell short of the golden Augustan era. It might be fairer to say that the self-confidence of the Augustan writers did not last. As the permanence of monarchy became clear, many in the elite looked back to the Republic with nostalgia and bitterness. Silver Age writing often takes refuge in satire or rhetorical flourish.

The Silver Age was an era of interest in antiquities and in compiling handbooks and encyclopedias; it was also an era of self-consciousness and literary criticism. In the first two centuries A.D., Roman writers came from an ever greater diversity of backgrounds and wrote for an ever wider audience, as prosperity and educational opportunities increased.

Many writers of the era pursued public careers, which offered access to patronage. The historian **Tacitus**, for instance, became governor of the province of Asia. Prominent literary families emerged, such as that of Pliny (PLIH-nee) the Elder (A.D. 23–79), an encyclopedic author on natural science, geography, history, and art; and his nephew, Pliny the Younger (ca. A.D. 62–ca. 113), an orator and letter writer. The most notable literary family is that of Seneca the Elder (ca. 55 B.C.–A.D. 40), a historian and scholar of rhetoric; his son, Seneca the Younger (ca. 4 B.C.–A.D. 65); and Seneca the Younger's nephew, the epic poet Lucan (A.D. 39–65).

Born in Cordoba, Spain, the younger Seneca moved at an early age to Rome, where he became a successful lawyer and investor. He was banished in A.D. 41 for alleged adultery with a sister of Caligula. Recalled in 49, he was tutor to the young Nero. When Nero became emperor in 54, Seneca became one of his chief advisers and helped bring good government to the empire. Seneca eventually fell out of favor, however, and was forced first into retirement and then, in A.D. 65, into suicide. He had been the major literary figure of his age, a jack-of-all-trades: playwright, essayist, pamphleteer, student of science, and noted Stoic philosopher.

**Tacitus** Roman historian of the "Silver Age," his greatest works were *The Histories* and *The Annals*.

A literary career was safer under the Five Good Emperors. Consider Tacitus and his contemporary, the poet Juvenal (JOO-veh-nal) (ca. A.D. 55–130). Juvenal's *Satires* are bitter and brilliant poems offering social commentary. He laments the past, when poverty and war had supposedly kept Romans chaste and virtuous. Amid "the woes of long peace," he says, luxury and foreign ways had corrupted Rome. Like many a critic who blames society's troubles on marginal groups, Juvenal launches harsh attacks on women and foreigners. Tacitus, too, is sometimes scornful of women.

Yet, if he is biased on matters of gender, Tacitus is far from ethnocentric. Few historians have expressed graver doubts about the value of their country's alleged success. For example, Tacitus highlighted the simple virtues of the Germanic tribes, so different from the sophisticated decadence of contemporary Rome. Nostalgia for the Republic pervades his two greatest works, *The Histories*, which covers the civil wars of A.D. 69, and *The Annals* (only parts of which survive), chronicling the emperors from Tiberius through Nero. A masterpiece of irony and pithiness, Tacitus's style makes an unforgettable impression on the reader.

Plutarch (PLOO-tark) (ca. A.D. 50–120), whose *Parallel Lives of Noble Greeks and Romans* later captured the imagination of Shakespeare, is probably the best-known pagan writer of the first two centuries A.D. Plutarch was a Roman citizen from Greece who wrote in Greek. Like Livy, Plutarch emphasizes the moral and political lessons of history. A careful scholar, Plutarch found his true calling in rhetorical craftsmanship—polished speeches and carefully chosen anecdotes. As in Rome, rhetoric was the basis of much of Greek literary culture in this period.

Another star of Greek culture at this time was the physician Galen of Pergamum (A.D. 129–?199). In his many writings, Galen (GAY-len) was to medicine what Aristotle had been to philosophy: a brilliant systematizer and an original thinker. He excelled in anatomy and physiology and proved that the arteries, as well as the veins, carry blood. He was destined to have a dominant influence on European medicine in the Middle Ages.

## The Crisis of the Third Century, A.D. 235–284

Leaving the relative calm of the second century A.D. behind, the third-century Roman Empire descended into crisis. Barbarian invasions, domestic economic woes, plague, assassinations, brigandage, urban decline—the list of Rome's problems is dramatic. The empire went "from a kingdom of gold to one of iron and rust," as one writer put it, summing up Roman history after the death of Marcus Aurelius in 180, when the seeds of the **third-century crisis** were sown.

Stability first began to slip away during the reign of the last of the Antonines, Marcus Aurelius's birth son, Commodus (KOM-uh-dus) (r. 180–192), a man with Nero's taste for

**third-century crisis** Period from A.D. 235 to 284, when the Roman Empire suffered barbarian invasions, domestic economic problems, plague, assassinations, and urban decline.

**Hadrian's Wall** Built in A.D. 122–126, this extensive structure protected Roman England from raids by the tribes of Scotland. It represents the strategy of stationary frontier defense.
Roy Rainford/Robert Harding World Imagery

## Gladiators

Gladiators were literally men who carried a gladius, or sword. They fought to the death as entertainment, and they enraptured the Roman Empire.

Gladiators took part in so-called games or combat before large crowds. The audience, seated in rank order, ranged from slaves to senators to the emperor himself. There was nothing tame about what they had come to see. Consider the word *arena*, referring to the site of the games. It literally means "sand," which is what covered the floor—and soaked up the blood.

Our fascination with the gladiator is nothing compared to the Romans'. At **Pompeii**, graffiti celebrated a star of the arena whom "all the girls sigh for." Gladiatorial images decorated art around the empire, from mosaics to household lamps.

Look at this mosaic from a Roman villa in Germany, one of several mosaic panels on the floor of the building's entrance hall, depicting scenes from the arena. The illustration shows a *retiarius*, or net-and-trident bearer, fighting a better-armed *secutor*, literally "pursuer," under the watchful eyes of a *lanista*, or trainer. As was typical, the retiarius wears no armor except for a shoulder piece protecting his left side. To defend himself against the dagger wielded by the secutor (in the mosaic, hidden behind the shield), the retiarius had to be fit enough to be able to keep moving. The difference between various types of gladiators would have been as obvious to a Roman as the difference between a catcher and a pitcher is to a baseball fan today.

As for the amphitheaters where gladiatorial combats took place, they were common in Italy and in the western Roman Empire. Look, for example, at this photograph of the amphitheater in the city of El Djem in modern Tunisia (the

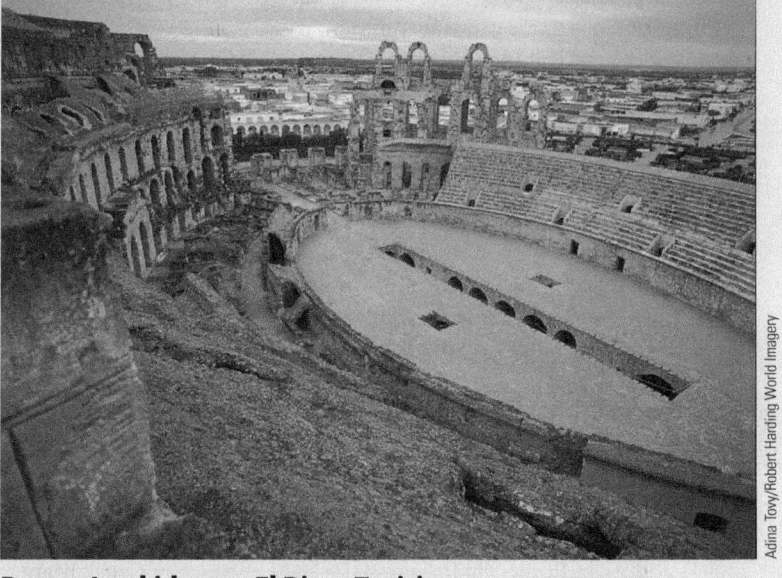

**Roman Amphitheater, El Djem, Tunisia**

Adina Tovy/Robert Harding World Imagery

Roman province of Africa). Built of high-quality local stone in the third century A.D., the structure was meant to have sixty-four arches, but it was never completed. The openings in the floor permitted animals to be released into the arena. A large amphitheater like this one held at least thirty thousand spectators, and the largest amphitheater of all, the Flavian Amphitheater—or Colosseum—at Rome, seated around fifty thousand. Amphitheaters were less common in the east, but the fans there also were loyal, so the games went on—in theaters.

Most gladiators were condemned criminals, prisoners of war, or slaves bought for the purpose. The most famous slave gladiator was Spartacus, a Thracian. Along with seventy-seven other gladiators in the Italian city of Capua, Spartacus instigated a slave rebellion that attracted thousands and shook Italy for two years (73–71 B.C.); see also page 135.

---

**Pompeii** Italian city destroyed in a volcanic eruption in A.D. 79; the ruins of Pompeii offer the best evidence of life in a Roman city in the era of the Roman Peace.

**Sassanids** A Persian dynasty (A.D. 224–651) that greatly strengthened Persian power and threatened Roman rule in western Asia.

decadence and penchant for terrorizing the senatorial elite. His predictable assassination led to civil war, after which Septimius Severus, commander of the Danube armies, emerged as the unchallenged emperor (r. 193–211). He founded the Severan dynasty, which survived until 235.

Severan reformers attempted to reestablish the empire on a firmer footing, but they only brought the day of crisis nearer. The main theme of Septimius's reign was the transfer of power—from the senate to the army and from Italy to the provinces. To extend the Roman frontier in North Africa and western Asia, Septimius expanded the army and improved the pay and conditions of service. These measures might have been necessary, but Septimius went too far by indulging in war with Parthia (197–199)—unnecessary war because the crumbling Parthian kingdom was too weak to threaten Rome. What the war did accomplish, however, was to inspire the enemy's rejuvenation under a new Eastern dynasty, the **Sassanids** (SASS-uh-nids).

The Sassanid Persians spearheaded increased pressure on Rome's frontiers. The Sassanids overran Rome's eastern provinces and captured the emperor Valerian himself in

**Gladiator Mosaic, Nennig, Germany**

Every gladiator took an oath to endure being burned, bound, beaten, and killed by the sword. They began each combat by greeting the official in charge (in Rome, the emperor) in this way: "We who are about to die salute you."

The games were brutal, but so was the empire. The arena kept Romans tough and warlike, or so an intellectual could argue, as does Pliny the Younger, who describes gladiatorial games:

"[The games] inspired a glory in wounds and a contempt of death, since the love of praise and desire for victory could be seen, even in the bodies of slaves and criminals" (*Panegyric* 33).

Arguably, the arena also contributed to public order. This was no small achievement, since the imperial army could not police a population of 50 million to 100 million, and few places had even the elementary police force that the city of Rome did. The violence that bloodied the amphitheater stepped into the breach by reminding criminals—or those defined as criminals—what punishment awaited them. Refuse to worship the emperor, and you might be fed to the lions, as Christians were from time to time. Rebel against Rome, and you might find yourself on a chain gang building a new amphitheater, as tradition says thirty thousand prisoners of the First Jewish Revolt (A.D. 66–70) did. The result was the Colosseum.*

Occasionally pagan, as well as Christian, writers condemned gladiatorial games. Yet, so popular was Rome's theater of power that gladiators and their games were not abolished until around A.D. 400.

## Questions

1. *What does the scene on the mosaic show, and what does it indicate about the Roman public's interest in gladiators?*

2. *What were the main features of the amphitheater at El Djem?*

3. *How might gladiatorial games have contributed to public order in the Roman Empire?*

---

* The preceding two paragraphs lean heavily on the fine discussion in Colin Wells, *The Roman Empire*, 2d ed. (Cambridge, Mass.: Harvard University Press, 1995), pp. 248–255.

260. (See the feature, "The Global Record: Syria Between Rome and Persia" on page 158.) The caravan city of Palmyra (in Syria) took advantage of Rome's weakness to establish independence; its most famous leader was the queen Zenobia. Meanwhile, three Germanic tribes, the Alamanni, the Franks, and the Goths, hammered the empire from the north.

Fending off invasions at opposite fronts stretched Rome to the breaking point. To pay for defense, the emperors devalued the currency, but the result was massive inflation. As if this were not bad enough, a plague broke out in Egypt at midcentury and raged through the empire for fifteen years, compounding Rome's military manpower problems.

Assassinations and civil wars shook the stability of the government. Between 235—when the last Severan emperor, Severus Alexander, was murdered—and 284, twenty men were emperor, however briefly in some cases. Civilians suffered in the resulting disorder.

Yet, the empire rebounded, which is a tribute to Roman resilience as well as a sign of the disunity and lack of staying power among the empire's enemies. Recovery began during

## SECTION SUMMARY

- The Flavian dynasty (A.D. 69–96) and the so-called Five Good Emperors (96–180) brought Rome a long era of stability and good government.

- A modest prosperity, an upturn in trade, and a flourishing city life all characterized the Roman Empire of the first two centuries A.D.

- Most of the empire's 50 to 100 million inhabitants lived in the countryside and had little contact with Rome, but the urban elite often adopted Roman ways.

- Pragmatic, orderly, and relatively fair, Roman law is one of antiquity's great legacies.

- The historian Tacitus, the poet Juvenal, the essayist and scholar Plutarch, and the man of letters and philosophy Seneca the Younger are among the great writers of Rome's so-called Silver Age.

- Invasions, plague, inflation, crime, and political assassination were among the many woes that made the third century A.D. a period of crisis for the Roman Empire.

the reign of Gallienus (r. 253–268), who instituted a series of reforms. Gallienus excluded senators from high military commands and replaced them with professionals. Moreover, he began a new, more modest policy of border defense. The Romans now conceded much of the frontier to the enemy and shifted to a defensive mode: Fortified cities near the frontier served as bases from which to prevent deeper enemy penetration into Roman territory. They also concentrated mobile armies at strategic points in the rear, moving them where needed. Thanks to his new policies, Gallienus inflicted defeats on the Alamanni and the Goths. By 275, Aurelian (r. 270–275) had checked the Goths decisively and reconquered the eastern provinces, including Palmyra.

Gallienus's new military and border policies pointed the way to imperial reorganization, but they remained to be completed by the two great reforming emperors at the end of the third century and the beginning of the fourth: Diocletian (r. 284–305) and Constantine (r. 306–337), subjects of the next chapter. When their work was done, the new Roman Empire of Late Antiquity might have been barely recognizable to a citizen of the Principate.

# Early Christianity

*What were the origins of Christianity, and how did it fare among the other religions of the Roman world?*

Increasing contact between Rome and its western provinces served to plant Roman cities, Roman law, and the Latin language (or its derivatives) in western Europe. As Rome, in turn, owed much to other Mediterranean peoples, so the Roman Empire transported ancient Mediterranean civilization to northern and western Europe. No feature of that civilization was to have a greater historical impact than the religion born in Tiberius's reign: Christianity.

Christianity began in the provincial backwater of Palestine among the Jews, whose language, Aramaic, was understood by few in Rome. It immediately spread to speakers of the two main languages of the empire, Greek and Latin, and the new movement addressed the common spiritual needs of the Roman world. By the reign of Diocletian, Christians had grown from Jesus's twelve original followers to perhaps millions, despite government persecution (see **Map 6.2** on page 162). In the fourth century A.D., Christianity unexpectedly became the official religion of the entire Roman Empire, replacing polytheism—one of the most momentous changes in Mediterranean history. We turn to that change in the next chapter; here we consider the career of Jesus and the early spread of the Christian Gospel (literally, "Good Tidings"). But first, to set the stage, we look at other religions of the Roman Empire.

## Mystery Religions

The Romans were polytheists. They did not try to impose one religion on the empire. Instead, Romans were usually willing to accept new gods, as long as their worshipers took part in the patriotic emperor cult. New religions spread widely during the first three centuries A.D. Besides Christianity and Judaism, the most important religions were Greek mystery cults, the cults of Isis and Mithras, and Manichaeism. These religions displayed a tendency toward syncretism, often borrowing rites, doctrines, and symbols from one another.

Greek mystery cults included the cults of Dionysus, the god of wine, and of Demeter, the goddess of grain, who was worshiped at annual ceremonies at Eleusis, a town outside Athens. The "mystery" consisted of secret rites revealed only to initiates. In the case of Demeter, the rites apparently had something to do with the promise of eternal life.

The cult of Isis derived from the ancient Egyptians' worship of Isis (see page 107), her brother and husband, Osiris, and their son, Horus. Like the cult of Demeter, its central theme was eternal life, through resurrection achieved by moral behavior in this life. Isis, the "Goddess of Ten Thousand Names," was portrayed as a loving mother, and elements of Isis were later syncretized in the cult of the Virgin Mary. Isis's followers marched in colorful, and at times terrifying, parades through Roman streets, flagellating themselves as a sign of penitence.

Although men joined in the worship of Isis, the cult appealed particularly to women. The goddess's popularity crossed class lines; devotees ranged from slaves to one Julia Felix, whose estate at Pompeii included a garden shrine to Isis and Egyptian statuettes. By contrast, the worship of Mithras (MYTH-rus) was dominated by men, and especially by soldiers. Mithras, a heroic Persian god of light and truth, also promised eternal life. His worshipers believed that Mithras had captured and killed a sacred bull, whose blood and body were the source of life. Accordingly, Mithraism focused on bull sacrifice carried out in a vaulted, cave-like temple called a *Mithraeum*. Initiates were baptized with bull blood and participated in various other rituals, among them a sacramental meal. Their moral code advised imitating the life of their hero.

Manichaeism (MAN-ih-kee-izm) also originated in Persia, but later, in the third century A.D. Its founder, the Persian priest Mani, was martyred by conservative religious authorities. Manichaeism attempted to be the true synthesis of the religious beliefs of the period, recognizing not only Jesus, but also Zoroaster and Buddha, as prophets. The main tenet of Manichaeism was philosophical dualism, which emphasized the universal struggle between good (light) and evil (darkness). According to believers, the world had been corrupted by Darkness, but eventually the Light would return. In the meantime, good Manichaeans were to attempt to lead pure lives. Manichaeism was a powerful religious force for two centuries, and its believers were spread as far as India. The great theologian Augustine even flirted with it before becoming a Christian.

A new philosophy that developed in the same intellectual world as these Roman religions was Neo-Platonism (nee-oh-PLAY-ton-ism), which was founded by Plotinus (ploh-TIE-nus) (A.D. 209–270). Using the works of Plato as a starting point, Plotinus developed a philosophy in which the individual could first seek inner unity and then achieve oneness with the supreme unity of what Plotinus called the One or the Good. By this, he meant an intangible and impersonal force that is the source of all values. Like the mystery cults, Plotinus's philosophy promised a kind of salvation. Neo-Platonism was destined to have a great influence on Western thought.

## Jesus of Nazareth

Christianity begins with **Jesus of Nazareth**. For all its historical importance, Jesus' life is poorly documented. The main source of information about it is the New Testament books of Matthew, Mark, Luke, and John. Jesus left no writings of his own. Early Christians, however, wrote a great deal. Between the second and fourth centuries A.D., Christians settled on a holy book consisting of both the Hebrew Bible, called the "Old Testament" by Christians, and a collection of writings about Jesus and his followers, called the "New Testament." The four **Gospels** provide commanding accounts, but they do not agree on all details. The Gospel according to Mark, probably the earliest Gospel, was most likely written about forty years after Jesus' crucifixion; several of the letters written by Paul of Tarsus (see pages 161–163) date from the 40s A.D.; and the earliest non-Christian sources are later in date and are scanty.

No personality has generated as much discussion among Western scholars as has Jesus. Many would distinguish the Jesus of theology, the object of faith, from the Jesus of history, the man who really lived in first-century Palestine. Recent work argues that the historical

## Syria Between Rome and Persia

Rome and Persia fought three great battles in western Asia in A.D. 244, 252, and 260, all resounding victories for Persia under King Shapur I (r. ca. 241–272). In the first selection Shapur celebrates his success in an inscription carved in rock near Persepolis. The second selection provides a Greek view of what Syria's inhabitants endured when Shapur "burned, ruined and pillaged" in A.D. 252. It comes from the Thirteenth Sibylline Oracle, a verse commentary on contemporary events, purporting to be ancient prophecy.

### The Persian Inscription

I, the Mazda worshipping lord Shapur, king of kings of Iran and non-Iran, whose lineage is from the Gods....

When at first we had become established in the empire, Gordian Caesar raised in all of the Roman Empire a force from the Goth and German realms and marched on Babylonia against the Empire of Iran and against us. On the border of Babylonia at Misikhe, a great "frontal" battle occurred. Gordian Caesar was killed and the Roman force was destroyed. And the Romans made Philip Caesar. Then Philip Caesar came to us for terms, and to ransom their lives, gave us 500,000 denars, and became tributary to us....

And Caesar lied again and did wrong to Armenia. Then we attacked the Roman Empire and annihilated at Barbalissos a Roman force of 60,000 and Syria and the environs of Syria we burned, ruined and pillaged all. In this one campaign we conquered of the Roman Empire fortresses and towns...a total of 37 towns with surroundings.

In the third campaign when we attacked Carrhae and Urhai [Edessa] and were besieging Carrhae and Edessa Valerian Caesar marched against us. He had with him a force of 70,000....

And beyond Carrhae and Edessa we had a great battle with Valerian Caesar. We made prisoner ourselves with our own hands Valerian Caesar and the others, chiefs of that army, the praetorian prefect, senators; we made all prisoners and deported them to Persis.

And Syria, Cilicia and Cappadocia we burned, ruined and pillaged....

And men of the Roman Empire, of non-Iranians, we deported. We settled them in the Empire of Iran....

We searched out for conquest many other lands, and we acquired fame for heroism, which we have not engraved here, except for the preceding. We ordered it written so that whoever comes after us may know this fame, heroism, and power of us.

### The Sibylline Oracle

...the evil Persians....

...the Persians, arrogant men....

...the arrow-shooting Persians...Now for you, wretched Syria, I have lately been piteously lamenting; a blow will befall you from the arrow-shooting men, terrible, which you never thought would come to you. The fugitive of Rome will come, waving a great spear; crossing the Euphrates with many myriads, he will burn you, he will dispose all things evilly. Alas, Antioch, they will never call you a city when you have fallen under the spear in your folly; he will leave you entirely ruined and naked, houseless, uninhabited; anyone seeing you will suddenly break out weeping....

Alas...they will leave ruin as far as the borders of Asia, stripping the cities, taking the statues of all and razing the temples down to the all-nourishing earth.

### Questions

1. According to Shapur's inscription, what were Rome's misdeeds toward Persia? According to the Sibylline Oracle, what were Persia's misdeeds toward Rome?

2. How did Persia retaliate, according to Shapur's inscription and according to the Sibylline Oracle? How and why do the two accounts differ?

3. Which account do you find more convincing? Why?

Sources: From History of Ancient Iran, translated by Richard N. Frye, Emeritus Professor of Iranian History, Harvard University (Munich: C.H. Beck'sche Verlagsbuchhandlung, 1984). Reprinted by permission of Richard N. Frye; From D.S. Potter, trans., Prophecy and History in the Crisis of the Roman Empire (Oxford: Clarendon Press, 1990), p. 175.

Jesus must be understood within the Judaism of his day—or rather the Judaisms, because it was an era of debate and disagreement about how to be a Jew. Within two centuries, the lines hardened. By A.D. 200, two new religions had emerged: Orthodox Christianity and **rabbinic Judaism**. The proponents of both religions claimed to be the rightful heirs of the biblical covenant. However, in Jesus' day, that outcome could hardly have been foreseen.

## The Jewish Background

**rabbinic Judaism** Main form of Judaism, which emerged during the first century A.D. under the leadership of the rabbis. It clarified Jewish practice, elevated the oral law to equal authority with the written Torah, and enabled Judaism to evolve flexibly.

Jesus was born a Jew. A speaker of Aramaic, he may also have known at least some Greek, widely spoken by both Jews and non-Jews in the several Hellenized cities of Palestine. To his followers, Jesus was Christ—"the anointed one" (from the Greek Christos), the man anointed with oil and thus marked as the king of Israel. They considered him the Messiah (from the Hebrew for "anointed one"), foretold in the Hebrew Bible, who would redeem the children of Israel and initiate the kingdom of heaven. The popularity of his teachings led to a clash with Jewish and Roman authorities in Jerusalem, the capital city of Judea, and to his execution. His mission began, however, in a corner of the Jewish world, in the northern region of Galilee (GAL-uh-lee), where he lived in the town of Nazareth (NAZ-uh-reth) (see inset, **Map 6.2)**. Jesus was probably born not long before the death in 4 B.C. of Herod, the Roman-installed client-king of Judea. (The date of A.D. 1 for Jesus's birth, a mistaken calculation of Late Antiquity, does not accord with the data in the New Testament.) At around age 30, Jesus was baptized by the mysterious preacher John the Baptist. Soon afterward, Herod Antipas, the Romans' client-king of Galilee, ordered the execution of John. John had preached that God's kingdom was about to arrive—a time of universal perfection and an end of misery. In preparation, sinful humankind needed to repent. Just how much influence John had on Jesus is a matter of debate.

The most popular group among Palestinian Jews, the Pharisees, focused on the spiritual needs of ordinary folk (see page 108). The Pharisees believed that the written law of the Hebrew Bible was supplemented by oral tradition, as interpreted by generations of Jewish sages and scholars. They saw themselves as the guardians of that tradition. The Pharisees emphasized charity toward the poor and spoke in parables—vivid allegories that made their teaching accessible.

Another movement within Judaism at the time was Essenes, who lived apart from society in pursuit of a new covenant with God. The community at Qumran in the Judean desert, whose history is documented in the Dead Sea Scrolls, ancient texts discovered in 1947, was probably Essene. The tenets of Qumran included frugality, sharing, participating in a sacred communal meal, and avoiding oath-taking. Adherents anticipated the coming of the Messiah and an end of days in which God would punish the wicked.

## Jesus' Teaching

There are both similarities and differences between Jesus' teaching and contemporary doctrines of Palestinian Judaism. Like the Essenes, he spoke of the Messiah, but he did not withdraw from the world as the Essenes did; instead, Jesus immersed himself in it. Like the Pharisees, Jesus strongly criticized the pillar of the Jewish establishment, the Sadducees, the priests and wealthy men who saw the Temple at Jerusalem and its rites as the heart of Judaism. Also like the Pharisees, Jesus rejected the growing movement of the Zealots (ZELL-ots), advocates of revolt against Roman rule, although there were Zealots among his followers. Unlike the Pharisees, however, Jesus believed that he could interpret the Hebrew Bible on his own authority, without the consent of the sages and scholars of Jewish tradition. Jesus rejected the need to follow the letter of Jewish law. Inward purity became the key principle, as reflected in Jesus' statement to his disciples (that is, his close followers): "Whoever does not accept the kingdom of God like a child will never enter it" (Mark 10:15). Only an adult could become expert in Jewish law, but it is probably easier for a child than for an adult to attain spiritual innocence.

Jesus argued that the kingdom of God, which John the Baptist had said was coming soon, was actually already beginning to arrive. Moreover, Jesus said that he himself, acting through the direct order of God, could forgive sins. He said, "the Son of Man has authority on earth to forgive sins" (Mark 2:10). He emphasized the notion of God as a loving and forgiving father. He often spoke in parables and announced himself through miracles, particularly faith healing. He welcomed marginalized groups, including prostitutes and lepers.

Jesus' teaching is typified in the Sermon on the Mount, addressed to his many followers in Galilee. He praised the poor and the humble and scorned the pursuit of wealth instead of righteousness. "Blessed are the poor in spirit;/the kingdom of Heaven is theirs" (Matthew 5:3). He called for generosity and forgiveness, recalling the traditional Jewish golden rule—to treat others as one would like to be treated. He said that prayer, fasting, and acts of charity should be conducted in private, not in public, in order to emphasize purity of motive. He called on his followers to endure persecution in order to spread his teachings: "You are light for all the world," he told them (Matthew 5:14).

Jesus spoke with conviction and persuasiveness—with "authority," as his followers said. He traveled from place to place; in Galilee, they greeted him as king. For some, this was a purely spiritual designation; others planned an overthrow of Roman rule, although Jesus rejected that course of action. In any case, his teachings won him hostility from some Pharisees, who considered his claim of authority to be heretical and his claim to be able to forgive sins blasphemous, and from Sadducees stung by his criticisms. Neither group accepted Jesus as the Messiah. It should be emphasized, nevertheless, that most of Jesus' followers were Jewish.

## Jesus in Jerusalem

Jesus challenged central authority by going to Jerusalem and teaching and healing in the Temple under the eyes of the men whom he criticized. Nor did he confine his opposition to words: He drove merchants and moneychangers away from the Temple precincts by overturning their tables and perhaps even threatening them with a whip. Jesus attracted large crowds of followers, at least some of whom were armed. Jewish authorities feared trouble, and so did the overlords of Judea, the Romans. The governor, Pilate (Pontius Pilatus), had already endured vehement Jewish objections to the display in Jerusalem of an imperial medallion and of an inscription that seems to have asserted Augustus's divinity. Pilate had no need of further uproar. Temple police and Roman soldiers were called on to arrest Jesus quietly.

Jesus' subsequent trial and execution have always been controversial. The New Testament emphasizes the role of the Jewish leadership and the Jerusalem mob in Jesus' death. Written after the First Jewish Revolt (A.D. 66–70), however, the Gospels may reflect anti-Jewish sentiment in the empire. Crucifixion, the method used to execute Jesus, was a Roman penalty (the traditional Jewish method was stoning), and Jesus was executed by Romans, not Jews. Jesus probably appeared in informal and hurried proceedings before both the Jewish Council and Pilate. He suffered slow death by crucifixion on Golgotha

**Mithras Sacrificing the Bull, Copy of a Roman Original (stone)** This sculpted relief comes from an underground sanctuary along the Rhine frontier (in modern Germany). It shows the hero-god Mithras sacrificing a bull, the central symbol of Mithraism. Actual bull sacrifices were carried out in a temple known as a Mithraeum. Saalburgmuseum, Romerkastell-Saalburg, Hessen, Germany/ Bildarchiv Steffens/The Bridgeman Art Library

(Calvary) Hill, just outside the city. It was a spring Friday, on the eve of the Passover festival, around A.D. 30.

## Paul of Tarsus

According to the Gospel writers, Jesus died on a Friday and rose from the dead on Sunday, an event commemorated by Christians at Easter. He is said to have then spent forty days on earth, cheering and commissioning his disciples in Galilee and working miracles, before finally ascending to heaven. Heartened, the disciples returned to Jerusalem and spread Jesus' teachings.

### The Apostles of Jesus

Jesus' followers preached in synagogues, private households, and even the Temple, and to speakers of Greek as well as of Aramaic. The "Jesus Movement," as many scholars today refer to it, spread, in the 30s and 40s A.D., throughout Palestine and into Syria. In Jerusalem, members of the movement were known as Nazarenes—that is, followers of Jesus of Nazareth; it was at Antioch in Syria that they were first called "men of Christ" (*christianoi*).

The leaders of the Jesus Movement were known as apostles, from the Greek *apostolos*, "one who is sent" and who enjoys the authority of the sender. The apostles believed that Jesus had sent them and given them authority. The apostles included Jesus' original followers, or disciples. The most prominent disciple was Peter, a Galilean fisherman whom Jesus endowed with particular authority. According to a reliable tradition, Peter eventually went to Rome, whose church he headed and where he died as a martyr in A.D. 64.

### Paul's Faith

It was not clear at first that Christians would form a new religion separate from Judaism. Although the Sadducees and Jewish civil officials were hostile, Christians found much support among the Pharisees. Some Christians, however, contemplated a radical break; among them no one was more important than **Paul of Tarsus** (d. A.D. 67?). Only Jesus himself played a greater role than Paul in the foundation of Christianity. A remarkable figure, Paul embodied three different and interlocking worlds. Born with the name of Saul, he was a Jew of the Diaspora from the southern Anatolian city of Tarsus. Paul was a native speaker of Aramaic and knew Hebrew and Greek. His father was one of the few Jews to attain Roman citizenship, a privilege that Paul inherited. Paul's heritage speaks volumes about the multiethnic and multicultural nature of the Roman peace, and his religious odyssey speaks volumes more (see **Map 6.2**).

At first, Paul joined in the persecution of the Christians, whom he considered blasphemous. Around A.D. 36, however, he claimed to see a blinding light on the road to Damascus, a vision of Jesus that convinced him to change from persecutor to believer. It was a complete turnaround, a *conversio* ("conversion"), to use the Latin word that would grow so important in years to come. Saul changed his name to Paul and became a Christian.

He also changed what being a Christian meant. The key to Paul's faith was not so much Jesus' life, although that was a model for Christian ethics, as it was Jesus' death and resurrection. Jesus' fate, Paul wrote, offered all humanity the hope of resurrection, redemption, and salvation. Paul retained his belief in Jewish morality and ethics but not in the rules of Jewish law. Following the law, no matter how carefully, would not lead to salvation; only faith in Jesus as Messiah would.

Such doctrines bespoke a break with Judaism, as did Paul's attitudes toward converts. Hellenistic Judaism had long reached out to Gentiles. Some became Jews. Others remained Gentiles: Scattered throughout the cities of the Roman Empire, they were known as "God-fearers"—that is, they accepted the moral teachings of Judaism but refrained from following strict dietary laws, circumcision, and other Jewish rituals. Seneca the Younger, writing in the 60s, complains about the spread of Judaism: "The customs of this accursed race have gained such influence that they are now received throughout the world."*

**Paul of Tarsus** Christian apostle and saint, under whom Christianity began its complete separation from Judaism.

---

*Seneca, "De Superstitione," trans. Menachem Stern, in *Greek and Latin Authors on Jews and Judaism*, vol. 1 (Jerusalem: Israel Academy of Sciences and Humanities, 1976), p. 431.

🌐 **Map 6.2 The Expansion of Christianity to A.D. 200** After its origin in Palestine, early Christianity found its main centers in the Greek-speaking cities of the Roman East. Missionaries such as Paul also brought the new faith to the Latin-speaking West, as well as to Ethiopia and Mesopotamia. © Cengage Learning 2014

The Jerusalem church baptized converts and considered them Jews, but Paul considered them not Jews but, rather, converts in Christ. For Pauline Christians, circumcision, dietary laws, and strict observance of the Sabbath were irrelevant. From the late 40s to the early 60s A.D., Paul tirelessly undertook missionary journeys through the cities of the Roman East and to Rome itself. He aimed to convert Gentiles, and so he did, but many of his followers were Hellenized Jews and "God-fearers."

## Judaism

Paul started Christianity on the road to complete separation from Judaism. Events over the next century widened the division. First, while Pauline churches prospered, departing ever more from Jewish customs, the Jerusalem church was decimated. Jewish authorities persecuted its leaders, and after Rome's suppression of the First Jewish Revolt and destruction of the Jerusalem Temple in A.D. 70, the rank and file of Palestinian Jews rallied to the Pharisees. Second, Jews and Christians, competing for converts, emphasized their respective differences. Third, although many Jews made their peace with Rome in A.D. 70, enough Jewish-Roman hostility remained to lead to uprisings in the Diaspora in 115 and to the Second Jewish Revolt in 132 to 135. Both were suppressed mercilessly by Rome, and Judaism became ever more stigmatized among Gentiles.

Bereft of the Temple at Jerusalem, Judaism nonetheless thrived as a religion. The rabbis, the religious leaders of the Pharisees, kept Judaism alive. After both A.D. 70 and 135, the Romans made the rabbis responsible for Jewish self-government in Palestine but Roman persecutions continued. The rabbis left their mark on history, however, not in administration, but in an intellectual movement. Continuing in the tradition of the Pharisees, the rabbis emphasized the notion of the "dual Torah," elevating the oral law to equal authority with the written law of the Hebrew Bible.

Because of the fragility of the Jewish community under the Romans, the rabbis decided to write the oral law down for the first time. The basic text of rabbinic Judaism is the Mishnah (MISH-nuh) (ca. A.D. 200), a collection of the oral law. During the next three centuries, rabbis would compile commentaries and analysis of the Mishnah in a collection known as the Gemara. Together, the Mishnah and the Gemara comprise the Talmud, which, for rabbinic Judaism, is the essence of the oral law. In rabbinic Judaism lies the basis of the medieval and modern forms of the Jewish religion.*

**The Good Shepherd**
This ceiling painting comes from a Christian catacomb in Rome dating before A.D. 284. The pastoral image, common in the early church, recalls Christ's ministry. It symbolizes both his beneficence and his sacrifice, as well as his closeness to ordinary people. Scala/Art Resource, NY

## Expansion, Divergence, and Persecution

Although Jesus' mission was mainly in the countryside, early Christianity quickly became primarily an urban movement. Through missionary activity and word of mouth, the religion slowly spread. It was concentrated in the Greek-speaking East, but by the second century A.D., Christian communities dotted North Africa and Gaul and, beyond Roman boundaries, appeared in Parthian Iraq and in Ethiopia (see **Map 6.2**).

By around A.D. 200, an orthodox (Greek for "right thinking") Christianity had emerged. Rooted in Judaism, it was nonetheless a distinct and separate religion that found most of its supporters among Gentiles. A simple "rule of faith," emphasizing the belief in one God and the mission of his son, Jesus, as savior, united Christians from one end of the empire to the other. Christianity attracted both rich and poor, male and female; its primary appeal was to ordinary, moderately prosperous city folk. Believers could take comfort from the prospect of salvation in the next world and in a caring community in the here and now. Christians emphasized charity and help for the needy, even for strangers; Greco-Roman society rarely helped those outside of the family. A Christian writer justly described a pagan's amazed comment on Christian behavior: "Look how they love each other." Most early Christians expected Christ's return—and the inauguration of the heavenly kingdom—to be about to happen.

Early churches were simple and relatively informal congregations that gathered for regular meetings. The liturgy, or service, consisted of readings from the Scriptures (the Old and New Testaments), teaching, praying, and singing hymns. Baptism was used to initiate converts. The Lord's Supper, a communal meal in memory of Jesus, was a major ritual. The most important parts of the meal were the breaking and distribution of bread at the beginning

**Christianity** Sect originally rooted in Judaism that emerged as a fully separate religion by around A.D. 200. It emphasized belief in one God and the mission of his son, Jesus of Nazareth, as savior.

*See Lawrence H. Schiffman, *From Text to Tradition: A History of Second Temple and Rabbinic Judaism* (Hoboken, N.J.: Ktav Publishing House, 1991), pp. 1-16.

and the passing of a cup of wine at the end; these recalled the body and blood of Christ. As organizational structures emerged (see pages 173–175), churches in different cities were in frequent contact with one another, discussing common concerns and coordinating doctrine and practice.

Just as Jewish women were not rabbis, so early Christian women did not hold the priesthood. Jewish women, however, did hold office in the synagogue, and Christian women likewise served as deaconesses. Both endowed buildings and institutions. For example, consider the Italian Jewish woman Caelia Paterna, an officeholder honored by her congregation as "mother of the synagogue of the people of Brescia." Or the two Christian deaconesses, both slaves, whom Pliny the Younger tortured during his governorship of the Anatolian province of Bithynia (buh-THIN-ee-uh) in about A.D. 110 in an attempt to extract information about the worrisome new cult. Deaconesses played an active part in church charities and counseling and could also preach sermons.

As Christianity spread, its troubles with the authorities deepened. For one thing, Christians met in small groups, a kind of assembly that conservative Romans had long suspected as a potential source of sedition. More troubling, however, was Christians' refusal to make sacrifices to the emperor. The Romans expected all subjects to make such sacrifices as a sign of patriotism. The only exception was the Jews, who were permitted to forgo the imperial cult because their ancestral religion prohibited them from worshiping idols. The Christians, however, were a new group, and the Romans distrusted novelty.

As a result, the emperors considered Christianity at best a nuisance and at worst a threat. Christians were tested from time to time by being asked to sacrifice to the emperor; those who failed to do so might be executed, sometimes in the arena. More often, however, the Romans tacitly tolerated Christians as long as they kept their religion private. As the emperor Trajan wrote about Christians to a provincial governor, "No search should be made for these people."* Christians could not proselytize in public places, put up inscriptions or monuments, or build churches. Christianity thus spread under severe restrictions, but spread it did, particularly in the cities of the East. The willingness of martyrs to die for the faith made a strong impression on potential converts. Although the number of Christians in the empire is not known, it is clear that by the late third century, they were a significant and growing minority.

## SECTION SUMMARY

- The cult of Demeter, the cult of Isis, Mithraism, and Manichaeism are among the mystery religions that spread in the Roman Empire during the first three centuries A.D.

- Jesus was born a Jew and was hailed by his followers as the Messiah, or redeemer, foretold in the Hebrew Bible.

- Jesus' teachings emphasized purity of soul, humility, charity, and the endurance of persecution to spread the word.

- Paul of Tarsus played an enormous role in spreading faith in Jesus outside the Jewish world, but Christianity took a long time to separate from its Jewish roots.

- By around A.D. 200, Orthodox Christianity had emerged as a systematic set of beliefs and a fully distinct religion from Judaism.

- The Roman peace provided the conditions for the spread of Christianity.

---

*Pliny the Younger, Correspondence. Translated by William Melmoth, revised by W.M.L. Hutchinson. Loeb Classical Library. (Cambridge, Mass.: Harvard University Press, 1915), slightly modified.

# Chapter Summary

◆ *How did Augustus establish a new imperial government to replace the Roman Republic? Why was he so successful?*

The Roman Republic collapsed under the weight of political maneuvering, judicial murders, gang skirmishes, and civil war. A shrewd and sickly outsider, Octavian, confounded expectations by creating a new empire that would enjoy two centuries of stability; as Augustus, he served as its first emperor. Augustus reconciled the senatorial class by sharing a degree of power, but he guaranteed peace by keeping most of the armies in his own hands. He wisely reduced military spending and compromised with Rome's enemies to stabilize the frontiers. He solved the problem of rebellious soldiers by raising taxes to provide farms for veterans. Perhaps most important, he began a new policy toward the provinces, which were slowly raised to equality with Italy. In short, Augustus initiated the prosperous Roman peace. Under imperial patronage, culture flourished in the Augustan Age, including such writers as Virgil, Horace, and Livy. Augustus's successors, the Julio-Claudian emperors, included scandalous figures like Nero, but nevertheless, they delivered peaceful and effective government.

◆ *What was life like in the era of the Roman peace? Why did peace end during the third century A.D.?*

The Flavian dynasty (A.D. 69–96) and the so-called Five Good Emperors (96–180) brought Rome a long era of stability and good government. In the provinces, the Roman peace made possible an era of architectural and literary flowering. It was a prosperous era, but not for everyone, as slavery remained widespread. Rome was a multiethnic empire whose inhabitants increasingly mixed with one another and exchanged ideas. Latin literature flourished in its so-called Silver Age, and so did the practical and relatively fair-minded system that was Roman law, one of antiquity's greatest legacies. The Roman peace did not last forever: invasions, plague, inflation, crime, and political assassination were among the many woes that made the third century A.D. a period of crisis for the Roman Empire.

◆ *What were the origins of Christianity, and how did it fare among the other religions of the Roman world?*

The cult of Demeter, the cult of Isis, Mithraism, and Manichaeism are among the mystery religions that spread in the Roman Empire during the first three centuries A.D. But the most important religion of the empire turned out to be Christianity, which began with Jesus of Nazareth. Born a Jew and hailed by his followers as the Messiah, Jesus taught humility, charity, and endurance of persecution to spread the word. The most important early Christian was Paul of Tarsus, who spread faith of Jesus outside the Jewish world. By around A.D. 200, Christianity had emerged as a systematic and fully distinct religion from Judaism.

# Key Terms

**Augustus** (p. 142)

**Principate** (p. 142)

**Virgil** (p. 146)

**Livia** (p. 146)

**Julio-Claudians** (p. 147)

**pax Romana** (p. 148)

**Flavian** (p. 148)

**Tacitus** (p. 152)

**third-century crisis** (p. 153)

**Pompeii** (p. 154)

**Sassanids** (p. 154)

**Jesus of Nazareth** (p. 157)

**Gospels** (p. 157)

**rabbinic Judaism** (p. 158)

**Paul of Tarsus** (p. 161)

**Christianity** (p. 163)

**CourseMate**

Go to the CourseMate website at www.cengagebrain.com for additional study tools and review materials—including audio and video clips—for this chapter.

**Santa Maria Maggiore** Santa Maria Maggiore (or Saint Mary Major) looks today much as it did when it was built. It was Rome's first church dedicated to Mary, the mother of Jesus. Erich Lessing/Art Resource, NY

# The World of Late Antiquity, 284–ca. 600

The reigns of Diocletian (284–305) and Constantine (306–337) inaugurated a period that scholars now label "Late Antiquity." For many years, educated people, often taking their lead from the influential *Decline and Fall of the Roman Empire* by the British historian Edward Gibbon (1737–1794), believed that, beset by insurmountable problems, the Roman Empire "fell" in the fifth century. With that fall, such a view insisted, the glories of classical civilization gave way to the gloom of the "Dark Ages." Today, on the contrary, specialists in the period from roughly 300 to 600 see vigor and achievement. They emphasize continuity and coherence over calamity and collapse. No one denies that the Roman world of 600 was different from the Roman world of 300. But recent scholarship stresses how the Romans themselves created a stable framework for change. No catastrophic time, place, or event marked the "fall of Rome."

The magnificent church of Santa Maria Maggiore in Rome was dedicated by Pope Sixtus III in 432. This building encapsulates many of the themes we will encounter in this chapter. How is it that a pope, a Christian bishop, had the power and resources to construct such a building in the empire's capital? For centuries, only emperors had built on such a scale. In architectural form, the building is a basilica, the traditional name for the rectangular halls that served the Romans well for public business. Now, the Christian church was adapting an old Roman form to its own purposes. Moreover, the beautiful mosaics and frescoes reveal ways in which the church was adapting Roman crafts and artistic motifs to its needs. In 410, Rome was sacked by barbarians and yet, within twenty years, the city's resources had rebounded sufficiently to make a building like this possible. In other words, this building itself testifies to the profound processes of continuity and change that are the hallmarks of Late Antiquity.

## Chapter Overview

### Rebuilding the Roman Empire, 284–395

◆ *What were the most important reforms of Diocletian, Constantine, and their successors, and what roles did those reforms play in saving and transforming the empire?*

### The Catholic Church and the Roman Empire, 313–604

◆ *How and why did a Roman and Catholic Church emerge in Late Antiquity?*

### The Rise of Germanic Kingdoms in the West, ca. 370–530

◆ *Who were the "barbarians," and what kinds of relations did Romans and barbarians have in Late Antiquity?*

### The Roman Empire in the East, 395–565

◆ *What challenges did the eastern empire face and what were some of its major contributions?*

### Society and Culture in Late Antiquity

◆ *How did women and men, elites and ordinary people, urban dwellers and farmers experience continuity and change in Late Antiquity?*

# Rebuilding the Roman Empire, 284–395

*What were the most important reforms of Diocletian, Constantine, and their successors, and what roles did those reforms play in saving and transforming the empire?*

The third-century Roman Empire had lurched from crisis to crisis. Decisive action was needed if Rome was to survive. The chronic civil wars had to be brought to an end. The army needed to be reformed and expanded to meet new threats on the frontiers. And the economy had to be stabilized to bring in the revenue the government needed for administrative and military reforms. Rome was fortunate in raising up two rulers, Diocletian (dy-oh-KLEE-shun) and Constantine, with more than fifty years of rule between them, who understood the empire's problems and legislated energetically to address them. Although these rulers thought of themselves as traditional Romans, they actually initiated a far-reaching transformation of the Roman Empire.

## The Reforms of Diocletian (r. 284–305)

The son of a poor Dalmatian farmer, Diocletian rose through the ranks of the army until he attained a key position in the emperor's elite guards. When the emperor was murdered, the soldiers elevated Diocletian to the imperial office.

🌐 **Map 7.1 Diocletian's Division of the Roman Empire, 286** Diocletian divided the Roman Empire into eastern and western halves; each half was divided into two prefectures. Thus, four regions, rulers, and bureaucratic administrations replaced the ineffective rule of **one man.** © Cengage Learning 2014

In about 293, Diocletian devised a regime that historians call the **tetrarchy** (see **Map 7.1**). Diocletian intended the tetrarchy (teh-TRAR-kee), "government by four," to address the empire's political instability and huge size, as well as to promote experienced men and provide an orderly succession to the imperial office. First, Diocletian decided to divide the empire into eastern and western halves, and he appointed an imperial colleague for the West. Ruling from Nicomedia and retaining the position of senior emperor, he took charge of the wealthy and militarily threatened eastern half of the empire. Diocletian and his colleague each selected a subordinate official who would eventually succeed to the imperial office. The advantage of the tetrarchy was that it yielded four men of imperial rank who could lead armies and make decisions in political and administrative matters.

Historians call the regime instituted by Augustus in 31 B.C. the "Principate" (see pages 142–143) because the emperor pretended to be the "first citizen" and heir of the Republican magistrates, even though his real power depended on control of the army. By contrast, Diocletian abandoned all pretense of being a magistrate. Scholars call his regime the "Dominate," from the Latin *Dominus*, "lord and master." Diocletian adopted Eastern, especially Persian, habits, such as wearing a gilded cloak and a jeweled diadem, sprinkling gold dust in his hair, sitting on an elevated throne, rarely appearing in public, and requiring those who approached to prostrate themselves before him. Diocletian succeeded in enhancing the prestige of the imperial office but did so at the price of making the emperor more remote from his subjects.

The empire had some fifty provinces, which varied greatly in size, population, wealth, strategic importance, and degree of Romanization, but the imperial administration was made up largely of aristocratic amateurs and numbered only a few hundred men when Diocletian ascended the throne. Rome had traditionally asked for relatively little from its empire—primarily taxes, military recruits, and loyalty. Local authorities generally did the tax collecting and military recruiting, with little interference from imperial agents.

## CHRONOLOGY

| | |
|---|---|
| 284–337 | Reforms of Diocletian and Constantine |
| 300–400 | Origins and spread of Christian monasticism |
| 324–360 | Foundation and development of Constantinople |
| 325–553 | First five ecumenical councils of the Christian church |
| 350s–ca. 600 | Age of the Church Fathers |
| 370s–530s | Beginnings of the Germanic kingdoms inside the Roman Empire |
| 379–395 | Reign of Theodosius I, last emperor of a united empire |
| 408–450 | Reign of Theodosius II; consolidation of eastern Roman Empire |
| 410 | Visigoths sack Rome |
| 412–418 | Visigoths settle in Gaul |
| 429 | Vandals begin conquest of North Africa |
| 440–604 | Development of the Roman papacy |
| 450–600 | Anglo-Saxons settle in Britain |
| 476 | Last Roman emperor in the West deposed |
| 481–511 | Clovis founds Frankish kingdom |
| 493 | Beginning of Ostrogothic kingdom in Italy |
| 527–565 | Reign of Justinian I |

**tetrarchy** Government ruled by four leaders. It was established about 293 by Emperor Diocletian to address the Roman Empire's political instability, huge size, and complexity.

Diocletian increased the number of officials and doubled the number of provinces by dividing old, large provinces into smaller ones. He then organized groups of provinces into thirteen dioceses and joined the dioceses into four prefectures. Diocletian subordinated each prefecture to a tetrarch and equipped each prefecture with a force of military, legal, financial, and secretarial officials headed by a praetorian prefect. By 350, the number of officers from the provincial to the prefectorial level had risen from a few hundred to thirty-five or forty thousand. Diocletian wished to fill the bureaucracy with trained administrators instead of with wealthy senators and equestrians, who viewed government service as a means of enriching themselves and advancing the interests of their families.

Diocletian also attended to Rome's military problems. His major initiative was to expand his army to 450,000 men. Diocletian also built new forts along the frontiers and improved the roads that supplied frontier defenders. He systematically incorporated barbarians into the army, a step that led to a blurring of the distinction between Romans and barbarians. Military service had long been attractive to people in the empire because it provided Roman citizenship as well as a secure income. After 212, almost every free man in the empire enjoyed automatic citizenship. As a result, noncitizen barbarians living along the frontiers found the army attractive. As the proportion of barbarian soldiers and officers in the army grew, its culture and ethos began to change.

**Tetrarchy** Ideal and reality are both evident in this sculpture of the tetrarchy. The rulers, depicted equal in size, embrace one another but also bare their weapons—to one another and to the world.

Scala/Art Resource, NY

Diocletian's reforms required more income from taxes. Thus, Diocletian attempted to regularize the tax system in the empire. The government conducted a census to identify all taxpayers and assessed the productive value of land. To address the mounting inflation of the third century, Diocletian issued, in 302, the Edict of Maximum Prices, which froze the costs of goods. Virtually the whole cost of the Roman system continued to fall on agriculture, in particular on small farmers. Diocletian's reform of the tax structure brought in more revenue, but it also caused hardships. A rising tax burden threatened those who were most vulnerable. And with more officials handling vastly greater sums of money, corruption ran rampant. Most people never saw the emperor, but they saw too much of his tax-gouging local minions.

The rationale behind Diocletian's reforms is easy to understand; their results were less easy to anticipate. The actions were costly in three unintended respects: moral, social, and economic. The emperors had always been military dictators, but Diocletian removed all pretenses that they served at the behest of the Roman people. His frankness may have enhanced the aura of the imperial office, but it also loosened the ties between the ruler and his subjects. By reducing the official duties of the senatorial order, Diocletian alienated an influential group of about two thousand leading citizens. The enlarged imperial administration necessarily impinged on the autonomy of cities and their local leaders, for three centuries the key components of the imperial system. Finally, the expanded administration and army cost dearly in real cash. That cash had to be extracted from an empire that was in serious economic distress.

## The Reforms of Constantine I (r. 306–337)

Diocletian's careful plans for the imperial succession collapsed almost immediately after his voluntary retirement in 305. When Diocletian's Western colleague (Constantine I) died in 306, his troops reverted to the hereditary principle and declared his son, Constantine, emperor. Until 324, Constantine's power was shared or contested, and from 324 to 337, he ruled alone over a reunited empire, although he made his sons subordinates in various parts of the empire. This compromise between the hereditary and tetrarchal systems persisted for the next two centuries.

Constantine continued the eastward shift of power by creating a second imperial capital in the East. In 324, he selected an old Greek city, Byzantium (bizz-AN-tee-um), and renamed it after himself, "Constantine's polis," or Constantinople (modern Istanbul). Byzantium's location, more than its size, wealth, or fame, recommended it. The city straddled military roads between the eastern and western halves of the empire, overlooked crucial trade lanes to and from the Black Sea region, and was well sited to respond to threats along both the Balkan and the eastern frontiers (see **Map 7.1**).

In financial affairs, too, Constantine's work echoed his predecessor's. He issued a new gold *solidus*, the principal currency in the Roman Empire. This coin promoted monetary stability in the Mediterranean world for nearly a thousand years. Unfortunately, both a stable currency and Diocletian's price controls braked, but could not stop, the headlong rush of inflation.

In military affairs, Constantine believed that Rome's frontiers stretched too far to be held securely by garrisons, so he expanded the use of mobile field armies. These armies, recruited largely (as under Diocletian) from barbarians living along or beyond the frontiers, were stationed well inside the borderlands so that they could be mobilized and moved quickly to any threatened point. They were given their own command structures, under officers called "Masters of the Soldiers." The praetorian prefects were deprived of their military responsibilities and became exclusively civilian officials. The separation of civilian and military command made sense administratively and politically because it meant that no individual could combine the command of an army with the authority of a government post.

Whereas Diocletian will always be remembered for launching the last persecution of Christianity (303–305), Constantine legalized the new faith. Each man's motivation has evoked scholarly controversy. Diocletian was a Roman of conventional piety, who seems to have been convinced that the presence of Christian soldiers in his army offended the ancestral gods and denied victory to the Roman troops. Constantine's mother, Helena, was a devout Christian, and there were Christians in his father's court circle. In 312, while marching toward Rome to fight one of his rivals, Constantine believed that he saw in the sky a cross accompanied by the words "In this sign you shall conquer." Persuaded, Constantine put a chi-rho (from the first two letters of *Chrestos*, "Christ" in Greek) monogram on his soldiers' uniforms. He defeated his foe at the Milvian Bridge near Rome, and, certain that Christ had assured his victory, he and his Eastern colleague issued the **Edict of Milan** in 313, granting Christianity full legal status in the empire.

Diocletian's persecution had been harsh and systematic. He ordered churches to be closed and the Scriptures seized, arrested members of the clergy, and required all citizens to make a public act of sacrifice in a temple. Constantine did far more than merely stop the persecution or legalize Christianity. He granted the church tax immunities, exempted the clergy from military and civic obligations, and provided money to replace books and buildings that had been destroyed in the persecution. He and his mother sponsored the construction of impressive churches, such as the Lateran in Rome and the Church of the Holy Sepulcher over the traditional site of Christ's tomb in Jerusalem.

Erich Lessing / Art Resource, NY

**Monumental Head of Constantine**   Nearly eight feet tall itself, this head once topped a statue more than thirty feet high. Constantine placed it in the basilica completed by Maxentius, whom he defeated at the Milvian Bridge. Note the impression it creates as the Dominate supplanted the Principate.

Scholars have long debated the strategic and political wisdom of Constantine's arrangements. Moving experienced troops away from the frontiers may have invited, rather than deterred, attacks. Recruiting barbarians into the field armies and leaving frontier defenses to barbarian auxiliaries may have created divided loyalties and conflicts of interest. One certain result of the reforms of Diocletian and Constantine was the militarization of Roman society—the transformation of the Roman Empire into a vast armed camp. The financial resources of that empire were now largely devoted to maintaining an expensive military establishment that was socially diverse and potentially politically volatile. Christians were still a minority of the population in Constantine's lifetime, so his legalization and patronage of the new faith may have been visionary but offended the elites of his day.

Diocletian and Constantine responded with imagination to the third-century crisis. They created a new kind of rulership and a new type of imperial regime. Constantine erected a statue of himself in Rome that was more than 30 feet high; its head alone was about 8 feet tall. This statue is an indicator of the late antique imperial ideology. Constantine's size in stone serves to emphasize a distance that the viewer cannot articulate but cannot help feeling. The huge statue does not so much depict Constantine as proclaim emperorship. The

**Edict of Milan**  Issued jointly by Constantine and his colleague Licinius, it granted freedom of worship to all and restored properties seized from the Christian church during Diocletian's persecution.

majesty of Constantine and his long, productive reign, in conjunction with Diocletian's success and longevity, stands in stark contrast to the troubles of the third century. But we may ask, as contemporaries did, whether order was purchased at too high a price in terms of personal freedom.

## The Fourth-Century Empire: A Fragile Stability

Diocletian and Constantine considered themselves to be Roman traditionalists, but their wide-ranging reforms had actually introduced deep changes in the Roman system. When Constantine died in 337, the Roman Empire was more peaceful and stable than it had been throughout the crisis-ridden third century. But Rome's rulers were now more despotic; Rome's government was bigger, more intrusive, and more expensive; and Rome's military was larger and increasingly barbarian in composition. The open question in 337 was whether Rome would revert to the chaos of the third century or continue along the path marked out by the reforms of Diocletian and Constantine.

Succession to the imperial office remained a troubling issue, despite the introduction of the tetrarchy. Constantine had employed a combination of the tetrarchal and dynastic systems. He had three subordinates, all of them his sons. Constantine's sons had no heirs of their own, and when the last of them died in 361, the army turned to Julian (331–363), Constantine's nephew. Julian was a great leader and a man who looked out for his troops. Julian ruled for only two years before he was killed fighting in Mesopotamia. Because Julian had no heirs, the army controlled the succession. The choice fell on Valentinian (r. 364–375) and his brother, Valens (r. 364–378). Valentinian ruled in the west, his brother in the east. Valentinian established a dynasty that ruled the Roman world for ninety-one years (364–455). In 378, when Valens was killed in battle, Valentinian's sons sent their brother-in-law, Theodosius (thee-oh-DOE-zhus) I (r. 379–395), who had risen through the military ranks in Spain, to the east to restore order.

Until his own death in 395, Theodosius was the most powerful man in the Roman world and, after 392, sole ruler. He enjoyed the confidence of the people and the army—the former because he was exceptionally competent and honest and the latter because he was an old military man and a superb general. He divided the empire between his two sons without dynastic or military challenge. His branch of the family lived on until the deaths of Theodosius II in the East in 450 and Valentinian III in the West in 455.

Following the reforms of Diocletian and Constantine, the army was supposed to protect the empire, not play a role in Roman politics. Events proved otherwise. In the 340s, the Romans faced a renewed threat in the east from Persia, where an ambitious king sought to revive the glories of his ancestors. The Romans did not take this Persian threat lightly, for they knew that in the Persians, they faced an old and formidable foe. In the west, Rome faced one serious challenge from the Visigoths (discussed later in this chapter). These military provocations inevitably enhanced the role of the army in public life and elevated military concerns over civilian ones.

The fourth century did not witness the kinds of intensive reforms that characterized the reigns of Diocletian and Constantine, but emperors did introduce many modest measures, some of which had outcomes very different from those intended by their implementers. One example may stand for many.

Valentinian I wanted to make military careers more attractive and soldiers' lives more comfortable. To achieve these ends, he proposed providing soldiers with plots of land and seed grain. He aimed to supplement soldiers' pay, to tie them more securely to a particular region, and to make them more loyal to him. This creative idea complemented earlier military reforms.

Nonetheless, Valentinian's program angered the senators, who were still rich and influential. They agitated against the reform because, they said, the emperor was spending too much time worrying about the army, and he was depriving them of lands they desired. The senators also complained that the new program was expensive. They were right. To pay for land and seed, Valentinian had to raise taxes.

Higher taxes were especially unpopular in the cities, where the burden of collecting them fell on the *decurions*, the main local officials who composed the town councils. From the time of Valentinian in the late fourth century, evidence points to a steady decline in loyalty to Rome among these provincial urban elites. One great success under the Principate involved the regime's ability to win over local elites all over the empire. Now, a military reform whose rationale was clear and defensible actually provoked suspicion and disloyalty among senators and decurions.

In the late fourth century, the empire may have numbered 50 million to 60 million inhabitants. Of these, not more than 5 million to 10 million lived in towns. Because Roman government was based on towns, the actual capacity of the Roman administration to keep track of, tax, coerce, and Romanize the population as a whole was limited. Nevertheless, as the Roman Empire became an increasingly militarized state, its towns were being dominated by central authorities as never before, and its rural population was being pressed hard by tax policies necessitated by larger civil and military structures. The reforms of Diocletian and Constantine continued to provide the framework within which these changes took place.

When Theodosius died in 395, the Roman world seemed reasonably secure. The families of Constantine and Valentinian had produced effective rulers. Frontiers faced ominous threats, but for the moment, conditions appeared stable. Programs of institutional and economic reform continued, generally along the lines marked out by Diocletian and Constantine.

> **SECTION SUMMARY**
>
> - Diocletian and Constantine enhanced the prestige of the imperial office but made it more remote and despotic.
> - Diocletian and Constantine expanded and redeployed the army but turned the empire into an armed camp.
> - Diocletian and Constantine increased taxes and stabilized the currency.
> - Diocletian and Constantine expanded the government and made it more effective, yet also more intrusive.
> - Diocletian persecuted, but Constantine legalized Christianity.

# The Catholic Church and the Roman Empire, 313–604

*How and why did a* **Roman** *and* **Catholic** *Church emerge in Late Antiquity?*

While Rome's rulers were trying to stabilize the state during the fourth century, the empire was experiencing a dynamic process of religious change. The formerly small and persecuted communities of Christians were achieving majority status in the Roman world. The Christianization of the empire's population (see **Map 7.2**), first in towns and then in the countryside, and the emergence of the Catholic Church as an institutional structure were two of the greatest transformations of the ancient world. Many Christians, now able to practice their faith publicly, discovered that they had sharp disagreements with one another on points of doctrine. Attempts to resolve those controversies entangled the church with the Roman authorities and strengthened the bishops of Rome. Moreover, numerous Christians—monks and nuns—sought a life of perfection away from the bustle of the world.

## Emperors, Bishops, and Heretics

Constantine discovered that his support of the church drew him into heated disputes over doctrine and **heresy**. *Heresy* comes from a Greek word meaning "to choose." Heretics are persons who choose teachings or practices that religious or state authorities deem wrong. The two greatest and most difficult heresies of Late Antiquity involved the central doctrines of Christianity: the deity of Jesus Christ and the relationship between his divine and human natures.

Christian belief holds that there is one God, who exists as three distinct but equal persons: Father, Son, and Holy Spirit. But around 320, a priest of Alexandria, Arius (AIR-ee-us) (ca. 250–336), began teaching that Jesus was the "first born of all creation." Christians had long been stung by the charge that their monotheism was a sham, that they really worshiped three gods. **Arianism**, as the faith of Arius and his followers is called, preserved monotheism by making Jesus slightly subordinate to the Father. Arianism won many adherents.

**heresy** An opinion that goes against religious or political doctrine and beliefs.

**Arianism** A term for the teaching of Arius and the beliefs of his followers, who believed that Jesus Christ, as "the first born of all creation," was generated by the Father, not coeternal with him. Their teachings challenged the doctrine of the Trinity.

🌐 **Map 7.2 The Spread of Christianity to A.D. 600** From its beginnings in Palestine (see **Map 6.2** on page 162), Christianity, while still illegal, spread mainly in heavily urbanized regions. After Constantine legalized Christianity (313), the faith spread into every corner of the Roman world. © Cengage Learning 2014

**Council of Nicaea** The first "ecumenical" or "all-the-world" council. Several more ecumenical councils would meet in Late Antiquity to deal with major heresies.

Constantine was scandalized by disagreements over Christian teachings and distressed by riotous quarrels among competing Christian factions. He dealt with religious controversies by summoning individual theologians to guide him and by assembling church councils to debate controversies and reach solutions. In 325, at Nicaea (Ny-SEE-uh), near Constantinople (see **Map 7.2**), the emperor convened a council of more than three hundred bishops, the largest council that had met up to that date. The **Council of Nicaea** condemned Arius and his teachings. The bishops issued a creed, or statement of beliefs, which maintained that Christ was "one in being with the Father," coequal and coeternal.

Religious unity remained elusive, however. The Council of Nicaea's attempt to eliminate Arianism was unsuccessful in the short term. Constantius II (r. 337–361), Constantine's son and successor in the eastern half of the empire, was an avowed Arian, as were some later emperors. For more than forty years, Rome's rulers occasionally embraced a faith that had been declared heretical. It was during this time that the Visigothic priest Ulfilas entered the empire, was converted to Arian Christianity, and returned to spread this faith among his people. Arian Christianity spread widely among the barbarian peoples living along the empire's frontiers. By the time those people began to enter the empire in significant numbers (see pages 179–180), catholic Christianity, universal (for that is what *catholicos* means) Christianity proclaimed by councils and emperors, had triumphed over Arianism, leaving the barbarians as heretics.

One emperor—Constantine's nephew Julian—made a last-ditch attempt to restore paganism during his short reign. He did not resort to persecution but forbade Christians to hold most government or military positions or to teach in any school. Although Christianity had been legalized only in 313, by the 360s, it was too well entrenched to be barred from the public sphere, and Julian's pagan revival died with him.

In the fifth century, Miaphysitism (literally one-nature-ism) emerged as a result of bitter quarrels between Christian thinkers in Alexandria and Antioch. Theologians were struggling to find a way to talk about the divine and human natures in Christ. Some emphasized one nature, some the other. In 451, an emperor called a new council at Chalcedon (KAL-see-dun) to deal with the issue of Miaphysitism. At Chalcedon, the theologians condemned the Miaphysites, who emphasized Christ's divine nature, and pronounced that Jesus Christ was true God and true man—that he had two authentic natures. By 451, the Roman world had a Catholic majority that derived its teachings from Nicaea and Chalcedon and a large community of Miaphysites spread from the Mediterranean to central Asia who believed themselves to be the true Catholics. (See the feature, "The Global Record: Cosmas Indicopleustes Finds Christians in South Asia" on page 178.)

## The Institutional Development of the Catholic Church, ca. 300–600

The earliest Christian communities were urban and had three kinds of official, whose customary titles in English are *bishop*, *priest*, and *deacon*. Deacons were responsible for charitable works and for arranging meetings. Bishops and priests presided at celebrations—most prominently the Eucharist (or Holy Communion, as it came to be called)—preached, and taught. Distinctions between bishops and priests developed over time. Towns often had many independent Christian groups, each headed by a priest. By about 200, as a sign of unity and authority, the eldest priest came to be called "overseer," the literal meaning of *bishop*. As more people converted, as the church acquired property, and as doctrinal quarrels began to cause divisions among the faithful, bishops began to be influential local officials. By the late fourth century, the bishops in the major cities of the empire were called *metropolitan bishops*, or sometimes *archbishops*, and they had responsibility for territories often called *dioceses*. The church was adapting to its own purposes the administrative geography of the Roman Empire—another sign of change and continuity in Late Antiquity.

### The Emergence of the Roman Papacy

From its earliest days, the Christian community had espoused the doctrine of *apostolic succession*. In other words, just as Jesus had charged his apostles with continuing his earthly ministry, that ministry was passed on to succeeding generations of Christian bishops and priests through the ceremony of ordination. When one or more bishops laid their hands on the head of a new priest or bishop, they were continuing an unbroken line of clerics that reached back through the apostles to Jesus himself. The bishops of Rome coupled this general notion of apostolic succession with a particular emphasis on the original primacy of Peter, in tradition, the leader of the apostles and the first bishop of Rome. The theory of "Petrine Primacy" was based on Matthew's Gospel (16:16–18), where Jesus said: "Blest are you Simon . . . you are 'Rock," (*petras* in Greek) and on this Rock I will build my church and the gates of Hell shall not prevail against it. I will entrust to you the keys of the kingdom of heaven. Whatever you declare bound on earth will be bound in heaven; whatever you declare loosed on earth shall be loosed in heaven." The theory held that just as Peter had been the leader of the apostles, so the successors to Peter, the bishops of Rome, continued to be the leaders of the church as a whole. By the late fourth century, the bishop of Rome was usually addressed as *papa*, or "pope" in English. The growing authority of the bishop of Rome within the church is the most striking organizational process of the fourth and fifth centuries.

Growing numbers of Christians, the increasing prominence of the clergy, and doctrinal quarrels drew emperors more deeply into the public life of the church. Between 378 and 381, Theodosius virtually outlawed the pagan cults, thereby making Christianity and Judaism the only legal religions, and required all Christians to believe as the bishop of Rome did, in the hope of imposing religious unity. Unity under Roman leadership was essential, Theodosius said, because Peter had transmitted the unblemished faith directly to Rome, and Peter's successors had preserved it there. The bishops of Rome took an ambivalent view of Theodosius's laws. They were glad to have the emperor's support but they did not wish for their authority or teaching to rest on imperial decrees. Theodosius's actions reflect the growing power of the bishop of Rome and demonstrate the degree to which the state and the church were becoming intertwined. The decrees themselves failed to achieve the unity Theodosius desired.

Ever since Nicaea, councils, with active participation by the emperors, had settled major disagreements in the church. Pope Leo I (r. 440–461) began to assert papal prerogatives. He had sent representatives to the Council of Chalcedon bearing his doctrinal formulation. Leo insisted that, as the bishop of Rome, he had full authority to make decisions in doctrinal controversies. The emperor skillfully steered Leo's "Tome" to acceptance by the council, but to appease many Eastern bishops, who felt that too much authority was being claimed by the pope, the emperor also encouraged the council to assert that the bishop of Constantinople (or patriarch, as he was often called) was second in eminence and power to the bishop of Rome. Leo, the greatest exponent of "Petrine Primacy" though not its originator, objected strenuously to the Council of Chalcedon's procedures. He disliked the prominent role of the emperor, complained that Eastern bishops had no right to challenge his doctrinal authority, and particularly opposed the elevation of Constantinople's status.

A generation later, Pope Gelasius I (r. 492–496) sent a sharply worded letter to the emperor Anastasius (r. 491–518), who had intervened in a quarrel between the Catholics and the numerous Miaphysites. Gelasius protested the emperor's intervention. He told the emperor that the world was governed by the "power" of kings and by the "authority" of priests. Ordinarily, the pope said, the jurisdictions of kings and priests are distinct. In a controversy between them, however, priestly authority must have precedence because priests are concerned with the salvation of immortal souls, whereas kings rule only mortal bodies. Gelasius was telling the emperor to stay out of theology, but he was implying much more. His opposition of the words *power*—meaning mere police power, the application of brute force— and *authority*—legitimacy, superior right—was of great importance. Gelasius elevated the church, with the pope at its head, above the whole secular regime, with the emperor at its head. But Gelasius had no means of coercing emperors. Moreover, many clergy in the eastern Mediterranean refused to accept the idea that the pope had supreme authority in either doctrine or church government.

Pope Gregory I "the Great" (r. 590–604) exemplifies the position of the papacy as Late Antiquity drew to a close. Gregory was the scion of an old senatorial family. He had risen through several important positions in the Roman administration, but then decided to abandon public life, sell off his family's property, and pursue a life of spiritual retreat. Soon, however, the Roman people elected him pope. His reputation for holiness was important to his election, but so too were his impeccable social credentials and wide political connections. Rome was threatened by the Lombards (a barbarian group that had entered Italy in the 560s), the local economy was in a shambles, and relations with the imperial government had been strained. Gregory did not wish to be elected pope, but given his conventional Roman sense of duty and obligation, he had little choice but to accept the office. Immediately, he undertook dangerous diplomatic measures to ward off the Lombard threat, sought improved relations with the emperor, and put the local economy on surer footing. He reorganized the vast estates of the church to place their products and revenues at the disposal of the Romans. In the absence of effective imperial administration in and around Rome, Gregory also began to attend to urban services and amenities, such as streets, aqueducts, and baths.

## The Role of the Elite

The rise of the pope in the church as a whole was paralleled by the rise of bishops throughout the empire. By the year 400, members of the social elite were everywhere entering the clergy and rising to its highest offices. This capture of the elite was the final, decisive factor in the triumph of Christianity.

The clergy was an outlet for the talents and ambitions of the elite. For some time, senators had been excluded from military offices and reduced in civilian influence, and decurions were growing dissatisfied with public service. The *episcopal* office (that is, the office of bishop) was desirable to prominent men for many reasons. It was prestigious. Bishops wore distinctive clothing when officiating and were addressed by special titles—traditional Roman marks of respect. They had opportunities to control patronage in the way that prominent Romans always had done. They could intervene on behalf of individuals at the imperial court. They controlled vast wealth, as the generosity of pious Christians put more resources at their disposal. By the middle of the fifth century, the dominant person in most towns was the bishop, not a civilian official. The bishops, however, were the same persons, from the same families, who had once dominated local society through civic service. The overall effect of these social changes was dramatic in the long run, but it happened very gradually.

The change from a secular to an ecclesiastical elite in Roman cities even led to alterations of the topography of the cities themselves. The elite usually financed local building projects, such as temples, basilicas, forums, and amphitheaters. Such benefactions declined sharply during the tumultuous third century. The fourth century at first saw little building on private initiative, but then came the construction of Christian cathedrals (a bishop's church, from *cathedra*, the chair or seat of the bishop's authority), episcopal residences, and other churches. Such buildings, as a rule, were not placed in the old city centers, which had associations with the pagan past. Instead, they were placed on the edges of populated districts. In the future, these Christian centers served as poles around which ancient towns were reconfigured. The Roman elites built to show pride in their cities and to promote themselves. This did not change in Late Antiquity, but this time, the elites were bishops or rich Christians, and the buildings were religious—look again at Santa Maria Maggiore on page 166.

## The Rise of Christian Monasticism

For some men and women, the call of the Gospel was radical. They yearned to escape the world and everything that might come between them and God. To do so, many of them embraced a new way of life—**monasticism**. Christian monks and nuns developed a theology and an institution that were among the most creative and long-lived achievements of Late Antiquity.

The practice of rigorous self-denial (*askesis*) was common to several religious and philosophical sects in antiquity—for example, the Pythagoreans and the Stoics—and was well known among the Jews in the time of Christ, as the Essenes show (see page 159). Ascetics believed that if they could conquer the desires of the body, they could commune with the supernatural beings who were greater and purer than humans, who were encumbered by lust for food, drink, knowledge, sex, and adventure. Sometimes ascetic practices were adopted by tightly knit groups, sometimes by heroic solitaries.

The founder of Christian monasticism was a young Egyptian layman, named Anthony (d. 356). At age 19, Anthony gave away all his possessions and took up, in the Egyptian desert, a life of prayer and renunciation. His spiritual quest became famous, and many disciples flocked to him. Finally, he decided to organize these seekers into a very loose community. His followers remained in solitude except for worship and meals. Anthony's form of monasticism is called **eremitic**, from the Greek *heremos*, or "desert," hence, the word *hermit*.

Pachomius (pack-OH-mee-us) (290–346) created a more communal form of monastic life. A former Roman soldier, he was baptized a Christian in 313 and retired to the Egyptian desert, where he studied with a hermit. Eventually Pachomius founded a community, which before long had grown to thousands of members. Perhaps because of his military background, or because his religious instincts favored order and unity, Pachomius wrote the first monastic rule, or code for daily living in community. He organized most aspects of his community by designing a common life based on routines of private prayer, group worship, and work. By the time of his death, Pachomius led nine male and two female communities. Pachomius's pattern of monasticism is called **cenobitic** (sen-oh-BIT-ik), from the Greek for "common life." People living this common life were called *monks*, and the place where they lived was called a *monastery*. The head of the community was designated the *abbot*, a word meaning

**monasticism** A way of life involving the renunciation of worldly pleasures and the embrace of a life of prayer and solitude. Monasticism arose in fourth-century Egypt and spread all over the Roman world.

**eremitic monasticism** An especially austere, solitary form of asceticism.

**cenobitic monasticism** From the Greek *koinos bios*, common life, this form of monasticism was communal.

## Cosmas Indicopleustes Finds Christians in Asia

*Cosmas Indicopleustes (the India-Navigator) set out from Alexandria around 554 and sailed in the Indian Ocean. He left an account that blends theology, biblical commentary, and travelogue.*

Matthew said, "The Gospel shall be preached throughout the whole world" . . . and we see that these predictions have been fulfilled. . . . Even in Ceylon, an island in further India, where the Indian Sea is, there is a church of Christians, with clergy and a body of believers, but I know not whether there be any Christians in the parts beyond it. In the country called Malabar, where the pepper grows, there is also a church, and another at a place called Calliana there is moreover a bishop, who is appointed from Persia. In the island, again, called the Island of Dioscorides [Socotra], which is situated in the same Indian Sea, and where the inhabitants speak Greek, having been originally colonists sent hither by the Ptolemies who succeeded Alexander the Macedonian, there are clergy who receive their ordination from Persia. . . .

I sailed along the coast of this island but did not land upon it. I met, however, with some of its Greek-speaking people who had come over into Ethiopia. And so likewise among the Bactrians and Huns and Persians, and the rest of the Indians, Persarmenians, and Medes and Elamites there is no limit to the number of churches with bishops and very large communities of Christian people, as well as many martyrs, and monks also living as hermits.

### Questions

1. *What hints does Cosmas provide about relations between the Mediterranean world and the land of south and central Asia?*

2. *Can you figure out what kinds of Christians Cosmas encountered?*

3. *Did Cosmas find church structures like those in the Roman world?*

The Christian Topography of Cosmas an Egyptian Monk, Workd Issued by the hakluyt Society, no. 98, trans. J. W. McCrindle (London: Hakluyt Society, 1897), pp. 118-20.

---

"father." In later times, the term *abbess*, meaning "mother," was coined for the woman who led a female community.

Monasticism spread from Egypt by means of texts, such as the *Life of Anthony* (a late antique "best seller"), collections of the wise sayings of famous desert abbots, and books written by persons who went to Egypt seeking a more perfect life—among whom were several prominent women. One attraction of monasticism among the devout was that it seemed to be a purer form of Christian life, uncorrupted by the wealth, power, and controversy of the hierarchical church. Many pious women embraced monasticism at least partly because they could not be ordained priests. Positions in monasteries, including that of abbess, provided responsible roles for talented women. Monasticism gave women a chance to choose a kind of family life different from the one available in households dominated by fathers and husbands.

Initially eremitic monasticism was prominent in Palestine and Syria and eventually throughout the Greek-speaking world. Eremitic monasticism arrived in the West in the person of Martin of Tours (336–397). Like Pachomius, Martin was a Roman soldier who, after his military service, embraced both Christianity and asceticism. Even though he was elected bishop of Tours, Martin kept to his rigid ascetic life. Martin's form of monasticism influenced many in the western regions of the Roman world but set especially deep roots in Ireland. There, the whole organization of the church was based on monasteries. At Kildare, the abbess Brigid (d. 523) had more authority than the local bishop. (See the feature, "The Global Record: Cosmas Indicopleustes Finds Christians in South Asia" above).

In both East and West, cenobitic monasticism became the dominant pattern. Eastern monasticism produced a great legislator in Basil (330–379), whose monastic rule was the most influential in the Orthodox Church (see page 192). Combining eremitic and cenobitic principles, these monks assembled only for weekly worship and otherwise ate, prayed, and worked alone. Benedict of Nursia (480–545) abandoned his secular career to pursue a life of solitary prayer in a mountain cave. Benedict's piety attracted a crowd of followers, and in about 520, he established a monastery at Monte Cassino, 80 miles south of Rome. The rule he drafted for his new community is marked by shrewd insights into the human personality. It emphasizes the bond of mutual love among the monks and obedience to the abbot. The Benedictine rule assigns the abbot wide powers but exhorts him to exercise them gently. The rule allows monks a reasonable diet and decent, though modest, clothing. Although providing for discipline and punishment, the rule prefers loving correction. In later centuries, Benedict's rule dominated monastic life.

Monasticism was a conscious alternative and an explicit challenge to the civic world of classical antiquity. Monks and nuns did not seek to give their lives meaning by serving the state or urban communities. They went into remote places to serve God and one another. They sought not to acquire but to abandon. Spiritual wisdom was more important to them than secular learning, and they yearned to achieve true holiness, not recognition of their social status. Still, monasticism was sometimes controversial. Whereas many people admired and emulated these holy men and women, others disputed their claims to elite spiritual status.

At the dawn of Late Antiquity, the church was persecuted and struggling. By the end of the period, the church was rich and powerful, its leaders were prominent and prestigious, and in the monasteries, at least, its spiritual fervor was deep. This change was gradual but fundamental.

**SECTION SUMMARY**

- Imperial legislation and church councils imposed a universal, a catholic, form of Christianity.
- The church developed a hierarchy of officers over which the bishops of Rome gradually achieved preeminence.
- Christians disagreed strongly on basic teachings, such as the Trinity (God is Father, Son, and Holy Spirit) and the divine and human natures of Jesus Christ.
- Some men and women rejected the values of the late antique world and embraced the monastic life of prayer, service, and renunciation, achieving in the process a new kind of status: holiness.

# The Rise of Germanic Kingdoms in the West, ca. 370–530

*Who were the "barbarians," and what kinds of relations did Romans and barbarians have in Late Antiquity?*

The years from the 370s to the 530s were decisive in the history of the Roman Empire in the West. This period saw the transformation of Rome's western provinces into several Germanic kingdoms, most of which maintained some formal relationship with the eastern Roman Empire. Roman encounters with the barbarians took many forms, ranging from violent conflict to peaceful accommodation. The key point to understand is that although the barbarians supplanted Roman rule in the West, they did so slowly and often with Roman collaboration (intentional or unwitting).

## Invasions and Migrations

Individual groups of barbarians did invade the empire in various places at different times, but there was never a single, coordinated barbarian invasion of the Roman world. The Romans and barbarians did not face one another as declared enemies. Indeed, peaceful encounters outnumbered violent confrontations in the history of Romano-barbarian relations. The Romans had long traded with the barbarian peoples, carried out complicated diplomacy with them, and recruited them into their armies. Barbarian veterans were settled in most provinces of the empire.

If we cannot label one grand movement as "the barbarian invasions," we must also avoid the idea that the barbarians were naturally nomadic and migratory. Holding this view would tempt us to see the entry of the barbarians into the empire as one stage in a long process of human movement. Archaeological evidence collected to date makes it clear that the barbarians were settled agriculturists. They lived in villages, farmed the surrounding country, and raised livestock. If barbarians moved from one place to another, their movement must be explained with reference to specific developments and cannot be attributed to migratory habits.

Few images of the ancient world are more fixed in the popular imagination than the overrunning of the Roman Empire by hordes of barbarians who ushered in a dark age. The Romans inherited the word *barbarian* from the Greeks, who had divided the world between those who spoke Greek and those who did not. Barbarians were literally babblers, foreigners who spoke an unknown language.

Who were the barbarians? Linguists classify them as speakers of Germanic languages. The Germanic peoples can be differentiated from the Celts and Slavs with whom they shared much of central and eastern Europe, but apart from some minor linguistic variations, it is difficult to distinguish one Germanic group from another.

What are we to make of the profusion of names offered to us by our sources: Franks, Saxons, Vandals, Visigoths, Ostrogoths, Lombards, Burgundians? The Romans referred to the Germanic peoples as tribes, but that does not mean that they were actually groups of related people. Every Germanic "tribe" was a confederation, and these confederations formed, dissolved, and re-formed many times. The confederations were formed either by powerful leaders who coerced less powerful people to join them or by groups of villages that banded together to protect themselves from aggressive neighbors. As a tribe was forming, its constituent peoples would intermarry and adopt the language, law, and lifestyle of the dominant group.

## Incorporating the Barbarians

The transformation of the western Roman Empire began as a result of an unexpected set of events involving the Huns, nomadic warriors from the central Asian steppes. Here is how one Roman author describes the Huns:

> From the moment of their birth they make deep gashes in their children's cheeks, so that when in due course hair appears its growth is checked by the wrinkled scars; as they grow older this gives them the unlovely appearance of beardless eunuchs. They have squat bodies, strong limbs, and thick necks, and are so prodigiously ugly and bent that they might be two-legged animals. Their shape, however disagreeable, is human.[*]

After plundering the frontiers of Persia and China for centuries, they turned west in search of plunder and tribute. In 374 or 375, they fell on the Ostrogoths, who lived near the Black Sea, and frightened the **Visigoths**, who requested permission to cross the Danube and enter the empire.

Because of dynastic quarrels and military challenges, the Romans delayed responding to the Visigoth request. Fearful of the Huns, the Visigoths crossed the Danube on their own and requested permission to settle in the Balkans. Reluctantly, Valens (VAY-lenz) (r. 364–378) agreed but postponed permanent arrangements. While the government considered how to deal with the Visigoths, local authorities sold them food at exorbitant prices and even traded dog meat for Gothic children, who were then enslaved. When the Visigoths revolted, Valens foolishly marched north to meet them with a small force. The Visigoths defeated his army and killed him at Adrianople in 378.

The history of the Visigoths presents an instructive example of Romano-Germanic relations. They had served as auxiliary troops entrusted with defending a stretch of the Danube frontier for a long time when they requested permission to enter the empire in 376. They did not cross the border as part of a massive invasion but because they were sorely threatened. In 382, Theodosius marched east to pacify the situation. He agreed to grant the Visigoths what they had been demanding: land to settle on and a Roman military title—that is, official status—for their king. A spokesman for Theodosius explained the emperor's motives: "Which is better: To fill Thrace with corpses or with farmers? To fill it with graves or with people? To travel through wilderness or cultivated land? To count those who have perished or those who are ploughing?"[**]

For about thirty years, the Visigoths struggled to improve the terms of their settlements in the Balkans. Alaric (AL-uh-rik), the Visigothic king after 395, grew tired of unfulfilled promises and forced matters by attacking Italy. In 410, the Visigoths sacked Rome. The

**Visigoths** A "West" Germanic people who coalesced along the Danube frontier in the fourth century, allied with the Romans, eventually entered the empire, sacked Rome in 410, and finally established a kingdom in Gaul.

---

[*]From Ammianus Marcellinus, *The Later Roman Empire* (A.D. 354-378), 31.2, ed. and trans. Walter Hamilton, 1986, pp. 411-412
[**]Themistius, Oration 16, 211 a-b, trans. L. Daly, in "The mandarin and the Barbarian: The Response of Themistius to the Gothic Challenge," *Historia,* 21 (1972), p. 373.

taking of the city for the first time in eight hundred years shocked the entire Roman world and has loomed large for centuries in people's ideas about the "fall" of the Roman Empire. Actually, it was a ploy by Alaric to improve the terms of his already official status. Alaric died in 410, and his brother led the Visigoths north into southern Gaul. For good measure, the new Visigothic king captured the Western emperor's sister, Galla Placidia, and forced her to marry him. However objectionable this act must seem, the Visigoths viewed it as a further demonstration of their loyalty to Rome and their determination to effect a satisfactory new treaty.

In 418, the Roman government gave in. A treaty permitted the Visigoths to settle in southern Gaul, with Toulouse as their base of operations. They were assigned the task of protecting the area from marauding bands of brigands. In return for their service, the Visigoths were given land allotments and a portion of Roman tax receipts as pay.

The Visigoths' treaty with Rome made theirs the first Germanic kingdom on Roman soil. From 418 to 451, the Visigoths served Rome loyally and earned the respect of the Gallo-Roman aristocrats among whom they ruled. Between 466 and 484, the Visigothic kingdom in Gaul reached its high point and continued to receive official recognition from Roman rulers. Southern Gaul, one of Rome's oldest provinces, gradually passed from the hands of the Roman bureaucracy and the local nobility into the control of the Visigoths.

While they were dealing with the Visigoths, the Roman authorities realized that the Huns, who had settled in the Danube basin after driving the Visigoths into the empire, were a serious menace. They raided the Balkans, preyed on trade routes that crossed the region, and demanded tribute from the Eastern emperor. In 434, the fearsome warrior Attila murdered his brother and became sole ruler of the Huns. In return for a huge imperial subsidy, he agreed to cease raiding the Balkans. At the same time, a Roman general in Gaul concluded an alliance with the Huns in an attempt to use them to check the expansion of the Burgundians, an allied people who lived in the central Rhineland.

Together, Attila and the Romans routed the Burgundians, but Attila realized the weakness of the Roman position in the West. He attacked Gaul in 451 and was stopped only by a combined effort of Romans, Visigoths, Burgundians, and Franks. The sources call the soldiers who defeated the Huns "Romans."

## More Kingdoms: The End of Direct Roman Rule in the West

To meet threats in Gaul and elsewhere, the Romans had begun pulling troops out of Britain in the fourth century and abandoned the island to its own defense in 410. Thereafter, raiding parties from Scotland and Ireland, as well as seaborne attackers—called "Saxons" by contemporaries because some of them came from Saxony in northern Germany—ravaged Britain. The British continually appealed to the military authorities in Gaul for aid, but to no avail. Between 450 and 600, much of southern and eastern Britain was taken over by diverse peoples whom we call the "Anglo-Saxons." The newcomers jostled for position with the Celtic Britons, who were increasingly confined to the north and west of the island. Amid these struggles was born the legend of King Arthur, a Briton who defended his people and led them to victory. Gradually, several small kingdoms emerged. Although Britain retained contacts with Gaul, the island had virtually no Roman political or institutional inheritance.

Through most of the fifth century the western empire was ruled by a series of forgettable and ineffective rulers. The last of them, Romulus Augustulus (note that he bore, in diminutive form, the names of the founders of Rome and of the empire) was deposed by a Germanic general in 476. Ruling in Italy, he simply sent the imperial regalia to Constantinople and declared that the West no longer needed an emperor. This is all that happened in 476, the traditional date for the "fall" of the Roman Empire.

After the vast coalition defeated the Huns in Gaul in 451, the remaining Roman authorities in the Paris region discovered that the Visigoths were expanding north of the Loire River into central Gaul. To check this advance, the Roman commander in Paris forged an alliance with the Franks. The Franks, long Roman allies, had been expanding their settlements from the mouth of the Rhine southward across modern Holland and Belgium since the third century.

The fortunes of the Frankish kingdom, indeed of all of Gaul, rested with Clovis. He became king of one group of Franks in 481 and spent the years until his death in 511 subjecting all the other bands of Franks to his rule. He gained the allegiance of the Frankish people by leading them to constant military victories that brought territorial gains, plunder, and tribute. The greatest of Clovis's successes came in 507, when he defeated the Visigoths and drove them over the Pyrenees into Spain.

Clovis was popular not only with the Franks but also with the Gallo-Roman population for three reasons. First, Clovis and the Romans had common enemies: Germanic peoples still living beyond the Rhine and pirates who raided the coast of Gaul. Second, whereas most of the Germanic peoples were Arian Christians, the Franks, after dallying with Arianism, converted to Catholicism. Thus, Clovis and the Gallo-Romans had a shared faith that permitted Clovis to portray his war against the Visigoths as a kind of crusade against heresy. Third, Clovis eagerly sought from Constantinople formal recognition and titles, appeared publicly in the dress of a Roman official, and practiced such imperial rituals as distributing gold coins while riding through crowds. The Frankish kingdom under Clovis's family—called "Merovingian," from the name of Merovech, one of his semilegendary ancestors—became the most successful of all the Germanic realms.

Several early Germanic kingdoms were short-lived. The Burgundian kingdom, which had once prompted the Romans to ally with the Huns, was swallowed up by the Franks in the 530s. The Vandals, who crossed the Rhine in 406 and headed for Spain, crossed to North Africa in 429 (see **Map 7.3**). They were ardent Arians who persecuted the Catholic population. They refused imperial offers of a treaty on terms similar to those accepted by other Germanic peoples, and they constantly plundered the islands of the western Mediterranean and the Italian coast, even sacking Rome in 455. Roman forces from Constantinople eliminated the Vandals in 534.

🌐 **Map 7.3 The Germanic Kingdoms, ca. 530** By 530, the western provinces of the Roman Empire (compare **Map 6.1** on page 142) had evolved into Germanic kingdoms. Just as Roman provincial boundaries had changed numerous times, the existence and extent of Germanic kingdoms were also impermanent.

The Ostrogoths, who had been living in Pannonia since the 370s as subjects of the Huns, began to pose a threat to the eastern empire after Attila's death. In 493, the emperor decided to send them to Italy to recover that area for the imperial government. The government at Constantinople was familiar with the Ostrogoths' king, Theodoric, because he had been a hostage there for several years

Theodoric conquered Italy quickly and set up his capital in Ravenna, the swamp-surrounded and virtually impregnable city that had sheltered the imperial administration for much of the fifth century. Through the force of his personality, and by a series of marriage alliances, Theodoric became the dominant ruler in western Europe. In Italy, he promoted peace, stability, and good government. Still, Theodoric had two strikes against him. First, he and his people were Arians. Second, although the population of Italy was accustomed to having an imperial court dominated by barbarians and to having Germanic military men as the real powers in the state, they had never been directly ruled by a barbarian, and some of them could not accept Theodoric. By the 520s, Theodoric grew increasingly suspicious and dictatorial.

When Theodoric died, his daughter Amalasuntha (498–535) served as regent for her son Athalaric from 526 to 534 and then briefly served as queen. A contemporary said that she was beautiful and well educated. She favored the Romans in Italy and promoted cultural fusion. For this, she angered the Goths, who deposed and then murdered her. Her death was Justinian's pretext to launch the Gothic Wars (535–554), which put an end to the Ostrogothic kingdom.

By the 530s, the western Roman Empire had vanished, the conclusion of a process initiated by the entry of the Visigoths into the Balkans in 376. Of all the peoples who had contested for a share of Rome's legacy, only the Franks in Gaul, the Visigoths in Spain, and the Anglo-Saxons in Britain had created durable political entities.

Why did the Roman government perish in the West? Beginning with Diocletian, Rome's best rulers were resident in and concerned mainly about the East. The Visigoths and other peoples were settled in their own kingdoms on Roman soil instead of being enrolled in and dispersed among Roman army units. Also during Diocletian's rule, the army was increasingly Germanized, and Germanic military men gained high offices in the state. Those leaders often dominated imperial courts and negotiated the series of treaties that submitted former provinces to barbarian peoples. Provincial elites had long been accustomed to having prominent Germans in their midst. The new situation was not unusual to them. Churchmen readily embraced the Catholic Franks and tolerated Arians, such as the Visigoths, when they promoted peace and good government without abusing the Catholic population.

Kunsthistorisches Museum, Vienna

**Amalasuntha, Daughter of Theodoric** This ivory plaque (ca. 530) depicts Amalasuntha in the way that Roman consuls and emperors had long been depicted on their assumption of office. Since the late fifth century, empresses had been depicted this way, too. Amalasuntha projects an image of legitimacy.

## Old and New in the West

Each realm was led by a king who usually appeared in two distinct guises. To his people, the king was the military leader. The essential bond of unity among each Germanic people was loyalty to the leader, who repaid his followers in booty, tribute, land, legal protection, and military security. To the Romans, the king appeared as an ally and magistrate. Almost all Germanic kings bore Roman titles, such as *consul* or *patrician*, and in these officially conferred titles resided the authority necessary to govern Roman populations. The kings also succeeded to a long line of Germanic Masters of the Soldiers, the title of the highest military officers in a prefecture. Each monarchy was led by a dynasty—for example, the Merovingians among the Franks—that was preeminent in wealth and possessed a sacral aura not unlike that of the Roman emperors.

The most common local officials were counts, a combined civilian-military position that made its first appearance in the fifth century. Initially a direct representative of the emperor, a count had financial, judicial, and military responsibilities. Local notables, usually great landowners, initially resented counts but gradually aspired to the office. Kings were careful to promote important locals, both Romans and their own people, to the office of count.

Local administration remained based in cities and towns. Taxes continued to be paid to royal governments throughout the sixth century. Provincial populations did not find this policy odd or unjust. Their taxes had always gone primarily to pay for the Roman military establishment, and the monarchies were the heirs of that establishment. Latin persisted as the language of administration, law, and the church. Until the end of Late Antiquity, notaries continued to draw up wills, records of land transactions, and legal documents of all kinds. Law codes issued by the Germanic kingdoms were largely adaptations of Roman provincial law. The legal conditions under which most people lived stayed pretty much the same. In sum, people's daily lives changed surprisingly little as a result of the replacement of Roman provinces by Germanic kingdoms.

## SECTION SUMMARY

- The Romans had long-standing relations with the Germanic barbarians living beyond their frontiers.
- The barbarian "tribes" were actually loose confederations of peoples, which achieved coherence only in kingdoms inside the empire.
- The Visigoths' change from allies, to enemies, and back to allies of the Romans is an instructive example of Romano-barbarian relations.
- The barbarian kingdoms retained many public and private aspects of Roman life.

# The Roman Empire in the East, 395–565

*What challenges did the eastern empire face and what were some of its major contributions?*

The creation of the tetrarchy at the end of the third century separated the eastern and western halves of the Roman Empire administratively. In theory, there was only one empire, ruled by one senior emperor, but in practice, the Eastern and Western courts followed different policies in many areas, notably in their relations with the barbarians. Fundamental cultural differences also distinguished East from West. The East was more populous, more heavily urbanized, and more prosperous. The eastern Mediterranean was Greek in culture and livelier intellectually than the West. The eastern empire survived while the western empire was being parceled out into kingdoms.

## Constantinople and Its Rulers

Constantius II (r. 337–361), Constantine's son and successor in the East, began making Constantinople a truly imperial city. He gave "New Rome" its own senate and urban magistrates, placing the city on an equal constitutional footing with Rome. Constantinople did not have an ancient aristocracy, so Constantius had to create a senatorial order. This he did by recruiting some Romans and promoting prominent and cultivated persons from cities in the eastern half of the empire, thereby forging bonds between the capital and its hinterland. Constantius and his successors also built palaces, public buildings, and churches to give the city a truly imperial character (see **Map 7.4**).

Theodosius II (r. 408–450) enjoyed the longest imperial reign in Roman history. Through skillful diplomacy and the occasional application of force, he managed to keep the eastern empire free of serious Germanic incursions and the Persians at bay in Mesopotamia. To protect his capital on the landward side, he built massive walls, whose ruins are impressive even today. He promoted learning in the city and both added and beautified important buildings. Theodosius and his family made the new capital a real intellectual center.

Born in 401, Theodosius ascended the throne as a child. Throughout his life, the two greatest influences on him were his sister, Pulcheria (399–453), and his wife, Athenais-Eudoxia

● **Map 7.4**
**Constantinople in Late Antiquity**
Protected by the sea, the Golden Horn, and its massive landward walls, Constantine's new city was an impregnable fortress for a thousand years. Note how the city was equipped with palaces, forums, wide thoroughfares, and other urban amenities.

Source: Robert Fossier, ed., *The Cambridge Illustrated History of The Middle Ages*, trans. Janet Sondheimer. Copyright © 1989. Used by permission of Cambridge University Press.

(ca. 400–460). Theodosius's moderate religious policy owed much to his wife, while his deep personal piety seems attributable to his sister. Pulcheria achieved the appointment and dismissal of imperial officers, guided foreign policy, and patronized scholars and churchmen. Only rarely do surviving sources permit us to observe the activities of imperial women. The cases of Pulcheria and Eudoxia hint at how much we do not know.

Theodosius's greatest achievement was his law code of 438. The most comprehensive collection of Roman law yet produced, this code brought together all Roman laws issued since Constantine and arranged them in systematic fashion. The principal Germanic kingdoms were established just after the Theodosian code was issued. From this text, and from the Roman institutional structures that employed it, the barbarians were taught the rule of law and regulations for the conduct of daily affairs.

## The Emperor Justinian (r. 527–565)

After Theodosius II died in 450, the eastern empire endured seventy-seven years of rule by military men who lacked the culture, vision, or administrative capacity of their predecessors. But they preserved the empire and kept its government functioning. It was from these rough soldiers that **Justinian** emerged to become the greatest ruler of Late Antiquity. (See the feature, "The Visual Record: The Ravenna Mosaics" on pages 188–189.)

Justinian was born in an Illyrian village (Croatia, today), entered the army, and secured high office under his illiterate uncle Justin, who had likewise risen from the peasantry to the imperial office (r. 518–527). Justinian surrounded himself with remarkable people and gave them considerable latitude. In 525, he flouted convention by marrying the actress Theodora (ca. 497–548). A woman of intelligence, imagination, and great courage, Theodora

**Justinian** Emperor of the eastern empire, he is best known for his law code and for overseeing the construction of the Church of Hagia Sophia.

**Theodosian Walls** By 413, Theodosius II had erected a massive set of walls, extending more than four miles, to protect Constantinople on the landward side. The wall system consisted of a double set of walls with brick facings and rubble-filled interiors. The main walls (shown here) were about 35 feet high with towers about every 240 feet. Sonia Halliday Photographs

was one of Justinian's key advisers. Contemporaries believed that she guided the emperor's religious policy. She certainly spent lavishly on charitable activities, not least, on homes for former prostitutes. Justinian also identified and promoted such previously obscure figures as the gifted general Belisarius (bel-uh-SAR-ee-us), the administrative genius John the Cappadocian, and the greatest legal mind of the age, Tribonian (tree-BONE-ee-un).

Almost immediately on assuming the throne, Justinian put John the Cappadocian to work reforming an administration that had been little altered in two centuries, despite vast changes in the scope of the empire. John worked particularly to secure tighter control of provincial administrators, to ensure a steady flow of tax revenue, and to eliminate official corruption. Tribonian and a commission were assigned the task of producing the first comprehensive collection of Roman law since that of Theodosius II in 438. Between 529 and 533, Justinian issued his code, the *Corpus Iuris Civilis* in several parts. Justinian's code, based on the idea that law should "give everyone his due," is the most influential legal collection in human history. It summarizes a thousand years of legal work, remained valid in the eastern empire until 1453, and has subsequently influenced almost every legal system in the modern world.

Not long after undertaking his legal and administrative reforms, Justinian launched an ambitious attempt to reunite the empire by reconquering its lost western provinces. Belisarius retook Africa from the Vandals and Italy from the Ostrogoths. Justinian also landed an army in Spain in an unsuccessful attempt to wrest Iberia from the Visigoths.

Justinian's ability to sustain major campaigns in the West was limited by the need to ward off constant threats in the East. The empire faced new enemies—Bulgars and Slavs—in the Balkans and a resurgent old foe—the Persians—in Mesopotamia. Costly treaties and humiliating subsidies bought a

**Hagia Sophia** Interior view of Hagia Sophia, the church of "Holy Wisdom," built by Justinian between 527 and 532. The church combines traditional Roman features and stunning new elements. When Constantinople fell to the Turks in 1453, this church became a mosque, an Islamic house of worship. In the early twentieth century, it became a museum. Werner Forman/Art Resource, NY string of cease-fires but no definitive settlements in these areas. The emperor's campaigns were so expensive that his administrative reforms wound up looking like contrivances to make more money for the emperor to waste. In 532, violent mobs coursed through the streets of Constantinople demanding the dismissal of John the Cappadocian and other imperial agents. Justinian almost fled, but Theodora steeled his resolve, telling him "the purple makes a good burial shroud." The revolt was put down. In 542, the Mediterranean world was visited by the most devastating plague in centuries, one more blow to the empire.

Justinian's religious policy also met with sharp opposition. A genuinely pious man, Justinian legislated frequently on behalf of the church and, along with Theodora, made charitable donations to the church and populace. Still, by both personal conviction and a sense of official duty, Justinian desired religious unity. Justinian was mildly Miaphysite, and his wife was enthusiastically so. Justinian tried again and again to find a compromise that would bring all parties together. His church council of 553 assembled amid high hopes, but his proposed doctrinal compromises alienated the clergy in Syria, Egypt, and Rome.

To create a monument equal to his lofty vision of the empire, Justinian sought out two great mathematicians, Anthemius of Tralles and Isidore of Miletus. He charged them to design a church that would represent the place where heaven and earth touched; the result was the Church of Hagia Sophia (AYE-yuh so-FEE-yuh). Regular meetings in this place of the emperor, the patriarch, and the people gave repeated symbolic confirmation of the proper ordering of the state. There is no evidence that Justinian dictated the form of his church, but the fact that he did not turn to any of the city's regular builders suggests that he was not looking for a conventional basilica. Tradition says that when Justinian first saw his new church, he said, "Solomon, I have outdone thee." The contemporary historian Procopius said the church was "extraordinary to those who saw it, quite unbelievable to those who merely heard about it."*

**Hagia Sophia** was the largest Christian church until the construction of new Saint Peter's in Rome (1503–1614). The building begins with a square just over 100 feet on a side, 70 feet above which are four great arches. Two of the arches are solid and form the nave walls of the church; the other two give way to semicircular continuations of the nave. Above the main square is a dome that seems to float on the blaze of light that pours through its windows. The inside is a riot of color, achieved by marble fittings in almost every imaginable hue and by the mysterious play of light and shadow. The effect of the whole is disorienting. The space in most basilicas is ordered, controlled, and elegant. The space in Hagia Sophia is horizontal and vertical, straight and curved, square and round. The inside is by turns dark and light, purple and green, red and blue. It is indeed as if one has entered a realm that is anchored to this world but gives access to another.

**Hagia Sophia**
Constructed during the reign of the emperor Justinian, this church in Constantinople was the largest Christian church until the construction of Saint Peter's in the sixteenth century.

## SECTION SUMMARY

- As the western empire was disappearing, the eastern empire experienced two centuries of capable, enlightened leadership.
- Constantinople was developed into a magnificent capital city.
- East Roman rulers continued to reform the administration and tax system.
- Both Theodosius II and Justinian made important contributions to the development of Roman law.

# Society and Culture in Late Antiquity

*How did women and men, elites and ordinary people, urban dwellers and farmers experience continuity and change in Late Antiquity?*

It is appropriate that in assessing his church, Justinian should have looked backward to Solomon, the Hebrew king who built Jerusalem's Temple. Justinian was a traditional, backward-looking ruler. His concern for the administrative minutiae of his empire would have made perfect sense to Diocletian. His combination of military and diplomatic initiatives would have been appreciated by Theodosius I, whose namesake, Theodosius II, would

---

*Procopius, *Buildings*, Loeb Classical Library. Trans. H. B. Dewing (Cambridge, MA: Harvard University Press, 1940), p. 13.

## The Ravenna Mosaics

*Propaganda.* The word has unsavory connotations. It suggests that someone is trying to convince someone else to do or to believe what is wrong. Actually, the word means only "things to be propagated," a message to be gotten out. The message itself may be good or bad, true or false.

When we think of propaganda, we must consider both the message and the medium in which it is conveyed. In antiquity, governments had several means of getting their messages out. Almost all the means were public, visible, and striking.

Mosaics are among the most spectacular art forms of Late Antiquity, and in the churches of Ravenna, they attained the summit of their propagandistic power. A mosaic is a picture formed by the intricate arrangement of thousands of tiny bits (called *tesserae*) of glass, stone, or metal. An artist created a rough sketch of the intended picture and then laid out the tesserae to conform to the sketch. Next, the artist applied wet plaster to a small section of the surface, usually a wall or a floor, that was to receive the picture and then embedded that section's tesserae into the plaster. This process was repeated until the mosaic was completed. The result was a durable art form of great beauty and visual interest. In the picture on the opposite page, you can see the tesserae and even some of the sparkle produced by the effect of sunlight and candlelight reflecting off the mosaic.

Mosaics were sometimes placed in private homes by the very wealthy, but more often they were put in conspicuous public places. Churches commonly received them in Late Antiquity. As more of society became Christian, aristocrats in particular were happy to spend lavishly to adorn their places of worship with beautiful decorations. Masses of people saw those decorations, reflected on who had financed them, and pondered the meaning of the images themselves.

The greatest patron of all was the emperor. By putting up any work of art, the emperor proclaimed his power and influence. His reach was vast even if he never left Constantinople. Nothing shows this better than the Ravenna mosaics erected by Justinian.

Let us recall the situation. The Arian Ostrogoths had taken over Italy in 493. Ruling from Ravenna, they claimed to be imperial allies and representatives. Down to 535, there were strains between Ravenna and Constantinople, and in that year, Justinian launched the twenty-year-long Gothic Wars. During and after the wars, churches were erected as symbols of the imperial restoration.

The mosaic pictured here is located on the left-hand side of the sanctuary, above and behind the altar, in the Church of San Vitale in Ravenna. Its central figure is the emperor Justinian. Immediately opposite it is another mosaic focusing on the empress Theodora. San Vitale was a monument to the defeat of the Arian Goths. Any worshiper who raised his or her eyes from the altar saw immediately both Justinian and Theodora. These images made a powerful statement in a city that had been ruled by a Gothic king for thirty-three years. Justinian was leaving no doubt about who was in charge. Consider, too, the prominence accorded to Theodora. Justinian really did view her as a partner in his rule.

That the emperor and empress were in charge is indicated in several distinct ways. They are slightly larger and are standing in front of their attendants. They are not quite like the other humans shown in the mosaic. They wear crowns and rich purple—that is to say, imperial—garments. They present gifts—he, a gold paten holding the Eucharistic bread and she, a golden chalice containing the Eucharistic wine. Thus, the emperor and empress are represented as the donors of the church and as the guarantors of authentic worship.

Justinian tried throughout his reign to promote *homonoia* ("concord"). He tried to reconcile many political and religious factions. Notice the figure to Justinian's

have admired Justinian's legal code. In his religious policies, especially his quest for unity, Justinian drew from a deep well of imperial precedent. Even in his attempt to restore direct rule in Rome's former western provinces, Justinian showed himself a traditionalist.

During these centuries of the ascendancy of the eastern Roman Empire, and the splintering of the western, the daily lives of men and women of every social class changed relatively little in terms of power relationships and economic opportunities. Nevertheless, provincial elites, members of the clergy, and barbarians gained unprecedented influence. Ordinary farmers, the overwhelming majority of the population, experienced changes in their legal status but not in their material well-being. Secular intellectual life lost most of its vitality, but a vibrant Christian culture flourished in the writings of the Church Fathers. Christianity added yet another element to the diversity that always characterized the Roman world.

## Social Hierarchies and Realities

Roman society had long been hierarchical, and from Republican times Rome had been governed by a hereditary class. Although the members of this class affected a style of life that set them apart, they were never a closed caste. First, they did not reproduce themselves very

**Justinian and His Courtiers, Sanctuary Mosaic, San Vitale, Ravenna**

We may note one more piece of propaganda. Look at the man standing to the left of Justinian and slightly behind him—between Justinian and Maximianus. This is Julianus Argentarius, a wealthy layman who was in all things the emperor's agent in Ravenna. He helped finance and oversaw the construction of not only San Vitale but also several other churches in Ravenna. His presence signifies *homonoia*, the traditional concord between the emperor and the elite throughout the empire. Relations between the court and the Italian elite had been very strained under the Ostrogoths. Julianus's presence signaled that all was well once again. Vanity played a role, too. Julianus paid for the art, so he had himself included in it.

The Church of San Vitale was itself a propaganda statement. Theodoric was buried in a grand octagonal tomb. Justinian's builders chose an octagonal form for San Vitale. This church is also a sepulcher—a shrine for the remains of Saint Vitalis, an early Ravenna Christian who was martyred for the true faith.

left (your right), over whose bald head you can read MAXIMIANUS. This man was the archbishop of Ravenna, a close ally of the emperor and the person responsible both for eradicating Arianism and for reconciling Arians. His prominent position next to the emperor, and the fact that he alone is named, assured everyone of the correct doctrinal position. And in case anyone needed a further reminder, Maximianus holds in his hand the cross of Christ: There would be no more Arian subordination of the second person of the Trinity to the first.

### Questions

1. Mosaics are public and visible. They convey messages. What images or monuments can you think of that convey messages?

2. How many propaganda "messages" can you find in this picture?

3. What do you think of Justinian as a propagandist?

effectively. About two-thirds of the Roman aristocracy was replaced every century—a typical pattern in premodern societies. This turnover created significant opportunities for social mobility. Second, just as the empire had been born in a social transformation that brought the Italian aristocracy into the Roman governing class, so Late Antiquity was characterized by a transformation that brought provincial elites and barbarians into the framework of power. Paradoxically, social change was always masked as social continuity because when new men reached the top, they tried to embrace the culture and values of those whom they had replaced.

Three ideals guided the lives of elite men: *otium*, *amicitia*, and *officium*. *Otium*, "leisure," meant that the only life worth living was one of withdrawal in which the finer things in life—literature especially—could be cultivated. *Amicitia*, "friendship," implied several things. It could mean the kinds of literary contacts that the thousands of surviving letters from Late Antiquity reveal. Friendship also could mean patronage. The doorstep of every noble household was crowded every morning with hangers-on who awaited their patron's small offerings and any commands as to how they might do his will. *Officium*, "duty," was the sense of civic obligation that Roman rulers communicated to the provincial upper classes.

Aristocrats governed in both public and private ways. Though gradually excluded from key military and administrative posts, nobles did not lose their influence. They used their wealth to win or reward followers, bribe officials, and buy verdicts. In towns, decurions controlled local market privileges, building trades, police forces, fire brigades, and charitable associations. Their public and private means of persuasion and intimidation were immense. In the West, in the growing absence of an imperial administration, Roman public power did not so much "decline and fall" as find itself privatized and localized. Patronage and clientage in Roman society had a benevolent dimension, but they also revealed the raw realities of power.

In Roman society, power was everything, and those who lacked power were considered "poor," regardless of their financial status. On this reckoning, much of the urban population was poor because they lacked access to the official means of coercion and security that the notables enjoyed. Merchants, artisans, teachers, and others were always vulnerable because their social, political, or economic positions could change at a moment's notice. They lacked the influence to protect themselves.

Most citizens of the late antique world can be classed as farmers, but this categorization is misleading because it lumps together the greatest landowners and the poorest peasants. Late Antiquity saw a trend in the countryside that continued into the Middle Ages: Freedom and slavery declined simultaneously. In uncertain times, many small farmers handed over their possessions to local notables and received them back in return for rents in money or in kind. They became *coloni*, "tenants." Their patrons promised to protect them from lawsuits and from severe economic hardship. More and more, these coloni were bound to their places of residence and forced to perform services or pay fees that marked their status as less than fully free. At the same time, many landlords who could no longer afford to house, feed, and equip slaves gave them their freedom and elevated them to the status of coloni. Probably, the day-to-day lives of the great mass of the rural population and their position at the bottom of the social hierarchy changed very little.

Women's lives are not as well known to us as men's. "Nature produced women for this very purpose," says a Roman legal text, "that they might bear children and this is their greatest desire." Ancient philosophy held that women were intellectually inferior to men, science said they were physically weaker, and law maintained that they were naturally dependent. In the Roman world, women could not enter professions, and they had limited rights in legal matters. Christianity offered women opposing models. There was Eve, the eternal temptress through whom sin had fallen on humanity, and then there was Mary, the virginal mother of God. The Bible also presented readers with powerful, active women, such as Deborah and Ruth, and loyal, steadfast ones, such as Jesus' female disciples.

Girls usually did not choose their marriage partners. Betrothals could take place as early as age 7 and lawful marriages at 12. Most marriages took place when the girl was around 16; husbands were several years older. A daughter could reject her father's choice only if the intended man was unworthy in status and behavior. Women could inherit property from their fathers and retained some control over their marital dowries. Divorce was possible but only in restricted cases. A divorced woman who had lost the financial security provided by her husband and father was at a distinct disadvantage legally and economically unless she had great wealth. (See the feature, "The Written Record: Divorce Roman Style" on page 191.)

Christianity brought some interesting changes in marriage practices. Since the new faith prized virginity and celibacy, women now had the option of declining marriage. The church at Antioch supported three thousand virgins and widows. Christian writers tried to attract women to the celibate life by emphasizing that housework was drudgery. Christianity required both men and women to be faithful in marriage, whereas Roman custom had permitted men, but not women, to have lovers, prostitutes, and concubines. Christianity increased the number of days when men and women had to abstain from sex. Ancient cultures often prohibited sexual intercourse during menstruation and pregnancy, but Christianity added Sundays and many feast days as forbidden times. Further, Christianity disapproved of divorce, which may have accorded women greater financial and social security, although at the cost of staying with abusive or unloved husbands.

Traditionally women were not permitted to teach in the ancient world, although we do hear of women teachers, such as Hypatia of Alexandria (355–415), renowned for her knowledge of philosophy and mathematics. Until at least the sixth century, the Christian church

## Divorce Roman Style

*The codes of both Theodosius and Justinian addressed the subject of divorce.*

### Theodosian Code

3.16.1 It is Our pleasure that no woman, on account of her own depraved desires, shall be permitted to send a notice of divorce to her husband on trumped up grounds, as, for instance, that he is a drunkard or a gambler or a philanderer, nor indeed shall a husband be permitted to divorce his wife on every sort of pretext. When a woman sends a notice of divorce, the following criminal charges only shall be investigated, that is, if she should prove that her husband is a homicide, a sorcerer, or a destroyer of tombs . . . if she should send a notice of divorce to her husband on grounds other than these three criminal charges, she must leave everything, even her last hairpin, in her husband's house, and, as punishment for her supreme self-confidence, she shall be deported to an island. In the case of a man also, if he should send a notice of divorce, inquiry shall be made as to the following three criminal charges, namely, if he wishes to divorce her as an adulteress, a sorceress, or a procuress. If he should cast off a wife who is innocent of these crimes, he must restore her entire dowry, and he shall marry no other woman.

### Justinian, *Novella 22*

2.3 Reciprocal affection constitutes marriage, without it being necessary to enter into a dotal contract; for when the parties are once agreed and have been influenced by pure affection, it is not requisite to stipulate a dowry, or a donation on account of marriage.

22.4 Marriages are occasionally dissolved by common consent during the lives of the contracting parties . . . at other times they are dissolved for some good reason.

22.5 Divorce takes place without blame whenever the husband or the wife enters monastic life, and desires to live in chastity.

22.6 Marriage is dissolved for a necessary and not unreasonable cause, when the husband is incapable of copulation with his wife, and cannot do what nature created him for.

22.7 The effect of captivity is to dissolve marriage by mutual consent, where one of the two married persons is in the hands of the enemy; for where the husband suffers a misfortune of this kind, and the wife remains at home; or, on the other hand, the wife is reduced to captivity, and her husband remains in the country, the marriage is dissolved for a reason derived from the condition of slavery; as, where a person is once reduced to servitude, the inequality of condition does not permit the marriage state to continue to exist. Considering cases of this kind from a humane point of view, we desire that the marriage remain undissolved as long as it is clear that either the husband or the wife is still living.

### Questions

1. *Do these rules seem just and balanced to you?*
2. *Do women or men have greater burdens in Roman law?*
3. *How many of these cases would be relevant today?*

Theodosian Code and Corpus Iuris Civilis, from Michael Maas, Readings in Late Antiquity (London: Routledge, 2000), pp. 231-33

had deaconesses, who had important responsibilities in the instruction of women and girls. Medical knowledge was often the preserve of women, particularly in areas such as childbirth, sexual problems, and "female complaints."

Christianity also affected daily life. Churchmen were concerned that women not be seen as sex objects. They told women to clothe their flesh, veil their hair, and use jewelry and cosmetics in moderation. Pious women no longer used public baths and latrines. Male or female, Christians thought and lived in distinctive new ways. All Christians were sinners, and so all were equal in God's eyes and equally in need of God's grace. Birth, wealth, and status were not supposed to matter in this democracy of sin. Theological equality did not, however, translate into social equality.

The church also introduced some new status distinctions. Holiness became a badge of honor, and holy men and women became Late Antiquity's greatest celebrities. After their deaths, they were venerated as saints. Sanctuaries were dedicated to them, and people made pilgrimages to their tombs to pray and seek healing from physical and spiritual ailments. Thus, in some ways, Christianity produced a society the likes of which the ancient world had never known, a society in which the living and the dead jockeyed for a place in a hierarchy that was at once earthly and celestial. But in other ways, Christianity reoriented traditional Roman patron-client relations so that client sinners in this world were linked to sanctified patrons in heaven.

## The Quest for a Catholic Tradition

By the middle of the fifth century, the Nicene Creed, first spelled out in 325, had taken definitive shape; it is still recited regularly in many Christian churches. With the Council of Nicaea, we see the first clear evidence that people were striving for a *catholic*, a universal, form of Christianity. Strictly speaking, catholic Christianity would be the one form professed by all believers. It is no accident that the Catholic Church grew up in a Roman world steeped in ideas of universality. The most deeply held tenet of Roman ideology was that Rome's mission was to civilize the world and bend it to Roman ways. As we have seen, however, it proved impossible to attain or impose a single set of beliefs.

One intriguing development in Late Antiquity is the emergence of several Christian communities claiming fidelity to a universal, or catholic, tradition. The Latin Christian church in the West clung tightly to the doctrinal formulations of Nicaea and Chalcedon and took its bearings from Latin church writers. In the eastern Mediterranean, writers tended to use the word *Orthodox*, which means "right believing" but also carries clear implications of catholicism, or "universality." The Orthodox Church centered primarily on the emperors and patriarchs, used Greek, and followed Greek Christian writers. The Coptic Church in Egypt was Miaphysite, followed the teachings of the patriarchs of Alexandria, and used the Coptic language. The Jacobite Church, mildly Miaphysite, was originally strong in Syria, from which it spread to Mesopotamia and beyond. Each of these churches produced a literature, art, and way of life that marked its members as a distinct community. These traditions did not reflect the emergence of something new in Late Antiquity so much as a Christian reinterpretation of very old cultures and ideals. Each of these traditions exists today.

Christianity drew much from the pagan and Jewish environments within which it grew, but its fundamental inspiration was the collection of writings called in modern times the Bible. It was understood to be a collection of sacred writings, and the individual items in that collection had different meanings. From the second century, Christian writers began trying to define a canon, a definitive list of genuine Old and New Testament scriptures. It was widely recognized that without an official, standardized set of Christian writings, there could be no uniformity of Christian belief. This process of determining authentic Scripture was not completed until the middle of the fifth century.

While the search was underway for an authoritative list of books, it was also necessary to try to get uniform versions of the books that were being pronounced canonical. The Greek East used the Greek version of the Old Testament and the Greek New Testament. But that version was unsuitable in the West, where Latin was the principal tongue. Late in the fourth century, Pope Damasus (DAM-uh-sus) commissioned Jerome (331–420), a man who had renounced his wealth for a life of monasticism and scholarship, to prepare a Latin version based on a new translation of the Hebrew Scriptures and Greek New Testament. Jerome's version is called the **Vulgate Bible** because it was the Bible for the "people" (*vulgus*) who knew Latin.

**Vulgate Bible** Prepared by Jerome in the late fourth century, it was a Latin translation of the Hebrew Scriptures (Old Testament) and the Greek New Testament.

The development of a scriptural canon paralleled the elaboration of a creedal statement that would set down precisely what Christians believed. As we have seen, the Councils of Nicaea and Constantinople defined the nature of the Trinity, and Chalcedon formulated the relationship between the human and divine natures of Christ. There were also debates about the nature of the priesthood, the structure and authority of the church, and the problem of human free will. Practical questions came up, too. How could Christians fulfill the moral demands of their faith while living in a world whose values were often at odds with church teachings?

Answers to these kinds of questions were provided by a group of Greek and Latin writers who are called the "Church Fathers" and whose era is called "patristic" (from *patres*, the Latin word for "fathers"). In versatility and sheer output, they have few rivals at any time. Their intellectual breadth was matched by their elegant style and trenchant reasoning.

Many Christian writers addressed the problems of moral living in the world. In his treatise *On Duties*, Ambrose of Milan (339–397) attempted to Christianize the public ethos that Cicero had spelled out many years before in his book of the same name. Cicero talked of citizens' obligations to one another and to the law and the need for those in power to be above reproach in the conduct of their personal lives. Ambrose reinterpreted these obligations as duties that Christians owed to one another because of their common worship of God.

Pope Gregory I (540–604) wrote *The Pastoral Rule* to reformulate Cicero's and Ambrose's ideas in ways that made them relevant to society's Christian leaders, the clergy. John Chrysostom (KRIH-sus-tum) (347–407), a patriarch of Constantinople and one of the most popular and gifted preachers of Late Antiquity (his name means "golden tongued"), bitterly castigated the immorality of the imperial court and aristocracy: By setting a bad example, they endangered the souls of their subjects. John's sermons infuriated the elite and he was exiled.

Boethius (bow-EE-thee-us) (480–524) illustrates contemporary themes well. Descended from one of Rome's oldest families, he held high offices but eventually earned the enmity of Theodoric the Ostrogoth, who imprisoned and executed him. He was a prolific writer, whose Latin translations of Greek philosophical texts bequeathed those writings to the Middle Ages. In his most famous book, *The Consolation of Philosophy*, written while he was in prison, Boethius describes how the soul could rise through philosophy to a knowledge of God. Once again, we see the classical and the Christian blended in a new synthesis.

**Sarcophagus of Junius Bassus** Junius Bassus, prefect of Rome, died in 359 and was laid to rest in this splendid sarcophagus (from the Greek "body eater"). Three points are important: First, as members of the Roman elite became Christian, they could afford to employ the finest craftsmen. Second, as Christianity became legal, it could search for artistic expression. Third, these Old and New Testament scenes proclaim Christ's divinity but, in an age of intense theological quarrels, glide over his humanity. Compare Santa Maria Maggiore on page 166. Scala/Art Resource, NY

## Saint Augustine and the Christian Tradition

The most influential Christian thinker after Saint Paul was **Augustine of Hippo** (354–430). Augustine was born in North Africa to a pagan father and a Christian mother. His family was of modest means, but at great sacrifice, they arranged for him to receive the best education available. He embarked on a career as a professor of rhetoric. Augustine fell under the spell of Ambrose and embraced the Christianity that his mother, Monica, had been urging on him throughout his life. Later, Augustine chronicled his quest for truth and spiritual fulfillment in his *Confessions*, a classic of Western literature. In 395, Augustine became a bishop and, until his death, served the wider Christian world and produced a torrent of writings.

Not a systematic thinker, Augustine never set out to provide a comprehensive exposition of the whole of Christian doctrine. Instead, he responded to problems as they arose. Crucial among these were the relationship between God and humans, the nature of the church, and the overall plan of God's creation.

In the early fifth century, some people believed that they could achieve salvation by the unaided operation of their own will. Augustine responded that although God did indeed endow humankind with free will, Adam and Eve had abused their will to rebel against God. Ever since that first act of rebellion, a taint, called by theologians "original sin," predisposed all humans to continual rebellion, or sin, against God. Only divine grace can overcome sin, and only by calling on God can people receive grace. Here was a decisive break with the classical idea of humanity as good in itself and capable of self-improvement, perhaps even perfection, in this world.

Some North African heretics taught that sacraments celebrated by unworthy priests are invalid. Augustine believed that the validity of the church's sacraments—those ritual celebrations that are considered to be channels for the communication of grace, of God's special aid and comfort to the faithful—does not depend on the personal merit of the minister. They depended on the grace of God. To Augustine, God alone is perfect. Clergy, rulers, and churches are all human institutions, all more or less good in particular circumstances.

To many adherents of the traditional Roman religion, the sack of Rome by the Visigoths in 410 was repayment for Rome's abandonment of its traditional gods. To refute them, Augustine wrote the most brilliant and difficult of all his works, *The City of God*. This book is a theology of history. Augustine sees time not as cyclical—the traditional classical view—but as linear. Since the creation of the world, a plan has been in operation—God's plan—and that plan will govern all human activity until the end of time. History is the struggle between

**Augustine of Hippo** North African bishop and influential Christian thinker, he authored the *Confessions* and *The City of God*.

those who call on divine grace, who are redeemed, who are citizens of the City of God, and those who keep to the ways of the world, who persist in sin, who live in the earthly city. One may observe the unfolding of the divine plan by seeing how much of the earthly city has been redeemed at any given time.

Even though the Roman Empire was officially Christian, Augustine refused to identify his City of God with it. Nor would he say that the church and the City of God were identical. What he did say was that the sack of Rome was a great irrelevance because many kingdoms and empires had come and gone and would continue to do so, but only the kingdom of God was eternal and, in the long run, important. To a Roman people whose most cherished belief held that the world would last exactly as long as Rome's dominion, Augustine's dismissal of Rome's destiny sounded the death knell of the classical worldview.

Augustine also addressed the problem of education. He regarded salvation as the goal of life but realized that people have to carry on with their ordinary occupations. He also knew that almost the entire educational establishment was pagan in design and content. Education was confined mainly to the elite, who sought schooling partly to orient themselves within their cultural tradition and partly to gain employment, often in the imperial or urban service. This education had three mainstays. Latin or Greek grammar—rarely both—was the first. Augustine, for instance, knew little Greek, and by the sixth century, few people in the East knew Latin. The second mainstay of education was rhetoric, once the art of public speaking but now, increasingly, literary criticism. The third was dialectic, or the art of right reasoning. In Late Antiquity, public schools were fast disappearing as the need for them slipped away. But the church still needed educated persons, so it provided schools in cathedrals and monasteries.

In a treatise entitled *On Christian Doctrine*, Augustine expressed some ideas about education that proved influential for a millennium. He argued that everything a person needs to know to achieve salvation is contained in the Bible. But the Bible, written in learned language, is full of difficult images and allusions. How is an ordinary person to learn what he or she needs to know in order to master this great book of life? Only by getting some schooling, and that education would inevitably be in the classical languages and literatures. Augustine's attitude toward classical learning was that it was useful only to the extent that it equipped individuals to read the Bible, to understand it, and to seek salvation. Classical culture had no intrinsic merit. It might give pleasure, but it was equally likely to be a distraction or a temptation to immorality.

The Italian writer Cassiodorus (ca. 485–580) gave this Augustinian interpretation of the classical heritage its definitive statement in his treatise, *On Divine and Human Readings*. His treatise served as a kind of annotated bibliography and curriculum of the major writings on school subjects, such as grammar, rhetoric, and dialectic, and on biblical commentary. For centuries, schools organized on Augustine's and Cassiodorus's model did an estimable job of preparing the clergy to carry out their functions.

## SECTION SUMMARY

- Despite dramatic political changes, Late Antiquity witnessed relatively little social or economic change.
- Christianity did, however, introduce many changes in morals and values.
- Late Antiquity presents us with the paradox of multiple "Catholic" traditions, that is, different Christian groups who believed that their tradition was universal.
- In the Latin and Greek churches, a catholic tradition was built upon a canon of sacred writings, a creed, and the writings of the Church Fathers.
- The greatest intellectual of Late Antiquity was Saint Augustine, who wrote on theology, history, and education.

# Chapter Summary

◆ *What were the most important reforms of Diocletian, Constantine, and their successors, and what roles did those reforms play in saving and transforming the empire?*

When the late antique period opened, Rome's vast and diverse empire was beset with innumerable political, military, and economic problems. The classical culture that had evolved over centuries in the Mediterranean world seemed to have lost much of its vigor and appeal. But energetic rulers, such as Diocletian and Constantine, undertook half a century of intense military, economic, and administrative reform. On religious issues, the rulers differed—Diocletian persecuted Christians while Constantine legalized the new faith. Their reforms put the empire on firm footing while simultaneously changing forever the basic nature of the Roman state.

◆ *How and why did a* Roman *and* Catholic *Church emerge in Late Antiquity?*

The fourth century was a period of religious change for the empire. Church officials attempted to resolve disagreements over Christian teachings with ecumenical councils, but religious unity was never fully achieved. Further attempts to resolve controversies strengthened the power of the bishops and created the new role of the papacy. As the power of the pope increased, so too did the role of the elite. However, some men and women yearned to escape the trappings of the world and turned toward a new way of life—monasticism.

◆ *Who were the "barbarians," and what kinds of relations did Romans and barbarians have in Late Antiquity?*

In 300, barbarians were a worrisome threat along the northern frontiers of the empire. By 600, barbarians had created, from Britain to Spain, a succession of kingdoms, the most successful of which owed great debts to Rome. The barbarians did not appear suddenly in Late Antiquity. Rome knew these people and had traded, fought, and allied with them for centuries. The barbarians did not come to destroy Rome but to join it, to benefit from it, to learn its ways. The creation of the barbarian kingdoms was, in many ways, one of Rome's most creative political acts.

◆ *What challenges did the eastern empire face and what were some of its major contributions?*

In the eastern empire, Constantinople rose to become a truly imperial city under the emperors Theodosius and Justinian. Justinian's code, which collected and organized Roman law, is the most influential legal collection in history. Equally impressive was the construction of a new Christian church, the Hagia Sophia. Yet despite these achievements, Justinian had to deal with new enemies, expensive military campaigns, and a devastating plague.

◆ *How did women and men, elites and ordinary people, urban dwellers and farmers experience continuity and change in Late Antiquity?*

While these centuries were a period of great political and religious change, the daily lives of men and women stayed remarkably unchanged. Society was hierarchical and most of the population was categorized as poor. Christianity brought some changes to social practices, such as marriage and relationships between men and women. Believers strived for a universal, or catholic, form of Christianity and this led to the development of a scriptural canon. New writings on Christianity, from Saint Augustine and others, also helped to shape beliefs.

## Key Terms

tetrarchy (p. 169)

Edict of Milan (p. 171)

heresy (p. 173)

Arianism (p. 173)

Council of Nicaea (p. 174)

monasticism (p. 177)

eremitic monasticism (p. 177)

cenobitic monasticism (p. 177)

Visigoths (p. 180)

Justinian (p. 185)

Hagia Sophia (p. 187)

Vulgate Bible (p. 192)

Augustine of Hippo (p. 193)

CourseMate

Go to the CourseMate website at **www.cengagebrain.com** for additional study tools and review materials—including audio and video clips—for this chapter.

**The Great Mosque of Cordoba** Christopher Rennie/Robert Harding World Imagery

# Early Medieval Civilizations, 600–900

This chapter treats three areas and histories: the Islamic East, the Byzantine Empire, and the Latin West. For each, the seventh century was an era of dramatic change, the eighth century a period of reform and consolidation, and the ninth century a time of upheaval. A new imperial tradition developed in all three areas. Muslims, Orthodox Christians, and Catholics all believed themselves to be chosen by God, and their rulers defined themselves as God's earthly agents. In all three realms, the interaction of local traditions and the Roman past produced new forms of central government that would prove influential for centuries. Commercial ties began to transform the Mediterranean world into a community of peoples who needed to balance mutual interests with bitter rivalries.

The Great Mosque of Cordoba, erected by Abd ar-Rahman in 786–787, at first glance appears much like a late antique building: elegant columns, arches arranged in arcades, rectangular space. But this is an Islamic house of worship, and it was built in Spain, one of Rome's oldest provinces. We saw in Chapter 7 that Spain had fallen to the Visigoths in the sixth century and that Justinian had been unable to reconquer the region. Between 711 and 716, an army of Arabs and North African tribesmen overwhelmed Spain and inaugurated seven centuries of Islamic rule on the Iberian Peninsula. A time traveler transported to the Mediterranean world of 600 would almost certainly have predicted only two heirs to Rome: the eastern empire and the kingdoms of the barbarian West. It is extremely unlikely that our intrepid wanderer would have foreseen one of the most dramatic developments in the history of Western civilization: the rise of the Arabs and their Islamic faith.

The Great Mosque serves as a remarkable reminder of how much changed—and how much remained the same—in the early Middle Ages. Arches and arcades graced classical architecture for more than a millennium. But Cordoba's arches are horseshoe shaped, a minor innovation. The arches incorporate alternating bands of red and cream-colored stone. These shapes and colors may be local traditions, an imitation of the Roman aqueduct at Mérida, Byzantine imports, or Syrian characteristics. The building's shape is basilican. In a basilica, the space is oriented to the area where officials presided—to an

## Chapter Overview

### The Islamic East
- *What were the most important factors in the rise of the Arab peoples and the Islamic faith?*

### The Byzantine Empire
- *Why did a distinctive civilization that can be called "Byzantine" emerge?*

### The Rise of the Carolingian Empire
- *What were the greatest achievements of the Carolingians and why were they so successful compared to the other states that survived Rome's collapse in the West?*

### Early Medieval Economies and Societies
- *What were the chief similarities and differences among the early medieval civilizations?*

altar when the basilica is a church. In a mosque, the space is oriented to the *quibla*—a place in the wall facing Mecca, the birthplace of Muhammad and Islam. The elements of the Great Mosque were old, but the overall effect was new.

The period from 600 to 900 is commonly called the "early Middle Ages." What does this term mean? In the seventeenth century, a Dutch scholar wrote of the "Middle Times" that lay between antiquity and the dawning modern world. The name stuck. As a label for the post-Roman world, "Middle Ages" (whose adjectival form is "medieval") has become traditional. The fact that we no longer talk of an abrupt and catastrophic "fall" of the Roman Empire means that we no longer use the word in negative ways.

# The Islamic East

*What were the most important factors in the rise of the Arab peoples and the Islamic faith?*

**Muhammad** Prophet and founder of Islam. He began receiving revelations to preach about Allah around 610. Before his death, he had converted most of Arabia.

Ancient writers took little notice of the Arabs, who inhabited the Arabian peninsula and lands to the north. Around 600, the prophet Muhammad (570–632) appeared among them preaching a faith old in its basic elements but new in its formulation. With unprecedented spiritual and military fervor, converts to that new faith conquered territories from Spain to the frontiers of China. Slowly, they built an imperial system with a coherent government and ideology. At the same time, cultural elites began forging a new civilization out of the ethnic, religious, and historical diversity of that vast realm.

The Arab world in 600 was large and turbulent. Long dominated by the Roman and Persian Empires, the region had no large-scale political entities. People belonged to close-knit clans, or extended families, that formed tribes. In theory, tribes were groups of people who traced their descent from a known ancestor; in reality—and in this, Arab and Germanic peoples were alike—tribes were complex groups of relatives, allies, and political or economic clients.

The Arab East was also economically intricate and fragile. Bedouins (Arabs who were nomadic pastoralists) provided for their own needs from their herds of sheep and goats, from small-scale trading in towns, and from regular raids on one another and on caravans. Some farmers worked the land, but in many areas soils were too poor and rain was too infrequent to support agriculture. Cities supported traders who carried luxury goods, such as spices, incense, and perfumes, from the Indian Ocean region and southern Arabia along caravan routes to the cities of the eastern Mediterranean. These traders formed the economic and political elite of Arabia, and they led the tribes. Mecca, dominated by the powerful Quraysh (KOOR-aysh) tribe, was the foremost city of Arabia.

A solution to the competition among tribes and towns for control of trade routes was the institution of *harams* (HAR-ahms), or sanctuaries—places where contending parties could settle disputes peacefully. Mecca was one of the chief harams in Arabia, and its founding was attributed to the Israelite patriarch Abraham and one of his sons, Ishmael. The focus of the sanctuary was the black stone shrine known as the Kaaba (KAH-bah), founded by Abraham, according to Arab tradition. For centuries, people from all over Arabia had made pilgrimages to Mecca, to the Kaaba, supposedly following Abraham's example.

The region's ethnic and religious composition was complicated, too. The Roman world was overwhelmingly Christian, although there were many kinds of Christian. The Persian realm was officially Zoroastrian, but it had Jewish, Christian, Manichaean, and Buddhist minorities. The Arabs themselves were generally pagans, but Arabia had Jewish and Christian minorities.

## The Prophet and His Faith

Muhammad was born in 570 to a respectable, though not wealthy or powerful, clan of the Quraysh tribe. His father died before he was born, his mother shortly afterward, leaving Muhammad under the care of his grandparents and an uncle. Like many young Meccans, he entered the caravan trade. By the time he was 20, Muhammad had such a reputation for competence and moral uprightness that he became financial adviser to a wealthy Quraysh widow, Khadija (KAH-dee-ah) (555–619). Though older than Muhammad, she became his wife in 595, and they had a loving marriage until her death.

In 610, Muhammad received the first of many revelations that commanded him to teach all people a new faith that called for an unquestioned belief in one god, Allah, and a deep commitment to social justice for believers. Muhammad began teaching in Mecca, but he converted few people outside his own circle; his wife was his first convert. Some Meccans were envious of Muhammad. Others feared that his new faith and new god might call into question the legitimacy of the shrines in Mecca and jeopardize the traditional pilgrimages to the Kaaba and the trade that accompanied them. By 619, Muhammad's well-connected wife and uncle were dead, and his position was precarious.

At this juncture, citizens from Medina, a smaller trading community wracked by dissension among pagan Arabs, Jews, and followers of Muhammad, asked Muhammad to establish a haram there. In the summer of 622, small groups of Muhammad's disciples made their way to Medina and, in September, Muhammad joined them. His journey from Mecca to Medina, the *hijra* (HEEZH-rah), marks the beginning of a new era, symbolized to this day in the Arab world by a calendar that dates "In the year of the Hijra."

Although Muhammad was fully in control in Medina, Mecca retained his attention. In addition to his sentimental attachment to Mecca, its political and economic importance was critical to his emerging desire to convert all of Arabia. His followers began attacking Meccan caravans and battled with the Meccans several times in the 620s. In 630, Muhammad and many of his followers returned to Mecca in triumph. Muhammad left the Quraysh in control, and he retained the Kaaba as a focus of piety. After making local arrangements, he returned to Medina and set about winning over the bedouins of the Arabian desert. By the time Muhammad died in 632, he had converted most of Arabia (see **Map 8.1**).

To what exactly had Muhammad and his followers converted? At the most basic level, people were asked to surrender completely to Allah, the one true God—that is, they were asked to make *al-Islam*, "the surrender." Those who surrendered became *Muslims* and joined the *umma muslima* (OO-mah MOOSE-lee-mah), a completely new kind of community in which membership depended only on belief in Allah and acceptance of Muhammad as Allah's prophet. No longer were one's bonds confined to a particular clan, tribe, or town. All members of the umma were understood to have personal and communal responsibility for all other members. Because of the experience of the hijra, Islam was a religion of exile, of separation from the ordinary world, and of reliance on God.

The basic teachings of Islam are traditionally described as **Five Pillars**: (1) the profession of faith, "There is no God but Allah and Muhammad is His Prophet"; (2) individual prayer five times daily, plus group prayer at noon on Friday in a *mosque*, a Muslim house of prayer; (3) the sunup-to-sundown fast for one month per year; (4) the donation of generous alms to the poor; and (5) a pilgrimage to Mecca at least once in a person's lifetime. These pillars are still the central requirements of Islam.

In the early decades the pillars sustained a faith that stressed strict monotheism and practices that affirmed Islam and built up a sense of community. At certain times of the day, all Muslims everywhere bowed in prayer, with their heads facing toward Mecca. Everyone

## CHRONOLOGY

| | |
|---|---|
| 570–632 | Life of Muhammad |
| 597 | Pope Gregory I sends missionaries to England |
| 610–641 | Reign of Heraclius in Byzantium |
| 622 | Hijra |
| 632–733 | Muslim conquests |
| 661–750 | Umayyad caliphate |
| 664 | Council of Whitby |
| 711–716 | Muslim conquest of Spain |
| 726–787, 815–842 | Byzantine iconoclasm |
| 750 | Founding of Abbasid caliphate |
| 751 | Lombard conquest of Ravenna |
| 755–756 | Foundation of Papal States |
| 755–774 | Frankish conquest of Lombards |
| 757–796 | Reign of Offa of Mercia |
| 768–814 | Reign of Charlemagne |
| 780s–860s | Carolingian Renaissance |
| 786–809 | Reign of Harun al-Rashid |
| 800 | Imperial coronation of Charlemagne |
| 843 | Treaty of Verdun creates three Frankish kingdoms |
| 867–886 | Reign of Basil I |

**Five Pillars** The basic beliefs and practices of Islam.

🌐 **Map 8.1 Arab Conquests to 733** This map vividly illustrates the spectacular gains by the Arabs in the time of Muhammad, under the first caliphs, and under the Umayyads. Later slow, steady gains in Africa, central Asia, and India expanded the empire even farther. Muslim conquest did not at first mean widespread conversion to Islam; Egypt, for example, was not majority Muslim before the tenth century. © Cengage Learning 2014

paid alms, creating thereby a feeling of solidarity among all members of the umma. Mecca itself and the experience of pilgrimage were central to all Muslims.

Originally, there was no elaborate theology, intricate doctrinal mysteries, creed, or clergy. Men called *imams* led the Friday prayers in the mosque and usually offered sermons that applied Muslim teaching to the issues of the day, but Islam involved no ordained priesthood, as in Judaism and Christianity, and no hierarchy, as in the Christian churches.

Muhammad always insisted that he transmitted a direct, verbal revelation, not his own interpretations. That revelation came in the form of "recitations" that make up the **Quran** (koo-RAHN), the Scriptures of Islam. Not long after Muhammad's death, his closest followers arranged the recitations into 114 *Suras*, or chapters. The Quran contains legal and wisdom literature, like the Hebrew Scriptures, and moral teaching, like the Christian New Testament. It also prescribes regulations for diet and for personal conduct.

For example, the Quran forbids alcohol and gambling, censures luxury and ostentation, and imposes strict sexual restraints on both men and women. (See the feature, "The Written Record: The Message of the Quran" on page 201.) The Quran permitted a man to have up to four wives if he could care for them and would treat them equitably. A Muslim woman, however, was given her dowry outright, and multiple marriages may have meant that relatively more Muslim women could gain a measure of security, since a woman without a dowry or husband was in a vulnerable position.

Initially, the Quran was interpreted rather freely within the umma, doubtless because there was no clergy to impose a uniform interpretation. After the Prophet's death, some people felt the need for an authoritative teaching—as early Christians had felt the need for a canon of Christian scripture and teaching—and their efforts resulted in the collections called the *sunna*, which means roughly "good practice"—that is, the words and customs of Muhammad himself. Crucial in the development of the sunna were the *hadith*, the "sayings"

**Quran** Containing Allah's revelations to Muhammad, it constitutes the scriptures of Islam.

## The Message of the Quran

*The Quran consists of 114 Suras, literally the "steps" (we might say chapters) by which one rises to knowledge of Allah. The earliest versions of the Quran were equipped with a running commentary. The first four extracts here illustrate the simplicity and elegance of Muslim prayer and the absolute transcendence of Allah. The last two extracts demonstrate the profound sense of religious continuity that marked Muhammad's teaching.*

### Sura 1

In the name of Allah, Most Gracious, Most Merciful. / Praise be to Allah, the Cherisher and Sustainer of worlds; / Most Gracious, Most Merciful. / Master of the Day of Judgment. / Thee do we worship and Thine aid we seek. Show us the straight way, the way of those on whom Thou hast bestowed Thy grace, Thou whose portion is not wrath, and who do not go astray.

### Sura 4.171

O People of the Book! Commit no excesses in your religion, nor say of Allah anything but truth. Christ Jesus the son of Mary was a messenger of Allah . . . so believe in Allah and in His messengers. Say not "Trinity" . . . for Allah is One God. Glory be to Him for He is exalted above having a son. To Him belong all things in the heavens and on earth.

### Sura 3.84

Say ye: We believe in Allah, and the revelation given to us, and to Abraham, Ismail, Isaac, Jacob and the descendants (children of Jacob), and that given to Moses and to Jesus and that given to all prophets from their Lord, but we make no difference between one and another of them, and we bow to Allah.

### Sura 2.87

We gave Moses the book and followed him up with a succession of messengers; We gave Jesus the son of Mary clear signs and strengthened him with the Holy Spirit.

### Sura 48

If the People of the Book rely upon Abraham, let them study his history. His posterity included both Israel and Ismail. Abraham was a righteous man of Allah, a Muslim, and so were his children. Abraham and Ismail built the Kaaba as the house of Allah and purified it, to be a centre of worship for all the world: For Allah is the God of all peoples.

### Sura 56

God's truth is continuous, and His prophets from Adam, through Noah and Abraham, down to the last of the prophets, Muhammad, form one brotherhood. Of Imran father of Moses and Aaron sprang a woman, who devoted her unborn offspring to Allah. That child was Mary the mother of Jesus. Her cousin was the wife of the priest Zakariya, who took charge of Mary. To Zakariya, in his old age, was born a son Yahya, amid prodigies: Yahya was the herald of Jesus the son of Mary and was known as John the Baptist.

### Questions

1. What can you discern from these suras about the similarities and differences among Islam, Christianity, and Judaism?

2. Who are the "people of the book"? Why do you think they matter?

3. How is Allah portrayed in these suras?

*The Meaning of the Holy Qur'an*, new edition with revised translation, commentary, and newly compiled comprehensive index by Abdullah Yusuf Ali (Beltsville, Md.: Amana Publications, 1988), pp. 14, 40, 51, 55–56, 134–135.

---

of the Prophet, the comments he sometimes made about how God's revelation was to be understood and applied. Extant compilations of the sunna date from the ninth century, and scholars are not sure what portion of them derives authentically from the age of the Prophet.

## The Arab Conquests

Muhammad's death brought a crisis. Who or what was to succeed him? In 632, the Meccan elite chose Abu Bakr as *caliph* (KAY-lif), or "successor to the Prophet." Abu Bakr was elderly, an early convert to Islam, and a former secretary to Muhammad. He and his three successors down to 661 (Umar, Uthman, and Ali) were all Meccans, relatives of the Prophet by marriage, and early converts. Islamic tradition calls them the "Rightly Guided Caliphs."

Abu Bakr left his successor, Umar, a united Arabia (see **Map 8.1**), no small feat in that fractious world. Umar began the lightning conquests by the Arabs of much of the Roman and Persian Empires. He initiated the policy of granting choice positions in the expanding **caliphate**, the Arab empire, to old converts and of ranking them according to precedence in conversion. As the old elite divided up the new provinces of the caliphate, some of them became *emirs* (governors), and others became lower administrators. Arab administrators then collected from

**caliphate** The name for the territory conquered by Muhammad's successors and for the governmental regime they established.

all conquered people personal taxes and land taxes. Converts to Islam paid only land taxes. Arab settlers paid no taxes and received salaries from the taxes paid by others.

Umar was murdered by a slave in 644, leaving his successor, Uthman, a huge empire to administer. A great centralizer, Uthman chose emirs, regulated the finances of the provinces, and authorized the preparation of the definitive text of the Quran. In attempting to preserve the advantages of the old Meccan elite, Uthman alienated many people, particularly in Egypt, Syria, and Iraq, who had benefited from conquest and who guarded jealously their newfound local wealth and power. Uthman was murdered in 656 and replaced by Ali, Muhammad's son-in-law, whose goal was to create a truly Islamic government by emphasizing the religious side of the caliph's office as the leader of the umma. Ali was in turn killed by a disillusioned follower in 661. Years later, some Muslims looked back to Ali as the true model for the caliph. These Muslims formed the *Shi'a,* the "Party of Ali."

When Ali was killed, the caliphate passed to Mu'awiya (MOO-ah-wee-uh), a Meccan who was the governor of Syria and commander of the finest army in the Arab world. That army ensured Mu'awiya's position. From 661 to 750, the Umayyads (OO-my-ahdz), as Mu'awiya's family is called, built many of the caliphate's institutions.

The Umayyads instituted greater centralization. This involved the introduction of a unified coinage, the Arabization of the administration (granting all key positions to Arabs), and taking tight control of provincial government and taxation. The Umayyads moved the capital of the caliphate to Damascus in their own power base of Syria, more centrally located than the old towns of Mecca and Medina and closer to the militarily active zones in eastern Iran and along the Byzantine frontier in Syria. In addition, the Umayyads presided over the final territorial expansion of the caliphate (see **Map 8.1**).

Rome's empire expanded for 350 years, but the caliphate reached its zenith in scarcely 100. How can we account for the astonishingly rapid creation of such a vast empire? Byzantium and Persia had financially and militarily weakened themselves in a series of wars that ended just as the caliphate of Umar commenced. Moreover, the Byzantine and Persian states were exceedingly diverse, and the Arab armies dismantled them piecemeal. Both old empires, but especially the Byzantine, had deep religious divisions. The Byzantines and Persians tended to depend on static frontier garrisons and large armies that could not be quickly mobilized and moved long distances. The Arabs rarely risked great pitched battles. They preferred a gradually expanding military frontier gained by numerous lightning strikes.

The Prophet himself had believed firmly in the need to expand the faith, and his successors shared that belief. Muslim ideology divided the world into the "House of Islam" and the "House of War." In the House of Islam, the justice of Allah reigned supreme. In the House of War, *jihad,* or holy war, was the rule. Christians and Jews, as fellow "Peoples of the Book"—sharers in a scriptural tradition reaching back to Abraham—were spared the choice of conversion or death, but "infidels" were expected to submit and convert. The Arab conquests were carefully planned and directed to channel violence out of Arabia, to populate much of western Asia with loyal Muslims, and to reward members of the umma.

## The Abbasid Revolution

Despite their military and administrative successes, the Umayyads were not popular. Many people resented their bureaucratic centralization. Such resentment was acute in areas heavily populated by recent converts, who had always disliked the old Arabian elites, and in frontier provinces, where Arab immigrants along with local converts desired autonomy. The secular nature of Umayyad rule also offended those pious Muslims who expected a high standard of personal morality from their rulers. The opposition came to a head in a series of rebellions that culminated in the naming of a rival caliph, Abu'l Abbas, in 749. In 750, he defeated his Umayyad opponent.

The Abbasids (uh-BASS-idz) reigned until the thirteenth century. Initially, they brought the Islamic world its first golden age. Harun's reign (786-809) was marked by political stability, economic prosperity, and cultural achievements.

With their frontier origins, the Abbasids were sympathetic to the caliphate's provincial populations. Thus, they created a more international regime. Non-Arabs and recent converts felt toward Islam, the Prophet, and the Prophet's family a loyalty that they would not grant to the old Arabian potentates who had led and initially benefited from the Arab conquests. The Abbasid polity was based on the idea of the fundamental equality of all believers. Local persons got more choice positions than Meccan or Syrian aristocrats. The capital of the caliphate was moved from Syria to Iraq, but to avoid favoring any existing group or region, the Abbasids built a new city, Baghdad, which they called "the navel of the universe." By addressing regional and ethnic sensitivities in an effective way, they were able to maintain, even extend, the centralized state of the Umayyad period.

The first caliphs chose administrators from loyal Arabs and from experienced Christian subjects. Under the Umayyads, the regime was Arabized. Under the Abbasids, the government became international, professional, and hereditary. The chief agency of government was the treasury, which had separate branches dealing with Muslim alms, land and poll taxes paid by subjects, and land taxes paid by converts. Alone among early medieval governments, the caliphate could draw up annual budgets. Alongside the treasury in exerting power was a prestigious group of palace servants. They did not hold major offices, but their informal influence on the caliph and his family was great. The army was another prominent body within the state.

**Dome of the Rock** This magnificent mosque in Jerusalem (built in 691–692) is the third-holiest shrine of Islam—after the Kaaba in Mecca and the Prophet's mosque in Medina. Muslims believe that Muhammad ascended to heaven from this spot.

The central government had several links to the provinces. In addition to controlling the army and provincial governorships, the caliph employed a network of regular envoys and spies. The court, especially under the Abbasids, drew able young men from all over into the service of the caliph and created hopes among provincial elites that they, too, might be chosen. In every district and city, there were judges, or *qadi* (KAH-dee), to oversee the application of Islamic law. Qadi were under the authority of the caliph.

The ninth century was a troubled time. Intense family rivalries touched both the succession to the caliphate and the possession of key provincial positions. The bureaucracy became an increasingly influential pressure group, and the palace servants began to foment intrigues. The army became more and more a professional body comprising non-Arabs, especially Turks, hired from the frontiers and beyond because Arabs, enjoying their salaries, declined to serve. The parallel with the Germanization of the late Roman army is striking. The army, the bureaucracy, and the courtiers all had different and conflicting interests and did not hesitate to press their own advantages. Religious divisions persisted, even intensified. Many felt that the Abbasids had not gone far enough in erecting a truly Islamic regime, but some felt that the caliphs had gone too far in claiming both the political and religious authority of the Prophet. After the early tenth century, the Abbasid caliphs had little effective power.

## The Emergence of Islamic Culture

Two currents are apparent in the culture of the Islamic East: One is the elaboration of religious thought; the other is the assimilation of multiple cultural heritages. Both were influenced by the spread of Islam that mixed Greek, North African, Iranian, Turkish, and even Hindu elements into a culture already rich with Arab, Christian, and Jewish ingredients.

Muslims assembled for prayer in mosques, the often beautiful buildings usually modeled on the original mosque in Medina. The worshipers—with men and women in separate areas—arrayed themselves in parallel rows and were led in prayer by an imam. Muslim judges began to issue opinions on how the Quran and sunna might be applied to the daily lives of believers. Teachers in mosque schools also were influential. Together, these authority figures, collectively the *ulama*, developed a body of religious thought.

The late ninth and early tenth centuries saw the emergence of a religious split in the Islamic world that persists to this day. The opposing groups are Shi'ite and Sunni Muslims. Shi'ites believe that caliphs should be chosen only according to strict standards of moral and

## SECTION SUMMARY

- Muhammad was a great teacher who emphasized *al-Islam*, surrender to Allah.
- The Islamic faith may be summarized in the "Five Pillars."
- Internal and external factors contributed to the lightning conquests of Islam in the century after Muhammad's death.
- Islamic culture was rooted in the religious teachings of the *ulama* and in the scholarship of those who tackled Greek and Persian learning.

spiritual worthiness. Further, they insist that the only way to ensure such worthiness is to choose caliphs from the line of Ali, the fifth caliph, husband of Muhammad's daughter Fatima and, in 661, a victim of assassination. Moreover, they believe that the whole ulama should measure up to Shi'ite standards. Sunni Muslims, always the vast majority, proclaim that only they adhere to the sunna, the "good practice," of Muhammad himself. Sunnis accept the legitimacy of the whole line of Umayyad and Abbasid caliphs and the teachings of the ulama.

In 832, an Abbasid caliph endowed the "House of Wisdom," an academy for scholars in Baghdad (compare Charlemagne's palace school; see pages 216–217), and from this point on, Muslim scholars had the leisure and wherewithal to begin tackling the corpus of Greek thought, especially the scientific writers. Greek, Persian, and Indian works were collected and translated, manuscripts were copied, and libraries were built.

Was the Islamic caliphate part of the West or not? From the vantage point of 900, the answer we might give to that question—"largely Western"—differs from the answer we might give today—"largely Eastern." In later chapters, we will see how the Islamic world became less Western and more Eastern.

# The Byzantine Empire

*Why did a distinctive civilization that can be called "Byzantine" emerge?*

The century after Justinian's death in 565 was difficult for the eastern Roman Empire. Attacks by Persians, Bulgars, and Muslims; riots and rebellions; plagues and famines; and some weak rulers imperiled the empire. Two fundamental changes transformed the eastern Roman Empire into a new civilization that is called "Byzantine" from "Byzantium," the ancient Greek name for the capital city, Constantinople. The empire experienced a sharp geographic contraction until it stabilized into the shape it would hold into the thirteenth century and the empire changed both its basic administrative structures and its cultural orientation.

**Greek Fire** Invented in the seventh century by Callimachus, a Syrian engineer, Greek fire was a mixture formed from petroleum, sulfur, saltpeter, and lime that ignited on contact with water. It was first used to repel the Muslim siege of Constantinople in 678.

Prado, Madrid/The Bridgeman Art Library

## Shifting Frontiers

In 600, the empire still laid claim, along the southern and eastern shores of the Mediterranean, to most of the lands that Rome had ruled for centuries. But in the East, the empire had been suffering recurrent losses to Persia. In 610, Heraclius (her-ACK-lee-us), a gifted ruler, ascended the throne. Between 622 and 629, Heraclius campaigned brilliantly and defeated the Persians. But he faced a cruel irony. When the Arab expansion began, Heraclius's empire was militarily and financially exhausted. As the seventh century wore on, Arabs captured Syria, Palestine, and Mesopotamia and began a centuries-long push into Anatolia. Eventually, they threatened Constantinople.

In the Balkans, Heraclius and his successors fought constant battles, with mixed results. They checked the advance of the Slavic peoples, who had been expanding southward. The Slavic advance was partly generated by social and political forces among the Slavs themselves and partly a result of pressure from the Avars and Bulgars. These peoples, who were related to the Huns, had begun penetrating into the Danube basin in the late sixth century. The empire tried hard to check their forward march.

Where the West was concerned, Heraclius and his successors were powerless to stop the Arab advance in North Africa and Spain. In Italy, imperial control was confined to a few outposts around Rome, Ravenna, and Sicily. Italy was too far away and strategically insignificant to attract much attention from the imperial government.

By around 700, the empire was assuming the basic geographic shape it would hold for centuries. In contrast to the vast lands once ruled by Rome, the empire was now confined to the eastern Balkans and western Anatolia. In 717, Leo III became emperor in a moment of acute crisis. Arab armies had seized much of Anatolia and had laid siege to Constantinople. Leo repulsed the attack and then ruled successfully until 741. He was followed by his able and charismatic son, Constantine V (r. 741–775). Constantine held the line in Anatolia and enjoyed decades of military success along the Balkan frontier.

In Italy alone, Byzantine (BIZZ-un-teen) policy was unsuccessful. When Justinian reconquered Italy from the Ostrogoths (see page 186), his armies devastated the region and left it poor and weak. Into the gap stepped the Lombards, who gradually built a kingdom in the north of Italy—Lombardy still bears their name—and set up a series of duchies in the center and south of Italy. The Byzantines prudently dedicated their resources to holding their Balkan and Anatolian frontiers, but this strategy left their subjects in Italy clamoring for aid. Eventually, the popes put themselves at the head of a movement in Italy that turned to the Franks for protection. In 755 and 756, the Frankish king marched to Italy, defeated the Lombards, and donated the territories he seized from them to the pope. This inaugurated the **Papal States**, the ever-changing set of lands in Italy whose current remnant is Vatican City, and put an end to effective Byzantine control in Italy, except for the areas around Naples and Sicily. In 827, Muslims attacked Sicily, and in the ensuing decades, they subjected southern Italy to continuous raids and occasional conquests.

After Constantine V's death, unsettled conditions prevailed until Irene (ca. 752–803) succeeded in 780, first as regent for her son and then as empress—the only woman to rule Byzantium in her own right. Irene was a skilled politician, but under her, the army grew restive because she preferred to make treaties, sometimes on unfavorable terms, than to send troops into the field. She did not trust the military's loyalty. Moreover, Irene had to contend with a foolish son who spent his time trysting with ladies of the court rather than attending to his official duties. In 797, Irene had him blinded, ironically in the very palace chamber where she had given birth to him. This was not a barbaric act in the Byzantine way of thinking. By mutilating Constantine VI, she merely rendered him unfit to rule: Roman ideology held that only a physically intact person could reign; the alternative would have been to murder him. In any case, Irene's credibility sank to nothing, and in 802, she was deposed by a wily old soldier, Nicephorus (nye-SEFF-for-us) (r. 802–811).

For two generations, Byzantium suffered through short reigns, usurpations, political unrest, and military reverses. In 867, a rough soldier, Basil I (r. 867–886), seized the throne and, like Heraclius and Leo III before him, reversed the fortunes of the state. He established a new dynasty, the "Macedonian," and for the first time in years won important military victories. This dynasty ruled effectively until the eleventh century.

**Coin of Empress Irene**
This gold *nomisma* of the empress Irene was struck between 797 and 802. The text reads "Irene, Empress." Note the craftsmanship of the Byzantine moneyers. Courtesy of the Trustees of the British Museum

**Papal States** The lands in central Italy ruled by the popes, initially with Frankish help, from the eighth century to 1870.

## New Forms of Government

Even as its territory was shrinking, Byzantium undertook military and administrative reforms, revised its laws, and refocused its culture, particularly its religious practices. In the early Middle Ages, a distinctive "Byzantium" emerged in place of Rome.

Leo III and Constantine V are reminiscent of Diocletian and Constantine, or of Justinian. They energetically reformed the military and fiscal machinery of the state. By the 830s their efforts, and those of their successors, introduced a major administrative change which we call the "theme system."

For centuries, Rome had recruited, trained, and paid professional troops out of tax revenues; they even used tax revenues to settle barbarian soldiers in their midst. Under the theme system men from frontier regions were now recruited and settled on farms in military districts called *themes*. All themes, whether land-based army ones or sea-based naval ones, were under the command of a leader, called a *strategos*, who was simultaneously the civil and military chief of his theme. The strategos had under him fiscal officers whose primary responsibility was to secure local resources to provision the troops. The farmer-soldiers did not pay taxes on their farms but discharged their obligation to the state by personal service. Henceforth, the thematic armies (see **Map 8.2**) formed the backbone of the Roman system. The new system demanded less tax revenue and fewer bureaucrats. The empire was smaller than in the past and needed a different kind of army: Smaller squadrons concentrated near the threatened frontier regions in Anatolia and the Balkans rather than large armies that were expensive to maintain and cumbersome to transport over long distances.

There were other reforms, too. Leo issued the *Ecloga* (ECK-low-guh), the first major revision and updating of Roman law since Justinian's. Leo and Constantine also instituted far-reaching reforms in imperial administration, which had changed little in centuries. Roman bureaucracy had consisted of a few large departments headed by officials with immense responsibilities and power. The revised Byzantine system was characterized by a profusion of departments under officers who had little real power. The emperor neutralized the bureaucrats by drawing them from all social classes, paying them well, and giving them pompous titles and lots of public recognition, all the while dividing their responsibilities, curbing their influence, and making them dependent on himself.

## The Birth of Byzantine Culture

Byzantine culture came to be increasingly defined by the church. The massive Arab conquests that stripped Byzantium of so much territory also removed the ancient patriarchates of Alexandria, Jerusalem, and Antioch from effective contact with Constantinople. Often in the past, the empire had been disturbed by severe theological quarrels generated by the differing views held in the several patriarchates. These disputes had been disruptive, but they had also prompted a great deal of learned religious writing. Now, deprived of this stimulus, Byzantium turned inward.

Monasticism gradually assumed a more prominent place in religious life. So many members of elite families sought to become monks that some emperors actually tried to limit entry into the religious life. Byzantine monks tended to be deeply learned, intensely critical of the patriarchs of Constantinople—whom they regarded as worldly and political—and opposed to imperial interference in the church.

In 726, Emperor Leo III embarked on a bold new religious policy: **iconoclasm**. For centuries, a beautiful and inspiring religious art had been emerging that troubled the emperor. Leo, a man of simple but fervent piety, believed that the presence of religious images, called "icons," in churches and public places was offensive to God. Moreover, Leo was convinced that the military disasters suffered by the empire in recent years were attributable to divine displeasure at the violation of Moses' prohibition of "graven images." Accordingly, he and his son banned religious images. They and some of their more enthusiastic followers even destroyed a few of them. Hence, they were called "iconoclasts," which means "image breakers." Iconoclasm was officially proclaimed by a church

**iconoclasm** Literally means "image breaking"; it describes the rejection or destruction of religious pictures called "icons."

council in 754, repudiated by another council in 787, proclaimed again in 815, and then definitively rejected in 843.

Iconoclasm had several important consequences in its own time and reveals important aspects of emerging Byzantium to the modern observer. Iconoclasm was categorically rejected as heretical by the popes. This difference drove a sharp wedge between Eastern and Western Catholics. The debates over iconoclasm finally sharpened Byzantine thinking on the role and function of art in religious life. To this day, the icon plays a more prominent role in religious devotion in the East than in the West. (See the feature, "The Visual Record: Icons" on pages 208–209.) Moreover, the battle over iconoclasm evoked some of the most sophisticated Greek religious writing since Late Antiquity. Writers produced learned treatises in defense of religious art that drew on Greek patristic writing (see pages 201–202) and on ancient Greek philosophy in ways that sharply differentiated Byzantine and Western religious thought.

As the Byzantines turned more and more deeply into their own traditions, they exposed other differences between themselves and the West. Some of these were important, such as the dispute over the so-called *filioque*. In the East, people believed that the Holy Spirit proceeded "from the Father." In the West, people said that the Holy Spirit proceeded "from the Father *and from the Son*" (*filioque* in Latin). Greek monks shaved the front of their heads, whereas Western monks shaved a circlet on the top. The Greek church used leavened (with yeast) bread in worship, whereas the Western church used unleavened bread. Taken together, these differences amounted to a sharpening of the divide between Christian groups whom we may now label "**Orthodox**" and "Roman Catholic." Neither group wished to see a division in the Christian world, but physical separation and independent cultural evolution were producing two different traditions.

**Orthodox** The Christian faith of Byzantium. It is known for its use of Greek, inclusion of icons in worship, and adherence to the Greek Church Fathers.

🌐 **Map 8.2 The Byzantine Empire in the Eighth and Ninth Centuries** After suffering tremendous territorial losses to the barbarians and arabs, the Byzantine Empire transformed its military, institutional, and cultural structures to create a regime that lasted until it was conquered by Crusaders in 1204. This map shows Byzantium's major institutional innovation.

© Cengage Learning 2014

## Icons

The word icon comes from the Greek eikōn, which means "image." Scholarly conventions, however, tend to use the term to signify a particular kind of religious image that emerged in Late Antiquity and became prominent in Byzantium. Although large frescoes or mosaics can be called icons, the word is typically restricted to panel paintings painted with encaustic (en-COST-ik). This is a technique that involves mixing pigment with beeswax and then heating the painted surface to fuse the painting to the surface.

Icons portrayed saints, the Virgin Mary, and sometimes Jesus Christ. They were believed to be genuinely holy, to capture, in some mysterious way, the holiness of the person whom they represented. Icons may have arisen from funeral portraits or they may have been miniature versions of much larger images on the walls of churches. One of the earlier examples of icons relates to Saint Symeon Stylites (STILL-ee-tays) (ca. 390–459). Symeon was a recluse who lived for many years on top of a pillar in the Syrian desert. After his death, his reputation for holiness drew many people to worship at his tomb. Soon people began to take away pictures of Symeon. We hear that in far-off Rome, shopkeepers affixed icons of Symeon to the doorposts outside their shops to ward off evil.

Eventually, Byzantine armies carried icons into battle and hung them over the walls of Constantinople to repel enemy attacks. Some churches became famous for their icons. Individuals possessed icons, too, and carried them around in sacks or installed them in their houses. People touched, kissed, or caressed icons to invoke the power of the person who was at once portrayed and spiritually present in the icon. Icons were believed to ward off demons, to heal illnesses, to overcome complications in pregnancy, and to secure victory in lawsuits—among many other uses to which they were put.

Pictured here is an icon of Saint Peter from the monastery of Saint Catherine in Sinai. It is one of the oldest surviving icons, believed to date back to the sixth century. Let us note some of its formal characteristics. Peter is depicted frontally and the background is indistinct, as if Peter is removed from earthly time and space. Peter is represented holding keys, which symbolize the keys to the kingdom of heaven mentioned by Christ. Notice that Peter's eyes look out hauntingly, taking in everything, yet are not focused

**Icon of Saint Peter from Saint Catherine's Monastery, Mount Sinai** Roger Wood/Corbis

on anything in particular. This feature, too, gives the icon a sense of timelessness and of holiness. The style of this icon is very similar to that of a consular diptych. When the emperor named two men consuls each year, they often had portraits done. In such a portrait, one consul was front and

With its new geographic shape, institutional structure, and its Orthodox faith, Byzantium was at once something old and something new. In official Byzantine ideology, the Roman Empire had always been one and inseparable. With its indebtedness to classical and Christian traditions, there can be no question that Byzantium was a part of the West. But in its reduced

**Khludov Psalter**

of Saint Catherine, where the icon of Saint Peter was, and still is, was so remote that iconoclasm did not touch it (see **Map 2.2**, top, on page 42). Eventually, iconoclasm came to an end and icons were restored to their honored position in Byzantium, and later in all the lands religiously influenced by the Byzantines. For an example of a Russian Orthodox icon, see the Virgin of Vladimir in Chapter 9 (page 249).

Iconoclasm was a particularly bitter episode in Byzantine history. There were polemical writings on all sides. Byzantine artists also commented on the controversy. In this image from the early-ninth-century Khludov Psalter—a psalter is a book containing the psalms—you can see two pictures. One is of a crucifixion. It is placed opposite verse 22 in Psalms 68 (modern 69): "They gave me also gall for my food and vinegar for my thirst." Note the soldier on Jesus' left (the viewer's right) who is holding up a sponge soaked in vinegar. But note too the soldier on Jesus' right (the viewer's left). This is the figure, later named Longinus, who pierced Jesus' side with a spear. Now look at the lower image. Depicted here is a man whitewashing an icon of Christ. The message is clear and powerful. Just as Longinus had tortured Jesus, so too do the iconoclasts.

We learned in Chapter 7 (see "The Visual Record: The Ravenna Mosaics" on pages 188–189) that art could serve propaganda purposes. The Ravenna mosaics were large and public. Some icons were also large and public, but many more were small and private. And the picture from the Khludov Psalter is tiny and very private, very intimate. But it conveys well the depth of anger provoked by iconoclasm, by an attack on Byzantium's revered icons.

## Questions

1. *What kinds of ideas enter your mind when you hear words like* icon *and* iconic?

2. *How does the icon of Saint Peter compare with the diptych-like representation of Amalasuntha on page 183?*

3. *How well do the images from the Khludov Psalter convey their message?*

center, while medallions above or beside him depicted the other consul, the emperor, and the empress. In this icon, Peter is likewise shown with three medallions: Christ in the center, Mary on the viewer's right, and Saint John the Evangelist on the viewer's left. One can see right away how ancient artistic motifs were being adapted to new purposes in Christian art.

In the eighth century, Byzantium's emperors initiated a policy of iconoclasm, literally, "icon-breaking." Many icons were destroyed, some were simply removed from view, and still others were whitewashed. The emperors believed that icons violated the biblical prohibition of "graven images" (Exodus 20:4). They felt that God had forsaken the empire because of idolatry and that only by removing the offending pictures could divine favor be won again. The monastery

size, constantly threatened frontiers, and Orthodox traditions, Byzantium was going to have a somewhat different future than the portions of the West situated inside Rome's former western provinces. As was the case in the Muslim world, the seventh and ninth centuries were acutely tumultuous in Byzantium, whereas the eighth was marked by consolidation and achievement.

## SECTION SUMMARY

- The Byzantine Empire faced hard challenges from Persians and then Muslims in the east; from Slavs, Avars, and Bulgars in the Balkans; and from Lombards in Italy.

- The "theme" system was a comprehensive and effective revision of the empire's traditional governmental structure.

- Byzantine culture was based on the Greek language, the Greek Church Fathers, Orthodox religious traditions, and distinctive local practices.

# The Rise of the Carolingian Empire

*What were the greatest achievements of the Carolingians and why were they so successful compared to the other states that survived Rome's collapse in the West?*

In the West, the seventh century also was marked by challenges, the eighth century by innovation and accomplishment, and the ninth century by new threats and, in some areas, near collapse. The social and political heritages of both the Germanic and the Roman past interacted with Christianity and the church to produce the third early medieval civilization: Western Europe. Crucial to these developments were the evangelization of the countryside, the growth of an ecclesiastical hierarchy, the shift of papal interests away from the Mediterranean world toward Western Europe, and the evolving relationship between royal governments and the Catholic Church. The decisive political development in Western Europe was the rise, among the Franks, of the Carolingian family whose most famous member was Charlemagne. Yet, as the seventh century dawned, the Franks had several potential rivals. One by one, those rivals encountered insurmountable challenges.

## Medieval Europe Takes Shape

In Spain, the Visigothic monarchy never recovered from its devastating defeat by Clovis in 507 (see Chapter 7). The kings managed to create a capital at Toledo, to issue sophisticated law codes that owed much to Roman law, and to adopt symbolic trappings of rulership, such as thrones and crowns. In 589, the Visigoths formally converted from Arianism to Catholicism, a step that helped social and cultural cooperation. In the churchman Isidore of Seville (560–636) Visigothic Spain produced a scholarly polymath whose works were influential for centuries. Nevertheless, intense rivalries within the Visigothic aristocracy and between the aristocrats and the kings engendered constant struggles that left Spain vulnerable to an attack by Arab-led Berbers (North African tribesmen and recent converts to Islam). Between 711 and 716, Spain was almost completely overrun and conquered.

In Italy, the Lombards, who had entered the peninsula after the conclusion of the Gothic Wars, were never able to build a cohesive kingdom. No dynasty could establish itself permanently and the kings, ruling from Pavia in the north, could not control the large, powerful duchies of Benevento and Spoleto in the center and south. Lombard, Italy, produced memorable writers, impressive law codes, and influential art and architecture. But the Lombards could not contend with their foes. The Lombards confronted a Byzantine presence in parts of Italy and, as the Byzantine grip loosened, the popes began to rally the Italians and also turned to the Franks for help. Pippin III, Charlemagne's father, campaigned in Italy in 755 and 756 and forced the Lombards to hand over to the papacy the territories that they had conquered at Byzantium's expense. These campaigns fatally weakened the Lombards, and Charlemagne finally conquered their kingdom and took its crown for himself in 774. The lands, which the Franks guaranteed to the popes, formed the basis for the Papal States, a political entity in central Italy that endured many changes over time and survives today as Vatican City. The papal claim to territorial rule was based at least in part on the *Donation of Constantine*, a document probably written in the 760s but claiming to represent a donation to the papacy by Constantine of rule in the West after he departed for Constantinople.

The period between 600 and 900 saw only the faint beginnings of political consolidation in the British Isles. In Ireland, Wales, and Scotland, there were numerous tiny kingdoms that constantly struggled with one another. In England, the Anglo-Saxons were slowly settling into seven kingdoms (see **Map 8.3**). Leadership within England shifted from one of these kingdoms to another. In the late eighth century, one king, Offa of Mercia (r. 757–796) achieved near hegemony over the English. England may have been heading toward some form of political consolidation when, in 793, the Vikings began what would be more than a century of devastating raids and conquests. Continued political unification in England was delayed until Alfred the Great (r. 871–899) ascended the throne of Wessex. He rallied the English and began the long, slow political recovery that bore fruit in the tenth century.

In the areas of religion and culture, however, the British Isles were distinctive and influential. Isolated groups of Christians survived in Ireland from Roman times, but tradition says that St. Patrick (360?–431?) effectively Christianized the island and initiated its ecclesiastical organization. Political rivalries among Irish clans led one prominent exile, St. Columba, to flee Ireland, settle on the Isle of Iona off the coast of Scotland, and begin the conversion of the local Picts (as the inhabitants of Scotland were called). Working from this northern base, Irish missionaries began spreading Christianity southwards in England. Meanwhile, in 597, Pope Gregory I sent Augustine and a group of monks to Kent, in southeastern England, where they established a base at Canterbury. From that base, Augustine's successors began spreading Christianity northwards. In 664, a council was held at the monastery of Whitby, then under the powerful abbess Hilda (614–680). The council decided that Roman, and not Irish, customs would be accepted by the English church. A few years later, the pope sent Theodore (r. 668–690), as Archbishop of Canterbury, and he organized the English church along traditional Roman lines. All the while, nobles had been founding monasteries and from these centers the real work of converting the English countryside was underway. The conversion of England to Christianity was fostered by women. Most convents had aristocratic abbesses who presided over complex enterprises and often schools. The Vikings were eventually disruptive to the English church, as were warring kings, Irish and Roman adherents, and squabbling nobles.

Nevertheless, at several centers, and notably at the monasteries of Wearmouth and Jarrow, an impressive Christian culture emerged. Schools were established and libraries were built up. The greatest product of those schools was Bede (673–735). A profoundly learned man and prolific author, Bede wrote commentaries on the Bible and popularized the use of A.D. dating. He is best known for his *Ecclesiastical History of the English Church and People*, a comprehensive history of the emergence of both England's kingdoms and church. Bede commanded a superb Latin style.

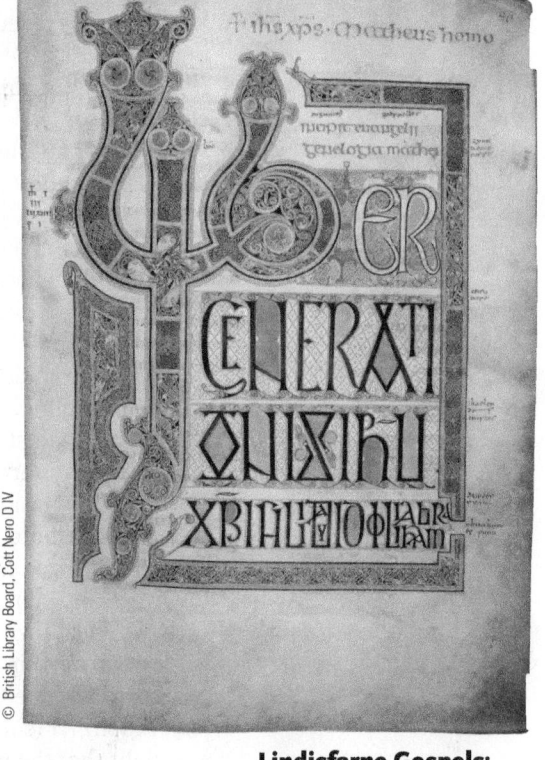

**Lindisfarne Gospels: Opening Page of the Gospel According to Matthew** In the last years of the seventh century in the north of England, scribes and painters produced this exquisite book, which combines the artistic styles of the Mediterranean and Celtic worlds.

© British Library Board, Cott Nero D IV

## The Carolingian Dynasty

Clovis and the Franks created the most effective of the early Germanic kingdoms. During the seventh century, that kingdom, too, experienced difficulties but did not disappear. Just as Roman aristocrats had borne the ancient heritage into the Middle Ages, so now a Frankish family, called "Carolingian" from the name of its greatest member, Charlemagne, assembled the talent and resources of the Frankish realm in a new way. Charlemagne reformed his government and church, patronized learning, and resurrected the western empire. Early medieval civilization reached its culmination in the work of Charlemagne and his dynasty.

When Clovis died in 511, his realm was divided among his sons, and thereafter several kingdoms coexisted. The Merovingian royal families feuded constantly, sought to expand at one another's expense, and drew local aristocracies into their battles. Nevertheless, the *idea* of a single kingdom of the Franks persisted. Kings and aristocrats in the small kingdoms competed for leadership of the realm as a whole. The flourishing culture of late antique Gaul was largely gone, but a creative Christian monastic culture was growing up in all parts of the Frankish kingdom. The seventh century, in other words, was a time when the late antique regime was slowly changing into the medieval regime.

The Carolingian family appeared in history just after 600 and thereafter monopolized the office of mayor of the palace (sort of a prime minister) to the king in Austrasia (the easternmost kingdom; see **Map 8.3**). The Carolingians were the boldest and wealthiest family in Austrasia (aw-STRAY-zhuh), perhaps in the Frankish world. Within two generations, they unified the Frankish realm and increased their own power.

The Carolingians formed alliances with powerful noble families in many regions. They waged war against the enemies of the Franks to restore the territorial integrity of the kingdom. Charles Martel (d. 741), Charlemagne's grandfather, led the Frankish forces that put an end to Arab raiding in Gaul, defeating a large force near Poitiers in 733. With booty from their wars, tribute from conquered peoples, spoils taken from recalcitrant opponents, and even lands seized from the church, the Carolingians attracted and rewarded more and more followers until no one was a match for them. The Carolingians also allied themselves very early with leading churchmen, both episcopal and monastic. They aided missionaries in the work of converting central Germany, thereby expanding Frankish influence in that area.

For years, the Carolingians were content with the office of mayor of the palace. Then in 749, Pippin III (son of Charles Martel) decided to send envoys to the pope to ask whether it was right that the person who had all the power in the land of the Franks was not the king. The pope responded that this situation ran counter to the divine plan. Accordingly, in 751, the last Merovingian king was deposed, and Pippin was elected in his place (r. 751–768). Pippin had prepared his usurpation very carefully with his Frankish supporters, but he appealed to the pope to make it appear that he had become king with divine approval and not by crude seizure. Three years later, the pope visited the Frankish kingdom, where he crowned and anointed Pippin and his sons, including Charlemagne. (The practice of anointing the head of a ruler with holy oil, which renders the recipient sacred, dates back to the kings of Israel. The head and hands of Catholic bishops also were anointed. The anointing of rulers and churchmen persisted throughout the Middle Ages and into the modern world.) The pope also forbade the Franks ever to choose a king from a family other than the Carolingians and received from their new favorites a promise of aid in Italy.

**Charlemagne** The greatest ruler of the early Middle Ages and a major figure in European lore and legend.

**Charlemagne** (Carolus Magnus, "Charles the Great" in Latin) was a huge man, and his stature has grown in European history and legend. Like all great leaders, Charlemagne (r. 768–814) was complex. He spoke and read Frankish, Latin, and some Greek but never learned to write. He promoted Christian morality but perpetrated unspeakable brutalities on his enemies and enjoyed several concubines. Many battles were fought in his name, but he rarely accompanied his armies and fought no campaigns that are remembered for strategic brilliance. Determination and organization were the hallmarks of his forty-six-year reign.

Charlemagne's first major achievement was the articulation of a new ruling ideology in the Latin West. In capitularies (kuh-PITCH-u-lar-eez)—royal executive orders—of 789, Charlemagne required all males to swear an oath of allegiance to him, and he compared himself to a biblical king in his responsibility to admonish, to teach, and to set an example for his people. He referred to the people of his realm as a "New Israel," a new chosen people. Interestingly, this chosen people was not exclusively Frankish. No distinctions were to be made among Franks or Bavarians or Saxons. Everyone was to be equal in allegiance to the king and in membership in a sort of Augustinian City of God.

Einhard (ca. 770–840), Charlemagne's friend and biographer, reports that Augustine's *City of God* (see page 193) was the king's favorite book. The king understood it to mean that two opposing domains contended for power on earth: a City of God consisting of all right-thinking Christians—the "New Israel"—and a City of Man consisting of pagans, heretics, and infidels. This idea is similar to the Islamic umma (see page 199). To Charlemagne and his advisers, it was obvious that as God was the sole legitimate ruler in heaven, Charlemagne was the sole legitimate and divinely appointed ruler on earth.

Modern readers may think that Charlemagne had crossed a boundary between church and state. It is crucial to understand that to Charlemagne, as to his Muslim and Byzantine contemporaries, no such boundary existed. Church (or religion) and state were complementary attributes of a polity whose end was eternal salvation, not military security or personal fulfillment. Charlemagne's ideological legacy was twofold: It created possibilities for bitter struggles later in the Middle Ages between secular rulers and ecclesiastical powers about the leadership of Christian society and it made it hard to define the state and its essential purposes in other than religious terms.

The most disputed event in the reign of Charlemagne was his imperial coronation in Rome on Christmas Day in 800. It is important to separate how this event happened from what it meant to the participants. In April 799, some disgruntled papal bureaucrats and their supporters attacked Pope Leo III (r. 795–816) in an attempt to depose him. Leo escaped and then traveled all the way to Saxony, where the king was camped with his army. Charlemagne agreed to restore the pope to Rome and, as his ally and protector, to investigate those who had attacked him. No real offenses could be proved against the pope, who appeared publicly in Rome to swear that he had done nothing wrong. Everything was handled to avoid any hint that the pope had been put on trial. When Charlemagne went to Saint Peter's Basilica on

🌐 **Map 8.3 The Carolingian World** The territory over which Charlemagne exerted direct or indirect control was vast. The areas beyond the Rhine and Danube, never part of the Roman Empire, became under the Carolingians a permanent part of Western civilization. The Treaty of Verdun (see inset), signed by Charlemagne's grandsons in 843, was the first and most important of many divisions of the Carolingian Empire that eventually led to the emergence of France and Germany. © Cengage Learning 2014

Christmas, he prayed before the main altar. As he rose from prayer, Pope Leo placed a crown on his head, and the assembled Romans acclaimed him as emperor.

Debate over this coronation arises from a remark of Einhard, who said that if Charlemagne had known what was going to happen, he would not have gone to church that day, even though it was Christmas. Einhard's point was not that Charlemagne did not wish to be emperor. For at least fifteen years, prominent people at the Carolingian court had been addressing Charlemagne in imperial terms in letters, treatises, and poems. Moreover, some were saying that because of Irene's usurpation (see page 205), the imperial throne was vacant—implying that a woman could not truly rule. What Einhard did mean was that Charlemagne saw himself as a Frankish and Christian emperor, not as a *Roman* emperor. The imperial office dignified his position as leader of the Frankish "Israel." Charlemagne did not wish to be beholden to the pope or to the Romans.

Charlemagne continued his program of legal and ecclesiastical reform and put the finishing touches on some military and diplomatic campaigns. In 806, he divided his empire among his three legitimate sons. Two of them died, so in 813, he made Louis his sole heir and successor. Charlemagne outlived most of the friends and companions of his youth and middle age. He outlived four wives and many of his children. Old and alone, ill and lame, he died in early 814.

Charlemagne's legacy was great. He brought together the lands that would become France, Germany, the Low Countries, and northern Italy and endowed them with a common ideology, government, and culture. He provided a model that Europeans would look back to for centuries as a kind of golden age. His vast supraregional and supra-ethnic entity, gradually called "Christendom," drew deeply on the universalizing ideals of its Roman, Christian, and Jewish antecedents but was, nevertheless, original. With its Roman, Germanic, and Christian foundations, the Carolingian Empire represented the final stage in the evolution of the Roman Empire in the West. (See the feature, "The Global Record: 'Persian' Visitors to the Court of Charlemagne" on page 215.)

## Carolingian Government

Charlemagne accomplished much through the sheer force of his personality and his boundless energy. But he also reformed and created institutional structures. These helped him to carry out his tasks, guaranteed a measure of permanence to his reforms, and created government patterns that lasted in many parts of Europe until the twelfth century.

The king (or emperor—the offices differed little in practical importance) was the heart of the system. In theory, the king ruled by God's grace and did not have to answer for his conduct to any person. In reality, the king necessarily sought consensus through a variety of means. The king controlled vast lands, which gave him great wealth of his own and also the means to reward loyal followers. By controlling appointments to key positions, the king required men to come to him for power, wealth, and prestige.

The Eastern contemporaries of the Carolingians relied on large numbers of carefully trained, paid civil servants. In contrast, the Carolingians employed a limited number of men who were tied to them by bonds of familial and personal allegiance. The Carolingian court included several ceremonial officers and a domestic staff, all desirable positions. For example, the constable, an officer in charge of transporting the royal entourage, was usually a great aristocrat; the real work of the office was carried out by underlings. The treasurer was the keeper of the king's bedchamber, where the royal treasure chest was kept. Several chaplains, whose primary duty was to see to the spiritual needs of the court, kept official records. The queen controlled the domestic staff and the stewards who managed the royal estates.

Local government was mainly entrusted to counts. About six hundred counts, and several times that number of minor officials, managed the empire. As in Merovingian times, the counts were administrative, judicial, and military officials. Most came from prominent families, and the office increased the wealth and importance of its holders. Counts had to promulgate and enforce royal orders and preside in regular sessions of local courts. They got one-third of the fines, so the zealous pursuit of justice was in their interest.

The royal court and the localities were linked in several ways. Under Charlemagne and his successors, it became usual for all major officers, whether secular (counts and their

## "Persian" Visitors to the Court of Charlemagne

*In the 880s a monk named Notker wrote the Deeds of Charles the Great. The work is not a continuous historical narrative but instead a lengthy series of anecdotes, including this one about some "Persian" (probably, in fact, Arab) envoys to Charlemagne. The story is fanciful but revealing of attitudes prevalent in the West. In reading, one has to work through the flattery and exaggeration.*

Envoys of the Persians were sent to him. They arrived in the last week of Lent. They were announced to the emperor but he put off seeing them until the eve of Easter. On the special feast that incomparable man was decked out incomparably and he ordered the people from the race that had once seemed terrible to all the world to be introduced. To them the most excellent Charles seemed amazing before all others, as if they had never seen a king or an emperor. He received them kindly and bestowed on them this gift: As if they were one of his children they had permission to go wherever they wished, look over anything whatsoever, and ask about or investigate anything. They jumped excitedly at the chance to be near him, to look upon him, to admire him; they valued this more than the riches of the East. They climbed up to the balcony that ran around the basilica and looked down on the clergy and soldiers but coming back again and again to the emperor they were unable to keep from laughing on account of their immense joy and they clapped their hands, saying "Before we have only seen men of clay but now we have seen men of gold."

At dawn Charles, unable to tolerate idleness or leisure, prepared to go hunting in the forest for bison or wild oxen, and to take along the Persian envoys. When they saw those huge animals they were struck with terror and turned in flight. But the hero Charles was unperturbed and sat on his bold horse as he approached one of them, drew his sword, and tried to cut right through its neck. But his blow was in vain. The monstrous beast tore through the boot and legwrap of the king and grazed his leg with the tip of his horn, rendering him a little slower than he was before. Angered by this slight wound, the beast fled safe and sound into a valley made tough by trees and rocks. Just about everyone in the service of the lord wanted to take off their leggings but he stopped them.

The Persians also brought the emperor an elephant, monkeys, balsam, nard, and various ointments, spices, perfumes, and different medicines to such an extent that the East seemed emptied and the West filled. When they had begun to become extremely familiar with the emperor, one day they were a little sillier than usual, heated up with strong white-beer, and they spoke these words in jest to Charles, who was always armed with seriousness and sobriety: "Your power, O Emperor, is very great but much less than the report of your power that is spread in the eastern kingdoms." On hearing this, Charles concealed his great indignation and asked them with a smile "Why do you speak so, my sons? Or why do things seem so to you?" So they went back to the beginning and told him everything that had happened to them in these lands across the sea saying, "We Persians, or Medes, and Armenians, Indians, Parthians, Elamites, and all the peoples of the East, fear you much more than our own ruler Harun. What should we say about the Macedonians or Achaeans? Nowadays they fear the pressure of your greatness more than they do the waves of the Ionian Sea. The peoples of all the islands through which we passed on our journey were as ready and determined in your service as if they had been raised in your palace and honored with huge favors."

### Questions

1. *How likely do you think it is that "Persian" visitors would have been so dazzled by Charlemagne?*

2. *Reading between the lines, so to speak, what does this document tell you about Frankish attitudes toward Arabs?*

3. *What aspects of this story seem most credible to you?*

Notker Balbulus, Gesta Karoli, 2.8, ed., Reinhold Rau (Darmstadt: Wissenschaftliche Buchgesellschaft, 1975), pp. 386-390. Translated by Thomas F.X. Noble.

subordinates) or ecclesiastical (bishops and abbots), to be **vassals** of the king. Vassals solemnly pledged loyalty and service to the king. Vassalage drew on both Roman and Germanic customs. Patron-client ties had always been socially and politically important among the Romans, and the allegiance of warriors to a chief was a key Germanic bond. But by connecting personal loyalty with public office, Charlemagne created something essentially new. Only a few thousand men, a tiny fraction of the total population, were vassals at any time. They constituted the political and social elite.

Another connection between the king and his local agents was the assembly that met in various places once or twice a year. In theory, all free men could attend these gatherings, which sometimes had separate secular and ecclesiastical sessions, to advise the king on matters of great importance, such as war and peace or legal reforms. In practice, only the vassals had the means or the interest to ensure their presence. Most of the great Carolingian reforms were formulated in these assemblies by cooperation between the king and his most important

**vassals** Generally high-status men who pledged personal loyalty to a lord in return for public offices and material benefits.

subjects. The assemblies served to defuse dissension, but the king also brought his power to bear locally by traveling widely. The monarchy possessed estates all over the heartlands of the kingdom, and the royal entourage often moved from one place to another. Monasteries and cathedrals provided hospitality to the king. As the royal party traveled about the realm, they were able to check on local conditions and to compel local officials to comply with royal wishes.

In 788, Charlemagne began to build a palace at Aachen (AH-ken), and in the last twenty years of his life, he usually resided there (see **Map 8.3**). The later Carolingian rulers all tended to have fixed residences, as did the Byzantines and the Abbasids. In adopting fixed residences and elaborate court rituals, the Carolingians may have been returning to Roman precedents or copying their contemporaries to appear as sophisticated as they. Elegant courts and intricate rituals project an aura of grandeur that enhances people's respect for their rulers. It is no accident that a key innovation of Charlemagne's reign coincided with his permanent residence in Aachen. In the late 780s, he began to send out pairs of roving inspectors, or *missi dominici* (MISS-ee doe-MEE-nee-kee), envoys of the lord king. Their function was to see that royal orders were being observed, that counts were dispensing justice honestly, and that persons of power were not oppressing the powerless.

## The Carolingian Renaissance

Charlemagne's reforms culminated in a revival of learning that scholars have named the **Carolingian Renaissance** (*renaissance* is French for "rebirth"). Charlemagne's fundamental ideas are revealed by the constant use in contemporary sources of words, such as *rebirth, renewal, reform,* and *restoration.* Charlemagne, his advisers, and his successors looked back for inspiration to Christian and papal Rome, to Saint Peter and Constantine, and to the Church Fathers. To them, the rebirth of Western society as a "New Israel" was equivalent to the theological rebirth of an individual in baptism. The Carolingians were the driving force behind intellectual growth in their era.

**Carolingian Renaissance** Major revival of learning, combined with reform of religious and political institutions, that occurred under Charlemagne and his successors.

To accomplish his objectives, Charlemagne required every cathedral and monastery to establish a school. To set up and run those schools, he summoned to his court many of the most able and influential intellectual figures of the day, among them Franks, such as his biographer Einhard, grammar teachers from Italy, and Visigothic theologians from the Spanish border. His most famous recruit was the Anglo-Saxon Alcuin (AL-kwin) (735–804), the most learned man of his day and the heir of Bede and of the brilliant culture of Northumbria.

Much of the work of Alcuin and his associates was devoted to producing textbooks and to teaching elementary knowledge. Charlemagne was convinced that people needed to be taught the basic truths of Christianity if he were to accomplish his task of leading them to salvation. A massive effort was thus undertaken to copy manuscripts of the Bible and the writings of the Latin Church Fathers. These books, the essential resources for the whole program, needed to be disseminated as widely as possible. The process of copying was facilitated by a new script, Caroline minuscule. The Frankish convent at Chelles was a renowned center for the copying of manuscripts.

Alcuin recognized that Charlemagne could place more resources at his disposal than anyone else and had the will to do so. Alcuin also saw the long-term benefits that would come from his work. Alcuin's pupils spread out in the next generation to create a network of schools that went right on multiplying across the ninth century. That is a powerful legacy. And Alcuin did more than just teach. He wrote learned works and poetry and was for twenty years Charlemagne's most trusted adviser.

With his plan, personnel, and schools in place, Charlemagne took many concrete steps. He secured from Rome a copy of the authoritative canon law of the church. Charlemagne also got from the pope a *sacramentary,* a service book for worship in cathedral churches. Charlemagne sought an authoritative copy of the *Rule of St. Benedict,* and after study and commentary, this rule was imposed on all monasteries in the kingdom.

Secular reforms mirrored religious ones. Orders regularized the management of all royal estates. Charlemagne attempted to update local law codes and to make them as uniform as possible. Not since Rome had governments possessed either the interest in or the means to promote such centralization. It is striking that in the eighth century the caliphate, the

Byzantine Empire, and the Carolingian Empire were engaged in similar centralizing activities.

Versatility was a hallmark of Carolingian learning. In the Frankish world, aristocratic women secured some learning, and one, Dhuoda, wrote in 841 a manual of advice for her son that conveys biblical and patristic teachings as well as practical wisdom. Various scholars excelled at poetry, history, and biography. Biblical studies and theology attracted a lot of attention. One figure who personifies the Carolingian Renaissance is the Visigoth Theodulf (ca. 760–821). He came to court in about 790 and served thereafter as a missus (singular form of *missi*), royal adviser, abbot of several monasteries, and bishop of Orléans. He issued important legislation for his diocese. He was the foremost Old Testament expert of his day and the only one who knew Hebrew. He wrote the official Frankish response to Byzantine iconoclasm. He also composed theological treatises, many letters, and dozens of poems. At Germigny (JHER-mee-nee), he designed a church that is a masterpiece of early Carolingian architecture.

Carolingian art is a crowning glory of the age. Several distinct currents inspired and informed Carolingian art. Most prominent were the animal and geometric decorative motifs of Irish and Anglo-Saxon art; the elegance, formality, and sense of composition of classical art; basic elements of style from Byzantine painting; actual scenes from papal Rome; and the mysteries of Christian theology. Every element was borrowed, but the finished product was new.

Architecture shows the same trends. Charlemagne's palace complex at Aachen has parallels in imperial Constantinople, papal Rome, and Ostrogothic Ravenna. Workers and building materials were fetched from all over the empire. From 768 to 855, 27 cathedrals were built, along with 417 monasteries and 100 royal residences. For basic buildings, the Carolingians adapted the basilica. The classical basilica was a horizontal building, but the Carolingians, by altering the western end and façade (the "westworks"), added the dimension of verticality. In Romanesque and Gothic architecture this innovation would have a long career (see pages 282–286).

**Ivory Cover of the Lorsch Gospels** In 810, the monks at Lorsch produced a Gospel book and probably its covers, too. This cover is now in London. It depicts an enthroned Mary with Jesus on her lap, flanked by Zacharias and his son, John the Baptist. The ivory carving is of such exquisite quality that scholars long refused to believe that this was not a late antique work.

*V&A Images, London/Art Resource, NY*

## The Fragmentation of Charlemagne's Empire, 814–887

The Carolingian Empire did not outlive the ninth century. By the end of the ninth century, small political entities had replaced the unified Carolingian Empire. Size and ethnic complexity contributed to the dissolution of the empire, as did dynastic squabbling and new waves of attacks.

The empire included many small regions—Saxony, Bavaria, Brittany, and Lombardy, for example—that had their own resident elites, linguistic traditions, and distinctive cultures, which had existed before the Carolingians came on the scene and persist to this day. The Merovingian and Carolingian periods were basically a unifying intrusion into a history characterized by regional diversity. The Carolingians made heroic efforts to build a common culture and to forge bonds of unity, but the obstacles were insuperable.

Another key issue in the breakup of the Carolingian Empire was political and dynastic. The Carolingians regularly tried to create subkingdoms for all their legitimate sons while preserving the imperial title for one of them. Unfortunately, younger sons rarely yielded to their older brothers, and the bonds of loyalty among cousins, nephews, and grandchildren grew weak. Frequent divisions of the empire, or of segments of it, placed local nobilities in the difficult position of changing their allegiances frequently and of jeopardizing their offices and landholdings.

In the Treaty of Verdun in 843 (see inset, **Map 8.3**), the three grandsons of Charlemagne—Charles the Bald, Louis the German, and Lothair—divided the empire into three realms: the West Frankish, the East Frankish, and the Middle Kingdoms. After fierce battles among the brothers, each appointed forty members to a study commission that traversed the empire to identify royal properties, fortifications, monasteries, and cathedrals so that an equitable division of these valuable resources could be made. Each brother needed adequate resources to solidify his rule and to attract or hold followers. The lines drawn on the map at Verdun did not last even for a generation. Nevertheless, large West Frankish and East Frankish Kingdoms emerged, swallowed the Middle Kingdom, and created a framework for the future France and Germany.

On the frontiers of the Carolingian Empire, new political entities began to appear. Before the ninth century, Scandinavia had known only small-scale political units under local chieftains and their trusted followers. Economic and political pressure from the Carolingians gradually began to push both Denmark and Norway in the direction of greater political consolidation. A single Danish monarchy has a continuous history from the late ninth century, and Norway's monarchy dates from the early tenth.

To the east of the Carolingian Empire lay a vast swath of Slavic lands. The Carolingians fought, allied, and traded with these peoples for decades. Charlemagne destroyed the Avar khanate in the Danube basin in campaigns between 788 and 804. By the middle of the ninth century, the princes of Great Moravia dominated the region and played a complicated diplomatic game between the East Frankish rulers and the Byzantine emperors. To the east of the Moravians, the Bulgarians profited from the Avar, and then the Carolingian, collapse to expand their kingdom. For two centuries, the Bulgarians dominated the northern Balkans and threatened Byzantium.

The most durable consequence of this political restructuring along the eastern frontier of the Frankish world was religious. In 863, on an invitation from Moravia and in hopes of countering the Franks, the Byzantine emperor sent the missionaries Cyril (826–869) and Methodius (805–884) into eastern Europe. The emperor hoped to erect an Orthodox union of his own realm, the southern Slavs, and the newly converted Bulgarians. Likewise, he was seeking a diplomatic bulwark between the Bulgarians in the East and the Franks in the West. Unfortunately for Byzantium, Cyril and Methodius agreed with the pope to introduce Roman Catholic Christianity in return for the pope's permission to use the Slavonic language in worship. Cyril and Methodius were formidable linguists who created a religious literature in "Church Slavonic" that went far toward creating a new cultural realm in central Europe.

Finally, a new wave of attacks and invasions contributed decisively to the fragmentation of the Carolingian Empire. In the middle decades of the ninth century, Muslims, Magyars, and Vikings wreaked havoc on the Franks.

Based in North Africa and the islands of the western Mediterranean, Muslims attacked Italy and southern France. The Byzantines lost Sicily to raiders from North Africa in 827 and found themselves seriously challenged in southern Italy. In the 840s, Muslims raided the city of Rome. These same brigands preyed on trade in the western Mediterranean and even set up camps in the Alps to rob traders passing back and forth over the mountains.

Magyars, relatives of the Huns and Avars who had preceded them into eastern Europe, were accomplished horsemen whose lightning raids, beginning in 889, hit Italy, Germany, and even France. East Frankish Carolingians tried to use the Magyars as mercenaries against the troublesome Moravians. In the end, the Magyars destroyed the incipient Moravian state and raided with impunity.

"From the fury of the Northmen, O Lord, deliver us," was a plaintive cry heard often in ninth-century Europe. Those Northmen were Vikings, mainly Norwegians and Danes, but later Swedes too. The name Viking is a shorthand for Vik-men, *vicus* being the Latin for "a place" or "a port." By 750 Norwegians had begun raiding and then settling in western Scotland and in the adjacent islands. Within a century they expanded into the Irish Sea. Between 790 and the 830s bands of Danes conducted small-scale raids along the northern and western rims of Britain and the Frankish world. Late in the ninth century Swedes raided down along the great rivers of Russia.

We saw in Chapter 7 that there was no coherent barbarian "other" to the settled Roman world. So too we must avoid thinking in terms of a single "Viking" phenomenon. As Anglo-Saxon kingdoms achieved a measure of consolidation and as the Carolingian realm expanded to the north, commercial relations expanded and so did countless small-scale raids. Viking leaders were bold adventurers who sought plunder, tribute, and glory. As they acquired more of each, they acquired more followers and became more dangerous.

In the middle decades of the ninth century major Viking bands began to settle in larger numbers and to undertake the conquest of large territories. Norwegian groups established stations in Dublin and Waterford in Ireland. The "Great Army" began the systematic conquest of Britain in 865. Within a few decades the army destroyed Mercia and Northumbria, establishing a major Danish kingdom centered on York. When Alfred the Great, from his base in Wessex, began to push the Danes northward past the Thames River, some Viking groups began to attack the Continent. In 911 one band captured and settled in Normandy—the "land of the Northmen." Swedish bands created a permanent settlement at Kiev in what is now the Ukraine, founding in the process the basis for primitive "Rus"—the ancestor of Russia.

In the unsettled political conditions of the ninth century, the Vikings were the great opportunists. The Vikings never defeated a Frankish army in a pitched battle and recoiled in Britain when they faced concerted opposition. Sometimes kings hired Viking bands to fight rebellious nobles and noble factions employed Vikings against one another. It is often difficult to disentangle raiding and settling, plunder and trade. For example, when Viking leaders built coastal settlements to extract tribute from surrounding regions, they contributed to drawing those regions into large-scale commercial networks. Owing to their superior seamanship, the Vikings had the advantage of mobility and surprise. Their attacks were unpredictable and caused local regions to fall back on their own resources rather than look to the central government. Commerce was disrupted everywhere. Schools, based in ecclesiastical institutions, themselves rich and defenseless, suffered severe decline. The raids represented a thousand pinpricks, not a single deadly sword stroke. Eventually they contributed to redrawing the map of post-Carolingian Europe.

Even though the Carolingian Empire itself disintegrated, the idea of Europe as "Christendom," as a single political-cultural entity, persisted. The Latin Christian culture, promoted by Carolingian schools and rulers, set the tone for intellectual life until the twelfth century. Likewise, Carolingian governing structures were inherited and adapted by all of the successor states that emerged in the ninth and tenth centuries. In these respects, the Carolingian experience paralleled the Roman, and the Islamic and Byzantine, too. A potent, centralizing regime disappeared but left a profound imprint on its heirs. For hundreds of years, Western civilization would be played out inside the lands that had been Charlemagne's empire and between those lands and their Byzantine and Muslim neighbors.

## SECTION SUMMARY

- The Carolingian family rose steadily to power, first as mayors of the palace, then as kings, and finally, as emperors.
- Charlemagne instituted far-reaching governmental innovations and reforms intended to make his power effective and to unify the lands under his rule.
- Carolingian rulers launched a cultural revival, called the Carolingian Renaissance, which aimed to master and then communicate basic Christian teachings.
- The Carolingian Empire broke down because of geographic diversity, political disunity, and new waves of invasion.

# Early Medieval Economies and Societies

*What were the chief similarities and differences among the early medieval civilizations?*

The economic and social history of the early Middle Ages provides additional evidence of the similarities among the three early medieval civilizations while also revealing differences. Overall, the world remained rural, society was hierarchical, and women were excluded from public power. Although broad political frameworks changed, the lives of most people changed rather little.

## Trade and Commerce

In the simplest terms, trade is a mechanism for exchanging goods from one person or group to another. There are many such exchange mechanisms. The Roman government, for example, moved large amounts of goods from the center of the empire to the frontiers to supply its armies. Roman, Byzantine, and Islamic governments raised taxes in one place, bought goods in another, and then consumed their purchases someplace else. Tribute and plunder were also effective exchange mechanisms, as were diplomatic gifts: A caliph, for example, sent Charlemagne an elephant.

The most common exchanges were intensely local, but several major trading networks operated during the early Middle Ages. In the East, Mesopotamia was linked by rivers to the Persian Gulf, East Africa, and southern Asia; by land and sea to Byzantium; and by land and rivers to the Black Sea region, Slavic Europe, and the Baltic. Byzantines traded mainly by sea. The whole Mediterranean was open to them, and from the Black Sea, they received the products of the Danube basin. The Muslim world was fundamentally a land empire that had relatively poor roads and primitive wheeled vehicles, so transport considerations were crucial: A caravan of some five hundred camels could move only one-fourth to one-half the cargo of a normal Byzantine ship.

The West had many trade routes. The Rhône-Saône river system carried goods, as did the land routes through the Alpine passes. The North and Baltic Seas were the hubs of a network that linked the British Isles, the whole of the Frankish north (by means of its rivers), the Rhineland, Slavic Europe, Byzantium, and the Muslim world. The Danube was also a major highway. The major trade networks intersected at many points. Despite religious and ideological differences, Rome's three heirs regularly traded with one another. Recent research has documented hundreds of east-west and north-south contacts across the early medieval period.

Food and other bulk goods never traveled very far because the cost was prohibitive. Most towns were supplied with foodstuffs by their immediate hinterlands, so the goods that traveled long distances were portable and valuable. Cotton and raw silk were transported to the Mediterranean, where they were made into cloth in, respectively, Egypt and Byzantium. Paper and pottery were transported around the caliphate. Asian spices and perfumes were avidly sought everywhere. The Byzantines traded in silk cloth, fine ivories, delicate products of the gold- and silversmiths' art, slaves, and naval stores. Byzantium, with its large fleet, usually controlled the Black and Mediterranean Seas. Reduced in prosperity, the empire could no longer dictate trade terms to subject peoples and competed badly with the Muslims. Trade in the West was partly in high-value luxury goods but mainly in ordinary items, such as plain pottery, raw wool, wool cloth, millstones, weapons, and slaves. Some Anglo-Saxon nuns owned ships and invested in commercial activities to support their convents. Almost all aspects of the cloth industry were in women's hands.

## Town and Countryside

To think of the ancient world is to think of cities, but to think of the medieval world is to envision forests and fields. Actually, 80 to 90 percent of people in antiquity lived in rural settings, and in the early Middle Ages, the percentage was not much higher. What changed was the place occupied by towns in the totality of human life. Fewer government functions were based in towns, cultural life was less bound to the urban environment, and trade in luxuries, which depended on towns, declined.

Towns in the West often survived as focal points of royal or, more often, ecclesiastical administration. A cathedral church required a large corps of administrators. Western towns were everywhere attracting *burgs*, new settlements of merchants, just outside their centers. Few Western towns were impressive in size or population. Rome may have numbered a million people in the time of Augustus, but only about thirty thousand lived there in 800. Paris had perhaps twenty thousand inhabitants at that time. These were the largest cities by far in Catholic Europe.

In the Byzantine East, apart from Constantinople, the empire had a more rural aspect after the Muslims took control of the heavily urbanized regions of Syria, Egypt, and parts of Anatolia in the seventh century. The weakening of the caliphate in the second half of the ninth century was a spur to renewed urban growth in the Byzantine Empire. In provincial cities, population growth and urban reconstruction depended heavily on military conditions: Cities threatened by Arabs or Bulgarians declined.

The Arabs were great city-builders. Baghdad—four times larger in area than Constantinople, with a million residents to the latter's 400,000—was created from scratch. The most magnificent city in the West was Cordoba, the capital of Muslim Spain. Its population may have reached 400,000, and its Great Mosque, begun in 786, held 5,500 worshipers, more than any Latin church except Saint Peter's. The city had 900 baths, 1,600 mosques (Rome had about 200 churches), 60,000 mansions, and perhaps 100,000 shops. Its libraries held thousands of books, while the largest Carolingian book collections numbered a few hundred.

Agriculture nevertheless remained the most important element in the economy and in the daily lives of most people in all three realms. Farming meant primarily the production of cereal grains, which provided diet staples such as bread, porridge, and beer. Regions tended to specialize in the crops that grew most abundantly in local circumstances. For example, olives and grapes were common in the Mediterranean area, whereas cereals predominated around the Black Sea and in central Gaul. Animal husbandry was always a major part of the rural regime. English sheep provided wool and meat. In Frankish and Byzantine regions, pigs, which were cheap to raise, supplied meat, but for religious reasons, pork was almost absent in the Muslim East—Islam adopted the Jewish prohibition against it.

A key development in the Frankish West was the appearance of a bipartite estate, sometimes called a **manor**. On a bipartite estate, one part of the land was set aside as *demesne* [duh-MEEN]), and the rest was divided into tenancies. The demesne, consuming from one-quarter to one-half of the estate's territory, was exploited directly for the benefit of the landlord. The tenancies were generally worked by the peasants for their own support. The bipartite estate provided the aristocrats with a livelihood while freeing them for military and government service.

Estates were run in different ways. A landlord might hire laborers to farm his reserve, paying them with money exacted as fees from his tenants. Or he might require the tenants to work a certain number of days per week or weeks per year in his fields. The produce of the estate might be gathered into barns and consumed locally or hauled to local markets. The reserve might be a separate part of the estate, a proportion of common fields, or a percentage of the harvest. The tenants might have individual farms or work in common fields. Although the manor is one of the most familiar aspects of European life throughout the Middle Ages, large estates with dependent tenants also were evolving in the Byzantine and Islamic worlds.

**Oseberg Ship**
Discovered in 1880, the Oseberg ship was buried in Norway in (probably) the tenth century. The ship may have belonged to a king and contained the remains of Queen Asa. It is 70 feet long and 16 feet wide. Its crew would have been thirty to forty men.
Christophe Boisvieux/Terrra/Corbis

**manor** A common term for an agricultural estate that typically had its lands divided between the manor's lord and dependent peasants.

## Social Patterns

Most of the surviving medieval records were written by elite members of society and reveal little about the middle and lower orders of society. Nevertheless, certain similarities are evident in the social structures of all levels in all three societies. The elites tended to be large landholders, to control dependent populations, and to have access to government offices. There were regional differences, too. Scholars ranked higher in Byzantium and the caliphate than in the West; churchmen, especially bishops, were powerful in Christian societies but had no counterparts in Muslim ones. Literature, surely reflecting social realities, portrays the cultivated Muslim gentleman in the Abbasid period. This social type, marked by learning, good manners, and a taste for finery, does not appear in Byzantium or in the West until the twelfth century.

Women were bound to the same social hierarchies as men. Predictably enough, women had few formal, public roles to play. Their influence, however great, tended to function in the private sphere, rarely revealed to us by sources that stem from the public realm of powerful men. Aristocratic women had opportunities and power that were denied ordinary women. Irene ruled at Byzantium as empress. Frankish and Anglo-Saxon queens were formidable figures in their realms. Carolingian queens managed the landed patrimony of the dynasty— dozens of huge estates with tens of thousands of dependents. The combination of a lack of evidence and the rigorous exclusion of women from public life in the Islamic world means that virtually no Muslim women emerge as distinct personalities in the early Middle Ages.

One example of the problems in the evidence concerning women relates to church roles. Women could not hold priestly office, and although deaconesses served at Hagia Sophia in the sixth century, they disappeared soon after and had long before vanished in the West. Religious power could come from personal sanctity as well as holding office. One study of some 2,200 saints from the early Middle Ages finds only about 300 females. It was hard for women to gain recognition as saints. And if a woman became a saint, her holiness was inevitably described either as "manly"—an extreme ascetic was praised for having the strength and courage of a man—or as beautiful, virginal, and domestic—in other words, with female stereotypes.

The middling classes show some disparities among the regions. Merchants, for example, often rose through the social ranks to become great aristocrats in Muslim society. Islamic society often evinced great mobility because of its restless, expanding nature and because Islamic ideology rejected distinctions in the umma. In Byzantium, traditional Roman prejudices against merchants and moneymaking activities persisted. Thus, rich merchants whose wealth gave them private influence frequently lacked public power and recognition. In the West, merchants were neither numerous nor powerful in the Carolingian period. In some towns, moreover, commerce was in the hands of Jews, always outsiders in a militantly Christian society.

Merchants were not the only people occupying the middle rungs of the social ladder. All three societies, in fact, possessed both central elites and provincial elites. Service at the Carolingian, Byzantine, or Abbasid court counted for more than service in a provincial outpost. It was one thing to be abbot of a great monastery and quite a different thing to preside over a poor, tiny house. The thematic generals in Byzantium were lofty personages; their subordinates held inferior positions. The vassals of a Carolingian king formed a real aristocracy, but vassals of local officials were of decidedly lower rank.

Degrees of freedom and local economic and political conditions shaped the lives of peasants. In all three societies, some farmers were personally free and owed no cash or labor services to anyone but the central government. In areas such as Abbasid Iraq, ordinary free farmers led a comfortable life. In the Frankish world, most peasants existed outside the dawning manorial system. They were free, and if they lived in areas of good land and political security, such as the Paris basin, their lives most likely were congenial. Byzantine peasants, though free, often lived in areas of military danger, and in some parts of the Balkans, they eked out a living from poor soils. Highly taxed and perpetually endangered, they may have viewed their freedom as small compensation for their economic and personal insecurity. All peasants were alike in their subjection to political forces over which they had no control.

At the bottom of the social scale everywhere were slaves. Christianity did not object to slavery in general but forbade the enslavement of Christians. Islam likewise prohibited Muslims from enslaving other Muslims. Slaves, therefore, tended to be most common in pagan societies—Scandinavia, for example—or in frontier regions where neighboring pagans could be captured and sold. There were more slaves in the Muslim world than in Byzantium, which had, in turn, more than the West.

The domestic sphere is a difficult realm to enter. In Byzantium and the West, families rarely arranged marriages for more than one or two daughters. Others remained single or entered convents. Women at all social levels tended to pass from the tutelage of their fathers to that of their husbands. In antiquity, a suitor usually paid a fee, or "bride price," to his prospective wife's father and then endowed his wife with a "morning gift," money or possessions of her own. Gradually, this practice changed to a system whereby a bride's father paid a dowry to her future husband. Thus, a wife who was cast aside could be left impoverished, for in most places, the law did not permit her to inherit land if she had brothers. Females were such valuable property in the marriage market that rape was an offense not against a girl but against her father. A man could divorce, even kill, his wife for adultery, witchcraft, or grave robbing and then marry again. A woman could usually gain a divorce only for adultery, and she could not remarry. For the vast majority of women, daily life was hedged about with legal limitations and personal indignities.

## SECTION SUMMARY

- The early Middle Ages witnessed the elaboration of several major trading networks that made ordinary and luxury goods available over long distances.
- Cities continued to play important roles in the life of the Islamic and Byzantine worlds but played comparatively little role in western Europe.
- Arab, Byzantine, and European societies were elitist and hierarchical. Merchants were less important in Europe than elsewhere. Agriculture was dominant everywhere.
- Women played important political, social, and economic roles in all societies, but women's lives were hedged with restrictions.

# Chapter Summary

We have traced three parallel histories in the development of early medieval civilizations: that of the Arabs and Islam; that of the Byzantines; and that of Western Europe and the Carolingians.

◆ *What were the most important factors in the rise of the Arab peoples and the Islamic faith?*

Muhammad was a great teacher who emphasized *al-Islam*, surrender to Allah. He taught a faith that may be summarized in the "Five Pillars" of Islam. Both internal and external factors contributed to the lightning conquests of Islam in the century after Muhammad's death, spreading Islam and Arab rule from Spain to the frontiers of China. Islamic culture was rooted in the religious teachings of the *ulama* and in the scholarship of those who tackled Greek and Persian learning.

◆ *Why did a distinctive civilization that can be called "Byzantine" emerge?*

The Byzantine Empire faced hard challenges from Persians and then Muslims in the east, from Slavs, Avars, and Bulgars in the Balkans, and from Lombards in Italy. The Byzantine Empire in the early Middle Ages was much smaller than the Roman Empire that preceded it. The "theme" system was a comprehensive and effective revision of the empire's traditional governmental structure. A distinctive Byzantine culture was based on the Greek language, the Greek Church Fathers, Orthodox religious traditions, and distinctive local practices.

Visigothic Spain suffered from religious, political, and military disunity, while Italy developed three stable regions: a Lombard and then Frankish north; a papal center; and a Byzantine and then Muslim south. In the British Isles, the conversion to Catholic Christianity and the development of ecclesiastical organization were forces for unity and cultural achievement. In the British Isles, political development in the Celtic regions was slow, but England began emerging as a coherent political entity under ambitious and effective kings.

◆ *What were the greatest achievements of the Carolingians and why were they so successful?*

The Carolingian family rose steadily to power, first as mayors of the palace, then as kings, and finally as emperors. The greatest Carolingian, Charlemagne, instituted far-reaching governmental innovations and reforms intended to make his power effective and to unify the lands under his rule. Carolingian rulers launched a cultural revival, called the Carolingian Renaissance, which aimed to master and then communicate basic Christian teachings. The Carolingian Empire broke down because of geographic diversity, political disunity, and new waves of invasion.

◆ *What were the chief similarities and differences among the early medieval civilizations?*

The early Middle Ages witnessed the elaboration of several major trading networks that made ordinary and luxury goods available over long distances. Cities continued to play important roles in the life of the Islamic and Byzantine worlds but played comparatively little role in western Europe except as ecclesiastical centers. Arab, Byzantine, and European societies were elitist and hierarchical. Merchants were less important in Europe than elsewhere. Agriculture was dominant everywhere. Women played important political, social, and economic roles in all societies, but women's lives were hedged by legal limitations, social conventions, and religious restrictions.

# Key Terms

**Muhammad** (p. 198)

**Five Pillars** (p. 199)

**Quran** (p. 200)

**caliphate** (p. 201)

**Papal States** (p. 205)

**iconoclasm** (p. 206)

**Orthodox** (p. 207)

**Charlemagne** (p. 212)

**vassals** (p. 215)

**Carolingian Renaissance** (p. 216)

**manor** (p. 221)

CourseMate

Go to the CourseMate website at **www.cengagebrain.com** for additional study tools and review materials—including audio and video clips—for this chapter.

**Bayeux Tapestry** The tapestry (ca. 1077) depicts the fleet of William the Conqueror of Normandy sailing to England in 1066. Erich Lessing/Art Resource, NY

# The Expansion of Europe in the High Middle Ages, 900–1300

The picture to the left represents one small section of the Bayeux Tapestry, a narrative account—in words and illustrations—of the conquest of England in 1066 by Duke William of Normandy. This scene is an apt introduction to the central theme of this chapter: expansion.

This section of the 230-foot-long tapestry depicts William setting sail for England. Already successful in Normandy, William was about to claim the throne of England. He gathered soldiers from all over western France and boldly crossed the English Channel. Leaving nothing to chance, he transported horses, too, as you can see in the picture.

One group of Normans conquered England, while another seized control of southern Italy. Still other Normans played a decisive role in the period's most prominent manifestation of expansion: the Crusades. Meanwhile, certain Scandinavians settled Iceland and Greenland to the west, while others founded the first state on Russian soil. Spanish Christians pushed back the Muslims in Iberia. From the Baltic to the Balkans, Slavic rulers founded new states and pressed hard against their neighbors. German rulers crossed the Alps into Italy, French kings reached the Pyrenees, and English monarchs pushed into Wales, Scotland, and Ireland. Seldom has Europe's political geography expanded so dramatically as during the High Middle Ages.

Between 900 and 1300, Europe's population began one of its longest periods of sustained growth. People brought more land under cultivation, introduced new crops, and made agriculture more efficient. Villages, towns, and cities grew in number and size. Trade expanded in every material and in every direction.

Europe witnessed the reemergence of centralizing monarchies in France, England, and Spain. Some new realms, such as Denmark and Hungary, built strong central governments. And an explosion of new states occurred along the frontiers of the old Carolingian Empire.

The "West" began taking on a more *western European* character. The Crusades complicated relations between Christian Europeans and Muslims, and both the Crusades

## Chapter Overview

### Economic Expansion

◆ *In how many different realms of life do you see signs of growth and innovation, of expansion?*

### The Heirs of the Carolingian Empire: Germany, Italy, and France

◆ *What did Germany, Italy, and France owe to the Carolingian past? How alike and different were these areas by 1300?*

### The British Isles

◆ *What were the chief dynamics in the development of medieval Britain?*

### The Growth of New States

◆ *How did new states emerge in Spain, Scandinavia, and the Slavic world, and how do those states compare with their western neighbors?*

### The Crusades

◆ *What basic factors contributed to the rise, persistence, and eventual decline of the crusading movement?*

and increasing religious differences alienated western Europe from Byzantium, and Roman Catholics from Orthodox believers. The center of Western civilization became more and more anchored to northwestern Europe. And that same western Europe was expanding to influence lands in Scandinavia and the Slavic world that had played no role at all in the West's classical, Mediterranean phase. The High Middle Ages repeatedly posed the question: Where is the West?

# Economic Expansion

*In how many different realms of life do you see signs of growth and innovation, of expansion?*

The economic expansion of Europe is manifest in many kinds of evidence that are more often qualitative than quantitative. Medieval people did not keep the records of births, deaths, population, or business activity that modern states routinely accumulate. After about 1000, every available indicator points to a growing population and an expanding scale and sophistication of economic activity.

## The Growing Population

The population of Europe began rising slowly in the Carolingian period and may have doubled between 1000 and 1200 to 60 million. In regions where family size can be estimated, fertile marriages were producing on the average 3.5 children in the tenth century and an average of 6 or 7 children per family in the twelfth. People were also living longer than their forebears. Studies of aristocrats, high clergy, and soldiers show that a surprising 40 percent of them were over 40 years old. Male life expectancy was surely longer than female because of the dangers of childbirth, always the great killer of women in the premodern world. The general trend is clear: more babies being born, more infants living into adulthood, more adults living longer.

Everywhere in Europe new land was brought into cultivation. More than half of the French documents relating to land in the twelfth century show new land being brought under the plow. Thousands of acres of forest were cut down. Marshes were reclaimed from the sea. Some 380,000 acres were drained along the western coast of France and probably twice that amount in both Flanders and England. This activity is inexplicable without assuming a growing number of mouths to feed.

Agriculture benefited from a warmer and drier climate through this whole period. Not a single vegetable blight was recorded. Food was more abundant and more nutritious. Animals were increasingly reared for their meat, and higher meat consumption meant more protein in the diet. Beans and other legumes, also rich in protein, were more widely cultivated. People of every class and region were almost certainly eating better and living longer and healthier lives.

## Technological Gains

The eleventh century was a decisive period in the spread of new technologies in Europe. Innovations occurred in agriculture, transportation, mining, and manufacturing. Agricultural changes came first as a rising population created an increased demand for food that could be met only by new practices. By the late twelfth century, an acre of farmland in a fertile region was probably yielding a crop three to four times larger than in the Carolingian era. Given the combination of more land under cultivation and more yield per acre, the overall gains in the food supply were enormous.

The increases can be accounted for in several ways. Horses were more frequently used as draft animals. They did, in a day, a third or half again as much work, hauling loads farther and faster than oxen. Thus, fewer people with horses could cultivate more land than their predecessors managed with oxen. In addition, they could cultivate the land more frequently and increase yields because more seed would fall on more finely plowed soil. The dissemination of the horse collar made possible the expanded use of horses—older forms of harnesses suitable for the low-slung, broad-shouldered ox would have choked a horse.

Plows, too, were improved. The light wooden scratch plow used by the Romans was satisfactory for the thin soils of the Mediterranean region but barely disturbed the heavy soils of northern Europe. The invention of a heavy wheeled plow with an iron plowshare and a moldboard was a real breakthrough. The iron plowshare cut deep furrows, and then the moldboard turned and aerated the soil. This heavy plow allowed farmers to exploit good soils more fully without exhausting the ground too rapidly. Perhaps introduced into Carolingian Europe from the Slavic world, this plow was widely adopted from the eleventh century.

Wider adoption of nitrogen-fixing crops, such as peas and some kinds of beans, retarded soil exhaustion and also put more protein in the diet. Leaving land fallow also avoided soil exhaustion. In the early Middle Ages, this meant setting aside about half of the arable land every year (the two-field system) or working the land intensively for a few years and then moving on. By the twelfth century, three-field schemes of crop rotation were common. Under the three-field system, two-thirds of the arable land saw nearly constant use. The amount of an estate under cultivation rose from 50 to 67 percent.

Surplus produce was intended mainly for the growing towns. To supply that market, improvements in transportation were necessary. Kings often passed laws to secure the safety of highways, and popes three times (in 1097, 1132, and 1179) threatened highwaymen—robbers who preyed on travelers—with excommunication. Landlords required their dependents to maintain roads and bridges. Many stone bridges were constructed in France between 1130 and 1170 because wooden bridges were so vulnerable to fire. Indeed, fire destroyed the bridge at Angers (in western France) five times between 1032 and 1167.

## CHRONOLOGY

| | |
|---|---|
| 862 | Founding of Kiev |
| 870–930 | Settlement of Iceland |
| 962 | Imperial coronation of Otto I |
| 987 | Accession of Hugh Capet in France |
| 988 | Kievan Rus accept Orthodox Christianity |
| 1016 | Conquest of England by Cnut |
| 1066 | Norman Conquest of England |
| 1073–1085 | Pontificate of Gregory VII |
| 1078 | Decree against lay investiture |
| 1085 | Spanish reconquest of Toledo |
| 1086 | *Domesday Book* |
| 1096–1099 | First Crusade |
| 1122 | Concordat of Worms |
| 1171 | Henry II of England invades Ireland |
| 1176 | Battle of Legnano |
| 1198–1216 | Pontificate of Innocent III |
| 1202–1204 | French drive English out of Normandy |
| 1203 | Fourth Crusade |
| 1212, 1214 | Battles of Las Navas de Tolosa and Bouvines |
| 1215 | Magna Carta |
| 1265 | First Parliament in England |
| 1294–1303 | Quarrel between Boniface VIII and Philip IV |
| 1295 | Model Parliament |

Transport improved not only because of safer roads but also thanks to better vehicles. The old two-wheeled cart, drawn by oxen, began giving way to the sturdy four-wheeled, horse-drawn wagon. Because greater quantities of foodstuffs could be moved farther and faster, urban communities could be supplied from larger areas. This was a crucial factor in enabling cities to grow and in providing urban residents with a predictable and diverse range of foods.

Seaborne trade expanded, too. The stern rudder, better sails, the compass (in use by 1180), and better navigational charts facilitated sea travel, as did the growing use of larger ships. An Italian fleet sailed to Flanders in 1277, and within a few years the old overland trade routes began a decline that was not reversed until the invention of the railroad in the nineteenth century.

At any time of year, travel was difficult and costly. Few dared to venture across the Alps in the winter, and the northern seas, especially the passage around Denmark, were treacherous in cold weather. Even in the relatively calm Mediterranean, the Venetians refused to send out their trading fleet between November and March. Overland trade was impeded by snow, rain, mud, and highwaymen, who would rob travelers on the road. Governments tried to restrain robbers, but no one could change the weather.

There were notable improvements in both the quarrying of stone and the mining of metals. Mines were not deep because people lacked the means to keep the shafts and galleries free of water. Still, the exploitation of surface veins of ore—principally iron, but also tin and silver—intensified, to supply the increased demand for plowshares, tools, weapons, construction fittings, and coins. Stone quarrying, the most common form of mining in the Middle Ages, benefited directly from more efficient stone saws and indirectly from improvements in transport. Better techniques in stonecutting, construction, and conveyance help to explain, for example, the increase in the number of England's stone religious buildings from sixty to nearly five hundred in the century after 1050.

## Signs of Growth

Agricultural specialization became common. People began to cultivate intensively those crops that were best suited to local conditions. The area around Toulouse, for example, concentrated on herbs from which blue and yellow dyes were made. The central regions of France focused on cereal grains, while the Bordeaux and Burgundy regions emphasized the grapes that produced wine. Northern Germany specialized in cattle raising; northern England favored sheep.

Agricultural specialization helps to explain the growth in trade everywhere (see **Map 9.1**). For certain commodities, local trade continued to flourish. Italian wines and olive oil, for example, only moved from countryside to town within a region. The same was true of French and English grains. However, French wines were much prized throughout Europe, especially in England, and certain products, such as English wool and Flemish cloth, were carried far and wide. Salt fish from the Baltic found its way all over the continent. Lumber traveled across the Mediterranean to the wood-poor Muslim world. Spain produced warhorses. Southern Europe supplied the northern demand for spices, oranges, raisins, figs, almonds, and other exotic foodstuffs. Caen, in Normandy, sent shiploads of its beautifully colored and textured stone to England for the construction of churches and monasteries. Rising population, higher productivity, and greater prosperity added up to a larger volume of goods moving farther and more frequently.

A novelty of the twelfth century was the emergence of the Champagne fairs as a meeting point for the commerce of north and south. Since the early Middle Ages, a few locations hosted permanent fairs, and many places sponsored occasional fairs. By the middle of the twelfth century, however, the spices, silks, and dyes of the Mediterranean, the wool of England, the furs and linens of Germany, and the leather products of Spain began to be sold in a series of six fairs held in the Champagne region of France from spring to autumn.

Whether for fuel, or for ships and buildings, the demand for wood grew steadily. Wood exemplifies the expansion and interconnectedness of the medieval economy and society. Forests were essential to daily life, providing the wood for houses, fences, and fuel in villages and towns. Animals, especially pigs, were grazed at the edges of the forest to permit as much land as possible to be dedicated to food crops. Wild animals were hunted in the forest. For aristocrats, hunting was as much for sport as for food. For poorer rural people, however, wild game made up a significant part of the regular diet. The forest was also a plentiful source of fruits, nuts, and honey. Thus, the decision to cut down a stand of trees was a serious one.

**Heavy Wheeled Plow** In the high Middle Ages the more widespread use of the wheeled plow with an iron plowshare, and often with a moldboard (not pictured here), made farmers more productive at a time when increasing population elevated the demand for food. The Art Archive / Biblioteca Capitolare Verona / Gianni Dagli Orti

**Map 9.1 European Resources and Trade Routes, circa 1100** In an age of expansion, some products were consumed locally, but many others were transported over longer and longer distances. Commercial connections expanded, too, creating several interlocking networks. © Cengage Learning 2014

Major route of trade and commerce

Grain-growing region

Wine-producing region

Coal Primary product

**229**

| Table 9.1 | Population Increases in Italian Cities, 1200–1300 | | |
|---|---|---|---|
| | 1200 | 1300 | Percentage Increase |
| **City** | | | |
| **Florence** | 15,000 | 96,000 | +640% |
| **Siena** | 19,000 | 52,000 | +274% |
| **Pisa** | 20,000 | 38,000 | +190% |

*Source*: Adapted from Malcolm Barber, *The Two Cities: Medieval Europe, 1050–1320*, p. 270. Copyright © 1992. Reprinted by permission of the publisher, Routledge, an imprint of the Taylor & Francis Group.

## The Roles of Cities and Towns

All over Europe, towns grew impressively in size and importance. **Table 9.1** shows the growth of three Italian cities. Such growth also occurred in cities in Flanders, such as Bruges and Ghent, and in Paris, London, and other cities that were becoming national capitals. Ghent expanded its city walls five times between 1160 and 1300, a sure sign of growth even in the absence of population figures. Similar forces were operating in the countryside. In 1100, about 11 fortified villages surrounded Florence, but by 1200, the city was ringed by 205 such villages.

For the first time since Late Antiquity, cities were becoming centers for many activities. Governments, which required larger staffs of trained personnel, settled in towns. Schools and eventually universities (see pages 277–279) were urban institutions. Mercantile, industrial, ecclesiastical, and legal organizations were located in towns. Towns began to compete with royal and aristocratic courts as literary centers, and cathedrals, the great buildings of the age, were exclusively urban.

**guilds** Voluntary associations of people who shared common crafts or trades.

One distinctive urban phenomenon was the rise of **guilds**. The guilds had many functions. Their main purpose was economic: to regulate standards of production, to fix prices, and to control membership in their respective trades. But as towns grew larger and more impersonal, these associations of people engaged in similar occupations fostered a sense of belonging, a feeling of community. Members tended to live in the same areas and to worship together in a parish church. Growing wealth in general, coupled with fierce local pride, produced building competitions whose results are still visible in the huge neighborhood churches that survive in most European towns. The guilds indulged in elaborate festivals and celebrations, which sometimes turned into drunken debauches despite being held to honor saints. The guilds also assisted members who fell on hard times, saw to their funeral expenses, and provided for widows and orphans.

The guilds had a damaging impact on women. As more economic activity came under the umbrella of the guild structures, women were more systematically excluded from guild membership. Usually, women could become guild members only as wives or widows. They could not open economic enterprises of their own, although they were workers in many trades. Despite a growing, diversifying economy, women were increasingly denied opportunities, although later centuries would find women establishing their own guilds.

## Changing Economic Attitudes

As medieval society generated more wealth and populations concentrated in cities, people who were relatively well-off became more conscious of those who were less fortunate. Moralists began to argue that the poor were a special gift of God to the rich, who could redeem their own souls by generous charitable benefactions. Most towns established schemes of poor relief. But the numbers of poor people grew so rapidly, particularly in large towns, that helping seemed hopeless, and some gave up trying. Hospitals, for example, began to refuse abandoned babies for fear that they would be deluged with them.

Efforts to alleviate the condition of the poor constituted one ethical concern of medieval thinkers, but two issues attracted even more attention. First, theologians and lawyers alike discussed the "just price," the price at which goods should be bought and sold. Christian teaching had long held that it was immoral to hoard food during a famine or knowingly to sell a damaged item. But what was the correct price in ordinary circumstances? A theological view, often dismissed as unrealistic, held that items could be sold for only the cost of the materials in them and the labor absolutely necessary to produce them. A commercial view, often dismissed as immoral, insisted that a fair price was whatever the market would bear, regardless of costs or consequences. A working consensus held that a just price was one arrived at by bargaining between free and knowledgeable parties.

The other ethical issue concerned usury, the lending of money at interest. Christian writers were always hostile to commercial enterprise, and they had plenty of biblical warrant for their view. Psalm 15 warned that no one can be blameless "who lends his money at usury." Luke's Gospel admonished Christians to "give without expecting to be repaid in full." Luke actually forbade the profit that makes most commercial enterprises possible. In the twelfth century, churchmen began to be much more assiduous in their condemnations of usury, a practice that had been winked at for centuries. Gradually, thinkers began to defend usury on the grounds that a person who lent money incurred a risk and deserved to be compensated for that risk.

Investment demands credit, and credit requires some payback for the lender. Even in the face of deep hostility, credit mechanisms spread in thirteenth-century Europe. They were held up to minute scrutiny by theologians and popular preachers and were found to be evidence of man's sinfulness, acquisitiveness, and greed. But all these practices persisted, fueled by the expansion of the European economy, and began putting individual profit alongside community interest at the heart of social and economic thought.

## SECTION SUMMARY

- Europe's population grew dramatically until the late 1200s, owing to better diets and more plentiful foods.
- Technological gains came with wider use of horses, improved plows, and more productive farming techniques.
- Many regions began to specialize in growing or manufacturing products, and this local specialization prompted larger-scale trade.
- Economic growth widened the gap between rich and poor and induced theologians to write about the just price and usury.

# The Heirs of the Carolingian Empire: Germany, Italy, and France

*What did Germany, Italy, and France owe to the Carolingian past? How alike and how different were these areas by 1300?*

The scope of political and institutional life expanded everywhere between 900 and 1300. In 900, the Carolingian Empire was collapsing. By 1300, France had emerged as a large, stable kingdom, and Italy had turned into several reasonably coherent regional entities. The most surprising political development within the old Carolingian lands, indeed within Europe as a whole, was Germany's rise to a premier position in the tenth century and then its long, slow decline. The states that evolved out of the Carolingian Empire faced common challenges: the achievement of territorial integrity; the growing responsibility of the central government; complicated political relations among kings, aristocrats, and churchmen; and the elaboration of new ideas about the state and its responsibilities.

## Germany and the Empire, 911–1272

From the ninth century to the present, no state in Europe has been less stable territorially and politically than Germany and the German Empire. Two issues are paramount: the role of dynastic and territorial instability in German history and German rulers' complex, contentious relations with the leaders of the church.

### Germany's Land and Rulers

The Treaty of Verdun (see page 217) created something essentially new in 843: an East Frankish kingdom. Before 843, no unified kingdom had ever existed in the territories east of the Rhine River (see **Map 9.2**). The lands had no tradition of unity and there was no single "German" people. Roman culture had barely penetrated into German lands, and Christian culture was recent. "Germany" had—has—no natural frontiers.

After the last East Frankish Carolingian died in 911, the dukes, or leaders, of Germany's major regions chose one of their number as king. Under varying circumstances, the dukes chose kings from different families several times: Saxons (or Ottonians) in 919, Salians in

🌐 **Map 9.2 Germany and Its Duchies, circa 1000–1200** The chief political dynamic in Germany was a contest for power between the kings and the dukes. The duchies emerged in the ninth and tenth centuries and outlived one dynasty of kings after another.

1024, and Staufer in 1138. This record of frequent dynastic change might be contrasted with the situation in France (see pages 240–242), where one family reigned from 987 to 1328.

At the beginning of Saxon rule, Germany comprised five duchies: Saxony, Franconia, Lorraine, Swabia, and Bavaria. German romantic tradition regarded the dukes as the heroic leaders of distinct ethnic communities, the so-called Tribal Duchies. The dukes were actually the descendants of local rulers introduced by the Carolingians. They were wealthy and powerful; they contested with kings for control of the bishops and abbots in their duchies; and sometimes they managed to make vassals out of the lower ranks of the aristocracy in their territories, effectively denying kings connections with these people. In sum, the dukes were extremely jealous of their independence.

When the Saxons came to power, they attempted, from their base in Saxony, to control one or more of the other duchies. Hoping to win new territories and distract troublesome aristocrats, the Saxons began Germany's centuries-long drive to the east, into Slavic Europe. In 955, Otto I gained power and prestige when he led a combined German force to victory against the Magyars at Lechfeld.

The Saxons also tried to control the church, especially bishops and abbots, to gain the allegiance of powerful and articulate allies. In 962, Otto I, who had begun expanding into Italy in 952, was crowned emperor in Rome by the pope. The imperial title conferred two benefits on the German kings: It gave them immense prestige and power that owed nothing to the dukes, and it raised the possibility of securing huge material resources in Italy, where, as emperors, they did not have to share power the way they did in Germany. The marriage of Otto II to a Byzantine princess was a sign of Germany's growing stature. Their son, Otto III, sponsored a brilliant court, patronizing writers and painters. When he died in 1002, Germany was the preeminent land in Europe.

After 1002, dynastic instability plagued Germany. For example, when Henry III died in 1056, he left behind a 6-year-old heir and a decade of civil war. Military expansion virtually ceased, and powerful aristocrats struggled with one another and with their kings. Chief among these aristocrats were the dukes, who had chafed under Saxon and Salian efforts to control them. When Henry IV came of age in 1066, he faced opposition on all sides, controlled no duchies, was not yet emperor, and had lost much of his father's control of the church. When he tried to make church appointments in the traditional way, he encountered the fierce opposition of the newly reformed papacy in the person of Pope Gregory VII (r. 1073–1085). Their battles inaugurated the so-called investiture controversy (discussed later in this chapter), which lingered on until 1122, when both of the original foes were long dead.

In the twelfth century, the Salian dynasty died out. With the accession of Frederick Barbarossa ("Red Beard") in 1152, a new family, the Staufer, consolidated its hold on the German throne. Frederick, based in Swabia, patiently worked to get other dukes to recognize his overlordship, even though he was powerless to demand payments or services from them. His plan was to build up slowly the idea that the king was the highest lord in the land (a plan that his French and English contemporaries used effectively). In 1158, Frederick summoned representatives of the major Italian cities to demand full recognition of his regalian, or ruler's, rights. These included military service; control of roads, ports, and waterways; administration of tolls, mints, fines, vacant fiefs, and confiscated properties; appointment of magistrates; construction of palaces; and control of mines, fisheries, and saltworks. Frederick's attempts to control northern Italy resulted in the creation of the Lombard League, a union of Italian cities that inflicted a humiliating defeat on German forces at Legnano (len-YAN-oh) in 1176.

Frederick also struggled for more than twenty years to get the popes to recognize his claim to the imperial office, which he viewed as a source of prestige and as a legitimation of his right to rule Italy. When he spoke of his "Holy Roman Empire," he meant that his power came from God himself and from the Romans via Charlemagne. The handsome, energetic, and athletic Frederick accomplished much, and he might have done more had he not drowned in Anatolia in 1190, while on his way to the Third Crusade.

In 1197, Germany's heir was an infant, Frederick II (r. 1212–1250), who had been born in Sicily. His mother, Constance, had no standing in Germany and little influence in Italy. Accordingly, she placed her son under the tutelage of Pope Innocent III (r. 1198–1216). By the time Frederick came of age, he so despaired of governing Germany that he conceded the "Statute in Favor of the Princes," which lodged royal power in ducal hands in return for a vague acknowledgment of his overlordship. Frederick concentrated his own efforts in Italy. Although he made good progress, he faced constant opposition from the popes, who were unwilling to trade a German ruler with interests in Italy for an essentially Italian ruler with interests in Germany. When Frederick II died in 1250, effective central authority in both Germany and Italy collapsed.

A long-lived dynasty might have made a difference. Germany did have great rulers: Otto I, Otto III, Frederick Barbarossa, and even Frederick II were the equals of any contemporary ruler. But repeated changes of ruling family in the context of a fragile political regime

| Table 9.2 Rulers of Medieval Germany |
| --- |
| **Saxons** |
| Henry I (919–936) |
| Otto I (936–973) |
| Otto II (973–983) |
| Otto III (983–1002) |
| Henry II (1002–1024) |
| **Salians** |
| Conrad II (1024–1039) |
| Henry III (1039–1056) |
| Henry IV (1056–1106) |
| Henry V (1106–1125) |
| **Staufer** |
| Conrad III (1138–1152) |
| Frederick Barbarossa (1152–1190) |
| Henry VI (1190–1197) |
| Frederick II (1212–1250) |

© Cengage Learning 2014

provided repeated opportunities for fragmentation. The German monarchy had a very limited territorial base and unimpressive government institutions. The Saxons were based in the north, the Salians in the center, and the Staufer in the south. Thus, continuity of rule was constantly threatened by huge dynastic, institutional, and geographical challenges. Germany's involvement with Italy and quest for the imperial title have occasioned no end of controversy. To some, royal involvement in Italy signals a failure to deal imaginatively with Germany itself. To others, the quest for prestige, power, and money in Italy was actually a creative solution to the monarchy's relative impotence in Germany.

## The Investiture Controversy

The key issue in the relations between Germany's rulers and the church is the investiture controversy. In the middle of the eleventh century, a group of ardent church reformers, who were committed to improving the moral and intellectual caliber of the clergy all over Europe, targeted the chief impediment to reform: the control of church appointments by laymen—or **lay investiture**, as they called it. Gregory VII prohibited lay investiture. This brought the reformers into direct conflict with the Salians, who, like their predecessors back to Charlemagne, believed that they reigned supreme in the "City of God." These German rulers stood, in their own view, nearest to God in a great hierarchy; the clergy occupied the rungs beneath them in human society. Thus, the king was God's specially chosen agent on earth, and the higher clergy were the king's natural helpers in governing the realm. To the reformers, the proper organization of society was just the opposite: The clergy, with the pope at its head, stood nearest to God, with secular monarchs subordinate to the church.

Alongside ideological struggles, the particular quarrel over the appointment of churchmen mushroomed into a general struggle for leadership in Christian society. In Germany, the struggle between Henry IV and Gregory VII became a pretext for ducal and aristocratic opposition to the king. Henry expended time and resources in Italy trying in vain to control Rome and the pope. (See the feature, "The Written Record: The Issues in the Investiture Controversy" on page 235.)

The Concordat of Worms (VORM), concluded in 1122 between Henry V (r. 1106–1125) and Pope Calixtus II (r. 1119–1124), brought the investiture controversy to an end. The decree stipulated that the election of bishops should be free and conducted according to church law. Only after a man had been duly elected bishop could a king, or emperor, invest him with the symbols and offices of secular authority. The Concordat was a blow to the German political system as it had existed for centuries. When Otto III died in 1002, Germany was powerful and confident. When Henry V died in 1125, Germany was weak, disunited, and searching for new bases of authority. With its promise, undoubted achievements, and yet ultimate failure, Germany is the political mystery of medieval Europe.

## The Varying Fortunes of Italy

The history of Italy has always been played out in three regions: north, central, and south. The Carolingians and the Germans after them laid a heavy hand on northern Italy. In the center of the peninsula, the Papal States was the key player. Outsiders always dominated the south, but their identities changed often.

## The Communal Movement

The rise of **communes** (see **Map 9.3**) owed much to the period's economic expansion. Merchants and artisans were gaining in wealth and anxious to have some say in the government of their cities. At the same time, bishops and counts contested

**lay investiture** A term for the appointment ("investiture") of members of the clergy by laymen.

**communes** Self-governing Italian towns.

Biblioteca Apostolica Vaticana, Vatican City/Flammarion/The Bridgeman Art Library

**Henry IV, Duchess Matilda of Tuscany, and Abbot Hugh of Cluny** The embattled Henry IV here implores Matilda, a tremendously wealthy landowner and ally of Pope Gregory VII, to intercede with the pope. The powerful abbot of Cluny looks over the scene protectively. Written documents do not portray women's power as vividly as this image does.

## The Issues in the Investiture Controversy

*These two documents illustrate the range of issues involved in the conflict between the emperor Henry IV and Pope Gregory VII. The first excerpt is from a long letter written by Henry in 1076. The second is a decree issued by Gregory in 1078.*

### Henry Denounces the Pope

Henry, king not by usurpation but by the holy ordination of God, to Hildebrand, not now pope but false monk:

Such greeting as this you have merited through your disturbances, for there is no rank in the church on which you have brought, not honor but disgrace, not blessing but curse. To mention only a few notable cases, you have dared to assail the holy rulers of the church, archbishops, bishops, and priests, and you have trodden them underfoot like slaves ignorant of what their master is doing; . . . you have regarded them as knowing nothing, yourself as knowing all things. . . .

We have endured all this in our anxiety to save the honor of the apostolic see, but you have mistaken our humility for fear and have ventured to attack the royal power conferred on us by God, and threatened to divest us of it. As if we had received our kingdom from you! As if the kingdom and empire were in your hands, not God's! For our Lord Jesus Christ did call us to the kingdom. . . . You have assailed me who, though unworthy of anointing, have nevertheless been anointed to the kingdom and who, according to the traditions of the holy fathers, are subject to the judgment of God alone. . . . The true pope Peter exclaims "Fear God, honor the king." But you, who do not fear God, dishonor me, His appointed one . . .

### Gregory Strikes Back

Inasmuch as we have learned that, contrary to the ordinances of the holy fathers, the investiture of churches is, in many places, performed by lay persons, and that from this cause many disturbances arise in the church by which the Christian religion is degraded, we decree that no one of the clergy shall receive the investiture of a bishopric, abbey, or church from the hand of an emperor, or king, or of any lay person, male or female. If anyone shall presume to do so, let him know that such investiture is void by apostolic authority, and that he himself shall lie under excommunication until fitting satisfaction shall have been made.

### Questions

1. On what foundations does Henry IV challenge Gregory VII?

2. How does Gregory see the issues?

3. What aspects of medieval thought and politics made this quarrel possible?

Slightly adapted from James Harvey Robinson, *Readings in European History*, vol. 1 (Boston: Ginn, 1904), pp. 279-281, 275.

---

each other for power and began to grant fiefs to vassals in the town's surrounding country-side. Landed and commercial wealth produced a volatile mix.

Communes began as sworn associations of the local nobility—landed lords—and their vassals. Commune members swore to uphold one another's rights and called themselves the *popolo*, or "people," although the people as a whole had nothing to do with the early communes. A commune accorded a high degree of participation to its members in choosing leaders and in assembling to vote on matters of common concern. The leaders of the early communes were usually called *consuls*—a deliberate attempt to evoke the Roman past. Usually elected for a single year, the consuls varied in number from four to twenty in different cities. The consuls proposed matters to an assembly for ratification. By the 1140s, every significant city in northern and central Italy had a commune. One by one, cities either refused to recognize papal or imperial overlordship or else renegotiated the terms under which they would acknowledge the rule of their historic masters. The working out of this ongoing relationship was a major development in the history of the Italian cities in the twelfth century.

By the late twelfth century, the consular communes were still governed by oligarchies of men whose wealth and power came from land, trade, and industry. Guild interests, however, gained in prominence at the expense of the landed groups among whom the communal movement had arisen, and ordinary workers began to clamor for participation. The communes were becoming increasingly volatile and violent.

One solution to this potential crisis was the introduction of the *podestà* (poe-des-TAH), a sort of city manager chosen by the local oligarchy. The podestà often came from the outside, served for a set period (usually six months or a year), and underwent a careful scrutiny

**Map 9.3 The Communal Movement in Italy** Beginning in the late eleventh century, many towns in northern Italy, some in the central regions, and a very few in the south erected communal forms of government. This distribution reflects the relative wealth of north and south and the power of the popes in the center. North of the Alps, only Flanders and northern France experienced comparable communal movements.

| **Table 9.3** Important Popes During the High Middle Ages |
| --- |
| Gregory VII (1073–1085) |
| Urban II (1088–1099) |
| Innocent III (1198–1216) |
| Boniface VIII (1294–1303) |

© Cengage Learning 2014

at the conclusion of his term. He was expected to police the city as well as defend it. Normally, he could not be a property owner in the town, marry into local society, or dine privately with any citizen. By the middle of the thirteenth century, some podestàs were becoming virtual professional administrators. One man, for example, was elected sixteen times in nine cities over a period of thirty-four years, four times in Bologna alone.

The Italian commune was a radical political experiment. Everywhere else in medieval Europe, power was thought to radiate downward—from God, the clergy, the emperor, the king. In a commune, power radiated upward from the popolo to its leaders. For several centuries, the Italian city was arguably the most creative institution in the Western world.

## The Papal Monarchy

**Papal Monarchy** A term meant to signify the enlarged and centralized papal government beginning in the twelfth century.

The key power in central Italy was the papacy, and the main political entity was the Papal States. In the political turmoil of the tenth and eleventh centuries, the papacy lost a great deal of territory. Throughout the twelfth and thirteenth centuries, therefore, a basic objective of papal policy was to recover lost lands and rights. This quest to restore the territorial basis for papal power and income helps explain why the popes so resolutely opposed German imperial influence in Italy.

The most striking development pertaining to the papacy is the expansion of its institutions. The **Papal Monarchy** is meant to characterize a church whose power was increasingly centralized in the hands of the popes. In Rome, the pope presided over the *curia*, the papal court. The College of Cardinals, potentially fifty-three in number, formed a kind of senate for the church. They elected the popes (by majority after 1059 and by a two-thirds majority after 1179), served as key advisers, headed the growing financial and judicial branches of the papal government, and often served as legates, papal envoys. Lateran Councils met often and gathered the clergy from all over Europe to legislate for the church as a whole. The hierarchical structure of the church became more visible as ecclesiastical business tended to accumulate in Rome.

High medieval popes built a sophisticated legal system (see page 273) and also reserved to themselves certain jurisdictional and coercive prerogatives. Popes could excommunicate persons—that is, exclude them from the sacraments of the church and the community of Christians. This was a form of social death in that excommunicated persons could not eat, converse, or socialize with others. Popes could lay a territory under interdict. This decree forbade all religious services except baptisms and burials and was designed to bring maximum pressure to bear on a particular individual. Finally, popes could invoke the inquisition. Despite horror stories about the inquisition, this was a judicial mechanism fully rooted in Roman law and widely used in the medieval West. Basically, an inquisition involved churchmen taking sworn testimony in an attempt to discover heresy.

Effective government, a network of legates, law, the Investiture Controversy, successful battles with many rulers, leadership in the Crusades (see pages 250–252), and Europe-wide councils (Lateran IV in 1215 was the largest council of the Catholic Church until the sixteenth century) made the papacy the premier institution in high medieval Europe.

## The Fate of Southern Italy

From the ninth century on, the region south of Rome was contested among Byzantines, North African Muslims, and local potentates. In 1026, Norman pilgrims, bound for the Holy Land, landed in southern Italy, where local people enlisted them in the fight against the Muslims. Initially opposed to the Normans, the papacy later allied with their leader as a counterweight against the Germans.

From his capital at Palermo, Roger II "the Great" (r. 1130–1154) ruled a complex state that blended Byzantine, Lombard, and Norman structures. Perched advantageously at the juncture of the Latin, Greek, and Arab worlds, the Norman court was more advanced in finance and bureaucratic administration than any of its European contemporaries. No one forgot for a moment, however, that the Normans were primarily great warriors. A chronicler said of the Normans, "They delight in arms and horses."

Once the popes had defeated Frederick II, they decided to look for more pliant allies in the south. They invited a succession of French and Spanish princes to assume the Crown, thus touching off long-standing rivalries in the area. A profusion of outsiders always dominated southern Italy.

## *Capetian France, 987–1314*

When the Treaty of Verdun created the West Frankish Kingdom in 843, no one knew what the future of France might be. Referring to France's tremendous diversity, the twentieth-century French leader Charles de Gaulle once quipped, "It is impossible to govern a country with 325 kinds of cheese." During the late ninth century and much of the tenth, the area suffered cruelly from constant waves of Viking attacks and from repeated failures of the

Scala/Art Resource, NY

**Coronation of Roger II in Sicily, 1130**  Roger's coronation by Jesus Christ makes a powerful ideological statement: He owes his office to no earthly power. The cultural crosscurrents of Sicily are visible: Roger is depicted more like a Byzantine emperor than a Western king. The inscriptions above his head ("Rogerios Rex") and next to Christ's are in Greek, not Latin. Beside Christ's head are the customary Greek abbreviations **IC** (the first and last letters of Iesu**S**) and **XP**, for **ChR**istos. (The original surely contains the full XP symbol.)

Carolingian family to produce adult heirs to the throne. At the end of the tenth century, however, the Carolingians were replaced by the Capetians (kuh-PEE-shunz), the family of Hugh Capet (r. 987–996). The Capetians ruled France for more than three hundred years—an impressive achievement in light of the repeated failure of German dynasties.

## Capetian Prestige

From the very beginning, the Capetian kings of France sought to preserve the royal office, increase its prestige, and consolidate its political base. Hugh Capet inaugurated the tradition of crowning his son as his successor during his own lifetime. This meant that when the old king died, a new king was already in place and the nobility could not easily meddle in the succession. Robert II (r. 996–1031) displayed the "royal touch," a ceremony in which the king was believed to be able to cure people of scrofula (a common respiratory ailment) by touching them. No French nobleman ever laid claim to such miraculous powers. Capetian kings capitalized on their control of the old, rich, prestigious, and centrally located city of Paris. The kings promoted the shrine of Saint Denis, the legendary first bishop of Paris, as a kind of "national" shrine for France. Louis VII (r. 1137–1180) began to make elegant tours of the country to put himself, his office, and his sparkling entourage on display. In Louis IX (r. 1226–1270), the Capetian family actually produced a saint of the Catholic Church—Saint Louis.

## Building the Capetian Kingdom

The Capetians initially controlled no more than Paris and its immediate region. They contested for control of this region with a number of ambitious and aggressive families, finally ground them down, and made the Île-de-France one of the best-governed regions in all of France. The kings also controlled about two dozen bishoprics and some fifty monasteries in northern France. This power base gave the kings unrivaled opportunities to extend their influence and, in turn, to build up a cadre of loyal and articulate supporters. Although French kings provoked a few battles with the papacy, France experienced no investiture controversy.

France's territorial expansion was tightly connected to military success. The background to French military success is complicated. The counts of Anjou (see **Map 9.4**), through war and marriage, secured control of almost two-thirds of France. Decisive was the marriage of Henry of Anjou to Eleanor of Aquitaine. To make things even more complicated, in 1154, Henry became king of England through his mother, a granddaughter of William the Conqueror (see below). For two generations, the king of France hammered away at this "Angevin Empire." In 1204, Philip II of France (r. 1180–1223) defeated King John of England (r. 1199–1216) and laid claim to the French holdings of the Angevins—but not to England.

Southeastern France was gained by wars of a different kind. In the last decades of the twelfth century, much of the south became a hotbed of the Albigensian (al-buh-JEN-see-un) heresy—an important religious movement (see page 268). Some Catholic locals and many churchmen urged the kings to undertake military action against the heretics. The French kings bided their time until they had the resources to deal with this turbulent region. Under Louis VIII (r. 1223–1226) and Louis IX, the French monarchy finally extended its authority to France's Mediterranean coast.

| Table 9.4 The Capetian Kings of France | |
|---|---|
| Hugh Capet (987–996) | Philip II (1180–1223) |
| Robert II (996–1031) | Louis VIII (1223–1226) |
| Henry I (1031–1060) | Louis IX (1226–1270) |
| Philip I (1060–1108) | Philip III (1270–1285) |
| Louis VI (1108–1137) | Philip IV (1285–1314) |
| Louis VII (1137–1180) | |

© Cengage Learning 2014

## Strategies of Capetian Government

The chief political dynamic in France was the contest for power between the kings and the territorial princes (see **Map 9.4**). At stake was the monarchy's ability to introduce effective rule into the lands won in all those battles. The territorial princes were locally powerful magnates, rather like the German dukes. But whereas Germany comprised five major duchies, France had a dozen or more territorial principalities.

© Cengage Learning 2014

🌐 **Map 9.4 French Territorial Principalities, circa 1200** As the Carolingian West Frankish Kingdom (see **Map 8.3** on page 213) broke down and feudal bonds proliferated, many territories arose under counts and dukes. Their struggles to impose control locally and to fight off royal supervision animated French history.

The territorial princes also faced localized rivalries for power and influence. Countless individuals built castles (see the feature, "The Visual Record: The Medieval Castle" on pages 242–243), brutally subjected local peasants, and became lords. Sometimes these individuals were the vassals of the territorial princes—say, the dukes of Normandy or the counts of Anjou—and sometimes they had vassals of their own. In the Carolingian world, the number of vassals was small, their fidelity reasonably solid, and their services reliable. By 1100, the number of vassals was immense, their fidelity was constantly shifting, and they tended to provide only local military service. Scholars call this shift from effective Carolingian government to myriad local lordships a **feudal revolution**. For the kings of France to re-create central government, they had to overcome the disruptive tendencies of this revolution and then consolidate institutions.

In the twelfth and thirteenth centuries, the Capetians followed a few basic policies to increase their ability to govern. They circumvented the local lords as much as possible. When they won military victories, the kings did not dole out the seized lands to lords as new fiefs but instead kept them in their own hands, or in the hands of family members. The kings introduced into these lands new officials, called bailiffs or provosts, who were of modest social background, had no personal ties to their assigned regions, often had some schooling in law, and were intensely loyal to the kings. By the time of Louis IX, officials called *enqueteurs* (on-KEH-tur) were sent around the country to inspect the work of bailiffs and provosts. Such roles had been unheard of since the Carolingian *missi dominici* (see page 216). Louis also began to issue *ordonnances*, what might be called executive orders,

**feudal revolution** A term that refers to the proliferation of lord-vassal bonds as key elements of governmental and social control.

## SECTION SUMMARY

- German political development was impeded by short-lived dynasties, territorial complexity, and battles with the papacy.
- Italy experienced the communal movement in the north, the consolidation of the Papal States and Papal Monarchy in the center, and the continued fragmentation of the south, where foreigners ruled.
- France had a prestigious and long-lived royal dynasty, patient territorial expansion, and a slowly, steadily centralizing government.

which were binding on all the land under the king's control. These precepts are reminiscent of Carolingian capitularies (see page 212).

If in 1000 France was a land of innumerable tiny lordships, then by 1300 it was the best-governed kingdom in Europe. Indicative of France's position is the outcome of two battles between King Philip IV (r. 1285–1314) and Pope Boniface VIII (r. 1294–1303). First, Philip attempted to tax the French clergy, and then he sought to bring a bishop before his court. Boniface angrily objected to Philip's intervention in ecclesiastical affairs. But things had changed drastically since the fateful confrontation between Henry IV and Gregory VII. Boniface had to back down. In 1300, France was the largest, richest, and best-governed kingdom in Europe. French culture and language were increasingly dominant. Considering France's situation in 900, and compared with Germany's in 1300, these were impressive achievements.

# The British Isles

*What were the chief dynamics in the development of medieval Britain?*

In the British Isles, expansion had three dimensions: the tremendous growth of the English government, England's relentless push into the Celtic world, and the emergence of Irish, Scottish, and Welsh states in the Celtic world (see **Map 9.5**). England is smaller than France or Germany and more homogeneous in population, culture, and language than either of them, or than Italy. Nevertheless, England faced some acute dynastic, military, and political challenges.

## Viking and Norman Invasions in England

Alfred's (see page 211) descendants ruled England for more than a century. They gradually rolled back the frontier of the "Danelaw," the areas of eastern and northern England controlled by Danish settlers. Alfred and his successors built strong central institutions. All free men in the realm owed allegiance to the king and could, in principle, be called to the militia, or *fyrd* (FEERD). The great men of the realm attended meetings of the royal council, or *witan* (WHIT-un), which was partly a court of law and partly a deliberative body. The king could issue writs—executive orders rather like Carolingian capitularies. The Danegeld—literally "money for the Danes"—was originally collected solely in times of danger and then slowly transformed into a regular tax. All of England was divided into shires, and each shire had a royally appointed officer, the *shire-reeve* (or sheriff).

Late in the tenth century, English leadership failed in the face of a severe threat from a new generation of Vikings. The powerful king of Denmark, Swein Forkbeard, conquered England in 1014 but survived his conquest by only two years. His son Cnut then ruled from 1016 to 1035, at which point power passed to Cnut's sons. Cnut was simultaneously king of Denmark and England, and for a time of Norway, too. He wed his daughter to Emperor Henry III and himself to Emma, the widow of the last English king. He was cultured, Christian, and an acquaintance of the pope.

When Cnut's sons died in 1042, without heirs, the English nobles called over from Normandy Edward, called "the Confessor," the son of the last English king. Edward, who was unusually pious, had taken a vow of chastity. Because he was not going to have an heir, claimants to the English throne began jockeying for position. Edward seems to have promised his throne to William, the duke of Normandy. Most of the English nobles preferred Harold of Wessex, one of their number. In Norway, Harald Hardrada ("Hard-Ruler") made a claim as Cnut's rightful heir. Harold of Wessex defeated Hardrada, only to be defeated in turn at Hastings by William.

Neither Cnut nor William, known as "the Conqueror" (r. 1066–1089), desired to dismantle or replace the old English institutions. But William had won England by conquest, and he did introduce some changes. He turned most of the estates in England into fiefs and distributed them among some 180 of his most loyal followers. Each of these vassals held his fief in return for a fixed quota of soldiers for the royal army. To raise the approximately five thousand soldiers required by William, each of his vassals had to create vassals of his own. The technical name for this process of vassals creating vassals is *subinfeudation*. In 1087, William exacted the Salisbury Oath, which established the principle of liege homage (LEEGE AHM-idge), according to which the king was the final lord of all vassals. To avoid creating territorial principalities on the French model, William scattered his vassals' holdings around the kingdom. Finally, to learn as much as he could about his new kingdom and about the fiefs he had assigned to his followers, William conducted a massive survey of England that resulted in 1086 in the *Domesday Book*, named for the Day of Judgment, against which there was no appeal. No comparable survey of any state was accomplished until the American census of 1790.

| Table 9.5 Important Kings of England | |
|---|---|
| Alfred (871–899) | William II (1089–1100) |
| Ethelred II (978–1016) | Henry I (1100–1135) |
| Cnut (1016–1035) | Stephen I (1135–1154) |
| Edward the Confessor (1042–1066) | Henry II (1154–1189) |
| Harold of Wessex (1066) | John (1199–1216) |
| William I (the Conqueror) (1066–1089) | Edward I (1272–1307) |

© Cengage Learning 2014

## The Development of English Law and Government

William was succeeded by two of his sons in turn, William II (r. 1089–1100) and Henry I (r. 1100–1135). Henry's only son drowned in a shipwreck, and the English nobles would accept neither his daughter Matilda as their queen nor her husband, Geoffrey of Anjou, as their king. Most of the English elite were Normans, and the Normans and Angevins were old foes. Consequently, the English turned in 1135 to a French prince, Stephen of Blois, who was a grandson of William the Conqueror through a daughter. Stephen I died childless in 1154 and bequeathed his kingdom to Henry of Anjou, the son of Geoffrey and Matilda, who ruled as Henry II (r. 1154–1189).

Henry was as much a French prince as an English king. From his father, mother, and wife (Eleanor of Aquitaine; see page 238), he had inherited a large part of France and was much preoccupied with his continental realm. He constantly battled his four sons for control of these vast French holdings. Two of these sons eventually became king. Richard I, also known as "Richard the Lionhearted" (r. 1189–1199), was a dashing prince who spent only ten months in England, preferring to pass his time on crusade or campaigning in France. John (r. 1199–1216) was defeated by France's Philip II, inducing contemporaries to mock him as "John Lackland" and "John Softsword."

Just as Viking and Norman rulers built on the solid foundations of the Anglo-Saxon state, so the Anglo-Normans and Angevins retained and expanded those very foundations. They refined the financial machinery of the English government, the Exchequer, named for the checkerboard table on which the accounts were reckoned. They

**Swift and Certain Justice** This picture from about 1130 depicts some of the forty-four thieves hung by Sheriff Ralph Basset in 1124. As a common law spread throughout England, criminals were more likely to be caught and punished.

## The Medieval Castle

Storybook castles, in the manner of Disneyland, figure prominently in almost everyone's idea of the Middle Ages. The reality was different. Medieval castles were generally small, stark, and uncomfortable, not beautiful and romantic.

Castles represent a stage in the history of both dwellings and fortifications. Initially, castles were private, residential, and military. A consideration of these three elements will place the castle in historical context and illustrate what historians learn from the impressive ruins that dot the landscape of Europe and the crusader states.

The first medieval castles were constructed in the tenth century. The French word *château* (from the Latin *castellum*) means "great house," signifying the castle's residential purpose. Powerful aristocrats erected castles not just as their principal dwellings but also as a base for securing and extending their social and political influence. From his castle, a lord could dominate the surrounding region. The castle also sheltered the lord's immediate dependents, who would come from surrounding villages, temporarily in the event of an attack and his military retainers more or less permanently.

A few castles were built exclusively for military purposes. In 1110, Crusaders captured a strategic plateau rising 2,000 feet above the main road from inner Syria to the Mediterranean. Between 1142 and 1205, Crusaders continually expanded the fortifications of the castle pictured here, the "Krak des Chevaliers" (from Syriac *karka*, meaning "fortress," and the Old French word for "horsemen"). This castle fell to Muslim attackers in 1271. The techniques of fortification developed in the crusader East influenced castle building in Europe.

The medieval city of Murviedro, Spain, takes its name from the Latin *mures veteres* (old walls). In 1871, the city was given back its ancient name, Sagunt. The hilltop above ancient Saguntum (attacked by Hannibal, thus affronting the Romans and providing a pretext for the Second Punic War between Rome and Carthage; see pages 124–126) reveals fortifications from the prehistoric, Carthaginian, Roman, Visigothic, and Muslim periods. The most spectacular visible remains date from the Muslim period, between 900 and 1098, when El Cid captured the site.

**Krak des Chevaliers, Syria, circa 1200**

Robert Harding World Images

Castles took many forms. From 900 to 1200, the "motte and bailey" castle was the most common. A lord commanded his dependents to dig a circular ditch and heap the dirt into a mound (the motte). The ditch, together with a wooden palisade—a fencelike wall—was the bailey. A wooden tower was often built atop the mound. Some castles included an elaborate series of mounds, ditches, and wooden walls, but usually these structures were quite simple.

As siege techniques improved (catapults could hurl projectiles weighing 600 pounds), the wooden building of the bailey began to be replaced by stone. By 1150 or 1200, stone towers (*donjons*, from the Latin *dominium* for "lordship") were only the inner portion—the "keep"—of a more complicated structure of walls, towers, and gates. It was not unusual for walls to be 75 or 100 feet high. Because of the growing power of bombarding engines, castle walls often had to be made thicker. Towers built at 40- or 50-foot intervals projected beyond the walls so that defenders armed with bows and arrows could fire at attackers along the length of a castle wall. Look at the spacing of the towers in

vastly improved the judicial institutions. Henry I began to send itinerant justices around the realm. He brought the royal court, with its swift, fair, and competent justice, within the reach of most people, and he made royal justice more attractive than the justice available in local lords' courts. This expansion of the work of the royal courts led to the emergence of a common law in England—a law common to all people, courts, and cases.

England's relations with the church fell somewhere between Germany's and France's in both intensity and outcome. Anglo-Saxon kings generally enjoyed cordial relations with the church on a traditional Carolingian model. William the Conqueror controlled the church with an iron hand but introduced reforms and reformers who were acceptable to Rome. Archbishop Anselm of Canterbury and Henry I had a quarrel that lasted several years, but

Much can be learned from the number of castles in a particular area. The presence of numerous small castles across the countryside suggests an extreme decentralization of power in that place and time. Remains of several hundred castles have been found in France alone; and England, in 1100, boasted a castle every 10 miles. Conversely, areas with only a few large, strategically sited castles were likely subject to greater central control. Careful mapping of the known locations of castles can tell historians a great deal about the structure of social and political relationships.

Castles both contributed and responded to developments in military technology, such as more powerful catapults. Stone castles proliferated as Europe grew wealthier and as quarrying technology improved. Castles grew larger as monarchies, rather than private individuals, built them. Like cathedrals,

**Muslim Fortress of Murviedro, Valencia, Spain, Eleventh Century**

the castles pictured here. At Krak des Chevaliers, we see one of the earliest examples of a double ring of walls. Two walls made it more difficult for attackers to take the keep and permitted defenders to battle invaders from inside both the inner and the outer walls.

To allow people to enter and leave, castles had gate towers, usually with two gates, one on the outside and one on the inside. Intricate systems of winches, cranks, and counterweights regulated the raising and lowering of the gates. Speedy operation was essential. Some castles had small "sally ports" from which soldiers could make a rapid dash to attack a besieging enemy.

When possible, lords sited their castles on the edges of cliffs, because fewer sides were open to assault and a garrison of modest size could defend the remaining walls. Krak sits on an impressive natural site. The fortress of Murviedro, perched on a hilltop, commands the surrounding territory. Rulers and conquerors from Roman to modern times have exploited this dominating site. To walls and natural defenses were sometimes added ditches.

massive state-funded castles tended to be built by professionals rather than by local laborers.

Both fortifications and magnificent dwellings have existed in Western civilization for millennia. From about 900 to 1200, the castle met the needs of a politically dominant warrior-aristocracy for a private residence with military significance. In later centuries, the castle, as a château, retained its private and residential nature but lost much of its military character to garrisoned fortresses in the service of kings and princes.

## Questions

1. *Who built castles and why did they build them?*
2. *What were the essential characteristics of a castle?*
3. *How does a castle differ from a residence?*

they finally mended their differences in a settlement that anticipated the terms of the Concordat of Worms. Henry II was always anxious to extend the influence of his courts. In 1164, he decided that "criminous clerks," or members of the clergy who had committed a crime, should be judged in royal courts. The archbishop of Canterbury, Thomas Becket (ca. 1118–1170), protested that clerics could be tried only in church courts. Although the two sides came to a reconciliation, a band of overly zealous knights murdered Becket, believing that they were doing the king's bidding. In fact, the crime so outraged the church and the public that Henry had to back down on criminous clerks and give up some authority to Rome. Despite these religious quarrels, however, England experienced no investiture controversy.

*The National Library of Wales*

**Howell the Good**   This picture of Howell, from a manuscript of his laws, depicts him wearing a crown, holding a scepter, and sitting on a tufted throne that looks like a palace. These are key symbols of rule.

**Magna Carta** 1215
English document that sets limits on the power of the king.

*parliaments*   Initially expanded meetings of the royal court intended to secure consensus for royal policies.

John's conflict with the church resulted in far more dramatic changes for England. The loss of Normandy had been costly in terms of prestige and resources. In difficult circumstances, John got into a row with Pope Innocent III because he refused to admit to England the pope's candidate for archbishop of Canterbury. Eventually, he submitted because Innocent had laid England under interdict and John needed the pope's support for his planned war of revenge against Philip II of France. True to his nickname, "Softsword," John lost and thus ended his quarrel with Rome.

With John's defeat and capitulation, the barons of England had had enough. These barons (a general name for the upper ranks of English society) were increasingly upset that an expanding royal government limited their influence. In 1215, a large group of disgruntled barons forced King John to sign the **Magna Carta**, or "Great Charter" (so called because it was written on an unusually large sheet of parchment). This document required the king to respect the rights of feudal lords, not abuse his judicial powers, and consult his "natural" advisers—that is, the barons.

John tried to wiggle out of the Magna Carta, but he died in 1216, leaving only a minor heir, and the barons exacted many concessions from the regency government. When Henry III came of age in 1234, he struggled to win a limited application of the Magna Carta. The barons, on the contrary, wanted a voice in devising royal policy, especially military policy, in light of recent defeats. They also wished to have some say in naming the king's closest advisers and in controlling the work of the king's agents, especially judges. This tension between king and barons led to several meetings of the royal court, often called *parliaments*, a French word meaning, roughly, "talking together." Initially, these meetings had no fixed rights or procedures, no set group of attendees, and no defined role. The kings viewed them as clever political devices to win support for royal policies. The barons viewed them as opportunities to play a real role in a government that had been marginalizing them. The English were groping to find a way to build consultation into their system.

The reign of Edward I (1272–1307) sums up the achievements of England's rulers in the High Middle Ages. He issued numerous statutes, laws that bear comparison with Louis IX's *ordonnances* (see pages 239–240)—which earned him the nickname "the English Justinian." He worked skillfully with the newly emerging Parliament. And like other English rulers before him, Edward balanced political and military accomplishments, bravely fighting for years on the Welsh and Scottish frontiers.

## The Celtic Realms

When the Romans appeared on the scene, Celtic peoples could be found in virtually every region from Ireland to Anatolia. Most Celts were absorbed by more numerous and powerful Germanic and Slavic peoples. It was in the British Isles that the most durable and distinctive Celtic regions evolved into Ireland, Wales, and Scotland. Two essential dynamics characterized each of these regions: Tiny political entities gradually turned into larger kingdoms; and relations between England and the Celtic realms were everywhere contentious (see **Map 9.5**).

In each of the Celtic realms, the movement toward greater unity was opened by the efforts of powerful, ambitious leaders to subjugate numerous well-entrenched local potentates, many of whom had expanded their power during the period of Viking invasions. In Ireland, Brian Boru (r. 976–1014) became the first ruler to exercise real authority over most of the island. In Wales, Rhodri the Great (d. 898) and Howell the Good (d. 950) were the

🌐 **Map 9.5  Northern and Eastern Europe, circa 1200**    Apart from Germany, the core states of Europe emerged inside the former Roman frontiers or right alongside them. After 900, an arc of new states emerged, from the Celtic realms and Iceland in the west, to Scandinavia in the north, to the western, southern, and eastern Slavs in eastern Europe. © Cengage Learning 2014

first rulers to gain at least nominal authority over the whole of the land. Although disunity is a continuous theme of Scottish history, the centuries after the reign of Kenneth MacAlpin (843–858) reveal the slow creation of a national tradition.

The course of development in the Celtic lands was disrupted by the English in the eleventh and especially the twelfth centuries. The Norman Conquest of England brought adventurers to the frontiers of Wales and Scotland. Sometimes these continental knights advanced with the support of William the Conqueror and his sons, but more often, they looked to wild frontier regions for opportunities to escape tight control. In Wales, some Normans allied with various local princes who resented the growing power of the Welsh kings. Henceforth, the actual power of Welsh rulers varied greatly, and English kings usually claimed some authority over the region. Scottish kings managed to enlist a good many Norman knights into their service, but this recruitment effort angered the English kings and spurred them to greater intervention. Civil disturbances in Ireland induced King Rory O'Connor (r. 1156–1186) to turn to King Henry II of England for mercenaries to help him establish his power. But by 1171, Henry had invaded Ireland himself and inaugurated the complicated English involvement that persists to this day.

## SECTION SUMMARY

- England's kings survived several changes of dynasty (compare Germany) without making fundamental changes in English society or government.
- English kings built on Anglo-Saxon precedents to secure revenues, extend the work of the royal courts, and limit the power of the barons.
- English kings brought constant pressure to bear on the Celtic realms that surrounded England, in the process retarding political development in these regions.

Edward I of England intervened repeatedly in the Celtic world. In 1277, he invaded Wales with the intention of totally subduing the Welsh. He built immense castles, whose ruins are still impressive today. Edward also made his son the Prince of Wales—still the title of the heir to the British throne. Between 1100 and 1260, England and Scotland went to war four times, and Edward resolved to put an end to this struggle by annexing Scotland. The Scots, however, rallied to the standard of Robert Bruce (r. 1306–1329), a dashing knight who managed to free Scotland for centuries.

# The Growth of New States

*How did new states emerge in Spain, Scandinavia, and the Slavic world, and how do those states compare with their western neighbors?*

The proliferation of new states constitutes one of the most remarkable examples of expansion in high medieval Europe. In Spain, Christian rulers waged a steady war of reconquest against the Islamic caliphate of Cordoba that led to the emergence of the kingdoms of Portugal, Castile, and Aragon. In Scandinavia, mighty leaders built durable kingdoms in Denmark, Norway, and Sweden. Local rulers created a band of new Slavic states running from the Baltic to the Balkans. To the east of those Slavic realms, around the city of Kiev, the Scandinavian Rus founded the first state on Russian soil. Between 900 and 1300, the geographic range of Europe's political entities more than doubled.

## Reconquista and Kingdom Building in Spain

Historians perceive two driving forces in the rich and colorful history of medieval Spain. One is the bloody experience of several centuries of war along an expanding frontier. The other is the constant interplay within the Iberian Peninsula of three vibrant cultures: Christian, Jewish, and Muslim. We describe the first of these forces in this chapter and the second in the next.

After 1002, unified Muslim rule in Spain began breaking down, affording an unprecedented opportunity to the Christians living in the north of the peninsula. King Sancho I (r. 1000–1035) of Navarre launched an offensive against the Muslims. This war, carried on intermittently until the fifteenth century, is called the **Reconquista** (ray-con-KEE-stuh), the "Reconquest."

Before Sancho died, he divided his realm among his sons; thus, the kingdoms of Aragon and Castile arose alongside Navarre. Castile advanced the Reconquista. In 1085, its forces captured the Muslim stronghold and old Visigothic capital of Toledo, an important moral and strategic victory. Now, the Reconquista began moving on three fronts (see **Map 9.6**). In the east, the emerging kingdom of Aragon-Catalonia advanced along the Mediterranean coast. In the center, León-Castile pressed hard against al-Andalus. In the west, the nascent kingdom of Portugal became a factor in Iberian politics. Christian successes, and the reconquest of Toledo, led the retreating Muslims to summon aid in the 1150s from militant North African Muslims. The Christian advance temporarily stopped.

In the early thirteenth century, Pope Innocent III stirred up crusading zeal and lent encouragement to clerics and nobles in Spain who wished to reopen hostilities against the Muslims. In 1212, a combined Castilian-Aragonese army won a decisive victory at Las Navas de Tolosa, south of Toledo. The victory of Las Navas de Tolosa was a great turning point in Spanish history. The outcome of the Reconquista, which did not conclude until the fifteenth century, was never again in doubt.

**Reconquista** The name for the centuries-long battle of Christians against Muslims in Spain.

© Cengage Learning 2014

🌐 **Map 9.6 The Christian Reconquista of Muslim Spain** From slow beginnings in the ninth century to the epochal Battle of Las Navas de Tolosa (1212), the Christians in Spain pushed back the Muslim frontier and built durable states behind it.

Twelfth-century Spanish kings, especially in Castile, imposed hereditary rule and exacted oaths of allegiance from their free subjects. The kings tried to force powerful nobles to become their vassals. In the thirteenth century, Spain produced kings of genius, especially Alfonso X (r. 1252–1284) of Castile. These rulers were pious men, genuinely inspired by the ideal of the Crusades (discussed later in this chapter) and zealous in the promotion of the church. They also were hardheaded rulers. Aragon-Catalonia became the greatest naval power of the western Mediterranean and a formidable economic power. Military victories brought as well a flow of booty and a supply of lands to reward the nobles who spent their energy on the frontier rather than on attacking the king. These kings built strong central governments. Increasingly, they used professional officers in key government posts and dispatched roving officials from the court to check on local rulers. Alfonso issued a major law book for the whole of Castile. The Cortes, a representative assembly made up primarily of urban notables, began forging an alliance between the king and the towns. Iberia was not united in the thirteenth century, but it had evolved into four coherent blocks: a small and impotent Muslim region in Valencia and Granada, and three vibrant kingdoms centered on Portugal, Castile, and Aragon.

## Scandinavia

Europe's expanding map saw new states in Scandinavia, the Roman name for the lands that became Denmark, Norway, and Sweden. Although the faint beginnings of political consolidation in Denmark can be traced to the Carolingian period, actual development of the states of Scandinavia dates from the tenth and eleventh centuries. Overseas expansion played one key role in northern political development. Another was the slow achievement of political unity by kings who had to overcome powerful local interests (see **Map 9.5**).

**Alfonso the Wise**
The Spanish king Alfonso X, depicted here in a thirteenth-century manuscript from Spain, is judging his Muslim and Christian subjects. Alfonso's reputation for impartiality was important in his culturally diverse realm. The Granger Collection, New York

The sea, not the land, is the great fact of Scandinavian history. Norway has more than 1,000 miles of coastline, and no point in Denmark is more than 35 miles from the sea. Scandinavia did not offer opportunities for large, land-based kingdoms or empires, but the sea provided Scandinavians with a wide scope for activities.

Because the sea made exit from Scandinavia so easy and because the whole region had absolutely no tradition of unified government, kings had a hard time establishing their power. Essentially, kings were war leaders with loyal bands of followers. Territorial states were thus built up as powerful leaders persuaded or forced more and more men to join them. Denmark's was the first of the northern monarchies to emerge in the early tenth century. Norway's monarchy arose a little later in the tenth century, but for much of the eleventh century, Norway was under Danish control. As the Danes fell more and more under German influence in the eleventh century, Norway managed to break free. Sweden's monarchy was the last to emerge in the northern world; it was not fully stable until the twelfth century, but by 1300, it had become the most powerful.

Christianity came rather late to Scandinavia, with the first missionaries entering the region in the ninth century and widespread conversion ensuing in the eleventh. Norway's King Olaf (r. 1016–1028), affectionately remembered as Saint Olaf, was the first northern king who actively promoted Christianization. Scandinavian kings viewed the church as a useful adjunct to their power. They cooperated in creating bishoprics on the assumption that members of the high clergy would be educated, talented allies in the process of building central governments. Ironically, the church was a stabilizing force in Scandinavia during the very years when the investiture controversy wreaked havoc in Germany.

## The Slavic World

In eastern Europe, between the Elbe and Dnieper (NEE-per) Rivers, lived numerous peoples customarily called Slavs. Partly because of language differences and partly because of the areas in which these people settled, scholars divide them into western, southern, and eastern Slavs. These peoples were never conquered by the Romans, assimilated few influences from the classical world, and received Christianity later than western Europe. Still, as states began emerging in eastern Europe, they exhibited many of the same problems that older and more westerly states had encountered: shifting frontiers, clashes between ambitious rulers and powerful nobles, and outside military and cultural influences (see **Map 9.5**).

The first western Slavic state was Great Moravia, created in the 830s by capable dukes, while the Carolingian Empire was experiencing civil wars. Moravia's early promise was cut short in 906 by the Magyars. Also in the late ninth century, the Přemysl (PURR-em-ih-sill) dynasty forged a kingdom in Bohemia that lasted through the Middle Ages, although for long periods it was under German domination.

The greatest of the western Slavic states was Poland. In the 960s and 970s, Duke Mieszko (mee-ESS-koe) (d. 992) unified a substantial territory and received Christianity from Rome. The first action created the Polish state, and the second anchored Poland firmly within the orbit of the Latin West. Mieszko's descendants, the Piast dynasty of kings, ruled until the kingdom was divided in 1138. For more than two centuries, Polish development was retarded as weak rulers contested for power with local magnates, who themselves were successfully subordinating both peasants and men of middling status.

The creation of a Hungarian state played a decisive role in dividing the western and southern Slavs. The Magyars were disruptive raiders from the 880s until their defeat by Otto I in 955. After that disaster, the Magyars concentrated on building a state within the Danube basin, the home base from which they had launched their raids. The Magyars blended with the local Slavs. King (later Saint) Stephen (r. 997–1038), who received Christianity from Rome, was the real founder of Hungary. Like Poland, Hungary was attached to the Latin West. Stephen's family, the Arpads, ruled in Hungary for centuries. They built ruling centers at Buda and Esztergom, created an impressive territorial organization, and promoted the growth of the church.

The southern Slavs built a band of states that extended across the Balkans. The first, reaching back to the seventh century, was Bulgaria. The Bulgars were a Turkic people who first led and then merged into the local Slavic population. The first Bulgarian state lasted until the early eleventh century, when the Byzantines, who had suffered many defeats at Bulgarian hands, destroyed it. By the late twelfth century, when Byzantium itself had weakened, a new Bulgarian state emerged, but its rulers never had the firm control that their predecessors had wielded. Under Khan Boris (r. 852–879), Bulgaria made the momentous decision to accept Orthodox Christianity from Constantinople instead of Roman Catholicism, despite the pope's best efforts. To the west of Bulgaria lay Serbia, a region dominated until the fourteenth century by Bulgaria and Byzantium. The region accepted Orthodox Christianity. To the west of Serbia lay Croatia. Croatia managed to preserve itself and evade the clutches of Hungary, Byzantium, and Venice. By 1107, however, Croatia was incorporated by Hungary. Owing to Italian and Hungarian influences, Croatia became Roman Catholic.

The creation of the major eastern Slavic state is shrouded in mystery and legend. It seems that in 862, a Swedish Viking named Rurik and his followers, called Varangians, established or seized a trading camp at Novgorod. A few years later, Oleg (r. 879–912) took over Kiev and made it his base of operations. Thus was founded Kievan Rus, a state that, like Hungary and Bulgaria, began with an outside, elite leadership over a local Slavic majority.

Kiev was ruled by grand dukes who pursued four basic policies. They created a vast trading network that linked Germany, Scandinavia, Byzantium, and the caliphate. They shared power with regional nobles who built up several important towns of their own. They received Orthodox Christianity from Constantinople in 988. And, finally, they

Scala/Art Resource, NY

**Virgin of Vladimir** The holiest icon of Russia, once the miraculous protector of the city of Vladimir and later of Moscow, this image was painted in Constantinople in 1131. Rus, and later Russian, icons tended to follow Byzantine traditions very closely.

## SECTION SUMMARY

- The Reconquista motivated Spanish kings to military victories and political consolidation.
- Although Scandinavian Vikings were influential and disruptive, large-scale states began to emerge in Denmark, Norway, and Sweden.
- Slavic states emerged from resolute local action (Poland, Bohemia) or from a fusion of elite outsider and dependent local populations (Hungary, Bulgaria, Rus).
- Christianity expanded everywhere, sometimes Roman Catholic (Spain, Scandinavia, Poland, Hungary) and sometimes Orthodox (Bulgaria, Rus).

struggled to defend Kiev, indeed Rus territory as a whole, from wave after wave of invaders from the eastern steppes.

Kievan Rus was destroyed by the Mongols. These were a loose coalition of pastoral nomads from Mongolia (lands lying east of the Caspian Sea and north of China) and Turkic soldiers. The charismatic leader Jenghiz Khan (1154–1227) turned the Mongols into an invincible fighting force. He and his successors built an empire stretching from China to eastern Europe. In 1221, the Mongols began their attacks on Rus, and in 1240, Kiev fell. Jenghiz Khan's empire was divided into several khanates on his death, with Rus dominated by the Golden Horde, so called because of the splendid golden tent from which they ruled. Throughout the West, people were alarmed by the Mongol onslaught.

# The Crusades

*What basic factors contributed to the rise, persistence, and eventual decline of the crusading movement?*

In 1096, an army of Christian knights who called themselves pilgrims left Europe to liberate the Holy Land from the Muslim "infidel." Although no one knew it at the time, this was the first of many **Crusades**, so called because the warriors were *crucesignati*, "signed by the cross." Normally we think of Crusades as expeditions to the Holy Land but in high medieval Europe there were also Crusades against political foes in Italy, against heretics in France, and against pagans in the Baltic. There was never a single legal theory or definition of crusading. Nevertheless, Europe's expanding population, economic dynamism, political consolidation, and buoyant optimism made possible not only the First Crusade but also many more over the next two centuries.

**Crusades** Armed pilgrimages intended to recover the Holy Land from the "infidel."

## The Background: East and West

With the accession in 867 of the Macedonian dynasty in the person of Basil I, the Byzantine Empire experienced a period of vigorous, successful rule that lasted until 1025. Although the Macedonians fostered striking cultural achievements, carried out significant administrative reforms, and established the kind of tight control of the church that had been so elusive in the iconoclastic era (see page 206), they were primarily great soldiers. Along the Balkan frontier, the Macedonian rulers kept both the Bulgarians and Kievan Rus at bay while also neutralizing many smaller Slavic principalities. In the West, the Macedonians maintained an effective diplomacy with Venice that permitted lucrative commercial opportunities in the Adriatic. In the East, the Macedonian rulers profited from the gradual dissolution of the Abbasid caliphate by expanding their frontier in Anatolia.

By contrast, throughout the ninth and tenth centuries, the ability of the caliphs in Baghdad to control their vast empire declined precipitously. Egypt and North Africa escaped Baghdad's control almost completely, and religious strife between Sunni and Shi'ite Muslims further destabilized the Islamic state.

After Basil II's death in 1025, Byzantium suffered a long period of short reigns and abrupt changes in policy. In the capital, factional squabbling swirled around the imperial court, and in the person of Patriarch Michael Cerularius (r. 1043–1058), the church sought to break out from two centuries of domination. When, in 1054, Cerularius and Pope Leo IX (r. 1049–1054) quarreled so bitterly over ecclesiastical customs that they excommunicated each other, a deep schism opened between the Catholic and Orthodox Churches that still exists.

It was in these divisive circumstances that the Seljuk Turks appeared on the eastern frontier of Anatolia. Bands of Turks, peoples from central Asia, had been serving the caliphs

## Ahmad ibn Fadlan Describes the Rus

*Dispatched by the caliph in 922 to the Volga Bulgars, ibn Fadlan prepared a report on his travels that contains this remarkable description of the Scandinavians who were trading and settling in the lands that became Russia. This is a cultivated Muslim commenting on "Vikings" in the medieval "Wild West."*

I have never seen more perfect physiques than theirs—they are like palm trees, are fair and reddish. The man wears a cloak with which he covers one half of his body, leaving one of his arms uncovered. Every one of them carries an axe, a sword, and a dagger. . . . Each man, from the tip of his toes to his neck, is covered in dark green lines and pictures. Each woman has, on her breast, a disk of either iron, silver, copper, or gold, depending on her husband's financial and social worth. Around their necks they wear bands of gold and silver.

They are the filthiest of all Allah's creatures. They do not clean themselves after excreting or urinating, or wash themselves when in a state of ritual impurity [i.e., after coitus], and do not wash their hands after food. . . . Each day the slave girl arrives in the morning with a large basin containing water, which she hands to her owner. He washes his hands and his face and his hair in the water, then he dips his comb in the water and brushes his hair, blows his nose and spits in the basin. . . the slave girl takes the basin to the man beside him and he goes through the same routine as his friend.

When a chieftain dies, his family ask his slave girls and slave boys, 'Who among you will die with him?' [A slave girl says 'I will'] and they place two slave girls in charge of her . . . On the day when he and the slave girl were to be burned [they erected a ship-pyre with Byzantine brocades] . . . The 'Angel of Death' is responsible for having his garments sewn up and putting them in order, and it is she who kills the slave girls. I myself saw her: a gloomy, corpulent woman, neither young nor old. They placed him inside the ship. . . they brought alcohol, fruit and, herbs . . . bread, meat, and onions . . . a dog, which they cut in two, and all of his weaponry . . . two mounts which they made to gallop until they sweated, and cut them up into pieces and threw them onto the ship . . . They fetched two cows, and a cock, and a hen which they slaughtered and cast onto it. . . . Six men entered the pavilion and all had intercourse with the slave girl. They laid her down beside her master and two of them took hold of her feet and two her hands. The crone called the 'Angel of Death' placed a rope around her neck and handed it to two of the men . . . and advanced with a dagger and began to thrust it in and out between her ribs . . . until she died.

One of the Russians said, 'You Arabs are foolish. You purposely take those who are dearest to you and throw them under the earth, where they are eaten by the earth, by vermin, and by worms whereas we burn them in the fire so that they enter paradise immediately.'

### Questions

1. How much of this account strikes you as credible?
2. If you compare this account to the Roman description of the Huns (page 180), what conclusions would you draw?
3. What inferences can you draw about differences between Muslim and "Viking" culture?

Adapted from Ahmed ibn Fadlan, trans. James E. Montgomery, "Ibn Fadlan and the Russiyah," *Journal of Arabic and Islamic Studies*, 3 (2000): 1-25.

---

as mercenaries since the ninth century. With new leaders at their head, and with both the caliphate and the empire distracted, the Turks broke into Anatolia with a vengeance. In 1071 at Manzikert, a skirmish between Byzantine and Turkish soldiers turned into a rout in which Byzantium lost an army, an emperor, and the Macedonian reputation for military prowess.

Ever since the emergence of the Turkish threat in the early eleventh century, the Byzantines had been seeking mercenary help. The imperial defeat at Manzikert made their search more urgent and led to appeals to the West. In 1095, Emperor Alexius Comnenus (r. 1081–1118) pleaded with Pope Urban II (r. 1088–1099) for mercenary help against the Turks.

To most people in western Europe, the Turkish threat to Byzantium mattered little. What *did* alarm Westerners were Turkish attacks on pilgrims to Jerusalem. The eleventh century witnessed a tremendous surge in pilgrimage to Jerusalem. People of every rank and role from all over Europe set out on the arduous journey. A heightened piety motivated many pilgrims but so too did apocalyptic anxiety about the year 1000 and the possibility that the world was going to end.

The Reconquista in Spain, a war of Christians against Muslims, was itself gaining momentum in the eleventh century. In 1063 Pope Alexander II rallied an army from all over Europe to besiege the Muslim-controlled city of Barbastro in Spain. This was the first sign of papal interest in such campaigns.

A crusade was perfectly consonant with the ethos of the knights of western Europe, born and trained to fight. The age's literature glorified war and warriors. But churchmen had for some years been advancing an ideal of Christian knighthood that stressed fighting God's enemies. In the late tenth century, first in France and then in many other places, movements arose called the "Peace of God" or the "Truce of God." These movements sought to prevent war in certain seasons, such as around Christmas and Easter, and on Sundays. Peace movements also attempted to outlaw fighting near churches, protect noncombatants, and soften the treatment of enemies and captives. Together, the movements induced knights to fight non-Christians outside Europe. Along with religious zeal, a quest for fame and fortune motivated many men whose political prospects at home were limited.

## The "Pilgrimage" to Jerusalem

The popes saw in the plight of the Byzantines and of Western pilgrims some opportunities to manifest their leadership of the church. The papacy also wanted very much to heal the Roman-Orthodox rift. The popes, therefore, placed a high value on aiding the Byzantines. Pope Urban II received Alexius's envoys in 1095 and then left Italy for France. He was actually a fugitive because Henry IV controlled Rome. In November at Clermont, Urban delivered a rousing speech to a vast Christian assembly. He ignored the Eastern emperor's appeal for aid and instead promised salvation to soldiers who would enlist in a great struggle to free the Holy Land. The crowd acclaimed his words with a shout of "God wills it!"

By 1096, four large armies, which eventually swelled to perhaps a hundred thousand men—mostly French knights, with a smattering of troops from other parts of Europe—assembled under the leadership of the pope's legate. The forces were to rendezvous at Constantinople, where they seem to have expected a cordial imperial welcome and all necessary assistance. Alexius, however, took a rather different view. A ragtag band of ordinary people preceding the Crusaders had torn through the Balkans like a plague of locusts. The crusading armies themselves sorely taxed the imperial authorities, who spent a lot of time and money arranging their passage from the frontier of Hungary to the gates of Constantinople. Finally, Alexius wanted mercenaries to fend off Turks in Anatolia, not armed pilgrims intent on liberating Palestine (see **Map 9.7**).

After receiving nominal promises of loyalty and the return or donation of any lands captured, Alexius moved the Crusaders into Anatolia. Almost immediately, the Latin army defeated a Turkish force, thus earning a valuable, though short-lived, reputation for invincibility. The troops then entered Syria and laid siege to Antioch, which did not fall until 1098. At this point, rivalries among the Crusaders came into the open. One force went to the frontier of Armenia and carved out a principality. One of the Norman leaders kept Antioch for himself. The main army pressed on to Jerusalem and, after a short but fierce siege, conquered it in July 1099. A Muslim historian describes the scene:

> In the Masjid [Mosque] al-Aqsa the Franks slaughtered more than 70,000 people, among them a large number of Imams and Muslim scholars, devout and ascetic men who had left their homelands to live lives of pious seclusion in the Holy Place. The Franks stripped the Dome of the Rock [the Mosque of Umar, near the al-Aqsa mosque, pictured on page 203] of more than forty silver candelabra, each of them weighing 3,600 drams [almost 40 pounds], and a great silver lamp weighing forty-four Syrian pounds, as well as a hundred and fifty smaller candelabra and more than twenty gold ones, and a great deal more booty.[*]

Godfrey of Bouillon, leader of the troops that had "liberated" Jerusalem, was named "Advocate of the Holy Sepulcher" and became ruler of the Christians in the East. He lived only a short time, however, and was replaced by his brother, Baldwin, as king of Jerusalem in 1100.

Judged on its own terms, the First Crusade was a success. The Holy Land was retaken from the Muslims who had captured it in the seventh century, and the pilgrim routes were

---

*Slightly adapted from the Gesta Francorum, trans. August C. Krey, in *The First Crusade* (Princeton, N.J.: Princeton University Press, 1921), p. 257.

Map 9.7 The Crusades The long-standing Western interest in the Holy Land is vividly illustrated by the Crusades. Note the numerous routes taken, lands traversed, destinations attained, and points of cultural encounter. © Cengage Learning 2014

**Map legend:**
- First Crusade, 1096–1099
- Second Crusade, 1147–1149
- Third Crusade, 1189–1192
- Fourth Crusade, 1202–1204
- Crusade of Frederick II, 1228–1229
- Crusades of Louis IX, 1248–1254 and 1270
- Crusader kingdoms in the East
- Major battle

passable once more. Entirely uncertain, however, were the prospects of the crusader states, the future course of Western relations with Byzantium, and the reaction of the Islamic world once it recovered from its initial shock.

## The Later Crusades

Crusading was intended to protect the Holy Land and keep open the pilgrim routes to Jerusalem. The creation of the small crusader states in the hostile environment of Syria and Palestine made continued crusading almost inevitable. In 1144, the tiny crusader state at Edessa on the Armenian frontier fell to a Muslim army. Although the news saddened Europeans, it took immense efforts by the papacy and other religious leaders, especially the influential Bernard of Clairvaux (see Chapter 10) to launch another crusade. Finally, Conrad III of Germany and Louis VII of France agreed to lead it, but the Second Crusade (as we call it; Crusades had no numbers in the Middle Ages) accomplished little. The German army was destroyed almost as soon as it entered Anatolia. The French army was too small to attack Edessa and its remnants went on to Jerusalem. The Crusade's one achievement was an accident. In 1147, an army of English, French, and Flemish soldiers who were proceeding to the Holy Land by sea put in on the Iberian coast and captured Lisbon. This opened a new front in the Reconquista and laid the foundations for the later kingdom of Portugal (see **Map 9.7**).

The papacy called for the Third Crusade when Saladin (sah-lah-DEEN) (1138–1193), a powerful local leader typical of the disintegrating Abbasid caliphate, recaptured Jerusalem in 1187. The fall of Jerusalem was a real shock to Europeans. It is a measure of the force of the crusading ideal that the greatest crowned heads of the day—Frederick Barbarossa, Philip II, and Richard the Lionhearted—answered the call. Only Frederick did so enthusiastically, but he died en route in 1190, while Philip returned home in 1191, and Richard in 1192. The crusaders recaptured the strategic port of Acre but, despite defeating Saladin in a battle, Richard decided to return home. He concluded a treaty with Saladin that won access to Jerusalem for pilgrims.

Disappointed with the results of the Third Crusade, Innocent III began calling for another crusade immediately on his election in 1198. Popular preachers summoned an army, once again largely French, and the pope and the Fourth Crusade's military leaders engaged the Venetians to construct a fleet of war and transport ships. In less than eighteen months, they produced 50 galleys and 450 transports, a tribute to the awesome capabilities of the Venetian shipyards.

Ships, however, were expensive, and the Venetians drove hard bargains. When too few Crusaders and too little money appeared, the Venetians suggested that the Crusaders could discharge some of their debt by recapturing from the Hungarians the formerly Venetian port of Zara on the Dalmatian coast. This idea outraged the pope, but he could do little about it. Then into the camp of the Crusaders came a pretender to the Byzantine throne, who promised that if the Crusaders would help him to claim his patrimony, he would contribute to the cost of the Crusade. The Venetians urged the indebted Crusaders to accept this offer, and, to the horror of Innocent III, the Fourth Crusade turned to Constantinople.

Once in Constantinople, the Crusaders learned that their new ally had few friends in the Byzantine capital, but the venture hardly collapsed. The Venetians saw an opportunity to expand business opportunities in the East, and the soldiers welcomed a chance to plunder the Mediterranean's greatest city and to avenge what they regarded as a century of Byzantine perfidy. Thus, the Fourth Crusade captured not Jerusalem but Constantinople. Until 1261, the Eastern and Western churches were reunited under papal leadership, and substantial tracts of the Balkans fell to Western knights under a "Latin emperor" of Constantinople.

In later decades, popes began to take a more active role in planning crusades. No pope wanted to lose control of a crusade as Innocent had done, and all popes saw that the liberation of Jerusalem required a solid base of operations in the eastern Mediterranean. Egypt was the objective of the Fifth (1218–1221) and Sixth (1248–1250) Crusades. Despite a few victories, the Crusaders could not win a secure base. No further crusades to the East were organized in the thirteenth century. In 1291, Acre, the last Crusader stronghold, fell, and the original crusading era ended.

## Taking Stock

Why did the Crusades end? There are several reasons. They were never universal or obligatory. Despite much mythmaking about poor people, shepherds, women, and children, crusaders were men of substance. Eventually they found other outlets for their wealth and energy. By the late thirteenth century, more violence was being directed inward against heretics and political foes of the papacy than outward against the alleged enemies of Christendom itself. As rulers became more sophisticated and controlled more territory, they had less interest in the intangible benefits of crusading, such as prestige. Whereas the cities of Italy once needed to open up Mediterranean ports, now they wished to secure comparative advantage over one another. Literary images provide another insight into the decline of the Crusades. After 1300, we are less likely to read about a Christian knight fighting honorably for God and king than about a gentleman of manners seeking the favor of a fair lady.

Crusading was brutal. Soldiers and their clerical companions spent years away from their homes and families, endured scorching Mediterranean heat, and suffered shortages of food and basic supplies. The vulnerable crusader states never received enough settlers to be viable communities, and consequently, intermarriage with locals was common and gradually produced a hybrid culture that was neither European nor Middle Eastern. Warfare was constant on all sides. When Crusaders conquered a town, they executed many locals. When Muslims recaptured a town, they did the same.

An examination of the crusading movement as a whole reveals more losses than gains. The shipping and iron (think of all those weapons) industries gained. Some women, particularly in France, from which the majority

## SECTION SUMMARY

- Weakness and disunity in the Byzantine Empire and the caliphate were important background factors in the Crusades.

- Heightened religious zeal in western Europe along with growing papal leadership were also significant background factors.

- Mixed motives stood behind the initial Crusades: The Byzantines wanted mercenaries to fight in Anatolia, the popes wanted to extend their authority and free the Holy Land, urban Italians sought commercial opportunities, and western knights sought both worldly glory and eternal reward.

- The momentum of the early crusading movement could not be sustained over a long time, and the Holy Land was not definitively liberated.

of all Crusaders came, may have enjoyed momentary benefits in terms of control of land, wealth, and people while their husbands were away. The papacy grew in both power and prestige. The collection of crusading taxes enhanced the fiscal capabilities of some governments. The Crusades exported many violent men from Europe, but it is not clear that Europe became a less violent place. The Crusades complicated relations between Christian Europe and the Muslim world. The Fourth Crusade mortally wounded Byzantium and worsened the already tense standoff between the Catholic and Orthodox Churches. Crusading zeal was directed deliberately against heretics and coincidentally against Jews. The Jewish populations of several towns, especially in the German Rhineland, were massacred on the eve of the First and Second Crusades. The Crusades did not create anti-Semitism, but they aggravated it. Finally, the Crusades may have done as much to disrupt Mediterranean trade as to promote it. Italian urban rivalries took the place of Latin-Muslim-Byzantine ones.

# Chapter Summary

◆ *In how many different realms of life do you see signs of growth and innovation, of expansion in the High Middle Ages?*

Between 900 and 1300, Western civilization expanded as never before in human, material, geographical, and political terms. Europe's population grew dramatically until the late 1200s, owing to better diets and more plentiful foods. Technological gains came with wider use of horses, improved plows, and more productive farming techniques. Many regions began to specialize in the products that they grew or made, and this local specialization prompted larger-scale trade. Towns came to play a larger role in almost all aspects of economic and social life. Economic growth widened the gap between rich and poor and induced theologians to write about the just price and usury.

◆ *What did Germany, Italy, and France owe to the Carolingian past? How alike and how different were these areas by 1300?*

German political development was impeded by short-lived dynasties, territorial complexity, and battles with the papacy. From being Europe's greatest state in the tenth century, Germany declined into weakness in the thirteenth. Italy experienced the communal movement in the north, the consolidation of the Papal States and Papal Monarchy in the center, and the continued fragmentation of the south, where foreigners ruled. Differences among these three zones are characteristic of Italian history. France had a prestigious and long-lived royal dynasty, patient territorial expansion, and a slowly, steadily centralizing government. By 1300, France was the most powerful state in Europe.

◆ *What were the chief dynamics in the development of medieval Britain?*

England's kings survived several changes of dynasty (compare Germany) without having to make fundamental changes in English society or government. English kings built on Anglo-Saxon precedents to secure revenues, extend the work of the royal courts, and limit the power of the barons.

English kings brought constant pressure to bear on the Celtic realms that surrounded England, in the process retarding political development in these regions and involving themselves in dangerous and costly ventures. By 1300, England was a unified and well-governed kingdom.

◆ *How did new states emerge in Spain, Scandinavia, and the Slavic world, and how do those states compare with their western neighbors?*

The growth of new states is an impressive achievement of the High Middle Ages. The Reconquista motivated Spanish kings to military victories and political consolidation. Although Scandinavian Vikings were influential and disruptive, large-scale states began to emerge in Denmark, Norway, and Sweden. Slavic states emerged from resolute local action (Poland, Bohemia) or from a fusion of elite outsider and dependent local populations (Hungary, Bulgaria, Rus). Christianity expanded everywhere, sometimes Roman Catholic (Spain, Scandinavia, Poland, Hungary) and sometimes Orthodox (Bulgaria, Rus). The "West" was a lot bigger in 1300 than it had been in 900.

◆ *What basic factors contributed to the rise, persistence, and eventual decline of the crusading movement?*

The Crusades represent a key sign of western Europe's expansion. Weakness and disunity in the Byzantine Empire and the caliphate were important background factors in the Crusades. Heightened religious zeal in western Europe along with growing papal leadership were also significant background factors. Mixed motives stood behind the initial Crusades: The Byzantines wanted mercenaries to fight in Anatolia, the popes wanted to extend their authority and free the Holy Land, urban Italians sought commercial opportunities, and western knights sought both worldly glory and eternal reward. The momentum of the early crusading movement could not be sustained over a long time, and the Holy Land was not definitively liberated.

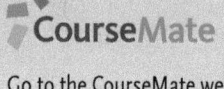

# Key Terms

**guilds** (p. 230)

**lay investiture** (p. 234)

**communes** (p. 234)

**Papal Monarchy** (p. 236)

**feudal revolution** (p. 239)

**Magna Carta** (p. 244)

*parliaments* (p. 244)

**Reconquista** (p. 246)

**Crusades** (p. 250)

**The Confirmation of the Rule of Saint Francis, 1223** Pope Honorius III confirms the revised version of Francis's Rule. Scala/Art Resource, NY

# Medieval Civilization at Its Height, 900–1300

**10**

This painting by Giotto di Bondone depicts Pope Honorius III confirming the Rule of Saint Francis in 1223. Saint Francis kneels humbly before the pope, along with several of his Franciscan followers. Note the simplicity of their dress, especially compared with the regal clothing worn by the pope and his bishops. The plain brown robes are recognized as the traditional clothing of Franciscans, who lived according to the scriptural ideals of poverty, preaching, and service. Unlike monastic orders who withdrew from the world, the Franciscans pledged themselves to working among Europe's outcasts—the poor, the sick, and the old.

The Franciscans, and similar orders, such as the Dominicans, led one of the most powerful religious movements of the Middle Ages. Yet, they were just one part of the religious climate of the period. Several social and religious movements, including heretical movements and religious communities of women, also emerged during the twelfth and thirteen centuries.

We know about Saint Francis and others from many Latin documents and from Italian ones. The culture of the High Middle Ages saw Latin cede some space to the *vernacular* languages. Religious themes were still foremost in writings of all kinds, but adventures, romances, and other works dedicated to secular themes were gaining in prominence. Intellectual life was broadened by encounters with long-lost Greek texts and with the writings of Jewish and Muslim scholars. Universities owed much to earlier cathedral and monastic schools but were new institutions—one of medieval Europe's greatest, and most durable, inventions.

The previous chapter concentrated on the economic foundations of society and on the ways in which people organized themselves politically. This chapter begins by introducing the increasingly complex social structures within which people lived and then turns to a study of what those people thought, wrote, and built.

## Chapter Overview

### The Traditional Orders of Society

◆ *Into what principal social groups were the people of high medieval Europe organized?*

### Social and Religious Movements, circa 1100–1300

◆ *Why did some spiritual movements result in heresy, while others ended in new religious orders?*

### Latin Culture: From Schools to Universities

◆ *What signs do you find of an expanding intellectual climate in high medieval Europe?*

### The Vernacular Achievement

◆ *What were the hallmarks of vernacular culture?*

# The Traditional Orders of Society

*Into what principal social groups were the people of high medieval Europe organized?*

Alfred the Great (r. 871–899) of England and two French bishops said that a kingdom needed "men of prayer, men of war, and men of work." This threefold division reveals the way the elite looked at the world. It provided neat places for the clergy, warrior-aristocrats, and peasants. The clergy and the nobility agreed that they were superior to the "workers," but fierce controversies raged over whether ultimate leadership in society belonged to the "prayers" or the "fighters."

By the time this three-part view of society was fully established in the West, it had begun to fit social realities less well. It excluded townspeople, who were becoming ever more important. Town residents worked for a living, of course, but only farmers were considered "workers." Alfred and the bishops did not speak about women, and they consciously excluded minorities, chiefly Jews.

## Those Who Pray: The Clergy

As the church promoted its own vision of the three-part ordering of society, it assigned primacy to the prayers—its own leaders. Within the clergy, however, sharp disagreements arose over whether the leading prayers were the monks in the monasteries or the bishops in their cathedrals. Whereas in the Carolingian world the clergy served occasionally as an avenue of upward social mobility for talented outsiders, in the High Middle Ages church offices were usually reserved for the younger sons of the nobility.

In the aftermath of the Carolingian collapse, a great spiritual reform swept Europe. It began in 910 when Duke William of Aquitaine founded the monastery of **Cluny** (CLUE-nee) in Burgundy on land that he donated (see **Map 9.4**). At a time when powerful local families dominated almost all monasteries, Cluny was a rarity because it was free of all lay and episcopal control and because it was under the direct authority of the pope. Cluny's abbots were among the greatest European statesmen of their day and became influential advisers to popes, French kings, German emperors, and aristocratic families.

**Cluny** A monastery in France that became a model for religious reform.

Cluny placed great emphasis on liturgical prayer. The monks spent long hours in solemn devotions and did little manual work. Because Cluniac prayer was thought to be especially effective, nobles all over Europe donated land to Cluny and placed local monasteries under Cluniac control. Many independent monasteries also appealed to Cluny for spiritual reform. By the twelfth century hundreds of monasteries had joined a Cluniac order. Individual houses were under the authority of the abbot of Cluny, and their priors had to attend an annual assembly. Although the majority of houses reformed by Cluny were male, many convents of nuns also adopted Cluniac practices.

Cluny promoted two powerful ideas. One was that the role of the church was to pray for the world, not to be implicated deeply in it. The other was that freedom from lay control was essential if churches were to concentrate on their spiritual tasks.

The same spiritual forces that motivated the Cluniacs inspired Bishop Adalbero of Metz in 933 to promote the restoration of Benedictine practices in the dilapidated Lorraine monastery of Gorze (GORTZ-eh). Customs at Gorze resembled those at Cluny, and they spread widely in Lorraine, Germany, and England. The Gorze reform was well received by kings and nobles; its aim was not so much to withdraw from the world as to improve it. Monks from the Gorze and Cluniac traditions bitterly condemned clerical immorality and inappropriate lay interference in the church. They preached against clerical marriage and simony, the buying and selling of church offices.

Reformers in the more ascetic eremitic tradition (see pages 177–178) desired more profound changes. They criticized the monastery at Cluny, saying that it had become too opulent and successful, and the monastery at Gorze because it seemed too immersed in worldly affairs. A desire to build new communities according to their vision of the apostolic church, featuring a life of poverty, self-denial, and seclusion, captivated the ascetics. Thus, the eleventh and early twelfth centuries saw a proliferation of both male and female experiments in eremitic monasticism. Other Europeans believed that the apostolic calling demanded not only an austere regimen of personal renunciation but also an active life of Christian ministry. Cathedral clergy, called canons, adapted the Rule of Saint Augustine so that they could live a communal life and also carry out priestly duties.

The greatest critics of the Cluniac tradition, and the real monastic elite of the early twelfth century, were the Cistercians. In 1098, Abbot Robert left his Burgundian monastery of Molesme (MOE-lem) because he believed it had abandoned the strict teachings of Saint Benedict. He founded a new monastery at Cîteaux (SEE-toe) in Burgundy. This house was to follow the Benedictine Rule literally and to refuse all secular entanglements: lands, rents, and servile dependents. So rigorous and poor was the community that it struggled until a charismatic young Burgundian nobleman named Bernard (1090–1153) joined in 1112. Through his writing, preaching, and personal example, Bernard dominated the religious life of Europe in his lifetime. By the end of the twelfth century, there were about five hundred Cistercian (from the Latin for *Cîteaux*) monasteries in Europe. Initially, the Cistercians wished to be an order of adult men. They successfully avoided admitting young boys, but by 1200, they had authorized about one hundred convents of Cistercian nuns.

And it was not just the Cistercians and the traditional Benedictines who attracted women. The twelfth century saw many new communities of women from England to eastern Europe. The age's growing prosperity and population contributed both potential nuns and healthy endowments, but the key factor was that women were responding to the spiritual forces of the age in the same way men were.

With the monastic clergy gaining so much in prestige and visibility, the episcopal clergy countered with its own view of society. Surely, the bishops agreed, spiritual, moral, and intellectual improvement were desirable. Likewise, it was time to end the grossest examples of lay interference in the church. But precisely because so many bishops came from great families and were so well connected, they were less inclined to be rigid about the line of demarcation between lay and clerical responsibilities. In Germany, for example, the king's chapel recruited young noblemen to train them as clerics and to inculcate in them the policies and ethos of the court. Many of these chaplains were appointed to bishoprics and then advanced the king's interests in their new ecclesiastical areas of authority. They were often men of spiritual depth and resented what they regarded as monastic carping about their worldliness.

It was the special responsibility of the clergy to look after the moral order of society. In the turbulent world of gentlemen warriors, the church had its own ideas about what a perfect "fighter" should do. The English bishop and scholar John of Salisbury (d. 1180), reflecting on knighthood in the twelfth century, concluded that it existed "to protect the church, to attack infidelity, to reverence the priesthood, to protect the poor, to keep the peace, to shed one's blood and, if necessary, to lay down one's life for one's brethren."

Turning large numbers of violent men into servants of the church was a tall order for the clergy, and they had only limited success. One strategy that worked was the creation of military orders. The Palestine-based Knights of St. John, or Hospitallers, and Knights of the Temple, or Templars, are the major examples. The Hospitallers started near Jerusalem as a foundation under Benedictine auspices dedicated to charitable works and care of the sick. They evolved into a monastic order using a version of the Rule of Saint Benedict and devoted themselves to the defense of pilgrims to the Holy Land. The Templars were men

## CHRONOLOGY

| | |
|---|---|
| ca. 900 | *Beowulf* |
| 910 | Foundation of Cluny |
| 940–1003 | Gerbert of Aurillac |
| 960–1028 | Fulbert of Chartres |
| d. 970 | Roswitha of Gandersheim |
| 1000–1088 | Berengar of Tours |
| ca. 1033–1109 | Anselm of Canterbury |
| ca. 1050–1150 | Maturation of the Romanesque |
| 1079–1142 | Peter Abelard |
| 1090–1153 | Bernard of Clairvaux |
| 1098 | Foundation of Cîteaux |
| 1098–1179 | Hildegard of Bingen |
| ca. 1100 | *Song of Roland* |
| 1135–1183 | Chrétien de Troyes |
| 1170–1221 | Dominic de Guzman |
| ca. 1177–1213 | Mary of Oignies |
| 1181–1226 | Francis of Assisi |
| 1184 | Waldensians declared heretics |
| 1194–1253 | Clare of Assisi |
| 1208 | Albigensian Crusade launched |
| 1210–1280 | Mechtild of Magdeburg |
| 1225–1274 | Thomas Aquinas |
| 1265–1321 | Dante Alighieri |

living under religious rule and sworn to protect the small states created by the Crusaders (see pages 253–254). These military orders measured up very well to the clergy's idea of what a perfect knight should be.

The clergy could also regulate disputes in society. For example, when a community was divided by a difficult conflict that demanded resolution, it might turn to the *ordeal*—a judicial procedure that sought divine judgment by subjecting the accused to a physically painful or dangerous test. An accused person might walk a certain distance carrying hot iron or plunge a hand into a boiling cauldron to pluck out a pebble. The resulting wounds would be bandaged for a set time and then examined. If they were healing, the person was considered innocent; if they were festering, the person was considered guilty. The clergy officiated at ordeals until the papacy forbade their participation in 1215.

## Those Who Fight: The Nobility

In recent years, scholars have spilled a sea of ink trying to define the medieval nobility. The matter is important because even though the nobility constituted only a small minority of the total population, nobles were the ruling class. To appreciate their crucial role, we need to consider the nobles' lifestyle and ethos.

In English, the word *noble* can be either an adjective or a noun. More commonly, it is an adjective, as in a "noble sentiment" or a "noble deed." Before the twelfth century, the Latin *nobilis* was almost exclusively an adjective. The word pertained to certain desirable personal qualities. Then, gradually, the word became a noun and pertained to a certain kind of person.

In the ideal case, a noble was a well-born, cultivated, office-holding soldier. In the earlier Middle Ages, many men held offices without necessarily being considered noble. Virtually all free men were expected to be soldiers, but few of them ranked as nobles. It was in the century or so following the feudal revolution (see pages 238–240) that these distinct elements were fused into a single social order.

In a world in which lords were everywhere extending their power, military prowess became more valuable. At the same time, the need for horses and for more expensive arms

Based on a drawing from Cluny des Églises et la Maison du Chef d'Ordre, by R. J. Conant. Courtesy, Medieval Academy of America

215

**Reconstruction of Cluny** A view of the monastic complex at Cluny in the early twelfth century. Note the basilica (the largest church in Europe until the sixteenth century), the cloister (to the left, actually south, of the basilica, with its dormitory in the foreground and refectory opposite the basilica), and the workshops.

and armor made it almost impossible for ordinary freemen to be soldiers. Likewise, ambitious lords who wished to expand their influence were looking for ways to use their resources to gain followers. These trends came together as lords granted to their followers either military gear or lands, which would generate the income necessary to obtain arms and horses. We call those followers "vassals" and the lands they obtained "fiefs." Vassalage became a widespread institution all over Europe, and fief-holding became a normal accompaniment to vassalage.

Vassals and fiefs bring to mind the concept of *feudalism* or the term *feudal system*. As we saw in Chapter 9, England, France, and, to a lesser degree, Germany and Italy were in some respects feudal realms. That is, lords, right up to the king, secured some personal and political services from vassals in return for material rewards, often landed estates called fiefs. Today, historians are reluctant to use the term *feudal system* because across Europe, and through many centuries, there was nothing systematic about how services were obtained or discharged.

Contemporary sources often call vassals "knights." Knights rarely boasted high birth or venerable ancestry, nor were they initially officeholders appointed by kings or emperors. Moreover, they were not wealthy and did not enjoy the lavish lifestyle that one might expect from nobles. Across the eleventh and twelfth centuries, knights saw their status change, in part because they mimicked the behavior of the nobles, who themselves accepted the necessity of military ability.

All over Europe, especially where royal power was ineffective, both knights and nobles secured tighter control of peasant labor. This process provided knights and nobles with the money to build castles and to acquire fine possessions. As governments expanded their competence, these nobles and knights often held high offices, or if they did not, they pressured kings to concede such offices to them. Lords also tended to gather their lands into coherent blocks and to name themselves after the castles they built on their lands. Families also began to produce genealogies tracing their ancestry to relatives in the distant past and to kings if at all possible. At the same time, families began to practice primogeniture—that is, reserving their lands, castles, and titles to the *primus genitus*, or "firstborn" son.

This allotment of the choicest inheritances to a shrinking group turned loose a large number of younger sons. Many of them entered the clergy, a tendency that helps to explain the rising aristocratic character of the church. This was not a punishment. Sons were not "dumped" on the church. Clerical careers were prestigious and relatively comfortable. But more numerous than clerics were the young men who were without an estate and who lacked the means to secure a bride and to form a family of their own. These men traipsed about Europe looking for fame and fortune, or failing that, a lord to serve. Many of these "young" men were 30 or 40 years old. They were called young because they had not yet established themselves.

By 1200, the nobility was a group identified by the profession of arms, the holding of office, a consciousness of family traditions, and an elevated lifestyle. A specific ethos—chivalry—belonged to the nobility. Today, chivalry is often thought of as either an elaborate code of conduct regulating relations between the sexes or the value system behind the literary image of dashing knights in shining armor saving damsels in distress from fire-breathing dragons. Actually, its very name derives from *cheval*, French for "horse," the classic conveyance of a knight. Chivalry began as the code of conduct for mounted warriors.

Chivalry highly esteemed certain masculine, militant qualities. Military prowess was the greatest of chivalric virtues. A knight who was not a great warrior was useless. Literature of the time exalts the knight who slays fearsome beasts or the hero who single-handedly overwhelms impossible numbers of the enemy. Openhanded generosity was another key virtue. The truly noble person engaged in sumptuous display to manifest his power, to show concern for his dependents, and to enlarge his entourage. Medieval literature is full of rich banquets and stunning presents. Knights were obsessed with their honor, their reputations. They sought glory, the better to win a lord or a bride or, if a lord already, to attract followers. Chivalry also emphasized loyalty, the glue that held feudal society together. The social realities of a knight's life probably differed considerably from the consistent and elegant descriptions of that life in literature. What is more, descriptions of chivalry, arising as they did just as cities and townspeople were becoming more prominent, may have represented idealized attempts to distinguish various kinds of men.

What role was left to noblewomen in a world of chivalry and lordship? By the late eleventh century, three developments adversely affected the position of aristocratic women. First, the elaboration of the chivalric ethos defined most key social and political roles as military and "manly" and thereby excluded women. By the middle of the twelfth century, it was rare for a woman to hold a castle and unheard of for one to ride to arms. Second, the consolidation of lineages by aristocratic families accompanied a moral campaign by the church to promote monogamous, unbreakable marriages. This situation subordinated women's freedom in the marriage market to the dynastic and patrimonial demands of great families. Third, the spread of lordship, with its intricate network of personal and proprietary relationships based on military service, tended to deprive women of independent rights over land.

But every rule has its exceptions. As noble families married off fewer of their daughters to noblemen, "extra" daughters accounted in part for the dramatic increase in the number and size of convents. Convents of aristocratic nuns were places where women could be highly educated and almost entirely in control of their own affairs. Matilda, daughter of the German empress Adelaide, was abbess of Quedlinburg, mistress of vast estates in northern Germany, and a dominant figure in German politics. But knights looking for brides would often marry the younger daughters of noblemen because if they could establish a household, any children born of that marriage could lay claim to the noble lineage of their maternal grandfathers.

Less predictably, Gaita, wife of a Norman prince in Italy, fought in helmet and armor alongside her husband, as did Duchess Agnes of Burgundy. And let us reflect on the career of Adela of Blois (ca. 1067–1137). She was the daughter of William the Conqueror, the wife of a powerful French count, and the mother of King Stephen I of England. In addition to regularly accompanying her husband as he administered his county, Adela founded monasteries, promoted religious reform, hosted Pope Paschal II, helped to reconcile her brother Henry I with the archbishop of Canterbury (thus averting an English investiture controversy), issued formal legal judgments, held fairs, and skillfully negotiated the aristocratic politics of western France after her husband's death. Adela is unusual because we know so much about her. In other words, noblewomen in high medieval society may often have led interesting, active lives, but there are few surviving records to document this.

## Those Who Work: The Peasants

The peasants were the "workers" in the three-part model. An extremely diverse segment of society, "peasants" ranged from slaves to free persons of some means. Except in frontier zones, where victims were available and religious scruples diminished, slaves declined in numbers during the tenth and eleventh centuries (as illustrated by the shift in meaning of the classical Latin *servus* from "slave" to "serf"). Serfs, persons bound to the soil, constituted a significant minority of the peasants. Serfdom was a mixture of economic, legal, and personal statuses. The serf could be flogged in public, could be set upon by dogs, was excluded from many judicial proceedings, required approval to contract a marriage, and was denied the right to bear arms.

The tenth and eleventh centuries were decisive in the reshaping of rural society. As lordships of all kinds and sizes formed in the countryside, they drew communities of people. Castles were critical. Powerful men generally sited their castles in close proximity to wood, water, and iron. (See the feature, "The Visual Record: The Medieval Castle" on pages 242–243 in Chapter 9.) People from a fairly wide area settled in the vicinity of the castle. Many, originally free, commended themselves to the local lord by handing over their properties and receiving them back in return for rents or personal services. Other people fell into dependent status through military or economic misfortune. What eventually emerged was the manor, an institution best described as a powerful lord controlling the lives of an often large number of dependents. He required payments and services from them and regulated their ordinary disputes.

A minor castellan, or lord of a castle, might control only a small manor and would probably be the vassal of a great lord. A powerful landed lord, on the other hand, would generally control many manors and would often give some of them to retainers as fiefs. In other words, the reorganization of the countryside affected the nobility and the peasantry and created parallel sets of vertical bonds of association: feudal lords and vassals entered into political bonds; lords and peasants entered into economic bonds.

The structure of individual manors, and the dues owed by peasants, varied tremendously across Europe. As the economy expanded, as trade brought more and different products into Europe, and as a more consciously aristocratic lifestyle spread, the nobility began to want disposable cash. Thus, in many places corvées (KOR-vay) (labor services) were commuted into cash payments. Peasants were required to pay rent from their own holdings instead of working on the lord's lands. But lords still needed provisions, so they sometimes split peasant payments into cash and kind. The lord could also extract money from his peasants by requiring them to use his mill and oven and then charging them gristing and baking fees.

The trend everywhere, however, was for labor services to diminish. In one region in northern France, twelfth-century peasants owed only three corvées of two days each per year for harvesting and haymaking. Elsewhere, peasants might still be required to haul crops to market or to keep roads, bridges, and buildings in repair. On many estates where the menfolk had been largely freed from corvées, the women might still have to work in the lord's house washing laundry, sewing, plucking fowl, cooking, minding dogs, and tending to other household chores.

In the expanding economy of the eleventh and twelfth centuries, the peasants grew more prosperous, and their lords constantly sought new ways to extract the fruits of that prosperity. Peasants thus began to band together to demand that "customs" be observed. These customs were more or less formal agreements spelling out the terms under which work and fees would be arranged. In general, life improved for the peasants in terms of both legal status and living conditions.

The European village was a key product of the tenth and eleventh centuries. People who originally gathered together around a castle for security and livelihood began to form a durable human community. Their church and graveyard helped to reinforce the community by tying together the living and the dead and by giving the village a sense of memory and continuity. Peasants generally worked only 250 to 270 days per year, so they had a good deal of time for festivals and celebrations. Births, baptisms, betrothals, and deaths provided opportunities for the community to come together and affirm its mutual ties. Market days and sessions of the lord's court also assembled the village. Villagers needed to cooperate in many of the operations of daily life. They shared tools, plow teams, and wagons. They performed their corvées together. The peasants experienced much less social differentiation than the nobility, and so, less tension.

The status of women in peasant society tended to be, in legal theory and in daily reality, the same as that of men at a time when the status of aristocratic women was fragile. Marriage contracts from northern Italy show that brides often entered marriages with a complement of valuable tools. This suggests that peasant women retained some control over their own personal property and also reminds us that the huge gains in rural productivity were almost certainly attributable in part to the work and ingenuity of women.

## Those Left Out: Townspeople and Jews

The three-part model excluded two important groups of people. The first neglected group consisted of the increasingly numerous citizens of Europe's growing towns. Obviously, people in towns worked, but the prejudices of the aristocracy were rural, so the only "workers" deemed necessary to the smooth functioning of the social order were farmers. In the second group were Europe's principal religious minority, the Jews. Jews could be found almost everywhere, although they constituted only about 1 percent of the population as a whole and, outside of Rome and parts of Spain, formed no single community numbering more than 1,500 to 2,000.

The central factor in the growth of towns was the rise in the productivity and profitability of medieval agriculture. A regular and substantial farm surplus could support an urban population that did not produce its own food. Increased local exchange, coupled with the relentless growth of a money economy, meant there were fortunes to be made and cash to be spent. Some of that cash was spent on luxury and exotic products that increasingly became the objects of far-flung commercial networks. A good part of the cash was spent by rural nobles,

**San Gimignano** The towers of this Tuscan city reveal the concentrated and competitive nature of power in the Italian communes. Most of these towers date from around 1300.

who earned it from rents, booty, and the profits of the private exercise of public power. When those nobles moved into towns, they created opportunities for merchants, craftsmen, day laborers, domestic servants, and professional people, such as notaries and lawyers. This was particularly true in Europe's most heavily urbanized regions: Flanders, southern France, and northern Italy. The key point is that the growth of the medieval city and of its human community began in the medieval countryside.

Town society was hierarchical, but its structures were new, ill-defined, and flexible. Rich men built up bands of followers who supported them in urban politics, protected their neighborhoods, and occasionally raided the houses of their enemies in the next neighborhood. Relatives, friends, neighbors, people from a common rural district, or those engaged in similar trades tended to worship together in particular churches, observe certain festivals, and look after one another's families.

In the rapidly changing world of the tenth and eleventh centuries, towns provided numerous opportunities for women. In urban industries, such as clothmaking, tanning, laundering, and brewing, women sometimes managed and even owned enterprises. Apart, perhaps, from finance and the law, distinctions between male and female roles were not as sharp in towns as in rural areas.

If urban men and all women stood in an ambiguous relationship to the ideals of the male, rural, aristocratic elite, we can hardly imagine what it must have been like for Jews. Jewish communities had existed in most European towns since antiquity. Then, because the Byzantine and Islamic worlds vacillated between persecution and toleration, many Jews migrated to western Europe, with the largest numbers settling in northern France and the German Rhineland. Paris had northern Europe's largest Jewish community, perhaps two thousand people in the twelfth century. Many cities had Jewish populations numbering two hundred to three hundred, but groups of forty to fifty were common. Although some Jews in Italy, Spain, and Germany owned farms and vineyards, most Jews settled in cities, where they could live and worship in community with other Jews. Urban clusters also provided strength in numbers for people who could at any moment fall victim to persecution and whose power was not based on landholding.

Three of the most important developments in high medieval Europe were disastrous for Jews. First, the growth of the European economy, with its attendant urban and commercial expansion, brought countless Christians into the practice of trade, an occupation dominated by Jews since Late Antiquity. As Jews were excluded from commercial opportunities, they were more and more confined to moneylending. Jews had been moneylenders before the economic surge of the High Middle Ages, but the expanding economy made financial operations more widespread than ever before. Given that, as we saw in Chapter 9, Christian moralists considered handling money to be the Devil's work, the visibility of Jews as moneylenders brought them much criticism, although they were never alone in this practice.

The second phenomenon that adversely affected Jews was the reform of the church. With so much attention being paid to the proper Christian life and the correct organization of the church, it was inevitable that more attention would be directed to the one prominent group in Western society that was not Christian.

Third, the Crusades unleashed vicious attacks on Jews. As crusading armies headed east in 1096, they visited unspeakable massacres on the Jewish communities of several German towns. This awful process was repeated on the eve of the Second Crusade in 1146–1147 and again just before the third in 1189. Popular frenzy identified the Jews as Christ-killers and equated them with Muslims as the enemies of Christianity. In fact, and despite grotesque and groundless stories about Jews kidnapping and ritually killing Christian children, Jews everywhere wished to live in peace with their Christian neighbors and to be left alone to observe their distinctive religious, dietary, and social customs.

The Jews were not without sympathetic champions, however. From the time of Gregory I (r. 590–604), the papacy urged peaceful coexistence and prayers for Jewish conversion. In the twelfth and thirteenth centuries, popes forcefully reminded Christians that while converting Jews was highly desirable, Jews were to be tolerated and left in peace. The Carolingians protected the Jews, and some kings in succeeding centuries repeated or even expanded upon Carolingian legislation.

Jews were vulnerable to attack at almost any time from people who simply disliked them or who owed them money. In 1181, Philip II of France, always on the lookout for income, had his henchmen arrest Jews and confiscate their possessions. In 1182, he expelled them from royal lands. Across the thirteenth century, French kings accorded the Jews less and less protection and often abused them financially. In 1306, Philip IV expelled the Jews from France after confiscating their goods. In England, the story is much the same. The ever-needy Henry II laid crushing taxes on the Jews in 1171. In 1189 in London and in 1190 in York, massive riots stirred by false rumors raged against the Jewish populations. In 1290, Edward I seized Jewish possessions and expelled Jews from the country. Royal protection of German Jews was reasonably effective until the death of Frederick II in 1250, after which time local princes often repudiated debts to Jewish lenders and appropriated Jewish property.

## SECTION SUMMARY

- Among the elite, society was divided into "those who pray," "those who fight," and "those who work."
- Constant waves of monastic reform modeled good spiritual behavior.
- Warrior-nobles were the governing class, marked by chivalry, their distinctive ethos.
- Peasants did much of the "work" in medieval society and generally found their lives improving.
- Townspeople enjoyed expanding opportunities but always suffered under the prejudices of landholding elites.
- In religious life, urban occupations, and rural pursuits, women experienced some improvements in their conditions of life.
- The condition of Europe's Jews grew progressively dangerous.

# Social and Religious Movements, ca. 1100–1300

*Why did some spiritual movements result in heresy, while others ended in new religious orders?*

Twelfth- and thirteenth-century Europe witnessed several social movements unlike any that had occurred before. Spurred by increasingly intrusive governments, economic dislocation, and spiritual turmoil, they involved large numbers of people; cut across lines of gender, wealth, status, and occupation; and appeared in many places. Most of these movements had cohesive beliefs, even ideologies, and well-determined goals. They are the first large-scale social movements in European history.

## Heretics and Dissidents

The canon lawyer Gratian (see page 273) defined *heresy* as a situation in which "each man chooses for himself the teaching he believes to be the better one"—that is, he ignores official doctrines. For Gratian and his like-minded contemporaries, faith was not an individual matter. Unity of belief was crucial in a catholic ("universal") Christian Europe. In the twelfth century, the church reacted ever more strictly to challenges to its teachings or to its exclusive right to teach. The effort by the church to define its law, theology, and bureaucratic procedures with greater precision drew lines more sharply than ever before between what was and was not acceptable.

Heretics did not see themselves as secessionists from the true church. They saw themselves as its only representatives. Church teachings always encountered a degree of popular skepticism. Not everyone believed, for example, that Jesus was born of a virgin or that he was true God and true man. But such doubts had not previously led to mass defections. Before the middle of the twelfth century, challenges to the church came from men—as far as we can tell, the ringleaders were all men—who saw themselves as inspired reformers.

Tanchelm (TANK-elm) of Antwerp preached between 1100 and 1115 in the Netherlands. He scandalized the mainstream by calling churches brothels and clerics whores. He rejected the sacraments and the payment of tithes. Although Tanchelm was radical and pugnacious, his ideas constituted a fairly coherent program of criticism. Like many others, he was concerned about the immorality and wealth of the church. But Tanchelm and his followers went even further. The heretic distributed his nail and hair clippings as relics of a sort, and in a bizarre public ceremony he "married" a statue of the Virgin Mary.

Coherent movements of much larger proportions emerged later in the century. In 1173, Waldo, a rich merchant of Lyon, decided to sell all his property, give the proceeds to the poor, and embrace a life of poverty and preaching. Waldo was motivated by the same quest for the apostolic life that had animated the eremitic movement of the eleventh century. But there was a difference: He was a layman. Waldo attracted many followers (known as Waldensians), and in 1179, Pope Alexander III (r. 1159–1181) scrutinized him closely, found his beliefs to be essentially correct, and approved his vow of poverty. But the pope commanded Waldo to preach only when invited to do so by bishops. The bishops, jealous about their own power, extended no such invitations.

Waldo and his "Poor Men of Lyon" went right on preaching and in 1184 were formally declared heretics. Until this point it was not their ideas so much as their appropriation of a clerical duty, preaching, that had set the church against them. From this time on, however, the Waldensians became more radical in their attacks. Waldensian communities exist to this day.

The most serious of the popular heretical movements was Catharism (from the Greek *katharos*, meaning "pure"). Because there were numerous Cathars near the southern French town of Albi, the whole movement is sometimes called "Albigensian." In fact, Cathars could be found all over Europe, although they did cluster in northern Italy and southern France. Cathars were the religious descendants of Mani (see page 157), a third-century Persian who taught an extreme dualism that featured polarities in almost all things: good-evil, love-hate, flesh-spirit. Extreme Cathars abstained from flesh in all ways: They were vegetarians and renounced sexual intercourse so as not to produce offspring—that is, more flesh. Cathar ideas had spread widely in the West by the 1140s. Catharism attracted many converts when Nicetas, the Cathar bishop of Constantinople, visited northern Italy and southern France between 1166 and 1176. People of every station joined the new church, which, in its own view, was the only true church.

The Catholic Church sent isolated preachers against the Cathars but with little success. In 1198 and 1203, Pope Innocent III organized systematic preaching tours in southern France, but these, too, lacked solid results, and in 1208, the pope's legate was murdered by a man who was sympathetic to the Cathars. The killing led to the launching of the Albigensian

Crusade, a loosely structured military action that lasted into the 1260s. Although the crusade itself was largely over by the 1220s, violence against Albigensians sputtered for decades: a massacre in 1244 and inquisitorial campaigns in 1246 and again in 1256 to 1257. Isolated resisters struggled on into the fourteenth century.

Albigensians denounced the clergy of their day as rich and corrupt. These teachings attracted urban dwellers who resented the wealth and pretensions of the clergy—the same people who followed Waldo. Nobles may have been drawn to the movement because it gave them opportunities to take possession of extensive tracts of church lands, something the investiture controversy had denied them. In addition, embracing Catharism may have been a way for nobles to resist the increasing encroachment of the government of far-off Paris. The Albigensians also attracted many women. Unlike the Catholic Church, which denied clerical, preaching, and teaching offices to women, the heretical sects tended to permit women to hold leading roles.

The Albigensians, like the Waldensians, were driven by the same spiritual zeal and desire for ecclesiastical reform that moved many of their contemporaries. They differed from other would-be reformers in that they did not seek to reform the Catholic Church from within but departed from it or insisted that they alone represented it. Thus, these heretical movements marked the first serious challenge to the ideology of a uniformly "catholic" Christendom since Late Antiquity.

## Reform from Within: The Mendicant Orders

Traditional monastic orders continued to win adherents, but their interpretation of the apostolic life meant ascetic withdrawal from the world, not pastoral work and preaching. Laymen who wished both to embrace poverty and to preach fell under the suspicion of the ecclesiastical authorities. Early in the thirteenth century, a new movement arose, the mendicants (literally, beggars). Mendicants were men who aimed to preach, to be poor, and to create formal but noncloistered religious orders. Though similar to the heretics in many ways, they submitted willingly to ecclesiastical authority.

The mendicant phenomenon began when **Francis of Assisi** (1181–1226), the son of a rich Italian merchant, decided to renounce the wealth and status that were his birthright. He carried out his renunciation in a most public display before the bishop of Assisi (uh-SEE-zee) in 1206. Francis had gradually grown tired of a life of ease and luxury, but he also experienced a blinding moment of spiritual insight when, by chance, his eyes fell on the passage in the Scriptures in which Christ commanded the rich young ruler, "Go, sell all you have, and follow me." Francis stripped himself naked so that "naked he might follow the naked Christ."

**Francis of Assisi** An Italian layman who renounced his wealth and founded a religious order dedicated to charitable works.

For a few years, Francis wandered about Italy begging for his meager sustenance, repairing churches, caring for the sick, and preaching repentance to all who would listen. By 1210, he had attracted many followers, and together, they set out to see Innocent III to win approval. After considering the matter for a while, Innocent decided to approve the new order of friars (that is, "brothers," from the Latin *fratres*) as long as they would accept monastic tonsure—a ritual haircut signifying submission—profess obedience to the pope, and swear obedience to Francis. The pope was genuinely won over by Francis himself, but he also sensed that by permitting the formation of the Franciscan order, he could create a legitimate and controllable repository for the explosive spiritual forces of the age.

Francis prepared a simple rule for his new order based on his understanding of the scriptural ideals of poverty, preaching, and service. Alarmed by the vagueness of the first rule and by the extraordinary influx of new members, the papal curia in 1223 prevailed on Francis to submit a revision that stressed order, a hierarchy of officials, and a novitiate—a regularized period of training for new members. Somewhat disappointed by this regulated formality, Francis withdrew more and more from the world and lived reclusively in the hills near Assisi.

After Francis died, the issues of property, power, education, and ordination provoked deep controversies within his order. Usually called "Franciscan," Francis's order is technically the "Friars Minor." The movement had begun among laymen, but over time more Franciscan brothers became ordained priests. Franciscans established schools in most great cities, and by the middle of the thirteenth century, some of Europe's greatest intellects were

Franciscans. In the 1230s, papal legislation had alleviated strict poverty by permitting the order to acquire property to support its work. Nevertheless, the issue of property continued to spark controversy among the Franciscans.

The other major mendicant order was the Dominican, a product of very different experiences than the Franciscan. Its founder, **Dominic de Guzman** (1170–1221), was the son of a Spanish nobleman. He became a priest and later a cathedral canon. While traveling, he saw firsthand the Albigensian heresy in southern France, and in 1206, he went to Rome to seek permission to preach against the heretics. The Albigensian Crusade began in 1208, but Dominic's methods were those of persuasion, not coercion.

Albigensian criticisms of the ignorance, indifference, and personal failings of the clergy could never be applied to Dominic and his fellow preachers. Dominic and his followers were supported enthusiastically by the bishop of Toulouse, who saw how useful these zealous preachers of unblemished lives could be. In 1215, Dominic, with his bishop's assistance, attempted to form a new order, but by that time, Rome had forbidden the creation of new orders for fear of heresy or uncontrollable diversity. Thus, Dominic's "Order of Preachers" (the proper name for the "Dominicans") adopted the Rule of Saint Augustine, which many communities of cathedral canons had been using since the eleventh century.

In 1217, Dominic presided at the first general meeting of the order. The Dominicans decided to disperse, some going to Paris, some (including Dominic) to Rome, and some to other cities in Europe. Henceforth, the order saw its mission as serving the whole church. Dominican schools were set up all over Europe, and the order acquired a reputation for learning and scholarship. The Dominicans were voluntarily poor, but the order was never rent by a controversy over property as the Franciscans were.

Both the Franciscan and Dominican orders reflected a widespread desire to emulate the apostolic life of the early church by poverty and preaching. Both submitted to legitimate authority. Francis's religious vision of charity and service was the product of a heartfelt need for repentance and renewal. This concern for the soul often caused Franciscans to serve as missionaries. Dominic set out to save the church from its enemies. He desired preachers who were sufficiently learned that they could combat the errors of heretics. Both men saw the need for exemplary lives. Francis was a more charismatic figure than Dominic, and his apostolate to the urban poor was more compelling. By 1300, Franciscan houses outnumbered Dominican by 3 to 1. The mendicants were the greatest spiritual force in high medieval Europe.

### Communities of Women

The religious forces that attracted men drew women as well. Traditional orders, however, tended to be hostile toward women. Cluniacs and Cistercians struggled to keep women out of their ranks. The wandering preachers of the twelfth century, without exception, acquired women as followers, but the usual results were either segregation of the women in cloisters or condemnation of the whole movement.

In 1212, Francis attracted the aristocrat Clare of Assisi (1194–1253), who was fleeing from an arranged marriage. She wanted to live the friars' life of poverty and preaching, and Francis wanted to assist her. Aware that the sight of women begging or preaching would be shocking, in 1215, he gave Clare and his other female followers their own rule. Clare became abbess of the first community of the "Poor Clares." Though cloistered and forbidden to preach, the Clares lived lives of exemplary austerity and attracted many adherents.

Beguines (BAY-geenz) were communities of women who lived together, devoted themselves to charitable works, but did not take vows as nuns. The Beguine movement arose from the work of Mary of Oignies (ca. 1177–1213). She was drawn to the ideals of voluntary poverty and service to others. So strong was the pull that she renounced her marriage, gave away all her goods, worked for a while in a leper colony, and thought of preaching against the Cathars. Instead, she formed a community.

Groups of Beguines appeared all over the Low Countries, western Germany, and northern France. This was the first exclusively women's movement in the history of Christianity. Beguines sometimes vowed poverty and sometimes did not. They sometimes cloistered themselves into communities and sometimes taught and served the poor and outcast. They

**Dominic de Guzman**
A Spanish nobleman who preached against Albigensian heretics and founded a religious order dedicated to preaching.

**The Parting of Mary from the Apostles** Duccio di Buoninsegna lived from the middle of the thirteenth century to 1318 or 1319. He did his finest work in Siena, including a huge altarpiece, one of whose panels depicts the touching scene of Mary taking leave of the apostles just before her death. Note the clever way Duccio has arranged the figures and how he balances Saint Paul, standing in the doorway, with Mary, reclining on the bed.

Scala/Art Resource, NY

neither challenged the institutional church nor demanded a right to preach. As laywomen, they did not give rise to scandal as noncloistered nuns would have.

Thirteenth-century Europe knew more female than male mystics, and female mysticism tended to focus on Jesus, especially on His presence in the Eucharist. This is the first religious devotion that can be shown to have been more common to women than to men. Most of the mystics were either nuns or Beguines. As the clergy was defining its own prerogatives more tightly and excluding women more absolutely from the exercise of formal public power, female communities provided a different locus for women's activity.

Women who spent their lives in community with other women reveal, in their writings, none of the sense of moral and intellectual inferiority that was routinely attributed to women by men and often by women themselves. Women who were in direct spiritual communion with God acquired, as teachers, mediators, and counselors in their communities, power that they simply could not have had outside those settings.

**SECTION SUMMARY**

- Some men and women who opposed the wealth and immorality of some clerics, and who wished to preach and teach, veered off into heresy.

- The mendicant orders—Franciscans and Dominicans, chiefly—led holy lives, worked among the poor or preached against heretics, and always had the approval of the papacy.

- Several religious movements were especially popular among women and constituted the first women's movements in the history of Christianity.

# Latin Culture: From Schools to Universities

*What signs do you find of an expanding intellectual climate in high medieval Europe?*

As in the late antique and Carolingian periods, courts and churches were the greatest patrons of artists and authors. But in this age of expansion, the number and geographic spread of such patrons increased dramatically. By 1150, the church comprised 50 percent more bishoprics and about three times as many monasteries as it had in 900. In 1300, monarchies reigned in many places—Scandinavia and the Slavic world, for example—where none had

🌐 **Map 10.1 Europe, circa 1230** By the early thirteenth century, the European states that would exist into modern times were clearly visible, although each would continue to undergo changes. To gain a sense of the evolution of Europe, compare this map with Maps **6.1**, **7.3**, and **8.3**. © Cengage Learning 2014

existed in 900 (see **Map 10.1**). In addition to an increase in the sheer amount of cultural activity, the years between 900 and 1300 also witnessed innovations. Logic replaced grammar at the heart of the school curriculum. Latin letters remained ascendant but literature in many vernacular (native) languages began to appear in quantity and quality. Romanesque art and architecture were fresh and original interpretations of their Carolingian ancestors. Europe's incipient urbanization produced the first stirrings of a distinctively urban culture. In one of those cities, Paris, a new kind of academic institution emerged—the university— which was arguably the period's greatest legacy to the modern world.

## The Carolingian Legacy

Political dislocation and constant attacks in the ninth and tenth centuries initially deprived schools and masters of the Carolingian patronage that they had enjoyed for a century or more. The Carolingians left firm enough foundations in a few centers for intellectual life to continue, but the scale of activity between 900 and 1050 was smaller than before. Three examples serve to capture the spirit of the age that set the stage for the High Middle Ages.

Gerbert of Aurillac (DJAIR-bear of OR-ee-ak) (940–1003) was the most distinguished intellect of his age. He left his home in Aquitaine to study in Spain and Italy before settling in Reims, in northern France, where he was a teacher and then briefly a bishop. He attracted the attention of the emperor Otto III and spent some time at the German court, earning appointments as abbot of Bobbio, bishop of Ravenna, and, finally, pope. Gerbert followed Carolingian tradition in being a collector of manuscripts and critic of texts, but he departed from older traditions in his interest in mathematics and in his study of logic—the formal rules of reasoning that, in the Western tradition, trace back over many thinkers to Aristotle (see pages 78–79).

Fulbert of Chartres (FULL-bear of SHART), Gerbert's finest pupil, elevated the cathedral school of Chartres to the paramount place in academic Europe. Fulbert (960–1028) wrote letters in elegant Latin and composed fine poems. He carried on his master's literary interests more than his scientific ones, and well into the twelfth century Chartres remained a major center of literary studies.

Another figure of interest is the aristocratic German nun Roswitha of Gandersheim (d. 970). She wrote poems on saints and martyrs, as well as a story about a priest who sold his soul to the Devil. In her mature years, Roswitha wrote Latin plays in rhymed verse based on the Roman writer Terence. In these plays, she refashioned tales from Roman and biblical history to convey moral truths.

## The Study of Law

Law was a field of major innovation. The increasing sophistication of urban life demanded a better understanding of law. The growing responsibilities of the church called for orderly rules, and the church's frequent quarrels with secular rulers demanded careful delineations of rights and responsibilities. Governments issued more laws and regulations in the twelfth and thirteenth centuries than at any time since antiquity.

In eleventh-century Bologna, scholars began once again to study and teach Roman law based on Justinian's great compilation. By the thirteenth century, Roman law was widely taught, usually on the basis of the "Ordinary Gloss" by Accursius (d. 1263) who appended some 96,000 annotations to the *Corpus Iuris Civilis*.

The revival of Roman law led to the study of the **canon law** of the church. Over some twenty years (1120–1140) the Bolognese monk Gratian continually revised a work traditionally known as the *Decretum* (from papal decretals). Although he collected a vast amount of ecclesiastical legislation, Gratian's innovation was to base his book on case law, not on abstract principles. Throughout the twelfth century, canon lawyers studied and wrote commentaries on Gratian's *Decretum*. These legists are called "decretists." Several collections of new papal decretals were prepared in the thirteenth century, especially the *Liber Extra* (1234), and the scholars who studied these later decrees are called "decretalists."

England was precocious in creating a common law, a single law applied uniformly in its courts. But English law was based on the careful accumulation of legal decisions—or precedents—and not on the routine application of the provisions of a law code. There were many law codes elsewhere. Alfonso X of Castile issued the *Siete Partidas*, a comprehensive law code largely reliant on Roman law. Prince Iaroslav (d. 1054) is reputed to have issued the first version of the laws of Kievan Rus. Byzantine law was revised under the Macedonian dynasty.

**canon law** The law of the church (as distinguished from civil law). It is based on papal decrees and the rulings of church councils.

## Greek, Arab, and Jewish Contributions

Norman and German settlement in southern Italy and Sicily, the Reconquista in Spain, the Crusades, and the creation of Italian communities in many Mediterranean cities brought European thinkers face-to-face with the intellectual traditions of Classical Greece, Islam, and medieval Judaism. Between 1100 and 1270, almost the whole corpus of Aristotle's writings, virtually unknown in the West for a millennium, became available. Arab commentaries on Aristotle, as well as Jewish philosophical and theological works, began to circulate. The presence of all these texts and currents of thought was decisive in expanding the range and raising the level of Western thought.

**Muslim Scholars in a Garden** From a thirteenth-century Iraqi manuscript, this picture shows literary men in a pleasure garden. Beasts are driving a water wheel to refresh them, and a lute player accompanies their poetry with music.

Bibliothèque nationale de France

Prior to 1100, only a few of Aristotle's writings, primarily some of his texts on logic, had been available in the West. Gradually, scholars recovered Aristotle's full treatment of logic, then his scientific writings, and finally his studies of ethics and politics. Aristotle's books posed a number of problems for Christian scholars. What relationship exists between the Christian faith and reason? Aristotle taught that the universe is eternal and mechanistic. His thought left no room for creation or for the continuing role of a Creator. For Christian thinkers, Aristotle asked questions that demanded answers: Were the Scriptures true? Did God create the world as Genesis said? Did God continue to intervene in this world?

Two major Arab thinkers were particularly influenced by the vast Aristotelian corpus. Ibn-Sina (980–1037), called Avicenna (ah-vih-SENN-uh) in the West, was drawn to the fundamental problem of how to understand the relationship between objects that exist in the world and the knowledge of those objects that is formed and held in the human mind. (See the feature, "The Global Record: The Making of an Arab Scholar" on page 275.) Ibn Rushd (1126–1198), called Averroes (uh-VERR-oh-eese), wrote no fewer than thirty-eight commentaries on the works of Aristotle, and at least fifteen of these were translated into Latin in the thirteenth century. Among many contributions, Averroes particularly tried to clarify the relationship between truths acquired through the exercise of reason and truths that depend on divine revelation. His contemporaries and many later scholars understood him to teach the "double truth": Truths about the natural world are more or less accessible to everyone depending on a person's intellectual ability. Revealed truths, however, are available only to the most enlightened.

Spain and northern France were both important centers of Jewish thought. In Spain, some Jewish thinkers also grappled with Aristotle. Solomon ibn Gebirol (1021–1070), called Avicebron, wrote *The Fountain of Life*, a treatise that attempted to reconcile Aristotle with the Jewish faith by finding a role for God in communicating knowledge to every human mind. The greatest of all medieval Jewish thinkers, Moses ben Maimon (1135–1204), called Maimonides (my-MON-uh-deez), wrote *A Guide for the Perplexed*. The perplexed he had in mind were those who had trouble reconciling the seemingly opposed claims of reason and faith. Maimonides taught a doctrine very close to Averroes's double truth.

Solomon ben Isaac (1040–1105), called Rashi, was educated in Jewish schools in the Rhineland and then set up his own school in Troyes (TWAH). He became the most learned biblical and Talmudic scholar of his time, indeed one of the wisest ever. The Talmud is a detailed and erudite commentary on the scriptural studies of the ancient rabbis. Christian scholars who wished to know the exact meaning of passages in the Bible sometimes consulted Rashi and his successors.

From Persia to Spain to France, then, countless thinkers were engaged in serious reflection on the mechanics of knowing, the nature of reality, the relationship between reason and faith, and the meaning and significance of revelation. In the years just around 1100, Latin Christian scholars began to encounter this torrent of thought and writing.

## The Development of Western Theology

Carolingian schools had focused on grammar—that is, on the basic foundations of language. Gradually, logic supplanted grammar at the center of both intellectual interests and school curricula. Eventually, the wider application of logic produced a new intellectual style and also evoked bitter criticisms.

## The Making of an Arab Scholar

*These excerpts from the engaging life of Avicenna (980–1037) reveal not only his remarkable intellectual attainments but also his ongoing encounter with Greek thought. Avicenna was deeply influenced by Aristotle and, in turn, his writings influenced Jewish and Christian writers who were also coming to grips with the greatest of Greek philosophers. His writings on medicine were authoritative until the seventeenth century.*

My father was from Balkh and moved from there to Bukhārā [now Turkmenistan] . . . where I was given teachers of the Quran and polite letters [literature, especially poetry]. By the time I was ten years old I had mastered the Quran and so much of polite letters as to provoke wonderment. My father decided to send me to a certain grocer who knew Indian arithmetic so that I could learn it from him. Then Abu Abdallah al-Natili, who claimed to be a philosopher, came to Bukhara. My father lodged him in our house in the hope that I would learn something from him. Before he came I was studying jurisprudence . . . and I was one of the best pupils. Then, under the guidance of al-Natili, I began to study the *Isagogue* [a commentary on some of Aristotle's works]. Thus I learned from him the broad principles of logic, but he knew nothing of the subtleties. Then I began to read books and study commentaries on my own until I mastered logic. I also read the geometry of Euclid. Then I passed on to the *Almagest* [Ptolemy's second-century astronomical treatise]. Eventually I busied myself with the study of the [treatises] and other commentaries on physics and metaphysics [subjects treated at great length by Aristotle and by Avicenna's Arab predecessors, especially al-Farabi], and the doors of knowledge opened before me. Then I took up medicine and began to read books written on this subject. Medicine is not one of the difficult sciences, and in a very short time I undoubtedly excelled in it, so that physicians of merit studied under me. At the same time I carried on debates and controversies in jurisprudence. At this point I was sixteen years old.

I resumed the study of logic and all parts of philosophy. During this time I never slept a whole night through and I did nothing but study all day long. Whenever I was puzzled by a problem . . . I would go to the mosque, pray, and ask the Creator of All to reveal to me that which was hidden from me and to make easy for me that which was difficult. Then at night I would return home, put a lamp in front of me, and set to work reading and writing.

I returned to the study of divine science. I read the book called *Metaphysics* [by Aristotle] but could not understand it, the aim of its author remaining obscure for me. I read the book forty times, until I knew it by heart, but I still could not understand its meaning or its purpose. Then one afternoon I happened to be in the market of the booksellers, and a crier was holding a volume in his hand and shouting the price. I bought it and found that it was Abu'l Nasr al-Farabi's book explaining the meaning of the *Metaphysics*. I returned to my house and made haste to read it. Immediately the purposes of this book became clear to me because I already knew it by heart. I was very happy at this, and the next day I gave much alms to the poor in thanksgiving to Almighty God.

In my neighborhood there lived a man who asked me to write him an encyclopedic work on all the sciences. I compiled the *Majmu* for him and named it after him. In it I dealt with all sciences other than mathematics. I was then twenty-one years old.

### Questions

1. In what academic subjects was Avicenna particularly interested?

2. In what ways was Avicenna's education like and unlike that received by students in Europe?

3. How did faith and reason play complementary roles in Avicenna's education?

Bernard Lewis, ed., *Islam: From the Prophet Muhammed to the Capture of Constantinople*, vol. 2. Copyright © 1974 Oxford University Press. By permission of Oxford University Press. (pp. 177–181)

Berengar (ca. 1000–1088), master of the school of Tours, wrote a treatise that denied Christ's presence in the Eucharist—the Communion bread and wine received by Catholics and Orthodox Christians in the celebration of the mass. This position was heretical. Ordinarily, churchmen would have refuted Berengar simply by quoting various passages from the Scriptures or from the writings of the Church Fathers, along with conciliar pronouncements about the consecrated elements. Berengar's claim was finally proved false, at least to the satisfaction of his opponents, by Archbishop Lanfranc of Canterbury (1010–1089), who used Aristotelian logical argumentation to dispose of Berengar's heretical arguments.

Anselm (ca. 1033–1109), Lanfranc's successor as archbishop of Canterbury, developed an ingenious logical proof for the existence of God. The French theologian and philosopher Peter Abelard (1079–1142) used logic to reconcile apparent contradictions in the Scriptures and in the writings of the Church Fathers. Anselm and Abelard were not skeptics. Anselm's motto was "Faith seeking understanding."

For conservatives, such as **Bernard of Clairvaux** (see page 261) and **Hildegard of Bingen** (1098–1179), however, faith and immediate divine inspiration were primary. To

**Bernard of Clairvaux**
A church reformer, adviser to rulers, and conservative intellectual who opposed the wide application of logic.

**Hildegard of Bingen**
A German Benedictine abbess and prolific author.

them, logical approaches to divine truth were the height of arrogance. Hildegard—well educated, musically gifted, and knowledgeable in medical matters—was perhaps the most profound psychological thinker of her age. More than anyone before her, Hildegard opened up for discussion the feminine aspects of divinity. She, like Bernard, believed that God was to be found deep within the human spirit, not in books full of academic wrangling.

The future lay with Anselm and Abelard, however. Anselm was the most gifted Christian thinker since Augustine. He wrote distinguished works on logic, and his theological treatise, *Why God Became Man* (ca. 1100), served for three hundred years as the definitive philosophical and theological explanation of the incarnation of Christ, the central mystery of the Christian faith.

Peter Abelard was a more colorful figure. He argued rudely and violently with all his teachers, though in the end, he was probably more intelligent than any of them. He rose to a keener understanding of Aristotle than anyone in centuries, and he developed a sharper sense of both the power and the limitations of language than anyone since the Greeks. He concerned himself with ethics, too, and was one of the first writers to see intention as more important than simple action.

Abelard seduced and then secretly married Heloise, one of his pupils and the daughter of an influential Paris churchman. Heloise's relatives castrated Abelard for his refusal to live openly with his wife. Abelard then arranged for Heloise to enter a convent, and he joined a monastic community, where he continued writing and teaching. The two carried on a voluminous correspondence that reveals Heloise as a first-rate philosophical thinker and one of her age's most knowledgeable connoisseurs of Classical literature. Some of Abelard's more imaginative ideas earned him formal ecclesiastical condemnations in 1121 and 1140. He popularized the schools of Paris, however, and attracted to them promising scholars from all over Europe.

Abelard and several of his contemporaries engaged in one of the first widespread intellectual debates in Western history, the quarrel over "universals." *Universal* is the philosophical name for a concept that applies to more than one seemingly related object. To illustrate: May we agree that you are reading a book right now? May we further agree that the book you are reading is not identical to any other book on your bookshelf? And may we go one step further and agree that no book on your bookshelf is exactly like any other book on that shelf? So, why do we call all of these objects books? "Book" is here the universal that we are trying to understand.

A medieval "realist," whose thought may be traced back to Plato, would say that there is a concept, let us call it "bookness," that exists in our minds before we ever encounter any particular object that we label a book. Just as no book is ever identical to any other, so too, no specific book is a perfect representation of that concept "bookness." The concept is fully real, and all representations of it in the world are mere hints, suggestions of a more perfect reality.

A medieval "nominalist," on the contrary, would say that "book" is merely a name (*nomen* in Latin, whence nominalism) that we apply to objects that we deem to bear sufficient similarity to one another that they can be adequately captured by one name. But only each particular book is fully real.

With the emergence of the problem of universals, we enter fully into a new intellectual approach that has long been called "Scholasticism." This word has come to have many meanings, but at the most basic level it describes a movement that attempted to show that Christian theology is inherently rational, that faith and reason need not be contradictory or antithetical. Scholasticism also implies a certain systematization of thought. Gratian's and Accursius's legal work may be thought of as Scholastic exercises. Twelfth-century biblical scholars tried to produce a single, systematic commentary on the Bible. In 1160, Peter Lombard produced the *Four Books of Sentences*, a comprehensive treatment of all of Christian theology.

**Thomas Aquinas** (1225–1274) was the greatest of the Scholastics, the most sensitive to Greek and Arab thought and the most prolific medieval philosopher. A Dominican friar, Thomas was educated at Naples, Cologne, and Paris and he taught for some fifteen years in Paris. His two most famous works are the *Summa Contra Gentiles* and the *Summa Theologiae*. A *summa* is an encyclopedic compendium of carefully arrayed knowledge on a particular subject. One might think of, say, Gratian's and Peter Lombard's works as precursors to the great summas of the thirteenth century. Thomas's first summa addresses natural truth—that is, the kinds of things that any person can know through the operation of reason.

**Thomas Aquinas** A Dominican theologian and the greatest of the Scholastics.

*summa* A compendium of knowledge within a particular field.

His second summa is a summation of the revealed truths of the Christian faith.

Thomas's works are distinctive for two reasons. First, no one before him had so rigorously followed the dialectical method of reasoning through a whole field of knowledge, not just a particular problem. For thousands of pages, Thomas poses a question, suggests answers, confronts the answers with objections, refutes the objections, and then draws a conclusion. Then, he repeats the process. Second, Thomas carefully distinguishes between two kinds of truths. On the one hand are *natural truths*, truths (even theological ones) that anyone can know (or so Thomas thought)—for example, that God exists. On the other hand are *revealed truths*, truths that can be known (if not understood) only through faith in God's revelation—for example, the Trinity or the incarnation of Christ. Thomas maintains that natural and revealed truths simply cannot contradict one another because God is ultimately the source of both. If a natural truth—for example, Aristotle's contention that the world is eternal—appears to contradict a revealed truth, the natural truth is wrong. Thomas was accused by some contemporaries of applying reason too widely, and after his death some of his ideas were condemned by the church. But he actually steered a middle path between intellectual extremes. In this respect, Thomas was like Maimonides and Averroes.

## The University

In the early decades of the twelfth century, students gathered wherever famous teachers might be found. Such teach-

**The Triumph of St. Thomas**  This painting by Benozzo Gozzoli (1349) for the church of Santa Caterina in Pisa, Italy, is idealized but still reveals much that is true. Above Thomas are four evangelists and two church fathers; to Thomas's right and left stand Plato and Aristotle; at Thomas's feet Averroes crouches, vanquished. Thomas was seen as the great synthesizer of philosophical and theological knowledge.

ers—figures like Peter Abelard—clustered in a few centers, and the students congregated there as well. The last decades of the twelfth century saw a swarm of masters and students in

Paris. Like members of secular guilds (see page 230), the masters organized. The University of Paris was the result of their efforts. By 1300, universities had formed elsewhere in France, as well as in Italy, England, and western Germany.

Several forces drove masters to organize. They wanted to negotiate with the bishop's chancellor, the traditional head of all schools in an episcopal city. They wanted to regulate the curriculum that students followed and to prescribe the requirements for entry into their own ranks. They also desired to set the fees to be charged for instruction. By 1209, the bishop of Paris, the pope, and the king of France had granted formal recognition to the university.

In Bologna, the university developed a little differently. Here the students came primarily to study law, after already acquiring a basic education. These law students were usually older and more affluent than students elsewhere. Consequently, in Bologna, the university arose from a guild of students who united to set standards in fees and studies and to protect themselves against unscrupulous masters.

Universities were known for certain specializations: Paris for arts and theology, Bologna for law, Salerno in Italy and Montpellier in France for medicine, Oxford for mathematical and scientific subjects. Still, the basic course of study was similar. At Paris, a young scholar came to the city, found lodgings where he could, and attempted to find a master who would guide him through the arts curriculum. These boys might be in their early teens or several years older, depending on their earlier education and financial resources. The arts course, which was the prerequisite to all higher faculties, usually lasted from four to six years. The bachelor's degree was a license to teach, but a bachelor who wished to teach in a university needed to go on for a master's degree. The master's degree required at least eight years of study (including the baccalaureate years), which culminated in a public oral examination. Some masters went on to become doctors in theology, law, or medicine. A doctorate required ten to fifteen years of study.

Student life was difficult. In many ways, students were always foreigners. Although their presence in a town enhanced its prestige, townspeople exploited them by charging exorbitant prices for food and rent. Students' own behavior was not always above reproach. There was surely some truth in the frequently lodged charge that students were noisy, quarrelsome, given to drinking, and excessively fond of prostitutes. England's Oxford and Cambridge were unique in always providing residential colleges for students; Paris got one later, and the mendicants often established houses of study. Typically, though, students were on their own.

Students had to work very hard. The arts curriculum demanded a thorough acquaintance with all the famous texts of grammar, logic, and rhetoric. Higher studies added more Aristotle, particularly his philosophical writings. In theology, the students had to master the Scriptures, the principal biblical commentaries from patristic times to the present, and the *Four Books of Sentences*. In medicine, the ancient writings of Galen and Hippocrates were supplemented by Arab texts as well as by observation and experimentation.

The basic method of teaching provides yet another definition of Scholasticism—that is, the method of studying in the schools. The teacher started by reciting a short piece of a set text, carried on with the presentation and discussion of many authoritative commentaries on that text, and concluded with his own explanations. The teacher then presented another passage of the set text and repeated the whole process. This education focused on standard books and accepted opinions and required students to remember large amounts of material.

In principle, universities were open to free men, but in practice, they were restricted to those who had the means to attend them. Women were not accepted at universities, either as students or as teachers. It was generally thought, by men, that learning made women insubordinate. Lacking the required education, women were denied entry into the learned professions of theology, law, and medicine, despite the fact that many rural and some urban medical practitioners were women. Nevertheless, women commonly possessed and transmitted knowledge of both folk remedies

## SECTION SUMMARY

- Latin studies in literature, law, theology, and philosophy remained important.
- Europe's expansion brought scholars into increasing contact with ancient Greek, Jewish, and Arab thought.
- The increasing prominence of logic drove theology and philosophy to the center of the curriculum and led to the production of majestic summas.
- Formed as guilds of either masters or students, universities were among the most original and durable medieval achievements.

and scientific medicine. Trota of Salerno, who probably lived in the twelfth century, wrote a knowledgeable treatise, *On the Care of Women*. Documents from medieval Naples record the names of twenty-four women surgeons between 1273 and 1410. How these women were educated is utterly unknown.

# The Vernacular Achievement

*What were the hallmarks of vernacular culture?*

A major achievement of high medieval civilization, from Iceland to Kievan Rus, was the appearance of rich literatures in native tongues. Vernacular, from the Latin *vernaculus*, meaning "home-born" or "domestic," is the name for the languages other than Latin—say, English or French. Although Latin remained the language of the clerical elite, writers of vernacular prose and poetry produced some of the greatest works in Western literature.

## Literatures and Languages

The number of people who commanded Latin was always a minority in western Europe, just as native Greek-speakers were a minority in Byzantium. As Latin, beginning in Late Antiquity, slowly evolved into the Romance (from Roman) languages, people who used what eventually became French, Italian, and Spanish had some advantages over the people in Celtic, Germanic, and Slavic lands, where the languages bore no obvious relationship to Latin. Persons who spoke Old French in their towns and villages would have had an easier time learning Latin than people who spoke Irish or Polish. Nevertheless, vernacular literatures began to appear at roughly the same time all over Europe, between about 800 and 1000.

Many writers continued to use Latin for several centuries. University scholars continued to compose their learned treatises in the ancient tongue, but now often in a style that was less ornate than before. Most law books and public documents were still in Latin, but in a "vulgar" Latin that was reasonably close to the vernacular in areas where Romance languages were spoken. Technical manuals—on farming and animal husbandry, on warfare and armaments, or on law and government—were prepared in Latin, too, but again in a style that was far more accessible than that of their ancient models. Popular literature—poetry, history and biography, and romance and adventure—was still often written in Latin. Some of this material was serious, but some breathed a light and carefree spirit. The anonymous German known as the Archpoet (d. 1165) wrote poems about drinking and womanizing. These lines are typical of his work:

> In the public house to die
> Is my resolution;
> Let wine to my lips be nigh
> At life's dissolution:
> That will make the angels cry,
> With glad elocution
> "Grant this drunkard, God on high,
> Grace and Absolution!"*

No less insouciant were the authors of biting satires, such as the anonymous *The Gospel According to the Silver Marks*, which parodies the wealth and greed of the papal curia.

The literary masterpieces of the High Middle Ages are almost entirely written in vernacular languages. The epic poem *Beowulf* is the first classic of English literature. We do not know who wrote it or when it was written. Scholars now usually place it in the ninth or possibly the tenth century. The story focuses on three great battles fought by the hero, Beowulf. The first two are against the monster Grendel and Grendel's mother, who have been harrying the kingdom of an old ally of Beowulf's family; the third is against a dragon. *Beowulf* is a

---

*John Addington Symonds, *Wine, Women and Song: Medieval Latin Students' Songs* (reprint, New York: Cooper Square, 1966), p. 69.

poem of adventure and heroism, of loyalty and treachery. It treats lordship, friendship, and kinship. Themes of good and evil resound throughout. The poem is barely Christian, but nevertheless, deeply moral. It speaks, in a mature, vigorous, and moving language, to and for the heart of a warrior society.

*Beowulf* is the best-known Anglo-Saxon work but by no means the only one. Several volumes of elegiac and lyric poetry, mostly on religious themes, also survive. And Anglo-Saxon writers produced chronicles, legal materials and charters, and at least one large collection of homilies.

Some fragments of poetry in Old French survive from the ninth century, but the great *chansons de geste* ("songs of deeds," or celebrations of the great) appeared in the eleventh century. Undoubtedly, they were transmitted orally for a long time before they were written down. The best is the *Song of Roland*, written around 1100. In 778, as Charlemagne's army was returning from Spain, Basques raided the baggage train and killed Count Roland. By 1100, this obscure event, long kept alive in oral traditions, had been transformed into a heroic struggle between Charlemagne and his retinue and an army of countless thousands of "paynim," who are crude caricatures of Muslims.

Like *Beowulf*, the *Song of Roland* is a story about loyalty and treachery, bravery in the face of insuperable odds, and the kindness and generosity of leaders. Both take us into a man's chivalric world, where females are all but absent. The two works do not show us personal hopes, fears, or motivations. What pours forth is the communal ethos and the dominant values of the elite, male social group. Although *Beowulf* is lightly clothed in Christianity, the *Song of Roland* is thickly vested in the faith.

Southern France, in the middle and late twelfth century, added something new to Western literature: the love lyrics of the troubadours. This poetry, composed by both men and women, profoundly influenced an age and created the literary movement that has long been called "courtly love." **Chivalry** was initially a code for men interacting with other men. In the world of courtly love, chivalry became an elaborate set of rules governing relations between men and women.

**chivalry** Beginning as the dominant ethos of the warrior-nobility, it changed into rules governing relations between men and women.

Courtly love had several sources. The classical poet Ovid (43 B.C.–A.D. 17?), who wrote *The Art of Love*, a manual of seduction, was one. Another was the lyrical poetry of Muslim Spain. Ironically, feudal values such as loyalty and service played a critical role as men became, in effect, love vassals. Platonic ideas made some contribution, too, particularly the notion that any love in this world could be only a pale imitation of real love. The courtly poets sang of *fin' amours*, a pure love in contrast to the mere lust of the masses. A lover cherished an unattainable lady. He would do anything for the merest display of pleasure or gratitude on her part, as we see in these lines from Bernart de Ventadorn, court poet of the counts of Toulouse in the late twelfth century:

> *Down there, around Ventadorn, all my friends*
> *have lost me, because my lady does not love me;*
> *and so, it is right that I never go back there again,*
> *because always she is wild and morose with me.*
> *Now here is why the face she shows me is gloomy and full of anger:*
> *because my pleasure is in loving her and I have settled down to it.*
> *She is resentful and complains for no other reason.*[*]

Male troubadours placed women on pedestals and, in ballads, worshiped them from afar. Women troubadours took a different line. Women's poems were more realistic, human, and emotionally satisfying. Castellozza (KAHS-teh-lohtz-eh) (b. ca. 1200), the southern French wife of a Crusader, idealized not at all when she wrote these lines:

> *Friend, if you had shown consideration,*
> *meekness, candor and humanity,*
> *I'd have loved you without hesitation,*
> *but you were mean and sly and villainous.*

---

*From *The Lyrics of the Troubador, Trouveres*, translated by Frederick Goldin, copyright © 1973 by Frederick Goldin. Used by permission of Doubleday, a division of Random House, Inc.

## The Rules of Love

*Around 1190 an obscure writer, whom we know only as Andrew the Chaplain, wrote a book* De amore *("on Love") that is often referred to as* The Art of Courtly Love. *It seems that Countess Marie of Champagne was his patron. The first two books of the treatise constitute a sort of seduction manual heavily dependent on Ovid but the third book rejects love on moral and practical grounds. It is difficult to know how seriously to take the book. In Book 2 Andrew lists the rules of love.*

1. Marriage is no excuse for not loving.
2. He who is not jealous cannot love.
3. No one can be bound by two loves.
4. Love is always growing or diminishing.
5. It is not good for one lover to take anything against the will of the other.
6. A male cannot love until he has fully reached puberty.
7. Two years of mourning for a dead lover are prescribed for surviving lovers.
8. No one should be deprived of love without a valid reason.
9. No one can love who is not driven to do so by the power of love.
10. Love always departs from the dwelling place of avarice.
11. It is not proper to love one whom one would be ashamed to marry.
12. The true lover never desires the embraces of any save his lover.
13. Love rarely lasts when it is revealed.
14. An easy attainment makes love contemptible; a difficult one makes it more dear.
15. Every lover turns pale in the presence of his beloved.
16. When a lover suddenly has sight of his beloved, his heart beats wildly.
17. A new love expels an old one.
18. Moral integrity alone makes one worthy of love.
19. If love diminishes, it quickly leaves and rarely revives.
20. A lover is always fearful.
21. True jealousy always increases the effects of love.
22. If a lover suspects another, jealousy and the effects of love increase.
23. He who is vexed by the thoughts of love eats little and seldom sleeps.
24. Every action of a lover ends in the thought of his beloved.
25. The true lover believes only that which he thinks will please his beloved.
26. Love can deny nothing to love.
27. A lover can never have enough of the embraces of his beloved.
28. The slightest suspicion incites the lover to suspect the worse of his beloved.
29. He who suffers from an excess of passion is not suited to love.
30. The true lover is continuously obsessed with the image of his beloved.
31. Nothing prevents a woman from being loved by two men, or a man from being loved by two women.

### Questions

1. *How many of these rules seem to fly in the face of traditional Christian morality?*

2. *Do you think Andrew can be taken seriously, or is he ironic, satirical, even farcical?*

3. *How many of these rules seem relevant today?*

From *The Art of Courtly Love*, by Andreas Capellanus, trans. with an introduction and notes by John Jay Parry. Copyright © 1941 by Columbia University Press. Reprinted with permission of the publisher. (pp. 184–186)

---

And she did not assign the active role exclusively to the man:

> *Handsome friend, as a lover true*
> *I loved you, for you pleased me*
> *But now I see I was a fool*
> *for I've barely seen you since.**

Count William IX of Poitou (1071–1127) was among the first of the troubadours, and his daughter, Eleanor of Aquitaine, brought the conventions of this poetry and point of view to the French and Angevin courts. She and her daughters were the greatest literary patrons of the late twelfth century. The wives of kings and nobles, who were frequently away from home, maintained stunning courts and cultivated vernacular literature.

The courtly literature of northern France broke new ground in both form and content. The romance and the lay were the chief new forms. Both drew on Classical literature, the heroic Germanic past, and the Arthurian legends of the Celtic world to create stories of love and adventure. The romance usually develops a complex narrative involving several major characters over a long time. The lay is brief and focuses on a single incident. The most famous

---

*From lyrics by Castellozza in *The Women Troubadours* by Meg Bogin, (W.W. Norton, 1976). Copyright © 1976 by Magda Bogin. Reprinted by permission of Magda Bogin.

twelfth-century writer of romance was Chrétien de Troyes (1135–1183), the court writer of Marie of Champagne, the daughter of Eleanor of Aquitaine. The greatest writer of lays was Marie de France, who wrote at the Angevin court in the 1170s.

The romances and lays explore the contradictions and tensions in a variety of human relationships. Loyalty and honor make frequent appearances. Lancelot, a paragon of knightly virtue, desperately loves his lord Arthur's wife, Guinevere. What is he to do? How can he be loyal to his lord, to his love, and to himself? What will he do when a single course of action brings both honor and dishonor? In the epics, speeches are made to swords, to horses, or sometimes to no one in particular; the points being made are universalized. In the romances, credible human beings struggle to resolve powerful and conflicting emotional and moral dilemmas.

France led the way in the production of vernacular literature, but French models did not inspire slavish imitation. This is seen most clearly in the work of the master of all vernacular writers, Dante Alighieri (DAHN-tay ah-lih-GYAIR-ee). Dante (1265–1321) began as a poet in *la dolce stil nuova*, "the sweet new style," which came from France and captivated Italians. But he moved beyond it in many ways. Dante was a man of extraordinarily wide learning and reading. He is best known for one of the masterpieces of world literature, *The Divine Comedy*.

The secret of the *Comedy*'s success is not easy to grasp. It is a long and difficult poem, but it is also humorous, instructive, and moving. In an exquisitely beautiful Italian, Dante took the most advanced theology and philosophy of his time, the richest poetic traditions, a huge hoard of stories, many contemporary events, and a lot of common sense and wove them into an allegorical presentation of the journey of the whole human race and of the individual lives of all people.

Accompanied by the Roman poet Virgil (see page 146), Dante travels through Hell and Purgatory, commenting along the way on the condition of the people he meets. Then, because Virgil is a pagan and only Dante's true love can accompany Dante into Paradise, Beatrice, the love of Dante's youth, joins him for a visit to Heaven. The poet's central metaphor is love; the love he feels for Beatrice symbolizes the love God feels for the world. Dante canvasses humanity from the pits of Hell, which he reserved for traitors, to the summit of Paradise, where a man inspired by pure love might, despite his sinfulness, dare to look into the face of God.

Although the romances and lays were by no means the exclusive preserve of the elite, very little is known about popular literature. Two exceptions are the mystery play and women's devotional writing. Mystery plays made their first appearance in the eleventh century. The liturgy of the church, which formally reenacted the life of Christ, was confined to the clergy. But this limitation did not prevent troupes of actors from staging, on church porches or village greens, scenes from the life of Christ in simple, direct language. Such plays served as both a form of popular entertainment and a device for teaching elementary Christian ideas. The female religious movements of the age gave rise to works in the vernacular. Mechtild of Magdeburg (1210–1280), a German Beguine, wrote *The Flowering Light of Divinity*, a mystical, allegorical account of the marriage between God and a spiritual woman. The vernaculars opened avenues of expression to women, who were normally denied Latin learning.

## Innovations in Architecture

**Romanesque**, "in the Roman style," is a term that was coined in the nineteenth century to characterize the architecture and, to a lesser extent, the painting of the period between the waning of Carolingian art and the full emergence of **Gothic** art in the late twelfth century. Today, scholars view the Romanesque style as a transition between Carolingian and Gothic.

At several places in Ottonian Germany, a return of political stability led to the construction of churches. Ducal dynasties and women of the imperial family were among the most generous patrons. The Germans developed a distinctive architectural style marked by very thick walls, alternating piers and columns in the nave, and galleries. As this architectural style spread all over Europe in the eleventh century, it produced true Romanesque, a style that differed from Roman and Carolingian styles, mainly in the greater internal height and space made possible by vaulting (see **Figure 10.1**). To the rectangular elegance of the classical basilica and the height of the Carolingian westworks (see page 217), Romanesque builders added a refined verticality. Among the distinctive features of Romanesque churches are their wall paintings and frescoes, sculpture, reliquaries, pulpits, and baptisteries—in short, their exuberant decoration and ornament.

---

**Romanesque** The name assigned to architecture "in the Roman style" that dominated the period from about 900 to 1150.

**Gothic** The name assigned to the architecture that emerged in twelfth-century France, spread all over Europe, and dominated construction until the fifteenth century.

**Barrel vault**

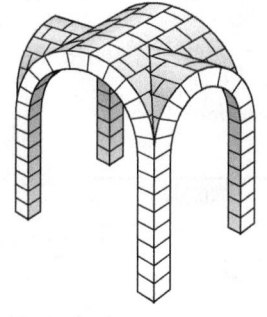

**Groin vault**

**Figure 10.1** The Structure of Romanesque Architecture   The basic structural element of Romanesque architecture was the barrel vault, which, when two were joined at right angles, formed a groin vault. These vaults produced great height and strength but gave buildings a massive, fortresslike appearance.

(Source: Anne Shaver-Crandell, *The Middle Ages*. Copyright © 1982 Cambridge University Press. Reprinted with permission of Cambridge University Press.)

**Romanesque Interior, Saint Sernin, Toulouse** The interior space of Saint Sernin is elegant, high, and well-ordered. But its typical Romanesque effect—from "barrel" vaulting—is that of a tunnel. Massive piers support the gallery and roofing above. Éditions Gaud

**Gothic Interior, Chartres Cathedral** Looking down the early-thirteenth-century nave of Chartres Cathedral provides an opportunity to visualize each of the major building components of Gothic architecture: pointed arch, ribbed vault, point support. The desired verticality is evident. Éditions Gaud

**Figure 10.2 The Structure of Gothic Architecture** The adoption of pointed arches, an import from the Islamic world, let Gothic builders join structures of identical height but different widths (something that barrel and groin vaulting could not do; see Figure 10.1 on page 282). The resulting structures were high, light, airy, and visually interesting.

(Source: Anne Shaver-Crandell, *The Middle Ages.* Copyright © 1982 Cambridge University Press. Reprinted with permission of Cambridge University Press.)

It is surely no coincidence that Gothic art and architecture emerged just as the West was absorbing the rediscovery of Euclid's mathematical writings and applying the intensely ordered logic of Aristotle to everything from legal problems to theological mysteries. One of the most familiar images of the Middle Ages is the inspiringly beautiful Gothic cathedral. It is thus ironic that the word *Gothic* first appeared in the sixteenth century as a term of derision for what was then regarded as an outmoded style so ugly that only the horrible conquerors of Rome, the Goths, could have been responsible for it. The name stuck, but today, it simply identifies a period in European architecture, sculpture, and painting that began in the middle of the twelfth century and that in some places lasted until the early sixteenth century.

Gothic is a French invention. It was Abbot Suger (SOO-jhay) (1085–1151) of Saint-Denis, a monastery outside Paris, who, in rebuilding his basilica beginning in 1135, consciously sought a new style. He desired to achieve effects of lightness, almost weightlessness, in the stonework of his church and to admit large amounts of light to create a dazzling and mysterious aura on the inside. The Bible often uses images of light to refer to God, and Suger wished to give expression to those images in the house of God for which he was responsible.

Suger produced something startlingly original by combining a number of elements that had long been in use—three in particular: A *pointed arch* is more elegant than a round one; it also permits the joining of two arches of identical height but different widths, which, in turn, permits complex shapes and sizes (see **Figure 10.2**). The *ribbed vault* is lighter and more graceful than the barrel and groin vaults characteristic of Romanesque architecture; it also exerts less stress and facilitates experimentation with shapes. Finally, *point support*—basically, the support of structural elements at only certain points—permits the replacement of heavy, stress-bearing walls with curtains of stained glass. (See the feature, "The Visual Record: Stained Glass" on pages 284–285.)

## Stained Glass

To walk into one of Europe's great churches is to enter a realm of mystery and beauty produced by the play of light—the brilliant light of the morning sun, the softer glow of the evening sun, the muted tones of a cloudy day—on thousands of square feet of colored glass. This mystery and beauty were created intentionally in Europe in the High Middle Ages. But the magnificent surviving medieval windows are not important solely for their beauty. Their images provide unique and crucial insights into religious and secular life.

Pictured here are two thirteenth-century cathedral windows. The one from Canterbury depicts that city's great bishop and martyr, Thomas Becket. A large window at Chartres depicts Saint Lubin, a sixth-century bishop of the city who was the patron saint of the town's inn and tavern keepers, and Noah, according to the Bible the first planter of grapevines. Here, in a window donated by the vintners guild, we see barrels of wine being hauled to market.

Many of Canterbury's windows represent aspects of the life of the murdered archbishop. The one pictured here shows Thomas as a bishop, not as a martyr. He is wearing a miter, the traditional headgear of a bishop. He also wears a *pallium*, a white wool band sent to a new archbishop by the pope. Becket's vestments are green, the most common liturgical color of the religious year (others are white, purple, and red). This window, then, would have served to remind people of their beloved bishop as he was in life, not martyrdom.

In Chartres, wine was important to the church because of its use in mass, and it was also a staple of the local economy. Accordingly, the vintners are portrayed in twenty-three of this window's forty-one panels. By comparison, most guilds are depicted only once in the windows they donated. These windows remind us, as they reminded contemporaries, of how these magnificent buildings fitted into the daily life of their communities. Religious devotions and secular preoccupations blended in one spot.

Glass is made by heating silica, found naturally in sand, flint, and quartz, to a very high temperature and then fusing the molten silicate with a borate or phosphate, often obtained from ashes produced by burning natural substances. Colored glass was made by adding metal oxides to the molten mixture. Iron oxide produced red, copper oxide produced green, and cobalt produced blue. Such glass, called "pot glass," tended to be opaque, obviously unsuitable for windows. To achieve greater translucency, glassmakers made "flashed glass" by fusing at low temperatures a layer of colored liquid to the surface of a panel of clear glass. Although fine glass vessels were made in a number of places, notably in Venice and the Rhineland, the large

**Canterbury, Thirteenth-Century Window: Thomas Becket**

Sonia Halliday Photographs

sheets of colored glass used for church windows were commonly manufactured in Lorraine and Normandy.

To make a stained glass window, a master glazier first drew a cartoon—a sort of rough draft—on a flat board, or perhaps on a piece of parchment. He then cut pieces of colored glass into various irregular shapes according to his design. To produce facial features, folds in garments, or other details, the glazier painted the inner sides of the colored glass pieces with dark-colored paints and then fired them at low temperatures to produce an enamel-like effect.

**Chartres, Thirteenth-Century Window:
Story of Saint Lubin**

You can see this patina on Thomas's face. Once the glazier had all his pieces cut and placed, he joined them by means of lead strips that were H shaped. If you look closely, you can see the pieces of glass, lead stripping, and painted details in the images on these pages. The whole picture was then fitted into a metal frame and mounted in a window opening.

Documents first mention the use of glass in church windows in the sixth century. The oldest surviving fragments of stained glass date from the ninth century, and the oldest complete windows from around 1100. With large Romanesque churches, and even more with the huge Gothic churches, came opportunities to use more and more glass. First, the greater height of Romanesque buildings meant that tall windows could be placed high up in the nave walls. Then, the structural innovations of Gothic architecture that removed stress, and hence stone, from the walls permitted them to become vast expanses of glass. Chartres Cathedral has 176 windows. Many high medieval churches had windows more than 50 feet high.

So far, we have looked at *how* medieval Europeans created stained glass and incorporated it into their greatest churches. But *why* did they undertake such time-consuming and costly decoration? Suger, the scholarly twelfth-century abbot of Saint-Denis outside Paris who rebuilt his basilica in the Gothic style, spoke of the spiritual force of his new glass windows:

> When . . . the loveliness of the many-colored gems has called me away from external cares . . . then it seems to me that I see myself dwelling in some strange region of the universe which neither exists entirely in the slime of the earth nor entirely in the purity of heaven; and that, by the grace of God, I can be transported from this inferior to that higher world.*

In the Greek philosophers, the Bible, and the Church Fathers, light always represents one way of imagining the unimaginable reality of God. For Suger and his contemporaries, the luminous effect of stained glass suggested the very presence of God. Earthquakes, fires, and wars have destroyed most of the glass that was installed in the Middle Ages. Today's visitor to Europe views more or less valid nineteenth-century reconstructions, except at Canterbury in England and Chartres in France, where almost all of the original glass survives. Usually medieval churches were laid out on an east-west axis. The western façade was normally pierced by tall "lancet" windows and by a single "rose" window. These windows typically portrayed scenes from the life of Christ and/or the Virgin Mary. The northern aisle windows usually contained Old Testament scenes, the southern windows New Testament scenes.

Stained glass played a key role, alongside sculpture, preaching, and churchyard dramas, in communicating the faith to ordinary people. Seldom has a teaching tool been so beautiful. Scholars also speak of stained glass as "painting with glass." Indeed, the art form most like stained glass is painting, especially the painting of illuminations on the pages of manuscripts.

## Questions

1. *How was stained glass made and assembled into windows?*

2. *What kinds of subjects were depicted on stained glass windows?*

3. *Who was the audience for stained glass windows?*

---

*Suger, *De rebus in administratione sua gestis*, 2d ed., ed. E. Panofsky, (Princeton, N.J.: Princeton University Press, 1979), pp. 63–65.

## SECTION SUMMARY

- Vernacular literature spread quickly and widely in high medieval Europe.
- Vernacular literature produced *chansons de geste*, romances, lays, sagas, and poetry.
- The High Middle Ages saw the full flowering of Romanesque architecture and then its eclipse by the Gothic style.

The points of support might be massive internal piers or intricate skeletal frameworks, called *buttresses*, on the outside of the church. These three elements—pointed arch, ribbed vault, and point support—produce a building that is characterized by verticality and translucency. The desired effect is one of harmony, order, and mathematical precision.

The thirteenth century was the most mature period for French Gothic architecture and also the time when Gothic spread most widely throughout Europe. Its popularity may be attributed to the superiority of French masons and stone-cutters and also to the tremendous prestige of French culture. By 1300, distinctive Gothic traditions shaped the urban landscape in almost all parts of Europe from Iceland to Poland.

## Chapter Summary

Comparisons between the Europe of 900 and the Europe of 1300 are instructive both as reminders of what had happened and as suggestions of what was to come. In 900, Carolingian Europe was being attacked on every side. By 1300, Europe was vastly larger than in Carolingian times; not only was its geography greater, but it also had expanded in economic, political, military, and cultural terms.

◆ *Into what principal social groups were the people of high medieval Europe organized?*

At least among the elite, society was divided into "those who pray," "those who fight," and "those who work." Constant waves of monastic reform modeled good spiritual behavior, and monks thought of themselves as society's natural leaders. Bishops embraced reform, too, but as they were often nobles, their views were more flexible than those held by monks. They also saw themselves as leaders. Warrior-nobles *were* the governing class, marked by chivalry, their distinctive ethos that emphasized prowess, courage, loyalty, and generosity. Peasants did much of the "work" in medieval society and generally found the conditions of their lives improving. Townspeople enjoyed expanding opportunities but always suffered under the prejudices of landholding elites. In religious life, urban occupations, and rural pursuits, women experienced some improvements in their conditions of life but always faced legal and social prejudices. The condition of Europe's Jews grew progressively dangerous.

◆ *Why did some spiritual movements result in heresy, while others ended in new religious orders?*

The High Middle Ages saw the birth of powerful religious movements. Some men and women who opposed the wealth and immorality of some clerics, and who wished to preach and teach, veered off into heresy. The mendicants—Franciscans and Dominicans, chiefly—led holy and blameless lives, worked among the poor or preached against heretics, and always had the approval of the papacy. Several religious movements were especially popular among women and constituted the first exclusively women's movements in the history of Christianity.

◆ *What signs do you find of an expanding intellectual climate in high medieval Europe?*

Latin studies in literature, law, theology, and philosophy remained important. Europe's expansion brought scholars into increasing contact with ancient Greek, Jewish, and Arab thought, which spurred new research and opened new questions. The increasing prominence of logic drove theology and philosophy to the center of the curriculum and led to the production of majestic summas, compendiums of knowledge in various fields. Formed as guilds of either masters or students, universities were among the most original and durable medieval achievements.

◆ *What were the hallmarks of vernacular culture?*

Vernacular literature, literature in "native" languages, spread quickly and widely in high medieval Europe, achieving visibility and prominence everywhere. Vernacular literature was written in many genres: *chansons de geste*, romances, lays, sagas, and poetry. The High Middle Ages saw the full flowering of Romanesque architecture and then its eclipse by Gothic. Magnificent cathedrals are testimony to the prosperity and pride of high medieval Europe.

# Key Terms

**Cluny** (p. 260)

**Francis of Assisi** (p. 269)

**Dominic de Guzman** (p. 270)

**canon law** (p. 273)

**Bernard of Clairvaux** (p. 275)

**Hildegard of Bingen** (p. 275)

**Thomas Aquinas** (p. 276)

*summa* (p. 276)

**chivalry** (p. 280)

**Romanesque** (p. 282)

**Gothic** (p. 282)

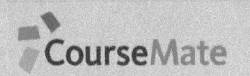 **CourseMate**

Go to the CourseMate website at **www.cengagebrain.com** for additional study tools and review materials—including audio and video clips—for this chapter.

**A Time of Judgment** On this cover for a fifteenth-century government account book, symbols of death—arrows, a scythe, and a horse—carry the angel of death from place to place. bpk, berlin/Kunstgewerbemuseum,Staatliche Museen, Berlin, Germany/Saturia Linke/Art Resource, NY

# Crisis and Recovery in Late Medieval Europe, 1300–1500

In the fourteenth century, Europeans sang an old Franciscan hymn, "Day of Wrath, Day of Burning." Its verses described the fear and disorder that would accompany the end of the world and God's judgment of the saved and the damned. That hymn could well have been in the mind of the painter of the facing illustration. When countless Europeans, such as these poor souls beneath the winged angel of death, fell victim to epidemic disease, many people thought they knew why. The illustrator seems to believe it was God's judgment against sinners, including these gamblers sickened by the angel's plague-tipped arrows. The flood, fire, and pestilence that ravaged late medieval Europe were thought to be premonitions of the breakdown of the world and a time of judgment.

The late Middle Ages (ca. 1300–1500) are often described as a period of continued crisis and decline that put an end to the growth and expansion of the previous three centuries. In truth, however, the years of crisis in the fourteenth and early fifteenth centuries gave way to a dramatic economic, social, and political recovery in the fifteenth century. The cultural and intellectual changes that accompanied the crisis and recovery are the focus of Chapter 12, "The Renaissance."

Questions of power and representation affected the Christian church as ecclesiastical claims to authority came under attack. Secular governments challenged church jurisdictions. Disputed papal elections led to the so-called Great Schism, a split between rival centers of control in Rome and Avignon (a city in what is now the south of France). In the aftermath of the crisis, the papacy was forced to redefine its place in both the religious life and the political life of Europe.

These crises were all intertwined. A struggle over church authority could only be solved through the intervention of secular powers. Yet the ability of these states to act was limited by war and dynastic claims.

Between 1337 and 1453, France and England fought a war that touched most of the states of western Europe. The Hundred Years' War, as it has come to be known, was fought primarily over English claims to traditionally French lands. Aristocrats in many parts of Europe challenged the hereditary rights of their rulers. In the towns of Germany

## Chapter Overview

### The Crisis of the Western Christian Church

- *How did the Great Schism change the church and the papacy?*

### War and the Struggle over Political Power, 1300–1450

- *What forces limited the political power of rulers in England, France, and Italy?*

### Crisis in Economy and Society

- *How were economic and social structures changed by plague and economic crisis?*

### The Consolidation of Political Power, 1450–1500

- *How did the political makeup of Europe in 1500 differ from that in 1300?*

and Italy, patrician classes moved to reduce the influence of artisans and laborers in government, instituting oligarchies or even aristocratic lordships in place of more demo-cratic governments.

A series of economic and demographic shocks worsened these political and religious difficulties. Part of the problem was structural: The population of Europe had grown too large to be supported by the resources available. Famine and the return of the plague in 1348 sent the economy into long-term decline. In almost every aspect of political, reli-gious, and social life, then, the fourteenth and early fifteenth centuries marked a pause in the growth and consolidation that had characterized the earlier medieval period.

Yet, out of the crises, a number of significant changes emerged. By 1500, the European population and economy were again expanding. England and France emerged strengthened by military and political conflicts, and the consolidation of the Spanish kingdoms, the Ottoman Empire, and the states of eastern Europe altered the political and social makeup of Europe. None of the transformations could have been predicted in 1300, as Europe entered a religious, political, and social whirlwind.

# The Crisis of the Western Christian Church

How did the Great Schism change the church and the papacy?

Early in the fourteenth century, the king of France attempted to kidnap the pope. His act initiated a series of crises that challenged traditional ideas about church government and the role of the church in the various countries of Europe. First, the popes and their entourages abandoned their traditional residences in central Italy and moved to Avignon, an imperial enclave in the south of modern France. Then, in the wake of a disputed election, two and later three rivals claimed the papal throne. Simultaneously, the church hierarchy faced challenges from radical reformers who wished to change it. At various times, all the European powers became entangled in the problems of the church. In the wake of the crisis, the papacy real-ized that it needed a stronger, independent base. Papal recovery in the fifteenth century was predicated on political autonomy in central Italy.

## The Babylonian Captivity, 1309–1377

The Christian church was in turmoil as a result of an attack on Pope Boniface VIII (r. 1294–1303) by King Philip IV (r. 1285–1314) of France. The king attempted to kidnap Boniface, intending to try him for heresy because of the pope's challenges to the king's authority within his own kingdom. The outstanding issues revolved around the powers of the pope and the responsibilities of the clergy to political leaders. It was, in fact, largely because of tensions with the northern kingdoms that the French archbishop of Bordeaux (bor-DOE) was elected Pope Clement V (r. 1305–1314). Clement, unlike Boniface, tried to work with the monarchs. He chose to remain north of the Alps in order to seek an end to warfare between France and England and to protect, to the extent possible, the wealthy religious order of the Knights of the Temple, or Templars (see page 261), which Philip was in the process of suppressing.

Clement's pontificate marked the beginning of the so-called Babylonian Captivity, a period from 1309 to 1378, when popes resided almost continuously outside of Italy. In 1309, Clement moved the papal court to Avignon, on the Rhône River in a region that was still part of the Holy Roman Empire—the name that, by the fourteenth century, was given to the medieval empire whose origin reached back to Charlemagne.

The papacy and its new residence in Avignon became a major religious, diplomatic, and commercial center. In the course of creating Europe's most magnificent court, the image of the papacy changed. Clement VI observed, "my predecessors did not know how to be pope."*

**Babylonian Captivity of the Papacy** Term used to describe the period from 1309 to 1378 when popes resided outside of Italy, relating the pontificate's move to the period when the tribes of Israel lived in exile.

*Quoted in L Pastor, *History of the Popes*, vol 1 (London, 1891), p. 92.

Thirteenth-century papal administration required only two hundred or so officials; the new court in Avignon required six hundred. It was not just the pope's immediate circle that expanded the population of Avignon. Artists, writers, lawyers, and merchants from across Europe were drawn to the new center of administration and hub of patronage. Papal administrators intervened actively in local ecclesiastical affairs, and the pope's revenues from annates (generally a portion of the first year's revenues from an ecclesiastical office granted by papal letter), court fees, and provisioning charges continued to grow.

Not everyone approved of this situation. It was the Italian poet and philosopher Francesco Petrarch (1304–1374) who first referred to the Avignon move as a **Babylonian Captivity of the Papacy**. Recalling the account in the Hebrew Bible of the exile of the Israelites and New Testament images of Babylon as the center of sin and immorality, he complained of

[an] unholy Babylon, Hell on Earth, a sink of iniquity, the cesspool of the world. There is neither faith, nor charity, nor religion. . . .*

Two of the most vigorous critics were Saint Catherine of Siena (1347–1380) and Saint Bridget of Sweden (1303–1373). They were part of a remarkable flowering of religious feeling among women who were strong moral critics within their communities. Unlike others, Catherine and Bridget left their homes and neighborhoods and led the call for religious reform and a return of the papacy to Rome. "Sweet Daddy," Catherine pleaded, "[God] demands justice. . . in his Holy Church."**

## The Great Schism, 1378–1417

In 1377, Pope Gregory XI (r. 1370–1378) bowed to critics' pressure and did return to Rome. He was shocked by what he found: churches and palaces in ruin and the city violent and dangerous. By the end of 1377, he had resolved to retreat to Avignon, but he died before he could flee Rome. During a tumultuous election, the Roman populace entered the Vatican Palace and threatened to break into the conclave itself, demanding that there be an Italian pope. The subsequent election of the archbishop of Bari, Urban VI (r. 1378–1389), was soon challenged by dissidents who then elected a French cardinal who took the name Clement VII (r. 1378–1394). The church now had two popes.

After some hesitation, Western Christians divided into two camps, initiating the **Great Schism** (SKIZ-em), a period of almost forty years during which no one knew for sure who was the true pope. This was a deadly serious issue for all. The true pope had the right to appoint church officials, decide important moral and legal issues, and allow or forbid taxation of the clergy by the state.

The crisis gave impetus to new discussions about church government: Should the pope be considered the sole head of the church? Representative bodies—the English Parliament,

## CHRONOLOGY

| | |
|---|---|
| 1303 | Pope Boniface VIII attacked at Anagni and dies |
| 1305 | Election of Pope Clement V |
| 1309 | Clement V moves papal court to Avignon; beginning of Babylonian Captivity |
| 1337 | Beginning of Hundred Years' War between England and France |
| 1348–1351 | Black Death |
| 1356 | German emperor issues Golden Bull |
| 1378 | Great Schism |
| 1381 | English Rising |
| 1397 | Union of Kalmar unites Denmark, Norway, and Sweden |
| 1410 | Battle of Tannenberg |
| 1414–1418 | Council of Constance |
| 1415 | Battle of Agincourt |
| 1420 | Treaty of Troyes |
| 1431 | Execution of Joan of Arc |
| 1438 | Pragmatic Sanction of Bourges |
| 1453 | End of the Hundred Years' War / Ottoman Turks conquer Constantinople |
| 1469 | Marriage of Ferdinand and Isabella unites kingdoms of Aragon and Castile |
| 1480 | Ivan III ends Tatar overlordship of Moscow |
| 1485 | Tudor dynasty established in England |
| 1492 | Spanish conquest of Granada / Jews expelled from Spanish lands / Columbus commissioned to discover new lands |
| 1494 | Charles VIII invades Italy |

**Great Schism** The period from 1378 to 1417 when there were two and eventually three claimants to the papal throne.

*Quoted in Guillaume Mollat, *The Popes at Avignon, 1305–1378* (London: Thomas Nelson, 1963), p. 112.
**Robert Coogan, *Babylon on the Rhone: A Translation of Letters by Dante, Petrarch, and Catherine of Siena on the Avignon Papacy* (Potomac, Maryland: Studia Humanitatis, 1983), p. 115.

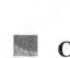

**Gregory XI Returns to Rome** This highly stylized painting conveys the hopes of European Christians when Gregory XI returned from Avignon in 1377. Saint Catherine of Siena, who had pleaded for the pope's return, is seen in the foreground.

the French Estates General, the Swedish Riksdag (RIX-dog)—already claimed the right to act for the realm, and in the city-states of Italy, ultimate authority was thought to reside in the body of citizens. Canon lawyers and theologians similarly argued that authority resided in the whole church, which had the right and duty to come together in council to correct and reform the church hierarchy. Even the most conservative of these **conciliarists** agreed that the "universal church" had the right to respond in periods of heresy or schism. More radical conciliarists argued that the pope as bishop of Rome was merely the first among equals in the church hierarchy and that he, like any other bishop, could be corrected by a gathering of his peers—that is, by an ecumenical council.

**conciliarists** People who argued that the pope was merely "the first among equals" and that therefore a council of church leaders could correct or discipline a pope.

The rival popes resisted international pressure to end the schism. In exasperation, the cardinals, the main ecclesiastical supporters of the rival popes, called a general council in Pisa, which deposed both popes and elected a new one. Since the council lacked the power to force the rivals to accept deposition, the result was that three men now claimed to be the rightful successor of Saint Peter. Conciliarists, by themselves, could not mend the split in the church.

Resolution finally came when the Holy Roman emperor Sigismund (r. 1411–1437) forced the diplomatically isolated third papal claimant, John XXIII (r. 1410–1415), to call a general council of the church. The council, which met from 1414 to 1418 in the German imperial city of Constance, could never have succeeded without Sigismund's support. At one point, he forced the council to remain in session even after Pope John had fled the city in an attempt to end deliberations.

## Heresy and the Council of Constance, 1414–1418

Sigismund hoped that a council could help him heal deep religious and civil divisions in Bohemia, the most important part of his family's traditional lands (see **Map 11.3**). Far from healing religious division, however, the actions of the council exacerbated tensions in central Europe and created a climate of religious distrust that poisoned relations for more than a century. Bohemia and its capital, Prague, were Czech-speaking. Prague was also the seat of the Luxemburg dynasty of German emperors and the site of the first university in German or Slavic lands. Religious and theological questions quickly became entangled with the competing claims of Czech and German factions. The preaching and teaching of the Czech reformer Jan Hus (ca. 1370–1415) were at the center of the debate. His criticisms of the church hierarchy, which in Prague was primarily German, fanned into flames the smoldering embers of Czech national feeling. It was Sigismund's hope that a council might clarify the orthodoxy of Hus's teachings and heal the rift within the church of Bohemia.

**Jan Hus** Czech reformer who attacked clerical privileges and advocated church reform. He was executed as a heretic at the Council of Constance in 1415.

The council's response to the theological crisis was based on the church's experience with heresy over the previous forty years, primarily the teachings of John Wyclif (1329–1384). In the 1370s, Wyclif, an Oxford theologian and parish priest, began to criticize in increasingly angry terms the state of the clergy and the abuses of the church hierarchy. By 1387, his ideas had been declared heretical and his followers were hunted out. Wyclif believed that the church could be at once a divine institution and an earthly gathering of individuals. Thus, in his opinion, individual Christians need not unquestioningly obey the pronouncements of the church hierarchy. Final authority lay only in the Scriptures, insisted Wyclif, who sponsored the first translations of the Bible into English. He gathered about himself followers called "Lollards," who emphasized Bible reading and popular piety; some even supported public preaching by women. According to one disciple, "Every true man and woman being in charity is a priest."[*]

Wyclif's influence continued on the Continent, especially in the circle of Jan Hus and the Czech reformers. By 1403, the German majority in the university had condemned Hus's teaching as Wycliffite, thus initiating almost a decade of struggle between Czechs and Germans, Hussites and Catholics. This was the impasse that Sigismund hoped the **Council of Constance** could settle. Accordingly, he offered a suspicious Hus a safe conduct pass to attend the council. The council, however, revoked the pledge of safe conduct and ordered Hus to recant his beliefs. He refused and the council condemned him as a heretic and burned him at the stake on July 6, 1415.

**Council of Constance** General council of the church convened by the Holy Roman emperor to deal with schism and church reform. It elected Pope Martin V to end the Great Schism.

Far from ending Sigismund's problems with the Bohemians, the actions of the council provided the Czechs with a martyr and hero. The execution of Hus provoked a firestorm of revolution in Prague. Czech forces roundly defeated an imperial army sent in to restore order. The Hussite movement gathered strength and spread throughout Bohemia. Moderate Hussites continued Hus's campaign against clerical abuses and claimed the right to receive both the bread and the wine during the sacrament of Communion. Radical Hussites argued that the true church was the community of spiritual men and women; they had no use for

---

*Quoted in Mary Aston, *Lollards and Reformers: Images and Literacy in Late Medieval Religion* (Ronceverte, W.V.: Hambledon, 1984), p. 60.

**The Execution of Jan Hus** Stripped of the signs of ecclesiastical office, Jan Hus was forced to wear a paper hat indicating he was a heresiarch, the leader of heretics. This and similar images were meant to show the legitimacy of his execution, but in Bohemia he was revered as a martyred saint.

ecclesiastical hierarchy of any kind. The German emperors were unable to defeat a united Hussite movement. In 1433, a new church council and moderate Hussites negotiated an agreement that allowed the Hussites to continue some of their practices, including receiving both bread and wine at Communion, while returning to the church. Radical Hussites refused the compromise, and the war dragged on until 1436. Bohemia remained a center of religious dissent, and the memory of Hus's execution at a church council would have a chilling effect on discussions of church reform during the Reformation in the sixteenth century.

## The Reunion and Reform of the Papacy, 1415–1513

To most of the delegates at the Council of Constance, the reunion and reform of the papacy were more important than the issue of heresy. And as we will see, attempts to deal with reform and reunion seemed in the eyes of the popes to threaten the political independence and the moral leadership of the papacy itself. This too would remain a problem well into the sixteenth century.

The council deposed two papal claimants and forced the third to resign. Then, in 1417, the council elected a Roman nobleman as Pope Martin V (r. 1417–1431). The council justified its actions in what was perhaps its most important decree, *Haec sancta synodus* ("This sacred synod"): "This sacred synod of Constance . . . declares . . . that it has its power immediately from Christ, and that all men . . . including even the pope himself are bound to obey it in those matters that pertain to the faith."* Popes could no longer expect to remain unchallenged; claims to ecclesiastical rights and jurisdictions increasingly were matters for negotiation.

---

*Quoted in Francis Oakley, *The Western Church in the Later Middle Ages* (Ithaca, N.Y.: Cornell University Press, 1979), pp. 65-66.

Reform was more difficult. Both the cardinals and the popes viewed any reforms to the present system as threats to their ability to function. The council, however, recognized the need for further reforms. A second reform council met at Basel from 1431 to 1449, but with modest results. The council again tried to reduce papal power, but this time it received little support from European governments.

Because of the continuing conciliarist threat, the papacy needed the support of the secular rulers of Europe. Thus, the papacy was forced to accept compromises on the issues of reform, on ecclesiastical jurisdictions and immunities, and on papal revenues. Various governments argued that it was they, and not the pope, who should be responsible for ecclesiastical institutions and jurisdictions within their territories.

Lay rulers wanted church officials in their territories to belong to local families. They wanted ecclesiastical institutions to be subject to local laws and administration. By the 1470s, it was clear that they wanted to have local prelates named as cardinal-protectors. These were not churchmen who could serve the church administration in Rome; rather they functioned as mediators between local governments and the papacy.

The reunited papacy had to accept claims it would have staunchly opposed a century earlier. One of the most important of these was the Pragmatic Sanction of Bourges of 1438. The papacy was unable to protest when the French clergy, at the urging of the king, abolished papal rights to annates, limited appeals to the papal court, and reduced papal rights to appoint clergy within France without the approval of the local clergy or the Crown. Similar concessions diminished church authority throughout Europe.

With reduced revenues from legal fees, annates, and appointments, the popes of the fifteenth century were forced to derive more and more of their revenue and influence from the Papal States. By 1430, the Papal States accounted for about half of the annual income of the papacy. Papal interests increasingly centered on protecting the papacy's influence as a secular ruler of a large territory in central Italy. Further, it saw political independence as essential to its continued moral leadership. Thus, the papacy had to deal with many of the same jurisdictional, diplomatic, and military challenges that faced other medieval governments.

### SECTION SUMMARY

- A political crisis forced the papacy to abandon central Italy and move to the south of France.
- A disputed papal election left two claimants—one French, the other Italian—and no clear way to resolve the issue.
- The religious beliefs of John Wyclif and Jan Hus challenged the basis of papal authority.
- In addition to resolving the disputed election, conciliarists claimed authority to correct and reform the papacy.
- By 1450, the papacy was reunited but weakened in relation to the European kingdoms.

# War and the Struggle over Political Power, 1300–1450

*What forces limited the political power of rulers in England, France, and Italy?*

A lawyer who served King Philip IV of France (r. 1285–1314) observed that "everything within the limits of his kingdom belongs to the lord king, especially protection, high justice and dominion."[*] Royal officials in England and France generally believed that "liberties"— that is, individual rights to local jurisdictions—originated with the king. These ideas were the result of several centuries of centralization of political power in royal hands. At almost the same time, however, an English noble challenged royal claims on his lands, saying, "Here, my lords, is my warrant," as he brandished a rusty long sword. "My ancestors came with William the Bastard [that is, William the Conqueror, in 1066] and conquered their lands with the sword, and by the sword I will defend them against anyone who tries to usurp them."[**] The views of the royal lawyer and the feisty earl exemplify the central tension over power in

---

*Quoted in Charles T. Wood, *Joan of Arc and Richard III* (New York: Oxford University Press, 1988), pp. 56-57.
**Quoted in Michael T. Clanchy, "Law, Government, and Society in Medieval England," *History* 59 (1974): 75.

**Hundred Years' War**
Series of conflicts, 1337–1453, fought over English claims within the French monarchy. It ended with the nearly complete expulsion of the English from French lands.

the late Middle Ages. The struggle over political power was played out in the context of the **Hundred Years' War**, which affected not just England and France but also most of western Europe, especially Italy, as mercenary soldiers traveled south during temporary lulls in the fighting. In England and France, the crisis led to strengthened monarchies. In Italy, however, local and regional entities exercised many of those liberties the old Englishman wanted to protect with his sword.

## The Hundred Years' War, 1337–1453

In the twelfth and thirteenth centuries, centralization of royal power in England and France had proceeded almost without interruption. In the fourteenth century, matters changed in both countries. Questions of the nature of royal power, common responsibility, and hereditary rights to rule challenged the power of the English and French monarchs. In both countries, competition began largely over dynastic issues, but by the mid-fifteenth century, resolution of the wars led to governments with a more distinctly national tone to them.

### England

In England, fears arising from the growing power of the English crown and the weakness of a gullible king brought issues to a head during the reign of Edward II (r. 1307–1327). By the early fourteenth century, the barons, the titled lords of England, feared that Edward II would continue many of the centralizing policies of his father, so they passed reform ordinances in 1311, limiting the king's right to wage war, leave the realm, grant lands or castles, or appoint chief justices and chancellors without the approval of Parliament, which they dominated. Special taxes or subsidies were to be paid to the public Exchequer rather than into the king's private treasury. Some of these ordinances were later voided, but the tradition of parliamentary consent remained a key principle of English constitutional history.

The baronial influence grew because Edward II was a weak and naive king, easily influenced by court favorites. After a humiliating defeat at the hands of the Scots at the Battle of Bannockburn (1314), his position steadily deteriorated until he was deposed in 1327 by a coalition of barons led by his wife, Queen Isabella. After a short regency, their son, Edward III (r. 1327–1377), assumed the throne. He was a cautious king, ever aware of the violence and rebelliousness of the baronage.

### France

French kings seemed significantly more powerful in the early fourteenth century. A complex succession crisis, however, made clear the limits of French kingship. In 1328, the direct Capetian line, which had sired the kings of France since the election of Hugh Capet in 987, finally died out. The last Capetians did produce daughters, but by the fourteenth century, many argued that according to custom the French crown should pass through the male line only. Thus, the French nobility selected as king Philip of Valois (Philip VI; r. 1328–1350), a cousin of the last king through the male line (Charles IV; r. 1322–1328). He was chosen in preference to the daughters of the last Capetian kings and, more significantly, in preference to King Edward III of England, whose mother, Isabella, was the daughter of King Philip IV (r. 1285–1314).

Controversy over succession was just one of the disputes between the French and English. An even longer-standing issue was the status of lands within France that belonged to the English kings. In 1340, climaxing a century of tensions over English possessions in France, Edward III of England formally claimed the title "King of France," and the Hundred Years' War was on.

The war was marked by quick English raids and only occasional pitched battles. With a population of about 16 million, France was far richer and more populous than England. On at least one occasion, the French managed to field an army of over 50,000; the English mustered only 32,000 at most. These armies were easily the largest ever assembled by a medieval European kingdom. In almost every engagement, the English were outnumbered. Their strategy, therefore, was to avoid pitched battles except on the most advantageous terms.

## FRENCH AND ENGLISH SUCCESSION IN THE FOURTEENTH CENTURY

© Cengage Learning 2014

Edward III engaged in extremely destructive raids, hoping to lure the French into ill-considered attacks. The English stole what they could, destroyed what they could not steal, and captured enemy knights to hold for ransom.

## Stages of the War

The war can be divided into four stages. The first stage (1337–1360) was characterized by a rapid series of English assaults and victories. The few pitched battles, including Crécy (1346) and Poitiers (1356), show how Edward's strategy worked (see **Map 11.1**). In these cases, the English gathered their forces in careful defensive positions and took advantage of an individualistic French chivalric ethos according to which, in the words of one knight, "who does the most is worth the most." The key to the English defensive position was the use of longbowmen and cannon. Arrows from the longbow had more penetrating power than a bolt from a crossbow, and the longbow could be fired much more rapidly. By 1300, Europeans had forged cannon for use in siege warfare and to protect defensive positions. Although there is a debate over how effective they were, when used in combination with the longbow, they effectively disrupted and scattered advancing troops.

In the second stage of the war (1360–1396), French forces responded more cautiously to the English tactics and slowly regained much of the territory they had lost. However, during this stage, the disruptions and expenses of war placed a huge burden on both French and English society. First, in the wake of the French defeat at Poitiers in 1356, France was rocked by a series of urban and rural revolts and protests. Later, in 1381, the English faced a similar series of protests over taxes and the costs of war. Finally, because of stress over the war and general noble dissatisfaction, Richard II was forced to abdicate the English throne. Parliament then elected as king Henry IV (r. 1399–1413), the first ruler from the House of Lancaster. Richard died in prison under mysterious circumstances in 1400.

A fateful shift occurred in the third stage of the war (1396–1422). King Charles VI (r. 1380–1422) of France suffered bouts of insanity throughout his long reign, which made effective French government almost impossible. The English king Henry V (r. 1413–1422) renewed his family's claim to the French throne. At Agincourt in 1415, the English (led by Henry himself) again enticed a larger French army into attacking an English position fortified by longbows and cannon. By the terms of the Treaty of Troyes (1420), Charles VI's son (the future Charles VII) was declared illegitimate and disinherited; Henry married Catherine, the daughter of Charles VI, and he was declared the legitimate heir to the French throne. A final English victory seemed assured, but both Charles VI and Henry V died in 1422, leaving Henry's infant son, Henry VI (r. 1422–1461), to inherit both thrones.

Bibliotheque nationale de France (BN Ms Fr 87 fol 138)

**The Introduction of Cannons** The Hundred Years war saw the first significant use of cannons. Although they initially were difficult to move, they were especially effective in siege warfare.

The kings' deaths ushered in the final stage of the Hundred Years' War (1422–1453), the French reconquest. In 1428, military and political power seemed firmly in the hands of the English and the great aristocrats. Yet, in a stunning series of events, the French were able to reverse the situation.

## Joan of Arc

In 1429, with the aid of the mysterious **Joan of Arc** (d. 1431), the French king, Charles VII, was able to raise the English siege of Orléans (or-lay-OHN) and begin the reconquest of the north of France. Joan was the daughter of prosperous peasants from an area of Burgundy that had suffered under the English and their Burgundian allies. Her "voices" told her to go to the king and assist him in driving out the English. Like many late medieval mystics, she

**Joan of Arc** Charismatic peasant who heard voices telling her to assist the French crown in its war against England. She was captured and executed as a heretic but eventually canonized.

**Map 1 (1337):**

ENGLAND
Southampton
Calais
FLANDERS
PONTHIEU
English Channel
50°N
NORMANDY
Paris
CHAMPAGNE
Seine R.
BRITTANY
MAINE
ANJOU
Loire R.
HOLY
ROMAN
EMPIRE
TOURAINE
BURGUNDY
POITOU
AUVERGNE
AQUITAINE
45°N
Bordeaux
Garonne R.
Saint-Sardos
DAUPHINÉ
Rhône R.
GASCONY
LANGUEDOC
Toulouse
SPAIN
Mediterranean
Sea
40°N

N

0  50 100 Km.
0  50  100 Mi.

**1337**
**(before the Battle of Crécy)**
☐ English holdings
☐ French holdings
☐ Extent of English holdings
after Treaty of Paris, 1259

**Map 2 (1360):**

ENGLAND
Calais
FLANDERS
English Channel
50°N
Rouen
NORMANDY
Paris
CHAMPAGNE
Seine R.
BRITTANY
MAINE
ANJOU
Loire R.
HOLY
ROMAN
EMPIRE
TOURAINE
BURGUNDY
Poitiers
1356
POITOU
AUVERGNE
AQUITAINE
Bordeaux
Garonne R.
DAUPHINÉ
Rhône R.
GASCONY
LANGUEDOC
Toulouse
SPAIN
45°N
Mediterranean
Sea
40°N

**1360**
**(after the Battle of Poitiers)**
☐ English holdings
☐ French holdings
★ Major battle

**Map 3 (ca. 1429):**

ENGLAND
Calais
FLANDERS
Agincourt
1415
English Channel
50°N
Rouen
Reims
NORMANDY
Seine R.
CHAMPAGNE
Paris
Domrémy
BRITTANY
MAINE
ANJOU
Orléans
Loire R.
HOLY
ROMAN
EMPIRE
Bourges
DUCHY OF
BURGUNDY
COUNTY OF
BURGUNDY
TOURAINE
POITOU
AUVERGNE
AQUITAINE
45°N
Bordeaux
Garonne R.
DAUPHINÉ
Rhône R.
GASCONY
LANGUEDOC
Toulouse
SPAIN
Mediterranean
Sea
40°N

**ca. 1429**
**(after the siege of Orléans)**
☐ English holdings      ☐ Burgundian lands allied
☐ French holdings          with England to 1435
★ Major battle

**Map 4 (1453):**

ENGLAND
BRABANT
Calais
FLANDERS
English Channel
50°N
LUXEMBOURG
NORMANDY
Paris
CHAMPAGNE
Seine R.
HOLY
ROMAN
EMPIRE
BRITTANY
MAINE
ANJOU
Loire R.
DUCHY OF
BURGUNDY
COUNTY OF
BURGUNDY
TOURAINE
POITOU
AUVERGNE
AQUITAINE
Castillon-sur-Dordogne
1453
Bordeaux
Garonne R.
DAUPHINÉ
Rhône R.
45°N
GASCONY
LANGUEDOC
Toulouse
40°N

**1453 (end of war)**
☐ English holdings
☐ French holdings
☐ Burgundian lands reconciled
with France after 1453
★ Last battle

© Cengage Learning 2014

🌐 **Map 11.1  England and France in the Hundred Years' War**   The succession of maps suggests both why hit-and-run tactics worked for the English early in the war and why the English were ultimately unable to defeat the French and take control of all of France.

# THE WRITTEN RECORD

## The Inquisition of Joan of Arc

*An important question at the trial of Joan of Arc was whether her acts had any authoritative value: Did the voices she heard originate with God or the Devil? The judges wanted to demonstrate to their own satisfaction that Joan was one of "the sowers of deceitful inventions" of which the Gospels warned. They fully expected that external signs could reveal hidden truths. The following memorandum is a summation of the commission's case against the maid.*

You said that your king received a sign by which he knew you were sent from God, that it was St. Michael, in the company of a host of angels.... You have said that you are certain of future and contingent events that you recognized men you had never seen, through the voices of St. Catherine and St. Margaret.... Regarding this article, the clergy find superstition, divination, ... and vain boasting.

You said that you wore and still wear man's dress at God's command and to His good pleasure, for you had instruction from God to wear this dress, and so you put on a short tunic, jerkin, and hose with many points. You even wear your hair cut above the ears, without keeping about you anything to denote your sex, save what nature has given you.... The clergy declare that you blaspheme against God, despising Him and His sacraments, that you transgress divine law, Holy Scripture and the canons of the Church, ... that you are given to idolatry and worship of yourself and your clothes, according to the customs of the heathen.

You have declared that you know well that God loves certain living persons better than you, and that you learned this by revelation from St. Catherine and St. Margaret; also that those saints speak French, not English, as they are not on the side of the English. And since you knew that your voices were for your king, you began to dislike the Burgundians.... Such matters the clergy pronounce to be a rash and presumptuous assertion, a superstitious divination, a blasphemy uttered against St. Catherine and St. Margaret, and a transgression of the commandment to love our neighbors....

You declared that to those whom you call St. Michael, St. Catherine and St. Margaret, you did reverence, bending the knee ... vowing them your virginity ... now touching these matters, the clergy affirm.. . You are an idolatress, an invoker of demons, an apostate from the faith, a maker of rash statements, a swearer of an unlawful oath.

And you have said ... That you know that all the deeds of which you have been accused in your trial were wrought according to the command of God and that it was impossible for you to do otherwise.... Wherefore the clergy declare you to be schismatic, an unbeliever in the unity and authority of the church, apostate and obstinately erring from the faith.... [The inquisitor admonished her,] "you have believed in apparitions lightly, instead of turning to God in devout prayer to grant you certainty; and you have not consulted prelates or learned ecclesiastics to enlighten yourself: although, considering your condition and the simplicity of your knowledge, you ought to have done so."

### Questions

1. What are the signs that indicated to the judges that Joan was a heretic?

2. Why do the judges believe that Joan's "voices" are false?

---

"The Inquisition of Joan of Arc" from *The Trial of Jeanne d'Arc*, trans. W.P. Barrett, 1932. Reprinted by permission of Gotham House.

---

reported regular visions of divine revelation. Even politically or militarily important female leaders depended initially on religious charisma. One of the tests that supported Joan's claim to divine direction was her identification of Charles, who had disguised himself among his courtiers. Dressed as a man, she was Charles's most famed and feared military leader. With Joan's aid, the king was crowned in the cathedral at Reims, the traditional site of French coronations. Joan was captured during an audacious attack on Paris itself and eventually fell into English hands. Because of her "unnatural dress" and her claim to divine guidance, she was condemned and burned as a heretic in 1431. (See the feature, "The Written Record: The Inquisition of Joan of Arc" above.) A heretic only to the English and their supporters, Joan almost instantly became a symbol of French resistance. Pope Calixtus III reversed the condemnation in 1456, and Joan was canonized in 1920. The heretic became Saint Joan, patron of France.

Despite Joan's capture, the French advance continued. By 1450, the English had lost all their major centers except Calais (ca-LAY). In 1453, the French armies captured the fortress of Castillon-sur-Dordogne (kasti-YON sir dor-DON-ya) in what was to be the last battle of the war (see **Map 11.1**). There was no treaty, only a cessation of hostilities.

The war touched almost every aspect of life in western Europe: political, religious, economic, and social. It ranged beyond the borders of France, as Scotland, Castile, Aragon, and

German principalities were, at various times, drawn into the struggle. French and English support for rival popes prevented early settlement of the Great Schism in the papacy (see page 291). Further, the war caused a general rise in the level of violence in society. As Henry V casually observed, "War without fire is as bland as sausages without mustard."* Because of the highly profitable lightning raids, this war was never bland.

## Italy

Compared with France and England, fourteenth- and fifteenth-century Italy was a land of cities. In northern Europe, a town of over 20,000 or 30,000 people was unusual; only Paris and London boasted more than 100,000 people in the fourteenth century. Yet, at one time or another, in the late Middle Ages, Milan, Venice, Florence, and Naples all had populations near or exceeding 100,000, and countless other Italian towns boasted populations of well over 30,000. Unlike northern European states with their kings or emperors, however, the Italian peninsula lacked a unifying force. The centers of power were in Italy's flourishing cities. Political life revolved around the twin issues of who should dominate city governments and how cities could learn to coexist peacefully.

## City-States

By the late thirteenth century, political power in most Italian towns was divided among three major groups. First was the old urban nobility that could trace its wealth back to grants of property and rights from kings, emperors, and bishops in the tenth and eleventh centuries. Second was the merchant families who had grown wealthy in the twelfth and thirteenth centuries, as Italians led the European economic expansion into the Mediterranean. Third, challenging these entrenched urban groups were the modest artisans and merchants who had organized trade, neighborhood, or militia groups and referred to themselves as the *popolo*, or "people." Townspeople gathered together in factions based on wealth, family, profession, neighborhood, and even systems of clientage that reached back into the villages from which many of them had come. "War and hatred have so multiplied among the Italians," observed one Florentine, "that in every town there is a division and enmity between two parties of citizens."

Riven with factions, townspeople often would turn control of their government over to a *signor* (sin-YOUR), a "lord" or "tyrant," often a local noble with a private army. Once firmly in power, the tyrant often allowed the government to continue to function as it had, requiring only that he control all major political appointments. The process might appear democratic, but it represented a profound shift in power. In the case of Milan, the noble Viscontis (vis-KON-tees) used support from the emperor Henry VII (r. 1308–1313) to drive their opponents out of the city. Eventually holding Milan and its territories as a duchy, the Viscontis, and later their Sforza successors, made marriage alliances with the French crown and created a splendid court culture. In a series of wars between the 1370s and 1450s, the dukes of Milan expanded their political control throughout most of Lombardy, Liguria, and, temporarily, Tuscany. The Viscontis maintained control of the city and much of the region of Lombardy until the last scion of the family died in 1447.

## The Republics

The great republics of Venice and Florence escaped domination by signori, but only by undertaking significant constitutional change. In both republics, political life had been disrupted by the arrival of immigrants and by the demands of recently enriched merchants and speculators for a voice in government. In 1297, reacting to increased competition for influence, the Venetian government began a series of reforms that would come to be known as the "Closing of the Grand Council." This enlarged the council to about eleven hundred members from those families eligible for public office, but its eventual effect was to freeze out subsequent

*A. Buchon, "Choix des Chroniques" (Paris, 1875), p. 565, as quoted in John Gillingham and J. C. Holt, eds., *War and Government in the Middle Ages* (Totowa, N.J.: Barnes & Noble, 1984), p. 85.

arrivals from ever rising to elite status. The Venetian patriciate became a closed urban nobility. Political, factional, and economic tensions were hidden beneath a veneer of serenity as Venetians developed a myth of public-spirited patricians who governed in the interests of all the people, leaving others free to enrich themselves in trade and manufacture.

In Florence, the arguments over citizenship and the right of civic participation disrupted public life. Violent wealthy families, immigrants, and artisans of modest background were cut off from civic participation. A series of reforms, culminating in the Ordinances of Justice of 1293 to 1295, restricted political participation in Florence to members in good standing of certain merchant and artisan guilds. Members of violence-prone families were defined as *Magnate* (literally, "the powerful") and disqualified from holding public office. In spite of the reforms, political power remained concentrated in the hands of the great families, whose wealth was based primarily on banking and mercantile investments. These families used their political influence and economic power to dominate Florentine life.

There were short-lived attempts to reform the system and extend the rights of political participation to include the more modest artisans and laborers. The most dramatic was in 1378, when the Ciompi (CHOMP-ee), unskilled workers in Florence's woolen industry, led a popular revolution hoping to expand participation in government and limit the authority of the guild masters over semiskilled artisans and day laborers. They created new guilds to represent the laborers who had no voice in government. Barely six weeks after the Ciompi insurrection, however, wealthy conservatives began a reaction suppressing, exiling, or executing the leaders of the movement and eventually suppressing the new guilds. Political and economic power was now even more firmly in the grip of influential patricians.

Following a crisis in 1434, brought on by war and high taxes, virtual control of Florentine politics fell into the hands of Cosimo de' Medici (day-MAY-di-chi), the wealthiest banker in the city. From 1434 to 1494, Cosimo, his son Piero, his grandson Lorenzo, and Lorenzo's son dominated the government in Florence. Although the Medicis were always careful to pay homage to Florentine republican traditions, their control was virtually as complete as that of the lords of towns such as Ferrara and Milan.

Indeed, by the middle of the fifteenth century, little differentiated the republics—Florence and Venice—from cities, such as Milan and Mantua, where lords held sway. Although Florentines maintained that they intervened to protect Florentine and Tuscan "liberty" when the Viscontis of Milan threatened Tuscany and central Italy, their interests went beyond simple defense. Relations among the great cities of Milan, Venice, Florence, Rome, and Naples were stabilized by the Peace of Lodi and the creation of the Italian League in 1454. In response to endemic warfare in Italy and the looming threat of the Ottoman Turks in the eastern Mediterranean (see pages 315–317), the five powers agreed to the creation of spheres of influence that would prevent any one of them from expanding at the expense of the others.

## The Italian Wars

The limits of these territorial states became clear when King Charles VIII of France invaded Italy in 1494 to assert his hereditary claim to the kingdom of Naples. The French invasion touched off a devastating series of wars called the Habsburg-Valois Wars (1496–1559). French claims were challenged by the Habsburg emperors and also by the

**The Journey of the Magi** The story of the journey of the Magi to Bethlehem to find the baby Jesus seemed a perfect image of the power and wisdom of rulers. This painting (a detail) of the Magi was commissioned for the private chapel of Cosimo de' Medici, the de facto ruler of Florence.

Scala/Art Resource, NY

Spanish, who themselves made claims on southern Italy and much of Lombardy. The cost of prolonged warfare kept almost all governments in a state of crisis.

In Florence, the wars destroyed the old Medici-dominated regime and brought in a new republican government. Anti-Medici efforts were initially led by the popular Dominican preacher Girolamo Savonarola (1452–1498). In the constitutional debates after 1494, Savonarola argued that true political reform required a sweeping purge of the evils of society. Gangs of youth flocked to his cause, attacking prostitutes and homosexuals. Many of his followers held "bonfires of vanities," burning wigs, silks, and other luxuries. In 1498, when his followers had lost influence in the government, Savonarola was arrested, tortured, and executed.

In spite of republican reforms, new fortresses, and a citizen militia, the Florentine government was unable to defend itself from papal and imperial armies. In 1512, the Habsburg emperor restored Medici control of Florence. The Medicis later became dukes and then grand dukes of Tuscany. The grand duchy of Tuscany remained an independent, integrated, and well-governed state until the French Revolution of 1789. Venice also managed to maintain its republican form of government and its territorial state until the French Revolution, but like the grand dukes of Tuscany, the governors of Venice were no longer able to act independently of the larger European powers.

The Habsburg-Valois Wars ended with the Treaty of Cateau-Cambrésis (kah-toe kam-bray-SEE) in 1559, which left the Spanish kings in control of Milan, Naples, Sardinia, and Sicily. Thus, the Spanish dominated Italy, but without the centralizing control typical of England and France. Venice, Tuscany, the Papal States, and even lesser republics and principalities retained significant influence, as Italy remained a land of regional governments.

## SECTION SUMMARY

- The Hundred Years' War was fought over English dynastic claims within the French kingdom.
- The costs of war contributed to social and political unrest in both countries.
- As a result of the war, the English lost all their significant possessions within the French kingdom.
- Italy was a land of populous, independent cities and regional states.
- By the fifteenth century, most Italian governments were dominated by merchant oligarchies or by lords.

# Crisis in Economy and Society

*How were economic and social structures changed by plague and economic crisis?*

After nearly three centuries of dramatic growth, Europe in 1300 was seriously overpopulated, with estimates ranging from about 80 million to as high as 100 million. In some parts of Europe, population would not be this dense again until the late eighteenth century. Opportunities dwindled because of overpopulation, famine, war, and epidemic, which also brought changes in trade and commerce. As the population began to decline, this trend, along with deflation and transformed patterns of consumption, affected agriculture, which was still the foundation of the European economy. Recovery from all these crises altered the structure and dynamics of families, the organization of work, and the culture in many parts of Europe. As a result of the crises, there had been a relative shift in economic and demographic vitality from Italy to England, France, and central Europe.

## Famine and Declining Births

People in many parts of Europe were living on the edge of disaster in 1300. Given the low level of agricultural technology and the limited amount of land available for cultivation, it became increasingly difficult for the towns and countryside to feed and support the expanding population.

Growing numbers of people competed for land to farm and for jobs. Farm sizes declined throughout Europe, as parents tended to divide their land among their children. Rents for farmland increased, as landlords found that they could play one land-hungry farmer against another. Competition for jobs kept urban wages low, and when taxes were added to high rents and low wages, many peasants and artisans found it difficult to marry and raise families. Thus, because of reduced opportunities brought on by overpopulation, poor townspeople and peasants tended to marry late and have smaller families. Life expectancy at birth was probably about forty. Persons who survived into their twenties may have lived to about sixty, at best. Figures would be lower for peasants and laborers.

More dramatic than this crisis of births were the deadly famines that occurred in years of bad harvests. The great famine of 1315 to 1322 marks a turning point in the economic history of Europe. Wet and cold weather repeatedly ruined crops in much of northern Europe. Food stocks were quickly exhausted, and mass starvation followed. At Ypres, in Flanders, 2,800 people (about 10 percent of the population) died in just six months and shortages continued. Seven other severe famines were reported in the south of France or Italy during the fourteenth century.

If Europe's problem had merely been one of famine brought on by overpopulation, rapid recovery should have been possible. However, the difficulties of overpopulation were exacerbated by war and plague. As noted previously, the devastation of cities and the countryside was a common tactic in the Hundred Years' War. It was also typical of the local wars in parts of Spain, Germany, and especially Italy. The destruction of trees and vineyards and the theft of livestock made it difficult for rural populations to survive. Then, in 1348, the **Black Death**, or "the great Mortality," as contemporaries called it, struck Europe.

> **Black Death** An epidemic, possibly of bubonic plague, that wiped out one-third or more of Europe's population between 1348 and 1351. It initiated almost three centuries of epidemics.

## The Black Death

Today there is no consensus as to what caused the Black Death. In the early twentieth century, after the bacillus that causes bubonic plague was identified by French and Japanese physicians in Hong Kong, it was assumed that bubonic plague was the cause. Yet, bubonic plague usually travels slowly and infects a relatively small portion of a given population. By contrast, the Black Death seemed to race across Europe, wiping out entire families and infecting whole cities. Because of this evidence, some historical epidemiologists have speculated that the cause may actually have been anthrax or even a "hemorrhagic plague" similar to the Ebola virus. Recently, however, researchers have isolated DNA fragments of plague bacillus from a number of mass graves that date to the period of the epidemics. It may be that plague was part of a deadly mix of diseases. But knowing as little as we do about clothing, sanitation, and parasites found in the typical house, we cannot say for sure what caused the deadly epidemics.

### The Spread of the Disease

Contemporaries, on the other hand, had little doubt about the source of the disease. Genoese traders, they believed, contracted the plague in Caffa, on the Black Sea coast. Infected sailors carried the disease south into Egypt and west into Sicily, then on to Genoa and Venice. From there, it followed established trade routes first into central Italy; later to the south of France, the Low Countries, and England; and finally, through the North and Baltic Seas, into Germany and the Slavic lands to the east (see **Map 11.2**).

Mortality rates varied, but generally 60 percent or more of those infected died. In the initial infestation of 1348 to 1351, 25 to 35 percent of Europe's population may have died. One French parish that recorded 30 deaths in a normal year reported 638 during 1348. In some of Europe's larger cities, the death rate may have been as high as 60 percent. In Florence, for example, the population probably declined from about 90,000 to about 50,000 or even less. The shock and disruption were immense. Governments in some towns simply ceased to function at the height of the epidemic. Chroniclers reported that no one could be found to care for the sick or bury the dead. Although abandonment of the sick was probably more a fear than a reality, the epidemic nonetheless significantly disrupted daily life.

Just as areas were rebounding from the initial outbreak of the plague, it returned between 1360 and 1363, and then, for three centuries thereafter, almost no generation could avoid it. It has been calculated that in central Italy, where the best records are available, the plague returned on average every eleven years between 1350 and 1400. Less is known about the plague in Muslim lands and in the eastern Mediterranean, but the situation seems to have been similar to the European experience. Because the plague tended to carry off the young, the almost generational return of the disease accounts for the depressed population levels found in many parts of Europe until the late fifteenth century and in western Asia until the late seventeenth or eighteenth century.

Lacking an understanding of either contagion or infection, fourteenth-century doctors depended on traditional theories inherited from the Greeks, especially the work of Galen (GAY-len), to treat the plague. In Galenic medicine, good health depended on the proper balance of bodily and environmental forces; it could be upset by corrupt air, the movement of planets, and even violent shifts in emotions. Yet, in the fifteenth and sixteenth centuries, as the rhythms of the infestations became clearer, towns and, later, territorial governments perceived the contagious nature of the disease. Officials instituted increasingly effective quarantines and embargoes to restrict the movement of goods and people from areas where the plague was raging. Some argue that it was the eventual extension of these efforts throughout Europe that led to the gradual reduction and then disappearance of the plague from western Europe by the early eighteenth century.

## Social and Cultural Responses

Alongside medical theory, however, another class of explanations developed. Taking a lead from biblical texts, many assumed pestilence was either a sign of the imminent Last Judgment or at least a sign of the severe judgment of God on a sinful world. Given that

🌐 **Map 11.2 The Progress of the Black Death** The Black Death did not advance evenly across Europe; rather, as is clear from the dates at which it struck various regions, it followed the main lines of trade and communication. © Cengage Learning 2014

Courtesy, Bayerisches Nationalmuseum

view, a traditional, and logical, religious response was to urge various moral reforms and penitential acts, such as charitable gifts, special prayers, and holy processions. (See the feature, "The Visual Record: A Painting of the Plague" on pages 308–309.) Many Muslim theologians also concluded that "the plague is part of Allah's punishment." Women were often thought to be a source of moral pollution and hence one of the causes of God's wrath. In Muslim Egypt, women were ordered off the streets; in Christian Europe prostitutes were driven out of towns.

A movement of penitents called "flagellants" arose in Hungary and spread quickly into Germany and across France and the Low Countries. In an imitation of Christ's life and sufferings, they sought to atone in their own bodies for the sins of the world. Following an ancient Christian tradition, they ritually beat (flagellated) themselves between the shoulders with metal-tipped whips. Through their processions and sufferings, these pilgrims hoped to bring about a moral and religious transformation of society. The arrival of flagellants was often an occasion for an end of feuds and political violence within a community. But their arrival, just as often, was an occasion for political and even religious unrest. Authorities recognized the flagellants and the leaders of the religious riots as dangerous and drove them from towns.

In a quest for a purer, truly Christian society, the flagellants brought suspicion on all those who were not Christian or who were otherwise suspect. Some parts of Europe witnessed murderous attacks on outsiders, especially lepers and Jews, who were suspected of spreading the contagion in an attempt to bring down Latin Christendom. These attacks probably have more to do with tensions and fears already existing in parts of Europe than with the provocations of the flagellants. Like many other anti-Semitic myths, the rumors of wells poisoned by lepers and Jews seemed to arise in the south of France and spread in their most virulent forms to German towns along the Rhine. In Strasbourg attacks on Jews preceded the arrival of the plague. Except in a few districts, officials opposed attacks on Jews, lepers, and heretics. Doctors and churchmen often observed that Jews were unlikely culprits, since the plague claimed Jewish as well as Christian victims. Despite official rejection of popular rumors and fears, from the mid-fourteenth century, life became more difficult for the Jews of Christian Europe.

It was a commonplace among contemporary chroniclers that "so many did die that everyone thought it was the end

**Saint Roch Cured by an Angel**   Saint Roch is often shown with an exposed plague bubo. This image offered Christians comfort since Roch himself was cured because of his faith and charity. It offers modern historians evidence that bubonic plague was responsible for at least some of the mortality.

of the world."* Yet it was the very young, the elderly, and the poor—those least likely to pay taxes, own shops, or produce children—who were the most common victims. And even in towns, such as Florence, where mortality rates were extraordinarily high, recovery from the initial epidemic was rapid. Government offices were closed at most for only a few weeks; markets reopened as soon as the death rate began to decline; and within two years, tax receipts were back at pre-plague levels. Yet plague, fear of plague, and social and economic disruption caused by epidemic disease became a regular feature of European life. Thus, famine, warfare, plague, and population decline fueled the economic and social transformations of the late Middle Ages.

## Trade and Agriculture

In the aftermath of plague, the economy of Europe changed in a number of profound ways. Disruptions brought on by population decline were accompanied by changes in the basic structure of economic life. In particular, Italy's domination of the European economy was challenged by the growth of trade and manufacturing in many other parts of Europe. Further, by 1500, the relative power of Italian bankers declined as they came to face competition from equally astute northern bankers.

### Italian and Northern Merchants

Discussions of the economy must begin with Italy because it was the key point of contact between Europe and the international economy. In 1300, Italian merchants sold woolens produced in Flanders and Italy to Arab traders in North Africa, who sold them along the African coast and as far south as the Niger Delta. The Italians used the gold that they collected in payment to buy spices and raw materials in Byzantium, Egypt, and even China. They resold these highly prized goods in the cities and at regional fairs of northern Europe. Italian traders also sold spices, silks, and other luxuries throughout Europe, from England to Poland.

Because of their expertise in moving bullion and goods and their ready sources of capital, Italian merchants, such as the Ricciardis of Lucca who flourished in England, were ideal bankers and financial advisers to the popes and European rulers, who appreciated sources of ready capital. In times of war, rulers tended to trade the rights to various revenues to Italian bankers, who had cash at hand. Merchants from Cremona, Genoa, Florence, and Siena forged commercial agreements with the kings of France, Aragon, and Castile, and with the papacy. The most powerful bank in fifteenth-century Europe was the Medici bank of Florence. Founded in 1397 by Giovanni de' Medici (1360–1429), the bank grew quickly because of its role as papal banker. Medici agents transferred papal revenues from all parts of Europe to Rome and managed papal alum mines, which provided an essential mineral to the growing cloth industry.

The dramatic career of the Frenchman Jacques Coeur (1395?–1456) demonstrates that by the mid-fifteenth century, Italian merchants were not the only Europeans who understood international trade. After making a fortune trading in southern France, Coeur managed the French royal mint and became the financial adviser of King Charles VII (r. 1422–1461). He put the French monarchy back on a solid financial footing after the Hundred Years' War, in the process becoming the wealthiest individual in France.

### New Trading Patterns

By 1500, Italians faced increased competition from local merchants throughout Europe. From as early as the late thirteenth century, trade along the North and Baltic Seas in northern Europe was dominated by the **Hanseatic League**, an association of over a hundred trading cities centered on the German city of Lübeck. By the late fourteenth and early fifteenth centuries, the Hansa towns controlled grain shipments from eastern Europe to England and

**Hanseatic League** An association of more than a hundred German trading towns, which dominated trade in the North Sea and Baltic Sea regions during the fourteenth and fifteenth centuries.

---

*Quoted in William M. Bowsky, *The Black Death* (Huntington, NY, 1978) p. 14.

## A Painting of the Plague

Writers who survived the coming of pestilential disease in 1348 described a world of terror in which things seemed changed forever. Look at this painting, *St. Sebastian Interceding for the Plague-Stricken*, created by the Flemish artist Josse Lieferinxe (lay-EEF-er-inks) between 1497 and 1499. One dying man seems to be falling terrified to the ground, while a female bystander in the background screams in alarm. Images of Christ, Saint Sebastian (pierced by arrows), a devil, and a priest seem to indicate that something terrifying and undreamed-of is happening. But what exactly was the terror, and what had changed?

The art of the later Middle Ages is an extremely valuable source for understanding social and religious values. As you look at *St. Sebastian Interceding for the Plague-Stricken*, the first step is to understand what men and women in the fourteenth and fifteenth centuries thought about death. After 1400 European Christians often depicted the universality of death in paintings showing the Dance of Death. The motif varies, but typically Death grasps the hands of men and women, rich and poor, noble and peasant, and leads them away. Deathbed scenes were another popular motif. In the late Middle Ages most people believed that at death the good and evil acts committed by an individual were tallied in the Book of Life and the person was either granted eternal life, first in Purgatory and then Paradise, or consigned to eternal suffering in Hell. Judgment scenes often depict the Virgin Mary or another saint pleading before God or contending with the Devil or demons over the souls of the dying.

It was essential for people to prepare for a good death. Individuals studied the *artes moriendi*, or "arts of dying." A lingering, painful illness was often interpreted as an opportunity for penitential suffering that would benefit the soul. At the point of death, the dying person could confess and receive absolution for sins and the last sacraments of the church. From that moment on, he or she needed to maintain a calm faith, free from fear. Salvation and eternal life depended on avoiding further sin, especially the questioning of God's forgiveness and mercy. Death was a public event. Clergy, family, religious societies, even neighbors helped the dying person to avoid losing faith at the end. The person might pray, "Virgin Mary, Mother of God, I have placed my hope in you. Free my soul from care, and from Hell, and bitter death."*

The concept of a good death is critical to understanding the European response to the plague. To be sure, individuals rarely look forward to death, then or now. Numerous writers and chroniclers lamented the suddenness of death and the lack of priests to hear confessions. Individuals who were healthy in the morning might be dead by nightfall. The suddenness, the lack of time to prepare for a good death, heightened the dread that accompanied the onset of the illness.

Medieval Christians turned to saints to represent them before God at the point of death and to stop the onslaught of the plague. Three patron saints were especially popular. The Virgin Mary was often shown using her cloak to shelter towns and individuals from arrows carrying pestilence. Saint Roch, himself a victim of the plague, was thought to intercede and protect those who prayed in his name. And Saint Sebastian, an early Christian who as part of his elaborate martyrdom survived being shot with arrows (later understood as symbols of death caused by the plague), was thought to be an especially effective patron during epidemics. In times of plague, people went on pilgrimages to local shrines dedicated to these or local saints, carried images of the saints in processions, and built churches and chapels in honor of the saints in thanks for deliverance from the plague.

With these issues in mind, what do we see in Lieferinxe's painting? The painting portrays an outbreak of the plague. We note first the body of the dead person, carefully shrouded. Ideally the dead, like the corpse here, were taken

---

Scandinavia. The league's domination waned in the second half of the fifteenth century, however, as Dutch, English, and even southern German merchants gained shares of the wool, grain, and fur trades.

In contrast to the Hanseatic League of towns, merchants in southern Germany adopted Italian techniques of trade, manufacture, and finance to expand their influence throughout central Europe. German merchants regularly bought spices in the markets of Venice and distributed them in central and eastern Europe. By the fifteenth century, the townspeople of southern Germany also produced linen and cotton cloth, which found ready markets in central and eastern Europe.

The Fugger (FOO-ger) family of Augsburg in southern Germany was the most prosperous of the German commercial families. Jacob Fugger (1459–1525) was a dominant figure in the spice trade and also participated in a number of unusually large loans to a succession of German princes. Jacob Fugger's wealth increased fourfold between 1470 and 1500. The Fuggers were indispensable allies of the German emperors. Jacob himself ensured the election of Charles V as Holy Roman emperor in 1519, making a series of loans that allowed Charles to buy the influence that he needed to win election.

**Lieferinxe:** *St. Sebastian Interceding for the Plague-Stricken*

to a church by friends and relatives and given a Christian burial. This was an important part of the ritual meant to ease the suffering of the soul in Purgatory. But chroniclers often reported that so many died, and died so quickly, that no one could be found to bury them properly. In many towns the dead were gathered on carts and hauled to gaping common graves outside the towns. We can see one such cart leaving the castle in the background. In a series of images, then, Lieferinxe shows what mattered most to people. In the foreground is the shrouded body attended by a priest and other clerics bearing a cross. This person experienced a good death. In contrast, the man who has fallen behind the body is suffering a bad death, one that caught him unaware. He is the object of the concern and grief of those near him. In the sky just above the castle walls, a white-robed angel and a horned, ax-wielding demon contend over the souls of the dead and dying. At the top of the painting Christ listens to the prayers of Saint Sebastian. The painting thus portrays the impact and horror of plague and also the way Christians were expected to respond to it.

Returning to our original question, we can conclude that the terror of epidemic plague was not entirely like a modern panic. Medieval people saw the Black Death, its ghastly devastation, and its only possible solution or meaning in terms of traditional religious values: The true terror was to be caught unaware.

## Questions

1. *What is a good death?*
2. *What responses to epidemic diseases can you find in this image?*
3. *Which parts of the image illustrate panic and which do not?*

*Quoted in Philippe Ariès, *The Hour of Our Death* (New York: Knopf, 1981), p. 108.

## The Rural Economy

As wealthy as the great merchants were, in most parts of Europe, prosperity was still tied to agriculture and the production of food grains. In northern and western Europe, foodstuffs were produced on the manorial estates of great churchmen and nobles. These estates were worked by a combination of farmers paying rents, serfs who owed a variety of labor services, and day laborers who were hired during planting and harvesting. In the face of a decimated population, landlords and employers found themselves competing for the reduced number of laborers who had survived the plague.

Cloth manufacture, not agriculture, was the part of the European economy that changed most dramatically in the late Middle Ages. First in Flanders, then later in England, Germany, and the rest of Europe, production shifted from urban workshops to the countryside. Industries in rural areas tended to be free of controls on quality or techniques. Rural production, whether in Flanders, England, or Lombardy, became the most dynamic part of the industry.

Rural cloth production was least expensive because it could be done as occasional or part-time labor by farmers, or by their wives or children, during slack times of the day or season. Merchants used a system called "putting out" in which they made arrangements with individual workers and moved the raw materials and then finished cloth from spinner to weaver. Because production was likely to be finished in the countryside (beyond guild supervision), the merchant was free to move the cloth to wherever it could be sold most easily and profitably; guild masters had no control over price or quality.

Two other developments also changed the woolen trade of the fifteenth century: the rise of Spain as an exporter of unprocessed wool and the emergence of England, long recognized as a source of prime wool, as a significant producer of finished cloth. Spain was an ideal region for the pasturing of livestock. By the fifteenth century, highly prized Spanish wool from merino sheep was regularly exported to Italy, Flanders, and England. By 1500, over three million sheep grazed in Castile alone, and revenues from duties on wool formed the backbone of royal finance.

In England, in contrast, economic transformation was tied to cloth production. During the fifteenth century, England reduced its export of its high-quality raw wool and began instead to export its own finished cloth. In 1350, the English exported just over 5,000 bolts of cloth. By the 1470s, exports had risen to 63,000 bolts, and they doubled again by the 1520s. The growth of cloth exports contributed enormously to the expansion of London. During the fourteenth and fifteenth centuries, English commerce became increasingly controlled by London merchant-adventurers. Soon after 1500, over 80 percent of the cloth for export passed through the hands of the Londoners. This development, coupled with the rise of London as a center of administration and consumption, laid the foundation for the economic and demographic growth that would make London the largest and most prosperous city in western Europe by the eighteenth century.

## Patterns of Economic Life

The new structures of agriculture, manufacture, and trade in the fifteenth century challenged customs and institutions by admitting new entrepreneurs into the marketplace. However, Europe was still a conservative society in which social and political influence was more prized than economic wealth. Patricians in many European towns acted to dampen competition and preserve traditional values. Great banking families, such as the Medicis of Florence, tended to avoid competition and concentrations of capital. They did not try to drive their competitors out of business because the leaders of rival banks were their political and social peers. In northern Europe, governments in towns, such as Leiden, restricted the concentration of resources in the hands of the town's leading cloth merchants. Their aim was to ensure full employment for the town's laborers, political power for the guild masters, and social stability in the town.

In the wake of plague, the patricians' role, literally as "city fathers," was challenged by artisans and laborers. As wages rose because of population decline, workers demanded more voice in public life. Famed revolts, like the English Rising of 1381 (see page 297) and the Ciompi Revolt in Italy (see page 302) are only the tip of the iceberg. Numerous other rebellions are recorded across Europe in the second half of the fourteenth century. Laborers attempted to use demand for labor to social and political advantage.

Full employment was not just for men. Although men had controlled the guilds and most crafts in the thirteenth and early fourteenth centuries, women's guilds existed in several European cities, including Paris and Cologne. In Italy, some women could be found among the more prosperous crafts. Women often practiced their trades in the context of the family. In Cologne, for instance, women produced the linen yarn and silk cloths that their husbands sold throughout Europe. Speaking of the silkmakers of Cologne, a report noted that "the women are much more knowledgeable about the trade than are the men." Unlike southern Europe, where women had no public roles, some northern towns apparently allowed women's guilds to protect their members' activities as artisans and even peddlers. Because they often worked before marriage, townswomen in northern Europe tended to marry at a later age than did women in Italy. Many women earned their own marriage dowries. Since they had their own sources of income and often managed the shop of a deceased husband, women could be surprisingly independent. They were consequently under less pressure to remarry at the death of a spouse. Although their economic circumstances varied considerably, up to a quarter of the households in northern towns such as Bern and Zurich were headed by

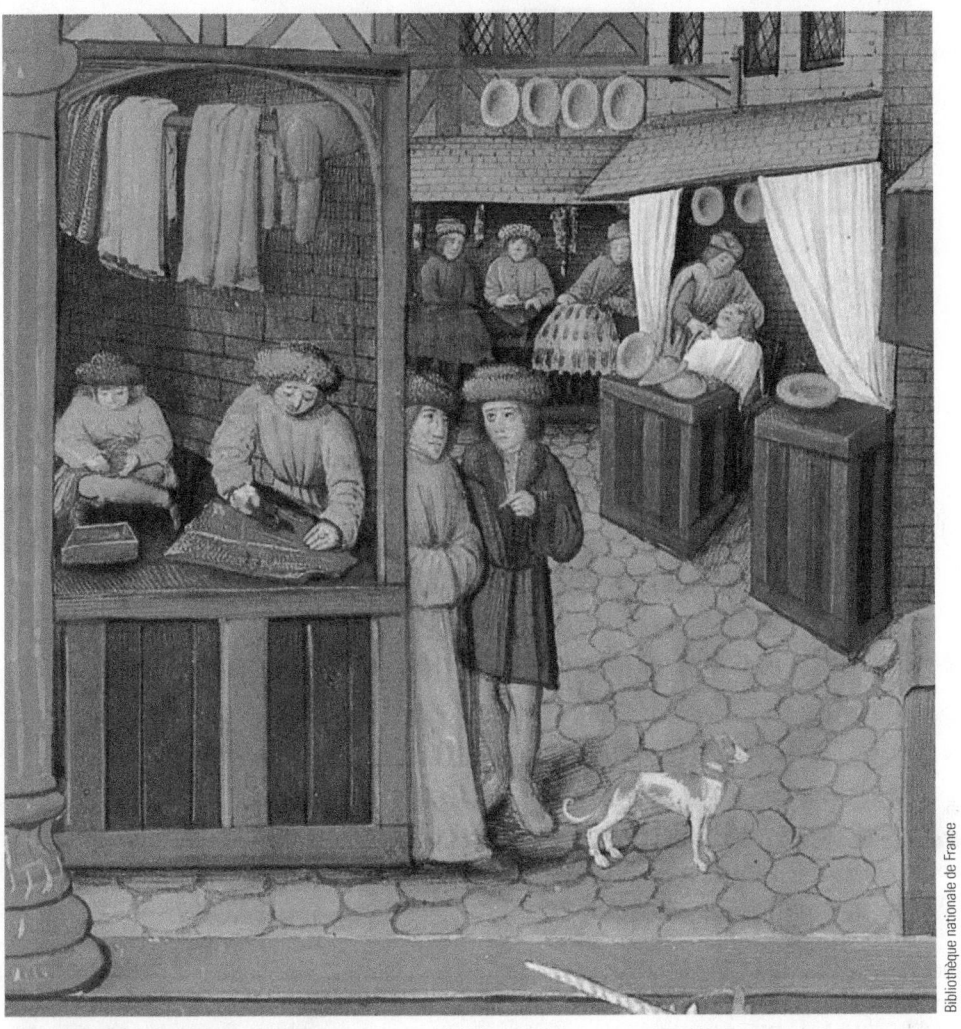

Bibliothèque nationale de France

**Street Life in Medieval Towns**    In a world dependent on natural lighting, shops were entirely open to the street. It made social and economic life much more public than it is in the modern world.

women. Many of them were widows, but many others, perhaps a third, were women who had never married.

If plague and population decline created new opportunities for women, the fifteenth century brought new restrictions to women's lives. In England, brewing ale had been a highly profitable part-time activity that women often combined with the running of a household. Ale was usually produced in small batches for household use and whatever went unconsumed would be sold. The introduction of beer changed matters. Because hops were added as a preservative during brewing, beer was easier to produce, store, and transport in large batches. Beer brewing became a lucrative full-time trade, reducing the demand for the alewife's product and providing work for men as brewers. At the same time, the rights of women to work in urban crafts and industries were reduced. Wealthy fathers became less inclined to allow wives and daughters to work outside the home. Guilds banned the use of female laborers in many trades and severely limited the rights of widows to supervise their spouses' shops.

Despite the narrowing of economic opportunities for women, the overall economic prospects of peasants and laborers improved. Lower rents and increased wages in the wake of the plague meant a higher standard of living for small farmers and laborers. Before the plague struck in 1348, most poor Europeans had subsisted on bread or grain-based gruel, consuming meat, fish, and cheese only a few times a week. A well-off peasant in England had lived on a daily ration of about two pounds of bread and a cup or two of oatmeal porridge washed down with three or four pints of ale. Poorer peasants generally drank water except on very special

Bibliothèque nationale de France

**Women at Work** Although guild records tend to ignore the contributions of women, many women worked in their husbands' shops. In this miniature, a woman is selling jewelry. Widows often managed the shops they inherited.

occasions. After the plague, laborers were more prosperous. Adults in parts of Germany may have consumed nearly a liter of wine, a third of a pound of meat, and a pound or more of bread each day. Elsewhere, people could substitute an equivalent portion of beer, ale, or cider for the wine. Hard times for landlords were good times for peasants and day laborers.

Landlords in England responded to the shortage of labor by converting their lands to grazing in order to produce wool for the growing textile market. In parts of Italy, landlords invested in canals, irrigation, and new crops in order to increase profits. In eastern Germany and Poland, landlords were able to take advantage of political and social unrest to force tenants into semi-free servile status. This so-called second serfdom created an impoverished workforce whose primary economic activity was in the lord's fields, establishing commercial grain farming. Increasingly in the second half of the century, grains cultivated in Poland and Prussia found their way to markets in England and the Low Countries. Europe east of the Elbe River became a major producer of grain, but at a heavy social cost.

The loss of perhaps a third of the urban population to the plague had serious consequences in the towns of Europe. Because of lower birthrates and higher death rates, late medieval towns needed a constant influx of immigrants to expand or even to maintain their populations. These immigrants did not find life in the cities easy, however. Citizenship in most towns was restricted to masters in the most important guilds, and local governments were in their hands, if not under their thumbs. In many towns, citizens constructed a system of taxation that worked to their own economic advantage and fell

## SECTION SUMMARY

- The Black Death may have killed one-third or more of Europe's population.

- In response to the epidemics, many groups attacked outsiders, lepers, and Jews.

- Italy's medieval bankers and merchants dominated trade between Europe, North Africa, and the eastern Mediterranean.

- By the late fifteenth century, north European merchants challenged Italian economic leadership.

- Cloth production, arranged by a putting-out system, was Europe's most important industry.

- By the end of the fifteenth century, women found it increasingly difficult to maintain a significant role in Europe's craft industries.

heavily on artisans and peasants living in territories controlled by the towns. Unskilled laborers and members of craft guilds depended for their economic well-being on personal relationships with powerful citizens who controlled the government and the markets. Peace and order in towns and in the countryside required a delicate balance of the interests of the well-to-do and the more humble. When that balance was shattered by war, plague, and economic depression, the result was often a popular revolt, such as the Ciompi insurrection of 1378 in Florence and the Rising of 1381 in England.

# The Consolidation of Political Power, 1450–1500

*How did the political makeup of Europe in 1500 differ from that in 1300?*

By 1500, it seemed that the French royal lawyer's claim that all within the kingdom belonged to the king was finally accepted. With the exception of Italy and Germany, strong central governments recovered from the crises of war and civil unrest that wracked the fourteenth and fifteenth centuries. The Hundred Years' War and the resulting disorganization in France and England seemed to strike at the heart of the monarchies. However, through the foundation of standing armies and the careful consolidation of power in the royal court, both countries seemed stronger and more able to defend themselves in the second half of the century. And as the Italians learned in the wars following the French invasion of 1494, small regional powers were no match for the mighty monarchies.

## France, England, and Scandinavia

In France, recovery from a century of war was based on a consolidation of the monarchy's power. A key to French military successes had been the creation of a paid professional army, which replaced the feudal host and mercenary companies of the fourteenth century. Charles VII created Europe's first standing army, a cavalry of about eight thousand nobles under the direct control of royal commanders. Charles also expanded his judicial claims. He and his son, Louis XI (r. 1461–1483), created new provincial *parlements*, or law courts, at Toulouse, Grenoble, Bordeaux, and Dijon. They also required that local laws and customs be registered and approved by the parlements.

A second key to maintaining royal influence was the rise of the French court as a political and financial center. While princes may have claimed their provinces were autonomous regions, they found themselves increasingly dependant on the crown. Through careful appointments and judicious offers of annuities and honors, Charles VII and Louis XI drew the nobility to the royal court and made the nobles dependent on it. "The court," complained a frustrated noble, "is an assembly of people who, under the pretense of acting for the good of all, come together to diddle each other; for there's scarcely anyone who isn't engaged in buying and selling and exchanging . . . and sometimes for their money we sell them our . . . humanity."* By 1500, France had fully recovered from the crisis of war and was once again a strong and influential state.

The fate of the English monarchy was quite different. Henry VI (r. 1422–1461) turned out to be weak-willed, immature, and prone to bouts of insanity—inherited, perhaps, from his French grandfather, Charles VI (see pages 297–298). The infirmity of Henry VI and the loss of virtually all French territories in 1453 led to factional battles known as the Wars of the Roses—the red rose symbolized Henry's House of Lancaster, the white stood for the rival House of York. Edward of York eventually deposed Henry and claimed the Crown for himself as Edward IV (r. 1461–1483). He faced little opposition because few alternatives existed. English public life was again thrown into confusion, however, at Edward's death. The late king's brother, Richard, duke of Gloucester, claimed the protectorship over the

---

*Quoted in Peter Shervey Lewis, *Later Medieval France: The Polity* (New York: Macmillan, 1968), p. 15.

13-year-old king Edward V (r. April–June 1483) and his younger brother. Richard seized the boys, who were placed in the Tower of London and never seen again. He proclaimed himself king and was crowned Richard III (r. 1483–1485). He withstood early challenges to his authority but in 1485 was killed in the Battle of Bosworth Field, near Coventry, by Henry Tudor, a leader of the Lancastrian faction. Henry married Elizabeth, the surviving child of Edward IV. Symbolically at least, the struggle between the rival claimants to the Crown appeared over.

Henry VII (r. 1485–1509), like Edward IV who preceded him, recognized the importance of avoiding war and taxation. Following Edward's example, Henry controlled local affairs through the traditional system of royal patronage. He also imitated Edward in emphasizing the dignity of the royal office. Henry solidified ties with Scotland and Spain by marrying his daughter, Margaret Tudor, to James IV of Scotland and his sons, Arthur and (after Arthur's death) Henry, to Catherine of Aragon, daughter of the Spanish rulers Ferdinand and Isabella. The English monarchy of the late fifteenth century departed little from previous governments. The success of Henry VII was based on several factors: the absence of powerful opponents; lower taxation thanks to twenty-five years of peace; and the desire, shared by ruler and ruled alike, for an orderly realm built on the assured succession of a single dynasty.

Public authority varied greatly across Scandinavia. In Norway, Denmark, and Sweden the power of the king was always mediated by the influence of the council, made up of the country's leading landowners. Power was based on ownership or control of lands and rents. All the Scandinavian countries were home to a significant class of free peasants, and they were traditionally represented in the popular assemblies that had the right to elect kings, authorize taxes, and make laws. Scandinavians spoke similar Germanic languages and were linked by close social and economic ties. Thus, it is not surprising that the crowns of the three kingdoms were joined during periods of crisis. In 1397, the dowager queen Margaret of Denmark was able to unite the Scandinavian crowns by the Union of Kalmar, which would nominally endure until 1523.

## Eastern Europe and Russia

Two phenomena had an especially profound effect on the governments of eastern Europe. One was the emergence of a newly important ruling dynasty. The other was the decline of Mongol, or Tatar, influence in the region. Since the thirteenth century, much of eastern Europe had been forced to acknowledge Tatar dominion and pay annual tribute. Now, the Tatar subjugation was challenged and finally ended.

As in much of Europe, political power was segmented and based on personal relationships among family members, communities, clients, and friends. Life in the East was further complicated by the mix of languages, cultures, and religions. Native Catholic and Orthodox Christian populations were further diversified in the fourteenth century by the arrival of Muslims in the Balkans and Ashkenazi Jews throughout most of the region. Escaping growing persecution in their traditional homelands in France and western Germany, the Ashkenazim migrated to Poland, Lithuania, and Ruthenian lands (parts of modern Russia), where they lived under their own leaders and followed their own laws.

### Poland and Lithuania

This mix of cultures and religions played a role in the growth of new states. Under the pretext of converting their pagan neighbors to Christianity, the mostly German Teutonic knights sought to expand eastward against the kingdom of Poland and the Lithuanian state. They were thwarted, however, by a profound dynastic shift. In 1386, Grand Duke Jagiello (yahg-YELL-loh) of Lithuania, who reigned from 1377 to 1434, converted to Catholic Christianity and married Hedwig, the daughter and heir of King Louis of Poland (r. 1370–1382). The resulting dynastic union created a state with a population of perhaps six million that reached from the Baltic nearly to the Black Sea. Polish-Lithuanian power slowed and finally halted the German advance to the east. The descendants of Jagiello, called Jagiellonians, had no hereditary right to rule Poland, and the Lithuanians opposed any Polish administrative influence in their lands. Yet, because of Jagiellonian power, the Poles continued to select them as kings. At various times, Jagiellonians also sat on the thrones of Bohemia and Hungary.

Poland and Lithuania remained more closely tied to western Europe than to the Russian East. They tended to be Catholic rather than Orthodox Christians. They wrote in a Roman rather than a Cyrillic script, and their political institutions resembled those of western Europe. Polish nobles managed to win a number of important concessions, the most significant being freedom from arbitrary arrest and confinement. This civil right was secured in Poland well before the more famous English right of habeas corpus. It was during this period, and under the influence of the Polish kings, that Cracow emerged as the economic and cultural center of Poland. Cracow University was founded in 1364, in response to the foundation of Prague University by the emperor Charles IV in 1348. After the dynastic union of Poland and Lithuania, Polish language and culture increasingly influenced the Lithuanian nobility. This union laid the foundation for the great Polish-Lithuanian commonwealth of the early modern period.

## The Rise of Moscow

Lithuania had never been conquered by the Tatars, and its expansion contributed to the decline of Tatar power. The rise of Moscow, however, owed much to the continuing Tatar domination. Since the Mongol invasions in the thirteenth century, various towns and principalities of Kievan Rus had been part of a Tatar sphere of influence. This primarily meant homage and payment of an annual tribute.

A key to the emergence of Moscow occurred when Ivan I (r. 1328–1341), Prince of Moscow, was named Grand Prince and collector of tribute from the other Russian princes. It was not for nothing that he was called "the Moneybag." It was during this same period that the head of the Russian Orthodox Church was persuaded to make his home in Moscow, and in 1367, the princes began to rebuild the Kremlin walls in stone.

The decisive change for Moscow, however, was the reign of Ivan III (r. 1462–1505). By 1478, Ivan III, called "Ivan the Great," had seized the famed trading center of Novgorod. Two years later, he was powerful enough to renounce Mongol overlordship and refuse further payments of tribute. After his marriage to an émigré Byzantine princess living in Rome, Ivan began to call himself "Tsar" (Russian for "Caesar"), implying that in the wake of the Muslim conquest of Constantinople, Moscow had become the new Rome.

## *The Ottoman Empire*

The most profound political and cultural transformation of the late Middle Ages took place in the Balkans with the conquest of Constantinople (1453) and the emergence of the Ottoman Turks as a major European power (see **Map 11.3**). They solidified a fragmented and unstable area and from their base spread their influence throughout the Mediterranean and Europe.

The eastern Mediterranean region was a politically tumultuous area in the fourteenth century, when the Ottoman Turks were first invited into the Balkans by the hard-pressed Byzantine emperor. In the 1420s, as the Turks and the Hungarians fought for influence in Serbia, the Serbian king moved easily from alliance with one to alliance with the other. Elites often retained their political and economic influence by changing religion.

An Ottoman victory over a Christian crusading army at Varna, on the Black Sea coast, in 1444 changed the dynamics and virtually sealed the fate of Constantinople. It was only a matter of time before the Turks took the city. When Mehmed (MEH-met) II (r. 1451–1481) finally turned his attention to Constantinople in 1453, the siege of the city lasted only fifty-three days. The destruction of the last vestiges of Byzantine administration sent shock waves through Christian Europe and brought forth calls for new crusades to liberate the East from the evils of Islam. The response in the east was more complex. The Turks were clear that their conquered territories were part of the Muslim world; they were aware that they were not a majority of the population and that to many they were just another of the contending political and religious groups. The Ottoman government allowed a limited toleration of

🌐 **Map 11.3  Turkey and Eastern Europe**  With the conquest of Constantinople, Syria, and Palestine, the Ottoman Turks controlled the eastern Mediterranean and dominated Europe below the Danube River. The Holy Roman emperors, rulers of Italy, and kings of Spain had to be concerned about possible invasions by land or by sea. © Cengage Learning 2014

non-Muslim groups, but it could not prevent occasional anti-Christian outbreaks among the Turks. The rise of the Ottoman Empire transformed eastern Europe and led to a profound clash between Christian and Muslim civilizations.

After the fall of Constantinople, the Turks worked to consolidate their new territories. Through alliance and conquest, Ottoman hegemony extended through Syria and Palestine, and by 1517, to Egypt. Even the Muslim powers of North Africa were nominally under Turkish control. In short order, they expanded to the west and north, seizing Croatia, Bosnia, Dalmatia, Albania, eastern Hungary, Moldavia, Bulgaria, and Greece. Turkish strength was based on a number of factors. The first was the loyalty and efficiency of the sultan's crack troops, the Janissaries. (See the feature, "The Global Record: The Origins of the Janissaries" on page 318.) These troops were young boys forcibly taken from the subject Christian populations, trained in the Turkish language and customs, and converted to Islam. Although they functioned as special protectors of the Christian community from which they were drawn, they were separated from it by their new faith. Because the Turkish population viewed them as outsiders, they were particularly loyal to the sultan.

**Suleiman the Magnificent Riding Through the Ruins of the Hippodrome, Constantinople**   An important public act of the sultan was his procession to Friday prayers in one of the major mosques in the center of Constantinople. Petitioners, Muslim or non-Muslim, could approach him during the procession. Sultans were also quite aware that they were heirs of the Roman Empire. This detail from an image of the procession shows Suleiman with the Hagia Sophia, newly made into a mosque, and other ancient monuments in the background. Scala/Art Resource, NY

The situation of the Janissaries underlines a secondary explanation for Ottoman strength: the unusually tolerant attitudes of Mehmed, who saw himself not only as the greatest of the *ghazi* (crusading warriors who were considered the "instruments of Allah") but also as emperor, heir to Byzantine and ancient imperial traditions. Immediately after the conquest of Constantinople, he repopulated the city with Greeks, Armenians, Jews, and Muslims. Mehmed especially welcomed Sephardic Jews from Spain and Portugal to parts of his empire. Thessalonica (Salonika), for example, was second only to Amsterdam as a Sephardic Jewish center until the community was destroyed in World War II. Society was arranged according to what would be called the Millet System. Religious groups in the cities lived in separate districts centered on a church or synagogue, and each religious community retained the right to select its own leaders. They followed their own traditions, but it was understood that everyone retained the right to appeal to Muslim law, that is, the Sharia courts. Mehmed made Constantinople the capital of the new Ottoman Empire and by building mosques, hospitals, hostels, and bridges, he breathed new life into the city, which he referred to as Istanbul—that is, "the city." In the fifty years following the conquest, the population of the city grew an extraordinary 500 percent, from about 40,000 to over 200,000, making it the largest city in Europe, as it had been in Late Antiquity.

At a time when Christian Europe seemed less and less willing to tolerate non-Christian minorities, the Ottoman Empire's more open attitude toward outsiders seemed striking. Muslims and non-Muslims belonged to the same trade associations and traveled throughout the empire. Mehmed had no qualms about making trade agreements with the Italian powers in an attempt to consolidate his control. In Serbia, Bulgaria, Macedonia, and Albania, he left in place previous social and political institutions, requiring only loyalty to his empire.

## The Union of Crowns in Spain

While expanding across the Mediterranean, the Turks came in contact with the other new state of the fifteenth century, the newly unified kingdom of Spain. As in Poland-Lithuania, the Spanish monarchy was only a dynastic union. In 1469, Ferdinand, heir to the kingdom of Aragon and Catalonia, married Isabella, daughter of the king of Castile. Five years later, Isabella became queen of Castile, and in 1479, Ferdinand took control of the kingdom of Aragon. This union of Crowns eventually would lead to the creation of a united Spain, but true integration was still a distant dream in 1469.

## The Origins of the Janissaries

*The Janissary Corps was the highly effective Ottoman infantry. Recruits were collected from subject, usually Balkan Christian, populations and converted to Islam. They came to play a critical military and even political role in the empire. The process of mandatory levies on subject populations continued until the seventeenth century. This Anonymous Ottoman Chronicle offers and explanation of the institution and, by extension, an understanding of how the Ottomans understood the subject populations. Kara Rustem was a provincial officer from Anatolia and Çandarlı [pronounced chan-DAR-la] Halil eventually served as the first Grand Vizier under Murad I (d. 1364).*

One day a scholar called Kara Rüstem came from the land of Karaman. The Kara Rüstem went to Çandarlı Halil, who was military judge, and said, "Why do you let so much state income go [to] waste?" The military judge Kara Halil asked, "What income is this that is going [to] waste? Tell me at once." Kara Rüstem said, "Of those prisoners that the warriors in the holy war bring back, one-fifth, according to God's command, belongs to the Sultan. Why do you not take this share?" The military judge Kara Halil said, "I will submit the matter to the Sultan!" He submitted it to Gazi Murad [Sultan Murad I], who said, "If it is God's command, then take it." They called Kara Rüstem and said, "Master, carry out God's command." Kara Rüstem went away and stayed in Gallipoli and collected twenty-five aspers from each prisoner. This innovation dated from the time of these two men. To collect a tax from the prisoners in Gallipoli has become the practice since Çandarlı Kara Halil and Kara Rüstem. After that he also instructed Gazi Evrenos to take one out of every five prisoners captured in the raids and, if anyone had only four prison-ers, to take twenty-five aspers from him. They acted according to this rule. They collect-ed the young men. They took one in every five prisoners captured in the raids and deliv-ered them to the Porte [the Sultan's court]. Then they gave these young men to the Turks in the provinces so that they should learn Turkish, and then they sent them to Anatolia. The Turks let these young men work in the fields for a while and made use of them until they learned Turkish. After a few years they brought them to the Porte and made them janissaries, giving them the name "New Troops." Their origin goes back to this time.

### Questions

1. *Why does the chronicler believe that the Sultan has the right to create Janissaries?*

2. *How do the Turks insure that the Janissaries will be loyal to the Sultan?*

"The Anonymous Chronicle" as translated by Bernard Lewis, ed. *Islam from the Prophet Muhammad to the Capture of Constantinople* (New York and London: Harper & Row, Publishers, 1974) 1: 226-27.

## Castile and Aragon

The permanence of the union was remarkable because the two kingdoms were so different. Castile was a much larger and more populous state. It had taken the lead in the Reconquista, the fight begun in the eleventh century to reclaim Iberia from Muslim rule. As a result, economic power within Castile was divided among the groups most responsible for the Reconquista: military orders and nobles. The military orders of Calatrava, Santiago, and Alcantara were militias formed by men who had taken a religious vow similar to that taken by a monk, with an added commitment to fight against the enemies of Christianity. In the course of the Reconquista, the military orders assumed control of vast districts. Lay nobles who aided in the Reconquista also held large tracts of land and proudly guarded their independence.

Castile's power stemmed from its agrarian wealth. During the Reconquista, Castilians took control of large regions and turned them into ranges for grazing merino sheep, producers of the prized merino wool exported to the markets of Flanders and Italy (see page 310). To maximize the profits from wool production, the kings authorized the creation of the Mesta, a brotherhood of sheep producers. The pastoral economy grew to the point that by the early sixteenth century, Castilians owned over three million sheep.

Economic power in Castile lay with the nobility, but political power rested with the monarch. Because the nobility was largely exempt from taxation, nobles ignored the Cortes (cor-TEZ), the popular assembly, which could do little more than approve royal demands. The towns of Castile were important only as fortresses and staging points for militias, rather than as centers of trade and commerce.

The kingdom of Aragon was dramatically different. The center of the kingdom was Barcelona, an important trading center in the Mediterranean. In the fourteenth and fifteenth centuries, the kings of Aragon concentrated their efforts on expanding their influence in the

Mediterranean, especially south of France and Italy. By the middle of the fifteenth century, the Aragonese empire included the kingdom of Naples, Sicily, the Balearic (ba-LEER-ik) Islands, and Sardinia.

The power of the Aragonese king, in sharp contrast to the Castilian monarchy, was limited because the Crown was not unified. The ruler was king in Aragon and Navarre but only count in Catalonia. Aragon, Catalonia, and Valencia each maintained its own Cortes. In each area, the traditional nobility and the towns had a great deal more influence than did their counterparts in Castile. The power of the Cortes is clear in the coronation oath taken by the Aragonese nobility: "We who are as good as you and together are more powerful than you, make you our king and lord, provided that you observe our laws and liberties, and if not, not."* The distinction between Aragon and Castile could not be stronger.

Initially, the union of the crowns of Aragon and Castile did little to unify the two monarchies. Nobles fought over disputed boundaries, and Castilian nobles felt exploited by Aragonese merchants. Trade duties and internal boundaries continued to be disputed. The two realms even lacked a treaty to allow for the extradition of criminals from one kingdom to the other. Castilians never accepted Ferdinand as more than their queen's consort. After the death of Isabella in 1504, he ruled in Castile only as regent for his infant grandson, Charles I (r. 1516–1556). "Spain" would not emerge in an institutional sense until the late sixteenth century.

Nonetheless, the reign of Isabella and Ferdinand marked a profound change in politics and society in the Iberian kingdoms and in Europe in general. Ferdinand and Isabella married their daughter Joanna to Philip of Habsburg in 1496 to draw the Holy Roman Empire into the Italian wars brought on by the French invasion (see pages 302–303). The marriage of their daughter Catherine of Aragon to Prince Arthur of England in 1501 was designed to obtain yet another ally against the French. Those two marriages would have momentous consequences for European history in the sixteenth century.

**Alfonso de Espina's *Fortress of Faith* (1474)** The diatribe against heretics, Muslims, and Jews fanned religious tensions in Spain. In this image from the book, Jews, Muslims, heretics, and demons are depicted as related threats to Christianity. Blindfolded Jews (blind to Christian Truth), Muslim warriors, and the Devil himself are seen assaulting the fortress of faith.

## 1492: Muslims and Jews

The reign of Ferdinand and Isabella is especially memorable because of the events of 1492. In January of that year, a crusading army conquered Granada, the last Muslim stronghold in Iberia. In March, Ferdinand and Isabella ordered the Jews of Castile and Aragon to convert or leave the kingdom within four months. In April, Isabella issued her commission authorizing Christopher Columbus "to discover and acquire islands and mainland in the Ocean Sea" (see pages 370–371).

The conquest of Granada and the expulsion of the Jews represented a radical shift in the Spanish mentality. Until the beginning of the fifteenth century, Spain maintained a level of religious tolerance unusual in Christendom. In the fourteenth century, perhaps 2 percent of the population of Iberia was Jewish, and the Muslim population may have been as high as 50 percent. The various groups were inextricably mixed. The statutes of the Jewish community in Barcelona were written in Catalan, a Spanish dialect, rather than in Hebrew. *Maranos,*

---

*Quoted in Angus MacKay, *Spain in the Middle Ages: From Frontier to Empire, 1000–1500* (London: Macmillan, 1977), p. 105.

Jewish converts to Christianity, and *moriscos*, Muslim converts, mixed continuously with Christians and with members of their former religions. It was difficult at times to know which religion these converts, or *conversos*, actually practiced. One surprised northern visitor to Spain remarked that one noble's circle was filled with "Christians, Moors, and Jews and he lets them live in peace in their faith."

This tolerant mingling of Christians, Muslims, and Jews had periodically occasioned violence. All three communities, in fact, preferred clear boundaries among the groups. In 1391, however, a series of violent attacks had long-lasting and unfortunate effects on Iberian society. An attack on the Jews of Seville led to murders, forced conversions, and suppression of synagogues throughout Spain. In the wake of the assault, large portions of the urban Jewish population either converted to Christianity or moved into villages away from the large commercial cities. The Jewish population in Castile may have declined by a fourth. Although the anti-Jewish feelings were expressed in religious terms, the underlying cause was anger over the economic prominence of some Jewish or converso families. After 1391, anti-Jewish feeling increasingly became racial. As one rebel said, "The converso remains a Jew and therefore should be barred from public office."*

Hostility and suspicion toward Jews grew throughout the fifteenth century, until Ferdinand and Isabella concluded that the only safe course was to order all Jews to accept baptism. In the Alhambra Decree of 1492, the monarchs claimed that there were "bad Christians who Judaized and committed apostasy." Thus they ordered that Jews who would not convert would have to leave the kingdom within four months. The order was signed on March 31, 1492, and published in late April, after an unsuccessful attempt by converso and Jewish leaders to dissuade the monarchs from implementing it.

Many Jews could not dispose of their possessions in the four months allowed and so chose to convert and remain. But it is estimated that about ten thousand Jews left Aragon and that even more left Castile. Many moved to Portugal and then to North Africa. Some went east to Istanbul or north to the Low Countries. A number of others moved to the colonies being established in the New World in the vain hope of avoiding the Inquisition, which was already underway when the expulsion order was issued (see below). In 1504, the expulsion order was extended to include all Muslims.

The economic and social costs of the expulsion were profound. Not every Muslim or Jew was wealthy and cultured, but the exiles did include many doctors, bankers, and merchants. Spanish culture, long open to influences from Muslim and Jewish sources, became narrower and less willing to accept new ideas. After the expulsion, a chasm of distrust opened between the "Old Christians" and the "New Christians"—that is, those newly converted. As early as the first decades of the fifteenth century, some religious orders had refused to accept "New Christians." They required that their members demonstrate *limpieza de sangre*, a purity of blood. By 1500, the same tests of blood purity became prerequisites for holding most religious and public offices. Thus, by the end of the fifteenth century, the Iberian kingdoms had created more powerful, unified governments, but at a terrible cost to the only portion of Christendom that had ever practiced religious tolerance.

Complaints that led to the expulsion arose from a variety of sources. The fact that many of the most important financiers and courtiers were Jews or conversos bred jealousies and tensions among the communities. All three religious communities favored distinct dress and identifying behaviors. Old Christians seemed concerned that many of the conversos might reconvert to Judaism, and the fear of reconversion, or "judaizing," led many to advocate the institution of the **Spanish Inquisition**.

Inquisitions were well known in many parts of Europe, but the Spanish Inquisition was unique because in 1478, Pope Sixtus IV placed the grand inquisitor under the direct control of the monarchs. Like most Christian rulers, Ferdinand and Isabella believed that uniform Christian orthodoxy was the only firm basis for a strong kingdom. Inquisitors attacked those aspects of converso tradition that seemed to make the conversos less than fully Christian. They were concerned that many conversos and maranos had converted falsely and were

**Spanish Inquisition**
A church court under monarchical control established in 1478 to look for "false Christians" among the newly converted Muslims and Jews.

---

secretly continuing to follow Jewish or Muslim rituals—a fear that some recent scholars have argued was unfounded.

Because its administration, finances, and appointments were in Spanish, not papal, hands, the Spanish Inquisition quickly became an important instrument for the expansion of state power. Many inquisitors used their offices to attack wealthy or politically important converso families not just to drive them from public life but also to fill the royal treasury, which was where the estates of those judged guilty wound up. "This inquisition is as much to take the conversos' estates as to exalt the faith," concluded one despairing conversa woman.[*]

## The Limits of Consolidation: Germany

The issue of central versus local control played a key role in German affairs as well. The Holy Roman Empire of the late Middle Ages was dramatically different from the empire of the early thirteenth century. Emperors generally were unable to claim lands and preside over jurisdictions outside Germany, and within Germany, power shifted eastward. Imperial power had previously rested on lands and castles in southwestern Germany. These strongholds melted away as emperors willingly pawned and sold traditional crown lands in order to build up the holdings of their own families. Emperor Henry VII (r. 1308–1313) and his grandson, Charles IV (r. 1347–1378), for example, liquidated imperial lands west of the Rhine in order to secure the House of Luxemburg's claims to the crown of Bohemia and other lands in the east. The Habsburgs in Austria, the Wittelsbachs in Bavaria, and a host of lesser families staked out power bases in separate parts of the empire. As a result, Germany unraveled into a loose collection of territories. More seriously, the power of each emperor depended almost entirely on the wealth and power of his dynastic lands.

The power of regional authorities in the empire was further cemented by the so-called **Golden Bull** of 1356, the most important constitutional document of late medieval German history. In it, Charles IV declared that henceforth the archbishops of Cologne, Mainz, and Trier, plus the secular rulers of Bohemia, the Rhenish Palatinate, Saxony, and Brandenburg, would be the seven electors responsible for the choice of a new emperor. He further established that the rulers of these seven principalities should have full jurisdictional rights within their territories. The Golden Bull acknowledged the power of regional princes, but it did nothing to solve the inherent weakness of an electoral monarchy. Between 1273 and 1519, Germany elected fourteen emperors from six different dynasties and only once, in 1378, did a son follow his father. The contrast between Germany and the monarchies of Iberia, France, and England is striking. By 1350, Germany had no hereditary monarchy, no common legal system, no common coinage, and no representative assembly. Political power rested in the hands of the territorial princes.

Territorial integration was least effective in what is now Switzerland, where a league of towns, provincial knights, and peasant villages successfully resisted a territorial prince. The Swiss Confederation began modestly enough in 1291, as a voluntary association to promote regional peace. By 1410, the confederation had conquered most of the traditionally Habsburg lands in the Swiss areas. Though still citizens of the Holy Roman Empire, the Swiss maintained an independence similar to that of the princes. Their expansion culminated with the Battle of Nancy in Lorraine in 1477, when the Swiss infantry defeated a Burgundian army and killed Charles the Bold, the duke of Burgundy. From then on "turning Swiss" was a common threat made by German towns and individuals who hoped to slow territorial centralization.

**Golden Bull** Edict of Holy Roman Emperor Charles IV establishing the method of electing a new emperor. It acknowledged the political autonomy of Germany's seven regional princes.

### SECTION SUMMARY

- By the end of the fifteenth century, both England and France had stronger, more centralized governments.
- By the fifteenth century a strong Polish-Lithuanian state had emerged to halt German expansion to the east.
- The rise of Moscow marked the end of Tatar domination in eastern Europe.
- Ottoman Turks established a strong empire that came to dominate the eastern Mediterranean and the Balkans.
- The union of the Aragonese and Castilian crowns created a Spanish monarchy intent on enforcing political unity and religious uniformity.
- In German lands, regional powers emerged to challenge and limit the power of the empire.

---

*Haim Beinart, ed., "Records of the Trials of the Spanish Inquisition" in *Ciudad Real*, vol. 1, trans. Duane Osheim (Jerusalem: Israel Academy of Sciences and Humanities, 1974), p. 391.

# Chapter Summary

The Europe of 1500 was profoundly different from the Europe of two centuries earlier. The religious, political, and economic crises of the fourteenth and early fifteenth centuries seemed about to destroy the progress of the previous centuries. But the recovery of the second half of the fifteenth century was nearly as dramatic as the preceding disasters.

◆ *How did the Great Schism change the church and the papacy?*

In the aftermath of schism and conciliar reform, the church also was transformed. In 1300, the papacy was able to exercise considerable authority over the administration of the Church throughout Europe. It collected a broad range of taxes and payments. Because of conciliar challenges to papal authority, popes had to deal much more carefully with the governments of Europe. They found governments resistant to what they saw as papal interference. Recognizing that, in the end, popes could count on support only from those areas they controlled politically, the papacy became an Italian regional power.

◆ *What forces limited the political power of rulers in England, France, and Italy?*

In both England and France, the Hundred Years' War was more than just a dynastic struggle. Both countries experienced a noble reaction against royal power that exacerbated the struggle. The English won dramatic battles, but they could not control the territory. As a result, by the end the English lost all their significant possessions in France. The result contributed to the eventual centralization and growth of royal power in the two kingdoms. Until the French invasions at the end of the fifteenth century, public life in Italy was different. Urban magnates, merchants, and artisans competed for influence. As a result, most cities were dominated by lords who kept the peace among the factions. Florence and Venice were the primary exceptions. Those two towns remained republics controlled in the end by an urban oligarchy.

◆ *How were economic and social structures changed by plague and economic crisis?*

The economy had grown more complex in the wake of the epidemic disease and dramatic population decline. Changes included the relative decline of the Italian economy as new patterns of trade and banking and new manufacturing techniques spread throughout Europe. Commerce and manufacture were now more firmly rooted in northern Europe. Italian merchants and bankers faced stiff competition from local counterparts throughout Europe.

◆ *How did the political makeup of Europe in 1500 differ from that in 1300?*

Recovery was equally dramatic for the governments of Europe. After the Hundred Years' War and challenges from aristocrats, townsmen, and peasants, governments grew stronger as kings, princes, and town patricians used royal courts and patronage to extend their control. Yet recovery among the traditional Western powers was largely overshadowed by the emergence of the tsars in Moscow and the rise of the Ottoman and Spanish Empires. These three emergent powers upset the political and diplomatic balance in Europe and would dominate politics and diplomacy in the next century.

# Key Terms

**CourseMate**

Go to the CourseMate website at **www.cengagebrain.com** for additional study tools and review materials—including audio and video clips—for this chapter.

**Raphael: *School of Athens* (detail)**   Raphael created this classical setting by using the technique of linear perspective. Scala/Art Resource, NY

# The Renaissance

The painting on the left, *School of Athens* by Raphael (1483–1520), was commissioned for the Stanze (STAN-zay), the papal apartments in the Vatican. At the center, Plato and Aristotle advance through a church-like hall, surrounded by the great thinkers and writers of the ancient world. But Raphael portrayed more than just ancient wisdom. The figure of Plato is, in fact, a portrait of Leonardo da Vinci. A brooding Michelangelo leans on a marble block in the foreground. In a companion painting on the opposite wall, Raphael depicted a gathering of the greatest scholars of Christendom. In this way, he brought together Christian and classical, writers and artists, and captured the entire cultural reform plan of the Renaissance.

The revival these paintings celebrate was a response to the religious, social, economic, and political crises discussed in the previous chapter. Italians, and later Europeans, generally found themselves drawn to imitate Roman literature, ethics, and politics. The wisdom of antiquity seemed to offer an opportunity to perfect the theological ideas about moral and political life current in the earlier Middle Ages. As Raphael's two paintings imply, Renaissance writers were convinced that all knowledge, pagan and Christian, ancient and modern, could be combined into a single, uniform view of the world.

Renaissance Italians wrote of themselves and their contemporaries as having "revived" arts, "rescued" painting, and "rediscovered" classical authors. They even coined the phrases "Dark Ages" and "Middle Ages" to describe the period that separated the Roman Empire from their own times. They believed that their society saw a new age, a rebirth of culture. And, to this day, we use the French word for "rebirth," *renaissance*, to describe the period of intense creativity and change that began in Italy in the fourteenth century and then extended to all of Europe.

This view comes to us primarily from the work of the nineteenth-century Swiss historian Jacob Burckhardt. In his book, *The Civilization of the Renaissance in Italy* (1860), he argued that Italians were the first individuals to recognize the state as a moral structure free from the restraints of religious or philosophical traditions. Burckhardt believed that people are entirely free. Their success or failure depends on personal qualities of creative brilliance rather than on family status, religion, or guild membership. Burckhardt

## Chapter Overview

**Humanism and Culture in Italy, 1300–1500**

◆ *How did Italians use classical values to deal with cultural and political issues?*

**Painting and the Arts, 1250–1550**

◆ *What was "new" about Renaissance art?*

**The Spread of the Renaissance, 1350–1536**

◆ *In what ways did humanism outside Italy differ from Italian humanism?*

**Politics and Renaissance Culture**

◆ *How did European rulers use Renaissance art and culture?*

**Renaissance** A word that has come to define any period of intense creativity. In this case, it refers specifically to a cultural movement based on imitating classical culture.

thought he saw, in Renaissance Italy, the first signs of the romantic individualism and nationalism that characterized the modern world.

The Renaissance offers us an excellent opportunity to consider revolutionary cultural change. It was not simply a rejection of the immediate past. As we have seen, there were no "Dark Ages." Humanists and artists remained profoundly influenced by traditional Christian values, yet the culture they produced was in many ways a radical departure.

How, then, should we characterize the Renaissance in Europe? The Renaissance was an important cultural movement that aimed to reform and renew by imitating what the reformers believed were classical and early Christian traditions in art, education, religion, and political life. Italians, and then other Europeans, came to believe that the social and moral values, as well as the literature, of classical Greece and Rome offered the best formula for changing their own society for the better. This enthusiasm for a past culture became the vehicle for changes in literature, education, and art that established cultural standards that were to hold for the next five hundred years.

# Humanism and Culture in Italy, 1300–1500

*How did Italians use classical values to deal with cultural and political issues?*

Italians turned to models from classical antiquity in their attempts to deal with current issues of cultural, political, and educational reform. A group of scholars, who came to be known as humanists, began to argue the superiority of the literature, history, and politics of the past. As humanists discovered more about ancient culture, they were able to understand more clearly the historical context in which Roman and Greek writers and thinkers lived. And by the early sixteenth century, their debates on learning, civic duty, and the classical legacy had led them to a new vision of the past and a new appreciation of the nature of politics.

## *The Emergence of Humanism*

**humanism** Western European literary and cultural movement, which emphasized the superiority of Greek and Roman literature and especially its values of personal and public morality.

**Humanism** initially held greater appeal in Italy than elsewhere in Europe because the culture in central and northern Italy was significantly more secular and more urban than the culture of much of the rest of Europe. Members of the clergy were less likely to dominate government and education in Italy. Quite the reverse: Boards dominated by laymen had built and were administering the great urban churches of Italy. Religious hospitals and charities were often reorganized and centralized under government control. Italy was the most urbanized region of Europe. Even the powerful Italian aristocracy tended to live at least part of the year in towns and conform to urban social and legal practices.

Differences between Italy and northern Europe are also apparent in the structure of local education. In northern Europe, education was organized to provide clergy for local churches. In the towns of Italy, education was much more likely to be supervised by town governments to provide training in accounting, arithmetic, and the composition of business letters. Public grammar masters taught these basics, and numerous private masters and individual tutors were prepared to teach all subjects. Giovanni Villani, a fourteenth-century merchant and historian, described Florence in 1338 as a city of nearly 100,000 people, in which perhaps as many as 10,000 young girls and boys were completing elementary education and 1,000 were continuing their studies to prepare for careers in commerce. Compared with education in the towns of northern Europe, education in Villani's Florence seems broad-based and practical.

Logic and Scholastic philosophy (see page 276) dominated university education in northern Europe in the fourteenth and fifteenth centuries but had less influence in Italy, where education focused on the practical issues of town life rather than on theological speculation. Educated Italians of this period were interested in the *studia humanitatis*, which we now call humanism. By *humanism*, Italians meant rhetoric and literature—the arts of persuasion.

Poetry, history, letter writing, and oratory, based on standardized forms and aesthetic values, consciously borrowed from ancient Greece and Rome were the center of intellectual life.

By 1300, it was usual for towns to celebrate the feast days of their patron saints as major political, as well as religious, festivals. And town governments often supervised the construction and expansion of cathedrals, churches, and hospitals as signs of their wealth and prestige.

Literature of the early fourteenth century tended to emphasize the culture of towns. The most famous and most innovative work of the fourteenth century, *The Decameron* by Giovanni Boccaccio (1313–1375) (bo-KAH-cho), pondered moral and ethical issues but in the lively context of Italian town life. And he characterized the expectations of many Renaissance writers when one of his characters observed that "moral worth consists not just in recollection of the past and knowledge of the present, but through them an appreciation of the future."* Boccaccio hoped the colorful and irreverent descriptions of contemporary Italians, which make his *Decameron* a classic of European literature, would also lead individuals to understand both the essence of human nature and the folly of human desires. The plot involves a group of privileged young people who abandon friends and family during the plague of 1348 to go into the country. There, on successive days, they mixed feasting, dancing, and song with one hundred tales of love, intrigue, and gaiety. With its mix of traditional and contemporary images, Boccaccio's book spawned numerous imitators in Italy and elsewhere.

Like Boccaccio, the majority of educated Italians in the early fourteenth century were not particularly captivated by thoughts of ancient Rome. Italian historians chose to write the histories of their hometowns. Theirs was a practical world in which most intellectuals were men trained in notarial arts—the everyday skills of oratory, letter writing, and the recording of legal documents.

## CHRONOLOGY

| | |
|---|---|
| 1304–1314 | Giotto paints Arena Chapel in Padua |
| 1345 | Petrarch discovers Cicero's letters to Atticus |
| 1348–1350 | Boccaccio, *The Decameron* |
| 1393–1400 | Chaucer, *The Canterbury Tales* |
| 1401 | Ghiberti wins competition to cast baptistery doors, Florence |
| 1405 | Christine de Pizan, *The Book of the City of the Ladies* |
| 1427 | Unveiling of Masaccio's *Trinity* |
| 1434 | Van Eyck, *The Arnolfini Wedding* |
| 1440 | Valla, *On the Donation of Constantine* |
| 1440s | Vittorino establishes Villa Giocosa in Mantua |
| 1450s | Gutenberg begins printing with movable metal type |
| 1460 | Gonzaga invites Mantegna to Mantua |
| 1475 | Pope Sixtus IV orders construction of Sistine Chapel |
| 1494 | Dürer begins first trip to Venice |
| 1501 | Michelangelo, *David* |
| 1511 | Erasmus, *The Praise of Folly* |
| 1513 | Machiavelli, *The Prince* |
| 1516 | More, *Utopia* |
| 1528 | Castiglione, *The Book of the Courtier* |

## Petrarch and Early Humanism

The first Italians who looked back consciously to the literary and historical examples of ancient Rome were a group of northern Italian lawyers and notaries who imitated Roman authors. These practical men found Roman history and literature more stimulating and useful than medieval philosophy. Writers, such as Albertino Mussato of Padua (1262–1329), adopted classical styles in their poetry and histories. Mussato used his play *The Ecerinis* (1315) to tell of the fall of Can Grande della Scala, the tyrannical ruler of Verona (d. 1329), and to warn his neighbors of the dangers of tyranny. From its earliest, the classical revival in Italy was tied to issues of moral and political reform.

This largely emotional fascination for the ancient world was transformed into a literary movement for reform by **Francesco Petrarch** (1304–1374), who popularized the idea of mixing classical moral and literary ideas with the concerns of the fourteenth century. Petrarch was the son of an exiled Florentine notary living at the papal court in Avignon. Repelled by the urban violence and wars he had experienced on his return to Italy, Petrarch was highly critical of his contemporaries: "I never liked this age," he once confessed. He

**Francesco Petrarch**
Influential poet, biographer, and humanist who strongly advocated imitation of the literary and moral values of the leading Greek and Roman writers.

*Boccaccio, *Decameron*, Day 10 (Trans Duane Osheim)

criticized the papacy in Avignon, calling it the "Babylonian Captivity" (see pages 290–291); he supported an attempt to resurrect a republican government in Rome; and he believed that imitation of the actions, values, and culture of the ancient Romans was the only way to reform his sorry world.

Petrarch believed that an age of darkness—he coined the expression "Dark Ages"—separated the Roman world from his own time and that the separation could be overcome only through a study and reconstruction of classical values: "Once the darkness has been broken, our descendants will perhaps be able to return to the pure, pristine radiance."* Petrarch's program and, in many respects, the entire Renaissance, involved, first of all, a reconstruction of classical culture, then a careful study and imitation of the classical heritage, and finally a series of moral and cultural changes that went beyond the mere copying of ancient values and styles.

Petrarch labored throughout his life to reconstruct the history and literature of Rome. He learned to read and write classical Latin. In the 1330s, he discovered a number of classical works, including orations and letters by Cicero, the great philosopher, statesman, and opponent of Julius Caesar (see pages 137–138). Cicero's letters to his friend Atticus were filled with gossip, questions about politics in Rome, and complaints about his forced withdrawal from public life. They create the portrait of an individual who was much more complex than the austere philosopher of medieval legend.

Petrarch's humanism was not worldly or secular; he was and remained a committed Christian. He recognized the tension between the Christian present and pagan antiquity. He wrote a dialogue, *The Secret*, reflecting his own ambivalence. Did his devotion to reading and imitating classical authors involve a rejection of traditional Christian values? "My wishes fluctuate and my desires conflict, and in their struggle they tear me apart," he confessed.** Yet, he prized the beauty and moral value of ancient learning. He wrote *The Lives of Illustrious Men*, biographies of men from antiquity whose thoughts and actions he deemed worthy of emulation. He argued that ancient moralists were superior to Scholastic philosophers, whose work ended with the determination of truth, or correct responses. "The true moral philosophers and useful teachers of the virtues," he concluded, "are those whose first and last intention is to make hearer and reader good, those who do not merely teach what virtue and vice are but sow into our hearts love of the best . . . and hatred of the worst."†

## Humanistic Studies

Petrarch's program of humanistic studies became especially popular with the wealthy oligarchy who dominated political life in Florence. The Florentine chancellor Coluccio Salutati (1331–1406), and a generation of young intellectuals who formed his circle, evolved an ideology of **civic humanism**. Civic humanists wrote letters, orations, and histories praising their city's classical virtues and history. In the process, they gave a practical and public meaning to the Petrarchan program. Civic humanists argued, as had Cicero, that there was a moral and ethical value intrinsic to public life. In a letter to a friend, Salutati wrote that public life is "something holy and holier than idleness in [religious] solitude." To another he added, "The active life you flee is to be followed both as an exercise in virtue and because of the necessity of brotherly love."‡

More than Petrarch himself, civic humanists desired to create and inspire men of virtue who could take the lead in government and protect their fellow citizens from lawlessness and tyranny. In his *Panegyric on the City of Florence* (ca. 1405), Leonardo Bruni (ca. 1370–1444) recalled the history of the Roman Republic and suggested that Florence could re-create the best qualities of the Roman state. To civic humanists, the study of Rome and its virtues was the key to the continued prosperity of Florence and similar Italian republics.

**civic humanism** An ideology popular with the political leaders of Florence that emphasized Rome's classical republican virtues of duty and public service.

*Quoted in J. B. Trapp, ed., *Background to the English Renaissance* (London: Gray-Mills Publishing, 1974), p. 11.
**Quoted in N. Mann, *Petrarch* (Oxford: Oxford University Press), p. 67.
†Petrarch, "On His Own Ignorance and That of Many Others," in *The Renaissance Philosophy of Man*, ed. Ernst Cassirer, Paul Oskar Kristeller, and John H. Randall (Chicago: University of Chicago Press, 1948), p. 105.
‡Quoted in Benjamin G. Kohl and Ronald G. Witt, *The Earthly Republic* (Philadelphia: University of Pennsylvania Press, 1978), p. 111.

## The Education of Women

*Leonardo Bruni wrote this tract on education for Battista di Montefeltro. She was the daughter of a Duke of Urbino and the unhappy wife of Galeazzo Malatesta, briefly the ruler of Pesaro. She was learned and a poet. She exchanged letters and poems with her father-in-law and later when living as a widow in Urbino, she presented a Latin oration to the Holy Roman Emperor Sigismond when he visited. Bruni wrote this tract when she was a young woman and newly married. It represents both Bruni's ideas about humanistic education in general and those aspects of thought most appropriate for women.*

I am led to address this Tractate to you, Illustrious Lady, by the high repute which attaches to your name in the field of learning; and I offer it, partly as an expression of my homage to distinction already attained, partly as an encouragement to further effort. ... [T]he wider question now confronts us, that of the subject matter of our studies, that which I have already called the realities of fact and principle, as distinct from literary form. ... For instance, subtleties of Arithmetic and Geometry are not worthy to absorb a cultivated mind, and the same must be said of Astrology. You will be surprised to find me suggesting (although with much more hesitation) that the great and complex art of Rhetoric should be placed in the same category. ... To her neither the intricacies of debate nor the oratorical artifices of action and delivery are of the least practical use, if indeed they are not positively unbecoming. Rhetoric in all its forms—public discussion, forensic argument, logical fence, and the like—lies absolutely outside the province of women.

What disciplines then are properly open to her? In the first place she has before here, as a subject peculiarly her own, the whole field of religion and morals. The literature of the church thus will claim her earnest study. ... St Augustine affords her the fullest scope for reverent yet learned study. ... [In addition] Morals, indeed have been treated of by the noblest intellects of Greece and Rome. What they have left to us upon Continence, Temperance, Modesty, Justice, Courage, Greatness of Soul, demands your sincere respect. ... Let religion and morals, therefore, hold the first place in the education of a Christian lady.

But we must not forget that true distinction is to be attained by a wide and varied range of such studies. ... First among such studies I place History: a subject which must not on any account be neglected by one who aspires to true cultivation. ... From History, also, we draw our store of examples of moral precepts. ...

The great orators of antiquity must by all means be included. Nowhere do we find the virtues more warmly extolled, the vices so fiercely decried. ...

I come now to Poetry and Poets—a subject with which every educated lady must shew herself thoroughly familiar. ... For in their writings we find deep speculations upon nature, and upon the Causes and Origins of things. ... Besides these, many important truths upon matters of daily life are suggested or illustrated.

### Questions

1. *In what ways was education for women deemed to be different from education for men?*

2. *What did Bruni believe students could learn from a humanist education?*

"The Eduction of Women," The Tractate of Lionardo Bruni d'Arezzo, de Studiis et literis," in *Vittorino da Feltre and Other Humanist Educators.* Tr, William Harrison Woodward ( first published 1897, republished New York, The Teachers College of Columbia University, 1963) 123, 126-29.

## Educational Reform

One of Petrarch's most enthusiastic followers was Guarino of Verona (1374–1460), who became the leading advocate of educational reform in Renaissance Italy. After spending five years in Constantinople learning Greek and collecting classical manuscripts, he became the most successful teacher and translator of Greek literature in Italy. Greek studies had been advanced by Manuel Chrysoloras (1350–1415), who, after his arrival from Constantinople in 1397, taught Greek for three years in Florence. Chrysoloras was later joined by other Greek intellectuals, especially after the fall of Constantinople to the Turks in 1453. Guarino built on this interest in Greek culture.

Guarino emphasized careful study of grammar and memorization of large bodies of classical history and poetry. He was convinced that through a profound understanding of Greek and Latin literature and a careful imitation of the style of the great authors, a person could come to exhibit the moral and ethical values for which Cicero, Seneca, and Plutarch were justly famous. Although it is unclear whether Guarino's style of education produced such results, it did provide a thorough training in literature and oratory. In an age that admired the ability to speak and write persuasively, the new style of humanistic education pioneered by Guarino spread quickly throughout Europe. The elegy spoken at Guarino's funeral sums up Italian views of humanistic education, as well as the contribution of Guarino himself:

Prado, Madrid/Giraudon/The Bridgeman Art Library

***Private Reading*** Robert Campin's painting of Saint Barbara of 1438 shows a typical Flemish interior with a woman reading. It was not unusual for well-to-do women to read even if they could not write.

"No one was considered noble, as leading a blameless life, unless he had followed Guarino's courses."

Guarino's example was widely followed. One of his early students, Vittorino da Feltre (1378–1446), was appointed tutor at the Gonzaga court of Mantua. Like Guarino, he emphasized close literary study and careful imitation of classical authors. But the school he founded, the Villa Giocosa (jo-KO-sa), was innovative because he advocated games and exercises, as well as formal study. In addition, Vittorino required that bright young boys from poor families be included among the seventy affluent students normally resident in his school. Vittorino was so renowned that noblemen from across Italy sent their sons to be educated at the Villa Giocosa.

## The Limits of Humanism

Since Italians viewed humanistic education as a preparation for public life, it was not necessary for laborers, women, or others without political power. Leonardo Bruni of Florence once composed a curriculum for a young woman to follow. He emphasized literature and moral philosophy, but, he cautioned, there was no reason to study rhetoric: "For why should the subtleties of . . . rhetorical conundrums consume the powers of a woman, who never sees the forum? . . . The contests of the forum, like those of warfare and battle, are the sphere of men."* (See the feature, "The Written Record: The Education of Women" on page 329.) To what extent did women participate in the cultural and artistic movements of the fourteenth and fifteenth centuries? Some polemicists argued that women were intellectually and morally weaker than men. More often, Italian patricians felt it simply was improper for women to play an obvious and public role.

Thus, while many women did learn to read and even to write, they exhibited their learning in restricted ways. Religious women and wives of merchants read educational and spiritual literature. Some women needed to write in order to manage the economic and political interests of their families. Alessandra Macinghi-Strozzi (ma-CHIN-ghee STROT-zi) of Florence (1407–1471), for example, wrote numerous letters to her sons in exile, describing her efforts to find spouses for her children and to influence the government to end their banishments. She used her letters to relay information about the indirect contacts she had with social and political leaders. They demonstrate, in fact, the subtle, indirect power women used to influence politics.

Women acted with care because many men were suspicious of literate women. The career of Isotta Nogarola of Verona (b. 1418), one of a number of fifteenth- and sixteenth-century Italian women whose literary abilities equaled those of male humanists, show how women might participate in a household salon. She was educated by her father and Isotta quickly became known as a gifted writer. She exchanged letters with many humanists, but the letters had to take a particular form. Writers often began by praising her virginity and only later spoke of literary matters. In a polemical exchange, one critic

*Quoted in M. L. King, *Women of the Renaissance* (Chicago: University of Chicago Press, 1991), p. 194.

suggested that it was unnatural for a woman to have such scholarly interests and accused her of equally unnatural sexual interests. Guarino of Verona himself wrote warning her that if she was truly to be educated, she must put off female sensibilities and find "a man within the woman."*

Women did play a role, but it was always influenced by assumptions about what was proper for a female. In other words, a woman who had literary or cultural interests was expected to enter a convent. That was a friend's advice to Isotta Nogarola. It was wrong, he said, "that a virgin should consider marriage, or even think about that liberty of lascivious morals."** Isotta never married and did retreat from public life, but she continued to correspond with other humanists. Fathers and husbands continued to value the moral voice of female humanists, but only in the domestic setting. The virtues of humanism were public virtues, and Europeans of the Renaissance remained uncomfortable with the idea that women might act directly and publicly.

## The Transformation of Humanism

The fascination with education based on ancient authorities was heightened by the discovery in 1416, in the Monastery of Saint Gall in Switzerland, of a complete manuscript of Quintilian's *Institutes of Oratory*, a first-century treatise on the proper education for a young Roman patrician. The document was found by Poggio Bracciolini (PO-joe bra-cho-LEE-nee) (1380–1459), who had been part of the humanist circle in Florence. The discovery was hardly accidental. Like Petrarch, the humanists of the fifteenth century scoured Europe for ancient texts to read and study. In searching out the knowledge of the past, these fifteenth-century humanists made a series of discoveries that changed their understanding of language, philosophy, and religion. Their desire to imitate led to a profound transformation of knowledge.

### Lorenzo Valla and Historical Perspective

The career of Lorenzo Valla (1407–1457) illustrates the transformation that took place in the fifteenth century, as humanism swept Europe. Valla was born near Rome and received a traditional humanistic education in Greek and Latin studies. He spent the rest of his life at universities and courts lecturing on philosophy and literature. Valla's studies had led him to understand that languages change with time—that they, too, have a life and a history. In 1440, he published a work called *On the Falsely Believed and Forged Donation of Constantine*.

The donation purported to record the gift by the emperor Constantine (r. 311–337) of jurisdiction over Rome and the western half of the empire to the pope when the imperial capital was moved to Constantinople (see pages 170–172). In the High and late Middle Ages, the papacy used the document to defend its right to political dominion in central Italy. The donation had long been criticized by legal theorists, who argued that Constantine had no right to make it. Valla went further and attacked the legitimacy of the document itself. Because of its language and form, he argued, it could not have been written at the time of Constantine: Valla was correct; the *Donation* was an eighth-century forgery.

> Through his [the writer's] babbling, he reveals his most impudent forgery himself. . . . Where he deals with the gifts he says "a diadem . . . made of pure gold and precious jewels." The ignoramus did not know that the diadem was [like a turban and] made of cloth, probably silk. . . . He thinks it had to be made of gold, since nowadays kings usually wear a circle of gold set with jewels.[†]

Valla later turned his attention to the New Testament. Jerome (331–420) had put together the Vulgate edition of the Bible in an attempt to create a single accepted Latin version of the Hebrew Bible and the New Testament (see page 192). In 1444, Valla completed his *Annotations on the New Testament*. In this work, he used his training in classical languages

*On the Falsely Believed and Forged Donation of Constantine* This work demonstrated that an important papal claim to political rule of central Italy was based on an eighth-century forgery.

---

*Quoted in M. L. King, *Women of the Renaissance* (Chicago: University of Chicago Press, 1991), p. 222.
**Quoted in M. L. King, *Women of the Renaissance* (Chicago: University of Chicago Press, 1991), p. 198.
†K. R. Bartlett, *The Civilization of the Italian Renaissance* (Lexington, Mass.: D. C. Heath, 1992), p. 314.

**The Donation of Constantine** Pope Julius II commissioned Raphael to include this painting of Constantine's purported gift in the Stanze, the papal apartments in the Vatican. The classical and imperial images were meant to emphasize that the Church was the heir to Roman imperial authority.

Scala/Art Resource, NY

to correct Jerome's standard Latin text and to show numerous instances of mistranslations. His annotations on the New Testament were of critical importance to humanists outside Italy and were highly influential during the Protestant Reformation.

## Renaissance Philosophy

Like Valla, many other humanists anticipated that literary studies would lead eventually to philosophy. In 1456, a young Florentine began studying Greek with just such a change in mind. Supported by the Medici rulers of Florence, Marsilio Ficino (1433–1499) began a daunting project: to translate the works of Plato into Latin and to interpret Plato in light of Christian doctrine and tradition.

Ficino believed that Platonism, like Christianity, demonstrated the dignity of humanity. He wrote that everything in creation was connected along a continuum ranging from the lowliest matter to the person of God. The human soul was located at the midpoint of this hierarchy and was a bridge between the material world and God. True wisdom, and especially experience of the divine, could be gained only through contemplation and love. According to Ficino, logic and scientific observation did not lead to true understanding. Humans, he observed, know logically only what they can define in human language; individuals can, however, love things, such as God, that they are not fully able to comprehend.

Ficino's belief in the dignity of man was shared by Giovanni Pico della Mirandola (mi-RAHN-do-la) (1463–1494), who proposed to debate, with other philosophers, nine hundred theses dealing with the nature of man, the origins of knowledge, and the uses of philosophy. Pico extended Ficino's idea of the hierarchy of being, arguing that humans surpassed even the angels in dignity. Angels held a fixed position in the hierarchy, just below God. In contrast, humans could move either up or down in the hierarchy, depending on the extent to which they embraced spiritual or worldly interests. "Constrained by no limits," he observed, "in accordance with your own free will, . . . you shall independently determine the bounds of your own nature."* Pico further believed that he had proved that all philosophies contain at least some truth. He was one of the first humanists to learn Hebrew and to argue that divine wisdom could be found in Jewish as well as Christian and pagan mystical literature.

*"Oration on the Dignity of Man," in *The Italian Renaissance Reader*, ed Julia Bondanella & Mark Musa (New York, 1987) 181.

## The Unity of Knowledge

Pico's ideas were shared by other humanists, who contended that an original, unified, divine illumination—a "Pristine Theology," they called it—preceded even Plato and Aristotle. These humanists found theological truth in what they believed was ancient Egyptian, Greek, and Jewish magic. Ficino himself popularized the *Corpus Hermeticum* (the Hermetic collection), an amalgam of magical texts of the first century A.D. that was thought mistakenly to be the work of an Egyptian magician, Hermes Trismegistos. Humanists assumed Hermes wrote during the age of Moses and Pythagoras. Like many mystical writings of the first and second centuries, Hermetic texts explained how the mind could influence and be influenced by the material and celestial worlds.

Along with exploring Hermetic magic, many humanists of the fifteenth and sixteenth centuries investigated astrology and alchemy. All three systems posit the existence of a direct, reciprocal connection between the cosmos and the natural world. In the late medieval and Renaissance world, astrological and alchemical theories seemed reasonable. By the late fifteenth century, many humanists assumed that personality was profoundly affected by the stars and that the heavens were not silent regarding human affairs. It was not by accident that for a century or more after 1500 astrologers were official or unofficial members of most European courts.

Interest in alchemy was equally widespread, though more controversial. Alchemists believed that everything was made of a primary material and that, therefore, it was possible to transmute one substance into another. The most popular variation, and the one most exploited by hucksters and frauds, was the belief that base metals could be turned into gold. The hopes of most alchemists, however, were more profound. They were convinced that they could unlock the secrets of the entire cosmos. On a personal and religious, as well as on a material level, practitioners hoped to make the impure pure. The interest in understanding and manipulating nature that lay at the heart of Hermetic magic, astrology, and alchemy was an important stimulus to scientific investigations and, ultimately, to the rise of modern scientific thought.

## Humanism and Political Thought

The humanists' plan to rediscover classical sources meshed well with their political interests. Petrarch and the civic humanists believed that rulers, whether in a republic or a principality, should exhibit all the classical and Christian virtues of faith, hope, love, prudence, temperance, fortitude, and justice. A virtuous ruler would be loved as well as obeyed. The civic humanists viewed governments and laws as essentially unchanging and static. They believed that when change does occur, it most likely happens haphazardly, by chance—that is, because of fortune (the blind Roman goddess Fortuna). Humanists believed that the only protection against chance is true virtue, for the virtuous would never be dominated by fortune. Thus, beginning with Petrarch, humanists advised rulers to love their subjects, to be generous with their possessions, and to maintain the rule of law. Humanistic tracts of the fourteenth and fifteenth centuries were full of classical and Christian examples of virtuous actions by moral rulers.

The French invasions of Italy in 1494 (see pages 302–303), and the warfare that followed, called into question many of the humanists' assumptions about the lessons and virtues of classical civilization. Francesco Guicciardini (gwih-char-DEE-nee) (1483–1540), a Florentine patrician who had served in papal armies, suggested that, contrary to humanistic hopes, history held no clear lessons. Unless the causes of separate events were identical down to the smallest detail, he said, the results could be radically different. An even more thorough critique was offered by Guicciardini's friend and fellow Florentine, **Niccolò Machiavelli** (1469–1527). In a series of writings, Machiavelli developed what he believed was a new science of politics. He believed one could learn from the past but that the lessons had been misunderstood. He wrote *Discourses on Livy*, a treatise on military organization, a history of Florence, and even a Renaissance play titled *The Mandrake Root*. He is best remembered, however, for *The Prince* (1513), a small tract numbering fewer than a hundred pages.

**Niccolò Machiavelli** A government functionary and political theorist in Florence, whose most famous work, *The Prince*, emphasized that the successful ruler must anticipate and adapt to change.

Machiavelli was confident he could teach his contemporaries the lessons to be learned from history. Thus, in his discourses on Livy he comments on Roman government, the role of religion, and the nature of political virtue, emphasizing the sophisticated Roman analysis of political and military situations. A shortcoming more serious than ignorance of history, Machiavelli believed, was his contemporaries' ignorance of the true motivations for people's actions. His play, *The Mandrake Root*, is a comedy about the ruses used to seduce a young woman. In truth, however, none of the characters is fooled. All of them, from the wife to her husband, realize what is happening but use the seduction to their own advantage. As a corrupt friar remarks, "if there is profit here somewhere, I'll be shrewder than they."[*] In the play, Machiavelli implicitly challenges the humanistic assumption that educated individuals will naturally choose virtue over vice. He explicitly criticizes these same assumptions in *The Prince*. Machiavelli holds the contrary view: that individuals are much more likely to respond to fear and that power rather than morality makes for good government.

Machiavelli's use of the Italian word *virtù* led him to be vilified as amoral. Machiavelli deliberately chose a word that meant both "manliness" or "ability" and "virtue as a moral quality." Earlier humanists had restricted *virtù* to the second meaning, using the word to refer to upright qualities such as prudence, generosity, and bravery. Machiavelli tried to show that in some situations these "virtues" could have violent, even evil, consequences. If, for example, a prince was so magnanimous in giving away his wealth that he was forced to raise taxes, his subjects might come to hate him. Conversely, a prince who, through cruelty to the enemies of his state, brought peace and stability to his subjects might be obeyed and perhaps even loved. The able ruler must be mindful of the goals to be achieved—that is what Machiavelli really meant by the phrase often translated wrongly as "the ends justify the means."

Like Guicciardini, Machiavelli understood that governing required more than simple imitation of the past. Governing is a process that requires different skills at different times, he warned: "The man who adapts his course of action to the nature of the times will succeed and, likewise, the man who sets his course of action out of tune with the times will come to grief."[**] The abilities that enable a prince to gain power may not be the abilities that will allow him to maintain it.

With the writings of Machiavelli, humanistic ideas of intellectual, moral, and political reform came to maturation. Petrarch and the early humanists believed fully in the powers of classical wisdom to transform society. Machiavelli and his contemporaries admitted the importance of classical wisdom but also recognized the ambiguity of any simplistic application of classical learning to contemporary life.

## SECTION SUMMARY

- The culture of Italy was more urban and less clerical than the rest of Europe.
- Francesco Petrarch popularized cultural movements that attempted to use Roman learning to change moral values and public behavior in Europe.
- Because women lacked a role in public life, their relationship to the humanistic movement was limited.
- By the end of the fifteenth century, humanists had developed a sense of historical change.
- Political crisis in Italy led Machiavelli to challenge the assumptions about morality and public life.

# Painting and the Arts, 1250–1550

*What was "new" about Renaissance art?*

Townspeople and artists in Renaissance Italy shared the humanists' perception of the importance of classical antiquity. Filippo Villani (d. 1405), a wealthy Florentine from an important business family, wrote that artists had recently "reawakened a lifeless and almost extinct art." In the middle of the fifteenth century, the sculptor Lorenzo Ghiberti concluded that, with the rise of Christianity, "not only statues and paintings [were destroyed], but the books and commentaries and handbooks and rules on which men relied for their training." Italian writers and painters themselves believed that the recovery of past literary and artistic practices was

---

[*] "Mandragola" in *The Portable Machiavelli*, eds. Peter Bondanella and Mark Musa (New York, 1979), p. 456.
[**] "The Prince," in *The Portable Machiavelli*, ed. Peter Bondanella and Mark Musa (New York, 1979), p. 160.

essential if society was to recover from the "barbarism" that they believed characterized the recent past.

The Renaissance of the arts is traditionally divided into three periods. In the early Renaissance, artists imitated nature; in the middle period, they rediscovered classical ideas of proportion; in the High Renaissance, artists were "superior to nature but also to the artists of the ancient world," according to the artist and architect Giorgio Vasari (1511–1574), who wrote a famous history of the eminent artists of his day.

## Early Renaissance Art

The first stirrings of the new styles can be found in the late thirteenth century. The greatest innovator of that era was Giotto di Bondone of Florence (ca. 1266–1337). Although Giotto's background was modest, his fellow citizens, popes, and patrons throughout Italy quickly recognized his skill. He traveled as far south as Rome and as far north as Padua, painting churches and chapels. According to later artists and commentators, Giotto broke with the prevailing stiff, highly symbolic style and introduced lifelike portrayals of living persons. He produced paintings of dramatic situations, showing events located in specific times and places. The frescoes of the Arena Chapel in Padua (1304–1314), for example, recount episodes in the life of Christ. In a series of scenes leading from Christ's birth to his crucifixion, Giotto situates his actors in towns and countryside in what appears to be actual space. Even Michelangelo, the master of the High Renaissance, studied Giotto's painting. Giotto was in such demand throughout Italy that his native Florence gave him a public appointment, so that he would be required by law to remain in the city.

Scala/Art Resource, NY

**Giotto's Naturalism**    Later painters praised the naturalistic emotion of Giotto's painting. In this detail from the Arena Chapel, Giotto portrays the kiss of Judas, one of the most dramatic moments in Christian history.

Scala/Art Resource, NY

**The Doors of Paradise** Ghiberti worked on panels for the baptistery from 1401 to 1453. In his representations of scenes from the Old Testament, he combined a love of ancient statuary with the new Florentine interest in linear perspective.

**linear perspective** A revolutionary technique developed by early-fifteenth-century Florentine painters for representing three-dimensional objects on a two-dimensional plane.

Early in the fifteenth century, Florentine artists devised new ways to represent nature that surpassed even the innovations of Giotto. The revolutionary nature of these artistic developments is evident from the careers of Lorenzo Ghiberti (gi-BER-tee) (1378–1455), Filippo Brunelleschi (broon-eh-LES-key) (1377–1446), and Masaccio (ma-SAH-cho) (1401–ca. 1428). Their sculpture, architecture, and painting began an ongoing series of experiments with the representation of space through **linear perspective**. Perspective is a system for representing three-dimensional objects on a two-dimensional plane. It is based on two observations: (1) as parallel lines recede into the distance, they seem to converge; and (2) a geometric relationship regulates the relative sizes of objects at various distances from the viewer. Painters of the Renaissance literally found themselves looking at their world from a new perspective.

In 1401, Ghiberti won a commission to design door panels for the baptistery of San Giovanni in Florence. He was to spend much of the rest of his life working on two sets of bronze doors on which were recorded the stories of the New Testament (the north doors) and the Old Testament (the east doors). Ghiberti used the new techniques of linear perspective to create a sense of space into which he placed his classically inspired figures. Later, in the sixteenth century, Michelangelo remarked that the east doors were worthy to be the "Doors of Paradise," and so they have been known ever since.

In the competition for the baptistery commission, Ghiberti had beaten the young Filippo Brunelleschi, who, as a result, gave up sculpture for architecture and later left Florence to study in Rome. While in Rome, he is said to have visited and measured surviving examples of classical architecture—the artistic equivalent of humanistic literary research. According to Vasari, he was capable of "visualizing Rome as it was before the fall." Brunelleschi's debt to Rome is evident in his masterpiece, Florence's foundling hospital. Built as a combination of hemispheres and cubes and resembling a Greek stoa or an arcaded Roman basilica, the long, low structure is an example of how profoundly different Renaissance architecture was from the towering Gothic of the Middle Ages. But his experience in Rome was also critical to his famous plan for constructing a dome over the Cathedral of Santa Maria del Fiore in Florence. The Florentines were replacing their old cathedral with a vast new one. But until Brunelleschi, no one had been able to design a dome to cover the 180-foot space created by the vast new nave. He designed mutually supporting internal and external domes that were stronger and lighter than a single dome would have been.

In the first decade of the fifteenth century, many commentators believed that painting would never be as innovative as either sculpture or architecture. They knew of no classical models that had survived for imitation. Yet, the possibilities in painting became apparent in 1427 with the unveiling of Masaccio's *Trinity* in the Florentine Church of Santa Maria Novella. Masaccio built on revolutionary experiments in linear perspective to create a painting in which a flat wall seems to become a recessed chapel. The space created is filled with the images of Christ crucified, the Father, and the Holy Spirit.

In the middle years of the fifteenth century, artists came to terms with the innovations of the earlier period. In the second half of the fifteenth century, however, artists such as the Florentine Sandro Botticelli (bot-ti-CHEL-ee) (1445–1510) added a profound understanding of classical symbolism to the technical innovations of Masaccio and Brunelleschi. Botticelli's famous *Primavera* (*Spring*, 1478), painted for a member of the Medici family, is filled with Neo-Platonic symbolism concerning truth, beauty, and the virtues of humanity.

## High Renaissance Art

The high point in the development of Renaissance art came at the beginning of the sixteenth century. Artists in Venice learned perspective from the Florentines and added their own tradition of subtle coloring in oils.

The work of two Florentines, Leonardo da Vinci (1452–1519) and Michelangelo Buonarroti (1475–1564), best exemplifies the sophisticated heights that art achieved early in the sixteenth century. Leonardo, the bastard son of a notary, was raised in the village of Vinci outside of Florence. Cut off from the humanistic milieu of the city, he desired, above all else, to prove that his artistry was the equal of his formally schooled social superiors. In his notebooks, he confessed, "I am fully conscious that, not being a literary man, certain presumptuous persons will think they may reasonably blame me, alleging that I am not a man of letters."[*] But he defended his lack of classical education by arguing that all the best writing, like the best painting and invention, is based on the close observation of nature. Close observation and scientific analysis made Leonardo's work uniquely creative in all these fields. Leonardo is famous for his plans, sometimes prophetic, for bridges, fortresses, submarines, and airships. In painting, he developed chiaroscuro, a technique for using light and dark in pictorial representation, and showed aerial perspective. He painted horizons as muted, shaded zones rather than with sharp lines. It was Leonardo's analytical observation that had the greatest influence on his contemporaries.

Michelangelo, however, was widely hailed as the capstone of Renaissance art. In the words of a contemporary, "He alone has triumphed over ancient artists, modern artists and over Nature itself." In his career, we can follow the rise of Renaissance artists from the ranks of mere craftsmen to honored creators, courtiers who were the equals of the humanists—in fact, Michelangelo shared Petrarch's concern for reform and renewal in Italian society. We can also discern the synthesis of the artistic and intellectual transformations of the Renaissance with a profound religious sensitivity.

The importance of Michelangelo's contribution is obvious in two of his most important works: the statue *David* in Florence and his commissions in the Sistine Chapel of the Vatican in Rome. From his youth, Michelangelo had studied and imitated antique sculpture, to the point that some of his creations were thought by many actually to be antiquities. He used his understanding of classical art in *David* (1501). Florentines recalled David's defeat of the giant Goliath, saving Israel from almost certain conquest by the Philistines. *David* thus became a symbol of the youthful Florentine republic struggling to maintain its freedom against great odds. As Vasari noted, "Just as David had protected his people and governed them justly, so who ever ruled Florence should vigorously defend the city and govern it with justice."[**]

Michelangelo was a committed republican and Florentine, but he spent much of his life working in Rome on a series of papal commissions. In 1508, he was called by Pope Julius II (r. 1503–1513) to work on the ceiling of the Sistine Chapel. Michelangelo spent four years decorating the ceiling with hundreds of figures and with nine scenes from the Book of Genesis, including the famous *Creation of Adam*. In the late 1530s, at the request of Pope Clement VII (r. 1523–1534), he completed *The Last Judgment*, which covers the wall above the altar. In that painting, the techniques of perspective and the conscious recognition of debts to classical culture recede into the background as the artist surrounds Christ in judgment with saints and sinners. In the hollow, hanging skin of flayed Saint Bartholomew we can detect a psychological self-portrait of an artist increasingly concerned with his own spiritual failings.

Scala/Art Resource, NY

**David** Michelangelo's sculpture is an example of the multiple meanings of art. A masterpiece of Renaissance art, it was especially valued by the Florentines as a symbol of civic culture. It is for this reason it was placed in front of the city hall.

**Leonardo da Vinci** A famous painter, engineer, and scientist who rejected arguments and ideas based on imitation of the ancients. Rather, he advocated careful study of the natural world.

**Sistine Chapel** The chapel at the Vatican Palace, containing Michelangelo's magnificent paintings of the Creation and Last Judgment; it captures the cultural, religious, and ideological program of the papacy.

---

[*]Quoted in *The Notebooks of Leonardo da Vinci*, ed. J. P. Richter, vol. 1 (New York: Dover, 1883 and 1970), p. 14.
[**]Giorgio Vasari, *The Lives of the Artists*, trans. George Bull (Baltimore: Penguin, 1965), p. 338.

## Gentile Bellini Travels to Meet the Turkish Sultan

*Giovanni and Gentile Bellini were two of the leading Renaissance artists in Venice. Their fame spread throughout the Mediterranean and resulted in this unusual cultural meeting in 1479. A portrait of the emperor Mehmed II by Gentile now hangs in the National Gallery in London.*

Some portraits having been taken to Turkey to the Grand Turk [the sultan] by an ambassador, that emperor was so struck with astonishment that, although the Mohammedan laws prohibit pictures, he accepted them with great goodwill, praising the work without end, and what is more, requesting that the master himself be sent to him. But the Senate, considering that Giovanni could ill support the hardships, resolved to send Gentile his brother, and he was conveyed safely in their galleys to Constantinople, where being presented to Mehmed [II], he was received with much kindness as an unusual visitor. He presented a beautiful picture to the prince, who admired it much, and could not persuade himself to believe that a mortal man had in him so much of the divinity as to be able to express the things of nature in such a lively manner. Gentile painted the Emperor Mehmed himself from life so well that it was considered a miracle, and the emperor, having seen many specimens of his art, asked Gentile if he had the courage to paint himself; and Gentile having answered "Yes," before many days were over he finished a lifelike portrait by means of a mirror, and brought it to the monarch, whose astonishment was so great that he would have it a divine spirit dwelt in him. And had not this art been forbidden by the law of the Turks, the emperor would never have let him go. But either from fear that people would murmur, or from some other cause, he sent for him one day, and having thanked him, and given him great praise, he bade him to ask whatever he would and it should be granted him without fail. Gentile modestly asked for nothing more than that he would graciously give him a letter of recommendation to the Senate and Lords of Venice. His request was granted in as fervent words as possible, and then, loaded with gifts and honors, and with the dignity of a cavalier, he was sent away. Among the other gifts was a chain of gold of two hundred and fifty crowns weight, worked in the Turkish manner. So, leaving Constantinople, he came safely to Venice, where he was received by his brother Giovanni and the whole city with joy, every one rejoicing in the honors which Mehmed had paid him. When the Doge and Lords [of Venice] saw the letters of the emperor, they ordered that a provision of two hundred crowns a year should be paid him all the rest of his life.

### Questions

1. What seems to be the role of Renaissance art and artists in Venetian and Turkish diplomacy?

2. What does Bellini's trip to Constantinople suggest about relations between the Turks and Christians?

Source: *Stories of the Italian Renaissance from Vasari*, arranged and translated by E. L. Seeley (London and New York, 1908), pp. 135–137.

---

Michelangelo's self-portrait reminds us that the intellectual content of the artist's work is one of its most enduring traits. He was a Platonist who believed that the form and beauty of a statue are contained, buried, in the stone itself. The artist's job is to peel away excess material and reveal the beauty within. As he noted in one of his poems, sculpting is a process not unlike religious salvation:

> *Just as by carving . . . we set*
> *Into hard mountain rock*
> *A living figure*
> *Which grows most where the stone is most removed;*
> *In like manner, some good works . . .*
> *Are concealed by the excess of my very flesh.*[*]

The works of Italian artists were admired well beyond the borders of Italy. Even Sultan Mehmed II of Constantinople valued Italian painters. He attempted at various times to hire both Leonardo da Vinci and Michelangelo. He and his architects were quite aware of the artistic and architectural breakthroughs in Italy. And as he saw himself as a successor to the Roman emperors, his building programs included what he had learned from the West. (See the feature, "The Global Record: Gentile Bellini Travels to Meet the Turkish Sultan" above.) Italian painters, goldsmiths, and architects continued to work in the Ottoman Empire throughout the sixteenth century.

*Julia Bondanella and Mark Musa, eds., *The Italian Renaissance Reader* (New York: Meridian Books, 1987), p. 377.

## Renaissance Art in the North

Artistic innovation was not just found in Italy and the Mediterranean world. In the early fifteenth century, while Brunelleschi and Masaccio were revolutionizing the ways in which Italian artists viewed their world, artists north of the Alps, especially in Flanders, were making equally striking advances in the ways they painted and sculpted. Artistic innovation in northern Europe began with changes tied closely to the world of northern courts; only later did artists take up the styles of the Italian Renaissance. Northerners took Italian Renaissance art and fit it to a new environment.

Northern art of the late fourteenth and fifteenth centuries changed in two significant ways. In sculpture, the long, austere, unbroken vertical lines typical of Gothic sculpture gave way to a much more complex and emotional style. In painting, Flemish artists moved from ornate, vividly colored paintings to experiments with ways to create a sense of depth. Artists strove to paint and sculpt works that more faithfully represented reality. The sculptures of Claus Sluter (1350–1406), carved for a family chapel of the Burgundian dukes at Champmol, captured a lifelike drama unlike the previous Gothic sculpture. Court painters, such as Jan van Eyck (ca. 1390–1441), in miniatures, portraits, and altar paintings, also moved away from a highly formalized style to a careful representation of specific places. In van Eyck's portrait of the Italian banker and courtier Giovanni Arnolfini and his bride, the image of the painter is reflected in a small mirror behind the couple, and above the mirror is written, "Jan van Eyck was here, 1434." Whereas Italians of the early fifteenth century tried to re-create space through linear perspective, the Flemish used aerial perspective, softening colors and tones to give the illusion of depth.

The influence of Renaissance styles in the north of Europe dates from the reign of the French king Francis I (r. 1515–1547), when Italian artists in significant numbers traveled north. Francis invited Italian artists to his court—most notably Leonardo da Vinci, who spent his last years in France. The most influential of the Italian-style creations in France was doubtless Francis's château Fontainebleau, whose decorations contained mythologies, histories, and allegories of the kind found in the Italian courts. Throughout the sixteenth century, Italianate buildings and paintings sprang up throughout Europe.

Perhaps the most famous artist who traveled to Italy, learned Italian techniques, and then transformed them to suit the environment of northern Europe was Albrecht Dürer of Nuremberg (1471–1528). Son of a well-known goldsmith, Dürer became a painter and toured France and Flanders, learning the techniques popular in northern Europe. Then, in 1494, he left Nuremberg on the first of two trips to Italy, during which he sketched Italian landscapes and studied the work of Italian artists, especially in Venice. What he learned in Italy, combined with the friendship of some of Germany's leading humanists, formed the basis of Dürer's works, which blended northern humanistic interests with the Italian techniques of composition and linear perspective. Dürer worked in charcoal, watercolors, and paints, but his influence was most widely spread through his numerous woodcuts covering classical and contemporary themes. His woodcut, *Whore of Babylon*, prepared in the context of the debate over the reform of the church, is based on sketches of Venetian prostitutes completed during his first visit to Italy.

Numerous other artists and engravers traveled south to admire and learn from the great works of Italian artists. The engravings they produced and distributed back home

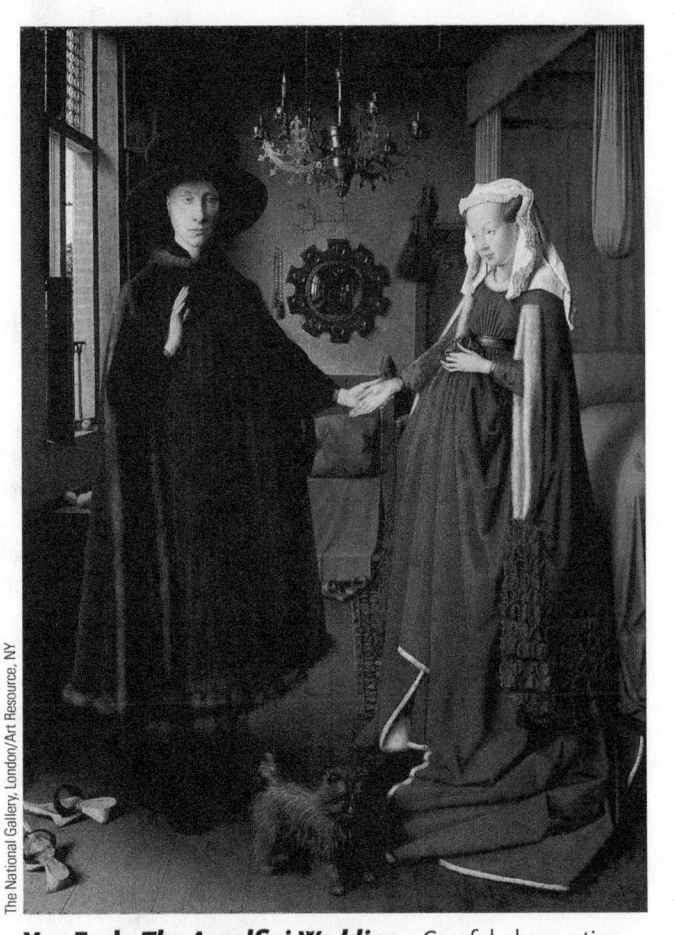

The National Gallery, London/Art Resource, NY

**Van Eyck: *The Arnolfini Wedding*** Careful observation of people and places was typical of the new art of both northern and southern Europe. Van Eyck seems to have re-created this scene to the smallest detail. His own image appears in the mirror on the wall.

**Portrait of a Black Man** Albrecht Dürer sketched this portrait in the early sixteenth century, most likely in a commercial center such as Venice or Nuremberg. By that time, it was common to show one of the three Magi as black, but such depictions, unlike Dürer's drawing here, were rarely based on portrait studies.

made the southern innovations available to those who would never set foot in Italy. In fact, some now lost or destroyed creations are known only through the copies engraved by northern artists eager to absorb Italian techniques.

## Art and Patronage

The variety and vitality of art in the Renaissance depended, in large measure, on the economic prosperity of Europe's cities and towns. Because of banking, international trade, and even service as mercenaries, Italians, and particularly Florentines, had money to spend on arts and luxuries. Thus, the Italians of the Renaissance, whether as public or private patrons, could afford to use consumption of art as a form of competition for social and political status.

It was not just the elite who could afford art. Surprisingly, modest families bought small religious paintings, painted storage chests, and decorative arts. Moralists advised families to buy small paintings of the Virgin Mary or the baby Jesus. Families also bought small paintings of saints considered special to their town or family. Wealthy and modest families alike bought brightly decorated terra-cotta pitchers, platters, and plates. Decorative arts were a critical social marker for families at all levels. (See the feature, "The Visual Record: Renaissance Marriage Chests" on pages 344–345.) Thus, the market for art steadily increased in the fourteenth and fifteenth centuries, as did the number of shops and studios in which artists could be trained.

Artists in the modern world are accustomed to standing outside society as critics of conventional ideas. In the late Middle Ages and Renaissance, artists were not alienated commentators. In 1300, most art was religious in subject, and public display was its purpose. Throughout Europe, art fulfilled a devotional function. Painted crucifixes, altarpieces, and banners were often endowed as devotional or penitential objects. The Arena Chapel in Padua, with its frescoes by Giotto, was funded by a merchant anxious to pay for some of his sins.

In the late Middle Ages and Renaissance, numerous paintings and statues throughout Italy (and much of the rest of Europe) were revered for their miraculous powers. During plague, drought, and times of war people had recourse to the sacred power of the saints represented in these works of art. (See the feature, "The Visual Record: A Painting of the Plague" in Chapter 11, pages 308–309.) The construction of the great churches of the period was often a community project that lasted for decades, even centuries. The city council of Siena, for example, voted to rebuild its Gothic Cathedral of Saint Mary, saying that the Blessed Virgin "was, is and will be in the future the head of this city" and that through veneration of her "Siena may be protected from harm." Accordingly, although the subject of art was clearly and primarily religious, the message was bound up in civic values.

## Art and the Commune

The first burst of artistic creativity in the fourteenth century was paid for by public institutions. Communal governments built and decorated city halls to house government functionaries and to promote civic pride. Most towns placed a remarkable emphasis on the beauty of the work. Civic officials often named special commissions to consult with a variety of artists and architects before approving building projects. Governments, with an eye to the appearance of public areas, legislated the width of streets, height limits, and even the styles of dwelling façades.

Public art in Florence was often organized and supported by various guild organizations. Guild membership was a prerequisite for citizenship, so guildsmen set the tone in politics, as well as in the commercial life of the city. Most major guilds commissioned sculpture for the Chapel of Or San Michele. This was a famous shrine in the grain market (its painting of the Virgin Mary was popularly thought to have wonder-working powers). The room above the chapel eventually became the seat of the Guelf Party, the city's most powerful political organization. Guilds took responsibility for building and maintaining other structures in the city as well. Guildsmen took pride in creating a beautiful environment that would reflect not only on the city and its patron saint but also on the power and influence of the guild itself.

## Individual Patrons

The princes who ruled outside the republics of Italy often had similarly precise messages that they wished to communicate. Renaissance popes embarked on a quite specific ideological program in the late fifteenth century to assert their dual roles as spiritual leaders of Christendom and temporal lords of a central Italian state (see pages 352–353). Rulers, such as the Este dukes of Ferrara and the Sforza dukes of Milan, constructed castles within their cities or hunting lodges and villas in the countryside and adorned them with pictures of the

**Men and Women Playing Cards**   This fresco painted in the early fifteenth century in Milan is typical of the art used to decorate the homes of the wealthy. It depicts one of the pastimes of noble families. Scala/Art Resource, NY

hunt or murals of knights in combat—scenes that emphasized their noble virtues and their natural right to rule.

By the mid-fifteenth century, patrons of artworks in Florence and most other regions of Italy were more and more likely to be wealthy individuals. Many of the patrons who commissioned and oversaw artists were women. Women paid for the construction of convents and chapels. In many cases, their patronage can simply be understood as an extension of their families, but in many other cases, it was not. One woman who had lived for years as a concubine of a merchant in Florence used her dead lover's bequest to commission a painting titled *Christ and the Adulteress*, making clear that even women in her situation could hope for God's mercy. Other women, like the duchess Isabella d'Este, used their power as patrons to create their own artistic worlds. Isabella created a studiolo, a private apartment where she could meet courtiers and diplomats when she ruled in the place of her absent husband.

Republics, in which all families were in principle equal, initially distrusted the pride and ambition implied by elaborate city palaces and rural villas. By the middle of the fifteenth century, however, such reserve was found in none but the most conservative republics, such as Venice and Lucca. Palaces, gardens, and villas became the settings in which the wealthy could entertain their peers, receive clients, and debate the political issues of the day. The public rooms of these palaces were decorated with portraits, gem collections, rare books, ceramics, and statuary. Many villas and palaces included private chapels. In the Medici palace in Florence, for example, the chapel is the setting for a painting of the Magi (the three wise men who came to worship the infant Jesus), in which the artist, Benozzo Gozzoli (1420–1498), used members of the Medici family as models for the portraits of the Magi and their entourage (see the painting on page 302). The Magi, known to be wise and virtuous rulers, were an apt symbol for the family that had come to dominate the city.

Artists at princely courts were expected to work for the glory of their lord. Often the genre of choice was the portrait. One of the most successful portraitists of the sixteenth century was Sofonisba Anguissola (1532–1625). Anguissola won renown as a prodigy because she was female and from a patrician family; one of her paintings was sent to Michelangelo, who forwarded it to the Medici in Florence. Since women would never be allowed to study anatomy, Anguissola concentrated her talents on portraits and detailed paintings of domestic life. Later, she was called to the Spanish court, where the king, queen, and their daughter sat for her. She continued to paint after her marriage and return to Italy. Even in her nineties, she welcomed painters from all parts of Europe to visit and discuss techniques of portraiture.

## SECTION SUMMARY

- Renaissance painters were especially prized for their ability to depict particular events in realistic, natural seeming settings.

- Beginning with Brunelleschi, artists consciously searched for ancient models for their work.

- Northern artists were keenly aware of Italian art, but they contributed a realism based on contrasts of dramatic colors.

- The work of Michelangelo shows the combination of artistic skill with humanistic moral and philosophical values.

# The Spread of the Renaissance, 1350–1536

*In what ways did humanism outside Italy differ from Italian humanism?*

By 1500, the Renaissance had spread from Italy to the rest of Europe. Well beyond the borders of the old Roman Empire, in Prague and Cracow, for example, one could find a renewed interest in classical ideas about art and literature. As information about the past and its relevance to contemporary life spread, however, the message was transformed in several important ways. Outside Italy, Rome and its history played a much less pivotal role. Humanists elsewhere in the West were interested more in religious than in political reform, and they responded to a number of important local interests. Yet, the Renaissance notion of renewal based on a deep understanding and imitation of the past remained at the center of the movement. The nature of the transformation will be clearer if we begin by considering the nature of vernacular literatures before the emergence of Renaissance humanism.

## Vernacular Literatures

The humanistic movement was not simply a continuation of practical and literary movements. The extent of its innovation will be clearer if we look briefly at the vernacular literatures (that is, written in native languages rather than Latin) of the fourteenth and fifteenth centuries.

As in Italy, fourteenth-century writers elsewhere were not immediately drawn to classical sources. Boccaccio's work, for example, influenced another vernacular writer, Geoffrey Chaucer (ca. 1343–1400), the son of a London burgher, who served as a diplomat, courtier, and member of Parliament. Chaucer's most famous work, *The Canterbury Tales*, consists of stories told by a group of thirty pilgrims who left the London suburbs on a pilgrimage to the shrine of Saint Thomas Becket at Canterbury Cathedral. The narrators and the stories themselves describe a variety of moral and social types, creating an acute, sometimes comic, portrait of English life. The Wife of Bath is typical of Chaucer's pilgrims: "She was a worthy woman all her life, husbands at the church door she had five." After describing her own marriages she observes that marriage is a proper way to achieve moral perfection, but it can be so only, she asserts, if the woman is master!

Although Chaucer's characters present an ironic view of the good and evil that characterize society, Chaucer's contemporary, William Langland (ca. 1330–1400), took a decidedly more serious view of the ills of English life. Whereas Boccaccio and Chaucer all told realistic tales about life as it truly seemed to be, Langland used the traditional allegorical language (that is, symbolic language in which a place or person represents an idea) of medieval Europe. In *Piers Plowman*, Langland writes of people caught between the "Valley of Death" and the "Tower of Truth." He describes the seven deadly sins that threaten all of society and follows with an exhortation to do better. Both Chaucer and Langland expected that their audiences would immediately recognize commonly held ideas and values.

Despite the persistence of old forms of literature, new vernacular styles arose, although they still dealt with traditional values and ideas. Letters like those of the Paston family in England or Alessandra Macinghi-Strozzi in Italy described day-to-day affairs of business, politics, and family life. Letters dictated and sent by Saint Catherine of Siena and Angela of Foligno offered advice to the troubled. Small books of moral or spiritual writings were especially popular among women readers in the fourteenth and fifteenth centuries, among them *The Mirror for Simple Souls* by Marguerite of Porete (d. 1310). Though Marguerite was ultimately executed as a heretic, her work continued to circulate anonymously. Her frank descriptions of love, including God's love for humans, inspired many other writers in the fourteenth and fifteenth centuries. Less erotic, but equally riveting, was the memoir of Margery Kempe, an alewife from England, who left her husband and family, dressed in white (symbolic of virginity), and joined other pilgrims on trips to Spain, Italy, and Jerusalem.

One of the most unusual of the new vernacular writers was Christine de Pizan (1369–1430), the daughter of an Italian physician at the court of Charles V of France. When the deaths of her father and husband left her with responsibility for her children and little money, she turned to writing. From 1389 until her death, she lived and wrote at the French court. She is perhaps best known for *The Book of the City of the Ladies* (1405). In it, she added her own voice to what is known as the *querelle des femmes*, the "argument over women." Christine wrote to counter the prevalent opinions of women as inherently inferior to men and incapable of learning or moral judgments. She argued that the problem was education: "If it were customary to send daughters to school like sons, and if they were then taught the natural sciences, they would learn as thoroughly and understand the subtleties of all the arts and sciences as well as sons." Christine described, in her book, an ideal city of ladies in which prudence, justice, and reason would protect women from ignorant male critics.

All these vernacular writings built on popular tales and sayings as well as on traditional moral and religious writings. Unlike the early humanists, the vernacular writers saw little need for new cultural and intellectual models.

## Renaissance Marriage Chests

The image here shows a marriage procession, including a servant carrying a large chest, or cassone. The picture is self-referential, since it was painted on the front of just such a cassone. We know that the painter of this image was Lo Scheggia (lo-SKED-ja) (1406–1486), the younger brother of Masaccio, and that he was recording a popular story of a marriage between the Bardi and Buondelmonte families of Florence. Lo Scheggia's work exhibits many of the characteristics we associate with Renaissance style. But historians often want to evaluate more than just painting technique. Historians of material culture are interested in the objects themselves and in the meanings that contemporaries gave to the possession and exhibition of them. To understand this, we need to know when and where cassoni were produced, why individuals prized them, and what the study of this image from a cassone can tell us about life in Renaissance Italy.

These highly practical chests were used by all but the poorest members of society. In houses that lacked closets, cabinets, and other kinds of storage space, everything was kept in wooden chests. Larger chests were used to store clothing, bedding, jewelry, and even weapons. Smaller chests were used for money, account books, and documents. Many of these chests had secret compartments where, for example, a businessman might keep his most sensitive papers. The most important chests made up the furnishings of the master of the house's bedroom. In a Renaissance palace the master's bedroom was also the room where he met with important allies and family members and conducted his most private business.

Cassoni took on new meaning between the late fourteenth and early sixteenth centuries. During that time, it was common for a groom to commission a matched set of chests: one for himself and the second to hold the fine clothes and jewelry that were part of his wife's dowry. These chests were decorated inside and out with scenes from classical mythology, medieval romances, and other popular stories. Classical Roman figures, such as Lucretia, who sacrificed her life to maintain her virtue, were common subjects. Some chests celebrated the virtues of chastity or fortitude—virtues thought to be essential in a proper wife. Thus, cassoni came to represent the taste, wealth, and social status of the families involved.

With these thoughts in mind, let us look closely at Lo Scheggia's cassone painting. The first thing we should notice is the procession at the left of the picture. We see a man accompanying a woman dressed in black into a house. The two are followed by others leading a horse (a sign of nobility) and carrying bedclothes and the chest. The procession testifies to the very public completion of the marriage process, which often stretched over months, if not years. It began with an engagement, followed by a promise of marriage, then a symbolic exchange of rings and physical consummation of the marriage, usually at the bride's home. The marriage was finalized by a procession to the groom's home. This procession celebrated publicly the alliance between the two families, as well as their standing in the community. Everyone noted carefully what and how much was carried in the procession, which was an indication of the size of the bride's dowry. The decoration of the marriage chest(s) in some way reflected the families involved.

What does the cassone image by Lo Scheggia indicate? The bride is the key to the story. Typically, a wealthy bride wore bright new clothes and jewelry, but this bride is dressed in black. The image tells a story not unlike that of Romeo and Juliet. The families of the bride and groom, Lionora de' Bardi and Ippolito Buondelmonte, had been

## The Impact of Printing

The spread of humanism beyond Italy was aided greatly by the invention of printing. In the fifteenth century, the desire to own and to read complete texts of classical works was widespread, but the number of copies was severely limited. Manuscripts required time and money to hand-copy and collate and to check each new copy. Poggio Bracciolini's letters are filled with complaints about the time and expense of reproducing the classical manuscripts he had discovered. One copy he had commissioned was so inaccurate and illegible as to be nearly unusable. Traveling to repositories and libraries was often easier than creating a personal library. It was rarely possible for someone who read a manuscript once to obtain a complete copy to compare with other works.

**Johann Gutenberg**
German inventor of movable metal type. His innovations led to the publication of the first printed book in Europe, the Gutenberg Bible, in the 1450s.

The invention of printing with movable lead type changed things dramatically. Although block printing had long been known in China, it was only in the late fourteenth century that it became a popular way to produce playing cards and small woodcuts in Europe. Bi Sheng experimented with moveable clay type in the eleventh century, but the Chinese concluded that carving an entire page on a single wooden block was more efficient for large print runs. **Johann Gutenberg** developed molds by which single letters or individual words could be cast in metal. These could be used to compose many different pages. They also were more durable. Metal fonts could produce many more copies before they had to be recast. And

**Lo Scheggia: The Bardi-Buondelmonte Wedding**  Alberto Bruschi di Grassina Collection, Florence/Bridgeman Art Library International

enemies for generations. Despite this fact, the two were in love. We can read the tale of their love in three scenes from right to left. In the first scene on the right, Ippolito is caught in Lionora's house. He refuses to declare his love for her because he wants to protect her reputation. In the middle scene, Lionora, dressed as a widow, interrupts Ippolito's trial and declares her love for him. By dressing as a widow, she symbolically declares that they have already made their wedding vows and are, in fact, married. The authorities accept her declaration, and in the final scene on the left, the marriage is made public. Ippolito leads Lionora in a marriage procession, complete with wedding chest, to their new home. According to tradition, their marriage ended the feud between the two families.

We do not know who commissioned this chest. Nonetheless, we can now step back and speculate a bit about what Florentines might have noticed when they viewed the procession in which this cassone was carried

through the streets of Florence. The image of the wedding couple and the servants carrying expensive dowry items, as well as the chest itself, testifies to the importance of the families involved. In a community such as Florence, where certain families were at the center of politics and public life, this image no doubt reminded those watching the procession of the power of prominent families and the critical role of marriage alliances in maintaining civic peace.

## Questions

1. *Look carefully at the image. Can you identify what seems most significant in the procession of the bride and groom?*

2. *How would this particular image influence the meaning that observers might give to the procession of the bride and groom?*

further, they could be reused to print different pages. Between 180 and 200 copies of the so-called Gutenberg Bible were printed in 1452 and 1453. It was followed shortly by editions of the Psalms. By 1470, German printing techniques had spread to Italy, the Low Countries, France, and England. It has been estimated that, by 1500, a thousand presses were operating in 265 towns (see **Map 12.1**). The output of the early presses was extremely varied, ranging from small devotional books and other popular and profitable literature to complete editions of classical authors and their humanistic and theological texts. Printing allowed for a dramatic expansion of libraries. Early humanists had to strive to create a library of several hundred volumes. The Venetian printer Aldus Manutius (1450–1515) himself printed and distributed over 120,000 volumes!

Printing allowed for the creation of agreed-upon standard editions of works in law, theology, philosophy, and science. Scholars in different parts of the European world could feel fairly confident that they and their colleagues were analyzing identical texts. Similarly, producing accurate medical and herbal diagrams, maps, and even reproductions of art and architecture was easier. Multiple copies of texts also made possible the study of rare and esoteric literary, philosophical, and scientific works. An unexpected result of the print revolution was the rise of the print shop as a center of culture and communication. The printers Aldus Manutius in Venice and Johannes Froben (d. 1527) in Basel were humanists. Both invited

🌐 **Map 12.1  The Spread of Printing**   Printing technology moved rapidly along major trade routes to the most populous and prosperous areas of Europe. The technology was rapidly adopted in peripheral areas as well as in highly literate centers such as the Low Countries, the Rhine Valley, and northern Italy. © Cengage Learning 2014

humanists to work in their shops editing their texts and correcting the proofs before printing. Print shops became a natural gathering place for clerics and laymen. Thus, they were natural sources of humanist ideas and later, in the sixteenth century, of Protestant religious programs.

## Humanism Outside Italy

As the influence of the humanist movement extended beyond Italy, the interests of the humanists changed. Although a strong religious strain infused Italian humanism, public life lay at the center of Italian programs of education and reform. Outside Italy, however, moral and religious reform formed the heart of the movement. Northern humanists wanted to renew Christian life and reinvigorate the church. Critics of the church complained that the clergy were wealthy and ignorant and that the laity were uneducated and superstitious. To amend those failings, northern humanists were involved in building educational institutions, in unearthing and publishing texts by Church Fathers, and in chronicling local customs and history. The works of the two best-known humanists, Thomas More and Desiderius Erasmus, present a sharp critique of contemporary behavior and, in the case of Erasmus, a call to a new sense of piety. The religious views of Erasmus were so influential that northern humanism has generally come to be known as "Christian humanism."

## Humanism and Universities

The intellectual environment into which humanism spread from Italy had changed significantly since the thirteenth century. The universities of Paris and Oxford retained the status they had acquired earlier but found themselves competing with a host of new foundations. Like Paris, almost all had theological faculties dominated by scholastically trained theologians. Nevertheless, the new foundations often had chairs of rhetoric, or "eloquence," which left considerable scope for those who advocated humanistic learning. These new universities, from Cracow (1367) to Uppsala in Sweden (1477), also reflected the increased national feeling in various regions of Europe. The earliest university in the lands of the German Empire, the Charles University in Prague (1348), was founded at the request of Emperor Charles IV, whose court was in Prague. The foundation of a new university at Poszony (1465) by Johannes Vitéz was part of a cultural flowering of the Hungarian court at Buda. A supporter of King Matthias Corvinus, Vitéz corresponded with Italian humanists, collected manuscripts, and tried to recruit humanist teachers to come to Buda. The universities in Vienna (1365), Aix (1409), Louvain (1425), and numerous other cities owed their foundations to the pride and ambition of local leaders.

The humanists associated with the new universities were often educated in Italy, but they brought a new perspective to their work. Humanists in Sweden wrote histories of the Goths, celebrating the contributions of Germans to European culture. Polish humanists wrote similarly, in one case trying to define where in eastern Europe one could draw the line between Europe and Asia.

Humanists on faculties of law at French universities used humanistic techniques of historical and linguistic study. Italian-trained French lawyers introduced what came to be called the "Gallican style" of jurisprudence. Because legal ideas, like language, changed over time, they argued that Roman law had to be studied as a historically created system and not as an abstract and unchanging structure. Humanists, like Guillaume Budé (1468–1540), moved from the study of law to considerations of Roman coinage, religion, and economic life in order to better understand the formation of Roman law. The desire to understand the law led other humanist-legists to add the study of society in ancient Gaul to their work on Rome, and then to examine the law of other societies as well.

## Humanism and Religion

The new universities often became centers of linguistic studies. Humanistic interest in language inspired the foundation of "trilingual" colleges in Spain, France, and the Low Countries to foster serious study of Hebrew, Greek, and Latin. Like Italian humanists, other humanists believed that knowledge of languages would allow students to understand more clearly the truths of Christianity. Typical of this movement was the archbishop of Toledo, Francisco Jiménez de Cisneros (1436–1517), who founded the University of Alcalá in 1508 with chairs of Latin, Greek, and Hebrew. He began the publication of a vast new edition of the Bible, called the "Polyglot ('many tongued') Bible" (1522) because it had parallel columns in Latin, Greek, and, where appropriate, Hebrew. Unlike Valla, Jiménez intended his translations not to challenge the Vulgate but merely to clarify its meaning. The university and the Bible were part of an effort to complete the conversion of Muslims and Jews and to reform religious practices among the old Christians.

To these humanists, the discovery and publication of early Christian authors seemed critical to any reform within the church. Jacques Lefèvre d'Étaples (le-FEV-ra du-TAHP-le) (1455–1536) of France was one of the most famous and influential of these humanistic editors of early Christian texts. After 1500, he concentrated on editing the texts of the early Church Fathers. The true spirit of Christianity, he believed, would be most clear in the works and lives of those who had lived closest to the age of the apostles. Christian humanists, inspired by Lefèvre, became key players in the later Reformation movements in France.

Tensions between the humanists and the advocates of Scholastic methods broke out over the cultural and linguistic studies that formed the heart of the humanist program. Taking to heart the humanistic belief that all philosophies and religions, not just Christianity, contained universal moral and spiritual truths, Johannes Reuchlin (RYE-klin) (1455–1522) of Württemberg embarked on a study of the Jewish Cabala. Johannes Pfefferkorn, a Dominican priest and recent convert from Judaism, attacked Reuchlin's use of Jewish traditions in the study of Christian theology. Sides were quickly drawn. The theological faculties of the German universities generally supported Pfefferkorn. The humanists supported Reuchlin. In his own defense, Reuchlin issued *The Letters of Illustrious Men*, a volume of correspondence he had received in support of his position. This work gave rise to one of the great satires of the Renaissance, *The Letters of Obscure Men* (1516), written by anonymous authors and purporting to be letters from various narrow-minded Scholastics in defense of Pfefferkorn. Although the debate arose over the validity of Hebraic studies for Christian theology and not over humanistic ideas of reform or wisdom, it indicates the division between the humanists and much of the Scholastic community. Many people initially misunderstood the early controversies of the Protestant Reformation as a continuation of the conflicts between humanists and Scholastic theologians over the uses of Hebrew learning.

## Humanists as Critics

The careers of two humanists in particular exemplify the strength—and the limits—of the humanistic movement outside Italy: Sir **Thomas More** (1478–1535) of London and **Desiderius Erasmus** (1466–1536) of Rotterdam. Their careers developed along very different paths. More was educated at St. Anthony's School in London and became a lawyer. He translated Lucan and wrote a humanistic history of Richard III while pursuing his public career. Erasmus, on the other hand, was born the illegitimate son of a priest in the Low Countries. Forced by relatives into a monastery, he disliked the conservative piety and authoritarian discipline of traditional monastic life. Once allowed out of the monastery to serve as an episcopal secretary, he never returned. He made his way as an author and editor.

**Thomas More** Well-known humanist and chancellor of England under Henry VIII. His best-known work, *Utopia*, describes a fictional land of peace and harmony that has outlawed private property.

**Desiderius Erasmus** Prominent Dutch humanist who is best known for his satire *The Praise of Folly*.

### Thomas More

More is most famous for his work *Utopia* (1516), the description of an ideal society located on the island of Utopia (literally, "nowhere") in the newly explored oceans. This powerful and contradictory work is written in two parts. Book I is a debate over the moral value of public service in a world dominated by powerful and autocratic monarchs. Morus, a well-intentioned but practical politician, tries to make the bureaucrat's argument about working for change from within the system. His friend Hythloday, a widely traveled idealist, rejects the argument out of hand. Thomas More himself seems to have been unsure, at that time, about the virtues of public service. He was of two minds, and the debate between Morus and Hythloday reflects his indecision. As part of his critique of injustice and immoral governments in Europe, Hythloday describes in Book II the commonwealth of Utopia, in which there is no private property but strict equality of possessions, and, as a result, harmony, tolerance, and little or no violence.

Since the publication of *Utopia*, debates have raged about whether More, or anyone, could ever really hope to live in such a society. Some scholars have questioned how seriously More took this work—he seems to have written the initial sections merely to amuse friends. Yet, whatever More's intentions, *Utopia*'s society of equality, cooperation, and acceptance continues to inspire social commentators.

Ironically, More, like his creation Morus, soon found himself trying to work for justice within precisely the sort of autocratic court that Hythloday criticized. Not long after the completion of *Utopia*, More entered the service of King Henry VIII (r. 1509–1547), eventually serving as chancellor of England. As a staunch Catholic and royal official, More never acted on utopian principles of peace and toleration. He was, in fact, responsible for the persecution of English Protestants in the years before the king's break with Rome (see pages 403–405). He implied that society could be reformed, yet, in the period after 1521, his humanism and his vision of utopian justice and tolerance had no influence on his own public life.

## Desiderius Erasmus

Unlike More, who was drawn to the power of king and pope, Erasmus always avoided working for authorities. Often called the "Prince of Humanists," he was easily the best-known humanist of the early sixteenth century. He lived and taught in France, England, Italy, and Switzerland. Of all the humanists, it was Erasmus who most benefited from the printing revolution. The printer Aldus Manutius invited him to live and work in Venice, and he spent the last productive years of his life at Johannes Froben's press in Basel.

Over a long career, Erasmus brought out repeated editions of works designed to educate Christians. His *Adages*, first published in 1500, was a collection of proverbs from Greek and Roman sources. The work was immensely popular, and Erasmus repeatedly issued expanded editions. He tried to present Greek and Roman wisdom that would illuminate everyday problems. *The Colloquies* was a collection of popular stories. Designed as primers for students, they presented moral lessons, even as they taught good language. His ironic *The Praise of Folly* (1511) was dedicated to Thomas More. An oration by Folly in praise of folly, it is satire of a type unknown since antiquity. Folly's catalog of vices includes everyone from the ignoramus to the scholar. But more seriously, Erasmus believed, as Saint Paul had said, that Christians must be "fools for Christ." In effect, human existence is folly. Erasmus's *Folly* adapts an observation first made by Plato and which Shakespeare would refine and make famous: "Now the whole life of mortal men, what is it but a sort of play in which . . . [each person] plays his own part until the director gives him his cue to leave the stage."[*]

Erasmus's greatest contributions to European intellectual life were his edition of and commentaries on the New Testament. His was a critical edition of the Greek text and a Latin translation independent of the fourth-century Latin Vulgate of Jerome. Unlike Jiménez, Erasmus corrected parts of the Vulgate. He rejected the authority of tradition, saying, "The sin of corruption is greater, and the need for careful revision by scholars is greater also, where the source of corruption was ignorance."[**] What was revolutionary in his edition was his commentary, which emphasized the literal and historical recounting of human experiences. Erasmus's Bible was the basis of later vernacular translations of Scripture during the Reformation.

Underlying Erasmus's scholarly output was what he called his "Philosophy of Christ." Erasmus was convinced that the true essence of Christianity was to be found in the life and actions of Christ. Reasonable, self-reliant, truly Christian people did not need superstitious rituals or magic. In his *Colloquies*, he tells of a terrified priest who, during a shipwreck, promised everything to the Virgin Mary if only she would save him from drowning. But, Erasmus observed, it would have been more practical to start swimming!

Erasmus believed that a humanistic combination of classical and Christian wisdom could wipe away violence, superstition, and ignorance. Yet, his philosophy of Christ, based on faith in the goodness and educability of the individual, was swamped in the 1520s and 1530s by the sectarian claims of both Protestants and Catholics. Although Erasmus's New Testament was influential in the Reformation, his calls for reforms based on tolerance and reason were not.

---

## SECTION SUMMARY

- Vernacular literatures of northern Europe emphasized religious and moral themes drawn from daily life.

- The development of printing using movable type made books more widely available. Humanists in northern Europe were more closely linked to university life and less tied to ideas of Roman public life.

- Thomas More and Desiderius Erasmus used their humanistic learning to develop a sophisticated critique of contemporary life.

---

[*]Quoted in A. Rabil, Jr., *Renaissance Humanism: Foundations, Forms, and Legacy*, vol. 2 (Philadelphia: University of Pennsylvania Press, 1988), p. 236.
[**]Quoted in A. Rabil, Jr., *Renaissance Humanism: Foundations, Forms, and Legacy*, vol. 2 (Philadelphia: University of Pennsylvania Press, 1988), p. 229.

# Politics and Renaissance Culture

*How did European rulers use Renaissance art and culture?*

The educational reforms of the humanists and the innovations in the arts between 1300 and 1550 provided an opportunity for rulers and popes alike to use culture to define and celebrate their authority. Art, literature, and politics merged in the brilliant life of the Renaissance Italian courts, both secular and papal. To understand fully the Renaissance and its importance in the history of Europe, we need to examine the uses of culture by governments, specifically investigating the transformation of European ideas about service at court. We will take as a model the politics and cultural life at one noble court: the court of the Gonzaga family of Mantua. Then, we will see how the Renaissance papacy melded the secular and religious aspects of art, culture, and politics in its glittering court in Rome. Finally, we will discuss the development of the idea of the Renaissance gentleman and courtier made famous by Baldassare Castiglione (ka-stee-lee-OH-nay), who was reared at the Gonzaga court.

## The Elaboration of the Court

The courts of northern Italy recruited artists and humanists inspired by classical civilization, and they closely imitated many of the values and new styles that were developing in the courts of northern Europe, such as the court of Burgundy. Throughout Europe, attendance at court became increasingly important to members of the nobility as necessary for high-paying administrative appointments and political influence. Kings and the great territorial lords were equally interested in drawing people to their courts as a way to influence and control the noble and the powerful.

Rulers in most parts of Europe instituted monarchical orders of knighthood to reward allies and followers. The most famous in the English-speaking world was the Order of the Garter, founded in 1349 by King Edward III. The orders were but one of the innovations in the organization of the court during the fourteenth and fifteenth centuries. The numbers of cooks, servants, huntsmen, musicians, and artists employed at court jumped dramatically in the late Middle Ages. In this expansion, the papal court was a model for the rest of Europe. The popes at Avignon, in the fourteenth century, already had households of nearly six hundred persons. If all the bureaucrats, merchants, local officials, and visitors who continually swarmed around the elaborate papal court were also counted, the number grew even larger.

Courts were becoming theaters built around a series of widely understood signs and images that the ruler could manipulate. Culture was meant to reflect the reputation of the ruler. On important political or personal occasions, rulers organized jousts or tournaments around themes drawn from mythology. The dukes of Milan indicated the relative status of courtiers by inviting them to participate in particular hunts or jousts. They similarly organized their courtiers during feasts or elaborate entries into the towns and cities of their realms.

The late fourteenth and fifteenth centuries were periods of growth in the political and bureaucratic power of European rulers. The increasingly elaborate and sumptuous courts were one of the tools that rulers used to create a unified culture and ideology. At the court of the Gonzagas in Mantua, one of the most widely known of the fifteenth-century courts, the manipulation of Renaissance culture for political purposes was complete.

## The Court of Mantua

The city of Mantua, with perhaps 25,000 inhabitants in 1500, was small compared with Milan or Venice—the two cities with which it was most commonly allied. Located in a rich farming region near the Po River, Mantua did not have a large merchant or manufacturing class. Most Mantuans were involved in agriculture and regional trade in foodstuffs. The town had been a typical medieval Italian city-state until its government was overthrown by the noble Bonacolsi family in the thirteenth century. The Bonacolsis, in turn, were ousted in a palace coup in 1328 by their former comrades, the Gonzagas, who ruled the city until 1627.

The Gonzagas faced problems typical of many of the ruling families in northern Italy. The state they were creating was relatively small, their right to rule was not very widely recognized, and their control over the area was weak. The first step for the Gonzagas was to construct fortresses and fortified towns that could withstand foreign enemies. The second step was to gain recognition of their right to rule. In 1329, they were named imperial vicars, or representatives in the region. Later, in 1432, they bought the title "marquis" from the emperor Sigismund for the relatively low price of £12,000—equivalent to a year's pay for their courtiers. By 1500, they had exchanged that title for the more prestigious "duke."

Presiding over a strategic area between the Milanese and Venetian states, the Gonzagas maintained themselves through astute diplomatic connections with other Italian and European courts and through service as well-paid mercenaries in the Italian wars of the fifteenth and sixteenth centuries.

The family's reputation was enhanced by Gianfrancesco (jan-fran-CHES-ko) (d. 1444) and Lodovico, who brought the Renaissance and the new court style to Mantua. By 1500, as many as eight hundred or more nobles, cooks, maids, and horsemen may have gathered in the court. Critics called them idlers, "who have no other function but to cater to the tastes of the Duke." It was under the tutelage of the Gonzagas that Vittorino da Feltre created his educational experiment in Villa Giocosa, which drew noble pupils from throughout Italy. It would be hard to overestimate the value for the Gonzagas of a school that attracted sons of the dukes of Urbino, Ferrara, and Milan and of numerous lesser nobles. The family also called many artists to Mantua. Lodovico invited Antonio Pisano, called Pisanello (ca. 1415–1456), probably the most famous court artist of the fifteenth century. Pisanello created a series of frescoes on Arthurian themes for the Gonzaga palace. In these frescoes, Lodovico is portrayed as a hero of King Arthur's Round Table.

The Gonzagas are best known for their patronage of art with classical themes. The Florentine writer and architect Leon Battista Alberti (1404–1472) redesigned the façade of the Church of Sant'Andrea for the Gonzagas, in the form of a Roman triumphal arch. The church, which long had been associated with the family, became a monument to the Gonzaga court, just as the Arch of Constantine in Rome had celebrated imperial power a thousand years earlier. In the 1460s, Lodovico summoned Andrea Mantegna (1441–1506) to his court. Trained in Padua and Venice, Mantegna was, at that time, the leading painter in northern Italy. His masterwork is the *Camera degli Sposi* (literally, "the room of the spouses"), completed in 1474. It features family portraits of Lodovico Gonzaga and his family, framed in imitations of Roman imperial portrait medallions. One scene shows Lodovico welcoming his son, a newly appointed cardinal, back from Rome. Lodovico even included the portrait of the Holy Roman emperor who had never been to Mantua but was related to Lodovico's wife, Barbara of Brandenburg. As Mantegna finished the work, diplomats and rulers throughout Italy carefully monitored it—proof to all of the new status of the Gonzagas.

The Gonzaga court, like most others, was both public and private. On the one hand, finances for the city, appointments to public offices, and important political decisions were made by the men who dominated the court. On the other hand, as the prince's domestic setting, it was a place where women were expected to be seen and could exert their influence. Women were thus actively involved in creating the ideology of the court. Through the patronage of classical paintings, often with moral and political messages, wives of princes helped make the court better known and more widely accepted throughout Italy and Europe.

The arrival at court of Isabella d'Este (1494–1539), as the wife of Francesco Gonzaga, marked the high point of the Renaissance in Mantua. Isabella had received a classical education at Ferrara and maintained an interest in art, architecture, and music all her life. Isabella was also an accomplished musician, playing a variety of string and keyboard instruments. She and others of the Gonzaga family recruited Flemish and Italian musicians to their court. By the end of the sixteenth century, Mantua was one of the most important musical centers of Europe. As a patron of the arts, she knew what she wanted. Isabella used the general interest in the cultural life of Mantua as a way to increase contacts with the Italian and European powers. She used these informal cultural connections to further the family's political and diplomatic goals.

In the fourteenth century, Petrarch had complained that however enjoyable feasting in Mantua might be, the place was dusty, plagued by mosquitoes, and overrun with frogs. By the end of the fifteenth century, the Gonzagas had transformed their city and secured a prominent place for themselves on the Italian, and the European, stage.

## The Renaissance Papacy

The issues of power and how it is displayed had religious as well as secular dimensions. After its fourteenth- and fifteenth-century struggles over jurisdiction, the papacy found itself reduced, in many respects, to the status of an Italian Renaissance court. But popes still needed to defend their primacy within the church from conciliarists, who had argued that all Christians, including the pope, were bound to obey the commands of general councils. The ideological focus of the revived papacy was Rome.

### The Transformation of Rome

The first step in the creation of a new Rome was taken by Pope Nicholas V (r. 1446–1455), a cleric who had spent many years in the cultural environment of Renaissance Florence. Hoping to restore Rome and its church to their former glory, Nicholas and his successors patronized the arts, established a lively court culture, and sponsored numerous building projects. Nicholas was an avid collector of ancient manuscripts that seemed to demonstrate the intellectual and religious primacy of Rome. He invited numerous artists and intellectuals to the papal court, including Leon Battista Alberti. He based his treatise, *On Architecture* (1452), on his research in topography and reading done in Rome. This was the most important work on architecture produced during the Renaissance. It was probably under Alberti's

**Giving of the Keys to Saint Peter**   Pietro Perugino's painting of Saint Peter receiving from Christ the keys to "bind and loose" on earth and in heaven illustrates the basis of papal claims to authority within the Christian church. This is the central message of the decorative plan of the Sistine Chapel. Scala/Art Resource, NY influence that Nicholas embarked on a series of ambitious urban renewal projects in Rome, which included bridges, roads, and a rebuilt Saint Peter's Basilica.

The transformation of Rome had an ideological purpose. As one orator proclaimed, "Illuminated by the light of faith and Christian truth, [Rome] is destined to be the firmament of religion . . . , the secure haven for Christians."* Thus, the papal response to critics was to note that Rome and its government were central to political and religious life in Christendom. By reviving the style and organization of classical antiquity, the church sought to link papal Rome to a magnificent imperial tradition, reaching back to Augustus and even to Alexander the Great. To papal supporters, only one authority could rule the church. Early tradition and the continuity of the city itself, they assumed, demonstrated papal primacy.

## The Sistine Chapel

One particular monument in Rome captures most vividly the cultural, religious, and ideological program of the papacy: the Sistine Chapel in the Vatican Palace. The chapel is best known for the decoration of the ceiling by the Florentine artist Michelangelo (see pages 337–338) and for the striking images in his painting of the Last Judgment. The chapel, however, was commissioned by Pope Sixtus IV in 1475. It was to be an audience chamber in which an enthroned pope could meet the representatives of other states. In addition, it was expected that the college of cardinals would gather in the chapel for the election of new popes.

The decorations done before Michelangelo painted the ceiling reflect the intellectual and ideological values that Sixtus hoped to transmit to the ambassadors and churchmen who entered the chapel. Along the lower sidewalls are portraits of earlier popes, a feature typical of early Roman churches. More ideologically significant, however, are two cycles of paintings of the lives of Moses and Christ, drawing parallels between them. To execute the scenes, Sixtus called to Rome some of the greatest artists of the late fifteenth century: Sandro Botticelli, Domenico Ghirlandaio, Luca Signorelli, and Pietro Perugino. The works illustrate the continuity of the Old Testament and New Testament and emphasize the importance of obedience to the authority of God. The meaning is most obvious in Perugino's painting of Saint Peter receiving the keys to the Kingdom of Heaven from Christ. The allusion is to Matthew 16:18: "Thou art Peter and upon this rock I shall build my church." The keys are the symbol of the claim of the pope, as successor to Saint Peter, to have the power to bind and loose sinners and their punishments. Directly across from Perugino's painting is Botticelli's *The Judgment of Corah*, which portrays the story of the opponent who challenged the leadership of Moses and Aaron while the Israelites wandered in the wilderness. Corah and his supporters, according to Numbers 16:33, fell live into Hell. Various popes recalled the fate of Corah and the rebels. The pope was bound to oppose the council, Pope Eugenius argued, "to save the people entrusted to his care, lest together with those who hold the power of the council above that of the papacy they suffer a punishment even more dire than that which befell Corah."** The meaning of the painting and the entire chapel could not be clearer.

The effects of Renaissance revival were profound. Rome grew from a modest population of about 17,000 in 1400 to 35,000 in 1450. By 1517, the city had a population of over 85,000, five times its population at the end of the Great Schism. The papal program was a success. Rome was transformed from a provincial town to a major European capital, perhaps the most important artistic and cultural center of the sixteenth century. Visitors to the Sistine Chapel, like visitors to the papal city itself, were expected to leave with a profound sense of the antiquity of the papal office and of the continuity of papal exercise of religious authority. Because the building and decorating were being completed as the Protestant Reformation was beginning in Germany, some historians have criticized the expense of the political and cultural program undertaken by the Renaissance popes. But to contemporaries on the scene, the work was a logical and necessary attempt to strengthen the church's standing in Christendom.

---

*Raffaele Brandolini, quoted in Charles L. Stinger, *The Renaissance in Rome* (Bloomington: Indiana University Press, 1985), p. 156.
**Quoted in Leopold D. Ettlinger, *The Sistine Chapel Before Michelangelo* (Oxford: Oxford University Press, 1965), p. 105.

## *Castiglione and the European Gentleman*

Renaissance ideas did not just spread in intellectual circles. They also were part of the transformation of the medieval knight into the early modern "gentleman." In 1528, Baldassare Castiglione (1478–1529) published *The Book of the Courtier*. The work, which describes the ideal behavior of a courtier, was based on Castiglione's own distinguished career serving in Italian courts. Set at the court of Urbino, the book chronicles a series of fictional discussions over the course of four nights in March 1507. Among the participants are the duchess of Urbino, Elizabeth Gonzaga; Emilia Pia, her lady-in-waiting; and a group of humanists, men of action, and courtiers. In four evenings, members of the circle try to describe the perfect gentleman of court. In the process, they debate the nature of nobility, humor, women, and love.

Castiglione describes, in many respects, a typical gathering at court, and the discourses reflect contemporary views of relations between men and women. The wives of princes were expected to be organizers of life at court but also paragons of domestic virtues. Women were expected to manage the household and even the financial interests if her husband was away. Noble and elite women also played an important, but indirect, role in political and diplomatic negotiations. Women communicated informally ideas and information that could not be passed in public dispatches. But even powerful women had to be careful about public appearances. In Castiglione's book, for example, the women organize the discussion, and the men discuss. Although the women direct and influence the talk by jokes and short interventions, they cannot afford to dominate the debate. As Emilia Pia explains, "[women] must be more circumspect, and more careful not to give occasion for evil being said of them . . . for a woman has not so many ways of defending herself against false calumnies as a man has."*

---

*Quoted in R. M. San Juan, "The Court Lady's Dilemma: Isabella d'Este and Art Collecting in the Renaissance," *Oxford Art Journal* 14 (1991): 71.

**Federigo da Montefeltro's Studiolo**   The duchy of Urbino was a showpiece of Renaissance court life and was the eventual locale for Castiglione's *Book of the Courtier*. It owed much of its fame to Duke Federigo da Montefeltro. Federigo's study is decorated with an expensive inlaid wooden design. Its illusion of great space and the expense of its construction were meant to celebrate Federigo's wealth and power.

Thus, in debate, as in politics and diplomacy, the influence of women was most effective when it was indirect.

The topics of such discussions were not randomly chosen. Castiglione explains that he wished "to describe the form of courtiership most appropriate for a gentleman living at the courts of princes." Castiglione's popularity was based on his deliberate joining of humanistic ideas and traditional chivalric values. Although his topic is the court with all its trappings, he tells his readers that his models for the discussion were Latin and Greek dialogues, especially those of Cicero and Plato. As a Platonist, he believed that all truly noble gentlemen have an inborn quality of "grace." It has to be brought out, however, just as Michelangelo freed his figures from stone.

What struck Castiglione's readers most was his advice about behavior. Francesco Guicciardini of Florence once remarked, "When I was young, I used to scoff at knowing how to play, dance, and sing, and other such frivolities. . . . I have nevertheless seen from experience that these ornaments and accomplishments lend dignity and reputation even to men of good rank."* Guicciardini's comment underlines the value that readers found in Castiglione's work. Grace may be inbred, but it must be brought to the attention of those who control the court. Courtiers should, first of all, study the military arts. They have to fight but only on occasions when their prowess will be noticed. Castiglione adds practical advice about how to dress, talk, and participate in music and dancing: Never leap about wildly when dancing as peasants might but dance only with an air of dignity and decorum. Castiglione further urges the courtier to be careful in dress: the French are "overdressed"; the Italians too quickly adopt the most recent and colorful styles. Bowing to the political, as well as social realities of Spanish domination of Italy, Castiglione advises black or dark colors, which "reflect the sobriety of the Spaniards, since external appearances often bear witness to what is within."

According to Castiglione, the courtier must take pains "to earn that universal regard which everyone covets." Too much imitation and obvious study, however, lead to affectation. Castiglione counsels courtiers to carry themselves with a certain diffidence or unstudied naturalness (*sprezzatura*) covering their artifice. Accomplished courtiers should exhibit "that graceful and nonchalant spontaneity (as it is often called) . . . so that those who are watching them imagine that they couldn't and wouldn't even know how to make a mistake." Thus, Castiglione's courtier must walk a fine line between clearly imitated and apparently natural grace.

Castiglione's book was an immediate success and widely followed even by those who claimed to have rejected it. By 1561, it was available in Spanish, French, and English translations. The reasons are not difficult to guess. It was critical for the courtier "to win for himself the mind and favour of the prince," and even those who disliked music, dancing, and light conversation learned Castiglione's arts "to open the way to the favour of princes." Many of the courtly arts that Castiglione preached had been traditional for centuries. Yet, Castiglione's humanistic explanations and emphasis on form, control, and fashion had never seemed so essential as they did to the cultured gentlemen of the courts of the Renaissance and early modern Europe.

## SECTION SUMMARY

- Rulers found Renaissance art and culture to be convenient vehicles to explain or justify political power.
- The Gonzaga rulers of Mantua followed a conscious policy of recruiting famous artists to work at their court.
- The papacy used art and culture to explain and justify their predominance in Rome and the Christian church.
- Castiglione's dialogue on behavior at court became a European bestseller because of its explanation of how to succeed at court.

*Quoted in R. W. Hanning and D. Rosand, eds., *Castiglione: The Ideal and the Real in Renaissance Culture* (New Haven, Conn.: Yale University Press, 1983), p. 17.

# Chapter Summary

◆ *How did Italians use classical values to deal with cultural and political issues?*

The Renaissance was a broad cultural movement that began in Italy in response to a series of crises in the early fourteenth century. It was a cultural and ideological movement based on the assumption that study and imitation of the past was the best method for reform and innovation in the future. The impulse for change arose from the belief, shared by thinkers from Petrarch to Machiavelli, that a great deal could be learned from study of the Roman past. This was the basis for humanistic innovations in language, history, and politics. Even revolutionary thinkers, such as Lorenzo Valla and Niccolò Machiavelli, began with the study of classical literature and history.

◆ *What was "new" about Renaissance art?*

The same transformation is evident among the artists. Early in the fifteenth century, Florentines who experimented with perspective were intent on recovering lost Roman knowledge, and Michelangelo was praised not only for mastering but also for surpassing Roman norms. The artistic innovations of Italy were noted and valued throughout the Mediterranean and northern Europe. Artists like Albrecht Dürer combined their understanding of Italian art with northern ideas. Throughout Europe, art was an important component of religious and political culture.

◆ *In what ways did humanism outside Italy differ from Italian humanism?*

Humanistic studies outside of Italy were less tied to public life. Moral and spiritual issues were more important. Yet, the same movement from imitation to transformation is evident. Erasmus and More valued humanistic learning from Italy, but in *The Praise of Folly* and *Utopia*, the use of past ideas and models was neither simple nor direct. Both authors, however, shared with Italian humanists the idea that humanistic values could lead to a transformation of individuals and society as a whole.

◆ *How did European rulers use Renaissance art and culture?*

The integration of art, literature, and public life was most evident in the ways that governments used art. The Gonzaga court and the papacy clearly recognized the value of artistic and literary works as vehicles for explaining and justifying power and influence. The beauty of Mantegna's painting and the power of Michelangelo's frescoes do not obscure their messages about power and authority.

# Key Terms

**CourseMate**

Go to the CourseMate website at **www.cengagebrain.com** for additional study tools and review materials—including audio and video clips—for this chapter.

veyotlipan.

onca quamicos mtlatoque q maca qyxqch qualom.

**Hernán Cortés**   Cortés—here shown with Doña Marina—is greeted by local leaders during the march to Tenochtitlán. Trans. no. V/C 31[2]. Courtesy Department of Library Sciences, American Museum of Natural History

# European Overseas Expansion to 1600

Hernán Cortés's (kor-TEZ) march in 1519 through the Valley of Mexico toward Tenochtitlán (teh-NOCK-tit-lan), the Aztec capital, was recorded not only in Spaniards' journals but also by local witnesses. In the native portrayal shown here, an elegantly garbed Mexica leader brings food and supplies to Cortés. Behind the adventurer are his own Spanish soldiers and his native allies. Many native peoples saw the Spanish as their defenders against the Aztecs, their harsh, recently arrived overlords. The woman standing next to Cortés is Malintzin, who later adopted the Spanish name Doña Marina. She was an Aztec noblewoman, traded by her stepfather to the Maya and eventually given to Cortés. As a translator and interpreter, she was an essential ally during the conquest of Mexico.

The image, with its baskets of bread, meats, and fodder, is part of a pictograph telling the story of Cortés in the Nahuatl (na-HWAT-luh) language of the Mexica peoples. The arrival of the Spanish began a cultural exchange between the Spanish and the peoples of the Americas that was more complex than anyone initially imagined. The picture captures the contradictory aspects of European contact with Asia and the Americas. Europeans called it discovery, but they were encountering sophisticated, fully functioning political and cultural worlds. Doña Marina's presence also reminds us of a more complex truth—that without allies, pilots, and interpreters among the native peoples, Europeans would have been lost both in the New World and in the Old.

Cortés's meeting with the Mexica peoples was part of a program of European overseas expansion that began in the last decade of the fifteenth century and would eventually carry Europeans to every part of the world. It would change how Europeans thought of themselves and how they understood their own connections to the rest of the world. Their expansion unified the "Old World" continents of Asia, Africa, and Europe with a "New World"—the Americas and the islands of the Pacific.

Those who focus on the transfer of European religion and culture view exploration and settlement as marking the creation of a new world with new values. However, the descendants of the native peoples who greeted the newly arriving Europeans—the Amerindians and the Aborigines, Maori, and Polynesians of the Pacific islands—remind us that the outsiders invaded another world. Their arrival brought modern warfare and epidemic diseases that virtually destroyed indigenous cultures.

Spain sent its explorers west because the Portuguese already controlled the eastern routes to Asia around the African coast and because certain technological innovations made long open-sea voyages possible. Thus, the story includes national competition, the development of navigational techniques, and strategic choices.

Finally, the Europeans overthrew the great empires of the Aztecs and the Inca, but the transfer of European culture was never as complete as the Europeans thought or expected. As our image suggests, the language and customs of the conquered peoples, blanketed by European language and law, survived, though the lands colonized by the Europeans would never again be as they had been before their encounter with the Old World.

# The European Background, 1250–1492

*What did Europeans know about the wider world in the Middle Ages?*

By 1400, Europeans already had a long history of connections with Africa and Asia. They regularly traded with Arabs in North Africa, traveled through the Muslim lands on the eastern edge of the Mediterranean, and eventually reached India, China, and beyond. After 1400, however, Europeans developed the desire and the ability to travel overseas to distant lands in Africa and Asia. Three critical factors behind the exploratory voyages of the fifteenth and early sixteenth centuries were technology, curiosity and interest, and geographic knowledge. A series of technological innovations made sailing far out into the ocean less risky and more predictable than it had been. The writings of classical geographers, myths and traditional tales, and merchants' accounts of their travels fueled popular interest in the East and made ocean routes to the East seem safe and reasonable alternatives to overland travel.

## Early Exploration and Cultural Interactions

Medieval Europeans knew there were lands to their west. Irish monks and Norse settlers traveled there. Indeed, by the late ninth century, Norse sailors, primarily Norwegians, had constructed boats combining oars and sails with strong-keeled hulls, which they used to travel to Iceland, Greenland, and eventually Vinland—the coast of Labrador and Newfoundland. The Norse traveled in families. A woman named Gudridr gave birth to a son in North America before returning to Iceland and eventually going on a pilgrimage to Rome. Although the settlements in North America and Greenland ultimately failed, the Norse were followed by English, French, and Spanish fishermen who regularly visited the rich fishing grounds off North America.

## Contacts Through Trade

The Greeks and Romans had cultivated contacts with the civilizations of Asia and Africa, and despite the nation-building focus of the Middle Ages, interest in the lands beyond Christendom had never been lost. In the thirteenth and fourteenth centuries, European economic and cultural contacts with these lands greatly increased. The rising volume of trade between Europe and North Africa brought with it information about the wealthy African kingdoms of the Niger Delta. The Mongols, in the thirteenth century, allowed European merchants and missionaries to travel along trade routes extending all the way to China, opening regions formerly closed to them by hostile Muslim governments.

Trade in the Mediterranean also kept Christians and Muslims, Europeans and North Africans, in close contact. Europeans sold textiles to Arab traders, who carried them across the Sahara to Timbuktu, where they were sold for gold bullion to residents of the ancient African kingdoms of Ghana and Mali, located just above the Niger River. European chroniclers recorded the pilgrimage to Mecca of Mansa Musa, the fabulously wealthy fourteenth-century emperor of Mali. Italian merchants tried unsuccessfully to trade directly with these African kingdoms, but Arab merchants prevented any permanent contact.

Europeans enjoyed more successful trade connections farther east. The discovery in London of a brass shard inscribed with a Japanese character attests to the breadth of connections in the early fourteenth century. Since the Roman period, the Mediterranean had been connected to Asia by the Silk Road, in reality, a network of roads that carried people, ideas, and commerce. In the Middle Ages, European access to the Silk Road had been restricted by local rulers. After the rise of the Mongols, Italian merchants regularly traveled east through Constantinople and on to India and China. By the fourteenth century, they knew how long travel to China might take and the probable expenses along the way.

## Geographic Knowledge

European intellectuals also maintained an interest in the lands beyond Christendom. The work of the greatest of the classical geographers, Ptolemy (TOL-eh-mee) of Alexandria (ca. A.D. 127–145), was known only indirectly until the early fifteenth century, but medieval thinkers read avidly and speculated endlessly about the information contained in the works of authors from Late Antiquity. For instance, one author reported that snakes in Calabria, in isolated southern Italy, sucked milk from cows and that men in the right circumstances became wolves—the earliest mention of werewolves. By the twelfth century, fictitious reports circulated widely in the West of a wealthy Christian country in the East or possibly in Africa. Chroniclers, at that time, talked of Prester John, who some thought was a wealthy and powerful descendant of the Magi, the wise men from the East who Scripture says visited the baby Jesus. The legend of the kingdom of Prester John probably reflects some knowledge of the Christian groups living near the shrine of Saint Thomas in India or the Christian kingdom of Ethiopia. In the fifteenth century, European Christians looked to Prester John for aid against the rising Turkish empire.

More reliable information became available in the thirteenth century, largely because of the arrival of the Mongols. Jenghiz Khan (JEN-gus KAHN) and his descendants created an empire that reached from eastern Hungary to China (see page 250). This *pax Mongolica*, or area of Mongol-enforced peace, was a region in which striking racial and cultural differences were tolerated. In the 1240s and 1250s, a series of papal representatives traveled to the Mongol capital at Karakorum near Lake Baikal in Siberia. The letters of these papal ambassadors, who worked extensively to gain converts and allies for a crusade against the Turks, were widely read and greatly increased accurate knowledge about Asia. Other missionaries and diplomats journeyed to the Mongol court, and some continued farther east to India and China. By the early fourteenth century, the church had established a bishop in Beijing.

## CHRONOLOGY

| | |
|---|---|
| ca. 1400 | Portuguese reach Azores |
| 1444 | Prince Henry "the Navigator" discovers Cape Verde Islands |
| 1487 | Dias becomes first European to sail around Cape of Good Hope |
| 1492 | Columbus reaches New World |
| 1494 | Treaty of Tordesillas |
| 1497 | Da Gama sails to India around Cape of Good Hope |
| | Cabot sights Newfoundland |
| 1501 | Vespucci concludes Columbus discovered a new continent |
| 1507 | Waldseemüller issues the first map showing "America" |
| 1510 | Portuguese capture Goa |
| 1513 | Balboa becomes first European to see Pacific Ocean |
| 1519–1522 | Magellan's expedition sails around the world |
| 1519–1523 | Cortés conquers the Aztecs, destroys Tenochtitlán |
| 1533 | Pizarro conquers Cuzco, the Inca capital |
| 1534 | Cartier discovers St. Lawrence River |
| 1542 | Charles V issues "New Laws" |
| 1545 | Spanish discover Potosí silver mines |

**Hereford Mappa Mundi** Like other medieval illustrations of eastern lands, this thirteenth-century map combines known fact with myth. It shows paradise at the top with Jerusalem in the center of the map. The dark area moving out from the center is the Mediterranean Sea, with Europe on the left and Africa on the right. That map is symbolic rather than geographical. Crete and Sicily are shown almost touching rather than separated into different parts of the sea.

Hereford Cathedral, Herefordshire, UK/The Bridgeman Art Library

Italian merchants followed closely on the heels of the churchmen and diplomats. The pax Mongolica offered the chance to trade directly in Asia and the adventure of visiting lands known only from travel literature. In 1262, Niccolò and Maffeo Polo embarked from Venice on their first trip to China. On a later journey, they took Niccolò's son, Marco (1255–1324). In all, they spent twenty-four years in China. Marco dictated an account of his travels to a Pisan as they both languished as prisoners of war in a Genoese jail in 1298. It is difficult to know how much of the text represents Marco's own observations and how much is chivalric invention by the Pisan. Some modern commentators even have speculated that Marco himself never traveled to China. His contemporaries, however, had no doubts. The book was an immediate success even among Venetians, who could have exposed any fraud. Christopher Columbus himself owned and extensively annotated a copy of Marco Polo's *Travels*, which combines a merchant's observations of ports, markets, and trade with an administrator's eye for people and organizations.

By 1300, a modest community of Italians had settled in China. By the late thirteenth and fourteenth centuries, Italian traders were traveling directly to the East in search of Asian silks, spices, pearls, and ivory. They, and other European merchants, could consult the *Handbook for Merchants* (1340), compiled by the Florentine Francesco Pegalotti (pey-gah-LOW-tee), which described the best roads, the most hospitable stopping points, and the appropriate freight animals for a trip to the East. Fragmentary reports of Europeans in the Spice Islands (also known as the Moluccas), Japan, and India indicate that many Europeans other than merchants traveled simply for the adventure of visiting new lands.

## Navigational Innovations

The invention of several navigational aids in the fourteenth and fifteenth centuries made sailing in open waters easier and more predictable. Especially important was the fly compass, consisting of a magnetic needle attached to a paper disk (or "fly"). The simple compass had been invented in China and was known in Europe by the late twelfth century, but because it was not initially marked off in degrees, it was only a rudimentary aid to navigation. By 1500, astrolabes and other devices enabling sailors to use the positions of the sun and stars to assist in navigation had also become available. An astrolabe allowed sailors to measure the altitude of the polestar in the sky and thereby calculate the latitude, or distance north or south of the equator, at which their ship was sailing. Still, until the general adoption of charts marked with degrees of latitude, most navigators sailed by relying on the compass, experience, and instinct.

The most common Mediterranean ship of the late Middle Ages was a galley powered by a combination of sails and oars. Such a vessel was able to travel quickly and easily along the coast, but it was ill suited for sailing the open seas. Throughout the Mediterranean, shipbuilders experimented with new designs, and during the fifteenth century, the Portuguese and Spanish perfected the caravel and adapted the European full-rigged ships. Large, square sails efficiently caught the wind and propelled these ships forward, and smaller triangular sails (lateens) allowed them to tack diagonally across a headwind, virtually sailing into the wind.

By the 1490s, the Portuguese and Spanish had developed the ships and techniques that would make long open-sea voyages possible. What remained was for Europeans, especially the Portuguese and Spanish, to conclude that such voyages were both necessary and profitable.

## The Revolution in Geography

Sea routes to Asia seemed more important by the end of the fourteenth century. With the conversion of the Mongols to Islam, the breakdown of Mongol unity, and the subsequent rise of the Ottoman Turks, the highly integrated and unusually open trade network fell apart. The caravan routes across southern Russia, Persia, and Afghanistan were abruptly closed to Europeans. Western merchants once again became dependent on Muslim middlemen.

The reports of travelers, however, continued to circulate long after the trade routes shut down, contributing to a veritable revolution in geographic knowledge in the decades before the Portuguese and Spanish voyages.

In 1375, Abraham Cresques (KRESK), a Jewish mathematician from the Mediterranean island of Majorca, produced what has come to be known as the *Catalan World Atlas*. He combined the traditional medieval *mappa mundi* (world map) with a Mediterranean *portolan*. The mappa mundi often followed the O-T form—that is, a circle divided into three parts representing Europe, Africa, and Asia, the lands of the descendants of Noah. Jerusalem—the heart of Christendom—was always at the center of the map. What the map lacked in accuracy, it made up in symbolism. The portolan, in contrast, was entirely practical. Sailors valued it because of its accurate outline of coasts, complete with sailing instructions and reasonable portrayals of ports, islands, and shallows along with general compass readings. The *Catalan World Atlas* largely holds to the portolan tradition but has more correct representations of the lands surrounding the Mediterranean.

In the fifteenth century, following Ptolemy's suggestions, mapmakers began to divide their maps into squares, marking lines of longitude and latitude. This format made it possible to show, with some precision, the contours of various lands and the relationships between landmasses. Numerous maps of the world were produced in this period. The culmination of this cartography was a globe constructed for the city of Nuremberg in 1492, the very year Columbus set sail. From these increasingly accurate maps, it has become possible to document the first exploration of the Azores, the Cape Verde Islands, and the western coast of Africa.

After his voyages, Columbus observed that maps had been of no use to him. True enough. But without the accumulation of knowledge by travelers and the mingling of that knowledge with classical ideas about geography, it is doubtful whether Columbus or the Portuguese seaman Vasco da Gama would have undertaken—or could have found governments willing to support—the voyages that so dramatically changed the relations between Europe and the rest of the world.

## SECTION SUMMARY

- Throughout the Middle Ages, Europe had indirect trade connections with Asia and Africa.
- In the fourteenth century, Italian merchants traveled widely in central and eastern Asia.
- Technological advances in ship design and navigation made it possible to sail far into the Atlantic.
- Restrictions on land routes between Europe and Asia made sailing to Asia a practical economic venture.

# Portuguese Voyages of Exploration, 1350–1515

*How did the Portuguese exploit their new connection to the East?*

Portugal, a tiny country on the edge of Europe, for a short time led the European overseas expansion. Portuguese sailors were the first Europeans to perfect the complex techniques of using the winds and currents of the South Atlantic, especially along the western coast of Africa (see **Map 13.1**). As the Portuguese moved down the African coast, and later, as they tried to compete commercially in Asia, they adapted traditional Mediterranean cultural and commercial attitudes to fit the new environment in which they found themselves. In some areas, the Portuguese created networks of isolated naval and trading stations to control the movement of goods. In other areas, they attempted to create substantial colonies, inhabited by Portuguese settlers. In still other areas, they used slaves to produce commercial products for the international market. Spain and the other European states would use these same strategies in Asia and the New World as they expanded their economic and political interests overseas.

## The Early Voyages

Portugal, like other late medieval European states, hoped that exploration and expansion would lead to "gold and Christians." The search for Christians was accelerated in the fifteenth century by the growing power of the Ottoman Turks. Europeans increasingly desired an alliance with the mythical Christian kingdoms of the East to open a second front against the militant Turks. Further, rediscovering the "lost" Christians and the hope of reclaiming Jerusalem fed Christian expectations that they were living in the last days before Christ's return.

For the Portuguese, facing the Atlantic and insulated from a direct Turkish threat, the lure of gold was always mixed with their religious motives. The nearest source of gold was well known to late medieval Christians: the African kingdoms of the Niger Delta. The problem for European traders and their governments was that overland contacts with this wealthy region remained controlled by the Muslim merchants of North Africa. The Portuguese and Spanish hoped to break the monopoly by taking control of the North African coast or by means of a flanking movement along the western coast of Africa.

Actual exploration of the Atlantic had begun long before Europeans recognized the extent of the Turkish threat. By 1350, the Madeiras and the Canaries, groups of islands off the western coast of Africa, regularly were included on European maps. By about 1365, Portuguese,

🌐 **Map 13.1  Winds and Currents**    Winds and ocean currents move in giant clockwise and counterclockwise circles that limit the directions in which ships can sail efficiently. It was impossible, for example, for the explorers to sail directly south along the entire western coast of Africa.

Spanish, and probably French sailors were visiting the Canary Islands. By 1400, the Azores (AY-zorz), a chain of islands one-third of the way across the Atlantic, were known and, from early in the fifteenth century, were routine ports of call for Portuguese ships (see **Map 13.2**). These voyages were no mean feat, calling for sophisticated ocean sailing out of sight of land for weeks at a time.

In the second decade of the fifteenth century, the Portuguese expansion began in earnest with the capture of the Muslim port of Ceuta (say-OO-tuh) on the coast of Morocco. From then on, the Portuguese moved steadily down the western coast of Africa. They were led by **Prince Henry "the Navigator"** (1394–1460), the younger son of King John I (r. 1385–1433). Legend has it that Prince Henry founded a school for the study of geography and navigation at Sagres, on the southwestern coast of Portugal. Whether he did or not,

**Prince Henry "the Navigator"**  The prince who directed Portuguese exploration and colonization along the west coast of Africa.

contemporaries agreed that Prince Henry was intent on reaching the "River of Gold"—that is, the Gold Coast of Africa and the Niger Delta. To accomplish this, he sponsored a series of expeditions down the African coast, reaching Senegal and the Cape Verde Islands by 1444. The Portuguese quickly established trading stations in the region and soon were exporting gold and slaves to Lisbon.

The islands off the coast of Africa were uninhabited, except for the Canaries, which the Portuguese tried unsuccessfully to keep from the Spanish. Thus, the Portuguese could not merely plant trading communities within a larger population. As a result, by the early 1440s, the Portuguese were bringing sheep, seed, and peasants to these hitherto unoccupied islands, and the Crown was granting extensive lordships to encourage reluctant nobles to relocate to the Azores. The islanders survived largely by exporting sheep and grain to Iberia.

A significant transformation occurred on Madeira in the 1440s, when the Portuguese introduced sugar cane to the island. A great many workers were needed to cut the cane, and expensive mills and lengthy processing were required to extract and produce sugar. On Madeira, most of the work was done by Portuguese peasants. However, when the Portuguese extended sugar cultivation to the newly discovered and colonized Cape Verde Islands in the 1460s, they found that Portuguese peasants would not work voluntarily in the sultry equatorial climate. Soon, the Portuguese introduced slave-based farming to maximize production and profits.

Slaves, imported from the Black Sea areas, had been used in agriculture since the introduction of sugar cultivation into the Mediterranean in the thirteenth century. The Portuguese had been trading in slaves along the western coast of Africa since the 1440s—the date from which black slaves appear in Lisbon. African slaves, along with slaves from northern and eastern Europe, could be found in Italy and throughout the Mediterranean in the fifteenth century, most often as domestics or laborers in small enterprises. Not since Roman times, however, had slave-based industries developed on the scale of the Portuguese sugar

🌐 **Map 13.2 World Exploration, 1492–1535** The voyages of Columbus, da Gama, and Magellan charted the major sea-lanes that became essential for communication, trade, and warfare for the next three hundred years. © Cengage Learning 2014 plantations. Sugar production in the New World eventually would be modeled on a plantation system begun by the Portuguese on their island colonies in the Atlantic.

## The Search for a Sea Route to Asia

Until the middle of the fifteenth century, the Niger Delta remained the focus of Portuguese interest. Only after securing control of the western coast of Africa did the Portuguese look seriously at sailing around Africa and discovering a sea route to Asia.

The fifteenth-century sailors who first tried to sail down the coast of Africa faced enormous difficulties. Water and wind currents tend to move in clockwise and counterclockwise circles, against which it is difficult for a sail-powered ship to make progress (see **Map 13.1**). Winds near the equator generally blow from the east; farther north and south, the westerlies prevail. Some zones, in certain seasons, are pockets of stillness—called doldrums—with few breezes to propel ships. A navigator had to find winds and currents moving in the direction he wished to travel. Sailing directly from port to port was virtually impossible.

Knowledge of winds and currents allowed Bartholomeu Dias (1450?–1500) to explore the coast of southern Africa in 1487. He followed the traditional Portuguese routes until southeasterly winds forced him to sail south and west, almost to the Brazilian and Argentine coasts. Then, he was able to ride the westerlies well past the southern tip of Africa, where he turned north. On his return, he sighted what he called the "Cape of Storms," later renamed the "Cape of Good Hope" by the Portuguese king. Dias had perfected the techniques for searching out currents in the Southern Hemisphere and opened the way to India.

A decade after Dias's return from the Cape of Good Hope, **Vasco da Gama** (1460?–1524) set sail on a voyage that would take him to Calicut on the western coast of India (see **Map 13.2**). Using the information gathered from countless navigators, travelers, and even spies sent into East Africa, da Gama set sail in 1497, with four square-rigged, armed caravels and over 170 men. He had been provided with maps and reports that indicated what he might expect to find along the eastern coast of Africa. He also carried textiles and metal utensils, merchandise of the type usually traded along the western coast of Africa. This was a trading mission and, in no sense, a voyage of discovery.

Da Gama followed established routes beyond the Cape of Good Hope and into the Indian Ocean. He traveled up the coast until he reached Malindi in Mozambique, where he secured an Arab pilot who taught him the route to Calicut. Although the goods the Portuguese traders presented were not appropriate for the sophisticated Asian market, da Gama did manage to collect a cargo of Indian spices, which he brought back to Portugal, arriving in 1499. From that pioneering voyage until the Portuguese lost their last colonies in the twentieth century (Goa in 1961; Mozambique in 1975), Portugal remained a presence in the Indian Ocean.

**Vasco da Gama**
Pioneering Portuguese trader, whose voyage to East Africa and India began the four-hundred-year presence of the Portuguese in the Indian Ocean.

## The Portuguese in Asia

Muslims predominated in the Indian Ocean, but in fact, a mixture of ethnic and religious groups—including Muslims, Hindus, Chinese, Jains, and Nestorian Christians—participated in the movement of cottons, silks, and spices throughout the region. There were numerous small traders, as well as prosperous long-distance merchants with connections reaching into central Asia, Africa, and China.

Less than a century before Vasco da Gama's arrival, the Chinese seaman Zheng He (JUNG HUH) made a series of voyages into the Indian Ocean. In 1405, he led a huge armada of 317 ships and over 27,000 sailors on an expedition designed to expand the trade and political influence of Ming China. He would make six subsequent trips before a new emperor, intent on concentrating his resources on China's internal development, ended the ventures. With the retreat of the Chinese, trade returned to its previous patterns.

The hodgepodge of trade reflected the political situation. Vasco da Gama's arrival coincided with the rise of the Moguls, Muslim descendants of Jenghiz Khan. By 1530, they had gained control of most of northern India, and during the sixteenth century, their influence increased in the south. The wealth and security of the Moguls depended on landed power.

**Portuguese in India**
This watercolor by a Portuguese traveler shows the varied peoples and customs and the great wealth to be found in India. Europeans were fascinated by all that seemed different from their own world.

Biblioteca Casanatense, Rome. Photo: Humberto Nicoletti Serra

They generally left traders and trading ports to themselves. Throughout the sixteenth century, the Moguls remained tolerant of India's religious, cultural, and economic diversity. Neither Muslim nor Hindu powers initially considered the Portuguese an unusual threat. The Indian Ocean was filled with trading communities that traded with each other, but which were separated by religion, language, and culture. The Portuguese seemed just another trading group

Asians may not have worried much about the Portuguese because, at first, they were so few and seemed so poor. (See the feature, "The Written Record: Vasco da Gama Arrives in India" on page 369.) Vasco da Gama arrived with only three ships. And the subsequent fleet of Pedro Alvares Cabral carried only fifteen hundred men. In the 1630s, after more than a century of emigration, probably no more than ten thousand Portuguese were scattered from modern Indonesia to the east coast of Africa. In addition to government officials, Portuguese settlers were likely to be petty traders, local merchants, and poorly paid mercenaries.

The Portuguese faced a number of problems as they attempted to compete in Eastern markets. There were very few of them and the trade goods they brought with them had little value in sophisticated, highly developed Asian markets. They could not profit from the India trade by competing with the indigenous traders. In response, they created a seaborne **trading-post empire**—an empire based on control of trade rather than on colonization. It was, in fact, a model that fit well with their crusading experience in North Africa and their desire to push back Muslim control.

Despite disadvantages, Portugal's commercial empire succeeded, thanks especially to fortified, strategically placed naval bases. As early as Vasco da Gama's second expedition in 1502, the Portuguese bombarded Calicut and defeated an Arab fleet off the coast of India. In the wake of their naval successes, they worked to control the coveted Spice Islands. By 1600, the Portuguese had built a network of naval bases that reached from Mozambique and Mombasa on the east coast of Africa to Goa on the west coast of India and the island of Macao off southeastern China (see **Map 13.2**).

The Portuguese established a royal trading firm, the Casa da India, to manage the booming market in cinnamon, ginger, cloves, mace, and a variety of peppers. Although their control was far from total, the Portuguese did become significant exporters of spices to Europe. More significant was the creation of the Portuguese Estado da India, or India office, to oversee Portuguese naval forces, administer ports, and regulate maritime trade. Under the

**trading-post empire**
A system developed by the Portuguese to allow them to use fortified naval bases to dominate commerce in the Indian Ocean.

## SECTION SUMMARY

- The Portuguese were especially interested in trade with the West African kingdoms along the Gold Coast.
- The Portuguese developed complex navigational techniques that allowed them to sail around the tip of Africa and into the Indian Ocean.
- Before the arrival of the Portuguese, the Muslim Mogul Empire left seaborne trade under the control of various ethnic and religious groups.
- The Portuguese established a trading-post empire that allowed them to dominate trade in the Indian Ocean.

## Vasco da Gama Arrives in India

*This anonymous account records Vasco da Gama's arrival in India. The Portuguese assumed that by moving beyond the Muslim states, they would encounter the Christian kingdom of Prester John. Further, they assumed that the new world into which they were traveling would be a commercial world like the Mediterranean and West Africa.*

The city of Calecut is inhabited by Christians. They are of a tawny complexion. Some of them have big beards and long hair, while others clip their hair short or shave the head, merely allowing a tuft to remain on the crown as a sign that they are Christians. They also wear mustaches. They pierce the ears and wear much gold in them. They go naked down to the waist, covering their lower extremities with very fine cotton stuffs. . . . When we arrived at Calecut the king was fifteen leagues away. The captain-major sent two men to him with a message informing him that an ambassador had arrived from the King of Portugal with letters. . . . The king presented the bearers of this message with much fine cloth. He sent word to the captain bidding him welcome, saying that he was about to proceed to Calecut. . . .

When we arrived [at Calecut] they took us to a large church [this would actually have been a Hindu temple] and this is what we saw:—

The large body of the church is as large as a monastery, all built of hewn stone and covered with tiles. At the main entrance rises a pillar of bronze as high as a mast, on the top of which was perched a bird, apparently a cock. In addition to this, there was another pillar as high as a man and very stout. In the center of the body of the church rose a chapel all built of hewn stone, with a bronze door sufficiently wide for a man to pass, and stone steps leading up to it. Within this sanctuary stood a small image which they said represented Our Lady [it is speculated that this could have been the Hindu goddess Gauri or Maya]. Along the walls, by the main entrance, hung seven small bells. In this church the captain-major said his prayers, and we with him. . . .

On Tuesday [May 29] the captain got ready the following things to be sent to the king, namely, twelve pieces of stripped cloth, four scarlet hoods, six hats, four strings of coral, a case containing six wash basins, a case of sugar, two casks of oil, and two of hone. As it was the custom not to send anything to the king without the knowledge of the Moor, his factor, and of the *bale*, the captain informed them of his intention. They came, and when they saw the present, they laughed at it, saying that it was not a thing to offer to a king, that the poorest merchant from Mecca, or any other part of India, gave more, and that if he wanted to make a present, it should be in gold, as the king would not accept such things.

### Questions

1. What does the chronicler observe when he arrives in Calecut?
2. Why might the Indians underestimate the impact the Portuguese would have on the Indian World?

*A Journal of the first Voyage of Vasco da Gama, 1497-1499, ed. and trans. E.G. Ravenstein (London: The Hakluyt Society, 1898), 49-50, 52-54, 60-61.*

---

Portuguese system, all merchants were expected to acquire export licenses and to ship products through Portuguese ports. Though a vigorous and highly profitable local trade remained out of Portuguese control, Asians still often found it more convenient to cooperate than to resist, and most agreed to pay for export licenses and trade through Portuguese ports. They even found it expedient to ship in European-style vessels and to use Portuguese as the language of commerce.

# Spanish Voyages of Exploration, 1492–1522

*Why did the Spanish choose to sail west in their attempt to find Asia?*

Spanish overseas expansion seems a logical continuation of the centuries-long Reconquista (see pages 246–247). In 1492, just before Columbus set sail, Castile was finally able to conquer the last Muslim kingdom of Granada and unify all of Iberia, with the exception of Portugal, under a single monarchy. Initially, in 1479, the Spanish kingdoms had agreed to leave the exploration and colonization of the African coast to the Portuguese, yet they watched nervously as the Portuguese expanded their African contacts. Portuguese successes led Castilians to concentrate their efforts on what came to be called the "Enterprise of the Indies"—that is, the conquest and settlement of Central and South America.

## The Role of Columbus

The story of the enterprise begins with Christopher Columbus (1451–1506), a brilliant seaman, courtier, and self-promoter who has become a symbol of European expansion. Columbus, however, was not a bold pioneer who fearlessly did what no others could conceive of doing. He benefited from long-standing interests in the world beyond European shores.

Columbus was born into a modest family in Genoa and spent his early years in travel and in the service of the Castilian and Portuguese crowns. His vision seems to have been thoroughly traditional and medieval. He knew the medieval geographic speculations inherited from Arab, and ultimately Classical Greek, sources. Medieval seafarers did not fear a flat earth; rather, the concern was whether a ship could cover the vast distances necessary to sail west to Asia. Studying information in *Imago Mundi* (*Image of the World*, 1410), by the French philosopher Pierre d'Ailly (die-YEE) (1350–1420), Columbus convinced himself that the distance between Europe and Asia was much less than it actually is. D'Ailly's estimate put the east coast of Asia within easy reach of the western edge of Europe. "This sea is navigable in a few days if the wind is favorable," d'Ailly concluded.

Columbus's own study convinced him that the distance from the west coast of Europe to the east coast of Asia was about 5,000 miles, instead of the actual 12,000. Columbus's reading of traditional sources put Japan in the approximate location of the Virgin Islands. (It is not surprising that Columbus remained convinced that the Bahamas were islands just off the coast of Asia.) When Amerindians told him of Cuba, he concluded that it "must be Japan according to the indications that these people give of its size and wealth."[*]

On the basis of first-century descriptions, Columbus assured Spanish authorities that King Solomon's mines were only a short distance west of his newly discovered islands. In addition to finding the gold of Solomon, Columbus expected that by sailing farther west he could fulfill a series of medieval prophecies that would lead to the conversion of the whole world to Christianity. This conversion, he believed, would shortly precede the Second Coming of Christ. In Columbus's own view, then, his voyages were epochal not because they were ushering in a newer, more secular world, but because they signaled the fulfillment of Christian history.

Columbus's enthusiasm for the venture was only partially shared by the Spanish monarchs, Ferdinand and Isabella. Vasco da Gama had been well supplied with a flotilla of large ships and a crew of over 170 men, but Columbus sailed in 1492 with three small vessels and a crew of 90. Da Gama carried extra supplies and materials for trade and letters for the rulers he knew he would meet. Columbus had nothing similar in his sea chest. His commission did authorize him as "Admiral of Spain" to take possession of all he should find, but royal expectations do not seem to have been great.

Yet, on October 12, about ten days later than he had expected, Columbus reached landfall on what he assumed were small islands in the Japanese chain. He had actually landed in the Bahamas. Because Columbus announced to the world that he had arrived in the Indies, the indigenous peoples have since been called "Indians" and the islands are called the "West Indies."

Columbus reported to the Spanish monarchs that the inhabitants on the islands were friendly and open to the new arrivals. He described a primitive, naked people eager, he believed, to learn of Christianity and European ways. Indeed, the Tainos, or Arawaks, whom he had misidentified, did live simple, uncomplicated lives. The islands easily produced sweet potatoes, maize, beans, and squash, which, along with fish, provided an abundant diet. Initially, these people shared their food and knowledge with the newcomers, who they seem to have thought were sky-visitors.

The Spanish, for their part, praised the Tainos. The visitors generally believed that they had discovered a compliant, virtuous people who, if converted, would be exemplars of Christian virtues to Europeans. Columbus himself observed:

---

*Quoted in William D. Phillips, Jr., and Carla Rahn Phillips, *The Worlds of Christopher Columbus* (Cambridge: Cambridge University Press, 1992), p. 163.

They are very gentle and do not know what evil is; nor do they kill others, nor steal; and they are without weapons. They say very quickly any prayer that we tell them to say, and they make the sign of the cross, †. So your Highnesses ought to resolve to make them Christians.[*]

The Spanish authorities changed their opinion quickly. The settlers Columbus left at his fortress set an unfortunate example. They seized food stocks, kidnapped women, and embarked on a frenzied search for gold. Those who did not kill one another were killed by enraged Tainos.

During succeeding voyages, Columbus struggled to make his discoveries the financial windfall he had promised the monarchs. He was utterly unable to administer this vast new land. He quickly lost control of the colonists and was forced to allow the vicious exploitation of the island population. He and other Spanish settlers claimed larger and larger portions of the land and required the Indians to work it. Columbus argued that there were profits to be made if "[p]ayments for these things could be made . . . in slaves."[**] He sent natives to Seville to be sold as slaves. He hoped for royal support, but the queen rejected slaving operations. Nonetheless, islands that easily supported a population of perhaps a million natives could not support those indigenous peoples and the Spanish newcomers and still provide exports to Spain. Scholars have estimated that the native population of the islands may have fallen to little more than thirty thousand by 1520, largely because of diseases (see pages 381–383). By the middle of the sixteenth century, the native population had virtually disappeared.

Columbus remained convinced that he would find vast fortunes just over the horizon. However, he found neither the great quantities of gold he promised nor a sea passage to Asia. With the islands in revolt and his explorations seemingly going nowhere, the Spanish monarchs stripped Columbus of his titles and commands. Once, he was returned to Spain in chains. Even after his final transatlantic trip, he continued to insist that he had finally found either the Ganges (GAN-jeez) River of India or one of the rivers that according to the Hebrew Bible flow out of the earthly paradise. Although Columbus died in 1506, rich and honored for his discoveries, he never did gain all the power and wealth he had expected. He remained frustrated and embittered by the Crown's refusal to support one more voyage, during which he expected to find the mainland of Asia.

In 1501, after sailing along the coast of Brazil, the Florentine geographer Amerigo Vespucci (1451–1512) drew the obvious conclusion from the information collected by Columbus's explorations. "Carefully considered," he wrote, "they appear truly to form another world, and therefore we have, not without reason, called it the New World."[†] He argued that Columbus had discovered a new continent unknown to the classical world. These claims were accepted by the German mapmaker Martin Waldseemüller (vald-SAY-mill-er), who, in 1507, honored Amerigo's claim by publishing the first map showing "America."

## Columbus's Successors

Columbus's explorations set off a debate over which nations had the right to be involved in trade and expansion. Portuguese claims were based on a papal bull of 1481, issued by Pope Sixtus IV (r. 1471–1484), that granted Portugal rights to all lands south of the Canaries and west of Africa. After Columbus's return, the Spaniards lobbied one of Sixtus's successors, Alexander VI (r. 1492–1503), whose family, the Borgias, was from the kingdom of Aragon. In a series of bulls, Pope Alexander allowed the Spanish to claim all lands lying 400 miles or more west of the Azores. Finally, in the **Treaty of Tordesillas** (tor-day-SEE-yas) (1494), Spain and Portugal agreed that the line of demarcation between their two areas should be drawn 1,480 miles west of the Azores. The treaty was signed just six years before Pedro Alvares Cabral (1467–1520) discovered the coast of Brazil. Thus, the Spanish unwittingly granted the Portuguese rights to Brazil.

**Treaty of Tordesillas** A treaty negotiated between Spain and Portugal dividing the newly explored lands in the New World and the Old. All New World lands except Brazil were given to the Spanish.

---

*Quoted in William D. Phillips, Jr., and Carla Rahn Phillips, *The Worlds of Christopher Columbus* (Cambridge: Cambridge University Press, 1992), p. 166.
**Ibid., page 202.
†*The Life and Voyages of Americus Vespuccius*, by Charles Edwards Lester, Andrew Foster, Amerigo Vespucci, (New York, Baker & Scribner, 1846) 203.

Adventurers and explorers worried little about the legal niceties of exploration. Even as Columbus lay dying in 1506, others, some without royal permission, sailed up and down the eastern coasts of North and South America. Vasco Nuñez de Balboa (1475–1519) crossed the Isthmus of Panama in 1513 and found the Pacific Ocean exactly where the natives living in the region said it would be.

## Ferdinand Magellan

**Ferdinand Magellan**
The Spanish explorer who established the routes by which ships could sail around the world.

The most important of the explorations that Columbus inspired was the voyage undertaken by **Ferdinand Magellan** in 1519 (see **Map 13.2**). Although his motives are unclear, Magellan (1480?–1521) may have planned to complete Columbus's dream of sailing to the Indies. By the 1510s, mariners and others understood that the Americas were a new and hitherto unknown land, but they did not know what lay beyond them or what distance separated the Americas from the Spice Islands of Asia. After sailing along the well-known coastal regions of South America, Magellan continued south, charting currents and looking for a passage into the Pacific. Late in 1520, he beat his way through the dangerous straits (now the Strait of Magellan) separating Tierra del Fuego (ti-AIR-ah del foo-WAY-go) from the mainland. These turbulent waters marked the boundary of the Atlantic and Pacific Oceans. It took almost four months to travel from the straits to the Philippines. The crew suffered greatly from scurvy and a shortage of water and, at times, had to eat the rats aboard ship to survive. One crew member reported, "We ate biscuit, which was no longer biscuit, but powder of biscuit swarming with worms, for they had eaten the good."* Nevertheless, Magellan managed to reach the Philippines by March 1521. A month later, he was killed by natives.

Spanish survivors, in two remaining ships, continued west, reaching the Moluccas, or Spice Islands, where they traded merchandise that they had carried along for a small cargo of cloves. A single surviving ship continued around Africa and back to Spain, landing with a crew of 15 at Cádiz in September 1522, after a voyage of three years and the loss of four ships and 245 men. Magellan completed and confirmed the knowledge of wind and ocean currents that European sailors had been accumulating. One of his sailors wrote of him, "More accurately than any man in the world did he understand sea charts and navigation."** The way was now open for the vast expansion of Europeans and European culture into all parts of the world.

## English and French Explorers

Although the pope seemingly divided the non-European world between the Spanish and the Portuguese, Spanish adventurers were not the only ones to follow in Columbus's wake. The French and the English never accepted the pope's right to determine rights of exploration. They did, however, concentrate their explorations farther north. Building on a tradition of fishing off the coast of Newfoundland, English sailors under the command of John Cabot (1450?–1499?) sighted Newfoundland in 1497, and later voyages explored the coast as far south as New England. Cabot initiated an intense period of English venturing that would lead to an unsuccessful attempt to found a colony on Roanoke Island in 1587 and eventually to a permanent settlement at Jamestown in 1607. French expeditions followed Cabot to the north. In 1534, Jacques Cartier (kar-ti-YAY) (1491–1557) received a royal commission to look for a northern passage to the East. He was the first European to sail up the St. Lawrence River and began the process of exploration and trading that would lead to a permanent presence in Canada beginning in the early seventeenth century. But British and French settlements in the New World came later. The sixteenth century belonged to the Spanish.

### SECTION SUMMARY

- Columbus was a brilliant seaman whose exploration was based on geographic knowledge accumulated in the previous centuries.
- The frenzied Spanish search for wealth destroyed the economies of the island peoples.
- Magellan's voyage around the world completed the geographic knowledge necessary for commerce connecting Europe, Asia, and the New World.
- It was only with the writings of Amerigo Vespucci that most Europeans accepted the idea that Columbus had sailed to a previously unknown continent.

---

*Quoted in J. H. Parry, ed., *The European Reconnaissance: Selected Documents* (New York: Harper & Row, 1968), p. 242.
**Quoted in Alfred W. Crosby, *Ecological Imperialism: The Biological Expansion of Europe, 900–1900* (Cambridge: Cambridge University Press, 1986), p. 125.

# Spain's Colonial Empire, 1492–1600

*How did the Spanish conquer and control the new world they entered?*

Spanish penetration of the New World was a far cry from the model of the Portuguese in Asia. The Spaniards established no complex network of trade and commerce, and no strong states opposed their interests. A trading-post empire could not have worked in the New World. To succeed, the Spaniards needed to colonize and reorganize the lands they had found.

Between 1492 and 1600, almost 200,000 Spaniards immigrated to the New World. "New Spain," as they called these newly claimed lands, was neither the old society transported across the ocean nor an Amerindian society with a thin veneer of Spanish and European culture. To understand the history of New Spain, it is essential to grasp what it replaced, and how: The Spaniards overthrew two major civilizations and created new institutions in the wake of conquest. The whole story is not conquest and extermination—many of the Spanish attempted to secure fair treatment for the indigenous peoples who were now part of the Spanish Empire.

## The Americas Before the European Invasion

The Spaniards, and later their European peers, entered a world vastly different from their own. It was a world formed by two momentous events—one geological, the other anthropological. The first was the creation of the continents of North and South America. The Americas, along with Africa and the Eurasian landmass, were once part of a single supercontinent. The breakup of this supercontinent left the Americas, Africa, and Eurasia free to evolve in dramatically different ways. The continental breakup occurred millions of years ago, long before the appearance of human beings and many other forms of mammalian life.

The second momentous event was the peopling of the Americas. Some migrants may have come over the seas. Most, though, arrived thanks to a temporary rejoining of the Americas to the Eurasian landmass by land and ice bridges that allowed Asians to cross over what is now the Bering Strait to the Americas in the period between 40,000 and 15,000 B.C. Their timing had a great impact. They arrived in the Americas long before the beginnings of the Neolithic agricultural revolution, which involved the domestication of numerous plants and animals. The agricultural revolution in the Americas occurred around 3000 B.C., perhaps six thousand years after similar developments in the Old World. The peoples of the Americas created complex societies, but those societies lacked large domesticated meat or pack animals (the llama was the largest), iron, other hard metals, and the wheel.

Nonetheless, by the time of Columbus's arrival, relatively populous societies were living throughout North and South America. Population estimates for the two continents range from 30 million to 100 million—50 million seems the most commonly accepted figure. North America saw the development of complex Mound Builder societies in the East and along the Mississippi River and pueblo societies in the deserts of the American Southwest. In Central and South America, there may have been 350 tribal or clan groups concentrated around fifteen or more cultural centers. But the greatest powers in the Amerindian world were the **Aztecs** in central and coastal Mexico and the **Inca** in the mountains of Peru.

## The Aztecs

When the collection of tribes, now known as the "Aztec" (or Mexica) peoples, appeared in central Mexico in the early fourteenth century, they found an already flourishing civilization concentrated around the cities and towns dotting the Valley of Mexico. The Aztecs conquered and united the many Nahuatl-speaking groups living in the valley, forming a confederation centered in Tenochtitlán, a city of perhaps 200,000 people built on an island in Lake Texcoco (see **Map 13.3**). In early-sixteenth-century Europe, only London, Constantinople, and Naples would have been as large as the Aztec capital. It literally rose out of the water of Lake Texcoco. Only Venice could have equaled the sight. The whole valley supported an unusually high population of about a million. Using canals along the edge of the lake and

**Aztecs** People who dominated the Valley of Mexico from the fourteenth to the sixteenth centuries and whose empire was destroyed by Cortés.

**Inca** A mountain empire that flourished in Peru. It was conquered for Spain by Pizarro.

**Tenochtitlán** The Aztec capital was built on an island. Its central temples and markets were connected to the rest of the city and the suburbs on the lakeshore by numerous canals. The city and its surrounding market gardens seemed to the Spanish to be floating on water.

other canals in Tenochtitlán itself, merchants easily moved food, textiles, gold and silver ornaments, jewels, and ceremonial feathered capes into the city markets. Spaniards later estimated that fifty thousand or more people shopped in the city on market days.

Religion was integral to the Aztecs' understanding of their empire. They believed that the world was finite and that they lived in the last of five empires. It was only regular human sacrifice to Huitzilopochtli (wheat-zeel-oh-POSHT-lee) that allowed the world to continue: The hearts of victims were necessary to sustain their god, to ensure that the sun would rise each morning. Thus, life for the Aztecs required a relentless parade of death.

Tenochtitlán was the center of an imperial culture based on tribute. Towns and villages under Aztec control owed ongoing allotments of food and precious metals to the Aztecs. To emphasize that Aztec power and dominance were complete, the Aztecs not only collected vast quantities of maize, beans, squash, and textiles but demanded payment in everything down to centipedes and snakes. The most chilling tribute, however, was in humans for sacrifice. When the wars of expansion that had provided prisoners came to an end, the Aztecs and their neighbors fought "flower wars"—highly ritualized battles to provide prisoners to be sacrificed. Five thousand victims were sacrificed at the coronation of Moctezuma II (r. 1502–1520) in 1502. Even more, reportedly twenty thousand, were sacrificed at the dedication of the great temple of Huitzilopochtli in Tenochtitlán.

Aztec society maintained a perpetual state of war with the peoples beyond the mountains that ringed the Valley of Mexico—especially the people along the Caribbean coast. Given this constant state of war, plus the heavy burdens in tribute placed on the nearby subject cities, it is no wonder that the Aztecs were obsessed by the contingencies of life. At the end of each calendar cycle of fifty-two years, all fires in the empire were extinguished until fire-priests ascertained that the world would continue. And the Aztec world did continue until August 1523 (see page 377).

## The Inca

The other great Amerindian empire of the fifteenth century, the empire of the Inca, was also of recent origin. During the fifteenth century, the Inca formed efficient armies and expanded their control beyond the central highlands of Peru. Fifteen thousand miles of roads and a sophisticated administrative system allowed the Inca to create a state that extended from modern-day Ecuador to Chile (see **Map 13.4**). As they expanded, they demanded political control and tribute but seem to have been tolerant of local traditions and language. The Inca perfected systems of irrigation and bridge building initiated by earlier inhabitants of the region. The empire, centered on the city of Cuzco high in the mountains of Peru, was able to sustain a population that may have reached 10 million by the end of the fifteenth century.

Human sacrifice, though not unknown to the Inca people, was not an essential part of their religious life. Their state was unsettled, however, by increasingly harsh tax exactions. Under the Inca system, the title Sapa Inca, or "Emperor," was inherited by the eldest son of the ruler's principal wife. The ruler's wealth, however, was retained by the rest of his family, who maintained the court as if the ruler still lived. Thus, each new ruler needed money to finance the creation of an entirely new court, and taxes were not only high but continuously climbing.

**Map 13.3 Mexico and Central America** The Valley of Mexico was a populous region of scattered towns, most of which were part of the Aztec Empire. As Cortés marched inland from Vera Cruz toward the valley, he passed through lands that for generations had been in an almost constant state of war with the Aztecs. © Cengage Learning 2014

Both great Amerindian empires, despite their brilliance, rested on uneasy conquests. Subject groups would be willing allies for any invader.

## The Spanish Conquests

**Hernán Cortés** (1485–1546) was ambitious to make something of himself in the New World. Of a poor but aristocratic background, from the Extremadura region of southwestern Spain, he had gone to the West Indies in 1504 to seek his fortune in the service of the governor of Cuba. The governor gave him a commission to lead an expeditionary force to investigate reports of a wealthy and prosperous mainland Indian civilization. From the beginning, Spanish authorities seem to have distrusted Cortés's aims. In fact, he departed hastily from Cuba to evade formal notification that the governor had revoked his commission because of insubordination.

Cortés landed in Mexico at the site of the city he would name Vera Cruz ("True Cross") early in 1519, with a tiny command of five hundred men, sixteen horses, eleven ships, and a few pieces of artillery. Aided by a devastating outbreak of smallpox and Amerindian peoples happy to shake off Aztec control, Cortés and his troops managed to destroy the network of city-states dominated by the Aztecs of Tenochtitlán in two years and lay claim to the Valley of Mexico for the king of Spain. The manner in which Cortés explained and justified his mission can serve as a model against which to measure the adventures of other sixteenth-century Europeans in the Americas.

## The Conquest of Mexico

Cortés, like Machiavelli (see page 333), believed in the power of truly able leaders (men of *virtù*) to overcome chance through bold acts. Even so, an attempt to capture a city of 200,000

**Hernán Cortés** The Spanish commander who conquered the Aztec Empire with a tiny force of Spaniards, reinforced by numerous Indian allies.

🌐 **Map 13.4 The Inca Empire** The Inca Empire was accessible from Spanish strongholds in Mexico only by sea. Spanish exploration and domination brought the destruction of Inca mountain citadels and the transfer of administrative power to the new Spanish city of Lima on the coast.

**Doña Marina**
An enslaved Mexica noblewoman who served as translator and guide for Cortés.

with an army of 500 appears more foolhardy than bold. Cortés seems to have attempted it simply because he found himself with very little choice. With his commission revoked by the governor of Cuba, Cortés arrived on the mainland as a rebel against both the governor of Cuba and the king of Spain. He burned his ships in Vera Cruz harbor, making clear to all his men that there was no turning back. Much of what he did and said concerning the great Aztec Empire was an attempt to justify his initial act of insubordination and win back royal support. He quickly found allies among native groups who, for their own reasons, wished to see the Aztec Empire destroyed. The allied forces moved toward Tenochtitlán.

Cortés was greatly aided by fortune in the form of Malintzin, a Mexica woman who, after her conversion to Christianity, called herself **Doña Marina** (ca. 1501–1550). Malintzin was Cortés's interpreter and, later, his mistress. Without her, one of Cortés's followers recalled, "we could not have understood the language of New Spain and Mexico." Her story illustrates many of the complex interactions at play in sixteenth-century Mexico. Born a noble Aztec, she was sold by her stepfather and mother, ending up in the hands of the Maya. They gave her, along with twenty other women, to Cortés. Knowing both the Maya and Mexica languages, and quickly learning Spanish, she was the one person who could mediate between Spaniard and native. After bearing Cortés a son, she finished her life in Spain as the wife of a Spanish gentleman. Like many of Cortés's native allies who felt no affection for the Aztecs of Tenochtitlán, she did not find it difficult to aid the Spaniards.

Despite the help of Malintzin and Spaniards who had previously lived with the natives, the meeting of Aztecs and Spaniards demonstrated the breadth of the chasm separating the Old World and the New. At first, the Aztec king Moctezuma was unconcerned about the coming of the Spaniards. Later, he seems to have attempted to buy them off. And finally, he and his successors fought desperately to drive them out of Tenochtitlán. The Aztecs' indecision was caused in large part by the fact that in neither words nor gestures did the two groups speak the same language. Hearing that the Spaniards were on the march, Moctezuma sent ambassadors bearing gold, silver, and other costly gifts, which they presented in a most humble fashion to the Spaniards. To a modern ear, the gifts sound like (and have often been interpreted to be) desperate attempts to buy off the invaders. To Cortés, or any European or Asian resident of the Old World, such gifts were a sign of submission. But to Moctezuma, and most Amerindians, the giving of gifts with great humility by otherwise powerful and proud people could be a show of status, power, and wealth. Seen in that light, Moctezuma's lavish gifts and apparent humility were probably meant to demonstrate the superiority of his civilization, and Cortés's acceptance of the gifts indicated to the Aztecs, at least, a recognition of Spanish inferior status.

Spaniards later explained that the Aztecs believed that Quetzalcoatl, the serpent-god symbolically conquered by Huitzilopochtli, had traveled to the east, promising one day to return and reclaim his lands, thus ending Aztec rule. The Spaniards believed that Moctezuma's ambivalence toward them was rooted in his belief in that myth.

The story does not hold up in light of the evidence; the myth of the return of Quetzalcoatl was first recorded in Spanish, not Mexica, sources long after the conquest. In truth, neither Cortés nor historians can satisfactorily explain, in Western terms, Moctezuma's initial response to the Spaniards. Cortés took the Aztec leader captive in 1521 and began what would be a two-year battle to take control of the capital and its empire. Although weakened by the arrival of smallpox and other virulent Old World diseases, the Aztecs continued to fight, even as more and more of the subject peoples joined the Spanish besiegers. The Spaniards cut off food and water to Tenochtitlán, but still the Aztecs fought.

Different understandings of the rules of war, different traditions of diplomacy, and different cultures prevented the Aztecs and Cortés from reaching any understanding. Warfare in pre-conquest America was highly ritualized. Armies captured enemies either to enslave them or to sacrifice them in one of the temples. The Spaniards, to Aztec eyes, killed indiscriminately and needlessly on the battlefield. Cortés later complained of the Aztecs' refusal to negotiate: "We showed them more signs of peace than have ever been shown to a vanquished people." It was a conflict that neither side could resolve in any other way; thus, by August 1523, Cortés and his allies had destroyed completely the garden city of Tenochtitlán.

## Later Conquests

Cortés's recurring insubordination was an unfortunate model. His own lieutenants later rebelled against his control and quickly found their own allies, so-called "Indian Conquistadors." The Spanish were in many respects catalysts, taking advantage of the patterns of warfare and conquest already established in the territories. In some cases they did violently search for riches and El Dorado, a mythical city of gold. Using private armies and torturing native peoples, some veterans of Cortés's army and newly arrived speculators hoped to find wealth that would allow them to live like nobles on their return to Spain. In other cases, however, generals like Don Antonio de Mendoza succeeded through careful negotiation with local Indian rulers.

Francisco Pizarro (1470–1541) was the most successful of the private adventurers. Poor and illegitimate at birth, he arrived in the Americas ambitious for riches and power. After serving in Balboa's army, participating in several slaving expeditions, and helping to found Panama City, Pizarro was prosperous but still not wealthy. Rumors of Inca wealth filtered through to Central America. Pizarro and two partners resolved in 1530 to lead an expedition down the west coast of South America in search of the Inca capital. Benefiting from disorganization, caused by a smallpox epidemic and ensuing civil war, Pizarro was able to find local sympathizers.

Like Cortés, he used numerous Indian allies in his most important battles. Aided by Amerindians, eager to throw off Inca domination, he captured and executed the Sapa Inca and conquered the capital of Cuzco by 1533. He later built a new capital on the coast at Lima (see **Map 13.4**), from which he worked to extend his control over all of the old Inca Empire. Pizarro and his Spanish partners seized vast amounts of gold and silver from the Inca. The Spanish eventually found silver mines at Potosí (po-to-SEE), which would be a critical source of revenue for the Spanish monarchy. Resistance to Spanish rule continued into the 1570s, when the last of the independent Inca strongholds was finally destroyed.

## Colonial Organization

The Spanish crown needed to create a colonial government that could control the actions of its headstrong adventurers and create an orderly economy. Although the Spaniards proclaimed that they would "give to those strange lands the form of our own [land]," the resulting political and economic organization of the new Spanish possessions was a curious mixture of old and new.

The head of the administration was the monarchy. As early as the reigns of Ferdinand and Isabella, Spanish monarchs had tried to curb the excesses of the explorers and conquerors who traveled in their name. As we have seen, Isabella initially opposed the enslavement of Amerindians and any slave trade in the new lands. Further, the monarchs promoted a broad-based debate about the rights of Amerindians and the nature of religious conversion. It was royal policy that native rights, even the right not to become Christian, were to be protected. Mexicans had to accept missionaries, but they did not have to convert. Royal control, however,

**Aztec Warrior** This watercolor, by a Mexican artist who was trained in European painting, depicts a pre-Aztec ruler. The dress and the stone-edged sword would have been typical of the Aztecs, too. Bibliothèque nationale de France

**Council of the Indies** An administrative body established in 1524 to oversee commerce and administration in Spain's colonial possessions.

**encomienda** A royal protectorship granted with the obligation to protect and Christianize the people. Instead, natives became virtual slaves.

was limited by the sheer distance between the court and the new provinces. On average, it took the Spanish fleet two years to complete a round-trip voyage. It could easily take two years for a royal response to a question to arrive at its destination. Things moved so slowly that as one viceroy ruefully noted, "If death came from Madrid, we should all live to a very old age." Given the difficulties of communication, the powers of local administrators had to be very broad.

By 1535, Spanish colonial administration was firmly established in the form it would retain for the next two hundred years. The king created the **Council of the Indies**, located at court, eventually in Madrid, which saw to all legal and administrative issues pertaining to the new possessions. The new territories themselves were eventually divided into the viceroyalty of New Spain (primarily Central America and part of Venezuela) and the viceroyalty of Peru.

In New Spain, royal administrators created Indian municipalities, or districts, in which Spaniards had no formal right to live or work. Government in these municipalities remained largely in the hands of pre-conquest native elites. Throughout the sixteenth century, official documents in these communities continued to be written in Nahuatl, the Aztec language. These native communities were, however, fragile. Colonists and local administrators often interfered in the hope of gaining control. (See the feature, "The Global Record: An Inca Nobleman Defends His Civilization" on page 379.)

## The Colonial Economy

The problem that most plagued the government was the conquerors' desire for laborers to work on the lands and in the mines that they had seized. From Columbus's first visit, the Spanish adopted a system of forced labor developed in Spain. A colonist called an *encomendero* (en-co-men-DARE-o) was offered a grant, or *encomienda* (en-co-mi-EN-da), of a certain number of people or tribes who were required to work under his direction. The Spanish government expected that the encomendero was to be a protector of the conquered peoples, someone who would Christianize and civilize them. In theory, Indians who voluntarily agreed to listen to missionaries or to convert to Christianity could not be put under the control of an encomendero. If natives refused to hear the missionaries, however, the Spaniards believed they had the right of conquest. In many areas, encomenderos allowed life to continue as it had, simply collecting traditional payments that the pre-conquest elites had claimed. In other cases, where the subject peoples were forced into mining districts, the conditions were brutal. The treatment of native peoples was "more unjust and cruel," one reformer concluded, "than Pharaoh's oppression of the Jews."

The pressures exerted by the encomenderos were worsened by the precipitous fall in the indigenous population. Old World diseases, such as smallpox and measles, swept through peoples with no previous exposure to them (see pages 381–383). In central Mexico, where we know most about population changes, the pre-conquest population was at least 10 million to 12 million and may have been twice that. By the mid-sixteenth century, the native population may have declined to just over 6 million, and it probably plunged to less than 1 million early in the seventeenth century, before beginning to grow again.

A large population was essential to the Spanish and the Portuguese. The Caribbean islands and Brazil were ideal for the production of sugar—a commercial crop in great demand throughout Europe. At first, plantations and mines were worked by Amerindians, but when their numbers shrank, the Spanish and Portuguese imported large numbers of slaves from Africa.

## An Inca Nobleman Defends His Civilization

*Felipe Guaman Poma was born into a noble Inca family with a long history of service first to the Inca kings and later to the Spanish administrators. Although Guaman Poma became a Christian and adapted to Spanish rule, he appealed to the king of Spain in 1613 to intervene on behalf of the Indian peoples. In this section he describes the evils he has seen and suggests how the king could remedy them.*

The aforementioned priests ... do not act like the blessed priests of Saint Peter.... Rather, they give themselves over to greed for silver, clothing, and things of the world.... [They] ask for Indians to carry to market their wine, peppers, coca, and maize. Some have Indians bring mountain wine and coca down from the high plains to the hot lowlands. Being highland people, they die from fever and chills.... [They] have thread spun and woven, oppressing the widows and unmarried women, making them work without pay.... And in this [dealing with the priests] the Indian women become notorious whores.... [The priests] clamor to involve themselves too much in judicial matters.... As a result they enter into disputes and initiate petitions and are bad examples for the pueblo [i.e., village].... They treat them so imperiously and thereby destroy the Indians of this kingdom.

The ancient [Andean] priests ... acted devoutly and gave good example, as with the virgins and nuns of the temples. And so the rest [of the Indians] submitted to their justice and law. They were Christians in everything but their idolatry.

Because of such damage and so many complaints lodged against them, these fathers and pastors should be appointed on an interim basis—for a year at a time if he is good; and if he is not, may he not remain a single day. He should be at least fifty years old because a child's or a young man's follies are not good.... They should be proven and tested for academic preparation as well as for humility, charity, love and fear of God and justice, and for knowledge of the Quechua [or] Aymara languages of the Indians, needed to reach them, confess them, and preach the Gospel and sermons [to them].

They should be examined by the reverend fathers ... who are great scholars and preachers in the world. Those [who pass the examinations] should be sent to Your Lordship and to the head viceroy for appointment as interim pastors, posting a guaranteed bond. With this they will lose their arrogance; they will obey your lordship.

In the time of the conquest of a province there was only one priest in charge of instruction; ... he demanded no silver and only enough to eat. Thus these first ones were exemplary saints. They ... did not pretend to be a bishop or a magistrate. Thus [the people] converted to God, giving themselves over to peace and to the royal Crown.

### Questions

1. What are the complaints about the behavior of Christian priests? What do these complaints imply about the place of a priest in a village?

2. What role does Guaman Poma expect priests to play in a village?

3. What are the benefits Guaman Poma expects villagers to receive from Spanish administrators?

Source: Used with permission of Scholarly Resources, Inc., from Kenneth Mills and William B. Taylor, eds., *Colonial Latin America: A Documentary History*, 2002; permission conveyed through Copyright Clearance Center, Inc.

Africans had participated in the initial stages of the conquest. (See the feature, "The Visual Record: The Mulattos of Esmeraldas," on pages 382–383.) Some had lived in Spain and become Christian; indeed, Amerindians called them "black whitemen." Most Africans, however, were enslaved laborers. African slaves were in Cuba by 1518; they labored in the mines of Honduras by the 1540s. After the 1560s, the Portuguese began mass importations of African slaves into Brazil to work on the sugar plantations. It has been estimated that 62,500 slaves were brought into Spanish America and 50,000 into Brazil during the sixteenth century. By 1810, when the movement to abolish the slave trade began to gather momentum, almost 10 million Africans had been involuntarily transported to the New World to work the fields and mines on which the colonial economy depended.

The conquerors had hoped to find vast quantities of wealth that they could take back to the Old World. In the viceroyalty of Mexico, the search for El Dorado remained largely unsuccessful. The discovery, in 1545, of the silver mines at Potosí in Peru, however, fulfilled the Spaniards' wildest dreams. Between 1550 and 1650, the Spanish probably sent back to Spain 181 tons of gold and 16,000 tons of silver, one-fifth of which was paid directly into the royal treasury.

The flood of silver and gold did have a significant impact on the Continent. The treasure represents one-quarter of the income of King Philip II of Spain in the 1560s and made him the richest monarch in Europe. The New World bonanza funded Spanish opposition to the

Protestant Reformation and Spain's attempts to influence the politics of most of its neighbors. And the Spanish coins, the *reales* (re-AL-es) and *reales a ocho* (re-AL-es a O-cho) (the "pieces of eight" prized by English pirates), became the common coin of European traders and even Muslim and Hindu traders in the Indian Ocean. In a world with limited commercial credit, the Spanish treasure was critical for a truly integrated system of world trade.

## The Debate over Indian Rights

To most conquerors, the ruthless pursuit of wealth and power needs little justification, but the more thoughtful among the Spaniards were uneasy. "Tell me," demanded Friar Antonio Montesinos (monteh-SEE-nos) in 1511, "by what right or justice do you hold these Indians in such cruel and horrible slavery? By what right do you wage such detestable wars on these people who lived idly and peacefully in their own lands?"*

Initially, the conquerors claimed the right to wage a just war of conquest if Amerindians refused to allow missionaries to live and work among them. Later, on the basis of reports of human sacrifice and cannibalism, written by Columbus and other early explorers, Europeans concluded that the inhabitants of the New World rejected basic natural laws. Juan Gines de Sepúlveda (HWAN HE-nays de se-PUL-ve-da), chaplain of King Charles I of Spain, argued that the idolatry and cannibalism of the Indians made them, in Aristotle's terms, natural slaves—"barbarous and inhuman peoples abhorring all civil life, customs and virtue." People lacking "civil life" and "virtue" clearly could not be allowed self-government. Other writers commented that nakedness and cannibalism were both signs of the lack of "civility" among the Amerindians. Sepulveda implied that Indians were merely "humanlike," not necessarily human.

Franciscan and Dominican missionaries were especially vocal opponents of views such as Sepúlveda's. Missionaries initially argued that Indians were innocents and ideal subjects for conversion to the simple piety of Christ and his first apostles. In their eyes, Indians were like children who could be converted and led by example and, where necessary, by stern discipline. The simple faith of the newly Christian native peoples was to be an example, the missionaries believed, for the lax believers of old Europe. These mendicants saw themselves as advocates for Indians; they desired to protect the natives from the depredations of the Spanish conquerors and the corruptions of European civilization.

The most eloquent defender of Indian rights was **Bartolomé de Las Casas** (1474–1566), a former encomendero who became a Dominican missionary and eventually bishop of Chiapas in southern Mexico. Las Casas passionately condemned the violence and brutality of the Spanish conquests. In a famous debate with Sepulveda, Las Casas rejected the "humanlike" argument. "All races of the world are men," he declared. All are evolving along a historical continuum. He assumed that all eventually would become Christian; indeed some have called him "an ecclesiastical imperialist." Nonetheless, it was wrong, he argued, to dismiss any culture or society as outside or beyond natural law. Like all other peoples, Indians had reason. That being the case, even the most brutal could be civilized and Christianized, but by conversion, not coercion. In the view of Las Casas, the argument for natural slavery was indefensible.

King Charles accepted Las Casas's criticisms of the colonial administration. In 1542, he issued "New Laws," aimed at ending the virtual independence of the most adventurous encomenderos. He further abolished Indian slavery and greatly restricted the transfer of encomiendas. We should have no illusion, however, that these measures reflected a modern acceptance of cultural pluralism. The very mendicants who protected the Indians assumed that Westernization and Christianization would quickly follow mercy. When it did not, as during revolts in the 1560s, the mendicants themselves sometimes reacted with a puzzled sense of anger, frustration, and betrayal.

**Bartolomé de Las Casas** A former encomendero and the first bishop of Chiapas, who passionately defended Indian rights and urged the passage of laws abolishing Indian slavery.

## SECTION SUMMARY

- Before the arrival of the Spanish, the Aztecs and Inca were large empires that dominated surrounding tribes and clans.
- Cortés found ready allies among the peoples dominated by the two empires.
- The conquest of Mexico set off a Spanish expansion, barely under the control of the Crown.
- The Crown eventually attempted to protect Amerindians by restricting encomiendas, outlawing Indian slavery, and forming Indian-controlled communities.

*Quoted in Mark A. Burkholder and Lyman L. Johnson, *Colonial Latin America* (Oxford: University Press, 1990), p. 29.

**Guaxtepec Map**   This detail from a map from 1580 shows the mixture of Spanish and Mexica that represents the ideal impact of Charles V's New Laws. The map shows a native village, but with a monastery at the center. The map is explained with Spanish captions and Nahuatl pictographic symbols. Nettie Lee Benson Latin American Collection, the University of Texas Libraries, The University of Texas at Austin

# The Columbian Exchange

*What changes did European expansion bring to the Old World and the New?*

The conquerors, adventurers, and traders who completed the expansion begun by the voyages of Christopher Columbus and Vasco da Gama profoundly altered the Old World and the New. A system of world trade had been in place before 1492, but now, as the Spanish proclaimed, Europe, and especially Spain, were at the center of economic and political life. As the Spanish and other Europeans moved throughout the world, they carried with them religions, ideas, people, plants, animals, and diseases—forever uniting the Old World and the New. This blending of cultures is known as the **Columbian Exchange**.

## Disease

Columbus, and those who followed him, brought not only people to the New World but also numerous Old World diseases. "Virgin-soil" epidemics—that is, epidemics of previously unknown diseases—are invariably fierce. Although it now seems certain that the New World passed syphilis to Spain, from which it quickly spread throughout the Old World, diseases transferred from the Old World to the New were much more virulent than syphilis. Smallpox

**Columbian Exchange**
A term used to describe the blending of cultures between the Old World and the New. Columbus, and others who followed, brought plants, animals, and diseases that transformed North and South America.

## The Mulattos of Esmeraldas

This painting, which is entitled *Los Mulatos de Esmeraldas*, is the earliest known signed colonial portrait, dating back to 1599. It was commissioned by Juan del Barrio de Sepúlveda, judge of the Audiencia of Quito. He sent it to the Spanish king in Madrid, where the painting still resides. The artist who painted this very European-styled painting was an Amerindian named Andrés Sánchez Galque who had trained with a Spanish Dominican. The resulting work is a striking mix of native and Spanish cultures and leads a historian to ask, "What does this image suggest about colonial Latin America?"

It demonstrates, first of all, how quickly even isolated areas became integrated into a complex international culture. In the center of the painting stands Don Francisco de Arobe, the head of one of two important Afro-Indian clans that dominated the region since the middle of the sixteenth century. He is flanked by his two sons, Don Petro (on his right) and Don Domingo (on his left). Don Francisco is of mixed ancestry—his father was African, his mother an enslaved Nicaraguan. The parents had escaped into the wild region of Esmeraldas, an isolated coastal area northwest of Quito (see **Map 13.2**). It was an area that the Spanish imagined was filled with gold and perhaps, as its name seemed to imply, emeralds. It was also an area that various missionaries and private adventurers attempted to control in the name of the Crown. They were convinced that had they subdued Esmeraldas, their reward would have been treasure and political power.

In the half-century before this portrait was painted, the mulatto groups had variously negotiated with, helped, and avoided the Spanish. Clan leaders regularly promised to become Christian, to give food to the explorers, and to help in the search for gold and other treasures. Throughout the sixteenth century, they regularly and successfully resisted incorporation into the empire. The leader of one clan had offered allegiance to the Spanish if they would name him governor "over your subjects and vassals and natives." And so, it is no doubt significant that the Spanish named Don Francisco governor. It was, in fact, his peaceful submission to the Audiencia that occasioned this surprising work. All this makes the portrait fascinating but ambiguous. Are the three, as some have suggested, "trophies, stuffed and mounted on a wall of blue" or perhaps crafty diplomats who preferred "Renaissance dissimulation to . . . rebellion?"*

The three figures have struck a pose typical in Renaissance portraits. Don Francisco looks directly at the viewer, while his sons look only at him. The three are wearing Spanish cloaks and ruffled collars, over what is probably a South American poncho, but the design of the material suggests it is European or Asian in origin. What is most striking is the gold jewelry—earrings and noseplugs. These very likely were scavenged from burial mounds left in the region by earlier native peoples. Spanish visitors to Esmeraldas often commented on the gold jewelry of the mulattos. The mulatto clans often used promises of gold to mesmerize the adventurers who came. The three also are wearing shell necklaces—a tradition among coastal peoples reaching back perhaps a millennium. And finally, they are carrying spears, probably a combination of local wood and imported steel tips.

But how to interpret the image? The first thing a historian must do is acknowledge that we cannot know for sure the thoughts of the painter, the patron, or the three who posed. But we can line up the visual evidence that might lead us to a tentative conclusion. First, notice the interesting mix of dress. The three men doubtless would not have worn so many layers of clothing at home, along the steamy seacoast. Are the Spanish additions indications that Don Barrio, the judge of the Audiencia in Quito, dressed them to look more subdued, Spanish, and civilized? All three are addressed as "don," an honorific title that suggests both Christian conversion and elevated social status. But if that is the case, why are there no crosses, no signs of deference? They continue to wear their coastal shells and their gold jewelry taken from

spread from Cuba to Mexico as early as 1519. It was soon followed by diphtheria, measles, trachoma, whooping cough, chickenpox, bubonic plague, malaria, typhoid fever, cholera, yellow fever, scarlet fever, amoebic dysentery, influenza, and some varieties of tuberculosis. Disease served as the silent ally of the conquerors. At critical points during the conquest of Tenochtitlán, smallpox was raging in the Aztec population. The disease later moved along traditional trade networks, often arriving in parts of North and South America decades before the Old World adventurers appeared. An epidemic shortly before Pizarro's expedition to Peru carried off the Sapa Inca and may have contributed to the unrest and civil war that worked to the advantage of the invaders.

Lacking sources, historians cannot trace accurately the movement of epidemic diseases or their effects on New World populations, yet many archaeologists and historians remain convinced that Old World diseases moved north from Mexico and ravaged and disrupted

The Mulattos of Esmeraldas

sites still unknown to the Spanish. Their hats are in their hands, perhaps a sign of respect or submission, but their eyes are not downcast or submissive. Don Francisco looks directly at the viewer and all three hold their spears. They may now be Spanish subjects, but Don Francisco does have the look of a governor.

In the end, it may be that Don Francisco and Judge Barrio would not have agreed on what the painting signified. But the ambiguity of the portrait does demonstrate to subsequent historians the extent to which understanding the Spanish role in Latin America requires more than simply ideas of conquest, domination, or rebellion. Identities may have been transformed, but persons like Don Francisco seem to be more than just obedient subjects.

## Questions

1. *Look at the portrait and try to identify those items that seem native or Spanish.*

2. *Can you find indications of either submission or independence in the portraits?*

---

*The first conclusion is from Kenneth Mills and William B. Taylor, eds., *Colonial Latin America: A Documentary History* (Wilmington, Del.: SR Books, 2002), p. 160; the second is from Kris Lane, *Quito, 1599* (Albuquerque: University of New Mexico Press, 2002), p. 33.

Amerindian populations in eastern North America long before the arrival of European immigrants. In most of the New World, 90 percent or more of the native population was destroyed by wave after wave of previously unknown afflictions. Explorers and colonists did not enter an empty land but rather an *emptied* one.

It was at least partially because of disease that both the Spanish and the Portuguese needed to import large numbers of African slaves to work their plantations and mines. With the settlement of southeastern North America, commercial agriculture was extended to include the production of tobacco and later cotton. As a result of the needs of plantation economies and the labor shortages caused by epidemics, African slaves were brought in by the thousands, then hundreds of thousands. In the Caribbean and along the coasts of Central and South America, the Africans created an African Caribbean or African American culture that amalgamated African, European, and American civilizations.

Spencer Collection, New York Public Library/Art Resource, NY

**Images of the New World** A mix of fact and fiction characterized many early images of the New World. The text below this illustration claims that these natives share everything, even wives; that they are cannibals; and that they have no government. The woodcut seems to justify Spanish domination.

## Plants and Animals

The impact of Old World peoples on native populations was immediately evident to all parties. However, scholars have recently argued that the importation of plants and animals had an even more profound effect than the arrival of Europeans. The changes that began in 1492 created "Neo-Europes" in what are now Canada, the United States, Mexico, Argentina, Australia, and New Zealand. The flora and fauna of the Old World, accustomed to a relatively harsh, competitive environment, found ideal conditions in the new lands. Like the rabbits that overran the Canary Islands and eventually Australia, Old World plants and animals multiplied, driving out many New World species.

The most important meat and dairy animals in the New World today—cattle, sheep, goats, and pigs—are imports from the Old World. Sailors initially brought pigs or goats aboard ship because they were easily transportable sources of protein. When let loose on the Caribbean islands, they quickly took over. The spread of horses through what is now Mexico, Brazil, Argentina, the United States, and Canada was equally dramatic. To the list of domesticated animals can be added donkeys, dogs, cats, and chickens. The changes these animals brought were profound. Cattle, pigs, and chickens quickly became staples of the New World diet. Horses enabled Amerindians and Europeans to travel across and settle the vast plains of both North and South America.

The flora of the New World was equally changed. Even contemporaries noted how Old World plants flourished in the New. By 1555, European clover was widely distributed in Mexico—Aztecs called it "Castilian grass." Other Old World grasses, as well as weeds such as dandelions, quickly followed. Domesticated plants, including apples, peaches, and artichokes, spread rapidly and naturally in the hospitable new environment. The Old World also

**Gardening in Spanish Mexico**   This closed Spanish-style garden is a mix of the old and the new. Workers use both a Spanish hoe and an indigenous spade to cultivate new plants introduced by the Spanish.

provided new and widely grown small grains such as oats, barley, and wheat. Early in the twentieth century, it was estimated that only one-quarter of the grasses found on the broad prairies of the Argentine pampas were native before the arrival of Columbus.

The exchange went both ways. Crops from the New World also had an effect on the Old. By the seventeenth century, maize (or American corn), potatoes, sweet potatoes, and many varieties of beans had significantly altered the diets of Europe and Asia. New crops supported the dramatic population growth that invigorated Italy, Ireland, and Scandinavia. With the addition of the tomato in the nineteenth century, much of the modern European diet became dependent on New World foods. The new plants and new animals, as well as the social and political changes initiated by the Europeans, pulled the Old World and the New closer.

## Culture

One reason for the accommodation between the Old World and the New was that the Europeans and Amerindians tended to interpret conquest and cultural transformation in the same way. The peoples living in the Valley of Mexico believed that their conquest was fated by the gods and that their new masters would bring in new gods. The Spaniards' beliefs were strikingly similar, based on the revelation of divine will and the omnipotence of the Christian God. Cortés, by whitewashing former Aztec temples and converting native priests into white-clad Christian priests, was in a way fulfilling the Aztecs' expectations about the nature of conquest.

Acculturation was also facilitated by the Spanish tendency to place churches and shrines at the sites of former Aztec temples. The shrine of the Virgin of Guadalupe (gwa-da-LOO-peh) (on the northern edge of modern Mexico City), for example, was located on the site of the temple of the goddess Tonantzin (to-NAN-tzin), an Aztec fertility-goddess of childbirth and midwives. The shrine of Guadalupe is a perfect example of the complex mixture of cultures. The shrine initially appealed to *creoles*—people of mixed Spanish and

Mexican descent. In the seventeenth century and after, it came to symbolize the connection of poor Mexicans to Christianity and was a religious rallying point for resisting state injustices.

The colonists tended to view their domination of the New World as a divine vindication of their own culture and civilization. During the sixteenth century, they set about remaking the world they had found. In the century after the conquest of Mexico, Spaniards founded 190 new cities in the Americas. Lima, Bogota, and many others were proudly modeled on and compared with the cities of Spain. In 1573, King Philip II (r. 1556–1598) established ordinances requiring all new cities to be laid out on a uniform grid with a main plaza, market, and religious center. In these cities, religious orders founded colleges for basic education, much like the universities they had organized in the Old World. In 1551, a century before English colonists founded Harvard University in Massachusetts, the Crown authorized the first universities in the New World. The universities in Mexico City and Lima mirrored the great Spanish university in Salamanca, teaching law and theology to the colonial elites. Colonists attempted to re-create in all essentials the society of Spain.

The experience of the Spanish and Portuguese in the sixteenth century seemed confirmed by the later experiences of the French and English in the seventeenth century. In seventeenth-century New England, the English Puritan John Winthrop concluded, "For the natives, they are nearly all dead of smallpox, so as the Lord hath cleared our title to what we possess."[*] A seventeenth-century French observer came to a similar conclusion: "Touching these savages, there is a thing that I cannot omit to remark to you, it is that it appears visibly that God wishes that they yield their place to new peoples."[**] Political philosophers believed that in the absence of evidence that the indigenous peoples were improving the land, the rights to that land passed to those who would make the best use of it. Thus, colonists believed that they had divine and legal sanction to take and to remake these new lands in a European image.

## SECTION SUMMARY

- Old World diseases, introduced into the New World, destroyed perhaps 90 percent of the indigenous population.
- Thousands of enslaved Africans were brought to the New World to replace the lost population.
- Old World plants and animals transformed the economy of the New World.
- The cult of the Virgin of Guadalupe shows how religious practices of the Old World were influenced by New World religious practices.

---

[*]Quoted in Alfred W. Crosby, *Ecological Imperialism: The Biological Expansion of Europe, 900-1900* (Cambridge: Cambridge University Press, 1986), p. 208.
[**]Ibid., page 125.

# Chapter Summary

◆ *What did Europeans know about the wider world in the Middle Ages?*

As we have seen, there was never a time when Europeans were unaware of or unconcerned about the outside world. In addition to traditional geographical knowledge, reaching back to the classical world, Europeans had valuable trade contacts via Muslim traders with both Africa and Asia. Further, in the thirteenth century, Italian merchants and adventurers began making regular trips through central Asia to China and even to Japan.

◆ *How did the Portuguese exploit their new connection to the East?*

Yet, the expansion begun by the Portuguese along the coast of Africa and then on to India began a fateful transformation of European economic, political, and cultural influence. The Portuguese voyages were almost never adventures of discovery. By rumor and careful reading, explorers had ideas about what they would find. Nonetheless, they were faced with challenges that led them to adapt their Mediterranean and European ways of organization. The Portuguese developed a trading-post system to control trade in Asia.

◆ *Why did the Spanish choose to sail west in their attempt to find Asia?*

Portuguese control of the African coast seemed to foreclose Spanish connections to Asian markets. Yet, based on a misunderstanding of classical texts, Columbus convinced the Spanish that the shortest route to Asia involved sailing west. Although Columbus never acknowledged it, by early in the sixteenth century, the Spanish knew that he had found a world unknown to the Old World.

◆ *How did the Spanish conquer and control the new world they entered?*

In the wake of savage conquest and exploitation by adventurers, the Spanish developed a system of law and administration that transformed the world they had found. In the New World, even as the Spanish conquered peoples and changed their languages, governments, and religions, many aspects of Amerindian culture survived in the local Indian municipalities.

◆ *What changes did European expansion bring to the Old World and the New?*

The meeting of the Old World and the New brought unexpected changes to both. The old empires of the Americas were replaced by a Spanish colonial government. They brought with them foods, livestock, religion, and traditional European culture. They also brought diseases that decimated populations and transformed economies.

  Modern historians have made us very aware of what was lost during the violent and tragic conquests that were part of European expansion. It is impossible to say whether the economic and technical benefits of the amalgamation of the Old World and the New outweigh the costs. Even those who celebrate the transformation of the New World would probably agree with the conclusions of a Native American in the Pacific Northwest: "I am not sorry the missionaries came. But I wish they had known how to let their news change people's lives from the inside, without imposing their culture over our ways."*

---

*Quoted in Maria Parker Pascua, "Ozette: A Makah Village in 1491," *National Geographic* (October 1991), p. 53.

# Key Terms

**Prince Henry "the Navigator"** (p. 365)

**Vasco da Gama** (p. 367)

**trading-post empire** (p. 368)

**Treaty of Tordesillas** (p. 371)

**Ferdinand Magellan** (p. 372)

**Aztecs** (p. 373)

**Inca** (p. 373)

**Hernán Cortés** (p. 375)

**Doña Marina** (p. 376)

**Council of the Indies** (p. 378)

*encomienda* (p. 378)

**Bartolomé de Las Casas** (p. 380)

**Columbian Exchange** (p. 381)

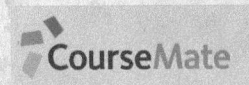
CourseMate

Go to the CourseMate website at **www.cengagebrain.com** for additional study tools and review materials—including audio and video clips—for this chapter.

**El Greco: *The Burial of the Count de Orgaz***   This traditional chapel painting shows the close connection between the earthly and celestial realms in traditional Catholic Christianity. Institut Amatller d'Art Hispanic

# The Age of the Reformation

El Greco's *The Burial of the Count de Orgaz* encapsulates the hopes and contradictions of the age of the Reformation. El Greco ("the Greek") first learned to paint on the island of Crete, then studied and worked in Venice and Rome before settling in Spain. This painting expresses the medieval Christian understanding of a good death. We see a saintly knight surrounded by clergy and witnesses as his soul (in the form of a cloud-wrapped body) is commended to Christ. But El Greco (1541–1614) painted during a period of social, political, and religious turmoil, when medieval assumptions about the unity of the Christian world and the nature of salvation were being challenged by religious reformers and their political supporters.

If we look more closely at the painting, we can see what El Greco and Roman Catholic Christians wished to emphasize. The two figures holding the count's body are Saint Stephen, the first Christian martyr, and Saint Augustine, perhaps the most important of the early Church Fathers. They represent the continuity of the Christian tradition. But just as important is the heavenly hierarchy of saints and angels reaching from the count upward to Christ. At the very top are Saint John the Baptist and the Virgin Mary, who are interceding with Christ for the count's soul. The hierarchy of saints and intercessors so vividly painted by El Greco represents one of the clearest differences between the two contending visions of Christian life and society. Most reformers rejected the idea that salvation depended on the intervention of others, no matter how saintly. Salvation was a simpler process. The hierarchy of saints and angels depicted by El Greco seemed unnecessary.

The crisis of the Reformation began with a challenge to the religious authority of the papacy. Debates over the power and status of the church that raged during this period, however, did not occur in a political vacuum. Support for the old church was an issue of state that profoundly affected the exercise of political authority in the Holy Roman Empire. In England and Scandinavia, by contrast, monarchs viewed the traditional church as a threat to strong royal government, and reformers soon found themselves with royal patrons. Elsewhere, especially in eastern Europe, no strong central governments existed to enforce religious unity, and so a variety of Christian traditions coexisted.

By the second half of the sixteenth century, political and religious leaders concentrated their energies on a process of theological definition and institutionalization that led to the formation of the major Christian religious denominations we know today. They created Roman Catholic, Anglican, Reformed (Calvinist), and Lutheran churches as clearly defined confessions, with formally prescribed religious beliefs and practices.

An important aspect of the reform movement was the emphasis on individual belief and religious participation. Far from freeing the individual, however, the Christian churches of the late sixteenth century all emphasized correct doctrine and orderliness in personal behavior. Although early Protestants rejected a system that they accused of oppressing the individual, the institutions that replaced the old church developed their own traditions of control. The increased moral discipline advocated by churches accompanied and even fostered the expansion of state power that would characterize the late sixteenth and seventeenth centuries.

# The Reformation Movements, ca. 1517–1545

*Why did the reformers feel it was necessary to establish entirely new churches outside the Roman Catholic Church?*

**Martin Luther** German theologian and religious reformer who began the Protestant Reformation in 1517 by questioning, and finally discarding, Catholic teaching about penance and salvation.

In 1517, **Martin Luther**, a little-known priest and professor of theology in eastern Germany, launched a protest against practices in the late medieval church. Luther's criticisms struck a responsive chord with many of his contemporaries and led to calls for reform across much of Europe. All the reformers, even the most radical, shared with Luther a sense that the essential sacramental and priestly powers claimed by the late medieval church were illegitimate. These reformers initially had no intention of forming a new church; they simply wanted to return Christianity to what they believed was its earlier, purer form. Although their various protests resulted in the creation of separate and well-defined religious traditions, the differences among the reformers became clear only in the second half of the sixteenth century. Thus, it is appropriate to speak of "Reformation movements" rather than a unified Protestant Reformation.

## The Late Medieval Context

In the flourishing religious life of the late Middle Ages, questions of an individual's salvation and personal relationship to God and to the Christian community remained at the heart of religious practice and theological speculation. Christians believed in a holy covenant in which God would save those who, by means of the church's sacraments and through penitential and charitable acts, were partners in their own salvation. Foremost among the penitential acts was the feeding of "Christ's Poor," especially on important feast days. The pious constructed and supported hospices for travelers and hospitals for the sick. Christians went on pilgrimages to shrines, such as the tomb of Saint Thomas Becket in Canterbury or the Church of Saint James of Compostela in Spain. They also endowed chapels, called chantry chapels, where prayers would be offered for their own souls. To moralists, work itself was, in some sense, a penitential and ennobling act.

## Popular Religion

The most common religious practice of the late Middle Ages was participation in religious brotherhoods. Urban brotherhoods were usually organized around a craft guild or neighborhood; rural brotherhoods were more likely to include an entire village or parish. Members vowed to attend monthly meetings, to participate in processions on feast days, and to maintain peaceful and charitable relations with fellow members.

The social and communal nature of traditional Christianity was evident in the most typical religious feast, that of *Corpus Christi* (the "Body of Christ"). It celebrated and venerated the sacrament of the mass and the ritual by which the bread offered to the laity became the actual body of Christ. Corpus Christi was popular with the church hierarchy because it emphasized the role of the priest in the central ritual of Christianity. The laity, however, equated Corpus Christi with the body of citizens who made up the civic community. Thus, religious identity seemed to be at the very heart of social identity. The most revered saint in the late Middle Ages, however, was the Virgin Mary, the mother of Jesus. The most popular new pilgrimage shrines in the north of Europe were dedicated to the Virgin. It was she, townspeople believed, who protected them from invasion, plague, and natural disasters. In such a society, it was impossible to distinguish between religion and society, church and state.

## Women and Religion

Women played a prominent role in late medieval religious life. Holy women who claimed any sort of moral standing often did so because of visions or prophetic gifts, such as knowledge of future events or discernment of the status of souls in Purgatory. The Italian Blessed Angela of Foligno (fo-LIN-yo) (ca. 1248–1309) had several visions and became the object of a large circle of devoted followers. She was typical of a number of late medieval religious women who, on the death of a spouse, turned to religion. They tended to gather "families" around them, people whom they described as their spiritual "fathers" or "children." They offered moral counsel and boldly warned businessmen and politicians of the dangers of lying and sharp dealings.

| CHRONOLOGY | |
|---|---|
| 1513–1517 | Fifth Lateran Council meets to consider reform of the Catholic Church |
| 1517 | Luther makes public his "Ninety-five Theses" |
| 1518 | Zwingli is appointed people's priest of Zurich |
| 1520 | Pope Leo X condemns Luther's teachings |
| 1521 | Luther appears at the Diet of Worms |
| 1524–1525 | Peasant revolts in Germany |
| 1527 | Imperial troops sack Rome |
| 1530 | Melanchthon composes the Augsburg Confession summarizing Lutheran belief |
| 1534 | Calvin flees Paris. Loyola founds the Society of Jesus |
| 1535 | Anabaptist community of Münster is destroyed |
| 1536 | Calvin arrives in Geneva and publishes *Institutes of the Christian Religion* |
| 1545–1563 | Council of Trent meets to reform Catholic Church |
| 1555 | Emperor Charles V accepts the Peace of Augsburg |
| 1559 | Parliament passes Elizabethan Act of Supremacy and Act of Uniformity |

In the late Middle Ages, religious houses for women probably outnumbered those for men. For unmarried or unmarriageable (because of poverty or disabilities) daughters, convents provided an economical, safe, and controlled environment. Moralists denounced the dumping of women in convents: "They give [unmarriageable daughters] to a convent, as if they were the scum and vomit of the world," Saint Bernardino of Siena (1380–1444) complained. The general public, however, believed that well-run communities of religious women promoted the spiritual and physical health of the general community. In a society in which women were not allowed to control their own property and, except among the nobility, lacked a visible role in political and intellectual life, a religious vocation may have had a compelling appeal. At the least, it permitted women to define their own religious and social relationships. Well-to-do or aristocratic parents also appreciated the fact that the traditional gift that accompanied a daughter entering a religious house was much smaller than a dowry.

Some women declined to join convents, which required vows of chastity and obedience to a community rule and close male supervision. They could be found among the many pilgrims who visited local shrines, the great churches of Rome, or even the holy city of Jerusalem. Many other women chose to live as anchoresses, or recluses, in closed cells beside churches and hospitals or in rooms in private homes. Men and women traveled from all parts of England seeking the counsel of the Blessed Julian of Norwich (d. after 1413), who lived in a tiny cell built into the wall of a parish church. The most controversial group of religious women was the Beguines, who lived in communities without taking formal vows and often with minimal connections to the local church hierarchy. By the early fifteenth century, Beguines were suspect because clerics believed that these independent women rejected traditional religious cloistering and the moral leadership of male clergy; consequently, it was thought, they were particularly susceptible to heresy.

A more conservative movement for renewal in the church was the Brothers and Sisters of the Common Life, founded by the Dutchman Geert Groote (HIRT HROW-ta) (1340–1384). A popular preacher and reformer, Groote gathered male and female followers into quasi-monastic communities at Deventer in the Low Countries. Members followed a strict, conservative spirituality that has come to be known as the *devotio moderna*, or "modern devotion." Although they called themselves "modern," their piety was traditional. They advocated the contrary ideals of fourteenth-century religious life: broader participation by the laity and strict control by clerical authorities.

Religious life in the late medieval period was broadly based and vigorous. Theologians, laypeople, and popular preachers could take heart that they were furthering their own salvation and that of their neighbors. Thus, the Reformation of the sixteenth century involved more than simple moral reform.

**Crowning with Thorns** Late medieval Christians meditated on Christ's sufferings and preferred images like this one, painted by Giovanni Canavesio, that shows a tortured Christ living in their own time. "Crowning with Thorns" by Giovanni Canavesio, 1492. © Francois Guenet/Art Resource, NY

## Martin Luther and the New Theology

Martin Luther (1483–1546) eventually challenged many of the assumptions of late medieval Christians. He seemed to burst onto the scene in 1517, when he objected to the way in which papal indulgences—that is, the remission of penalties owed for sins—were being bought and sold in the archbishopric of Magdeburg. Luther's father, a miner from the small town of Mansfeld, had hoped that his son would take a degree in law and become a wealthy and prestigious lawyer. Luther chose instead to enter a monastery and eventually become a priest.

### Justification by Faith

Luther recalled having been troubled throughout his life by a sense of his own sinfulness and unworthiness. According to late medieval theology, the life of a Christian was a continuing cycle of sin, confession, contrition, and penance. Luther came to believe that the church's requirement that believers achieve salvation by means of confession, contrition, and penance made too great a demand on the faithful. Instead, Luther said, citing the New Testament, salvation (or justification) was God's gift to the faithful. Luther's belief is known as **justification by faith**. Acts of charity were important products resulting from God's love, but in Luther's opinion, they were not necessary for salvation. In Luther's theology, the acts of piety so typical of the medieval church were quite unnecessary for salvation because Christ's sacrifice had brought justification once and for all. Justification came entirely from God and was independent of human works.

> **justification by faith** Luther's doctrine that Christians can be saved only by grace, a free gift of God, and independent of penitential or charitable acts.

Luther also attacked the place of the priesthood in the sacramental life of the church and, by extension, the power and authority a church might claim in public life. Priests, in Luther's view, were not mediators between God and individual Christians. John Wyclif and Jan Hus (see page 293) had argued against the spiritual authority of unworthy priests. Luther, however, challenged the role of all clergy, and of the institutional church itself, in the attainment of salvation. "The Pope or bishop anoints. . . , he may make a hypocrite of a man, . . . but never a Christian. . . ." Thus, he argued for a "priesthood of all believers."[*]

### Controversy over Indulgences

In the years before 1517, Luther's views on salvation and his reservations about the traditional ways of teaching theology attracted little interest outside his own university. Matters changed, however, when he questioned the sale of indulgences, rewards for pilgrimages or for noteworthy acts of charity or sacrifice. The papacy frequently authorized the sale of indulgences to pay various expenses. Unscrupulous priests often left the impression that purchase of an indulgence freed a soul from Purgatory. After getting no response to his initial complaints, Luther posted his "Ninety-five Theses" on the door of the Wittenberg Castle church, the usual way to announce topics for theological debates. His text created a firestorm when it was quickly translated and printed throughout German-speaking lands. His charges against the sale of indulgences encapsulated German feelings about unworthy priests and economic abuses by the clergy. Luther was acclaimed as the spokesman of the German people.

Responding to the crisis in Germany, Pope Leo X (r. 1513–1521) condemned Luther's teachings in 1520 and gave him sixty days to recant. Luther refused to do so and publicly burned the papal letter. In 1521, Emperor **Charles V** called an imperial diet, or parliament, at Worms to deal with the religious crisis. Charles demanded that Luther submit to papal authority. Luther, however, countered that religious decisions must be based on personal experience and conscience informed by a study of Scripture. Luther's refusal became a ringing statement of conscience, when a later editor added the famous, "Here I stand. I can do no other, may God help me."

> **Charles V** Holy Roman emperor and King Charles I of Spain. His empire included Spain, Italy, the Low Countries, Germany, and the New World.

---

[*]"To the Christian Nobility of the German Nation" in John Dillenberger, *Martin Luther Selections from his Writing* (New York: Random House, 1962) ebook accessed 12-20-2011 http://books.google.com/books?id=jEQ_X5CMh2MC&printsec=frontcover&dq=john+dillenberger&hl=en&sa=X&ei=o8DwTrbXJIrz0gGG37mjAg&ved=0CE0Q6AEwBTgK#v=snippet&q=pope%20or%20bishop%20anoints&f=false)

The emperor and his allies stayed firmly in the papal camp, and the excommunicated Luther was placed under an imperial ban—that is, declared an outlaw. As Luther left the Diet of Worms, friendly princes took him to Wartburg Castle in Saxony, where they could protect him. During a year of isolation at Wartburg, Luther used Erasmus's edition of the Greek New Testament as the basis of a translation of the New Testament into German, which became an influential literary as well as religious work.

## The Reformation of the Communities

Luther challenged the authority of the clerical hierarchy and called on laypeople to take responsibility for their own salvation. His ideas spread rapidly in the towns and countryside of Germany because he and his followers took advantage of the new technology of printing. (See the feature, "The Visual Record: A Reformation Woodcut" on pages 398–399.) Perhaps 300,000 copies of his early tracts were published in the first years of the protest. Luther's claim that the Scriptures must be the basis of all life and his appeal to the judgment of the laity made sense to the men and women in towns and villages, where councils of local people were accustomed to making decisions based on ideas of the common good.

The impact of Luther's ideas quickly became evident. If the active intercession of the clergy was not necessary for the salvation of individuals, then, according to Luther's followers, there was no reason for the clergy to remain unmarried and celibate, nor for men and women to cloister themselves in monasteries and convents. Because Luther's followers believed that penitential acts were not prerequisites for salvation, they tended to set aside the veneration of saints and give up pilgrimages to the shrines and holy places all over Europe.

Many historians have referred to the spread of these reform ideas as the "Reformation of the Common Man." Where Luther's own reform was individual and doctrinal, the reformation in towns and villages was led by the people and contained a strong communal sense. The message seems to have spread especially quickly among artisan and mercantile groups, which put pressure on town governments to press for reform. Agitation was often riotous. One resident of Augsburg exposed himself during a church service to protest what he believed was an evil and idolatrous service. Women on both sides of the reform stepped away from traditional ideas about male and female roles. One reformer demanded to be judged "not according to the standards of a woman, but according to the standards of one . . . filled with the Holy Sprit."[*] Women, like Katharina Schütz Zell of Strasbourg, who married a former priest, dedicated their lives to the social and moral work of community reform. Schütz Zell was more than just a strong moral voice in her community; she wrote an important work defending her own right to interpret Scripture and arguing for the moral role of the laity. Other women wrote tracts advocating reform or defending the old order, and still others used shovels and rakes to defend religious values.

**Huldrych Zwingli** Town preacher of Zurich and leading reformer in Switzerland and southwest Germany. He emphasized the role of the godly community in the process of individual salvation.

The process of reform in Zurich is instructive. **Huldrych Zwingli** (SVING-lee) (1484–1531), son of a rural official, received a university education and became a typical late medieval country priest, right down to his publicly acknowledged mistress. Yet, after experiences as a military chaplain and an acquaintance with the humanist writings of Erasmus, Zwingli began to preach strongly biblical sermons. In 1522, he defended a group of laymen in Zurich, who protested ecclesiastical authority by breaking the required Lenten fast. Later in the same year, he requested episcopal permission to marry. Early in 1523, he led a group of reformers in a public debate over the nature of the church. The city council declared in favor of the reformers, that is, in their words preaching should be based on the Word of God. Zurich became in effect a Protestant city.

Unlike Luther, Zwingli believed that reform should be a communal movement—that town governments should take the lead in bringing reform to the community. Zwingli explained that the moral regeneration of individuals was an essential part of God's salvation. In the years following 1523, the reformers restructured church services, abolishing the mass. In some places, they also removed religious images from churches and suppressed monastic institutions.

---

[*]Quoted in Merry Wiesner-Hanks, "Women and Religious Change," in *The Cambridge History of Christianity*, volume 6 *Reform and Expansion 1500–1660* (Cambridge: Cambridge University Press, 2007), p 467.

## The Twelve Articles

*Luther's emphasis on biblical authority and his example of defiance encouraged peasants to make their own set of demands for justice. The Twelve Articles of the Peasants in Swabia composed at the peasant parliament in Memmingen quickly became the most influential statement of peasant demands. Luther maintained peasants had misunderstood his message of Christian freedom. The articles do, however, outline long-standing grievances among the peasantry.*

There are many antichrists who, now that the peasants are assembled together, seize the chance to mock the gospel, saying, "Is this the fruit of the new gospel: to band together in great numbers and plot conspiracies to reform and even topple the spiritual and temporal powers—yes, even to murder them?" The following articles answer all these godless, blasphemous critics.

. . . [T]he gospel . . . tells of Christ, . . . whose words and life teach nothing but love, peace, patience, and unity. . . . [T]he peasants, whose articles demand this gospel as their doctrine and rule of life cannot be called "disobedient" or "rebellious.". . .

First of all, we humbly ask and beg . . . that henceforth we ought to have the authority and power for the whole community to elect and appoint its own pastor. . . . For the Scripture clearly teaches that we may come to God only through true faith and can be saved only through His mercy. This is why we need such a guide and pastor. . . .

[A]lthough the obligation to pay a just tithe prescribed in the Old Testament is fulfilled in the New, yet we will gladly pay the large tithe on grain. . . . From now on we want to have our church wardens, appointed by the community, collect and receive this tithe and have our elected pastor draw from it, with the whole community's consent. . . .

Third, it has until now been the custom for the lords to own us as their property. This is deplorable, for Christ redeemed and bought us all with his precious blood, the lowliest shepherd as well as the greatest lord. . . . Thus the Bible proves that we are free and want to be free. . . .

Fourth, until now it has been the custom that no commoner might catch wild game, wildfowl, or fish in the running waters, which seems to us altogether improper, unbrotherly, selfish and contrary to God's word. . . . When the Lord God created man, he gave him dominion over all creatures. . . .

[W]e believe and have decided that if any one or more of these articles is not in agreement with God's Word (which we doubt), then this should be proved to us from Holy Writ. We will abandon it, when this is proved by the Bible. . . . We, for our part, will live and exercise ourselves in all Christian teachings, for which we will pray to the Lord God. . . .

### Questions

1. *How do the peasants understand the principle of "by Scripture alone?"*

2. *How did the peasants envision church life within their parishes?*

3. *How might a "reformation" as outlined here have differed from the reformation advocated by Luther and Zwingli?*

"The Twelve Articles," in Peter Blickle, *The Revolution of 1525: The German Peasants' War from a New Perspective*, pp. 195–201. Copyright © 1981 by The Johns Hopkins University Press. Reprinted with permission.

---

The reform message spread from towns into the countryside, but often with effects that the reformers did not expect or desire. Many peasants and modest artisans believed that Luther's message of biblical freedom carried material, as well as theological, meaning.

In many parts of Germany, landlords and local governments had increased their claims for rents and services from villagers and peasants. Their tenants and subjects, however, argued that new tithes and taxes not only upset tradition but also violated the Word of God. Their demands that landlords and magistrates give up human ordinances and follow "Godly Law" soon turned violent. Peasants, miners, and villagers in 1524 and 1525 participated in a series of uprisings that began on the borderlands between Switzerland and Germany and spread throughout southwestern Germany, upper Austria, and even northern Italy. Bands of peasants and villagers, perhaps a total of 300,000 in the empire, revolted against their seigneurial lords or even their territorial overlords.

Luther initially counseled landlords and princes to redress the just grievances. As reports of riots and increased violence continued to reach Wittenberg, however, Luther condemned the rebels as "mad dogs" and urged that they be suppressed. Territorial princes and large cities quickly raised armies to meet the threat. The peasants were defeated and destroyed in a series of battles in April 1525. A townsman of Zurich noted the result, "Many came to a great hatred of the preachers, where before they would have bitten off their feet for the Gospel."*

---

*Quoted in Robert W. Scribner, *The German Reformation* (London: Macmillan, 1986), p. 32.

## John Calvin and the Reformed Tradition

The revolts of 1524 and 1525 demonstrated the mixed messages traveling under the rubric "true" or "biblical" religion. In the 1530s, the theological arguments of the reformers began to take on a greater clarity, mostly because of the Franco-Swiss reformer **John Calvin** (1509–1564). Calvin received a humanistic education in Paris and became a lawyer before coming under the influence of reform-minded thinkers in France. In 1534, he fled from Paris, as royal pressures against reformers increased. He arrived in Geneva in 1536, where he would remain, except for a short exile, until the end of his life.

The heart of Calvin's appeal lay in his formal theological writings. In 1536, he published the first of many editions of the *Institutes of the Christian Religion*, which was to become the summa of Reformed theology. Here he outlined his understanding of how only some were predestined to salvation. And, he added, there were ways to tell who was and who was not to be saved.

Like Luther, Calvin viewed salvation as a mysterious gift from God. Yet, Calvin differed from Luther in a crucial aspect. Salvation was by grace, but it was part of progressive sanctification. This was a critical difference, for Luther did not believe that human behavior could be transformed. We are, he said, "simultaneously justified and sinners." By contrast, Calvin believed that there could be no salvation "if we do not also live a holy life." Thus, the religious behavior of the individual and the community was evidence of justification. As a result, Calvin believed that it was the church's duty to promote moral progress. Public officials were to be "vicars of God." They had the power to lead and correct both the faithful and the unregenerate sinners who lived in Christian communities. In his years in Geneva, Calvin tried to create a "Christian Commonwealth," but Geneva was far from a theocracy.

Elders—the true leaders of the Genevan church—were selected from the patriciate who dominated the civil government of the city. Thus, it makes as much sense to speak of a church governed by the town as a town dominated by the church. The elders actively intervened in education, charity, and attempts to regulate prostitution. Consistories, or church courts, made up of preachers and community elders who enforced moral and religious values, became one of the important characteristics of Reformed (Calvinist) communities.

**John Calvin** A Franco-Swiss theologian whose *Institutes of the Christian Religion* was the key text of Reformed theology. He stressed the absolute power of God.

Private Collection/The Bridgeman Art Library

**Iconoclasm**   Calvinists believed that Christians had to live in communities in which "true religion" was practiced. Iconoclasts (image smashers) cleansed churches of all paintings and statuary that might lead people back to the worship of idols—that is, the medieval cult of saints. This illustration shows just how organized iconoclasm really was.

Reformed churchmen reacted promptly and harshly to events that seemed to threaten their vision of the Christian community. The most famous episode involved the capture, trial, and execution of Michael Servetus (1511–1553), a Spanish physician and radical theologian who rejected traditional doctrines such as the Trinity and specifically criticized many of Calvin's teachings in the *Institutes*. After corresponding with Servetus for a time, Calvin remarked that if Servetus were in Geneva, "I would not suffer him to get out alive." After living in various parts of Europe, Servetus eventually did come anonymously to Geneva. He was recognized and arrested. Calvin was as good as his word. After a public debate and trial, Servetus was burned at the stake for blaspheming the Trinity and the Christian religion. Calvin's condemnation of Servetus was all too typical of Christians in the sixteenth century. Lutherans, Calvinists, and Catholics all believed that protection of true religion required harsh measures against the ignorant, the immoral, and the unorthodox. All too few would have agreed with the humanist reformer Sebastian Castellio that "To burn a heretic is not to defend a doctrine, but to burn a man."*

## The Radical Reform of the Anabaptists

Michael Servetus was but one of a number who felt Luther, Zwingli, and Calvin had not gone far enough. Called **Anabaptists** (or "rebaptizers" because of their rejection of infant baptism) or simply "radicals," they tended to take biblical commands more literally than the mainline reformers. More interested in behavior and community standards than in learned theological arguments, they believed that only adults should be baptized, and then only after confession of sin. In their view, Christians should live apart in communities of the truly redeemed. Thus, civil oaths or public office were a compromise with "the Abomination," that is, unreformed civil society.

Radicals, such as the revolutionaries who took control of the northern German city of Münster, rejected infant baptism, adopted polygamy, and proclaimed a new "Kingdom of Righteousness." The reformers of Münster instituted the new kingdom in the city by rebaptizing those who joined their cause and expelling those who opposed them. They abolished private property rights and instituted new laws concerning morality and behavior. Leadership in the city eventually passed to a tailor, Jan of Leiden (d. 1535), who proclaimed himself the new messiah and lord of the world. After a sixteen-month siege, the bishop of Münster and his allies recaptured the city in 1535. Besieging forces massacred men, women, and children. Jan of Leiden was captured and executed by mutilation with red-hot tongs.

In the wake of the siege of Münster, leaders such as Menno Simons (1495–1561), who founded the Mennonites, and Jakob Hutter (d. 1536), who founded the Hutterian Brethren, or Hutterites, rejected their predecessors' violent attempts to establish truly holy cities. To varying degrees, they also rejected connections with civil society, military service, and even civil courts. They did, however, believe that their own communities were exclusively of the elect. They tended to close themselves off from outsiders and enforce a strict discipline over their members. The elders of these communities were empowered to excommunicate or "shun" those who violated the groups' precepts. Anabaptist communities have proved unusually durable. Hutterite and Mennonite communities continue to exist in western Europe, North America, and parts of the former Soviet Union.

Like Luther, all of the early reformers appealed to the authority of the Bible in their attacks on church tradition. Yet, in the villages and towns of Germany and Switzerland, many radicals were prepared to move far beyond the positions Luther had advocated. When they did so, Luther found himself in the odd position of appealing for vigorous action by the very imperial authorities whose previous inaction had allowed his own protest to survive.

**Anabaptists** Radical reformers in Germany and Switzerland who emphasized that baptism should only be of adults and that Christians should separate themselves into communities of the "truly redeemed."

### SECTION SUMMARY

- Women played an important role in popular religious observance in the Middle Ages.
- Luther's religious ideas challenged the late medieval church's understanding of sin and salvation rather than immoral behavior.
- The key to Luther's theology was his emphasis on the role of grace and biblical authority.
- Calvin's religious reforms centered on the role of the Reformed community in enforcing religious discipline.
- Radical reformers and Anabaptists formed small, tightly controlled communities suspicious of the outside world.

---

*Quoted in Carter Lindberg, *The European Reformations* (New York: Blackwell Publishers, 1996), p. 269.

## A Reformation Woodcut

Erhard Schön's 1533 woodcut, "There Is No Greater Treasure Here on Earth Than an Obedient Wife Who Desires Honor," and other broadsheets like it, informed and amused Europeans of all walks of life in the late fifteenth and sixteenth centuries. Schön's image of a henpecked husband and his wife followed by others would have been instantly recognizable to most people. Accompanying texts clarified the message implied in the woodcut itself. But how may we, centuries later, "read" this message? How does the modern historian analyze Schön's broadsheet to investigate popular ideas about social roles, religion, and politics? What do this and similar broadsheets tell us about popular responses to the social and religious tumults of the sixteenth century?

Look at the simple and clear lines of the woodcut. They give a clue about the popularity of broadsheets. They were cheap and easy to produce and were printed on inexpensive paper. Artists would sketch an image that an artisan would later carve onto a block. A printer could produce a thousand or more copies from a single block. Even famous artists, such as Albrecht Dürer (see page 339), sold highly profitable prints on religious, political, and cultural themes.

Almost anyone could afford broadsheets. Laborers and modest merchants decorated their houses with pictures on popular themes. In the middle of the fifteenth century, before the Reformation, most images were of saints. It was widely believed, for example, that anyone who looked at an image of Saint Christopher would not die on that day.

During the political and religious unrest of the sixteenth century, artists increasingly produced images that referred to the debates over religion. Schön himself made his living in Nuremberg producing and selling woodcuts. He and other artists in the city were closely tuned to the attitudes of the local population. One popular image was titled "The Roman Clergy's Procession into Hell."

Schön's "Obedient Wife" reflects a fear shared by both Protestants and Catholics: the rebellious nature of women. Evidence suggests that women in the late fifteenth and sixteenth centuries may have been marrying at a later age and thus were likely to be more independent-minded than their younger sisters. The ranks of single women were swollen by widows and by former nuns who had left convents and liberated themselves from male supervision. Thus, it was not difficult for men in the sixteenth century to spot women who seemed dangerously free from male control.

Let us turn again to the woodcut, to see what worried villagers and townspeople and how Schön depicted their fears. Notice the henpecked husband. He is harnessed to a cart carrying laundry. Both the harness and the laundry were popular images associated with women's duties. During popular festivals, German villagers often harnessed unmarried women to a plow to signify that they were shirking their duty by not marrying and raising children. Doing the laundry was popularly thought to be the first household chore that a powerful wife would force on her weak-kneed husband. Countless other images show women, whip in hand, supervising foolish husbands as they pound diapers with a laundry flail. "Woe is me," says the poor man, all this because "I took a wife." As if the message were not clear enough, look at what the woman carries in her left hand: his purse, his sword, and his pants. (The question "Who wears the pants in the family?" was as familiar then as it is now.) But the woman responds that he is in this position not because of marriage but because he has been carousing: "If you will not work to support me, then you must wash, spin, and draw the cart."*

The figures following the cart are commenting on the situation. The young journeyman is asking the maiden at his side, "What do you say about this?" She responds coyly, "I have no desire for such power." The woman dressed as a fool counsels the young man never to marry and thus to avoid anxiety and suffering. But an old man, identified as "the wise man," closes the procession and ends the debate. "Do not listen to this foolish woman," he counsels. "God determines how your life together will be, so stay with her in love and suffering and always be patient."

If we think about this woodcut's images and text, we can understand the contrary hopes and fears in sixteenth-century Germany. Like the young woman, the Christian wife was expected to eschew power either inside or outside the home. Martin Luther concluded that "the husband is the head of the wife even as Christ is head of the Church. Therefore as the Church is subject to Christ, so let wives

# The Empire of Charles V (r. 1519–1556)

*What political factors limited Charles V's ability to respond to the religious crisis?*

Luther believed that secular authorities should be neutral in religious matters. In his eyes, the success of the early Reformation was simply God's will:

> [W]hile I slept or drank Wittenberg beer with my friend . . ., the Word [of God] so greatly weakened the Papacy that no prince or emperor ever inflicted such losses on it.*

Luther's belief in the Word of God was absolute, yet he must have known, even as he drank his beer, that the Holy Roman emperor could have crushed the reform movements

*Quoted in Euan Cameron, *The European Reformation* (Oxford: Clarendon Press, 1991), pp. 106–107.

**"There Is No Greater Treasure Here on Earth Than an Obedient Wife Who Desires Honor," Erhard Schön**

be subject to their husbands in everything" (Ephesians 5:23–24). Authority was to be in the hands of husbands and fathers. But if the good wife was required to avoid power, the good husband was expected to follow Luther's precepts for the Christian family. As the wise old man observes, the husband must be a loving and forgiving master.

Schön's woodcut and others similar to it should remind you of the "argument over women" discussed in Chapter 12 (see page 343). The words of the wise man and the young maid bring to mind Christine de Pizan's *Book of the City of the Ladies* when they urge love and understanding, but their hopefulness is undercut by the power and immediacy of the image. As the broadsheet clearly demonstrates, suspicion of women characterized even the most simple literature of Reformation Europe.

### Questions

1. *What conclusion might a viewer draw about women from thinking about the three women pictured in this woodcut?*

2. *How does the image of the godly marriage differ in this woodcut and the picture of the holy household (see page 414)?*

---

*Keith Moxey, *Peasants, Warriors and Wives: Popular Imagery in the Reformation* (Chicago: University of Chicago Press, 1989), pp. 108–109; includes a translation of portions of the text in the broadsheet.

had he not faced a series of political and military challenges which made concerted action all but impossible. The eventual religious settlement required a constitutional compromise that preserved the virtual autonomy of the great princes of Germany. Charles had dreamed of using his imperial office to restore and maintain the political and religious unity of Europe. The realities of sixteenth-century Europe, however, made nobles afraid of the emperor, even when he tried to preserve the unity of the church.

## Imperial Challenges

Emperor Charles V (r. 1519–1556) was the beneficiary of a series of marriages that, in the words of his courtiers, seemed to re-create the empire of Charlemagne. From his father, Philip of Habsburg, he inherited claims to Austria, the imperial crown, and Burgundian lands that included the Low Countries and the county of Burgundy. Through his mother, Joanna,

🌐 **Map 14.1 The Global Empire of Charles V** Religious and political change were profoundly affected by the complexity of the empire of Charles V. German calls for reform had to be understood in the context of an immense empire. © Cengage Learning 2014

the daughter of Ferdinand and Isabella of Spain, Charles became heir to the kingdoms of Castile, Aragon, Sicily, Naples, and Spanish America (see **Map 14.1**). By 1506, he was duke in the Burgundian lands; in 1516, he became king of Aragon and Castile; and in 1519, he was elected Holy Roman emperor. Every government in Europe had to deal with one part or another of Charles's empire. His chancellor enthused, "[God] has set you on the way towards a world monarchy, towards the gathering of all Christendom under a single shepherd."

Charles seems sincerely to have desired such a world monarchy, but he faced challenges in each of the areas under his control. Between 1517 and 1522, when religious reform was making dramatic advances in Germany, many of the most important towns of Spain were in open rebellion against the Crown. In Castile, for example, grandees, townspeople, and peasants had many complaints. But most of all, they objected that too many of his officials were foreigners whom he had brought with him from his home in Flanders. Protests festered in the towns and villages of Castile and finally broke out into a revolt called the *Comunero* (townsmen's or citizens') movement. Charles's forces eventually took control of the situation, and by 1522 he had crushed the Comuneros. However, in the critical years between 1522 and 1530, he was careful to spend much of his time in his Spanish kingdoms.

Charles's claims in Italy, as well as in the Pyrenees and the Low Countries, brought him into direct conflict with the Valois kings of France. In the critical 1520s, the Habsburgs and the Valois fought a series of wars (see pages 302–303). Charles dramatically defeated the French at Pavia in northern Italy in 1525, sacked and occupied Rome in 1527, and became the dominant power in Italian politics. The Habsburg-Valois Wars, however, dragged on until, in exhaustion, the French king Henry II (r. 1547–1559) and the Spanish king Philip II (r. 1556–1598) signed the Treaty of Cateau-Cambrésis in 1559.

Charles was not the only ruler to claim the title "emperor" and a tradition of authority reaching back to the Roman Empire. After the conquest of Constantinople in 1453, the sultan

## THE HABSBURG SUCCESSION, 1493–1556

### HOLY ROMAN EMPERORS AND KINGS OF SPAIN

**Maximilian of Austria** ——— **Mary of Burgundy**
Holy Roman Emperor
(r. 1493–1519)

**Philip of Habsburg** ——— **Joanna of Spain**

**Charles V**
King of Spain (r. 1516–1556)
Holy Roman Emperor (r. 1519–1556)

**Ferdinand I**
Holy Roman Emperor
(r. 1556–1564)

**Philip II**
King of Spain (r. 1556–1598)

© Cengage Learning 2014

of the Ottoman Turks often referred to himself as "the Emperor." Sultans carefully culti-vated their connections with Christian rulers, playing off the suspicions and rivalries within Christendom. After consolidating control of Constantinople and the Balkans, Turkish armies under the command of the emperor Suleiman (r. 1520–1566), known as "the Magnificent," resumed their expansion to the north and west. After capturing Belgrade, Turkish forces soundly defeated a Hungarian army at the Battle of Mohács in 1526. Charles appealed for unity within Christendom against the threat. Even Martin Luther agreed that Christians should unite during invasion.

Suleiman's army besieged Vienna in 1529 before being forced to retreat. The Turks also deployed a navy in the Mediterranean and, with French encouragement, began a series of raids along the coasts of Italy and Spain. The Turkish fleet remained a threat throughout the sixteenth century. The reign of Suleiman marked the permanent entry of Turkey into the European military and diplomatic system. Turkish pressure was yet another reason Charles was unable to deal with German Protestants in a direct and uncompromising way. (See the feature, "The Global Record: The Sultan Suleiman" on page 403.)

## German Politics

The political configuration of Germany had an ongoing influence on the course of religious reform. In 1500, Germany was much less centralized than France or England. Indeed, the empire lacked a unified legal system, and the emperor himself had only one vote on the impe-rial council. In many respects, political centralization and innovation were characteristics of individual territories, not of the empire as a whole. The power of the emperor depended on his relations with the towns and princes of Germany.

In the first years after Luther issued his "Ninety-five Theses," he was defended by the elector Frederick of Saxony, who held a key vote in Charles's quest for election as Holy Roman emperor. As long as Frederick protected Luther, imperial officials had to proceed against the reformer with caution. When Luther was outlawed by the imperial Diet of Worms in 1521, Frederick and many other princes and towns refused to enforce the edict against him and his followers unless their own grievances against the emperor and their complaints about the church were taken up at the same time. At the Diet of Speyer in 1526, delegates passed a resolution empowering princes and towns to settle religious matters in their territories as they saw fit. In effect, this resolution legitimated the reform in territories where authorities chose to follow the new teachings and presaged the final religious settlement in Germany.

**The Capture of Belgrade, 1521** During the sixteenth century, Ottoman Turks dominated the Balkans militarily and were a significant force in European diplomacy. They were masters of coordinated attacks combining artillery and infantry.

Österreichische Nationalbibliothek

German authorities took advantage of the emperor's relative powerlessness and made choices reflecting a complex of religious, political, and diplomatic issues. Some rulers acted in ways that were even more consciously cynical and self-serving. The grand master of the religious order of the Teutonic Knights, Albrecht von Hohenzollern (1490–1568), who controlled the duchy of Prussia, renounced his monastic vows and secularized the order's estates (that is, he transferred them from church to private ownership), which then became East Prussia, hereditary lands of the Hohenzollern family. In other territories, rulers managed to claim the properties of suppressed religious orders. In the autonomous towns, many decisions about religion were often made with one eye on the choices made by neighbors and competitors.

Some rulers found their personal reservations about Luther reinforced by their fears of popular unrest. Luther's call for decisions based on personal conscience seemed to the dukes of Bavaria, for example, to repudiate princely authority and even to provoke anarchy. In the confused and fluid situation of the 1520s and 1530s, imperial interests were never the primary issue.

## The Religious Settlement

**Augsburg Confession** Document, written by Philipp Melanchthon, that became the most widely accepted statement of the Lutheran faith.

With the fading of the Turkish threat on Vienna in 1529, Charles V renewed his pressure on the German principalities at a meeting of the imperial diet at Augsburg in 1530. It was for this diet that Philipp Melanchthon (1497–1560), Luther's closest adviser, prepared the **Augsburg Confession**, which would become the basic statement of the Lutheran faith. Melanchthon hoped that the document would form the basis of compromise with Catholic powers, but that possibility was rejected out of hand by the imperial party. Charles aimed to end the reform movement and enforce bans on Luther's teachings.

Religious reform and political resistance to imperial power, however, remained closely connected. In the religious Peace of Augsburg of 1555, the emperor formally acknowledged the principle that sovereign princes could choose the religion to be practiced in their territories—*cuius regio, eius religio* ("who holds the territory, choses his religion"). There were limits, however: Leaders had only two choices—remain under papal authority or adopt the Augsburg Confession outlined by Melanchthon. Reformed churches associated with Zwingli or Calvin were not legally recognized (see **Map 14.2**).

## SECTION SUMMARY

- Charles V united under his personal rule Germany, the Low Countries, Spain, most of Italy, and Latin America.
- Political control in the area of Charles's empire was just weak enough that Charles was never able to act effectively against Luther and his allies.
- Throughout the sixteenth century, the Ottoman Turks were a major threat to the western European powers.
- The religious Peace of Augsburg (1555) recognized the political and religious autonomy of the independent princes and towns.

## The Sultan Suleiman

*The Venetians had the most sophisticated system of information gathering in the sixteenth century. Venetian ambassadors were expected to report regularly on the events they had witnessed and submit a full report at the end of their term of office. The report by ser Marco Minio, recorded in April 1522, included a report on Sultan Suleiman whose troops had captured Belgrade in 1521. The Venetians wanted both a report on the young sultan and information on how they could best deal with the Ottoman threat.*

The sultan has huge resources of manpower, authority, an income of three million in gold, and tax revenues of one million two hundred thousand in personal taxes [from Christians].... His Majesty spends a great deal on the 10,000 janissaries, who are paid quarterly and who cost him 75,000 ducats annually.... It is not known whether he has money in the treasury, but it is clear that he is assiduously obeyed. While I was there, he had a Salitar pasha hanged; he was one of the leaders of the Salitars, a group of cavalry, and had many slaves at his command. The sultan sent an agent to his house, who told him, "You, the sultan has decided that you will be hanged." Without further ado, he was led out and hanged while his company wept.... This is a person who informs himself, who does not like to be told what to do but who instead forms opinions that he clings to stubbornly. I do not believe he will be a peaceful person, but will soon show that he is most warlike. Now that he has taken Belgrade, he thinks that he holds the keys to Christendom in his hands. They say that Mustaphà Pasha, who is the governor in Greece and a friend of ours, wants to make war in Hungary. And in our discussions, this Mustaphà told me that our government should not show favor to that king.... [He] is plump, cheery, and warm hearted.... It is said that as far as the peace accord goes, the pashas were concerned with only two stipulations: that if our ships encounter the sultan's armada when they are at sea, they are to lower their sails, and that if any ship belonging to a subject of his causes damage [to a Venetian ship] and [the offending ship] is captured, it will be sent to the sultan, who will punish them [the captain and the crew]; if they happen to be pirates, justice is to be meted out on the spot.

### Questions

1. What does the ambassador believe is most important about the Sultan's power?

2. What are the important issues the Venetians need to consider in dealing with the Turks?

*"The Sultan Suleiman" Venice, città Excellentissima. *Selections from the Renaissance Diaries of Marin Sanudo*, pp. 208, 209, 210. Ed. by Patricia H. Langbalme and Laura Sanguineti White. Copyright © 2008 by The Johns Hopkins University Press. Reprinted with permission.

Shortly after the settlement, Charles abdicated his Spanish and imperial titles. Exhausted by years of political and religious struggle, he ceded the imperial crown to his brother, Ferdinand (r. 1556–1564). He transferred his possessions in the Low Countries, Spain, Italy, and the New World to his son, Philip II (r. 1556–1598). Charles had believed his courtiers when they had compared his empire to that of the ancient Romans. He had accepted that his duty as emperor was to unite Christendom under one law and one church. But in no part of his empire did he ever command the authority that would have allowed him to unite his lands politically, let alone to reestablish religious unity. Following his abdication, Charles retired to a monastery in Spain, where he died in 1558.

# The English Reformation, 1520–1603

*Why did the English monarchs take the lead in efforts to reform the English church?*

The Reformation in England is often called a monarchical Reformation. In contrast with Germany, where reform occurred in spite of imperial opposition, in England, the Crown instituted the reform. As in Germany, however, institutional change in the church followed from both secular issues and reform ideas. In England, an initially hostile monarch began to tolerate reform when he perceived the papacy as an unbiblical, tyrannical force blocking essential state policy. And by the middle of the sixteenth century, it was royal interest in compromise that brought a settlement that left England a curious hybrid of reformed and traditional religious practices.

🌐 **Map 14.2 Catholics and Protestants in 1555**   At the time of the Peace of Augsburg, Christendom in western Europe was divided into three major groups. Lutheran influence was largely confined to parts of Germany and Scandinavia, while Calvinist influence was strong in Switzerland, Scotland, the Low Countries, and parts of France. Most of the West remained within the Roman Catholic Church. © Cengage Learning 2014

## Henry VIII and the Monarchical Reformation

England had close economic ties to Germany. Reformers from Wittenberg and other Protestant towns influenced English merchants from London who traded and traveled on the Continent. One reformer, William Tyndale (ca. 1494–1536), served as a bridge between the Continent and England. He had a humanistic education in classical languages and began working on an English translation of the Bible in the 1520s. Forced by the church hierarchy to flee London, he visited Luther in Wittenberg before settling in Antwerp, where he completed his English New Testament. By 1526, copies of his translation and his religious tracts flooded England. By the 1520s, Lutheran influence was noticeable in London and Cambridge. There is still debate about just how strong this early influence was. To some extent, the ground may have been prepared for the reformers by the few surviving Lollards (see page 293), who tended to be literate and were an ideal market for Tyndale's English Bible and his numerous reformist tracts. But religious brotherhoods, lay piety, and traditional forms of penance remained an important part of religious life. If reform was to succeed, it required support from the king.

**Henry VIII** (r. 1509–1547) began his reign as a popular and powerful king. Handsome, athletic, and artistic, he seemed to be the ideal ruler. At first, he was quite hostile to Luther's reform ideas. He wrote *Defense of the Seven Sacraments*, which earned him the title "Defender of the Faith" from a grateful Pope Leo X. Throughout his life, Henry remained suspicious of many Protestant ideas, but he led the initial phase of the break with the papacy because of his political problems with the highly orthodox Holy Roman emperor Charles V. The first phase of the English Reformation was thus monarchical.

**Henry VIII** King of England who broke with the church over the issue of his divorce. In the end, Henry claimed that, as king, he was the head of the Church in England.

## Divorce

Religious change was initiated in response to what the English called "the King's Great Matter"—that is, Henry's determination to divorce his wife, Catherine of Aragon, emperor Charles's aunt. Recalling the unrest of the Wars of the Roses (see page 313), Henry believed that he needed a son to ensure that the Tudors could maintain control of the English crown. By 1527, Henry and Catherine had a daughter, Mary, but no living sons. Unfortunately for him, Leo X's successor, Pope Clement VII (r. 1523–1534), was a virtual prisoner of imperial troops who had recently sacked Rome and taken control of most of Italy. As long as Charles supported Catherine of Aragon and his forces occupied Rome, a papal annulment was out of the question.

The king's advisers quickly divided into two camps. Sir Thomas More, humanist writer (see page 348), royal chancellor, and staunch Catholic, urged the king to continue his policy of negotiation with the papacy and his efforts to destroy the growing Protestant party. Until his resignation in 1532, More led royal authorities in a vigorous campaign against the dissemination of the newly translated Tyndale Bible and against the spread of Protestant ideas. More was opposed and eventually ousted by a radical party of Protestants led by Thomas Cranmer (1489–1556) and Thomas Cromwell (1485?–1540), who saw in the king's desire for a divorce an effective wedge to pry Henry out of the papal camp. Cromwell, who eventually replaced More as chancellor, advised the king that the marriage problem could be solved by the English clergy without papal interference.

**Oxford Executions, 1555** Protestant images make clear the public nature of executions for heresy and the martyr's unbending faith. Here we see a public gathering of the citizens of Oxford. These often included a pulpit for a sermon before the execution as well as prominent seats for public authorities. In the background Thomas Cranmer prays, "O Lord strengthen them," and the two men on the pyre pray ". . . receive my soul" and ". . .into Thy hands."

## Monarchical Reformation

Between 1532 and 1535, Henry and Parliament took a number of steps that effectively left the king in control of the church in England. In 1533, Parliament ruled that appeals of cases concerning wills, marriages, and ecclesiastical grants had to be heard in England. In May, an English court annulled the king's marriage to Catherine. Four months later, Henry's new queen, Anne Boleyn, gave birth to a daughter, Elizabeth.

After the split, the king began to seize church properties. Parliamentary action culminated in the passage of the **Act of Supremacy** in 1534, which declared the king to be "the Protector and only Supreme Head of the Church and the Clergy of England." Henry meant to enforce his control by requiring a public oath supporting the act. Sir Thomas More refused to take the oath and was arrested, tried, and executed for treason.

Cromwell and Cranmer had hoped to use "the King's Great Matter" as a way to begin a Lutheran-style reform of the church. But Henry remained suspicious of religious change. Between 1534 and Henry's death in 1547, neither the Protestant nor the Catholic party was able to gain the upper hand at court or at Canterbury. Substantive changes in the English church would be made by Henry's children.

**Act of Supremacy** Act of the English Parliament, during the Protestant Reformation, that finalized the break with the Catholic Church by declaring the king to be head of the Church of England. Henry VIII required a public oath supporting the act, which Sir Thomas More refused to take; More was then executed for treason.

## Reform and Counter-Reform under Edward and Mary

Prince Edward, Henry's only surviving son in 1547, was born to Henry's third wife, Jane Seymour. He was only 10 years old when his father died. By chance, Edward Seymour, who was Prince Edward's uncle, and the Protestant faction were in favor at the time of Henry's death. Seymour was named duke of Somerset and Lord Protector of the young King Edward VI (r. 1547–1553). Under Somerset, the Protestants were able to make significant changes in religious life in England. Edward completed the "dissolution of the monasteries"—the process of confiscating properties belonging to chapels and shrines—that his father had begun. In an act of great symbolic meaning, priests were legally allowed to marry. Finally, Archbishop Cranmer introduced the first edition of the English *Book of Common Prayer* in 1549. The publication updated some late medieval English prayers and combined them with liturgical and theological ideas taken from Luther, Zwingli, and Calvin. In its beautifully expressive English, it provided the laity with a primer on how to combine English religious traditions with reform theology. If Edward had not died of tuberculosis in 1553, England's reform would have looked very much like the movement in Switzerland and southern Germany.

Protestant reformers attempted to prevent Mary Tudor (r. 1553–1558), Henry's Catholic daughter, from claiming the throne, but Mary and the Catholic party quickly took control of the court and the church. Mary immediately declared previous reform decrees to be void. Cardinal Reginald Pole (1500–1558), who had advocated reform within the Catholic Church, became the center of the Catholic restoration party in Mary's England. Pole rooted out Protestants within the church. More than eight hundred gentlemen, clerics, and students fled England for Protestant havens on the Continent. Some officials, including Cranmer, chose to remain and paid with their lives. In all, three hundred Protestants, mostly artisans and laborers, were tried and executed by church courts, earning the queen her nickname, "Bloody Mary."

The policies of the queen brought about an abrupt change in official policy. Many parishes quickly and easily returned to traditional Roman religious practices. Statues were removed from hiding and restored to places of honor in churches and chapels. In many others, there was an uneasy amalgam of traditional and reformed. The ease with which the queen restored Catholic practice indicates that Henry's reform was not deeply rooted. In fact, a Catholic reform led by Mary might have succeeded had the queen not died after little more than six years on the throne. At her death, the issue of the reform in England was far from certain.

## SECTION SUMMARY

- England's Reformation was monarchical because it was shaped and directed by the cultural and political needs and attitudes of the monarchs.
- Cranmer's *Book of Common Prayer* organized and introduced into England the ideas of the continental Reformation.
- Queen Mary might have succeeded in restoring much of traditional church practice had she not died after just a short reign.

# France, Scandinavia, and Eastern Europe, 1523–1560

*How did ideas of church reform influence social and political developments in the rest of Europe?*

In England and in the empire of Charles V, the success of the new religious reforms depended greatly on the political situation. It would be naive to conclude, as Luther claimed, that "the Word did everything." Yet, this complex religious reform movement cannot be reduced to the politics of kings and princes. The issues will be clearer if we survey politics and reform in the rest of Europe, noting whether and to what extent the new ideas took root (see **Map 14.2**). In France, for example, the widespread, popular support of the old religion limited the options of the country's political leaders. Similarly, in northern Europe, religious reform was an issue of both popular feeling and royal politics.

## France

Luther's work, and later the ideas of the urban reformers of southwestern Germany and Switzerland, passed quickly into France. Geneva is in a French-speaking area, close to the French border. Perhaps because of France's proximity to the Calvinists in French-speaking Switzerland or because of the clarity and power of Calvin's *Institutes*, French Protestants, known as Huguenots, were tied more closely to the Calvinists of Geneva than to the Lutherans of Germany.

At the height of the Reformation's popularity, Protestants probably represented no more than 10 percent of the population of France. Protestants seem to have comprised a diverse mix that included two of the three most important noble families at court: the Bourbon and Montmorency families. Clerics interested in moral reform and artisans who worked at new trades, such as the printing industry, also made up a significant portion of the converts. Perhaps reflecting the numerous printers and merchants in their numbers, Protestants tended to be of higher than average literacy. They were particularly well represented in towns and probably constituted a majority in the southern and western towns of La Rochelle, Montpellier, and Nîmes. Paris was the one part of the realm in which they had little influence, and this may have been their undoing.

The conservative theologians of the Sorbonne in Paris were some of Luther's earliest opponents. They complained that many masters at the University of Paris were "Lutheran." But, as in Germany, there was no clear understanding of who or what a Lutheran was. The Sorbonne theologians were also suspicious of a number of "pre-reformers," including the humanistic editor Jacques Lefèvre d'Étaples (1455–1536; see page 347), who, late in life, had come to an understanding of justification quite like Luther's. Others were clerics intent on religious reform within the traditional structures. Unlike Luther and the French Protestants, these pre-reformers did not challenge the priests' relationship to the sacraments. They were interested in the piety and behavior of churchmen. They never challenged the role of the clergy in salvation. King Francis's own sister, Margaret of Angoulême (1492–1549), gathered a group of religious persons, including several reformers, at her court. However, Margaret herself urged that theology be left to scholars; she believed that the laity should stick to simple pieties. Like Margaret, most French Christians had no clear sense that Protestant teachings required a complete break with medieval Christian traditions.

Like other monarchs, Francis I (r. 1515–1547) largely interpreted religious issues in the context of royal interests. Primarily engaged in the seemingly intractable wars with the Habsburgs, Francis generally ignored religious questions. He was not initially opposed to what seemed to be moral reform within the church. His own view was that the king's duty was to preserve order and prevent scandal, and at first, carrying out that duty meant protecting reformers whom the conservative militants persecuted. The king feared disorder more than he feared religious reform.

**The Great Cauldron**

In dramatic images, this French woodcut shows the Protestant expectation that the Bible carried down by the Holy Spirit will overturn the whole cauldron of false images and errors that supported the old church.

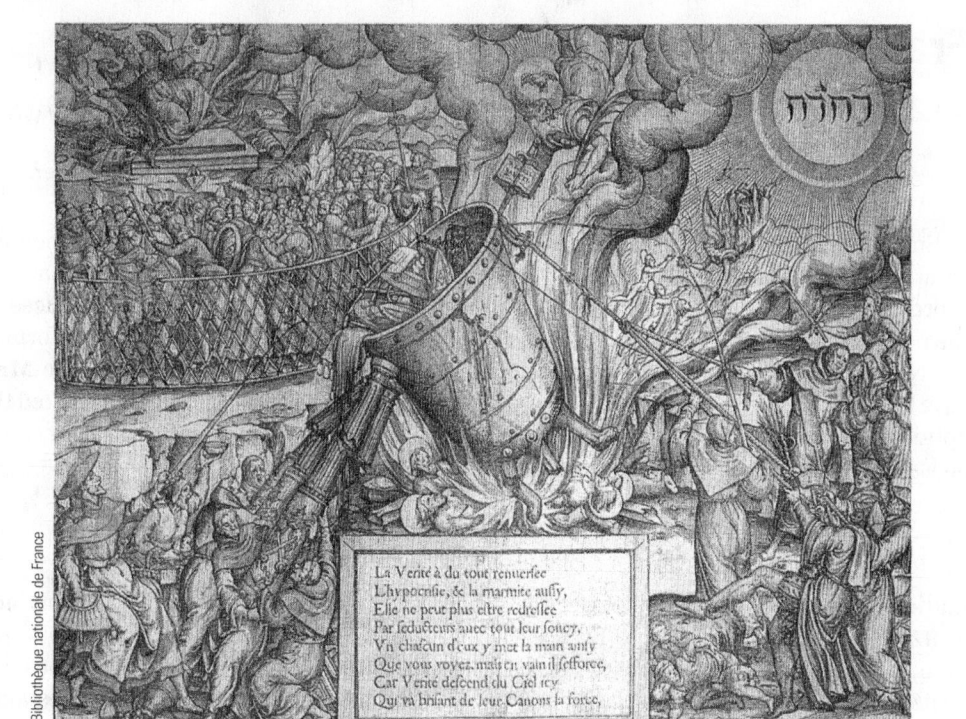

Bibliothèque nationale de France

La Verité à du tout renuersee
L'hypocrisie, & la marmite aussy,
Elle ne peut plus estre redressee
Par seducteurs auec tout leur soucy,
Vn chascun d'eux y met la main ainsy
Que vous voyez, mais en vain il sefforce,
Car Verité descend du Ciel icy
Qui va brisant de leur Canons la force,

On October 18, 1534, however, Francis's attitude changed when he and all Paris awoke to find the city littered with anti-Catholic placards containing, in the words of the writers, "true articles on the horrible, great and insufferable abuses of the Papal Mass." The "Affair of the Placards" changed Francis's ideas about the sources of disorder. Opposition to traditional religious practices became more difficult and more dangerous. John Calvin himself was forced to leave Paris, and eventually France, because he feared persecution. Between 1534 and 1560, some ten thousand Protestants fled France, many joining Calvin in Geneva.

By the middle of the sixteenth century, it was clear that neither Protestant nor Catholic factions would be able to control religious and political life in France. Francis I died in 1547, and the stage was set for a series of destructive factional struggles over religion and political power that would continue for the rest of the century (see Chapter 15).

## Scandinavia

All of Scandinavia became Lutheran. Initial influences drifted north from Germany, carried by Hanseatic merchants and students who had studied at the universities of northern Germany. Yet, the reform in Sweden and Denmark, even more than in England, was monarchical. In both Scandinavian kingdoms, the kings began with an attack on the temporal rights and properties of the church. Changes in liturgy and practice came later, as reformers gained royal protection.

In Sweden, the establishment of a strong monarch required concern for religious reform. Gustav Vasa, a leading noble, was able to secure the loyalty of most of the Swedes and in 1523 he was elected king of Sweden. Gustav's motto was "All power is of God." Like Henry VIII of England, Gustav (r. 1523–1560) moved carefully in an attempt to retain the loyalty of as many groups as possible. Although he never formally adopted a national confession of faith, the Swedish church and state gradually took on a more Lutheran character. In an effort to secure royal finances, the Riksdag, or parliament, passed the Västerås Ordinances, which secularized ecclesiastical lands and authorized the preaching of the "Pure Word of God." Olaus Petri (1493–1552), Sweden's principal reform preacher, was installed by royal order in the Cathedral of Stockholm.

In Denmark, the reformers also moved cautiously. Frederick I (r. 1523–1533) and his son, Christian III (r. 1534–1559), continued the policy of secularization and control that Christian I had initiated. Danish kings seemed interested in reform as a diplomatic means of attack on the Roman church. The kings tended to support reformers as a way to attack the political power of the bishops. In 1538, the Danes finally accepted the Augsburg Confession, which was becoming the most widely accepted exposition of Lutheran belief. The transformation of practice proceeded slowly over the next decades.

In the frontier regions of Scandinavia—Finland, Iceland, and Norway—the reform was undertaken as a matter of royal policy. Initially, only a handful of local reformers introduced and proselytized the new theology and practice. In many regions, resistance to the Reformation continued for several generations. One valley, hidden in the mountains of western Norway, continued to follow the old religion for three centuries after its contacts with Rome had been severed.

### Eastern Europe

In some respects, there was less opposition to the expansion of Protestantism in eastern Europe. The result was the creation of a unique religious culture. The church hierarchy was not in a position to enforce orthodoxy. Some Christian rulers were indifferent to religious debates, as were the Muslim Ottoman Turks, who controlled much of eastern Hungary and what is now Romania. Other rulers whose societies already contained Orthodox and Catholic Christians, as well as Muslims and Jews, offered toleration because they could ill afford to alienate any portion of their subject populations.

Protestant ideas initially passed through the German communities of Poland and the trading towns along the Baltic coast. But in the 1540s, Calvinist ideas spread quickly among the Polish nobles, especially those at the royal court. Given the power and influence of some of the noble families, Catholics were unable to suppress the various secret Calvinist congregations. During the first half of the sixteenth century, Protestantism became so well established in Poland that it could not be rooted out. Throughout the sixteenth century, Protestantism remained one of the rallying points for those Polish nobles opposed to the expansion of royal power.

Much was the same in Hungary and Transylvania. Among German colonists, Magyars, and ethnic Romanians, many individuals were interested first in Luther's message and later in Reformed theology. The situation was exacerbated after the Turkish victory at Mohács in 1526, which destroyed the traditional political and religious elite of Hungary. Because no one could hope to enforce uniformity, some cities adopted a moderate Lutheran theology, and others followed a Calvinist confession. In 1568, the Estates (representative assemblies) of Transylvania had decreed that four religions were to be tolerated—Catholic, Lutheran, Reformed (Calvinist), and Unitarian. Further, when various radical groups migrated from the west in search of toleration, they were able to create their own communities in Slavic and Magyar areas.

The Reformation was to have virtually no influence farther to the east, in Russia. The Orthodox Church in Russia was much more firmly under government control than was the church in the West. The Russian church followed the traditions of the Greek church, and Western arguments over justification made little sense in Orthodox churches. Given the historic suspicion of the Orthodox churches toward Rome, the Russians were more tolerant of contacts with the Protestants of northern Europe, but there would be no theological innovation or reform in sixteenth-century Russia.

**SECTION SUMMARY**

- Widespread support for traditional religious practices in France limited the spread of reformed ideas.

- Francis I tolerated religious dissent until it seemed that religious strife might lead to civil unrest.

- In Scandinavia, religious change was fostered by monarchs who wished to reduce the influence of the church in public life.

- Religious toleration was much more common in eastern Europe, where many rulers declined to support one religious movement over another.

# The Late Reformation, ca. 1545–1600

*How did Catholic and Protestant Christians differ by the end of the Reformation?*

In the first half of the sixteenth century, Catholics applied the term *Lutheran* to anyone critical of the papacy. As was clear from countless debates and attempts at compromise, there was real confusion about what Luther had meant. In parts of Germany by the late 1520s and across Europe by the 1550s, political and religious leaders struggled to explain to the people just what *Lutheran*, *Reformed (Calvinist)*, and *Catholic* had come to mean. And in many parts of Europe, individuals could leave or join a religious movement rather easily. Even Anabaptists often would rejoin the protestant or Catholic movements they had harshly criticized. It was only in the second half of the sixteenth century that these terms came to have any clarity. After the middle of the sixteenth century, it was true that along with theological and political changes, the Reformation represented a broad cultural movement.

The profound changes that began in the sixteenth century continued into the seventeenth. Central governments supported religious authorities who desired religious uniformity and control over individual Christians. In all parts of Europe, religious behavior changed. Both Protestants and Catholics became more concerned with the personal rather than the communal aspects of Christianity. After the sixteenth century, the nature of Christianity and its place in public life, whether in Protestant or in Catholic countries, differed profoundly from Christianity in the Middle Ages.

## Catholic Reform, 1512–1600

Historians commonly speak of both a movement for traditional reform and renewal within the Catholic Church and a "Counter-Reformation," which was a direct response to and rejection of the theological positions championed by the Protestants. It is certainly true that one can categorize certain acts as clearly challenging the Protestants. However, to do so is to miss the point that the energetic actions of the Roman Catholic Church during the sixteenth century both affirmed traditional teachings and created new institutions better fitted to the early modern world.

The idea of purer, earlier church practices to which the "modern" church should return had been a commonplace for centuries. In 1512, five years before Luther made his public protests, Pope Julius II (r. 1503–1513) convened another ecumenical council, the Fifth Lateran Council (1513–1517), which was expected to look into the problems of nonresident clergy, multiple benefices, and a host of other issues. This tradition of moral reform was especially strong in Spain, Portugal, and Italy, lands whose political rulers were either indifferent or opposed to Protestant reforms.

In the wake of the sack of Rome by imperial troops in 1527, one Roman cardinal, Bishop Gian Matteo Giberti (ji-BARE-ti) of Verona (1495–1543), returned to his diocese and began a thoroughgoing reform. He conducted visitations of the churches and other religious institutions in Verona, preached tirelessly, worked hard to raise the educational level of his clergy, and required that priests live within their parishes. Giberti believed that morally rigorous traditional reform and renewal could counter the malaise he perceived. Other reforming bishops could be found throughout Catholic Europe.

### The Role of Music and Mysticism

New religious foundations sprang up to renew the church. Members of the new orders set out to change the church through example. The Florentine Filippo Neri (1515–1595) founded the Oratorian order, so named because of the monks' habit of leading the laity in prayer services. Filippo was joined in his work by Giovanni Palestrina (ca. 1525–1594), who composed music for the modest, but moving, prayer gatherings in Rome. Palestrina's music combined medieval plainchants with newer styles of polyphony, creating complex harmonies without obscuring the words and meaning of the text. The popularity of the Oratorians and their services can be measured in part by the fact that oratories, small chapels modeled on those favored by Filippo, remain to this day important centers of musical life in the city of Rome.

The Catholic reform of the sixteenth century, however, was better known for its mystical theology than for its music. In Italy and France, but especially in Spain, a profusion of reformers chose to reform the church through austere prayer and contemplative devotions. Teresa of Avila (1515–1582), who belonged to a wealthy converso family (see page 320), led a movement to reform the lax practices within the religious houses of Spain. Famed for her rigorous religious life, her trances, and her raptures, Teresa animated a movement to reform the order of Carmelite nuns in Spain. Because of her writings about her mystical experiences,

**Society of Jesus**
(Jesuits) Religious group founded in 1534 by Ignatius Loyola; they were famed for their role in the Catholic Counter-Reformation.

she was named a "Doctor of the Church," a title reserved for the greatest of the church's theologians.

## Jesuits

The most important of the new religious orders was the **Society of Jesus**, or Jesuits, founded in 1534 by **Ignatius Loyola** (1491–1556). He initially meant to organize a missionary order directed at converting the Muslims. The structure of his order reflected his military experience. It had a well-defined chain of command, leading to the general of the order and then to the pope. To educate and discipline the members, Loyola composed *Spiritual Exercises*, emphasizing the importance of obedience. He encouraged his followers to understand their own attitudes, beliefs, and even lives as less important than the papacy and the Roman church. If the church commands it, he concluded, "I will believe that the white object I see is black." He prohibited Jesuits from holding an ecclesiastical office like bishop (unless ordered to accept it by the pope) that might compromise their autonomy. After papal approval of the order in 1540, the Jesuits directed their activities primarily to education in Catholic areas and reconversion of Protestants.

Throughout Europe, Jesuits gained fame for their work as educators of the laity and as spiritual advisers to the political leaders of Catholic Europe. In the late sixteenth and early seventeenth centuries, they were responsible for a number of famous conversions, including that of Christina (1626–1689), the Lutheran queen of Sweden, who abdicated her throne in 1654 and spent the rest of her life in Rome. Jesuits were especially successful in bringing many parts of the Holy Roman Empire back into communion with the papacy. They have rightly been called the vanguard of the Catholic reform movement.

## Catholic Reform

Catholic reformers were convinced that one of the reasons for the success of the Protestants was that faithful Christians had no clear guide to orthodox teachings. The first Catholic response to the reformers was to try to separate ideas they held to be correct from those they held to be incorrect. Successive popes made public lists of books and ideas that they considered to be in error. The lists were combined into the *Index of Prohibited Books* in 1559. The climate of suspicion was such that the works of humanists, such as Erasmus, were prohibited alongside the works of Protestants, such as Martin Luther. In times of religious tensions, the *Index* could be vigorously enforced. In Italy, for example, no editions of the Holy Bible in Italian translation were published in the late sixteenth and seventeenth centuries. In general, however, the *Index* could not prevent the circulation of books and ideas. It was finally suppressed in 1966.

## Council of Trent

During the first half of the sixteenth century, Catholics joined Protestants in calls for an ecumenical council that all believed would solve the problems dogging the Christian church. But in the unsettled political and diplomatic atmosphere that lasted into the 1540s, it was impossible to find any agreement about where or when a universal council should meet. Finally, in 1545, at a time when the hostilities between the Valois and Habsburgs had cooled, Pope Paul III (r. 1534–1549) was able to convene an ecumenical council in the city of Trent, a German imperial city located on the Italian side of the Alps.

The **Council of Trent** marked and defined Roman Catholicism for the next four hundred years. Reformers within the Catholic Church hoped that it would be possible to create a

Foto Marburg/Art Resource, NY

**Marian Shrine**   Shrines, such as this one in Regensburg dedicated to the Virgin Mary, remained important centers of Catholic piety. As we see here, shrines drew large crowds made up of individuals and religious groups who came in search of spiritual and physical healing.

**Ignatius Loyola**  A Spanish nobleman and founder of the Society of Jesus. Loyola's order vowed absolute authority to the papacy.

*Index of Prohibited Books*  A list of books banned by the Roman Catholic Church because of moral or doctrinal error. It was thought that this would inhibit the spread of Protestant ideas.

**Council of Trent**  An ecumenical council of the Roman Catholic Church called to both respond to the Protestant challenge and institute reforms in the Catholic Church. Its decrees established the basic tenets of Roman Catholicism for the next four hundred years.

**A Mystical Reformer** Saint Teresa of Avila came from a converso family. She believed that renewal within the Christian church would come through mysticism, prayer, and a return to traditional religious practices. She founded a reformed Carmelite order of nuns to further religious renewal in Spain.

broadly based reform party within the church and that the council would define theological positions acceptable to the Protestants, making reunion possible.

The Council of Trent sat in three sessions between 1545 and 1563. The initial debates were clearly meant to mark the boundaries between Protestant heresy and the orthodox positions of the Catholic Church. In response to the Protestant emphasis on Scripture alone, the council affirmed that Scripture has to be interpreted in the context of Church tradition. Delegates rejected the humanists' work on the text of the Bible, declaring that the Latin Vulgate edition compiled by Jerome in the late fourth century was the authorized text. In response to the widely held Protestant belief that salvation came through faith alone, the council declared that good works were not merely the outcome of faith but prerequisites to salvation. The council rejected Protestant positions on the sacraments, the giving of wine to the laity during Holy Communion, the marriage of clergy, and the granting of indulgences.

To assume that the council's decrees were merely negative, however, is to ignore the many ways in which the decrees of the council were an essential part of the creation of the Roman Catholic Church that would function for the next four centuries. The delegates at Trent generally felt that the real cause behind the Protestant movement was the lack of leadership and supervision within the church. Many of the acts of the council dealt with that issue.

First, the council affirmed apostolic succession—the idea that the authority of a bishop is transmitted through a succession of bishops, ultimately leading back through the popes to Saint Peter. Thus, the council underlined the ultimate authority of the pope in administrative as well as theological matters. The council ordered that local bishops should reside in their dioceses; that they should establish seminaries to see to the education of parish clergy; and that, through regular visitation and supervision, they should make certain that the laity participated in the sacramental life of the church. In the final sessions of the council, the nature of the Roman Catholic Church was summed up in the Creed of Pius IV, which, like the Lutheran Augsburg Confession, expressed the basic position of the church.

## Confessionalization

The labors of the Jesuits and the deliberations of the Council of Trent at midcentury proved that reconciliation between the Protestant reformers and the Catholic Church was not possible. Signs of the separation include the flight of important Protestant religious leaders from Italy in the late 1540s and the wholesale migration of Protestant communities from Modena, Lucca, and other Italian towns to France, England, and Switzerland. These actions signify the beginnings of the theological, political, and social separation of "Protestant" and "Catholic" in European society. Further, the states of Europe saw themselves as the enforcers of religious uniformity within their territories. It is from this time forward that denominational differences become clearer.

The theological separation was marked in a number of concrete and symbolic ways. Churches in which both bread and wine were distributed to the laity during the sacrament of Holy Communion passed from Catholic to Protestant. Churches in which the altar was moved forward to face the congregation but the statuary was retained were likely to be Lutheran. Churches in which statues were destroyed and all other forms of art were removed were likely to be Reformed (Calvinist), for Calvin had advised that "only those things are to be sculpted or painted which the eye is capable of seeing; let not God's majesty, which is far above the perception of the eyes, be debased through unseemly representations."* Even matters such as singing differentiated the churches. Although the Calvinist tradition tended to believe that

---
*Quoted in Carter Lindberg, *The European Reformations* (New York: Blackwell Publishers, 1996), p. 375.

music, like art, drew the Christian away from consideration of the Word, Luther believed that "next to the Word of God, music deserves the highest praise." Lutherans emphasized congregational singing and the use of music within the worship service. Countless pastors in the sixteenth and seventeenth centuries followed Luther in composing hymns and even theoretical tracts on music. This tradition would reach its zenith in the church music of Johann Sebastian Bach (1685–1750), most of whose choral works were composed to be part of the normal worship service.

Music had played an important role in Catholic services since well before the Reformation. It was really architecture that distinguished Catholic churches from Protestant churches in the late sixteenth and seventeenth centuries. In Rome, the great religious orders built new churches in the baroque style (see pages 447–449). Baroque artists and architects absorbed all the classical lessons of the Renaissance and then went beyond them, sometimes deliberately violating them. Baroque art celebrates the supernatural, the ways in which God is not bound by the laws of nature. The painting by El Greco that opens this chapter (see page 388) emphasizes the connection of heaven and earth. Whereas Renaissance art was meant to depict nature, baroque paintings and sculpture seem to defy gravity. The work celebrates the supernatural power and splendor of the papacy. This drama and power are clear in the construction of the Jesuit Church of the Gesù (jeh-ZOO) in Rome and even more so in Gianlorenzo Bernini's (1598–1680) throne of Saint Peter, made for Saint Peter's Basilica in the Vatican. The construction of baroque churches, first in Spain and Italy, but especially in the Catholic parts of Germany, created yet another boundary between an austere Protestantism and a visual and mystical Catholicism.

## The Regulation of Religious Life

Because of the continuing religious confusion and political disorder brought on by the reforms, churchmen, like state officials, were intent on maintaining religious order within their territories by requiring what they understood to be the practice of true Christianity. In an ironic twist, both Protestant and Catholic authorities followed much the same program. In both camps, regulation of religion became a governmental concern. Religious regulation and state power grew at the same time. This true religion was much less a public and communal religion than medieval Christianity had been. In the age of confessionalization, theologians—both Protestant and Catholic—became preoccupied with the moral status and interior life of individuals. Sexual sins and gluttony now seemed more dangerous than economic sins, such as avarice and usury. Even penance was understood less as a "restitution" that would reintegrate the individual into the Christian community than as a process of coming to true contrition for one's sins.

All of the major religious groups in the late sixteenth century emphasized education, right doctrine, and social control. In Catholic areas, it was hoped that a renewed emphasis on private confession by the laity would lead to a proper understanding of doctrine. During this period, Charles Borromeo, archbishop of Milan (1538–1584), introduced the private confessional box, which isolated priest and penitent from the prying ears of the community. This allowed confessors the time and opportunity to instruct individual consciences with care. As early as the 1520s, some Lutheran princes had begun church visitations in their territories to ensure that the laity understood basic doctrine.

Churchmen in both Protestant and Catholic areas used catechisms—handbooks containing instruction for the laity. The first and most famous was by Luther himself. Luther's *Small Catechism* includes the Lord's Prayer, Ten Commandments, and Apostles' Creed, along with simple, clear explanations of what they mean. More than Catholic rulers, Protestant rulers used church courts to enforce discipline within the community. Churchmen began to criticize semireligious popular celebrations, such as May Day, harvest feasts, and the Feast of Fools, whose origins lay in popular myths and practices that preceded Christianity. Such observances were now scorned for encouraging superstition and mocking the social and political order with, for example, parodies of ignorant clergy and foolish magistrates.

Religious authorities were also concerned by what seemed to be out-of-control mysticism and dangerous religious practices, especially among women. The impact of the Reformation on the status of women has often been debated. The Protestant position is that the Reformation freed women from the cloistered control of traditional convents. By rejecting clerical celibacy and emphasizing marriage as the highest spiritual state, Lutherans

**The Holy Household**
One of the most popular ideas among Protestants was that true religion should be taught and preserved in the Christian family, presided over by the father. The detail in this painting shows not only the interior of a Flemish home but also the role of the father and the symbolic importance of meals eaten together.

The Shakespeare Birthplace Trust

believed they were elevating the status of women. Further, the Protestant attack on state-controlled prostitution reduced one of the basest forms of exploitation. To the realists who argued that young, unmarried men would always need sexual outlets, Luther replied that one cannot merely substitute one evil practice for another. Critics of the Reformation counter that a convent was one of very few organizations that a woman could administer and direct. Women who took religious vows, Catholics point out, could engage in intellectual and religious pursuits similar to those enjoyed by men. The destruction of religious houses for women, Catholics argue, destroyed one of the few alternatives that women had to life in an authoritarian, patriarchal society.

In fact, in the late sixteenth and early seventeenth centuries, both Protestant and Catholic authorities viewed with suspicion any signs of religious independence by women. In the first years of the Reformation, some women did leave convents, eager to participate in the reform of the church. They wrote tracts concerning the morality of the clergy. And for a time, women served as deacons in some Reformed (Calvinist) churches. Yet, like the female witches discussed in Chapter 15, these religious women often seemed somehow dangerous. Lutheran and Calvinist theologians argued that a woman's religious vocation should be in the Christian care and education of her family. And even the most famous of the sixteenth- and seventeenth-century female Catholic mystics were greeted with distrust and some hostility. Religious women in Catholic convents were required to subordinate their mysticism to the guidance they received from male spiritual advisers. Calvinist theologians exhibited similar suspicions toward the theological and spiritual insights of Protestant women. For the laity, in general, and for women, in particular, the late Reformation brought increased control by religious authorities.

## SECTION SUMMARY

- Catholic reform emphasizing moral reform and renewed piety had begun before Luther's protests.
- The Council of Trent defined Catholic doctrine for the next four hundred years.
- During the second half of the sixteenth century, Protestant and Catholic churches became more clearly differentiated by architecture and ritual.
- Both traditions emphasized personal discipline and self-control, which became an important part of the early modern state.

# Chapter Summary

During the age of the Reformation, Europe experienced a number of profound shocks. The medieval assumption of a unified Christendom in the West was shattered. No longer could Europeans assume that, at heart, they held similar views of the world and the place of individuals in it. Charles V had begun his reign with hopes for one law, one faith, and one empire. He ended it by dividing his empire and retiring to a monastery.

◆ *Why did the reformers feel it was necessary to establish entirely new churches outside the Roman Catholic Church?*

The Protestant challenge did not simply attack the institutional structure or the moral lapses as previous heretical movements had done. The early Protestant reformers rejected the penitential system that was at the heart of the medieval church. Peasants and artisans argued that Luther's message of Christian freedom liberated them from both economic and spiritual oppression. Both Protestant and peasant claimed all authority must rest on Holy Scripture. They rejected the traditions of the late Middle Ages.

◆ *What political factors limited Charles V's ability to respond to the religious crisis?*

Emperor Charles V was opposed to Luther and wanted to maintain the unity of the church and of his empire. But he faced almost continuous problems in one part or another of his empire. Both the French and the Turks did all they could to reduce his power. Consequently, even after years of struggle, he was forced, in the religious Peace of Augsburg, to accept the principle that the towns and regional principalities had the right to accept either traditional Catholic worship or the new Lutheran reform.

◆ *Why did the English monarchs take the lead in efforts to reform the English church?*

In England, on the other hand, the monarchy was powerful enough that Henry VIII was able to shift religious debate and declare himself the head of the Church in England. But Henry's children were alternately Protestant, Catholic, and Protestant again. The result in England was a church that maintained certain aspects of traditional Catholic Christianity, even as it allowed a married clergy and accepted other Protestant reforms.

◆ *How did ideas of church reform influence social and political developments in the rest of Europe?*

Monarchies and republics throughout Europe came to view religious institutions and religious choices as matters of state. In Scandinavia, monarchs seemed to have favored the Lutherans as a way to weaken the power of the Catholic clergy. While in France, Francis I was willing to allow some Protestant protests, until it seemed that religious unrest threatened public order. At that point, he began to suppress Protestant worship, acknowledging the fact that France had largely remained Catholic. Much of the rest of eastern Europe followed no clear pattern. When faced with theological challenges and cries for moral reform, governments reacted in ways that offered religious change and bolstered the claims of secular authorities.

◆ *How did Catholic and Protestant Christians differ by the end of the Reformation?*

By the second half of the sixteenth century, Protestants and Catholics had largely adopted patterns that made clear which religion was favored. Calvinist churches were spare; Catholic churches, ornate; and Lutheran churches, filled with varieties of music. As a part of their reform movements, both Protestant and Catholic governments redoubled their efforts to regulate religion and moral life. In Catholic countries, the church hierarchy extended its control over the religious life of the laity. Thus, both Reformation and Counter-Reformation brought about a significant strengthening of religious and secular authorities.

# Key Terms

**Martin Luther** (p. 390)

**justification by faith** (p. 393)

**Charles V** (p. 393)

**Huldrych Zwingli** (p. 394)

**John Calvin** (p. 396)

**Anabaptists** (p. 397)

**Augsburg Confession** (p. 402)

**Henry VIII** (p. 404)

**Act of Supremacy** (p. 406)

**Society of Jesus** (p. 410)

**Ignatius Loyola** (p. 411)

*Index of Prohibited Books* (p. 411)

**Council of Trent** (p. 411)

**The Saint Bartholomew's Day Massacre** Scala/White Images/Art Resource, NY

# Europe in the Age of Religious Wars, 1560–1648

A dying man's body is thrown from a window. Below, three well-dressed gentlemen stand over a mutilated body; one of them holds up the severed head. Elsewhere, sword-wielding men engage in indiscriminate slaughter, even of babies. Corpses are piled up in the background. This painting memorializes the grisly events of August 24, 1572. A band of Catholic noblemen, accompanied by the personal guard of the king of France, had hunted down a hundred Protestant nobles, asleep in their lodgings in and around the royal palace, and murdered them in cold blood. The king and his counselors had planned the murders as a preemptive strike because they feared that other Protestant nobles were gathering an army outside Paris. But the calculated attack became a massacre when ordinary Parisians, overwhelmingly Catholic and believing they were acting in the king's name, turned on their neighbors. About three thousand Protestants were slain in Paris over the next three days.

This massacre came to be called the Saint Bartholomew's Day Massacre for the Catholic saint on whose feast day it fell. Though horrible in its scope, the slaughter was not unusual in the deadly combination of religious and political antagonisms it reflected. Religious conflicts were, by definition, intractable political conflicts, since virtually every religious group felt that all others were heretics who could not be tolerated and must be eliminated. Rulers of all faiths looked to divine authority and religious institutions to uphold their power.

In the decades after 1560, political tensions led to instability and violence, especially when newly reinforced by religious differences. Royal governments continued to consolidate authority, but resistance to royal power by provinces, nobles, or towns accustomed to independence now might have a religious sanction. Warfare over these issues had consumed the Holy Roman Empire in the first half of the sixteenth century. The conflict now spilled over into France and the Netherlands and threatened to erupt in England. In the early seventeenth century, the Holy Roman Empire once again was

## Chapter Overview

### Imperial Spain and the Limits of Royal Power

◆ *What circumstances permitted Spain's ambitious policies and to what degree were they successful?*

### Religious and Political Conflict in France and England

◆ *What conditions led to civil war in France? How did religious and political conflict develop differently in England?*

### The Holy Roman Empire and the Thirty Years' War

◆ *Why did war erupt again within the Holy Roman Empire and what was the significance of the conflict?*

### Economic Change and Social Tensions

◆ *What caused the economic stresses of these decades and how did ordinary people cope with them?*

### Writing, Drama, and Art in an Age of Upheaval

◆ *In what ways do the literature and art of this period reflect the political, social, and religious conflicts of the age?*

417

wracked by a war simultaneously religious and political in origin. Regardless of its roots, warfare itself had become more destructive than ever before thanks to innovations in military technology and campaign tactics. Tensions everywhere were also worsened by economic changes, especially soaring prices and unemployment. The political and religious struggles of the era took place against a background of increasing want, and economic distress was often expressed in both political and religious terms.

A period of tension, even extraordinary violence, in political and social life, the era of the late sixteenth and early seventeenth centuries was also distinguished by great creativity in some areas of cultural and intellectual life. The plays of Shakespeare, for example, mirrored the passions but also reflected on the dilemmas of the day and helped to analyze Europeans' circumstances with a new degree of sophistication.

# Imperial Spain and the Limits of Royal Power

*What circumstances permitted Spain's ambitious policies and to what degree were they successful?*

**Philip II** King of Spain (r. 1556–1598), son of Charles V, who ruled Spain at the height of its influence.

To contemporary observers, no political fact of the late sixteenth century was more obvious than the ascendancy of Spain. **Philip II** (r. 1556–1598) ruled Spanish conquests in the New World, as well as wealthy territories in Europe, including the Netherlands and parts of Italy. Yet imperial Spain did not escape the political, social, and religious turmoil of the era. Explosive combinations of religious dissent and political disaffection led to revolt against Spain in the Netherlands. This conflict revealed the endemic tensions of sixteenth-century political life: nobles, towns, and provinces trying to safeguard remnants of medieval autonomy against efforts at greater centralization—with the added complications of economic strain and religious division. The revolt also demonstrated the material limits of royal power, since even with treasure from American conquests pouring in, Philip could, at times, barely afford to keep armies in the field. As American silver dwindled in the seventeenth century, Philip's successors faced severe financial and political strains, even in their Spanish domains.

## The Revolt of the Netherlands

Philip's power stemmed in part from the far-flung territories he inherited from his father, the Habsburg king of Spain and Holy Roman emperor Charles V: Spain, the Low Countries (the Netherlands), the duchy of Milan, the kingdom of Naples, the conquered lands in the Americas, and the Philippine Islands in Asia. (Control of Charles's Austrian lands had passed to his brother, Ferdinand, Philip's uncle; see **Map 15.1**.) Treasure fleets bearing silver from the New World began to reach Spain regularly during Philip's reign. Spain was now the engine powering a trading economy unlike any that had existed in Europe before. To supply its colonies, Spain needed timber and other shipbuilding materials from the hinterlands of the Baltic Sea. Grain from the Baltic fed the urban populations of Spain (where wool was the principal cash crop) and the Netherlands, while the Netherlands, in turn, was a source of finished goods, such as cloth. The major exchange point for all of these goods was the city of Antwerp in the Netherlands, the leading trading center of all of Europe by 1550.

The Netherlands were the jewel among Philip's European possessions. These seventeen provinces (constituting mostly the modern nations of Belgium and the Netherlands) had been centers of trade and manufacture since the twelfth century. In the fourteenth and fifteenth centuries, they had enjoyed political importance and a period of cultural innovation under the control of the dukes of Burgundy. Like his father, Philip was technically the ruler of each province separately—that is, he was count of Flanders, duke of Brabant, and so forth. (See **Map 15.2**.) By Philip's reign, a sort of federal system of government had evolved to accommodate the various centers of power. Each province had an assembly (Estates) in which representatives of leading nobility and towns authorized taxation, but each also acknowledged a central administration in Brussels that represented Philip. Heading the council of state in Brussels was a governor-general, Philip's half sister, Margaret of Parma.

## Background to the Revolt

Philip's clumsy efforts to adjust this distribution of power in his favor pushed his subjects in the Netherlands into revolt. Born and raised in Spain, Philip had little real familiarity with the densely populated, linguistically diverse Netherlands, and he never visited there after 1559. Early in his reign, tensions in the Netherlands arose over taxation and Spanish insistence on maintaining tight control. Bad harvests and disruptions of trade, caused by wars in the Baltic region in the 1560s, depressed the Netherlands' economy and made it difficult for the provinces to pay the taxes Spain demanded. When the Peace of Cateau-Cambrésis (kahtoe kam-bray-SEE) of 1559 brought an end to the long struggle between the Habsburgs and the Valois (val-WAH) kings of France, the people of the Netherlands had reason to hope for lower taxes and reduced levels of Spanish control, yet neither was forthcoming. Indeed, Philip named to the council of state in Brussels officials who were Spaniards themselves or had close ties to the Spanish court, bypassing local nobles who had fought for Philip and his father before 1559.

Philip only added to the discontent by unleashing an invigorated repression of heresy. Unlike his father, Philip directed the hunt for heretics not just at lower-class dissenters but also at well-to-do Calvinists—followers of the French Protestant religious reformer John Calvin—whose numbers were considerable. Punishment for heresy now included confiscation of family property along with execution of the individual. By 1565, town councils in the Netherlands routinely refused to enforce Philip's religious policies, believing that their prosperity—as well as their personal security—depended on restraint in the prosecution of heresy. Leading nobles also stopped enforcing the policies on their estates.

Encouraged by greater tolerance, Protestants began to hold open-air meetings and attract new converts in many towns. In a series of actions called the "iconoclastic fury," Calvinist townsfolk around the provinces stripped Catholic churches of the relics and statues they believed idolatrous. At the same time, reflecting the economic strain of these years, some townsfolk rioted to protest the price of bread. One prominent nobleman warned Philip, "All trade has come to a standstill, so that there are 100,000 men begging for their bread who used to earn it . . . which is [important] since poverty can force people to do things which otherwise they would never think of doing."*

## CHRONOLOGY

| | |
|---|---|
| 1556–1598 | Reign of Philip II |
| 1558–1603 | Reign of Elizabeth I |
| 1559 | Act of Supremacy (England) |
| 1562–1598 | Religious wars in France |
| 1565 | Netherlands city councils and nobility ignore Philip II's law against heresy |
| 1566 | Calvinist "iconoclastic fury" begins in the Netherlands |
| 1567 | Duke of Alba arrives in the Netherlands |
| 1571 | Defeat of Turkish navy at Lepanto |
| 1576 | Sack of Antwerp |
| 1579 | Union of Utrecht |
| 1588 | Defeat of Spanish Armada |
| 1589–1610 | Reign of Henry IV |
| 1598 | Edict of Nantes (France) |
| 1609 | Truce between Spain and the Netherlands declared |
| 1618–1648 | Thirty Years' War |
| 1620 | Catholic victory at Battle of White Mountain |
| 1621 | Truce between Spain and the Netherlands expires; war between Spain and the Netherlands begins |
| 1629 | Peace of Alais |
| 1631 | Swedes under Gustav Adolf defeat imperial forces |
| 1635 | Peace of Prague |
| 1640–1653 | "Long Parliament" in session in England |
| 1648 | Peace of Westphalia |

*Geoffrey Parker, *The Dutch Revolt* (London: Penguin, 1985), p. 288, n. 5.

**⊕ Map 15.1 The Spanish Habsburgs and Europe, ca. 1556**  Philip II's control of territories in northern Italy permitted the overland access of Spanish troops to the Netherlands and heightened the Spanish threat to France. Lands bordering the western Mediterranean made the sea a natural sphere of Spanish influence as well. Habsburg lands in central Europe were controlled after 1556 by Charles V's brother Ferdinand and his descendants. © Cengage Learning 2014

## The Provinces Revolt

In early 1567, armed Calvinist insurgents seized two towns in the southern Netherlands in hopes of stirring a general revolt that would secure freedom of worship. Margaret of Parma quelled the uprisings by rallying city governments and loyal nobles, now fearful for their own property and power. But by then, far away in Spain, a decision had been made to send in the Spanish duke of Alba with an army of ten thousand men.

When Alba arrived in August 1567, he repeated every mistake of Spanish policy that had triggered rebellion in the first place. He billeted troops in friendly cities, established new courts to try rebels, arrested thousands of people, executed about a thousand rebels (including Catholics as well as prominent Protestants), and imposed heavy taxes to support his army.

Margaret of Parma resigned in disgust and left the Netherlands. Protestants from rebellious towns escaped into exile, where they were joined by nobles who had been declared traitors for resisting Alba's policies. The most important of these was William of Nassau (NAS-saw), prince of Orange (1533–1584), whose lands outside the Netherlands, in France and the Holy Roman Empire, lay beyond Spanish reach and so could be used to finance continued warfare against Spain. A significant community with military capability began to grow in exile.

In 1572, ships of exiled Calvinist privateers, known as the "Sea Beggars," began preying on Spanish shipping and coastal fortresses from bases in the northern provinces. These provinces, increasingly Calvinist, became the center of opposition to the Spanish, who concentrated their efforts against rebellion in the wealthier southern provinces. Occasionally, the French and English lent aid to the rebels.

The war in the Netherlands was a showcase for the new and costly technology of warfare in this period. Many towns were (or came to be, as a consequence of the revolt) equipped with "bastions," newly designed walled defenses that could resist artillery fire; such cities could not be taken by storm. Where bastions had been built, military campaigns consisted of grueling sieges, skirmishes in surrounding areas for control of supplies, and occasional pitched battles between besiegers and forces attempting to break the siege. Vast numbers of men were required, both for effective besieging forces and for garrisoning the many fortresses that controlled the countryside and defended access to major towns.

**The City of Antwerp**   Antwerp, in the southern Netherlands, was the point of sale for Portuguese spices brought around Africa from India; the selling and transshipping center for Baltic goods, including timber, fur, and grain; and the source for manufactured goods such as cloth. © Royal Museums of Fine Arts of Belgium Brussels

In an attempt to supply the Netherlands with veteran troops and materiel from Spain and Spanish territories in Italy, the Spanish developed the "Spanish Road," an innovative string of supply depots where provisions could be gathered in advance of troops marching to the Netherlands (see **Map 15.1**). Maintaining its large armies, however, taxed Spain's resources to the breaking point. Even with American silver at hand, Philip could, at times, barely afford to keep armies in the field. Inevitably, large numbers of troops also exhausted the countryside, and both soldiers and civilians suffered great privations. On occasion, Spanish troops reacted violently to difficult conditions and to delayed pay (American treasure dwindled badly between 1572 and 1578). In 1576, they sacked the hitherto loyal city of Antwerp and massacred about eight thousand people. Bitterly remembered as the "Spanish Fury," the massacre prompted leaders in the southern provinces to raise their own armies to protect themselves against the Spanish. Late in 1576, they concluded an alliance with William of Orange and the northern rebels.

## Formation of the United Provinces

**United Provinces** The seven northern provinces of the Low Countries that successfully revolted against Spanish rule in the late sixteenth century and became the modern nation of the Netherlands.

The alliance between northern and southern provinces did not last. The provinces were increasingly divided by religion, and their differences were skillfully exploited by Philip's new commander, Margaret of Parma's son Alexander Farnese (far-NAY-zee), duke of Parma. With silver from America filling the king's coffers again, Parma wooed the Catholic elites of the southern provinces back into loyalty to Philip, in return for promises to respect their provincial liberties and safeguard their property from troops.

In 1579, the northern provinces united in a defensive alliance, the Union of Utrecht (OO-trekt), against the increasingly unified south. Parma's forces could not push beyond the natural barrier of rivers that bisect the Low Countries (see **Map 15.2**), particularly as Spain diverted money to conflicts with England in 1588 and France after 1589. In 1609, a truce was finally concluded between Spain and the northern provinces. This truce did not formally recognize the "United Provinces" as an independent entity, though in fact they were. The modern nations of Belgium (the southern Spanish provinces) and the Netherlands are the distant result of this truce.

The independent **United Provinces** (usually called, simply, the Netherlands) was a fragile state, an accident of warfare at first. But commercial prosperity began to emerge as its greatest strength. Much of the economic activity of Antwerp had shifted north to Amsterdam in the province of Holland because of fighting in the south and a naval blockade of Antwerp by rebel ships. Philip's policies had created a new enemy nation and had enriched it at his expense.

In addition, the revolt of the Netherlands lured Spain into wider war, particularly against England. Spain and England had a common foe in France and common economic interests, and Philip had married Mary Tudor, the Catholic queen of England (r. 1553–1558). Even after Mary's death and the accession of her Protestant half sister, Queen Elizabeth (r. 1558–1603), Spanish-English relations remained cordial. Relations started to sour, however, when Elizabeth began tolerating the use of English ports by the rebel Sea Beggars and authorizing attacks by English privateers on Spanish treasure fleets. In response, Spain supported Catholic resistance to Elizabeth within England, including plots to replace her on the throne with her Catholic cousin, Mary, Queen of Scots. Greater Spanish success in the Netherlands, raids by the Spanish

🌐 **Map 15.2 The Netherlands, 1559–1609** The seventeen provinces of the Netherlands were strikingly diverse politically, economically, and culturally. © Cengage Learning 2014

and English on each other's shipping, and Elizabeth's execution of Mary in 1587 prompted Philip to order an invasion of England. A fleet (*armada*) of Spanish warships sailed in 1588.

"The enterprise of England," as the plan was called in Spain, represented an astounding logistical effort. The **Armada** was supposed to clear the English Channel of English ships in order to permit an invading force—troops under Parma in the Netherlands—to cross on barges. The sheer number of ships required—about 130—meant that some, inevitably, were slower supply ships, or vessels designed for the more protected waters of the Mediterranean. The English also had the advantage in arms, since they had better long-range artillery and better-trained gunners. Contemporaries were aware of the long odds facing Philip's forces. The Venetian ambassador in Spain reported, as the Armada set sail, that "here in all the churches they make constant prayers and the king himself is on his knees two or three hours every day. . . ," and, in a later dispatch, wondered why Philip insisted, "quite against his natural temper, that the Armada shall give battle to the English, who are known to be awaiting the attack with eager courage."* Spain's Armada was defeated partly by the English and partly by stormy weather that dispersed much of the fleet. The invasion failed and fewer than half of the 130-ship Armada ever made it back to Spain.

> **Armada** Massive fleet of Spanish warships sent against England by Philip II but defeated by the English navy and bad weather in 1588. The tactics used by the English helped set the future course of naval warfare.

## Successes at Home and Around the Mediterranean

Despite his overseas empire and his preoccupation with the Netherlands, many of Philip's interests still centered on the Mediterranean. In his kingdoms of Spain and their Mediterranean sphere of interest, Philip made his power felt more effectively, though not without effort.

Philip's father, Charles V, had tried to secure the western Mediterranean against the Ottoman Turks and their client states along the African coast, but it was under Philip that the Turkish challenge in the western Mediterranean receded. The Spanish allied temporarily with the papacy and Venice—both were concerned with Turkish naval power in the Mediterranean—and their combined navies inflicted a massive defeat on the Turkish navy at

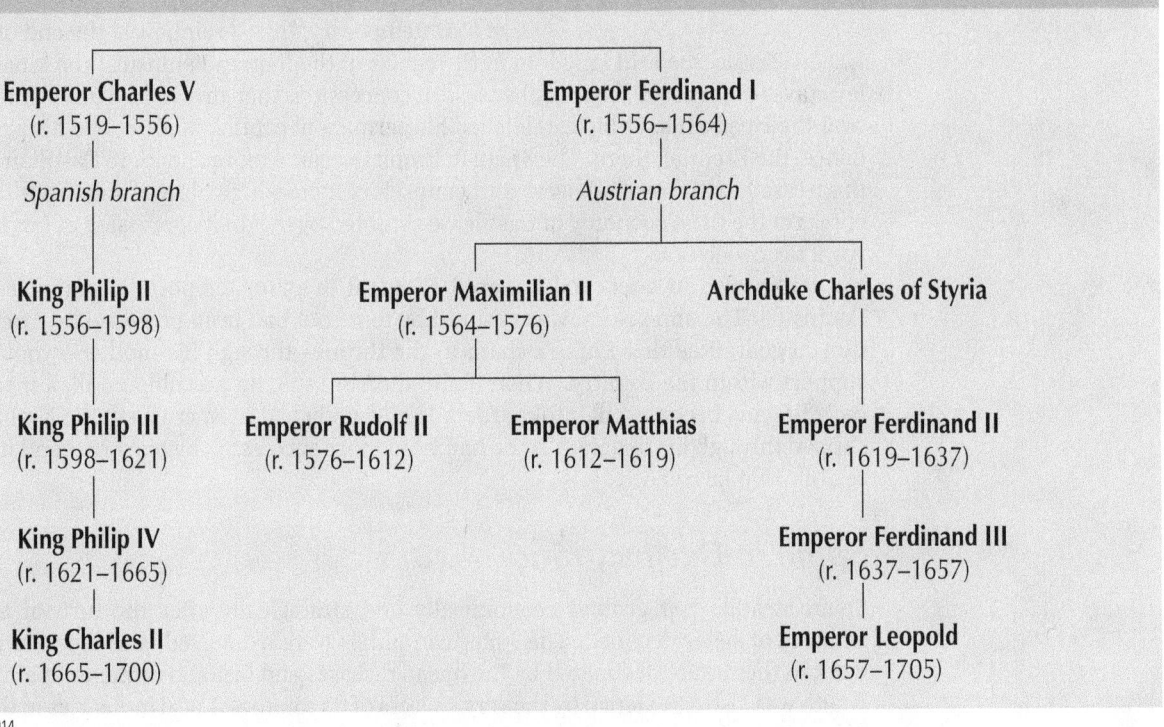

### THE SPANISH AND AUSTRIAN HABSBURGS, 1556–1700

**Emperor Charles V** (r. 1519–1556) — *Spanish branch*

**Emperor Ferdinand I** (r. 1556–1564) — *Austrian branch*

**King Philip II** (r. 1556–1598)

**Emperor Maximilian II** (r. 1564–1576)

**Archduke Charles of Styria**

**King Philip III** (r. 1598–1621)

**Emperor Rudolf II** (r. 1576–1612)

**Emperor Matthias** (r. 1612–1619)

**Emperor Ferdinand II** (r. 1619–1637)

**King Philip IV** (r. 1621–1665)

**Emperor Ferdinand III** (r. 1637–1657)

**King Charles II** (r. 1665–1700)

**Emperor Leopold** (r. 1657–1705)

© Cengage Learning 2014

*James C. Davis, ed., *Pursuit of Power: Venetian Ambassadors' Reports on Turkey, France and Spain in the Age of Philip II, 1560–1600* (New York: Harper and Row, 1970), pp.110–113.

Prado, Madrid/Giraudon/The Bridgeman Art Library

**Philip II in 1583** Dressed in the austere black in fashion at the Spanish court, Philip holds a rosary and wears the Order of the Golden Fleece, an order of knighthood, around his neck. Though conscientious to a fault, Philip was a rigid, unimaginative man ill suited to meet the challenges he faced.

Lepanto, off the coast of Greece, in October 1571 (see **Map 15.1**). The Turks remained the leading power in the eastern Mediterranean, but their ability to threaten Spain and Spanish possessions in the West was over.

To Philip and his advisers, the Turks represented an internal threat as well, since it was feared that they might incite rebellion among his Muslim subjects. These were the nominally Christian descendants of the Muslims of Granada, who had been conquered by the Spanish in 1492. Called *moriscos*, they had been forced to convert to Christianity in 1504 or be expelled from Spain. Yet no serious effort had been made to teach them Christian beliefs in their own language (Arabic), and they had not been assimilated into Spanish society. Philip inaugurated a new wave of persecution and provoked a massive rebellion by the moriscos that began on Christmas Day in 1568. The revolt took two years to suppress. After it was crushed, the moriscos of Granada were forcibly exiled and dispersed farther north in Spain.

Philip's power in each of his Spanish kingdoms was limited by the traditional privileges of towns, nobility, and clergy. In Aragon, for example, he could raise revenues only by appealing to local assemblies, the Cortes (core-TEZ). Philip made inroads into Aragonese independence by the end of his reign, however, because noble feuds and peasant rebellions during the 1580s provided an excuse to send in veteran troops from the Netherlands campaigns to establish firmer control. Philip was successful, in the long run, in Aragon, as he had not been in the Netherlands, because he used adequate force but tempered it afterward with constitutional changes that were cleverly moderate. He cemented the peace by appearing in Aragon in person, in the words of a contemporary, "like a rainbow at the end of a storm."*

In Castile, the arid kingdom in the center of the Iberian Peninsula, the king was able to levy taxes more easily, but only because of concessions that gave nobles undisputed authority over their peasants. Philip established his permanent capital, Madrid, and his principal residence, the Escorial, there. The Spanish Empire became more and more Castilian as the reign progressed, with royal advisers and counselors increasingly drawn only from the Castilian elite. Yet the rural economy of Castile was stunted by the dual oppression of landholders and royal tax collectors.

Philip also invaded and annexed Portugal in 1580, temporarily unifying the Iberian Peninsula. The annexation was ensured by force but had been preceded by careful negotiation to guarantee that Philip's claim to the throne—through his mother—would find some support within the country. When Philip died in 1598, he was old and ill, a man for whom daily life had become a painful burden. His Armada had been crushed; the Netherlands had slipped through his fingers. Yet, he had been more successful, by his own standards, in other regions that he ruled.

## Spain in Decline, 1600–1648

Spain steadily lost ground economically and strategically after the turn of the century. Imports of silver declined. The American mines were exhausted, and the natives forced to work in them were decimated by European diseases and brutal treatment. Spain's economic health was also threatened by the very success of its colonies: Local industries in the Americas began to produce goods formerly obtained from Spain. Also, Spanish colonists could now buy from English, French, and Dutch traders many of the goods they needed. Often, these

---

*Quoted in A. W. Lovett, *Early Habsburg Spain, 1517–1598* (Oxford: Oxford University Press, 1986), p. 212.

**The Battle of Lepanto**   On October 7, 1571, vessels of the Holy League (Spain, Venice, and the papacy) defeated the Ottoman fleet off the coast of Greece. Lepanto was the last great battle between galleys—the oared warships that had dominated Mediterranean waters since ancient times. National Maritime Museum/The Image Works

competitors' goods were cheaper than Spanish ones. Spanish productivity was low and prices were high because of the inflationary effects of the influx of American silver.

Spain renewed hostilities with the United Provinces in 1621, after the truce of 1609 had expired. Philip IV (r. 1621–1665) also aided his Habsburg cousins in the Thirty Years' War in the Holy Roman Empire (see pages 437–438). Squeezed for troops and revenue for these commitments, other Spanish territories revolted. The uprisings reflected both economic distress and unresolved issues of regional autonomy. Castile bore the brunt of the financial support of the state. When Philip IV's chief minister tried to distribute the burdens more equitably among the various regions of Spain, rebellions broke out in many of the territories controlled by the Spanish crown.

In Catalonia, a province of the kingdom of Aragon, Spain resumed control only in 1652, after years of fighting and promises to respect Catalan liberties. In Portugal, which had been under Spanish control only since 1580, a war of independence began in 1640, launched by an aristocratic revolt. Unlike his grandfather, Philip IV did not respect Portuguese autonomy. He had never visited Portugal, had appointed Spanish officials to govern there in place of Portuguese elites and had even demanded that Portuguese troops be sent to quash the Catalan rebels. In addition, the Portuguese economy was reeling from Spanish demands for revenue and from losses in their colonies, which Spain could not adequately protect, especially from the Dutch. John, duke of Braganza, the nearest living relative to the last king of Portugal, was proclaimed king in 1640 and, although war dragged on until 1668, the Portuguese succeeded in winning independence from Spain. In 1647, upheaval would shake Spain's Italian possessions of Sicily and Naples. By mid-century, Spain had lost its position as the preeminent state in Europe.

## SECTION SUMMARY

- Spain was the most powerful state in Europe in the second half of the sixteenth century because it controlled territory in Italy and in the Netherlands, as well as colonies in the Americas.

- The prosperous Netherlands revolted against Spanish control for political, economic, and religious reasons.

- The invention of new kinds of fortifications increased the cost and destructiveness of the war.

- The northern provinces in the Netherlands, called the United Provinces, won independence from Spanish control by 1609.

- Spain attempted, but failed, to invade England with the Armada.

- The Spanish state weakened economically and politically in the seventeenth century as its income from colonies declined.

# Religious and Political Conflict in France and England

*What conditions led to civil war in France? How did religious and political conflict develop differently in England?*

In the second half of the sixteenth century, France was convulsed by civil war that had both religious and political causes. A fragile peace was achieved by 1598, but the kingdom was still divided by religion and by military and political challenges to royal authority. England, in contrast, was spared political and religious upheaval in the second half of the century, in part because of the talents and long life of its ruler, Elizabeth I. But in the seventeenth century, religious dissent and political opposition combined to dramatically threaten royal power.

## The French Religious Wars, 1562–1598

Civil war wracked France from 1562 until 1598. As in the Netherlands, the conflicts in France had religious and political origins and international consequences. The French monarch, like Philip, was unable to monopolize military power. In 1559, the king of France, Henry II (r. 1547–1559), had concluded the Peace of Cateau-Cambrésis with Philip II, ending the Habsburg-Valois Wars but died in July of that year from wounds suffered at a tournament held to celebrate the new treaty. His death was a political disaster. Great noble families vied for influence over his young sons, Francis II (r. 1559–1560) and Charles IX (r. 1560-1574). The queen mother, Catherine de' Medici (day MAY-di-chi) (1519–1589), worked carefully and intelligently to balance the nobles' interests. But it proved impossible to keep the conflicts among the great courtiers from boiling over into civil war.

### Background to Civil War

In France, as elsewhere, noble conflict invariably had a violent component. Noblemen carried swords and daggers and were accompanied by armed entourages. Provincial land holdings, together with the royal offices they enjoyed, afforded enough resources to support private warfare, and the nobles assumed the right to wage it.

In addition, religious tension was rising throughout France. Public preaching by and secret meetings of Protestants (known as **Huguenots** in France) were causing unrest in towns. At court, members of leading noble families—including the Bourbons, princes of royal blood—had converted to Protestantism and worshiped openly in their rooms in the palace. In 1561, Catherine convened a national religious council to reconcile the two faiths. When it failed, she chose provisional religious toleration as the only practical course and issued a limited edict of toleration of Huguenots (HEW-guh-nots) in the name of the king in January 1562.

The edict solved nothing. Ignoring its restrictions, Protestants armed themselves, while townspeople of both faiths insulted and attacked one another at worship sites and religious festivals. In March 1562, the armed retainers of a Catholic duke killed a few dozen Protestants gathered in worship at Vassy (vah-SEE), near one of the duke's estates. The killing, bringing the military power of the nobility to bear on the broader problem of religious division, sparked the first of six civil wars.

### Decades of Civil War

In some ways, the initial conflict in 1562 was decisive. The Protestant army lost the principal pitched battle of the war in December. This defeat reduced the appeal of the Protestant movement to nobles. The limited rights granted by the peace edict in 1563 made it difficult for Protestants in towns—where the vast majority of them lived—to worship. But if the Huguenots were not powerful enough to win, neither were they weak enough to be decisively beaten.

**Huguenots** French Protestants, followers of the teachings of John Calvin.

Le Massacre fait a Vassy le premier iour de Mars. 1562.

A. Lagrange ou l'on preschoit ou estoyent enuiron 1200 per-
fonnes.
B. Monfieur de Guife qui commandoit.
C. Le Miniftre dedans la Chaire priant Dieu.
D. Le Miniftre fe cuydant fauuer eft bleflé en plufieurs lieux

& euft efté tué fi l'efpee ne fuft rompue en deux.
E. Le Cardinal de Guyfe appuyé fur 1; cimentiere de la pa-
roiffe.
F. Le toiĉt que les gens du prefche rompent pour eux fauuer.
G. Plufieurs qui fe rettans fur la muraille de la ville fe fauuent

aux champs.
H. Plufieurs qui fe cuydans fauuer fur le toiĉt font harque-
boufés.
I. Le tronc des poutres attaché,
k. Les trompettes qui fonnerent par deux diuerfes fois,

**Massacre at Vassy** This contemporary engraving by two Protestant artists depicts the Duke of Guise (center left) and his men coldly butchering Huguenot worshipers at Vassy. In a Catholic version of the event, the Protestants were killed by gunfire after pelting Guise's men with rocks when they tried to disperse the worshipers. HIP/Art Resource, NY

The turning point most obvious to contemporaries came a decade later. The Protestant faction, still represented at court by the Bourbon princes and their allies, pressed the king for war against Spain to aid Protestant rebels in the Netherlands. Opposed to another war against Spain and alarmed by rumors of Huguenot armies massing outside Paris, Charles IX (r. 1560–1574) and his mother authorized royal guards to murder the Protestant leaders on August 24, 1572—Saint Bartholomew's Day. These murders touched off a massacre of Protestants throughout Paris and, once news from Paris had spread, throughout the kingdom.

The Saint Bartholomew's Day Massacre revealed the degree to which religious differences had strained the fabric of community life. Neighbor murdered neighbor in an effort to rid the community of heretical pollution; bodies of the dead were mutilated. Gathered in the south of France, the remaining Huguenot forces vowed "never [to] trust those who have so often and so treacherously broken faith and the public peace."* Huguenot writers published tracts arguing that royal power was by nature limited and that rebellion was justified against tyrants who overstepped their legitimate authority.

*Quoted in R. J. Knecht, *The French Wars of Religion, 1559–1598* (London: Longman, 1989), p. 109.

Many Catholics also renounced reconciliation. Some noblemen formed a Catholic league to fight in place of the weakened monarchy. Charles's successor, his brother Henry III (r. 1574–1589), was forced to cooperate with first one of the warring parties and then another. In December 1588, he resorted to murdering two leaders of the ultra-Catholic faction; in turn, he was murdered by a priest in early 1589.

The heir to the throne, a distant cousin of the dead king, was the Bourbon prince Henry of Navarre, who became Henry IV (r. 1589–1610). He was a Protestant, and he had to fight for his throne. He faced Catholic armies now subsidized by Philip II of Spain, an extremist Catholic city government in Paris, and subjects who were tired of war but mainly Catholic. Given these obstacles, the politically astute Henry agreed to convert to Catholicism.

After his conversion in 1593, many of Henry's subjects believed that only rallying to the monarchy could save France from chaos. In any case, nobles were increasingly inclined to cooperate with the Crown. Service to a successful king was honorable and a source of patronage; Henry was personally esteemed because he was a talented general and brave, gregarious, and charming. The nobility forced the citizens of Paris and other cities to accept Henry's authority. The civil war period thus proved to be an important phase in the accommodation of the nobility to the power of the state.

In April 1598, Henry granted toleration for the Huguenot minority in a royal edict proclaimed in the city of Nantes (NAHNT). The **Edict of Nantes** was primarily a repetition of provisions from the most generous edicts that had ended the various civil wars. Nobles were allowed to practice the Protestant faith on their estates; townspeople were granted more limited rights to worship in selected towns in each region. Protestants were also guaranteed rights of self-defense—specifically, the right to maintain garrisons in about two hundred towns. About half of these garrisons would be paid for by the Crown.

The problem was that the Edict of Nantes, like any royal edict, could be revoked by the king at any time. Moreover, the provision allowing Protestants to keep garrisoned towns reflected concessions to Protestant aristocrats, who could support their followers by paid garrison duty. It also reflected the assumption that living peacefully amid religious diversity might prove to be impossible. Thus, although Henry IV ended the French religious wars, he had not solved the problem of religious and political division within France.

**Edict of Nantes** 1598 edict of Henry IV, granting France's Protestants (Huguenots) the right to practice their faith and maintain defensive garrisons.

## The Consolidation of Royal Authority in France, 1598–1643

During Henry IV's reign, France began to recover from the long years of civil war. Population and productivity began to grow; the Crown increased royal revenue by nibbling away at traditional local self-government and control of taxation.

Yet, Henry's regime was stable only in comparison with the preceding years of civil war. The power of the great nobility had not been definitively broken. Also, the king had agreed to a measure, known as the *paulette* (named for the functionary who first administered it), that allowed royal officeholders to own their offices and to pass on those offices to their heirs in return for the payment of an annual fee. The paulette was primarily a device to raise revenue after decades of civil war, but it also helped cement the loyalty of royal bureaucrats at a critical time, particularly that of the royal judges of the supreme law court, the Parlement of Paris, who had recently agreed to register the Edict of Nantes only under duress. However, the paulette made royal officeholders largely immune from royal control, since their posts were now in effect property, like the landed property of the traditional nobility.

In 1610, a fanatical Catholic assassinated Henry IV. Henry's death brought his 9-year-old son, Louis XIII (r. 1610–1643), to the throne with Louis's mother, Marie de' Medici, initially serving as regent. Within four years, Louis faced a major rebellion by his Huguenot subjects in southwestern France. Huguenots felt that Louis's policies, including his recent marriage to a Spanish princess, meant that royal support for toleration was wavering. The war persisted, on and off, for eight years, as the French royal troops, like the Spanish in the Netherlands, had difficulty breaching the defenses of even small fortress towns held by the Protestants. The main Huguenot stronghold was the well-fortified port city of La Rochelle, which had grown wealthy from European and overseas trade. Not until the king took the city, after a siege lasting more than a year, did the Protestants accept a peace on royal terms.

## THE FRENCH SUCCESSION, 1515–1715

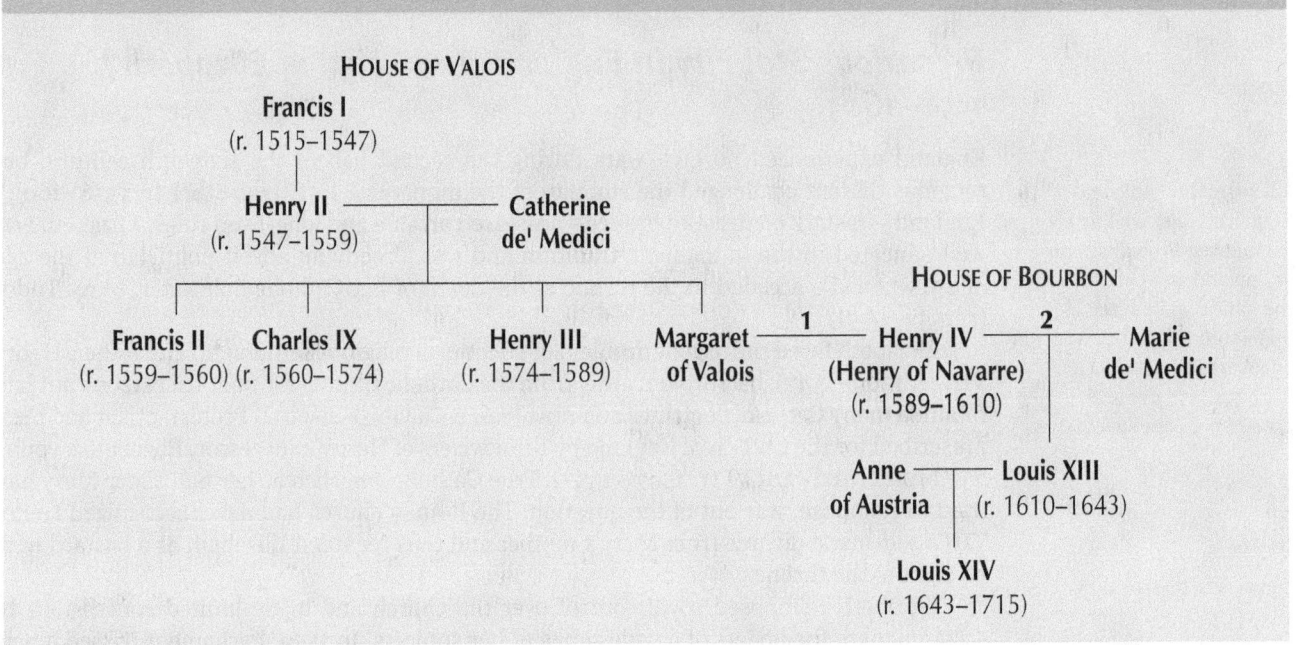

HOUSE OF VALOIS

**Francis I**
(r. 1515–1547)

**Henry II** ——— **Catherine
de' Medici**
(r. 1547–1559)

HOUSE OF BOURBON

**Francis II** | **Charles IX** | **Henry III** | **Margaret** —1— **Henry IV** —2— **Marie**
(r. 1559–1560) | (r. 1560–1574) | (r. 1574–1589) | of Valois | (Henry of Navarre) | de' Medici
(r. 1589–1610)

**Anne** ——— **Louis XIII**
of Austria | (r. 1610–1643)

**Louis XIV**
(r. 1643–1715)

© Cengage Learning 2014

The Peace of Alais (ah-LAY) (1629) reaffirmed the policy of religious toleration but rescinded the Protestants' military and political privileges. It was a political triumph for the Crown because it deprived French Protestants of the means for further rebellion, while reinforcing their dependence on the Crown for religious toleration. Most of the remaining great noble leaders began to convert to Catholicism.

The Peace of Alais was also a personal triumph for the king's leading minister, who crafted the treaty and had directed the bloody siege that made it possible. Armand-Jean du Plessis (1585–1642), Cardinal Richelieu (RISH-el-yiuh), came from a provincial noble family and rose in the service of the queen mother. He was admired and feared for his skill in the political game of seeking and bestowing patronage—a crucial skill in an age when elites received offices and honors through carefully cultivated relationships at court. He and the king—whose sensitive temperament Richelieu handled adeptly—formed a lasting partnership that had a decisive impact not only on French policy but also on the entire shape of the French state.

Richelieu favored an aggressive foreign policy to counter what he believed still to be the greatest external threat to the French crown: the Spanish Habsburgs. After war resumed between the Netherlands and Spain in 1621 (see pages 437–438), Richelieu attacked Spanish possessions in Italy, supported Catalan rebels against the Spanish monarchy, superintended large-scale fighting against Spain in the Netherlands itself, and subsidized Swedish and German Protestant armies fighting the Habsburgs in Germany.

Richelieu's policies were opposed by many French people, who saw taxes double, then triple, in just a few years. Many courtiers and provincial elites favored keeping the peace with Spain, a fellow Catholic state, and objected to alliances with German Protestants. They were also alarmed by the revolts that accompanied the peasants' distress. Their own status was also directly threatened by Richelieu's monopoly of royal patronage and by his creation of new offices, which undermined their power. In 1632, for example, Richelieu created the office of *intendant*. Intendants had wide powers for defense and administration in the provinces that overrode the established bureaucracy.

By 1640, Richelieu's ambitious foreign policy seemed to be bearing fruit. The French had won territory along their northern and eastern borders by their successes against Habsburg forces. But when Richelieu and Louis XIII died within five months of each other, in December 1642 and May 1643, Louis XIII was succeeded by his 5-year-old son, and the warrior-nobility, as well as royal bureaucrats, would waste little time before challenging the Crown's new authority.

## Precarious Stability in England: The Reign of Elizabeth I, 1558–1603

England experienced no civil wars during the second half of the sixteenth century, but religious dissent challenged the stability of the monarchy. In Elizabeth I (r. 1558–1603), England—in stark contrast to France—possessed an able and long-lived ruler. Elizabeth was well educated in the humanistic tradition and was already an adroit politician at the age of 25, when she acceded to the throne at the death of her Catholic half sister, Mary Tudor (r. 1553–1558).

Elizabeth faced the urgent problem of effecting a religious settlement. Her father, Henry VIII (r. 1509–1547), had broken away from the Catholic Church for political reasons but had retained many Catholic doctrines and practices. A Calvinist-inspired Protestantism had been prescribed for the Church of England by the advisers of Henry's successor, Elizabeth's young half brother, Edward VI (r. 1547– 1553). True Catholicism, such as her half sister Mary had tried to reimpose, was out of the question. The Roman church had never recognized Henry VIII's self-made divorce from Mary's mother and thus regarded Elizabeth as a bastard with no right to the throne.

Elizabeth reimposed royal control over the church and made limited concessions to accommodate the beliefs of a wide range of her subjects. In 1559, Parliament passed a new Act of Supremacy, which restored the monarch as head of the Church of England. Elizabeth dealt with opposition to the act by arresting bishops and lords whose votes would have blocked its passage by Parliament. The official prayer book, in use in Edward's day, was revised to include elements of both traditional and radical Protestant interpretations of Communion. But church liturgy, clerical vestments, and, above all, the hierarchical structure of the clergy closely resembled Catholic practices. The Act of Uniformity, also passed in 1559, required all worship to be conducted according to the new prayer book. Although uniformity was required in worship, Elizabeth was careful, in her words, not to "shine beacons into her subjects' souls."

Catholicism continued to be practiced, especially by otherwise loyal nobility and gentry in the north of England, who worshiped privately on their estates. But priests returning from exile beginning in the 1570s, most newly imbued with the proselytizing zeal of the Counter-Reformation (the Catholic response to the Protestant Reformation), practiced it more visibly and were zealously prosecuted for their boldness. In the last twenty years of Elizabeth's reign, approximately 180 Catholics were executed for treason, two-thirds of them priests. (By 1585, being a Catholic priest in itself was a crime.)

In the long run, the greater threat to the English crown came from the most radical Protestants in the realm, known (by their enemies initially) as Puritans. Puritanism was a broad movement for reform of church practice along familiar Protestant lines: an emphasis on Bible reading, preaching, and private scrutiny of conscience; a de-emphasis on institutional ritual and clerical authority. Most Puritans had accepted Elizabeth's religious compromise because they had no choice, but they grew increasingly alienated by her insistence on clerical authority and her refusal to change any elements of the original religious settlement. A significant Presbyterian underground movement began to form among them. Presbyterians wanted to dismantle the episcopacy—the hierarchy of priests and bishops—and to govern the church instead with councils, called "presbyteries," that included lay members of the congregation. Laws were passed late in the queen's reign to enable the Crown to prosecute more easily and even to force into exile anyone who attended "nonconformist" (non-Anglican) services.

The greatest challenge Elizabeth faced from Puritans came in Parliament, where they were well represented by many literate gentry. Parliament met only when called by the monarch. In theory, members could merely voice opinions and complaints; they could not initiate legislation and prescribe policy. However, only Parliament could vote taxes. Further, since it had in effect helped constitute royal authority by means of the two Acts of Supremacy,

**Elizabeth I** Able and long-lived ruler who firmly established Protestantism in England and defended the nation against the Spanish Armada, but who bequeathed financial, religious, and political problems to her successors.

**Puritans** Radical Protestants in late-sixteenth- and seventeenth-century England who became a majority in Parliament during the reign of Charles I and led opposition to the king.

Parliament's merely advisory role had been expanded by the monarchy itself. During Elizabeth's reign, Puritans capitalized on Parliament's enlarged scope, using meetings to press for further religious reform. In 1586, they went so far as to introduce bills calling for an end to the episcopacy and the Anglican prayer book. Elizabeth had to resort to imprisoning one Puritan leader to end debate on the issue and on Parliament's right to address it. Elizabeth won this early skirmish between Parliamentary and royal power, but her successors would face Parliaments more practiced at collective action and emboldened by such harsh efforts to control it.

Also during Elizabeth's reign, efforts at English expansion in the New World began, in the form of unsuccessful attempts at colonization and successful raids on Spanish possessions. However, the main focus of her foreign policy remained Europe itself. Elizabeth, like all her forebears, felt her interests tightly linked to the independence of the Netherlands, whose towns were a major outlet for English wool. Philip II's aggressive policy in the Netherlands increasingly alarmed her, especially in view of France's weakness. She began to send small sums of money to the rebels and allowed their ships access to southern English ports, from which they could raid Spanish-held towns on the Netherlands' coast. In 1585, in the wake of the duke of Parma's successes against the rebellions, she committed troops to help the rebels.

Her decision was a reaction, not only to the threat of a single continental power dominating the Netherlands but also to the threat of Catholicism. From 1579 to 1583, the Spanish had helped the Irish fight English domination and were involved in several plots to replace Elizabeth with her Catholic cousin, Mary, Queen of Scots. These threats occurred as the return of Catholic exiles to England peaked. The victory over the Spanish Armada in 1588 was quite rightly celebrated, for it ended any Catholic threat to Elizabeth's rule.

The success against the Armada has tended to overshadow other aspects of Elizabeth's foreign policy, particularly with regard to Ireland. Since the twelfth century, an Anglo-Irish state, dominated by transplanted English families, had been loosely supervised from

Woburn Abbey, Bedfordshire, UK/The Bridgeman Art Library

**Elizabeth I: The Armada Portrait**   Both serene and resolute, Elizabeth is flanked by "before" and "after" glimpses of the Spanish fleet; her hand rests on the globe in a gesture of dominion that also memorializes the circumnavigation of the globe by her famous captain, Sir Francis Drake, some years before.

England, but most of Ireland remained under the control of Gaelic chieftains. Just as Charles V and Philip II attempted to tighten their governing mechanisms in the Netherlands, so did Henry VIII's minister, Thomas Cromwell, streamline control of outlying areas such as Wales and Anglo-Ireland. Cromwell proposed that the whole of Ireland be brought under English control, partly by the established mechanism of feudal ties: The Irish chieftains were to pay homage as vassals to the king of England.

Under Elizabeth, this legalistic approach gave way to virtual conquest. Elizabeth's governor, Sir Henry Sidney, appointed in 1565, inaugurated a policy whereby Gaelic lords, by means of various technicalities, could be entirely dispossessed of their lands. Any Englishman capable of raising a private force could help enforce these dispossessions and settle his conquered lands as he saw fit. This policy provoked stiff Irish resistance, which was viewed as rebellion and provided the rationale for further military action, more confiscations of lands, and more new English settlers. Eventually the Irish, with Spanish assistance, mounted a major rebellion, consciously Catholic and aimed against the "heretic" queen. The rebellion gave the English an excuse for brutal suppression and massive transfers of lands to English control. The political domination of the Irish was complete with the defeat, in 1601, of the Gaelic chieftain Hugh O'Neill, lord of Tyrone, who had controlled most of the northern quarter of the island. Although the English were unable to impose Protestantism on the conquered Irish, to Elizabeth and her English subjects, the conquests in Ireland seemed as significant as the victory over the Spanish Armada.

The English enjoyed relative peace at home during Elizabeth's reign. However, her reign ended on a note of strain. The foreign involvements, particularly in Ireland, had been very expensive. Taxation granted by Parliament more than doubled during her reign, and local taxes further burdened the people. Price inflation related to government spending, social problems caused by returned unemployed soldiers, and a series of bad harvests heightened popular resentment against taxation. Despite her achievements, therefore, Elizabeth passed two problems on to her successors: unresolved religious tensions and financial instability. Elizabeth's successors would also find in Parliament an increasing focus of opposition to their policies.

## Rising Tensions in England, 1603–1642

In 1603, Queen Elizabeth died, and James VI of Scotland, the Protestant son of Mary, Queen of Scots, ascended to the English throne as James I (r. 1603–1625). Tensions between Anglicans and Puritans were briefly quieted under James because of a plot, in 1605, by Catholic dissenters. The Gunpowder Plot, as it was called, was a conspiracy to blow up the palace housing both king and Parliament at Westminster. Protestants of all stripes again focused on their common enemy, Catholics—though only temporarily.

### James I

Financial problems were James's most pressing concern. Court life became more elaborate and an increasing drain on the monarchy's resources. James's extravagance was partly to blame, but so were pressures for patronage from courtiers. To the debts left from the Irish conflicts and wars with Spain, James added new expenses to defend the claims of his daughter and her husband, a German prince, to rule Bohemia (see pages 435–437).

To raise revenue without Parliament's consent, James relied on sources of income that the Crown had enjoyed since medieval times: customs duties, wardship (the right to manage and liberally borrow from the estates of minor nobles), and the sale of monopolies, which conveyed the right to be sole agent for a particular kind of goods. James's increase of the number of monopolies for sale was widely resented. Merchants objected to the arbitrary restriction of production and trade; common people found that they could no longer afford certain ordinary goods, such as soap, under monopoly prices. Criticism of the court escalated, particularly by the nobility, as James indulged in extreme favoritism of certain courtiers. He even created a new noble title—baronet—which he sold to socially ambitious commoners.

When James summoned Parliament to ask for funds in 1621, Parliament used the occasion to protest court corruption and the king's financial measures. The members revived the medieval procedure of impeachment and removed two royal ministers from office. In 1624, still faced with expensive commitments to Protestants abroad, James again called Parliament, which voted new taxes but also openly debated the wisdom of the king's foreign policy.

## Charles I

Tensions between Crown and Parliament increased under James's son, Charles I (r. 1625–1649). Charles inherited a complicated and expensive foreign policy that included aiding Protestant armies in Germany which, in turn, meant conflict with Spain. In addition, trade conflicts led to war with France. The British fleets' efforts to raid the Spanish and French coasts were disastrous failures, and Charles' efforts to raise money for these ventures were also badly handled. In 1626, Parliament was dissolved without granting any monies, in order to stifle its objections to his policies. Instead, Charles levied a forced loan and imprisoned gentry who refused to lend money to the government.

Above all, Charles's religious policies caused controversy. Charles was personally inclined toward "high church" practices: an emphasis on ceremony and sacrament reminiscent of Catholic ritual. He also was a believer in Arminianism, a school of thought that rejected the Calvinist notion that God's grace cannot be earned and hence emphasized the importance of the sacraments and the authority of the clergy. Charles's views put him on a collision course with gentry and aristocrats who leaned toward Puritanism.

Charles's views were supported by William Laud (1573–1645), archbishop of Canterbury from 1633, and thus leader of the Church of England. He tried to impose changes in worship, spread Arminian ideas, and censor opposing views. He also challenged the redistribution of church property, which had occurred in the Reformation of the sixteenth century, and thereby alienated the gentry on economic as well as religious grounds.

Charles's style of rule worsened religious, political, and economic tensions. Cold and intensely private, he lacked the charm and the political skills to disarm his opponents. His court was ruled by formal protocol, and access to the king was highly restricted—a serious problem in an age when proximity to the monarch was a guarantee of political power.

Revenue and religion dominated debate in the Parliament of 1628–1629, which Charles had called, once again, to get funds for his foreign wars. Parliament presented the king with a document called the Petition of Right, which protested his financial policies, as well as arbitrary imprisonment. (Seventeen members of Parliament had been imprisoned for refusing loans to the Crown.) Though couched conservatively as a restatement of customary practice, the petition, in fact, claimed a tradition of expanded parliamentary participation in government. Charles dissolved Parliament in March 1629, having decided that the money he might extract was not worth the risk.

For eleven years, Charles ruled without Parliament. When he was forced to summon it again in 1640, the kingdom was in crisis. Royal finances were in desperate straits, even though Charles had pressed collection of revenues far beyond traditional bounds.

## 1640: The Kingdom in Crisis

The immediate crisis and the reason for Charles's desperate need for money was a rebellion in Scotland. Like Philip II in the Netherlands, Charles tried to rule in Scotland through a small council of men who did not represent local elites. Worse, he also tried to force his "high church" practices on the Scots. The Scottish church had been more dramatically reshaped during the Reformation and now was largely Presbyterian in structure. The result of Charles's policies was riots and rebellion. Unable to suppress the revolt in a

**Criticism of Monopolies**   Holders of royally granted monopolies were bitterly resented by English consumers and tradespeople alike, as this contemporary print reveals. The greedy beast pictured here controls even ordinary commodities such as pins, soap, and butter.

first campaign in 1639, Charles was forced to summon Parliament for funds to raise a more effective army.

But the Parliament that assembled in the spring of 1640 provided no help. Instead, members questioned the war with the Scots and other royal policies. Charles's political skills were far too limited for him to reestablish a workable relationship with Parliament under the circumstances. Charles dissolved this body, which is now known as the "Short Parliament," after just three weeks. Even more stinging than Charles's dissolution of the Parliament was the lack of respect he had shown the members: A number of them were harassed or arrested. Mistrust, fomented by the eleven years in which Charles had ruled without Parliament, thus increased.

Another humiliating defeat at the hands of the Scots, later in 1640, made summoning another Parliament imperative. Members of the "Long Parliament" (it sat from 1640 to 1653) took full advantage of the king's predicament. Charles was forced to agree not to dissolve or adjourn Parliament without the members' consent and to summon Parliament at least every three years. Parliament abolished many of the traditional revenues he had abused and impeached and removed from office his leading ministers, including Archbishop Laud. The royal commander deemed responsible for the Scottish fiasco, Thomas Wentworth, earl of Strafford, was executed without trial in May 1641.

The execution of Strafford shocked many aristocrats in the House of Lords (the upper house of Parliament), as well as some moderate members of the House of Commons. Meanwhile, Parliament began debating the perennially thorny religious question. A bare majority of members favored abolition of Anglican bishops as a first step in thoroughgoing religious reform. Working people in London, kept updated on the issues by the regular publication of parliamentary debates, demonstrated in support of that move. Moderate members of Parliament, in contrast, favored checking the king's power but not upsetting the Elizabethan religious compromise.

An event that unified public and parliamentary opinion at a crucial time—a revolt against English rule in Ireland in October 1641—temporarily eclipsed these divisions over religious policy but did not diminish suspicion of the king. Fearing that Charles would use Irish soldiers against his English subjects, Parliament demanded that it control the army to put down the rebellion. In November, the Puritan majority introduced a document known as the "Grand Remonstrance," an appeal to the people and a long catalog of parliamentary grievances against the king. It passed by a narrow margin, further inflaming public opinion in London against Charles. The king's remaining support in Parliament eroded in January 1642, when he tried to arrest five members on charges of treason. The five escaped, and the stage was set for wider violence. The king withdrew from London, unsure he could defend himself there, and began to raise an army. In mid-1642, the kingdom stood at the brink of civil war.

## SECTION SUMMARY

- France suffered through more than thirty years of civil war after 1562, caused by religious conflict, weak rulers, and powerful nobility.

- The French religious wars ended in the 1590s, when war-weary elites rallied behind the talented king Henry IV; Henry decreed religious toleration in the Edict of Nantes.

- After Henry, religious and political conflict broke out again, but the king's minister, Cardinal Richelieu, successfully reinforced royal authority.

- Elizabeth I of England weathered religious and political tensions at home and challenges from abroad during her long reign.

- James I and Charles I struggled with limited financial resources, unpopular policies, and religious division.

- Parliamentary resistance to Charles's authority and policies led England to a political crisis in 1640.

# The Holy Roman Empire and the Thirty Years' War

*Why did war erupt again within the Holy Roman Empire and what was the significance of the conflict?*

The Holy Roman Empire enjoyed a period of comparative quiet after the Peace of Augsburg halted religious and political wars in 1555. The 1555 agreement had permitted rulers of the various states within the empire to impose either Catholicism or Lutheranism in their lands. By the early seventeenth century, however, fresh causes of instability brought about renewed fighting. One factor was the rise of Calvinism, for which no provision had been necessary in 1555. Also destabilizing was the attempt by the Austrian Habsburgs to reverse the successes of Protestantism, both in their own lands and in the empire at large, and to solidify their control of their own diverse territories. The result was a devastating conflict known as the **Thirty Years' War** (1618–1648).

Like conflicts elsewhere in Europe, the Thirty Years' War reflected religious tensions, regionalism versus centralizing forces, and dynastic and strategic rivalries between rulers. As a result of the war, the empire was eclipsed as a political unit by the regional powers that composed it.

**Thirty Years' War**
Destructive war (1618–1648) involving most European countries but fought in Germany, resulting from religious tensions, regionalism versus centralizing forces, and dynastic and strategic rivalries between rulers.

## Fragile Peace in the Holy Roman Empire, 1556–1618

The Austrian Habsburgs ruled over a diverse group of territories in the Holy Roman Empire, as well as northwestern Hungary. On his abdication in 1556, Emperor Charles V granted the Habsburg lands in the Holy Roman Empire to his brother, Ferdinand (see the chart on page 423), who was duly crowned emperor when Charles died in 1558.

Though largely contiguous, Ferdinand's territories comprised independent duchies and kingdoms. In addition to the Habsburgs' ancestral lands (separate territories more or less equivalent to modern Austria in extent), Ferdinand also ruled the non-German lands of Bohemia (the core of the modern Czech Republic) and Hungary (see **Map 15.3**). Both kingdoms bestowed their crowns by election and had chosen Ferdinand, the first Habsburg to rule them, in separate elections in the 1520s and 1530s. Most of Hungary was now under Ottoman control, but the kingdom of Bohemia, with its rich capital, Prague, was a wealthy center of population and culture.

Unlike the Netherlands, each of these linguistically and culturally diverse lands was still governed by its own distinct institutions. Moreover, unlike their Spanish cousins, the Austrian Habsburgs made no attempt to impose religious uniformity in the late sixteenth century. Ferdinand was Catholic but tolerant of reform efforts within the church. Both he and his son, Maximilian II (r. 1564–1576), believed that an eventual reunion of the Catholic and Protestant faiths might be possible. During his reign, Maximilian worked to keep religious peace in the empire as a whole and granted limited rights of worship to Protestant subjects in the Habsburgs' own lands. Catholicism and many varieties of Protestantism flourished side by side in Maximilian's domains, particularly in Hungary and, especially, Bohemia, which had experienced a religious reform movement under Jan Hus in the fifteenth century.

Maximilian's son, Rudolf II (r. 1576–1612), shared the religious style of his father and grandfather. He patronized education and the arts and sponsored the work of scientists. Yet Rudolf was a weak leader politically and was challenged by his brother and ambitious cousins for control both of Habsburg lands and of the empire itself. Meanwhile, the resurgence of Catholicism in the wake of the Council of Trent (1545–1563) had begun to shift the religious balance. Members of the Jesuit order arrived in Habsburg lands in the reign of Maximilian. Tough-minded and well trained, they established Catholic schools and became confessors and preachers to the upper classes. Self-confident Catholicism emerged as a potent form of cultural identity among the German-speaking ruling classes and thus as a religious impetus to further political consolidation of all the Habsburg territories.

Resurgent Catholicism spread in the empire as a whole, too, and many Catholic princes believed they might now eliminate Protestantism, as their ancestors had failed to do. Like the English under Elizabeth, Habsburg subjects and peoples in the empire had enjoyed a period of calm in political and religious matters. Now, as in England, the stage was set for conflict of both kinds.

## The Thirty Years' War, 1618–1648

The Thirty Years' War was touched off in 1618 by a revolt against Habsburg rule in the kingdom of Bohemia. Rudolf II had made Bohemia's bustling capital, Prague, his imperial capital.

**Map 15.3  Europe During the Thirty Years' War, 1618–1648**   The Thirty Years' War was fought largely within the borders of the Holy Roman Empire. It was the result of conflicts within the empire as well as the meddling of neighbors for their own strategic advantages.
© Cengage Learning 2014

Its powerful Protestant community had wrested formal recognition of its right to worship from Rudolf and his younger brother, Matthias (r. 1612–1619).

Matthias was quickly succeeded by his cousin Ferdinand II (r. 1619–1637), who did not honor these agreements. Educated by the Jesuits, Ferdinand sincerely believed that reimposing Catholicism was his Christian duty; he once stated that he would "sooner beg than rule over heretics."* He would not tolerate the political independence of nobles and towns in

*Quoted in Jean Berenger, *A History of the Habsburg Empire, 1273–1700*, trans. C. A. Simpson (London and New York: Longman, 1990), p. 239.

**The Defenestration of Prague** This contemporary print memorializes the events of May 23, 1618. Bohemian Protestants "tried" two imperial officials for violating agreements that safeguarded their religious liberties. The two officials and their secretary were thrown out of the windows of Prague castle.

Bohemia or the religious pluralism that independence defended. As Philip II had done in the Netherlands, Ferdinand appointed a council to govern in his name, which enforced unpopular policies, such as denying the right to build Protestant churches and barring non-Catholics from serving in government.

On May 23, 1618, delegates to a Protestant assembly that had unsuccessfully petitioned Ferdinand to honor his predecessors' earlier guarantees marched to the palace in Prague where his officials met. After a confrontation over their demands, the delegates "tried" the officials on the spot for treason and, literally, threw them out of the palace window. The incident became known as the "Defenestration of Prague" (from the Latin *fenestra*, or "window"). (The officials survived because they fell into a pile of garbage in the moat.) The rebels set up their own government.

This upstart Bohemian government officially deposed Ferdinand and elected a new Bohemian king in 1619: Frederick, the Protestant elector of the Palatinate. His election had implications for the Holy Roman Empire as a whole because his territories in west-central Germany, called the Lower and Upper Palatinate, conveyed the right to be one of the seven electors who chose the emperor.

The revolt in Bohemia set off a wider war because foreign rulers also felt their interests to be involved. The English king, James I, supported Frederick because Frederick was married to his daughter. Spain's supply routes north from Italy to the Netherlands passed next to Frederick's lands in western Germany. France's first interest was its rivalry with Spain; thus, France kept its eye on the border principalities that were strategically important to Spain and wanted to keep Protestant, as well as Catholic, princes within the empire strong enough to thwart Austrian Habsburg ambitions. Thus, from the outset, the war was a conflict not only over the Habsburgs' power in their own lands but also over the balance of religious and political power in the empire and in Europe (see **Map 15.3**).

Ferdinand secured aid from Catholic princes, including his cousin, King Philip III (r. 1598– 1621) of Spain, by promising them Frederick's lands in the Palatinate. By the fall of 1620, a Catholic army faced Bohemian rebels who had received little support as yet from fellow Protestants. The Battle of White Mountain, in November, was a complete Catholic victory.

Despite the rout, fighting did not end but instead became more widespread. The 1609 truce between Spain and the Netherlands expired in 1621, and the nearby Lower Palatinate, now in Spanish hands, offered a staging point for Spanish forces and thus threatened the peace in that corner of the empire. Claiming to be a Protestant champion, the Protestant king of Denmark, Christian IV (r. 1588–1648), who was also duke of Holstein in northern Germany, entered the fight. He wanted to gain greater control over German Baltic seaports and to defend his northern German territories against any Catholic aggressors. Christian received little help from fellow Protestants, however. The Dutch were busy with Spain, the English were wary of fighting after Frederick's defeat, and Denmark's rival, the Swedes, were not interested in helping Danish ambitions in the Baltic.

Just as Protestant powers did not always support each other, neither did Catholic ones. When imperial forces defeated Denmark's armies in 1626, Catholic princes became alarmed at the possibility of greater imperial power in northern Germany. Led by the duke of Bavaria, they arranged a truce that resulted in Denmark's withdrawal from the fighting on relatively generous terms.

The Danish king's rival, Gustav Adolf, king of Sweden (r. 1611–1632), hoping to gain territory along the Baltic seacoast, now assumed the role of Protestant leader. Gustav Adolf was an innovative commander and his campaigns were capped by a victory over an imperial army at Breitenfeld, in Saxony, in 1631. However, the tide turned in favor of Ferdinand's forces when Gustav Adolf was killed in battle the following year; further imperial victories led to the Peace of Prague (1635), a general peace treaty favorable to Catholics.

The Peace of Prague brought only a temporary peace, however, because Ferdinand died shortly afterwards and French involvement increased now that other anti-Habsburg forces had been eclipsed. France seized imperial territory along its own eastern border and subsidized continued war within the empire by channeling monies to Protestant princes and mercenaries there. The fighting dragged on. By the end of the Thirty Years' War, order had disintegrated so completely in the wake of the marauding armies that both Catholic and Protestant rulers willingly allied with any power necessary, even religious enemies, to safeguard their states.

A comprehensive peace treaty became possible when France withdrew its sponsorship of the fighting in order to concentrate on its conflict with Spain, namely, the continued rivalry with the Spanish Habsburgs for control of territory along France's eastern and northern borders and in Italy. The French wanted only a workable balance of power in the empire, which had been achieved with a convincing defeat of imperial forces in 1645. Negotiations for peace began among war-weary states of the empire in 1643 and resulted in a group of agreements known as the **Peace of Westphalia** (west-FAIL-yuh) in 1648.

**Peace of Westphalia**
Treaty that ended the Thirty Years' War in 1648. The principalities within the Holy Roman Empire were recognized as virtually autonomous, severely weakening the power of the emperor.

## The Effects of the War

The Thirty Years' War ruined the economy and decimated the population in many parts of the empire and had long-term political consequences for the empire as a whole. One reason for the war's devastation was a novel application of firepower to warfare that increased both the size of armies and their deadly force in battle. This was the use of volley fire, the arrangement of foot soldiers in parallel lines so that one line of men could fire while another reloaded. This tactic, pioneered in the Netherlands around the turn of the century, was refined by Gustav Adolf of Sweden. He amassed large numbers of troops and increased the rate of fire so that a virtually continuous barrage was maintained. He also used maneuverable field artillery to protect the massed infantry from cavalry charges.

Following Gustav Adolf's lead, armies of all the major states adopted these new offensive tactics. But defensive expertise—as in holding fortresses—also remained important, and pitched battles still tended to be part of sieges. The costs in resources and human life of this kind of warfare reached unheard-of dimensions. Compounding these effects of battle was the behavior of troops hired by enterprising mercenary generals, for whom loyalty to the

**The Horrors of War**  The painter of this scene of soldiers plundering a farm in the Thirty Years' War was himself a veteran of Spanish campaigns in the Netherlands. The scene he depicts of soldiers pillaging a village was commonplace in this era of poorly supplied troops. The artist suggests that the soldiers, who were not content with food, murder villagers almost as sport.

princes who paid them took a back seat to personal advancement. They were contracted to provide and supply troops and thus were more willing than the princes would have been to allow armies to live "economically" on plunder. European states could field large armies but had not yet evolved the mechanisms fully to fund, and thus control, them. Popular printed literature and court drama both condemned the horrors of the war.

Where fighting had been concentrated, as in parts of Saxony, between one-third and one-half of the inhabitants of rural villages and major towns may have disappeared. Many starved, were caught in the fighting, or were killed by marauding soldiers. Some people migrated to other regions or joined the armies simply in order to survive.

The Peace of Westphalia was one of the most important outcomes of the war. The various individual treaties composing the Peace effectively put an end to religious war in the empire. Calvinism was recognized as a tolerated religion. The requirement that all subjects must follow their ruler's faith was retained, but some leeway was allowed for those who now found themselves under new rulers.

In political matters, the treaties reflected Swedish successes by granting them territory on the Baltic coast. France gained the important towns of Metz, Toul, and Verdun on its eastern border. Spain formally recognized the independence of the Netherlands. The son of Frederick, Protestant king of Bohemia, received back the smaller of the two Palatine territories that his father had held. The Upper Palatinate—as well as the right to be a new elector of the emperor—was given to the Catholic duke of Bavaria.

**SECTION SUMMARY**

- The Holy Roman Empire was relatively peaceful until destabilized by the spread of Calvinism and the ambition of the Austrian Habsburgs to extend their political and religious control within the empire.
- The Thirty Years' War started in Bohemia (modern Czech Republic) when local leaders challenged Habsburg policies.
- The Bohemian revolt led to a wider war because many rulers, inside and outside Germany, had a stake in the balance of religious and political power there.
- Large armies of mercenaries caused widespread devastation in certain areas of Germany.
- The Peace of Westphalia established a new balance of power between states within the Holy Roman Empire, but the empire itself declined as a political entity.

The most important political outcome of the Peace, however, was a new balance of power in the empire. Most of the major Catholic and Protestant rulers extended their territories at the expense of smaller principalities and cities. The principalities within the empire were acknowledged, in the Peace of Westphalia, to be virtually autonomous, both from the emperor and from one another. In addition, the constitution of the empire was changed to make it very difficult for one prince or a group of princes to disrupt the peace in their own interests. As a result, the agreements at Westphalia were the beginning of one hundred years of peace within the Holy Roman Empire.

Another outcome was that the Habsburgs, though weakened as emperors, were strengthened as rulers of their own hereditary lands on the eastern fringes of the empire. They moved their capital back to Vienna from Prague, and the government of their hereditary lands gained in importance as administration of the empire waned.

# Economic Change and Social Tensions

*What caused the economic stresses of these decades and how did ordinary people cope with them?*

Religious strife disrupted the everyday lives of whole communities in the late sixteenth and early seventeenth centuries. Wars devastated many areas of western Europe and contributed to severe economic decline in parts of the Low Countries (the Netherlands), France, and the Holy Roman Empire. But other factors, most notably a steady rise in prices, also played a role in the dramatic economic and social changes of the century after 1550. Economic changes altered power relations in cities, in the countryside, and in the relationship of both to central governments. Ordinary people managed their economic difficulties in a variety of ways: they sought new sources of work; they protested against burdensome taxes; sometimes they found scapegoats for their distress among their neighbors.

## Economic Transformation and Social Change

The most obvious economic change was an unrelenting rise in prices. Sixteenth-century observers attributed rising prices to the inflationary effects of the influx of silver from Spanish territories in the New World. Historians now believe that European causes may also have helped trigger this **price revolution**. Steady population growth caused a relative shortage of goods, particularly food, and the result was higher prices. Between 1550 and 1600, with local variations, the price of grain may have risen between 50 and 100 percent, and sometimes more, in cities throughout Europe. Wages did not keep pace with prices; historians estimate that wages lost between one-tenth and one-fourth of their value by the end of the century.

Wealth in the countryside was also becoming more stratified. Population growth caused many peasant farms to be subdivided for numerous children, creating tiny plots that could not support the families who lived on them. Countless peasants lost what lands they had to wealthy investors who lent them money to rent more land or to buy seed and tools and then reclaimed the land when the peasants failed to repay. Land rents rose because of high demand and some peasants were unable to rent land at all. To survive, they sought work as day laborers for rich landlords or more prosperous farmers. Many found their way to cities, where they swelled the ranks of the poor. In eastern Europe, peasants faced other dilemmas, for their lands had a different relationship to the wider European economy. The more densely

**price revolution** Steady rise in prices in the sixteenth and seventeenth centuries, resulting from population growth and the importation of precious metals from Spain's New World territories.

urbanized western Europe, whose wealth controlled the patterns of trade, sought bulk goods, particularly grain, from eastern Germany, Poland, and Lithuania. Thus, there was an economic incentive for landowners in eastern Europe to bind peasants to the land, just as the desire of their rulers for greater cooperation had granted the landlords more power. Serfdom now spread in eastern Europe, while precisely the opposite condition—a more mobile labor force—grew in the West.

The growth of markets around Europe and in Spanish possessions overseas, as well as population growth within Europe, had a marked effect on patterns of production and the lives of artisans. Production of cloth on a large scale for export, for example, now required large amounts of capital—much more than a typical guild craftsman could amass. Cloth production was increasingly controlled by new investor-producers with access to distant markets. These entrepreneurs bought up large amounts of wool and hired it out to be cleaned, spun into thread, and woven into cloth by wage laborers in urban workshops or by pieceworkers in their homes. Thousands of poor women and men in the countryside around towns supported their families in this way. In towns, guilds still regulated most trades but, as their share of production declined, they could not accommodate the numbers of artisans who sought to join them. Fewer and fewer apprentices and journeymen could expect to become master artisans. The masters began to treat apprentices virtually as wage laborers, at times, letting them go during slow periods.

Another consequence of the circumstances guild members faced was the effort to reduce competition at the expense of the artisans' own mothers, sisters, and daughters. Increasingly, widows were forbidden to continue their husbands' enterprises, though they headed from 10 to 15 percent of households in many trades. Women had traditionally practiced many trades, but rarely followed the formal progress from apprenticeship to master status, since they usually combined work of this kind with household production. Outright exclusion of women from guilds occurred as early as the thirteenth century but now began regularly to appear in guild statutes. Town governments also restricted women's participation even in work they had long dominated, such as selling in markets. Working women thus began to have difficulty supporting themselves if single or widowed and difficulty supporting their children.

Profits from expanding production and trade and from higher land values made more capital available to wealthy urban or landholding families to invest in the countryside, by buying land outright on which to live like **gentry** or by making loans to desperate peasants. Enterprising landholders raised rents on farming and grazing land wherever they could, or they converted land to the production of wool, grain, and other cash crops destined for distant markets.

> **gentry** Class of wealthy, educated, and socially ambitious families in western Europe, especially England, whose political and economic power was greatly enhanced during the sixteenth century.

As a result, a stratum of wealthy, educated, and socially ambitious "new gentry," as these families were called in England, began to grow. Many of the men of these families were royal officeholders. Many bought titles of nobility or were granted nobility as a benefit of their offices. They often lent money to royal governments. The monumental expense of wars made becoming a lender to government, as well as to individuals, an attractive way to live off personal capital.

No one would have confused these up-and-coming gentry with warrior-aristocrats from old families, but the social distinctions between them are less important (to us) than what they had in common: legal privilege, the security of landownership, and a cooperative relationship with the monarchy. Monarchs deliberately favored the new gentry as counterweights to independent aristocrats.

City governments also changed character. Town councils became dominated by small numbers of privileged families, now more likely to live from landed wealth, like gentry, than from trade or manufacture. By the beginning of the seventeenth century, traditional guild control of government had been eliminated in many places. The long medieval tradition of towns serving as independent corporate bodies had come to an end.

## Coping with Poverty and Violence

The common people of Europe did not submit passively to either the economic difficulties or the religious and political crises of their day. Whatever their religion, common people took the initiative in attacking members of other faiths to rid their communities of them. Heretics were considered to be spiritual pollution that might provoke God's wrath, and ordinary citizens believed that it was up to them to eliminate heretics if the state failed to do so.

Ordinary people fought in wars not only from conviction but also from the need for self-defense and from economic choice. It was ordinary people who defended the walls of towns, dug siege works, and manned artillery batteries. Although nobles remained military leaders, armies consisted mostly of infantry made up of common people, not mounted knights. Women were part of armies, too. Much of the day-to-day work of finding food and firewood, cleaning guns, and repairing clothing was done by women looking after their husbands and lovers among the troops. Landless farm hands, day laborers, and out-of-work artisans joined armies because having work was attractive enough to outweigh the dangers of military life. Desertion was common; nothing more than the rumor that a soldier's home village was threatened might prompt a man to abandon his post. Battle-hardened troops could threaten their commanders, not only with desertion, but with mutiny. Occasionally, mutinies were brutally suppressed; more often, they were successful and troops received some of their back wages.

The devastation of religious war led to both peasant rebellions and urban uprisings. Peasants and townspeople rebelled because of high taxes and food shortages. Elites participated too; former soldiers, prosperous farmers, or even noble landlords whose economic fortunes were tied to peasant profits led some rural revolts. Rebels sometimes seized property—for example, they might distribute looted bread among themselves—and occasionally killed officials. Their protests rarely generated lasting political change and were usually brutally quashed.

Governments at all levels tried to cope with the increasing problem of poverty by changing the administration and scale of poor relief. In both Catholic and Protestant Europe, caring for the poor became more institutionalized and systematic and more removed from religious impulses. Governments established public almshouses and poorhouses to dispense food or

**A Beggar Is Whipped Through the Streets**   In this sixteenth-century woodcut, probably made in England, a poor man is tied up and led through the streets of a town while being whipped on his bare back. The gallows in the distance, just outside the city gates, imply that the poor were now thought of as dangerous outlaws. Private Collection/The Bridgeman Art Library to care for orphans or the destitute in towns throughout Catholic and Protestant Europe. At first, these institutions reflected an optimistic vision of an ideal Christian community caring for its neediest members. But by 1600, the distribution of food was accompanied by attempts to distinguish "deserving" from "undeserving" poor, by an insistence that the poor work for their ration of food, and even by an effort to force the poor to live apart, in poorhouses.

These efforts were not uniformly successful. Although begging was outlawed by Catholic and Protestant city governments alike, it was never thoroughly suppressed. Catholic religious orders often resisted efforts at regulating their charitable work, even when they were imposed by Catholic governments. Nonetheless, the trend was clear. From viewing poverty as a fact of life and a lesson in Christian humility, European elites began to see it as a social problem and poor people as needing to be controlled.

## The Hunt for Witches

Between approximately 1550 and 1650, Europe saw a dramatic increase in the persecution of women and men for witchcraft. Approximately one hundred thousand people were tried and about sixty thousand executed. The surge in witch-hunting was closely linked to communities' religious concerns and also to the social tensions that resulted from economic difficulties.

Certain types of witchcraft had long existed in Europe. So-called black magic of various kinds—one peasant casting a spell on another peasant's cow—had been common since the Middle Ages. The practice now seemed dangerous, especially to elites, who linked black magic to Devil worship. Catholic leaders and legal scholars began to advance such theories in the fifteenth century, and by the late sixteenth century, both Catholic and Protestant elites viewed a witch not only as someone who might cast harmful spells but also as a heretic.

The impetus for most individual accusations of witchcraft came from within the communities where the "witch" lived—that is, from common people. Usually targeted were solitary or unpopular people whose difficult relationships with fellow villagers made them seem likely sources of evil. Often, such a person had practiced black magic (or had been suspected of doing so) for years, and the villagers took action only when faced with a community crisis such as an epidemic.

Because they were often prompted by village disasters, individual accusations of witchcraft increased in this period in response to the crises that beset many communities. In addition, isolated accusations often started localized frenzies of active hunting for other witches. These more widespread hunts were driven, in part, by the anxieties of local elites about disorder and heresy and were facilitated by contemporary legal procedures that they applied. These procedures permitted lax rules of evidence and the use of torture to extract confessions. Torture or the threat of torture led most accused witches to "confess" and to name accomplices or other "witches." In this way, a single initial accusation could lead to dozens of prosecutions. In regions where procedures for appealing convictions were fragile or nonexistent, witch-hunts could expand with alarming speed and dozens of "witches" might be identified and executed before the whirlwind subsided. Aggressive hunts were common, for example, in the small principalities and imperial cities of the Holy Roman Empire, which were largely

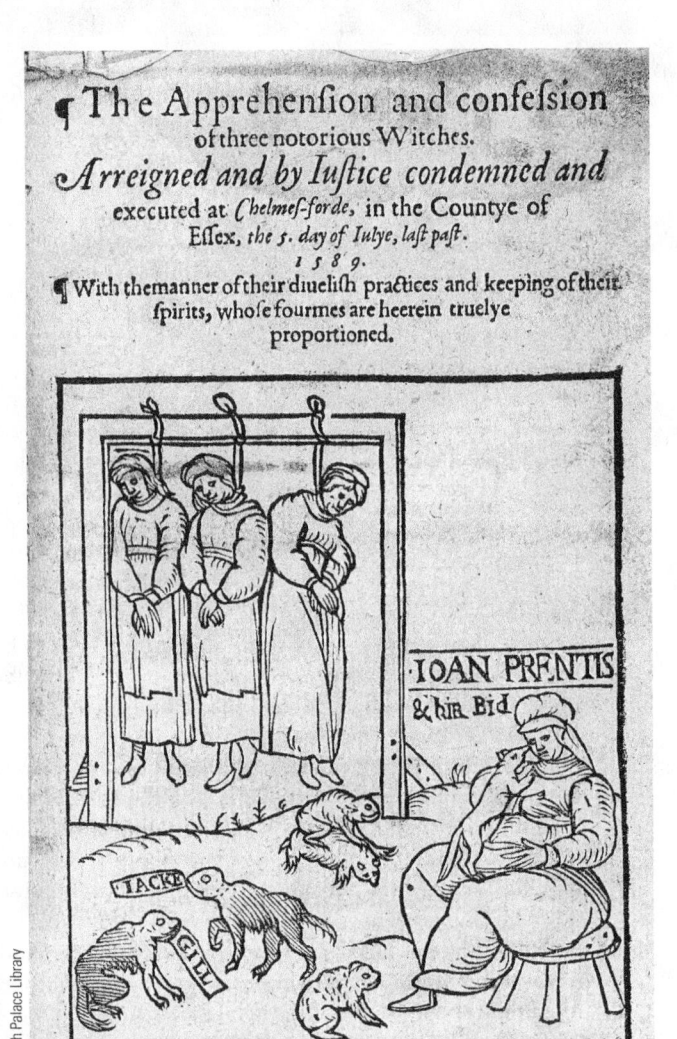

Lambeth Palace Library

**Publicizing Witch Trials**  Printed pamphlets, such as this one describing the execution of three women in Essex, England, spread the news of local "outbreaks" of witchcraft. One of the women, Joan Prentis, is also depicted surrounded by her animal familiars. The ferret in Joan's lap, the pamphlet relates, was the Devil himself in animal form.

# THE WRITTEN RECORD

## A City Official Worries About Witch-Hunting

*In this letter written to a friend in 1629, the chancellor to the prince-bishop of the German city of Würzburg describes the witch-hunt in his community.*

As to the affair of the witches, which Your Grace thinks brought to an end before this, it has started up afresh, and no words can do justice to it. Ah, the woe and misery of it—there are still four hundred in the city, high and low, of every rank and sex, nay, even clerics, so strongly accused that they may be arrested at any hour. It is true that, of the people of my Gracious Prince here, some out of all the offices and faculties must be executed: clerics, elected councilors and doctors, city officials, court assessors several of whom Your Grace knows. There are law students to be arrested. The Prince-Bishop has over forty students who are soon to be pastors; among them thirteen or fourteen are said to be witches. A few days ago a Dean was arrested; two others who were summoned have fled.

The notary of our Church consistory, a very learned man, was yesterday arrested and put to the torture. In a word, a third part of the city is surely involved. The richest, most attractive, most prominent of the clergy are already executed. A week ago a maiden of nineteen was executed, of whom it is everywhere said that she was the fairest in the whole city, and was held by everybody a girl of singular modesty and purity. She will be followed by seven or eight others of the best and most attractive persons. . . . And thus many are put to death for renouncing God and being at the witch-dances, against whom nobody has ever else spoken a word.

To conclude this wretched matter, there are children of three or four years, to the number of three hundred, who are said to have had intercourse with the Devil. I have seen put to death children of seven, promising students of ten, twelve, fourteen and fifteen of the nobles—but I cannot and must not write more of this misery. There are persons of yet higher rank, whom you know, and would marvel to hear of, nay, would scarcely believe it; let justice be done. . . .

P.S. Though there are many wonderful and terrible things happening it is beyond doubt that, at a place called the Fraw-Rengberg, the Devil in person, with eight thousand of his followers, held an assembly and celebrated mass before them all, administering to his audience (that is, the witches) turnip-rinds and pairings in place of the Holy Eucharist. There took place not only foul but most horrible and hideous blasphemies, whereof I shudder to write. It is also true that they all vowed not to be enrolled in the Book of Life, but all agreed to be inscribed by a notary who is well known to me and my colleagues. We hope, too, that the book in which they are enrolled will yet be found, and there is no little search being made for it.

### Questions

1. Which townspeople are victims of the witch-hunt?

2. Does the document reveal why the hunt is continuing? Who is in charge?

3. What is the author's attitude toward the events he describes? Does the chancellor believe that witchcraft exists?

*Source: Alan C. Kors and Edward Peters, eds., *Witchcraft in Europe, 1100-1700: A Documentary History* (Philadelphia: University of Pennsylvania, 1972), pp. 251-252. Reprinted by permission of the University of Pennsylvania Press.

independent of higher political and judicial authority. (See the box, "The Written Record: A City Official Worries About Witch-Hunting" above.)

The majority of accused witches were women. Lacking legal, social, and political resources, women may have been more likely than men to use black magic for self-protection or advancement. Women's work often made them vulnerable to charges of witchcraft, since families' food supplies and routine medicines passed through women's hands. The deaths of young children or of domestic animals, such as a milk cow, were among the most common triggers for witchcraft accusation. The increase in poverty during the late sixteenth and early seventeenth centuries made poor women frequent targets of witch-hunts.

Both Christian dogma and humanistic writing portrayed women as morally weaker than men and thus more susceptible to the Devil's enticements. Writings on witchcraft described Devil worship in sexual terms, and the prosecution of witches had a voyeuristic, sexual dimension. The bodies of accused witches were searched for the "Devil's mark"—a blemish thought to be Satan's imprint. In some regions, women accounted for 80 percent of those prosecuted and executed. A dynamic of gender stereotyping was not always at work, however; in other regions, prosecutions were more evenly divided between men and women, and occasionally men made up the majority of those accused.

The widespread witch-hunts virtually ended by the late seventeenth century, in part because the intellectual energies of elites shifted from religious to scientific thought. The practice of witchcraft continued among common folk, although accusations of one neighbor by another never again reached the level of these crisis-ridden decades.

## SECTION SUMMARY

- A price revolution caused a decline in the value of wages in the sixteenth century.
- Elites, particularly new gentry families, could grow rich by controlling increasingly scarce and valuable land.
- Economic hardship led common people to seek jobs in cities, join armies, and protest taxation.
- Persecutions for witchcraft dramatically increased between 1550 and 1650, reflecting both common people's search for scapegoats for their hard lives and elites' anxiety about controlling common people's religion.

# Writing, Drama, and Art in an Age of Upheaval

*In what ways do the literature and art of this period reflect the political, social, and religious conflicts of the age?*

Both imaginative literature and speculative writing, such as political theory, bear the stamp of their times. In the late sixteenth and early seventeenth centuries, political speculation concerned questions of the legitimacy of rulers and of the relationship of political power to divine authority—urgent problems in an age when religious division threatened the very foundations of states. Authors and rulers alike often relied on still-prevalent oral modes of communication to convey their ideas. Indeed, some of the greatest literature and some of the most effective political statements of the period were presented as drama and not conveyed in print. Nevertheless, literacy continued to spread and led to greater opportunities for knowledge and reflection. The medium of print became increasingly important to political life. In the visual arts, the dramatic impulse combined with religious purposes to create works that conveyed both power and emotion.

## Literacy and Literature

Traditional oral culture changed slowly under the impact of the spread of printing, education, and literacy. Works of literature from the late sixteenth and early seventeenth centuries incorporate material from traditional folktales and reflect the coexistence of oral and literate culture. In *Don Quixote* (key-HO-tay), by Spain's Miguel de Cervantes (sair-VAHN-tayz) (1547–1616), the title character and his companion, Sancho Panza, have a long discussion about oral and literate traditions. The squire Panza speaks in the style that was customary in oral culture—a rather roundabout and repetitive style, which enabled the speaker and listener to remember what was said. Much of the richness of *Don Quixote* is due to the interweaving of prose styles and topical concerns from throughout Cervantes' culture—from the oral world of peasants to the refined world of court life. Yet, what enabled Cervantes to create this rich portrayal was his own highly developed literacy and the awareness of language that literacy made possible.

Much literature in this period stressed the value of education—particularly by means of the humanist recovery of ancient wisdom, a new vision of what it meant to be a cultivated and disciplined man of the world. The French author Michel de Montaigne (1533–1592) was the epitome of the reflective gentleman. Montaigne (mon-TEN-yuh) was a judge in the parlement (law court) of Bordeaux. In 1570, he resigned from the court and retired to his small château, where he wrote his *Essais* (from which we derive the word *essays*), a collection of short reflections that were revolutionary in both form and content. Montaigne invented writing in the form of a sketch, an "attempt" (the literal meaning of *essai*) that enabled him to combine self-reflection with formal analysis.

Owing to the spread of printing, Montaigne had a virtually unparalleled opportunity to compare different events, values, and cultures through reading a wide variety of printed texts. His reflections range from the destructiveness of the French civil wars to the consequences of

European exploration of the New World. Toward all of these events, Montaigne was able to achieve an analytic detachment remarkable for his day. For example, he noted ironically that Europeans labeled New World peoples "savages," yet, they committed seemingly endless and wanton violence against those "savages" and one another. (See the feature "The Global Record: Montaigne Discusses Barbarity in the New World and the Old" on page 447.) Montaigne's essays also reveal self-reflection—a distancing from himself. This distancing was also the result of literacy and leisure, which enabled him to enjoy long periods of solitude and reflection in the company of other solitary, book-bound voices. Montaigne's works mark the beginning of what we know as the "invention" of private life, in which an individual is defined more by internal character and personality traits than by social role.

## The Great Age of Theater

The works of the great English poet and playwright William Shakespeare (1564–1616) are still compelling to us because of the profundity of the questions asked about love, honor, and political legitimacy; he asked these questions in terms appropriate to his own day. One of his favorite themes—evident in *Hamlet* and *Macbeth*—is the legitimacy of rulers. He also explored the contradictions in values between the growing commercial world he saw around him and the older, seemingly more stable world of feudal society. Subtle political commentary distinguishes Shakespeare's later writings near and shortly after the death of Elizabeth in 1603, when political and economic problems were becoming increasingly troublesome. In *Coriolanus*, he portrays commoners as poor but not ignorant; they are in fact fully rational and capable of analyzing their situation—perhaps more capable, Shakespeare hints, than their ruler. The play is safely set in ancient Rome, but the social and political tensions it depicts clearly applied to the Elizabethan present.

Shakespeare's extraordinary career was possible because his life coincided with the rise of professional theater. In the capitals of England and Spain, professional theaters first opened in the 1570s. Some drama was produced at court or in aristocratic households, but most public theaters drew large and very mixed audiences, including the poorest city dwellers. Playwrights, including Shakespeare, often wrote in teams, under great pressure to keep acting companies supplied with material. The best-known dramatist in Spain, Lope de Vega (LOW-pah day VAY-guh) (1562–1635), wrote more than fifteen hundred works on a wide range of topics. Although religious themes remained popular in Spanish theater, as an echo of medieval drama, most plays in England and Spain treated secular subjects and, as in *Coriolanus*, disguised political commentary.

Over time, theater became increasingly restricted to aristocratic circles. In England, Puritan criticism of the "immorality" of public performance drove actors and playwrights to seek royal patronage. The first professional theater to open in Paris, in 1629, quickly became dependent on Cardinal Richelieu's patronage. Inevitably, as court patronage grew in importance, the wide range of subjects treated in plays began to narrow to those of aristocratic concern, such as family honor and martial glory. These themes are depicted in the works of the Spaniard Pedro Calderón (kall-day-ROHN) (1600–1681), who wrote for his enthusiastic patron, Philip IV, and of the Frenchman Pierre Corneille (kore-NAY) (1606–1684), whose great tragedy of aristocratic life, *Le Cid*, was one of the early successes of the seventeenth-century French theater.

Drama's significance as an art form is reflected in its impact on the development of music: The opera, which weds drama to music, was invented in Italy in the early seventeenth century. The first great work in this genre is generally acknowledged to be *Orfeo* (*Orpheus*, 1607) by Claudio Monteverdi (mon-tay-VAIR-dee) (1567–1643). Opera, like drama, reflected the influence of humanism in its secular themes and in its emulation of Greek drama, which had used both words and music. The practice of music itself changed under the dramatic impulse. Monteverdi was the first master of a new musical style known as "monody," which emphasizes the progression of chords. Monodic music is inherently dramatic, creating a sense of forward movement, expectation, and resolution.

## Montaigne Discusses Barbarity in the New World and the Old

*In one of his most famous essays, the French jurist and essayist Michel de Montaigne (1533–1592) ironically compares the customs of Native Americans with the customs of his own society. Information about Native Americans came from published reports of European voyages and from news of individual Native Americans who had journeyed (usually forcibly) to Europe. Europeans' encounters with peoples in the New World gave Montaigne a vantage point from which to criticize his own society.*

They have their wars with [other] nations, to which they go quite naked, with no other arms than bows or wooden spears.... It is astonishing that firmness they show in their combats, which never end but in slaughter and bloodshed; for, as to routs and terror, they know nothing of either.

Each man brings back as his trophy the head of the enemy he has killed.... After they have treated their prisoner well for a long time with all the hospitality they can think of ... they kill him with their swords. This done, they roast him and eat him in common and send some pieces to their absent friends.

I am not sorry that we notice the barbarous horror of such acts, but am heartily sorry that ... we should be so blind to our own. I think there is more barbarity ... in tearing by tortures and the rack a body still full of feeling, in roasting a man bit by bit, having him bitten and mangled by dogs (as we have not only read but seen within fresh memory ... among neighbors and fellow citizens, and what is worse, on the pretext of piety and religion).

Three of these men (were brought to France) ... and [someone] wanted to know what they had found most amazing.... They said that in the first place they thought it very strange that so many grown men, bearded, strong and armed who were around the king ... should submit to obey a child [the young French king].... Second (they have a way in their language of speaking of men as halves of one another), they had noticed that there were among us men full and gorged with all sorts of good things, and that their other halves were beggars at their doors, emaciated with hunger and poverty; and they thought it strange that these needy halves could endure such injustice.

### Questions

1. What practices in the two cultures is Montaigne commenting on in this excerpt?

2. In what ways does he find Native American culture admirable by comparison to his own? What aspects of his own culture is he criticizing?

3. How are contemporary events and conditions in France reflected in Montaigne's remarks?

Source: Excerpts from *The Complete Essays of Montaigne* by Donald M. Frame, translator, pp. 153, 155–159. Copyright © 1958 by the Board of Trustees of the Leland Stanford Jr. University, renewed 1971, 1976. All rights reserved. Used with permission of Stanford University Press, www.sup.org.

## Drama, Art, and Political Thought

Whether produced on a public stage or at court or in a less formal setting, drama was a favored method of communication in this era because people responded to and made extensive use of the spoken word. Dramatic gesture and storytelling to get a message across were commonplace and were important components of politics.

What we might call "street drama" was a common event. When aristocratic governors entered major towns, such as when Margaret of Parma entered Brussels, an ostentatious formal "entry" was often staged. The dignitary would ride through the main gate, usually beneath a canopy made of luxurious cloth. Costumed townspeople staged brief symbolic dramas, such as of the story of David and Goliath, on the streets; the event might end with an elaborate banquet. A remnant of these proceedings survives today in the ceremony of giving distinguished visitors "the keys to the city," which, in the sixteenth century, really were functional.

Royalty made artful use of ceremony. Royal entries into towns took on an added weight, as did royal funerals and other such occasions. These dramas reinforced political and constitutional assumptions in the minds of witnesses and participants and, over time, there were revealing changes in the representations of royal power. In France, for example, the ritual entry of the king into Paris had originally stressed the participation of the leading guilds, judges, and administrators, symbolizing their active role in governing the city and the kingdom. But in the last half of the sixteenth century, the procession began to glorify the king alone.

## Baroque Art

If today you were to walk through the cathedral in the Belgian city of Antwerp and notice this painting, titled *The Raising of the Cross*, it might not strike you as remarkable. The crucifixion of Jesus is a frequent subject of religious painting, after all. But let us look at the image more carefully. First of all, this is a portrayal not of Jesus hanging on the cross but rather of the raising of the cross. In other words, it captures a moment of action, not its aftermath. The frame of the painting is filled with action as well. The figures on the left and at the center support the cross and push it up. At the bottom right, we see figures straining at ropes as they pull the cross upright. Our eye is drawn to the movement in the painting, partly by the use of light, which floods the figure of Jesus. We also note the unexpected diagonal position of the crucified figure, and we survey the image in order to make sense of it.

This is a dynamic painting and simultaneously an emotionally engaging one. We encounter Jesus not as a static, perhaps already dying, figure on the cross, but at the very moment of his crucifixion. There is also a striking similarity between the figure of Jesus and those of the men who are working hard to accomplish his crucifixion: They are all men, whose muscled bodies are more alike than not. The human pathos of the moment is brought to life.

The image you see before you is one of three panels in a triptych, or three-paneled altarpiece. The left-hand panel depicts Saint John, the Virgin Mary, and others witnessing Jesus' crucifixion. The panel on the right shows a Roman officer watching over his soldiers as they crucify two thieves. Whereas most triptychs of the period contained three unrelated images, here the panels combine to form a single story of the crucifixion.

This altarpiece was executed in 1610 by the influential painter Peter Paul Rubens (1577–1640), a native of Antwerp, in the southern Netherlands. Rubens was one of the great masters of what came to be called the baroque style. Baroque techniques were pioneered in the late sixteenth century in Italy, first in church design, and spread slowly, with many regional variations, especially throughout Catholic Europe, during the seventeenth century. The origin of the term *baroque* has been debated; it may have come from the Portuguese *barroco*, used to describe irregularly shaped pearls. The term as applied to the arts was initially derogatory, denoting distortion, illogic, and irregularity. Baroque painting was distinguished by the dramatic use of color and shading and by the dynamic energy of figures. Baroque artists based their work on Renaissance achievements in representing the human form in a convincing three-dimensional space. But with the strong use of light, movement, and more robust and realistic human figures, these artists enhanced the drama and emotional impact of what they depicted.

Like baroque artists, baroque architects modified the precision, symmetry, and orderliness of Renaissance architecture to produce a sense of greater dynamism in space. Baroque churches, for example, were impressively grand and monumental yet emotionally engaging at the same time. Façades and interiors were both massive and, through the clever use of architectural and decorative components, suggestive of movement. A good example of this is the work of Gianlorenzo Bernini (bare-NEE-nee) (1598–1680), who designed the portico outside Saint Peter's Basilica in Rome, as well as the highly ornate bronze canopy over the altar inside the basilica. Dramatic illusion in the interior of buildings—such as painting a chapel ceiling with figures receding as if ascending to heaven—was a common device in baroque architecture. One of the primary purposes of baroque architecture and art was to create simultaneously a display of power and an invitation to sensory experience. Baroque art encouraged piety that was not only emotionally involved, and thus satisfying, but also awe-inspired. In this way, it reflected the aims of the Counter-Reformation church, whose leaders were among its most important patrons.

Peter Paul Rubens's early training in Italy shaped him as an artist and established his secondary career as a diplomat. Throughout his life, he undertook diplomatic missions for the Habsburg viceroys in the Spanish Netherlands, gaining artistic commissions wherever he went. Rubens's subject matter varied widely, including church design and decoration, portraiture, and landscape painting, reflecting the fact that baroque art also had important secular applications. Indeed, magnificent baroque palaces symbolized the wealth and power of the elites (see the photos on pages 460 and 468).

Rulers began to employ artists as portrait painters, such as Rubens's pupil Anthony Van Dyck (1599–1641), whose painting of Charles I of England appears on page 450. Because portraits have become so common, we cannot fully appreciate how arresting this image would have been in its day. Like Rubens's *Raising of the Cross*, Van Dyck's image of Charles was an innovative rendering of familiar elements. The image of a ruler on horseback was well known, but it had

---

Speculation about and celebration of power, as well as dramatic emotion, also occurred in the visual arts—most notably in painting and architecture, in the style now known as **baroque**. Baroque (ba-ROKE) style was a new kind of visual language that could project power and grandeur and simultaneously engage viewers' senses. (See the feature "The Visual Record: Baroque Art" above.)

The very fact that rulers experimented with self-representation suggests that questions about the nature and extent of royal power were far from settled. Queen Elizabeth I had the

Onze Lieve Vrouwkwerk, Antwerp Cathedral, Belgium/Peter Willi/Bridgeman Art Library

never been exploited as fully by English monarchs as it had been by rulers on the Continent. This large portrait of the king was designed to be hung at the end of a long palace corridor so that, from a distance, a courtier would have the illusion of actually seeing the king riding proudly through a triumphal arch.* Compare this portrait with the much more stilted one of Elizabeth I on page 431. It is striking how effective the technical and stylistic innovations of baroque art and architecture were in expressing secular, as well as spiritual, power.

## Questions

1. *How does baroque art involve the viewer by appealing to senses and emotions?*

2. *Why was baroque painting effective for conveying political messages, as in Van Dyck's portrait of Charles I?*

---

*This discussion draws on the work of Roy Strong, *Van Dyck: Charles I on Horseback* (New York: Viking, 1972), pp. 20–25.

particular burden of assuming the throne in a period of great instability. Hence, she paid a great deal of attention to the image of herself that she conveyed in words and authorized to be fashioned in painting. Elizabeth styled herself variously as mother to her people and as a warrior-queen (drawing on ancient myths of Amazon women). More formal speculation about constitutional matters also resulted from the tumult of the sixteenth and seventeenth centuries. As we have seen, the Protestant faction in France advanced arguments for the limitation of royal power. Alternative theories enhancing royal authority were offered, principally in

**An Image of Royalty**   This dramatic painting of Charles I on horseback was one of several likenesses of the king painted by the baroque artist Anthony Van Dyck. This painting was originally hung at the end of a long gallery in one of the royal palaces, next to similarly triumphal images of Roman emperors. The Royal Collection © 2003, Her Majesty Queen Elizabeth II

**baroque** Style of European art and architecture popular from the late sixteenth to early eighteenth centuries. Baroque art modified Renaissance techniques, adding dynamism and emotional energy, which resulted in works that were both impressively grand and emotionally engaging.

support of the Catholic position, though also simply to buttress the beleaguered monarchy itself. The most famous of these appeared in *The Six Books of the Republic* (1576), by the legal scholar Jean Bodin (bo-DAHN) (1530–1596). Bodin was a Catholic but offered a fundamentally secular perspective on the purposes and source of power within a state. His special contribution was a vision of a truly sovereign monarch. Bodin offered a theoretical understanding that is essential to states today and is the ground on which people can claim rights and protection from the state—namely, that there is a final sovereign authority. For Bodin, that authority was the king. Contract theory, devised by French Protestants to legitimize resistance to the monarchy, was abandoned when Henry IV granted toleration to the Huguenots in 1598. In England, theoretical justification of resistance to Charles I was initially limited to invoking tradition and precedent. Contract theory, as well as other sweeping claims regarding subjects' rights, would be more fully developed later in the century.

Bodin's theory of sovereignty, however, was immediately echoed in other theoretical works, most notably that of Hugo Grotius (GROW-shus) (1583–1645). A Dutch jurist and diplomat, Grotius developed the first principles of modern international law. He accepted the existence of sovereign states that owed no loyalty to higher authority (such as the papacy) and thus needed new principles to govern their interactions. His major work, *De Jure Belli ac Pacis* (*On the Law of War and Peace*, 1625), was written in response to the turmoil of the Thirty Years' War. Grotius argued that relations between states could be based on respect for treaties voluntarily reached between them. In perhaps his boldest move, he argued that war must be justified, and he developed criteria to distinguish just wars from unjust ones.

## SECTION SUMMARY

- Literacy and access to printed books enabled new levels of self-consciousness and self-reflection, as in the work of Montaigne.
- The rise of professional theater began in the 1570s; drama was a favored means of communication by writers as well as political leaders.
- Shakespeare and other writers and artists reflected on many of the current concerns about legitimate authority, religion, and human life in this period.
- Baroque art appealed to viewers' emotions but also expressed power and grandeur.
- Political theorist Bodin developed the notion of sovereign authority within the state.

# Chapter Summary

◆ *What circumstances permitted Spain's ambitious policies and to what degree were they successful?*

The most powerful monarch of the day, the king of Spain, could not defeat a religious and political rebellion in the prosperous Netherlands, even with the resources of treasure from the New World.

◆ *What conditions led to civil war in France? How did religious and political conflict develop differently in England?*

France was torn apart by decades of civil war before the Crown was able to impose a workable peace and reassert royal authority. In England, political and religiously inspired challenges to royal authority were contained by Elizabeth I, but not as effectively addressed by her successors. Meanwhile, the various states of the Holy Roman Empire were engulfed in a thirty-year war that also had political and religious roots and which became one of the most bitter and complex conflicts of the period.

◆ *Why did war erupt again within the Holy Roman Empire and what was the significance of the conflict?*

The late sixteenth and early seventeenth centuries were an era of intense struggle over political and religious authority. Rulers everywhere, through a variety of means, tried to buttress and expand their power. They were resisted by traditional centers of power, such as independent-minded nobles and wealthy townspeople. But they were also resisted by the novel challenge of religious dissent, which empowered even common people both to claim a greater right to question authority and to risk more in their attempts to oppose it.

◆ *What caused the economic stresses of these decades and how did ordinary people cope with them?*

War itself became more destructive, owing to new technologies and increasing resources devoted to it. Ordinary people also coped with the price revolution, which caused their wages to lose value and many to lose their land. The difficult economic circumstances of these decades meant that working people, desperate for secure livelihood, rioted or took up arms out of economic, as well as religious, concerns. A surge in witch trials in this period was also partly the result of economic and social stress that was felt disproportionately by women.

◆ *In what ways do the literature and art of this period reflect the political, social, and religious conflicts of the age?*

However grim the circumstances people faced, the technology of print and the spread of literacy helped spur speculative and creative works by providing the means for reflection and the audiences to receive and appreciate it. Ironically, the increased importance and grandeur of court life, though a cause of political strain, resulted in a new wave of patronage for art, literature, and drama. Other works, such as Shakespeare's plays, both reflect and reflect on the conflicts in the society of the day. Baroque art expressed both the religious passions of the era and the claims to authority by rulers.

## Key Terms

**Philip II** (p. 418)

**United Provinces** (p. 422)

**Armada** (p. 423)

**Huguenots** (p. 426)

**Edict of Nantes** (p. 428)

**Elizabeth I** (p. 430)

**Puritans** (p. 430)

**Thirty Years' War** (p. 435)

**Peace of Westphalia** (p. 438)

**price revolution** (p. 440)

**gentry** (p. 441)

**baroque** (p. 450)

CourseMate

Go to the CourseMate website at **www.cengagebrain.com** for additional study tools and review materials—including audio and video clips—for this chapter.

**Louis XIV in Roman Armor** Scala/Art Resource, NY

# Europe in the Age of Louis XIV, ca. 1640–1715

The portrait of King Louis XIV of France as a triumphant warrior, to the left, was one of hundreds of such images of the king that decorated his palace at Versailles and other sites around his kingdom—where they made his subjects aware of his presence, regardless of whether he was in residence. In this painting, the contemporary artist Charles Le Brun depicts Louis as a Roman warrior, and his power is represented by a mixture of other symbols—Christian and pagan, ancient and contemporary. An angel crowns him with a victor's laurel wreath and carries a banner bearing the image of the sun. In his hand, Louis holds a marshal's baton—a symbol of military command—covered with the royal emblem of the fleur-de-lys (flur-duh-LEE). In the background, behind the "Roman" troops following Louis, is an idealized city.

These trappings symbolized the significant expansion of royal power during Louis's reign. He faced down the challenges of warrior-nobles, suppressed religious dissent, and tapped the nation's wealth to wage a series of wars of conquest. A period of cultural brilliance early in his reign and the spectacle of an elaborate court life crowned his achievements. In his prime, his regime was supported by a consensus of elites; such harmony was made possible by the lack of institutional brakes on royal authority. However, as his attention to symbolism suggests, Louis's power was not unchallenged. By the end of the Sun King's reign, the glow was fading: France was struggling under economic distress brought on by the many wars fought for his glory and had missed opportunities for commercial success abroad. Elites throughout France who had once accepted, even welcomed, his rule became critics, and common people, outright rebels.

In England, by contrast, the Crown faced successful rebellion by subjects claiming religious authority and political legitimacy for their causes. Resistance to the expansion of royal authority, led by Parliament, resulted in the execution of the king and the establishment of a short-lived republic, the Commonwealth. Although the monarchy was restored, it became permanently weaker after the civil war. After the Thirty Years' War, vigorous rulers in central and eastern Europe undertook a program of territorial expansion and state building that led to the dominance in the region of Austria, Brandenburg-Prussia,

## Chapter Overview

### France in the Age of Absolutism

◆ *How did Louis XIV successfully expand royal power in France and what were some of the achievements of his reign?*

### The English Civil War and Its Aftermath

◆ *What were the long-term consequences of the English civil war?*

### New Powers in Central and Eastern Europe

◆ *Which states began to dominate central and eastern Europe and why were they successful?*

### The Expansion of Overseas Trade and Settlement

◆ *How and why did Europe's overseas trade and colonization expand in the seventeenth century and what effects did this expansion have on Europe itself?*

and Russia. The power of these states derived, in part, from the economic relationship of their lands to the wider European economy. In all the major states of continental Europe, princely governments were able to monopolize military power for the first time, in return for economic and political concessions to noble landholders.

The seventeenth century also witnessed a dynamic phase of European expansion overseas, following on the successes of the Portuguese and the Spanish in the fifteenth and sixteenth centuries. The Dutch created the most successful trading empire. Eager migrants settled in the Americas in ever-increasing numbers, while forced migrants— enslaved Africans—were transported by the thousands to work on the profitable plantations of European colonizers. Aristocrats, merchants, and peasants back in Europe jockeyed to take advantage of—or to mitigate the effects of—the local political and economic impact of Europe's expansion.

# France in the Age of Absolutism

*How did Louis XIV successfully expand royal power in France and what were some of the achievements of his reign?*

**absolutism** Extraordinary concentration of power and symbolic authority in royal hands, achieved particularly by the king of France (Louis XIV) in the seventeenth century.

**Louis XIV** Longest-reigning ruler in European history, he imposed "absolute" rule in France and his reign witnessed a great flowering of French culture.

**Absolutism** is a term often used to describe the extraordinary concentration of power in royal hands achieved by the kings of France, most notably **Louis XIV** (r. 1643–1715), in the seventeenth century. Louis continued the expansion of state power begun by his father's minister, Cardinal Richelieu (see page 429). The extension of royal power, under Louis as well as his predecessor, was accelerated by his desire to sustain an expensive and aggressive foreign policy. The policy itself was partly traditional—fighting the perpetual enemy, the Habsburgs, and seeking military glory—and partly new—expanding the borders of France. Louis XIV's successes in these undertakings made him both envied and emulated by other rulers: The French court became a model of culture and refinement. But increased royal authority was not accepted without protest: Common French people as well as elites dug in their heels over the cost of Louis's policies to them.

## The Last Challenge to Absolutism: The Fronde, 1648–1653

Louis inherited the throne at the age of five in 1643. His mother, Anne of Austria (1601–1666), acted as regent, together with her chief minister and personal friend, Cardinal Jules Mazarin (mah-zah-RAHN) (1602–1661). They immediately faced revolts against the concentration of power in royal hands and the exorbitant taxation that had prevailed under Louis's father. The most serious revolt began in 1648, led by the Parlement (par-luh-MAWN) of Paris and the other sovereign law courts in the capital.

The source of the Parlement's leverage over the monarchy was its traditional right to register laws and edicts, which amounted to judicial review. Now, the Parlement attempted to extend this power by debating and even initiating government policy. The sovereign courts sitting together drew up a reform program abolishing most of the machinery of government established under Richelieu and calling for consent to future taxation. The citizens of Paris rose to defend the courts when royal troops were sent against them in October.

Civil war waxed and waned around France from 1648 to 1653. Fighting was led by great aristocrats in the name of the parlements and other law courts. At the same time, further reform proposals were offered. For example, middling nobles in the region around Paris worked on their own reform program and made preparations for a meeting of the Estates General—a representative assembly—to enact it.

These revolts begun in 1648 were derided with the name "Fronde," which was a popular children's game. However, the Fronde (FRAWND) was not child's play; it constituted a serious challenge to the legacy of royal government as it had developed under Richelieu. It ended without a noteworthy impact on the growth of royal power for several reasons. First, Mazarin made strategic concessions to individual aristocrats, who were always eager to trade their loyalty for the fruits of royal service. Meanwhile, the Parlement of Paris accepted a return to royal authority when the civil war caused starvation as well as threatened its control of reform.

Moreover, the Parlement of Paris was a law court, not a representative assembly. Its legitimacy derived from its role as upholder of royal law, and it could not sustain a challenge to the king on the pretext of upholding royal tradition in his name. Parlementaires saw the Estates General as a rival institution and helped quash the proposed meeting of representatives. They especially wanted to avoid reform that included abolition of the paulette, a fee guaranteeing the hereditary right to royal office (see page 428).

Unlike England, France had no single institutional focus for resistance to royal power. A strong-willed and able ruler, as Louis XIV proved to be, could counter challenges to royal power, particularly when he satisfied the ambitions of aristocrats and those bureaucrats who profited from the expansion of royal power.

## France Under Louis XIV, 1661–1715

Louis XIV fully assumed control of government in 1661, at a propitious moment. The Peace of the Pyrenees in 1659 had ended, in France's favor, the wars with Spain that had dragged on since the end of the Thirty Years' War. As part of the peace agreement, Louis married a Spanish princess, Maria Theresa. In the first ten years of his active reign, Louis achieved a degree of control over the mechanisms of government unparalleled in the history of monarchy in France or anywhere else in Europe. Louis was an extremely vigorous and diligent king. He put in hours a day at a desk, while sustaining the ceremonial life of the court, with its elaborate hunts, balls, and other public events.

### Government Reforms

Louis did not invent any new bureaucratic devices, but rather used existing ranks of officials in new ways that increased government efficiency and further centralized control. He radically reduced the number of men in his High Council, the advisory body closest to the king, to include only three or four great ministers of state affairs. This intimate group, with Louis's active participation, handled all policymaking. The ministers of state, war, and finance were chosen exclusively from non-noble men of bourgeois origin, whose training and experience fitted them for such positions. Jean-Baptiste Colbert (coal-BEAR) (1619–1683), perhaps the greatest of them, served as minister of finance and supervised most domestic policy from 1665 until his death. He was from a merchant family and had served for years under Mazarin.

Several dozen other officials, picked from the ranks of up-and-coming lawyers and administrators, drew up laws and regulations and passed them to the intendants for execution at the provincial level. Sometimes these officials at the center were sent to the provinces on short-term supervisory missions. The effect of this system was to bypass many entrenched provincial bureaucrats, particularly those known as tax farmers. Tax farmers were freelance

## CHRONOLOGY

| | |
|---|---|
| 1602 | Dutch East India Company formed |
| 1607 | Jamestown colony founded in Virginia |
| 1608 | Champlain founds Quebec City |
| 1613 | Michael becomes first Romanov tsar in Russia |
| 1620 | Pilgrims settle at Plymouth (Massachusetts) |
| 1642–1648 | Civil war in England |
| 1643 | Louis XIV becomes king of France |
| 1648–1653 | Fronde revolts in France |
| 1649 | Execution of Charles I |
| 1649–1660 | English Commonwealth |
| 1659 | Peace of the Pyrenees |
| 1660 | Monarchy restored in England |
| 1661 | Louis XIV assumes full control of government |
| 1672–1678 | Dutch War |
| 1682 | Peter the Great becomes tsar of Russia |
| 1685 | Edict of Nantes revoked |
| 1688 | Glorious Revolution |
| 1699 | Treaty of Carlowitz |
| 1700–1721 | Great Northern War |
| 1701–1714 | War of the Spanish Succession |
| 1713 | Peace of Utrecht |
| 1715 | Death of Louis XIV |

businessmen who bid for the right to collect taxes in a region in return for a negotiated fee they paid to the Crown. The Crown, in short, did not control its own tax revenues. The money Louis's regime saved by the more efficient collection of taxes (revenues almost doubled in some areas) enabled the government to streamline the bureaucracy: Dozens of the offices created over the years to bring cash in were bought back by the Crown from their owners.

The system still relied on the bonds of patronage and personal service—political bonds borrowed from aristocratic life. Officials rose through the ranks by means of service to the great, and family connection and personal loyalty still were essential. Of the seventeen different men who were part of Louis XIV's High Council during his reign, five were members of the Colbert family, for example.

## Economic Development

Colbert and the other ministers began to develop the kind of planned government policy-making that we now take for granted. Partly by means of their itinerant supervisory officials, they tried to formulate policy based on carefully collected information. How many men of military age were available? How abundant was this year's harvest? Answers to such questions enabled not only the formulation of economic policy, but also the deliberate management of production and services to achieve certain goals—above all, the recruitment and supply of the king's vast armies.

Colbert actively encouraged France's economic development in other ways. He reduced the internal tolls and customs barriers, which were relics of medieval landholders' rights. He encouraged industry with state subsidies and protective tariffs. He set up state-sponsored trading companies—the two most important being the East India Company and the West India Company, established in 1664.

**Mercantilism** is the term historians use to describe the theory behind Colbert's efforts. This economic theory stressed self-sufficiency in manufactured goods, tight control of trade to foster the domestic economy, and the absolute value of bullion. Both capital for development—in the form of hard currency, known as bullion—and the amount of world trade were presumed to be limited in quantity. Therefore, state intervention in the form of protectionist policies was believed necessary to guarantee a favorable balance of payments.

This static model of national wealth did not wholly fit the facts of growing international trade in the seventeenth century. Nevertheless, mercantilist philosophy was helpful to France. France became self-sufficient in the all-important production of woolen cloth, and French industry expanded notably in other sectors. Colbert's greatest success was the systematic expansion of the navy and merchant marine. By the end of Louis XIV's reign, the French navy was virtually the equal of the English navy.

**mercantilism** Economic policy pursued by western European states in the seventeenth and eighteenth centuries that stressed self-sufficiency in manufactured goods, tight government control of trade, and the absolute value of bullion.

## Religious Life

Beginning in 1673, Louis tried to bring the religious life of the realm more fully under royal control. He claimed some of the church revenues and powers of ecclesiastical appointment within France that the pope still exercised. Partly to bolster his position with the pope, he also began to attack the Huguenot community in France. First, he offered financial rewards for conversion to Catholicism. Then, he took more drastic steps, such as destroying Protestant churches and quartering troops in Huguenots' homes to force them to convert. In 1685, he revoked the Edict of Nantes. A hundred thousand Protestant subjects—including some six hundred army and navy officers—refused even nominal conversion to Catholicism and chose to emigrate.

Meanwhile, Louis faced resistance to his claims against the pope from within the ranks of French Catholics. These laypeople and clerics represented a movement within French Catholicism known as Jansenism, after Cornelius Jansen, a professor of theology whose writings inspired it. Jansenists practiced an austere style of Catholic religiosity that was akin to some Protestant doctrine in its notions about human will and sinfulness. Louis was wary of any challenge to either the institutional or symbolic unity of his regime and was particularly suspicious of Jansenism because its adherents included many of his political enemies, particularly among families of parlement officials. Late in Louis's reign, another pope obligingly declared many Jansenist doctrines to be heretical as part of a compromise agreement with Louis on matters of church governance and finance.

Despite these successes, the power of the Crown was still greatly limited by modern standards. The "divine right" of kingship, a notion formulated by Louis's chief apologist, Bishop Jacques Bossuet (BOS-soo-way) (1627–1704), did not mean unlimited power to rule; rather, it meant that hereditary monarchy was the divinely ordained form of government, best suited to human needs. *Absolutism* was not iron-fisted control of the realm, but rather the successful focusing of energy, loyalties, and symbolic authority in the Crown. The government functioned well in the opening decades of Louis's reign because his role as the focal point of power and loyalty was both logical, after the preceding years of unrest, and skillfully exploited. Much of the glue holding together the absolutist state lay in informal mechanisms, such as patronage and court life, as well as in the traditional hunt for military glory—all of which Louis amply supplied.

## The Life of the Court

An observer comparing the lives of prominent noble families in the mid-sixteenth and mid-seventeenth centuries would have noticed striking differences. By the second half of the seventeenth century, most sovereigns or territorial princes had the power to crush revolts. The nobility relinquished its former independence but retained economic and social supremacy and, as a consequence, considerable political clout. Nobles also developed new ways to symbolize their privilege by means of cultural refinement. This process was particularly dramatic in France.

One sign of Louis's success in marshaling the loyalty of the aristocracy was the brilliant court life that his regime sustained. No longer able to wield independent political power, aristocrats lived at court whenever they could. There, they competed for patronage and prestige—for commands in the royal army and for honorific positions at court itself. A favored courtier might, for example, participate in the elaborate daily *lever* (LEV-ay) (arising) of the king; he might be allowed to hand the king his shirt—a demeaning task, yet a coveted one for the access to the king that it guaranteed. Courtiers now defended their honor with private duels, not warfare, and relied on precise etiquette and clever conversation to mark their political and social distinctiveness. Wrote one critic from his court, "he felt that of real favors he had not enough to bestow; in order to keep up the spirit of devotion he therefore unceasingly invented all sorts of ideal ones, little preferences and petty distinctions, which answered his purpose well."* (See the feature, "The Visual Record: Table Manners" on pages 458–459.)

Noblewomen and noblemen alike began to reflect on their new roles in letters, memoirs, and the first novels. A prominent theme of these works is the increasing need for a truly private life of affection and trust, with which to counterbalance the public façade necessary to an aspiring courtier. The most influential early French novel was *The Princess of Clèves* by Marie-Madeleine Pioche de la Vergne (1634–1693), best known by her title, Madame de Lafayette. Mme. de Lafayette's novel treats the particular difficulties faced by aristocratic women who, without military careers to bring glory and provide distraction, were more vulnerable than men to gossip and slander at court and more trapped by their arranged marriages.

Louis XIV's court is usually associated with the palace he built at Versailles (vare-SIGH), southwest of Paris. Some of the greatest talent of the day worked on the design and construction of Versailles from 1670 through the 1680s. It became a masterpiece of luxurious but restrained baroque style—a model for royal and aristocratic palaces throughout Europe for the next one hundred years.

Before Louis's court, in his later years, withdrew to Versailles, it traveled among the king's other châteaux around the kingdom, and in this itinerant period, court life was actually at its most creative. These early years of Louis's personal reign were the heyday of French drama. The comedian Jean-Baptiste Poquelin, known as Molière (mole-YARE) (1622–1673),

---

*Duc de Saint-Simon, *Memoirs*, trans. Bayle St. John (London: Swan Sonnonschein & Co., 1900) p. 364.

## Table Manners

If you were to sit down in a fancy restaurant, order a juicy steak, and then eat it with your bare hands, other diners would undoubtedly stare, shocked by your bad manners. It has not always been the case that table manners meant very much—were able to signal social status, for example. In fact, table manners did not always exist at all in the sense that we know them. How did they evolve? How did they come to have the importance that they do? And why should historians pay any attention to them?

Imagine that you have been invited to dinner at a noble estate in the year 1500. As you sit down, you notice that there are no knives, forks, or spoons at your place, and no napkins either. A servant (a young girl from a neighboring village) sets a roast of meat in front of you and your fellow diners. The lords and ladies on either side of you hack off pieces of meat with the knives that they always carry with them, and then they eat the meat with their fingers. Hunks of bread on the table in front of them catch the dripping juices.

One hundred fifty years later, in 1650, dinner is a much more "civilized" meal. Notice the well-to-do women dining in this engraving by the French artist Abraham Bosse (1602–1676). The table setting, with tablecloths, napkins, plates, and silverware, is recognizable to us. The lady at the extreme right holds up her fork and napkin in a somewhat forced and obvious gesture. These diners have the utensils that we take for granted, but the artist does not take them for granted: They are intended to be noticed by Bosse's elite audience.

In the seventeenth century, aristocrats and gentry signaled their political and social privilege with behavior that distinguished them from the lower classes in ways their more powerful ancestors had found unnecessary. Historians have called this the invention of civility. As we have seen, proper courtesy to one's superiors at court was considered essential. Rituals of honor and deference were increasingly taking the place of armed conflict as the routine behavior of the upper classes. Also essential, however, were certain standards of physical privacy and delicacy. Something as seemingly trivial as the use of a fork became charged with symbolic significance. As the actual power of the aristocrats was circumscribed by the state, they found new expressions of status. Since the sixteenth century, new

kinds of manners had been touted in handbooks, reflecting changes that already had occurred at Italian courts. During the seventeenth century, these practices became more widespread and opened up a gulf between upper- and lower-class behavior.

Some of the new behaviors concerned bodily privacy and discretion. A nobleman now used a handkerchief instead of his fingers or coat sleeve, and he did not urinate in public. The new "rules" about eating are particularly interesting. Why did eating with a fork seem refined and desirable to aristocrats trying to buttress their own self-images? As any 3-year-old knows, eating with a fork is remarkably inefficient.

Using a fork kept you at a distance—literal and symbolic—from the animal you were eating. Napkins wiped away all trace of bloody juices from your lips. Interestingly, as diners began to use utensils, other eating arrangements changed in parallel ways. Sideboards had been in use for a long time, but pieces of meat were now discreetly carved on the sideboard and presented to diners in individual portions. The carcass was brought to the sideboard cut into roasts instead of unmistakably whole, and it was often decorated—as it is today—to further disguise it.

The new aristocrat was increasingly separated from the world of brute physical force, both in daily life and on the battlefield. In warfare, brute force was no longer adequate. Training, discipline, and tactical knowledge were more important and heightened the significance of rank, which separated officers from the vast numbers of common soldiers. Aristocrats now lived in a privileged world where violence—except for an occasional duel—was no longer a fact of life. Their new behavior codes signaled their new invulnerability to others. Above all, they worked to transform a loss—of the independence that had gone hand in hand with a more violent life—into a gain: a privileged immunity to violence.

Specific manners became important, then, because they were symbols of power. The symbolic distance between the powerful and the humble was reinforced by other changes in habits and behavior. A sixteenth-century warrior customarily traveled on horseback and often went from place to place within a city on foot, attended by his retinue. A seventeenth-century aristocrat was more likely to travel in a horse-drawn carriage. The presence of special

impressed the young Louis with his productions in the late 1650s and was rewarded with the use of a theater in the main royal palace in Paris. Like Shakespeare earlier in the century, Molière explored the social and political tensions of his day. He satirized the pretensions of the aristocracy and the social climbing of the bourgeoisie. Some of his plays were banned, but most were not only tolerated but extremely popular with the elite audiences they mocked. Their popularity is testimony to the confidence of Louis's regime in its early days.

Also popular at court were the tragedies of Jean Racine (rah-SEEN) (1639–1699), who was to the French theater what Shakespeare was to the English: the master of poetic language. His plays focus on the emotional and psychological lives of the characters and stress the unpredictable, usually unhappy, role of fate, even among royalty. The pessimism in Racine foreshadowed the less successful second half of Louis's reign.

**Table Manners of the Upper Class in the Seventeenth Century**

commodities from abroad—such as sugar—in the seventeenth century created further possibilities for signaling status.

It is interesting to note that other personal habits still diverged dramatically from what we would consider acceptable today. Notice the large, stately bed in the same room as the dining table in Bosse's engraving. Interior space was still undifferentiated by our standards, and it was common for eating, talking, sleeping, and estate management all to go on in a single room. The grand bed is in the picture because, like the fork, it is a mark of status. Like virtually everything else, what is "proper" varies with historical circumstance.

### Questions

1. *Why did elites become interested in table manners in the seventeenth century?*

2. *How did manners function as effective symbols of power?*

## The Burdens of War and the Limits of Power

Louis XIV started wars that dominated the attention of most European states in the second half of the seventeenth century. His wars sprang from traditional causes: the importance of the glory and dynastic aggrandizement of the king and the preoccupation of the aristocracy with military life. But if Louis's wars had familiar motives, they were far more demanding on state resources than any previous wars.

The new offensive tactics developed during the Thirty Years' War (see page 438) changed the character of armies in ways that demanded more resources for training. A higher proportion of soldiers became gunners, and their effectiveness lay in how well they operated as a unit. Armies began to train seriously off the field of battle because drill and discipline were

459

vital to success. France's victories in the second half of the seventeenth century are partly traceable to the regime's attention to these tasks, as well as to recruitment and supply, which together constituted another phase of the "military revolution." The numbers of men on the battlefield increased somewhat as training increased the effectiveness of large numbers of infantry, but the total numbers of men in arms supported by the state at any time increased dramatically once the organization to support them was in place. Late in the century, France kept more than 300,000 men in arms when at war (which was most of the time).

In 1667, Louis invoked rather dubious dynastic claims to demand from Spain lands in the Spanish Netherlands and the large independent county on France's eastern border called the Franche-Comté (FRAWNSH–con-TAY) (see **Map 16.1**). After a brief conflict, the French obtained only some towns in the Spanish Netherlands.

Louis's focus then shifted to a new enemy, the Dutch. The Dutch had been allied with France since the beginning of their existence as provinces in rebellion against Spain. But the French now turned against them because of Dutch dominance of seaborne trade in the growing international economy. At first, the French tried to offset the Dutch advantage with tariff barriers against Dutch goods. But confidence in the French army led Louis's generals to urge action against the vulnerable Dutch lands. "It is impossible that his Majesty should tolerate any longer the insolence and arrogance of that nation," rationalized the usually pragmatic Colbert in 1670.*

The Dutch War began in 1672, with Louis personally leading one of the largest armies ever fielded in Europe—perhaps 120,000 men. The English had also fought the Dutch over

*Quoted in D. H. Pennington, *Europe in the Seventeenth Century*, 2d ed. (London: Longman, 1989), p. 508.

**Versailles Palace, The Hall of Mirrors** This ornate gallery, more than 75 yards long, connects the two wings of the palace. Seventeen huge windows and opposing walled mirrors flood the gallery with light. In addition to these dramatic effects, the designers included many thematic details, such as miniature fleur-de-lys entwined with suns to symbolize the union of France and Louis, in the gilded work near the ceiling. Réunion des musées nationaux/Art Resource, NY trade in the 1650s and now Louis secretly paid the English king, Charles II, to join an alliance against the Dutch.

At first, the French were spectacularly successful, but the Dutch opened dikes and flooded the countryside, and the land war became a soggy stalemate. At the same time, the Dutch beat combined English and French forces at sea and gathered allies who felt threatened by Louis's aggression. The French soon faced German and Austrian forces along their frontier, and by 1674, the English had joined the alliance against France as well. A negotiated peace in 1678 gave France further territory areas in the Spanish Netherlands, as well as control of the Franche-Comté, but it was an illusion of victory only.

Ensconced at Versailles since 1682, Louis seemed to be at the height of his powers. Yet, the Dutch War had in fact cost him more than he had gained. Reforms in government and finance ended under the pressure of paying for war, and old habits of borrowing money and selling offices were revived. Other government obligations, such as encouraging overseas trade, were neglected. Colbert's death in 1683 dramatically symbolized the end of an era of innovation in the French regime.

## The Nine Years' War

A new war, now known as the Nine Years' War, or King William's War, was touched off late in 1688 by a French invasion of Germany to claim an inheritance there. In his ongoing dispute with the pope, Louis also seized the papal territory of Avignon (ah-veen-YOHN) in southern France. Boldest of all, he helped the exiled Catholic claimant to the English crown, James II, mount an invasion to reclaim his throne (see page 467). Louis's unforgiving Dutch opponent, William of Orange, king of England from 1689 to 1702, led an alliance of all the major powers—Spain, the Netherlands, England, Austria, and the major German states—against the French. As with the Dutch War, the Nine Years' War was costly and, on most fronts, inconclusive. This time, though, there was no illusion of victory for Louis. In the Treaty of Ryswick (1697), Louis gave up most of the territories he had claimed or seized, as well as his contentious claim to papal revenues. The terrible burden of war taxes, combined with crop failures in 1693 and 1694, caused widespread starvation in the countryside. French courtiers began to criticize Louis openly.

## The War of the Spanish Succession

The final and most devastating war of Louis's reign, called the War of the Spanish Succession, broke out in 1701. It was a straightforward dynastic clash between France and its perennial enemy, the Habsburgs. Both Louis and Habsburg Holy Roman emperor Leopold I (r. 1657–1705) hoped to claim, for their heirs, the throne of Spain, left open at the death in 1700 of the last Spanish Habsburg, Charles II. Charles II bequeathed the throne to Louis's grandson, Philip of Anjou, by reason of Louis's marriage to the Spanish princess Maria Theresa and Philip had quickly entered Spain to claim his new kingdom. War was made inevitable when, in an act of sheer belligerence, Louis renounced one of the conditions of Charles's will: Philip's accession to the throne of Spain, Louis insisted, did not prevent his becoming king of France as well. The Dutch and English responded to the prospect of so great a disruption of the balance of power in Europe by allying with the emperor against France. The Dutch and English also wanted to defend their colonial interests, since the French had already begun to profit from new trading opportunities with the Spanish colonies.

Again, the French fought a major war on several fronts on land and at sea. Again, the people of France felt the cost in crushing taxes that multiplied the effects of harvest failures. Major revolts inside France forced Louis to divert troops from the war. For a time, it seemed that the French would be soundly defeated, but they were saved by the superior organization of their forces and by dynastic accident: Unexpected deaths in the Habsburg family meant that the Austrian claimant to the Spanish throne suddenly was poised to inherit rule of Austria and the empire as well. The English, more afraid of a revival of unified Habsburg control of Spain and Austria than of French domination of Spain, quickly called for peace negotiations.

The Peace of Utrecht in 1713 helped to set the agenda of European politics for the eighteenth century. Philip of Anjou was recognized as Philip V, the first Bourbon king of Spain, but

🌐 **Map 16.1 Territorial Gains of Louis XIV, 1667–1715** Louis's wars, though enormously expensive for France, produced only modest gains of territory along France's eastern and northern frontiers.

on the condition that the Spanish and French crowns would never be worn by the same monarch. To maintain the balance of power against French interests, the Spanish Netherlands and Spanish territories in Italy were ceded by a second treaty in 1714 to Austria, which for many decades would be France's major continental rival. The Peace of Utrecht also marked the beginning of England's dominance of overseas trade and colonization. The French gave to England certain lands in Canada and the Caribbean and renounced any privileged relationship with Spanish colonies. England was allowed to control the highly profitable slave trade with Spanish colonies.

Louis XIV had added small pieces of territory along France's eastern border (see **Map 16.1**), and a Bourbon ruled in Spain. But the costs in human life and resources were great for the slim results achieved. The army and navy had swallowed up capital that might have fueled investment and trade; strategic opportunities overseas were lost, never to be regained. Louis's government had been innovative in its early years but remained constrained by traditional ways of imagining the interest of the state.

## SECTION SUMMARY

- The Fronde were revolts against royal power early in Louis XIV's reign.
- Louis successfully rebuilt royal power using control of taxation, a reformed bureaucracy, and traditional political bonds, such as aristocratic patronage.
- The power Louis wielded has been labeled "absolutism" because there were no formal institutional limits on his authority.
- Court life in Louis's reign sponsored artistic creativity and encouraged a new emphasis on cultural refinement in the aristocracy.
- Louis started a series of costly wars from which the French state gained little.

# The English Civil War and Its Aftermath

*What were the long-term consequences of the English civil war?*

In England, unlike in France, a representative institution—**Parliament**—became an effective, permanent brake on royal authority. The process by which Parliament gained a secure role in governing the kingdom was neither easy nor peaceful, however. As we saw in Chapter 15, conflicts between the English crown and its subjects, culminating in the Crown-Parliament conflict, concerned control over taxation and the direction of religious reform. Beginning in 1642, England was beset by civil war between royal and parliamentary forces. The king was eventually defeated and executed, and for a time, the monarchy was abolished altogether. It was restored in 1660, but Parliament retained a crucial role in governing the kingdom—a role that was confirmed when, in 1688, it again deposed a monarch and established limits on future monarchs' power.

> **Parliament** English legislative institution, which used control over monies to bargain with the Crown over foreign and domestic policies, leading to civil war and the deposition of Charles I.

## Civil War, 1642–1649

Fighting broke out between the armies of Charles I and parliamentary armies in the late summer of 1642. The Long Parliament (see page 434) continued to represent a broad coalition of critics and opponents of the monarchy, ranging from aristocrats, concerned primarily with abuses of royal prerogative, to radical Puritans, eager for thorough religious reform and determined to defeat the king. Fighting was halfhearted initially, and the tide of war at first favored Charles.

In 1643, however, the scope of the war broadened. Charles made peace with Irish rebels and brought Irish troops to England to bolster his armies. Parliament, in turn, received military aid from the Scots in exchange for promises that Presbyterianism would become the religion of England. Meanwhile, **Oliver Cromwell** (1599–1658), a Puritan member of the Long Parliament and a cavalry officer, helped reorganize parliamentary forces. The eleven-hundred-man cavalry, trained by Cromwell and known as the "Ironsides" and supported by parliamentary and Scottish infantry, defeated the king's troops at Marston Moor in July 1644. The victory made Cromwell famous.

> **Oliver Cromwell** English Puritan general, during the English civil war, who governed as Lord Protector during the interregnum from 1653 to 1658.

Shortly afterward, Parliament further improved its forces by creating the New Model Army, rigorously trained like Cromwell's Ironsides. Sitting members of Parliament were barred from commanding troops; hence, upper-class control of the army was reduced. This army played a decisive role not only in the war but also in the political settlement that followed the fighting.

The New Model Army won a convincing victory over royal forces at Naseby in 1645. In the spring of 1646, Charles surrendered to a Scottish army in the north. In January 1647, Parliament paid the Scots for their services in the war and took the king into custody. In the negotiations that followed, Charles tried to play his opponents off against one another, and, as he had hoped, divisions among them widened.

Most members of Parliament were Presbyterians, Puritan gentry who favored a strongly unified and state-controlled church along Calvinist lines. They wanted peace with the king in return for acceptance of the new church structure and parliamentary control of standing militias for a specified period. They did not favor wider political changes, such as extending the right to vote to ordinary people. These men were increasingly alarmed by the appearance of multiple religious sects and by the actual religious freedom that many ordinary people were claiming for themselves. With the weakening of royal authority and the disruption of civil war, censorship was relaxed, and public preaching by ordinary men, and even women, who felt divinely inspired was becoming commonplace.

Above all, Presbyterian gentry in Parliament feared more radical groups in the army and in London who had supported them up to this point but who favored more sweeping political and religious change. Most officers of the New Model Army, such as Cromwell, were Independents, Puritans who, unlike the Presbyterians, favored a decentralized church, a degree of religious toleration, and a wider sharing of political power among men of property, not just among the very wealthy gentry. In London, a well-organized artisans' movement known as the "Levellers" went even further; Levellers favored universal manhood suffrage, equality under the law, better access to education, and decentralized churches—in short, the separation of political power from wealth and virtual freedom of religion. Many of the rank and file of the army were deeply influenced by Leveller ideas.

In May 1647, the majority in Parliament voted to offer terms to the king and to disband the New Model Army—without first paying most of the soldiers' back wages. This move provoked the first direct intervention by the army in politics. Representatives of the soldiers were chosen to present grievances to Parliament; when this failed, the army seized the king and, in August, occupied Westminster, Parliament's meeting place. Independent and Leveller elements in the army debated the direction of possible reform to be imposed on Parliament. Leveller representatives argued for universal manhood suffrage while Independents called for political rights to be limited to men of property (see the feature, "The Written Record: The Putney Debates" on page 465).

In November, however, their common enemy Charles escaped from his captors and raised a new army with his former enemies, the Scots, who were also alarmed by the growing radicalism in England. Civil war began again early in 1648. Although it ended quickly with a victory by Cromwell and the New Model Army in August, the renewed war further hardened political divisions and enhanced the power of the army. The king was widely blamed for the renewed bloodshed, and the army did not trust him to keep any agreement he might now sign. When Parliament, still dominated by Presbyterians, once again voted to negotiate with the king, army troops, led by Colonel Thomas Pride, prevented members who favored Presbyterianism or negotiating with the king from attending sessions. The "Rump" Parliament that remained after "Pride's Purge" voted to try the king. A hasty trial followed and, on January 30, 1649, Charles I was executed for "treason, tyranny and bloodshed" against his people.

## The Interregnum, 1649–1660

A Commonwealth—a republic—was declared. Executive power resided in a council of state. The House of Lords was abolished and legislative power resided in the one-chamber Rump Parliament. Declaring a republic proved far easier than running one, however. The execution of the king shocked most English and Scots and alienated many elites from the new regime. The legitimacy of the Commonwealth government would always be in question.

The tasks of making and implementing policy were hindered by the narrow political base on which the government now rested. Excluded were the majority of the reformist Presbyterian or Anglican gentry who had been purged from Parliament. Also excluded were the more radical Levellers; Leveller leaders in London were arrested when they published tracts critical of the new government. Within a few years, many disillusioned Levellers would join a new religious movement called the Society of Friends, or Quakers, which espoused complete religious autonomy. Quakers declined all oaths or service to the state, and they refused to acknowledge social rank.

Above all, the new government was vulnerable to the power of the army, which had created it. In 1649 and 1650, Cromwell led punitive expeditions to Ireland and Scotland, partly for sheer revenge and partly to put down resistance to Commonwealth authority. In Ireland, where Cromwell's forces were particularly ruthless, the English dispossessed more Irish landholders, which served to pay off the army's wages. Meanwhile, Parliament could not agree on systematic reforms, particularly the one reform Independents in the army insisted on: more broadly based elections for a new Parliament. Fresh from his victories, Cromwell led his armies to London and dissolved Parliament in the spring of 1652.

In 1653, a cadre of army officers drew up the "Instrument of Government," England's first—and still, today, only—written constitution. It provided for an executive, the Lord Protector, and a Parliament to be based on somewhat wider male suffrage. Cromwell was the natural choice for Lord Protector. Cromwell was an extremely able leader who was not averse to compromise, either in politics or religion. He believed in a state church but, unlike his Presbyterian opponents, one that allowed for local control, including choice of minister,

## The Putney Debates

*In October 1647 representatives of the Leveller movement in the army ranks confronted Independents—largely comprising the officer corps—in formally staged debates in a church at Putney, outside London. In this exchange, the Leveller representative, Thomas Rainsborough, advocates universal manhood suffrage, whereas Cromwell's fellow officer, Henry Ireton, argues for a more restricted franchise. The staging of the debates reflects the importance of the army in deciding the scope of constitutional change in England at this moment of extraordinary political fluidity. Even more important were the views that were aired at the debates, which had in common the assertion that government should exist only by the consent of the governed. These ideas became reality very slowly. The poorest men (and all women) did not get the vote in Britain until the twentieth century.*

**Rainsborough**:. . . Really I think that the poorest he that is in England hath a life to live as the greatest he; and therefore truly, sir, I think it's clear, that every man that is to live under a government ought first by his own consent to put himself under that government; and I do think that the poorest man in England is not at all bound in a strict sense to that government that he hath not had a voice to put himself under; and I am confident that, when I have heard the reasons against it, that something will be said to answer those reasons, insomuch that I should doubt whether I was an Englishman or no, that should doubt of these things.

**Ireton**:. . . I think that no person hath a right to an interest or share in the disposing of the affairs of the kingdom, and in determining or choosing those that shall determine what laws we shall be ruled by here, no person hath a right to this that hath not a permanent fixed interest in this kingdom, and those persons together are properly the represented of this kingdom, who taken together, and consequently are to make up the representers of this kingdom, are the representers, who taken together do comprehend whatsoever is of real or permanent interest in the kingdom, and I am sure there is otherwise (I cannot tell what), otherwise any man can say why a foreigner coming in amongst us, or as many as will be coming in amongst us, or by force or otherwise settling themselves here, or at least by our permission having

a being here, why they should not as well lay claim to it as any other. We talk of birthright. Truly birthright there is thus much claim: men may justly have by birthright, by their very being born in England, that we should not seclude them out of England. That we should not refuse to give them air and place and ground, and the freedom of the highways and other things, to live amongst us, not any man that is born here, though he in birth, or by his birth there come nothing at all that is part of the permanent interest of this kingdom to him. That I think is due to a man by birth. But that by a man's being born here he shall have a share in that power that shall dispose of the lands here, and of all things here, I do not think it a sufficient ground, but I am sure if we look upon that which is the utmost, within man's view, of what was originally the constitution of this kingdom, upon that which is most radical and fundamental, and which if you take away, there is no man hath any land, any goods, you take away any civil interest, and that is this: that those that choose the representers for the making of laws by which this state and kingdom are to be governed, are the persons who taken together, do comprehend the local interest of this kingdom; that is, the persons in whom all land lies, and those in corporations in whom all trading lies. This is the most fundamental constitution of this kingdom, and which if you do not allow, you allow none at all.

### Questions

1. *On what grounds does Henry Ireton argue for restricting the right to participate in government? How does he counter Rainsborough's more sweeping claim that all men should be governed only with their own consent?*

2. *What social, religious, economic, and political conditions prevalent in seventeenth-century England help us to explain the origins of these ideas?*

3. *In what ways might the Putney debates have been important, even though the ideas aired in them were not enacted, in the main, for centuries to come?*

Source: From *The Levellers in the English Revolution*, edited by G. E. Aylmer, pp. 100–101. © 1975 G. E. Aylmer, reprinted by kind permission of Thames & Hudson Ltd., London.

by individual congregations. He also believed in toleration for Catholics and Jews, as long as no one disturbed the peace.

As Lord Protector, Cromwell oversaw impressive reforms in law that reflected his belief in the limits of governing authority. For example, contrary to the practice of his day, he opposed capital punishment for petty crimes. The government of the Protectorate, however, accomplished little, given Parliament's internal divisions. The population at large still harbored royalist sympathizers; after a royalist uprising in 1655, Cromwell divided England into military districts and vested governing authority in army generals.

Mary Evans Picture Library/The Image Works

**Popular Preaching in England** Many women took advantage of the collapse of royal authority to preach in public—a radical activity for women at the time. This print satirizes the Quakers, a religious movement that attracted many women.

After Cromwell died of a sudden illness in September 1658, the Protectorate could not survive the strains over policy and the challenges to its legitimacy. In February 1660, the decisive action of one army general enabled all the surviving members of the Long Parliament to rejoin the Rump. The Parliament summarily dissolved itself and called for new elections. The newly elected Parliament recalled Charles II, son of Charles I, from exile abroad and restored the monarchy. The chaos and radicalism of the late civil war and "interregnum"—the period between reigns, as the years from 1649 to 1660 came to be called—now spawned a conservative reaction.

## The Restoration, 1660–1685

Charles II (r. 1660–1685) claimed his throne at the age of 30. He had learned from his years of uncertain exile and from the fate of his father. He did not seek retribution but rather offered a general pardon to all but a few rebels (mostly those who had signed his father's death warrant), and he suggested to Parliament a relatively tolerant religious settlement that would include Anglicans as well as Presbyterians.

That the reestablished royal government was not more tolerant than it turned out to be was not Charles's doing, initially, but Parliament's. During the 1660s, the "Cavalier" Parliament, named for royalists in the civil war, passed harsh laws aimed at religious dissenters. Anglican orthodoxy was reimposed, including the reestablishment of bishops and the Anglican Book of Common Prayer. All officeholders and clergy were required to swear oaths of obedience to the king and to the established church. As a result, hundreds of non-Anglican Protestants were forced out of office. Holding nonconformist religious services became illegal, and Parliament passed a "five-mile" act to prevent dissenting ministers even from traveling near their former churches. Property laws were tightened and the criminal codes made more severe.

The king's behavior, however, began to mimic prerevolutionary royalist positions. Charles II began to flirt with Catholicism, and his brother and heir, James, openly converted. Charles promulgated a declaration of tolerance that would have included Catholics, as well as nonconformist Protestants, but Parliament would not accept it. In 1678, Charles's secret treaties with the French became known (see page 461), and rumors of a Catholic plot to murder Charles and reimpose Catholicism became widespread. No firm evidence of the "Popish Plot" was ever unearthed, although thirty-five people were executed for alleged participation. Parliament passed the Test Act, which barred all but Anglicans from public office. As a result, the Catholic James was forced to resign as Lord High Admiral.

When Parliament then moved to exclude James from succession to the throne, Charles dissolved it. A subsequent Parliament, worried by the possibility of a new civil war, backed down. But the legacy of the previous civil war and interregnum was a potent one. After two decades of religious pluralism and broadly based political activity, it was impossible to reimpose religious conformity or to silence all dissent, even with harsh new laws on the books. It was also impossible to silence Parliament. Though reluctant to press too far, Parliament tried to assert its policies against the desires of the king.

However, by the end of his reign, Charles was financially independent of Parliament, thanks to increased revenue from overseas trade and secret subsidies from France, his recent ally against the Dutch. If he had been followed by an able successor, Parliament might have lost a good measure of its confidence and independence. But his brother James's reign and its aftermath further enhanced Parliament's power.

## The Glorious Revolution, 1688

When James II (r. 1685–1689) succeeded Charles, Parliament was wary but initially cooperative. For example, it granted James customs duties for life, as well as funds to suppress a rebellion by one of Charles's illegitimate sons. James did not try to impose Catholicism on England as some had feared, but he did try to achieve toleration for Catholics in two declarations of indulgence in 1687 and 1688. However admirable his goal—toleration—he had essentially changed the law of the realm without Parliament's consent. He further undermined his position with heavy-handed tactics. When several leading Anglican bishops refused to read the declarations from their pulpits, he had them imprisoned and tried for seditious libel. However, a sympathetic jury acquitted them.

James also failed because of the coincidence of other events. In 1685, at the outset of James's reign, Louis XIV of France had revoked the Edict of Nantes. The possibility that subjects and monarchs in France and, by extension, elsewhere could be of different faiths seemed increasingly unlikely. Popular fears of James's Catholicism were thus heightened early in his reign, and his later declarations of tolerance, though they benefited Protestant dissenters too, were viewed with suspicion. Moreover, in Ireland, where Catholics had been subjugated by Protestant settlers and royal policies in previous reigns, James set about reversing the tide—most ominously, from the English perspective, by purging the Irish army of Protestants. Then, in 1688, the king's second wife, who was Catholic, gave birth to a son. The birth raised the specter of a Catholic succession. (James had two Protestant daughters by his first marriage, but a son would have the first claim on the throne.)

In June 1688, leading members of Parliament invited William of Orange, husband of James's Protestant daughter, Mary, to come to England to "preserve and maintain established laws, liberties and customs"—meaning, to support Parliamentary resistance to James. William's own interests as a leader in the Netherlands (see below, page 476) included influencing British policy away from an alliance with his nemesis, France. William mounted an invasion that became a rout when James abandoned his capital, then sought protection in France. William called Parliament, which declared the throne to be vacant and offered the throne jointly to him and to Mary. With French support, James invaded the British Isles in 1690 but was defeated by William's forces at the Battle of Boyne, in Ireland, that year.

The substitution of William (r. 1689–1702) and Mary (r. 1689–1694) for James, known as the **Glorious Revolution**, was engineered by Parliament and confirmed its power. Parliament presented the new sovereigns with a Declaration of Rights upon their accession in 1689 and, later that year, with a Bill of Rights that defended freedom of speech, called for frequent Parliaments, and required all future monarchs to be Protestant. Parliament's role in the political process was ensured by its power of the purse, since William called Parliament frequently to seek funds for his ambitious military efforts, particularly the Netherlands' ongoing wars with France.

The issues that had faced the English since the beginning of the century were common to all European states: religious division and elite power, fiscal strains and resistance to taxation. Yet, the cataclysmic events in England—the interregnum, the Commonwealth, the Restoration, the Glorious Revolution—had set it apart from other states. A representative institution had become a partner of the monarchy.

**Glorious Revolution**
Political coup in Britain in 1688–1689 in which Parliament replaced the Catholic King James II with William (of Orange) and his wife, Mary (James's Protestant daughter), and imposed on the new rulers a Bill of Rights that confirmed Parliament's power.

## SECTION SUMMARY

- In England, unlike in France, a representative institution controlled taxation and could effectively challenge royal policies.

- A civil war between Charles I and parliamentary forces ended with the defeat and execution of the king in 1649.

- Several groups, including wealthy gentry and ordinary townspeople, had allied to support Parliament, but they did not agree on a program of political and religious reform.

- The government of the interregnum did not last after the death of the Lord Protector, Oliver Cromwell, because too few of the original supporters of Parliament believed it legitimate or approved of its policies.

- The Crown was restored under Charles II but began to conflict again with Parliament over political and religious policy under his successor James II.

- The role of Parliament in English government was confirmed when William and Mary accepted the Crown under conditions stated in the Bill of Rights.

# New Powers in Central and Eastern Europe

*Which states began to dominate central and eastern Europe and why were they successful?*

By the end of the seventeenth century, three states dominated central and eastern Europe: Austria, Brandenburg-Prussia, and Russia. After the Thirty Years' War, the Habsburgs' dominance in the splintering empire waned, and they focused on expanding and consolidating their power in their hereditary possessions, centered in what became modern Austria. Brandenburg-Prussia, in northeastern Germany, emerged from obscurity to rival the Habsburg state. The rulers of Brandenburg-Prussia had gained lands in the Peace of Westphalia, and astute management transformed their relatively small and scattered holdings into one of the most powerful states in Europe. Russia's new stature in eastern Europe resulted in part from the weakness of its greatest rival, Poland, and the determination of one leader, Peter the Great, to assume a major role in European affairs. Sweden controlled valuable Baltic territory through much of the century but eventually was also eclipsed by Russia as a force in the region.

**Baroque Splendor in Austria** The Belvedere Palace (whose name means "beautiful view") was built near Vienna as the summer residence of the great aristocratic general Prince Eugene of Savoy, who had successfully led Habsburg armies against the Turks and had reaped many rewards from Leopold and his successors. The palace shares many features in common with Louis XIV's palace of Versailles. Erich Lessing/Art Resource, NY

The internal political development of states was dramatically shaped by their relationship to the wider European economy: They were sources of grain and raw materials for the more densely urbanized West. The development of and the competition among states in central and eastern Europe were closely linked to developments in western Europe.

## The Consolidation of Austria

The Thirty Years' War (see pages 434–440) weakened the Habsburgs as emperors but strengthened them in their own lands. The main Habsburg lands in 1648 were a collection of principalities comprising modern Austria, the kingdom of Hungary (largely in Turkish hands), and the kingdom of Bohemia (see **Map 16.2**). In 1714, Austria acquired the Spanish Netherlands (modern Belgium), which were renamed the Austrian Netherlands. Although language and ethnic differences prevented an absolutist state along French lines, Leopold I (r. 1657–1705) made political and institutional changes that enabled the Habsburg state to become one of the most powerful in Europe through the eighteenth century.

Much of the coherence that already existed in Leopold's lands had been achieved by his predecessors after the Thirty Years' War. The lands of rebels in Bohemia had been confiscated and redistributed among loyal, mostly Austrian, families. In return for political and military support for the emperor, these families were given the right to exploit their newly acquired land and the peasants who worked it. The desire to recover population and productivity after the destruction of the Thirty Years' War gave landlords further incentive to curtail peasants' autonomy, particularly in devastated Bohemia. Austrian landlords throughout the Habsburg domains provided grain and timber for the export market and foodstuffs for the Austrian armies, while elite families provided the army with officers. This political-economic arrangement provoked numerous serious peasant revolts, but the peasants were not able to force changes in a system that suited both the elites and the central authority.

Although Leopold had lost much influence within the empire itself, an imperial government including a war ministry, financial bureaucracy, and the like still functioned in his capital, Vienna. Leopold worked to extricate the government of his own lands from the apparatus of imperial institutions, which were staffed largely by Germans more loyal to imperial than to Habsburg interests.

In addition, Leopold used the Catholic Church as an institutional and ideological support for his state. Leopold's personal ambition was to reestablish devout Catholicism throughout his territories. Acceptance of Catholicism became the litmus test of loyalty to the Habsburg regime, and Protestantism vanished among elites. Leopold encouraged the work of Jesuit teachers and members of other Catholic religious orders. These men and women helped staff his government and administered religious life down to the most local levels.

Leopold's most dramatic success, as a Habsburg and a religious leader, was his reconquest of the kingdom of Hungary from the Ottoman Empire. Since the mid-sixteenth century, the Habsburgs had controlled only a narrow strip of the kingdom. Preoccupied with fighting France, Leopold did not himself choose to begin a reconquest. His centralizing policies, however, alienated nobles and townspeople in the portion of Hungary he did control, as did his repression of Protestantism, which had flourished in Hungary. Hungarian nobles began a revolt, aided by the Turks, aiming for a reunited Hungary under Ottoman protection.

The Habsburgs won, instead, in part because they received help from the Venetians, the Russians, and especially the Poles, whose lands in Ukraine were threatened by the Turks. The Turks overreached their supply lines to besiege Vienna in 1683. When the siege failed, Habsburg armies slowly pressed east and south, recovering Buda, the capital of Hungary, in 1686 and Belgrade (modern Serbia) in 1688. The **Treaty of Carlowitz** ended the fighting in 1699, after the first conference where European allies jointly dictated terms to a weakening Ottoman Empire. Austria's allies had also gained at the Ottomans' expense: The Poles recovered the threatened Ukraine, and the Russians gained a vital foothold on the Black Sea.

Leopold gave control of reclaimed lands to loyal Austrian officers but could not fully break the traditions of Hungarian separatism. Hungary's great aristocrats—whether they had defended the Habsburgs against Turkish encroachment or guarded the frontier for Turkish overlords—retained their independence. The peasantry, as elsewhere, suffered a decline in status as a result of the Crown's efforts to ensure the loyalty of elites. In the long

**Treaty of Carlowitz** Treaty imposed by the European allies on the Ottoman Empire, by which the Austrians, Venetians, Russians, and Poles gained territory at the Turks' expense.

run, Hungarian independence weakened the Habsburg state, but in the short run, Leopold's victory over the Turks and the recovery of Hungary were momentous events, confirming the Habsburgs as the preeminent power in central Europe.

## The Rise of Brandenburg-Prussia

Several German states, in addition to Austria, gained territory and stature after the Thirty Years' War. By the end of the seventeenth century, the strongest was **Brandenburg-Prussia**, a conglomeration of small territories held, by dynastic accident, by the Hohenzollern family. The two principal territories were electoral Brandenburg, in northeastern Germany, with its capital, Berlin, and the duchy of Prussia, a fief of the Polish crown along the Baltic coast east of Poland proper (see **Map 16.2**). In addition, the Hohenzollerns ruled a handful of small principalities near the Netherlands. These unpromising lands became a powerful state, primarily because of the work of Frederick William, known as "the Great Elector" (r. 1640–1688).

Frederick William used the occasion of a war to effect a permanent change in the structure of government. He took advantage of a war between Poland and its rivals, Sweden and Russia (described in the next section), to win independence for the duchy of Prussia from Polish overlordship. When his involvement in the war ended in 1657, he kept intact the general war commissariat, a combined civilian and military body that had efficiently directed the war effort, bypassing traditional councils and representative bodies. He also used the standing army to force the payment of high taxes. Most significantly, he established a positive relationship with the Junkers (YUNG-kurz), hereditary landholders, which ensured him both revenue and loyalty. The Junkers surrendered their accustomed political independence in return for greater economic and social power over the peasants who worked their lands. The freedom to control their estates led many nobles to invest in profitable agriculture for the export market. The peasants were serfs who received no benefits from the increased productivity of the land.

Frederick William further enhanced his state's power by sponsoring industry. These industries did not have to fear competition from urban producers because the towns had been frozen out of the political process and saddled with heavy taxes. Though an oppressive place for many Germans, Brandenburg-Prussia attracted many skilled refugees, such as Huguenot artisans fleeing Louis XIV's France.

Other German states, such as Bavaria and Saxony, had vibrant towns, largely free peasantries, and weaker aristocracies but were relative nonentities in international affairs. Power on the European stage depended on military force. Whether in a large state like France or in a small one like Brandenburg-Prussia, that power usually came at the expense of the people.

## Competition Around the Baltic

The rivers and port cities of the Baltic coast were conduits for the growing trade between the Baltic hinterland and the rest of Europe. Trade in grain, timber, furs, iron, and copper was vital to the entire European economy and caused intense competition, especially between Poland-Lithuania and Sweden, to control the coast and inland regions. In 1600, a large portion of the Baltic hinterland lay under the control of Poland-Lithuania, a vast state at the height of its power, but one that would prove an exception to the pattern of expanding royal power in the seventeenth century.

Poland and Lithuania had been jointly governed since a marriage united their ruling families in the late Middle Ages. Even so, the two states retained distinct traditions. Like some of the Habsburgs' territories, Poland-Lithuania was a multiethnic state, particularly the huge duchy of Lithuania, which included Ruthenia (modern Belarus and Ukraine). Poles spoke Polish, a Slavic language, and were primarily Catholic, although there were also large minorities of Protestants, Orthodox Christians, and Jews in Poland. Lithuanians, whose language was only distantly related to the Slavic languages, were mostly Catholic as well, although Orthodox Christianity predominated among the Ruthenians, who spoke a Slavic language related to both Russian and Polish.

**Brandenburg-Prussia**
Group of German territories ruled by the Hohenzollern family that became one of Europe's most powerful states in the seventeenth century.

**Map 16.2 New Powers in Central and Eastern Europe, to 1725** The balance of power in central and eastern Europe shifted with the strengthening of Austria, the rise of Brandenburg-Prussia, and the expansion of Russia at the expense of Poland and Sweden. © Cengage Learning 2014

Legend:
- French Bourbon lands
- Spanish Bourbon lands
- Austrian Habsburg lands
- Prussian lands
- Great Britain
- Boundary of the Holy Roman Empire
- Russian Empire
- Russian gains, by 1725
- Ottoman Empire, 1722

The state commanded considerable resources, including the ports of Gdansk and Riga on the Baltic and grain-producing lands in the interior. However, Poland-Lithuania had internal weaknesses. It was a republic of the nobility, with a weak elected king at its head. The great nobles, whose fortunes increased with the grain trade, ran the affairs of state through the national parliament, the Sejm (SAME). They drastically limited the ability of the Crown to tax and to grant new titles of nobility, as was the practice throughout Europe. These limitations meant that the king could not reward the loyalty of wealthy gentry or the small numbers of urban elites, so that they might be a counterweight to noble power. Limited funds also meant that the Polish crown would be hard put to defend its vast territories when challenged by its rivals.

Strains began to mount within Poland-Lithuania in the late sixteenth century. The spread of the Counter-Reformation, encouraged by the Crown, created tensions with both Protestant and Orthodox subjects in the diverse kingdom. As the power of landholding nobles grew with Poland's expanding grain exports, impoverished peasants were bound to the land, and lesser gentry, particularly in Lithuania, were shut out of political power. In Ukraine, communities of **Cossacks**, nomadic farmer-warriors, grew as Polish and Lithuanian peasants fled harsh conditions to join them. The Cossacks had long been tolerated because they served as a military buffer against the Ottoman Turks to the south, but now Polish landlords wanted to reincorporate the Cossacks into the profitable political-economic system they controlled.

In 1648, the Polish crown faced revolt and invasion that it could not fully counter. The Cossacks led a major uprising, which included Ukrainian gentry as well as peasants. In 1654, the Cossacks tried to assure their autonomy by transferring their allegiance to Moscow. They became part of a Russian invasion of Poland-Lithuania that, by the next year, had engulfed much of the eastern half of the dual state. At the same time, Poland's perennial rival, Sweden, seized central Poland in a military campaign marked by extreme brutality. Many Polish and Lithuanian aristocrats continued to act like independent warlords and cooperated with the invaders to preserve their own local power.

Operating with slim resources, Polish royal armies eventually managed to recover much territory—most important, the western half of Ukraine (see **Map 16.2**). But the invasions and subsequent fighting were disastrous. The population of Poland declined by as much as 40 percent, and vital urban economies were in ruins. The Catholic identity of the Polish heartland had been a rallying point for resistance to the Protestant Swedes and the Orthodox Russians, but the religious tolerance that had distinguished the diverse Polish kingdom and had been mandated in its constitution was now abandoned. In addition, much of its recovery of Lithuanian territory was only nominal.

The elective Polish crown passed in 1674 to the military hero Jan Sobieski (so-BYESS-key) (r. 1674–1696), known as "Vanquisher of the Turks" for his role in raising the siege of Vienna in 1683. Given Poland's internal weakness, however, Sobieski's victories, in the long run, helped the Ottomans' other foes—Austria and Russia—more than they helped the Poles. After his death, Poland would be vulnerable to the political ambitions of its more powerful neighbors. The next elected king, Augustus II of Saxony (r. 1697–1704, 1709–1733), dragged Poland back into war, from which Russia would emerge the clear winner in the power struggle in eastern Europe.

The Swedes, meanwhile, successfully vied with the Poles for control of the lucrative Baltic coast. Swedish efforts to control Baltic territory had begun in the sixteenth century, first to counter the power of its perennial rival, Denmark, in the western Baltic. Sweden then competed with Poland to control Livonia (modern Latvia) and its major port city, Riga. By 1617, under Gustav Adolf, the Swedes gained the lands to the north of Livonia surrounding the Gulf of Finland (the most direct outlet for Russian goods), and in 1621, they displaced the Poles in Livonia itself. Swedish intervention in the Thirty Years' War (see page 438) had been part of this campaign to secure Baltic territory. And the Treaty of Westphalia (1648, see page 438) confirmed Sweden's gains on the Baltic.

The port cities held by Sweden were profitable but simply served to pay for the costly wars necessary to seize and defend them. Indeed, Sweden did not have the resources to hold Baltic territory over the long term, and it gained little from its aggression against Poland in the 1650s. Owing to its earlier gains, Sweden managed to reign supreme on the Baltic coast until the end of the century, when it was supplanted by the powerful Russian state.

**Cossacks** Russian term meaning "free men" originally applied to people of central Asian origin in the hinterland of the Black Sea. After 1500, many peasants escaping serfdom in Poland-Lithuania and Russia fled and became "Cossacks."

## *Russia Under Peter the Great*

The Russian state grew dramatically in the sixteenth century, under Ivan IV (r. 1533–1584), the first Russian ruler to routinely use the title "Tsar" (Russian for "Caesar"). Ivan's use of the title reflected his imperial intentions. He expanded the territory under Moscow's control south to the Caspian Sea and east into Siberia. Within his expanding empire, Ivan ruled as an autocrat. The need to gather tribute money for Mongol overlords in medieval times had concentrated many resources in the hands of Muscovite princes. Ivan was able to bypass noble participation and create ranks of officials loyal only to him.

Ivan came to be called "the Terrible," from a Russian word meaning "awe-inspiring." Although a period of disputed succession to the throne, known as the "Time of Troubles," followed Ivan's death in 1584, the foundations of the large and cohesive state he had built survived until a new dynasty of rulers was established in the seventeenth century.

The Romanovs, an aristocratic family related to Ivan's, became the new ruling dynasty in 1613. Michael (r. 1613–1645) was named tsar by an assembly of aristocrats, gentry, and commoners who were more alarmed by the civil wars and recent Polish invasions than by a return to strong tsarist rule. Michael was succeeded by his son, Alexis (r. 1645–1676), who presided over the extension of Russian control to eastern Ukraine in 1654, following the wars in Poland, and developed an interest in cultivating relationships with the West.

A complete shift of the balance of power in eastern Europe and the Baltic, in Russia's favor, was achieved by Alexis's son, Peter I (r. 1682–1725), "the Great." **Peter the Great** accomplished this by military successes against his enemies and by forcibly reorienting Russian government and society toward involvement with the rest of Europe.

Peter was almost literally larger than life. Nearly 7 feet tall, he towered over most of his contemporaries and had physical and mental energy to match his size. He set himself to learning trades and studied soldiering by rising through the ranks of the military like a common soldier. He traveled abroad to learn as much as he could about western European economies and governments. He wanted the revenue, manufacturing output, technology and trade, and, above all, up-to-date army and navy that other rulers enjoyed.

Immediately on his accession to power, Peter initiated a bold series of changes in Russian society. His travels had taught him that European monarchs coexisted with a privileged, but educated, aristocracy and that a brilliant court life symbolized and reinforced their authority. So, he set out to refashion Russian society in what amounted to an enforced cultural revolution. He provoked a direct confrontation with Russia's traditional aristocracy over everything from education to matters of dress. He elevated numerous new families to the ranks of gentry and created an official ranking system for the nobility to encourage and reward service to his government.

Peter's effort to reorient his nation culturally, economically, and politically toward Europe was most obvious in the construction of the city of St. Petersburg on the Gulf of Finland, which provided access to the Baltic Sea (see **Map 16.2**). In stark contrast to Moscow, dominated by the medieval fortress of the Kremlin, St. Petersburg was a modern European city with wide avenues and palaces designed for a sophisticated court life.

Although Peter was highly intelligent, practical, and determined to create a more productive and better governed society, he was also cruel and authoritarian. Peasants already bore the brunt of taxation, but their tax burden worsened when they were assessed arbitrarily by head and not by output of the land. The building of St. Petersburg cost staggering sums in both money and workers' lives. Peter's

**Peter the Great**
Energetic and tyrannical Russian tsar who forcibly westernized Russian state and society and made Russia into a great power.

bpk, Berlin/Rijksmuseum, Amsterdam, The Netherlands/Hermann Buresch/Art Resource, NY

**Peter the Great** This portrait by a Dutch artist captures the tsar's "westernizing" mission by showing Peter in military dress according to European fashions of the day.

## SECTION SUMMARY

- After the Thirty Years' War, Austria, Brandenburg-Prussia, and Russia became the dominant states in central and eastern Europe.

- Central and eastern Europe provided raw materials for the wider European economy, which enhanced elites' power over peasants, increased revenues to states, and caused wars between states over these resources.

- The Austrian Habsburgs consolidated their power in their territories within the Holy Roman Empire and reconquered Hungary from the Ottoman Turks.

- Although composed of a collection of small principalities, Brandenburg-Prussia became a powerful state.

- Poland-Lithuania declined in the seventeenth century because the elective monarchy could not defend itself against independent aristocrats, rebellious Cossacks, or powerful neighboring states.

- Russia was forcibly modernized by Peter the Great and became the most powerful state in eastern Europe under his reign, eclipsing Sweden in control of Baltic territories.

entire reform system was carried out tyrannically; resistance was brutally suppressed. Victims included his own son, who died after torture while awaiting execution for questioning his father's policies. Peter faced rebellions by elites, as well as common people, against the exactions and the cultural changes of his regime.

A major reason for the high cost of Peter's government to the Russian people was his ambition for territorial gain—hence, his emphasis on an improved, and costly, army and navy. He recruited experienced foreign technicians and created the Russian navy from scratch. At first, ships were built in the south to contest Turkish control of the Black Sea. Later, they were built in the north to secure and defend the Baltic. Peter also modernized the Russian army by employing tactics, training, and discipline he had observed in the West. He introduced military conscription and built munitions plants. By 1709, Russia was able to manufacture most of the up-to-date firearms its army needed.

Russia waged war virtually throughout Peter's reign. He struck at the Ottomans and their client state in the Crimea. Peter was most successful against his northern competitor, Sweden, for control of the weakened Polish state and the Baltic Sea. The conflicts between Sweden and Russia, known as the Great Northern War, raged from 1700 to 1709 and, in a less intense phase, lasted until 1721. By the Treaty of Nystadt in 1721, Russia gained its present-day territory in the Gulf of Finland near St. Petersburg, plus Livonia and Estonia. These acquisitions gave Russia a secure window on the Baltic and, in combination with its gains of Lithuanian territory earlier in the century, made Russia the preeminent Baltic power, at Sweden's and Poland's expense.

# The Expansion of Overseas Trade and Settlement

*How and why did Europe's overseas trade and colonization expand in the seventeenth century and what effects did this expansion have on Europe itself?*

By the beginning of the seventeenth century, competition from the Dutch, French, and English was disrupting the Spanish and Portuguese trading empires in the New World and in Asia. During the seventeenth century, the Dutch not only became masters of the spice trade but also broadened the market to include many other commodities. In the Americas, a new trading system linking Europe, Africa, and the New World came into being with the expansion of tobacco and, later, sugar production. French and English colonists began settling in North America in increasing numbers. Overseas trade also had a crucial impact on life within Europe: on patterns of production and consumption, on social stratification, and on the distribution of wealth.

## The Growth of Trading Empires: The Success of the Dutch

By the end of the sixteenth century, the Dutch and the English were making incursions into the Portuguese-controlled spice trade with areas of India, Ceylon, and the East Indies. Spain had annexed Portugal in 1580, but the drain on Spain's resources, from its wars with the Dutch and French, prevented Spain from adequately defending its enlarged trading empire in Asia. The Dutch and, to a lesser degree, the English rapidly supplanted Portuguese control of this lucrative trade (see **Map 16.3**).

The Dutch were particularly well placed to dominate overseas trade. They already dominated seaborne trade within Europe, including the most important long-distance trade, which linked Spain and Portugal—with their wine and salt, as well as spices, hides, and gold from abroad—with the Baltic seacoast, where these products were sold for grain and timber produced in Germany, Poland-Lithuania, and Scandinavia. The geographic position of the Netherlands and the fact that the Dutch consumed more Baltic grain than any other area, because of their large urban population, help to explain their dominance of this trade. In addition, the Dutch had improved the design of their merchant ships to maximize their profits. By 1600, they had developed the *fluitschip* (flyship), a cheaply built vessel with a long, flat hull and simple rigging, that carried goods economically.

The Dutch succeeded in Asia because of institutional, as well as technological, innovations. In 1602, the **Dutch East India Company** was formed. The company combined government management of trade, typical of the period, with both public and private investment. In the past, groups of investors had funded single voyages or small numbers of ships on a one-time basis. The formation of the Dutch East India Company created a permanent pool of capital to sustain trade. After 1612, investments in the company were negotiable as stock. These greater assets allowed proprietors to spread the risks and delays of longer voyages among larger numbers of investors. In addition, more money was available for warehouses, docks, and ships. The English East India Company, founded in 1607, also supported trade, but more modestly. It had one-tenth the capital of the Dutch company and did not use the same system of permanent capital held as stock by investors until 1657. The Bank of Amsterdam, founded in 1609, became the depository for the bullion that flowed into the Netherlands with the flood of trade. The bank established currency exchange rates and issued paper money and instruments of credit to facilitate commerce.

**Dutch East India Company** Commercially innovative Dutch company, formed in 1602, that combined government management of trade with both public and private investment.

**Map 16.3 Dutch Commerce in the Seventeenth Century** The Dutch supplanted Portuguese control of trade with Asia, established significant colonies in the Americas, and dominated seaborne trade within Europe. © Cengage Learning 2014

A dramatic expansion of trade with Asia resulted from the Dutch innovations, so much so that by 1650, the European market for spices was glutted, and traders' profits had begun to fall. To control the supply of spices, the Dutch seized some of the areas where they were produced. The Dutch and English also responded to the oversupply of spices by diversifying their trade. The proportion of spices in cargoes from the East fell from about 70 percent at midcentury to just over 20 percent by the century's end. New consumer goods, such as tea, coffee, and silk and cotton fabrics, took their place. Eventually, the Dutch and the English, alert for fresh opportunities, entered the local carrying trade among Asian states. This enabled them to make profits even without purchasing goods, and it slowed the drain of hard currency from Europe—currency in increasingly short supply, as silver mines in the Americas were depleted.

## The "Golden Age" of the Netherlands

The prosperity occasioned by the Dutch trading empire created social and political conditions within the Netherlands unique among European states. The concentration of trade and shipping sustained a healthy merchant oligarchy and also a prosperous artisanal sector. Disparities of wealth were smaller here than anywhere else in Europe. The shipbuilding and fishing trades, among others, supported large numbers of workers with a high standard of living for the age.

The Netherlands appeared to contemporaries to be an astonishing exception to the normal structures of politics. Political decentralization in the Netherlands persisted. The Estates General (representative assembly) for the Netherlands as a whole had no independent powers of taxation. Each of the seven provinces retained considerable autonomy. Wealthy merchants in the Estates of the province of Holland, in fact, constituted the government for the entire nation for long periods because of Holland's economic dominance. The head of government was the executive secretary, known as the pensionary, of Holland's Estates.

Holland's only competition in the running of affairs came from the House of Orange, aristocratic leaders of the revolt against Spain (see pages 418–422). They exercised what control they had by means of the office of *stadtholder* (STAHT-hole-der)—a kind of military governorship—to which they were elected in individual provinces. Their principal interest, traditional military glory and dynastic power, accounted for some of their influence, since they led the Netherlands' defense against Spanish attacks until the Peace of Westphalia in 1648 and against French aggression after 1672. Their power also came from their status as the only counterweight within the Netherlands to the dominance of Amsterdam's (in Holland) mercantile interests. Small towns, dependent on land-based trade or rural areas dominated by farmers and gentry, looked to the stadtholders of the Orange family to defend their interests.

As elsewhere, religion was a source of political conflict. The stadtholders and the leading families of Holland, known as regents, vied for control of the state church. Regents of Holland generally favored a less rigid and austere form of Calvinism than did the stadtholders. Their view reflected the needs of the diverse urban communities of Holland, where thousands of Jews, as well as Catholics and various Protestants, lived. Dutch commercial dominance involved the Netherlands in costly wars throughout the second half of the century. Between 1657 and 1660, the Dutch fought the Swedes to safeguard the sea-lanes and port cities of the Baltic. The most costly conflicts came from the rivalry of England and France. Under Cromwell, the English attempted to close their ports to the Dutch carrying trade. In 1672, the English, under Charles II, allied with the French, hoping that together they could destroy Dutch commercial power and even divide the Netherlands' territory between them. The Dutch navy, rebuilt since Cromwell's challenge, soon forced England out of the alliance.

But there were long-term consequences of these wars for the Dutch state. As a result of the land war with France, the Estates in Holland lost control of policy to William of Nassau (d. 1702), prince of Orange, after 1672. William drew the Netherlands into his family's long-standing close relationship with England. Like previous members of his family, William had married into the English royal family: His wife was Mary, daughter of James II. After William and Mary assumed the English throne, Dutch commerce actually suffered more when allied with England than in its previous rivalry. William used Dutch resources for the land war against Louis XIV and reserved, for the English navy, the fight at sea. By the end of the century, Dutch maritime strength was being eclipsed by English sea power.

## The Growth of Atlantic Commerce

In the seventeenth century, the Dutch, the English, and the French joined the Spanish as colonial and commercial powers in the Americas. The Spanish colonial empire, in theory a trading system closed to outsiders, was in fact vulnerable to other European traders. Spanish treasure fleets were themselves a glittering attraction. In 1628, for example, a Dutch captain seized the entire fleet. But by then, Spain's goals and those of its competitors had begun to shift. The limits of an economy based on the extraction, rather than the production, of wealth became clear with the declining output of the Spanish silver mines during the 1620s. In response, the Spanish and their Dutch, French, and English competitors expanded the production of cash crops: tobacco, dyestuffs, and, above all, sugar.

The European demand for tobacco and sugar, both addictive substances, grew steadily in the seventeenth century. The **plantation system**—the use of forced labor to produce cash

**plantation system**
Agricultural system, first developed by the Portuguese, in which forced labor produced cash crops on large estates owned by absentee landlords.

Bridgeman-Giraudon/Art Resource, NY

**Vermeer: The Letter**    This is a later work by one of the great artists of the Dutch "Golden Age." Dutch art was distinguished by common rather than heroic subjects—here, a merchant-class woman writes a letter. The masterful use of lighting and perspective in paintings such as this one would not be equaled until the age of photography.

crops on vast tracts of land—had been developed on Mediterranean islands in the Middle Ages by European entrepreneurs, using slaves procured in Black Sea ports by Venetian and Genoese traders. Sugar production by this system had been established on Atlantic islands, such as the Cape Verde Islands, using African labor, and then in the Americas, by the Spanish and Portuguese. Sugar production in the New World grew from about 20,000 tons a year in 1600 to about 200,000 tons by 1770.

In the 1620s, while the Dutch were exploiting Portuguese weakness in the Eastern spice trade, they were also seizing sugar regions in Brazil and replacing Portuguese slave traders in African ports. The Portuguese were able to retake most of their Brazilian territory in the 1650s. But the Dutch, because they monopolized the carrying trade, were able to become the official supplier of slaves to Spanish plantations in the New World and the chief supplier of slaves, as well as other goods, to most other regions. (See the feature, "The Global Record: Dutch Colonies in the Americas" on page 480.) The Dutch made handsome profits dealing in human cargo until the end of the seventeenth century, when they were supplanted by the British.

The Dutch introduced sugar cultivation to the French and English after learning it themselves in Brazil. Sugar plantations began to supplant tobacco cultivation, as well as subsistence farming, on the Caribbean islands the English and French controlled. Beginning in the late sixteenth century, English and French seamen had seized islands in the Caribbean to use as provisioning stations and staging points for raids against or commerce with Spanish colonies. Some island outposts had expanded into colonies and attracted European settlers— some, as in North America, coming as indentured servants—to work the land. Sugar cultivation drastically transformed the character of these island settlements because it demanded huge outlays of capital and continual supplies of unskilled labor. Large plantations, owned by wealthy, often absentee landlords and dependent on slave labor, replaced smaller-scale independent farms. The most profitable sugar colonies were, for the French, the islands of Martinique and Guadeloupe and, for the English, Barbados and Jamaica.

**Sugar Manufacture in Caribbean Colonies** Production of sugar required large capital outlays, in part because the raw cane had to be processed quickly, on-site, to avoid spoilage. This scene depicts enslaved workers operating a small sugar mill on the island of Barbados in the seventeenth century. In the background, a press crushes the cane; in the foreground, the juice from the cane is boiled down until sugar begins to crystallize.

## Early Colonies in North America

Aware of the overwhelming Spanish advantage in the New World, and still hoping for treasures such as the Spanish had found, the English, French, and Dutch were also eager to explore and settle North America. From the early sixteenth century on, French, Dutch, English, and Portuguese seamen had fished and traded off Newfoundland. By 1630, small French and Scottish settlements in Acadia (near modern Nova Scotia) and on the St. Lawrence River and English settlements in Newfoundland were established to systematically exploit the timber, fish, and fur of the North Atlantic coasts.

## English Settlements

In England, rising unemployment and religious discontent created a large pool of potential colonists, some of whom were initially attracted to early farming and trading settlements in the Caribbean. The first of the English settlements to endure, in what was to become the United States, was established at Jamestown, named for James I, in Virginia in 1607. ("Virginia," named for Elizabeth I, the "Virgin Queen," was an extremely vague designation for the Atlantic coast of North America and its hinterland.)

The Crown encouraged colonization, but a private company, similar to those that financed long-distance trade, was established to organize the enterprise. The directors of the Virginia Company were London businessmen. Investors and would-be colonists purchased shares. Shareholders among the colonists could participate in a colonial assembly, although the governor appointed by the company was the final authority.

The colonists arrived in Virginia with ambitious and optimistic instructions: to open mines, establish profitable agriculture, and search for sea routes to Asia. But at first, the colonists struggled even to survive in the unfamiliar environment. "Though there be fish in the seas. . . . and beasts in the woods . . . they are so wild and we so weak and ignorant, we cannot trouble them much," wrote Captain John Smith from Virginia to the directors in London.[*] The native peoples in Virginia, unlike those in Spanish-held territories, were not organized in urbanized, rigidly hierarchical societies that, after conquest, could provide the invaders with a labor force. In fact, most of the native population was quickly wiped out by European diseases. The introduction of tobacco as a cash crop a few years later saved the colonists economically—although the Virginia Company had already gone bankrupt and the Crown had assumed control of the colony. With the cultivation of tobacco, the Virginia colony, like the Caribbean islands, became dependent on forced, eventually slave, labor.

Among the Virginia colonists were impoverished men and women who came as servants, indentured to those who had paid their passage—that is, they were bound by contract to pay off their debts by several years of labor. Colonies established to the north, in what was called "New England," also drew people from the margins of English society. Early settlers there were religious dissidents. The first to arrive were the Pilgrims, who arrived at Plymouth (modern Massachusetts) in 1620. They were a community of religious Separatists who had originally immigrated to the Netherlands from England for freedom of conscience.

Following the Pilgrims, came Puritans, escaping escalating persecution under Charles I. The first, in 1629, settled under the auspices of another royally chartered company, the Massachusetts Bay Company. Among their number were many prosperous Puritan merchants and landholders. Independence from investors in London allowed them an unprecedented degree of self-government once the Massachusetts Bay colony was established.

Nevertheless, the colonies in North America were disappointments to England because they generated much less wealth than expected. Shipping timber back to Europe proved too expensive, although New England forests did supply some of the Caribbean colonists' needs. The fur trade became less lucrative, as English settlement pushed the Native Americans, who did most of the trapping, west and as French trappers to the north encroached on the trade. Certain colonists profited enormously from the tobacco economy, but the mother country did so only moderately because the demand in Europe for tobacco never matched the demand

---

*Philip A. Barbour, ed., *The Complete Works of Captain John Smith (1580-1631)*, vol. 2 (Chapel Hill: University of North Carolina Press, 1986), p. 189.

## Dutch Colonies in the Americas: The Challenges of a Trading Empire

*This letter was sent in August 1659 by Matthias Beck, the Dutch vice-director of the island of Curacao, to Peter Stuyvesant, Director-General of New Netherland (the Dutch colony that was renamed New York when taken over by the English). The Dutch had seized the island of Curacao from the Spanish in 1634. Located in the Caribbean off the coast of Venezuela, this island and its neighbors in the Lesser Antilles had been attractive to the Dutch as a source of salt, vital to them for their fishing industry. Curacao became the center of salt production and trade and also, as this document shows, an important outpost in the slave trade. Though the vice-director at Curacao was supposed to take orders from the Director-General, in fact, as this letter also shows, the island had to manage its own affairs without much help from far-away New Netherland.*

My Lord. I am hereby sending the duplicates of the information which I sent your honor with Augustinus Heermans on the occasion of the galiot *Nieuw Amstel* and it would please us to be informed as soon as possible of its timely and safe arrival; just as I do not want to miss this good occasion and opportunity with skipper Jan Pietersen of the ship *Speramundij* to inform your honor further (praise God) of the condition of this island. Concerning commerce with our nearest neighbors, because until now we have received so few goods here that have been easily saleable or everything has been sold, and in particular the slave trade for which the West India Company has reserved this place: Presently there are two ships here almost ready to sail directly to the fatherland. They keep me so busy that I have no time left to write to your honor about these matters in detail. One of them is a Company ship named *Den Coninck Salomon* which arrived here on the 2nd of July with 331 slaves from Guinea, of which I have sold 300 for 150 pieces of eight each upon delivery to a certain Spanish merchant whom I have been expecting to arrive here any day now to pick them up. I hope this takes place before the departure of the aforesaid two ships so that I can send the proceeds thereof to the honorable lords-superiors.*

I have orders from the honorable lords-superiors to send your honor about 15 or 16 Negroes towards spring. They would have been able to come over now, but because we lack heavy cloth here with which to clothe them, we were afraid that they would not be able to survive there during the winter; and furthermore, because we cannot spare any Negroes here, we have decided, according to the orders of the honorable lords-superiors, to wait until spring. . .

We anxiously await here one or another ship which might bring us some provisions, because we are in need of everything here: bread as well as pottage, meat, bacon, etc.

I fear that the lords-superiors presume that the yacht *Diemen* is bringing us enough provisions from there, by which they and we shall be misled; and it will cause them

---

*Refers to the Dutch merchants who directed the West India Company, which controlled Dutch trade in the Americas after being chartered in 1624. Beck and Stuyvesant were employed by the company.

---

for sugar. The English settlements did continue to attract more migrants than other colonizers' outposts. By 1640, Massachusetts had some fourteen thousand European inhabitants. Through most of the next century, the growth of colonial populations in North America would result in an English advantage over the French in control of New World territory.

## French Settlements

The French began their settlement of North America at the same time as the English, in the same push to compensate for their mutual weakness in comparison to the Spanish (see **Map 16.4**). The French efforts, however, had very different results, owing partly to the sites of their settlements, but mostly to the relationship between the mother country and the colonies. The French hold on territory was always tenuous because of the scant number of colonists who could be lured from home. There seems to have been less economic impetus for colonization from France than from England. After the French crown took over the colonies, the religious impetus also evaporated, since only Catholics were allowed to settle in New France. Moreover, the Crown forced a hierarchical political organization on the French colonies. A royal governor directed the colony, and large tracts of land were set aside for privileged investors. Thus, North America offered little to tempt French people of modest means who were seeking a better life.

The first successful French colony was established in Acadia in 1605. This settlement was an exception among the French efforts because it was founded by Huguenots, not by Catholics. A few years later, the explorer Samuel de Champlain (1567–1635) navigated the more losses in the sale of the Negroes than the food which we require both for the maintenance of the garrison and in particular of those Negroes already arrived and still to come. If food does not come soon, which is worth tenfold [to us], I cannot understand why the honorable lords-superiors are so remiss in sending provisions...

I was hoping that your honor would have the opportunity to be able to return this ship or another one as soon as possible with as many unfinished timbers previously and once again required here as per memorandum for a reasonable cargo and with as much food as your honor can spare. If a load of salt from here or horses from Aruba is needed, they can be provided in return upon your honor's order.

It grieves me that I am embarrassed by not being able to supply provisions, necessary equipment and other repair materials for the Spanish ships that come into our harbor now and then. For this reason I submitted a proposal some time ago to our honorable lords-superiors in the fatherland to erect here, among other things, a dry dock provided with all kinds of necessary materials and equipment in order to be able to accommodate all such ships with everything, which would serve as a great incentive and inducement to come to our harbor with their ships, and thereby increase our trade. I also proposed that it was necessary to provide these places from now on with stronger garrisons than before as preservation and protection from all foreign designs...

It has been on our minds here that if England and Holland go to war again, may God mercifully prevent it, whether we would be attacked here first out of envy for these places and the incipient trade, which they are eager to do because they would like to monopolize trade everywhere and exclude the Hollanders from the same....

I had hoped to have the time and opportunity to be able to write to your honor in more detail, as well as to various other well-known friends there; however, because of the dispatching of the aforesaid ship and other Spanish ships and merchants presently here, I will delay doing so until the next time, God willing.

On account of the continuing drought here, we have not been able to send your honor any oranges or lemons; nevertheless, I am sending your honor herewith four ankers of lemon juice received from the coast of Africa, which I ask be kindly received, with another two barrels of salt for your honor's household. According to occasion and opportunity I shall not fail to provide your honor with more and better items.

## Questions

1. What does this letter reveal about the trade linking Curacao with other Netherlands' colonies?

2. What other trading relationships are revealed here? What, in particular, do you learn about the trade and transport of enslaved people?

3. What concerns does Matthias Beck have, beyond those related to trade? What do you learn, directly or indirectly, about conditions on the island, or conditions affecting communication, supplies, security?

Source: Charles T. Gehring and J. A. Schiltkamp, eds., *New Netherlands Documents*, vol. 17, pp. 124–127. Copyright © 1987 by Heart of the Lakes Publishing. Reprinted with permission.

St. Lawrence River and founded Quebec City (1608). He convinced the royal government, emerging from its preoccupations with religious wars at home, to promote the development of the colony. French explorers went on to establish Montreal, farther up the St. Lawrence (1642), and to explore the Great Lakes and the Mississippi River basin (see **Map 16.4**).

Such investment as the French crown was able to attract went into profitable trade, mainly in furs, and not into the difficult business of colonization. French trappers and traders who ventured into wilderness areas were renowned for their hardiness and adaptability, but they did not bring their families and establish settled, European-style towns. Quebec remained more of a trading station, dependent on shipments of food from France, than a growing urban community. Much of the energy of French colonization was expended by men and women of religious orders—the "Black Robes"—bringing their zeal to new frontiers. By the middle of the seventeenth century, all of New France had only about three thousand European inhabitants.

The seeming weakness of the French colonial effort in North America was not much noticed at the time. French and English fishermen, trappers, and traders competed intensely, and the French often reaped the greater share of profits, owing to their closer ties with Native American trading systems. Outright battles occasionally erupted between English and French settlements. But for both England and France, indeed for all colonial powers, the major profits and strategic interests in the New World lay to the south, in the sugar-producing Caribbean. For example, in 1674, the Dutch gave up their trading center, New Amsterdam (modern-day New York City) to the English in return for recognition of the Dutch claims to sugar-producing Guiana (modern Suriname) in South America.

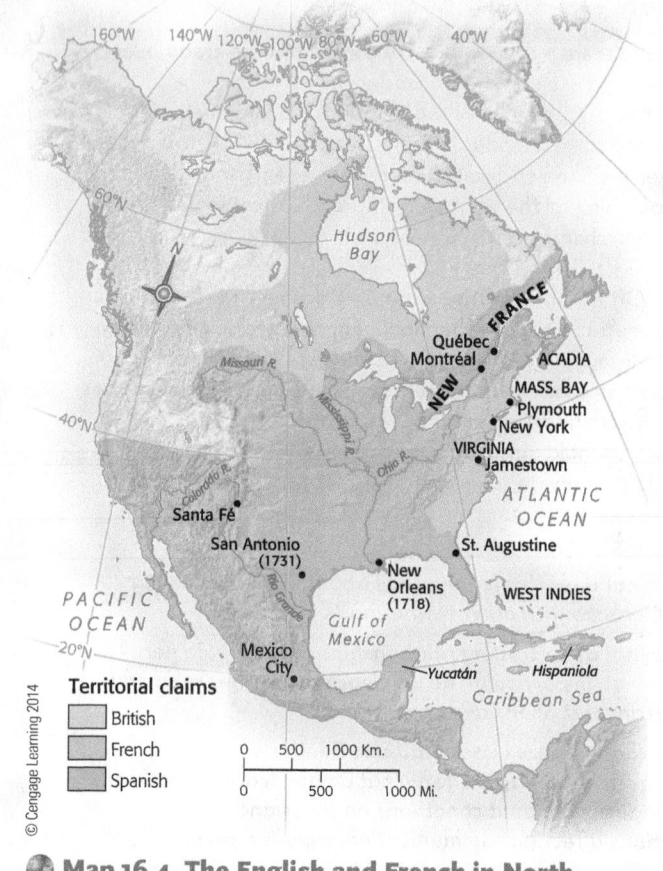

🌐 **Map 16.4 The English and French in North America, ca. 1700** By 1700, a veritable ring of French-claimed territory encircled the coastal colonies of England. English-claimed areas, however, were more densely settled and more economically viable.

The growth of the plantation system meant that, by far, the largest group of migrants to European-held territories in the Americas was forced migrants: African men and women sold into slavery and shipped, like other cargo, across the Atlantic to work on Caribbean islands, in South America and southern North America. A conservative estimate is that approximately 1.35 million Africans were forcibly transported as slave labor to the New World during the seventeenth century.

## The Impact of Trade and Warfare Within Europe

Within Europe, the economic impact of overseas trade was profound. Merchants and investors in a few of Europe's largest cities reaped great profits. Mediterranean ports, such as Venice, once the heart of European trade, did not share in the bonanza from the new trade with Asia or the Americas. Atlantic ports, such as Seville, through which most Spanish commerce with the New World flowed, and, above all, Amsterdam began to flourish. The population of Amsterdam increased from about 30,000 to 200,000 in the course of the seventeenth century.

All capital cities, not just seaports, however, grew substantially during the 1600s. Increasing numbers of government officials, courtiers and their hangers-on, and people involved in trade lived and worked in capital cities. These cities also grew indirectly from the demand such people generated for workers, such as carters and domestic servants, and products, ranging from fashionable clothing to exotic foodstuffs. For the first time, large numbers of country people found work in cities. Perhaps as much as one-fifth of the population of England passed through London at one time or another, creating the mobile, volatile community so active in the English civil war and its aftermath.

But social stratification intensified despite the expanding economy. Poverty increased in cities, even in vibrant Amsterdam, because cities attracted people fleeing rural unemployment with few skills and fewer resources. As growing central governments heaped tax burdens on peasants, many rural people were caught in a cycle of debt; the only escape was to abandon farming and flock to cities. Patterns of consumption reflected the economic gulf between city dwellers; most people could not afford to buy the spices or sugar that generated such profits.

Peasant rebellions occurred throughout the century as a result of depressed economic conditions and the heavy taxation that accompanied expanded royal power and extensive warfare. Some small-scale revolts involved direct action, such as seizing the tax collector's grain or stopping the movement of grain to the great cities. Urban demand often caused severe food shortages in rural areas in western Europe, despite the booming trade in grain with eastern Europe via the Baltic.

The scale of popular revolts, especially against taxation, meant that thousands of troops sometimes had to be diverted from a state's foreign wars. As a matter of routine, soldiers accompanied tax officials and enforced collection all over Europe. As the ambitions of rulers grew, so too did the resistance of ordinary people to the exactions of the state.

## SECTION SUMMARY

- The Dutch innovations in ship design and forms of investment helped them dominate overseas trade.

- The wealth from trade supported a higher standard of living, wider political participation, and more religious tolerance in the Netherlands than elsewhere in Europe.

- The Dutch, the English, and the French expanded their trade and colonization in the Americas, following Spain and Portugal's earlier successes.

- Most European profits from trade and settlement in the Americas came from plantation agriculture, using slave labor, established on Caribbean islands.

- Overseas trade, together with more centralized governments, resulted in the spectacular growth of coastal and capital cities, wider divisions between rich and poor, and increased peasant rebellions.

# Chapter Summary

◆ *How did Louis XIV successfully expand royal power in France and what were some of the achievements of his reign?*

Following the most powerful monarchy in Europe, France, most states had moved from internal division—with independent provinces and aristocrats going their own way—to greater coherence. In France, Louis XIV's brand of government, which has been labeled "absolutism," arose from successful use of traditional political mechanisms, such as patronage, plus the defeat of any institutional brakes on his authority. Court life in Louis's reign sponsored artistic creativity and encouraged a new emphasis on cultural refinement in the aristocracy. In the military realm, however, Louis started a series of costly wars from which the French state gained little.

◆ *What were the long-term consequences of the English civil war?*

In England, a civil war over the very issue of parliamentary participation in government led to the temporary abolition of the monarchy itself. The Crown was restored under Charles II, but conflicts arose again over political and religious policy under his successor James II. The year 1688 marked the "Glorious Revolution," in which Parliament helped bring William and Mary to the throne. Parliament's power was ensured by the Declaration of Rights and Bill of Rights, which have lasting significance today.

◆ *Which states began to dominate central and eastern Europe and why were they successful?*

States, troubled by religious and political turmoil or on the political margins early in the century, evolved into secure and dynamic centers of power: the Netherlands, the Habsburg domains, Brandenburg-Prussia, and Russia. This stability was both cause and consequence of rulers' desires to make war on an ever larger scale. The Austrian Habsburgs reconquered Hungary from the Ottoman Turks, while the power of Poland-Lithuania declined in the seventeenth century because it was unable to defend itself against independent aristocrats, rebellious Cossacks, or powerful neighboring states. Russia was forcibly modernized by Peter the Great and became the most powerful state in eastern Europe, eclipsing Sweden in control of Baltic territories. By the end of the century, only those states able to field massive armies were competitive on the European stage. The Netherlands, a stark exception to the pattern of centralized royal control, began more closely to resemble other states under the pressure of warfare by century's end.

◆ *How and why did Europe's overseas trade and colonization expand in the seventeenth century and what effects did this expansion have on Europe itself?*

At the beginning of the century, overseas trade and colonization had been the near monopoly of Spain and Portugal. At the end of the century, the English, French, and Dutch had supplanted them in controlling trade with Asia and were reaping many profits in the Americas, especially from the extension of plantation agriculture. The Dutch were a successful trading empire because of their innovations in ship design and forms of investment. With their wealth from trade, they supported a higher standard of living, wider political participation, and more religious tolerance. Beneath all these developments lay significant economic, social, and cultural shifts. One effect of the increased wealth generated by overseas trade and the increased power of governments to tax their subjects was a widening gulf between rich and poor. New styles of behavior and patterns of consumption highlighted differences between social classes.

# Key Terms

absolutism (p. 454)
Louis XIV (p. 454)
mercantilism (p. 456)
Parliament (p. 463)
Oliver Cromwell (p. 463)
Glorious Revolution (p. 467)

Treaty of Carlowitz (p. 469)
Brandenburg-Prussia (p. 470)
Cossacks (p. 472)
Peter the Great (p. 473)
Dutch East India Company (p. 475)
plantation system (p. 477)

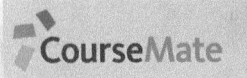

CourseMate

Go to the CourseMate website at **www.cengagebrain.com** for additional study tools and review materials—including audio and video clips—for this chapter.

**Descartes and Queen Christina** René Descartes (*second from the right*) instructs Queen Christina of Sweden and her courtiers. Réunion des musées nationaux/Art Resource, NY

# A Revolution in Worldview

The year is 1649. Queen Christina of Sweden welcomes us with her gaze and her gesture to witness a science lesson at her court. Her instructor, the French philosopher René Descartes, clutches a compass and points to an astronomical drawing. The young queen, 23 years old at the time, was already well known as a patron of artists and scholars. Christina had invited Descartes to her court because of his achievements in physics and philosophy. This painting depicts the fact that during Christina's lifetime, new theories in the field of astronomy revolutionized the sciences and required new definitions of matter to explain them. Descartes earned fame both for his new theories about matter and for his systematic approach to using human reason to understand the universe. This painting celebrates both Descartes's work and Christina's sponsorship of it.

The revolution within the sciences had been initiated in the sixteenth century by the astronomical calculations and hypotheses of Nicholas Copernicus, who theorized that the earth moves around the sun. The work of the Italian mathematician and astronomer Galileo Galilei, as well as others, added evidence to support this hypothesis. Their work overturned principles of physics and philosophy that had held sway since ancient times. Later generations of scientists and philosophers, beginning with Descartes, labored to construct new principles to explain the way nature behaves. The readiness of scientists, their patrons, and educated laypeople to push Copernicus's hypothesis to these conclusions came from several sources: their exposure to the intellectual innovations of Renaissance thought, the intellectual challenges and material opportunities represented by the discovery of the New World, and the challenge to authority embodied in the Reformation. They advanced and discussed scientific theories in print for the first time. Also, the new science offered prestige and technological advances to the rulers, such as Christina, who sponsored it.

By the end of the seventeenth century, a vision of an infinite but orderly cosmos appealing to human reason had, among educated Europeans, largely replaced the medieval vision of a closed universe centered on the earth and suffused with Christian purpose. Religion became an increasingly subordinate ally of science as confidence in an open-ended, experimental approach to knowledge came to be as strongly held as

## Chapter Overview

### The Revolution in Astronomy, 1543–1632

- *How did the Copernican theory challenge traditional views of the universe?*

### The Scientific Revolution Expands, ca. 1600–1700

- *How and why did new theories about astronomy lead to a broader Scientific Revolution?*

### The New Science in Context: Society, Politics, and Religion

- *How did the new scientific worldview lead people to challenge traditional notions of society, the state, and religion?*

religious conviction. It is because of this larger shift in worldview, not simply because of particular scientific discoveries, that the seventeenth century can be called the era of the Scientific Revolution.

Because religious significance had been attached to previous scientific explanations and religious authority had defended them, the new astronomy automatically led to an enduring debate about the compatibility of science and religion. But the revolution in worldview was not confined to astronomy or even to science generally. As philosophers gained confidence in human reason and the intelligibility of the world, they turned to new speculation about human affairs. They began to challenge traditional justifications for the hierarchical nature of society and the sanctity of authority, just as energetically as Copernicus and his followers had overthrown old views about the cosmos.

# The Revolution in Astronomy, 1543–1632

*How did the Copernican theory challenge traditional views of the universe?*

The origins of the seventeenth-century revolution in worldview lie, for the most part, in developments in astronomy. Because of astronomy's role in the explanations of the world and human life that had been devised by ancient and medieval scientists and philosophers, any advances in astronomy were bound to have widespread intellectual repercussions. By the early part of the seventeenth century, fundamental astronomical beliefs had been successfully challenged. The consequence was the undermining of both the material (physics) and the philosophical (metaphysics) explanations of the world that had been standing for centuries.

## The Inherited Worldview

Most ancient and medieval astronomers accepted the perspective on the universe that unaided human senses support—namely, that the earth is fixed at the center of the universe and the celestial bodies, such as the sun and the planets, rotate around it. The regular movements of heavenly bodies and the obvious importance of the sun for life on earth made astronomy a vital undertaking for both scientific and religious purposes in many ancient societies. Astronomers in ancient Greece carefully observed the heavens and learned to calculate and to predict the seemingly circular motion of the stars and the sun about the earth. The orbits of the planets were more difficult to explain, for the planets seemed to travel both east and west across the sky at various times and with no regularity that could be mathematically understood. Indeed, the word *planet* comes from a Greek word meaning "wanderer."

We now know that all the planets simultaneously orbit the sun at different speeds in paths that are at different distances from the sun. The relative positions of the planets constantly change; sometimes other planets are "ahead" of the earth and sometimes "behind." In the second century A.D., the Greek astronomer Ptolemy (TAHL-eh-mee) attempted to explain the planets' occasional "backward" motion by attributing it to "epicycles"—small circular orbits within the larger orbit. Ptolemy's mathematical explanations of the imagined epicycles were extremely complex, but neither Ptolemy nor medieval mathematicians and astronomers were ever able fully to account for planetary motion.

Ancient physics, most notably the work of the Greek philosopher Aristotle (384–322 B.C.), explained the fact that some objects (such as cannonballs) fall to earth but others (stars and planets) seem weightless relative to earth because of their composition: Different kinds of matter have different inherent tendencies and properties. In this view, all earthbound matter (like cannonballs) falls because it is naturally attracted to earth—heaviness being a property of earthbound things.

In the Christian era, the Aristotelian explanation of the universe was infused with Christian meaning and purpose. The heavens were said to be made of different, pure matter because they were the abode of the angels. Both the earth and the humans who inhabited it were changeable and corruptible. Yet, God had given human beings a unique and special place in the universe, which was thought to be a closed world with the stationary earth at the center. Revolving around the earth in circular orbits were the sun, moon, stars, and planets. The motion of all lesser bodies was caused by the rotation of all the stars together in the vast crystal-like sphere in which they were embedded.

A few ancient astronomers theorized that the earth moved about the sun. Some medieval philosophers also adopted this heliocentric thesis (*helios* is the Greek word for "sun"), but it remained a minority view because it seemed to contradict both common sense and observed data. The sun and stars *appeared* to move around the earth with great regularity. Moreover, how could objects fall to earth if the earth was moving beneath them? Also, astronomers detected no difference in angles from which observers on earth viewed the stars at different times. Such differences would exist, they thought, if the earth changed positions by moving around the sun. It was inconceivable that the universe could be so large and the stars so distant that the earth's movement would produce no measurable change in the earth's position with respect to the stars.

Several conditions of intellectual life in the sixteenth century encouraged new work in astronomy and led to the revision of the earth-centered worldview. The most important was the work of Renaissance humanists in recovering and interpreting ancient texts. Now able to work with new Greek versions of Ptolemy, mathematicians and astronomers noted that his explanations for the motion of the planets were imperfect and not simply inadequately transmitted, as they had long believed. Also, the discovery of the New World dramatically undercut the assumption that ancient knowledge was superior. The existence of the Americas specifically undermined Ptolemy's authority once again, for it disproved many of the assertions in his *Geography*, which had just been recovered in Europe the previous century.

## CHRONOLOGY

| | |
|---|---|
| 1543 | Copernicus, *De Revolutionibus Orbium Caelestium* |
| | Vesalius, *On the Fabric of the Human Body* |
| 1576 | Construction of Brahe's observatory begins |
| 1603 | Accademia dei Lincei founded in Rome |
| 1609 | Kepler's third law of motion |
| 1610 | Galileo, *The Starry Messenger* |
| 1620 | Bacon, *Novum Organum* |
| 1628 | Harvey, *On the Motion of the Heart* |
| 1632 | Galileo, *Dialogue on the Two Chief Systems of the World* |
| 1633 | Galileo condemned and sentenced to house arrest |
| 1637 | Descartes, *Discourse on Method* |
| 1651 | Hobbes, *Leviathan* |
| 1660 | Boyle, *New Experiments Physico-Mechanical* |
| | Royal Society of London founded |
| 1666 | Académie Royale des Sciences founded in France |
| 1686 | Fontenelle, *Conversations on the Plurality of Worlds* |
| 1687 | Newton, *Principia (Mathematical Principles of Natural Philosophy)* |
| 1690 | Locke, *Two Treatises of Government* and *Essay on Human Understanding* |
| 1702 | Bayle, *Historical and Critical Dictionary* |

The desire to explain heavenly movements better was still loaded with religious significance in the sixteenth century and was heightened by the immediate need for reform of the Julian calendar (named for Julius Caesar). Ancient observations of the movement of the sun, though remarkably accurate, could not measure the precise length of the solar year. By the sixteenth century, the cumulative error of this calendar had resulted in a change of ten days: The spring equinox fell on March 11 instead of March 21. An accurate and uniform system of dating was necessary for all rulers and their tax collectors and record keepers. And because the calculation of the date of Easter was at stake, a reliable calendar was the particular project of the church.

Impetus for new and better astronomical observations and calculations arose from other features of the intellectual and political landscape as well. Increasingly, as the century went on, princely courts became important sources of patronage for and sites of scientific activity. Rulers, eager to buttress their own power by symbolically linking it to dominion over nature, sponsored investigations of the world, as Ferdinand and Isabella had so successfully done, and displayed the marvels of nature at their courts. Sponsorship of science also yielded practical benefits: better mapping of the ruler's domains and better technology for mining, gunnery, and navigation.

Finally, schools of thought fashionable at the time, encouraged by the humanists' critique of tradition, hinted at the possibilities of alternative physical and metaphysical systems. The ancient doctrine of Hermeticism (named for the mythical originator of the ideas, Hermes Trismegistos), revived since the Renaissance, claimed that matter is universally imbued with divine (or magical) spirit. Drawing on Hermeticism was Paracelsianism, named for the Swiss physician Philippus von Hohenheim (1493–1541), who called himself Paracelsus (literally "beyond Celsus," an acclaimed Roman physician whose works had just been recovered). Paracelsus (pair-uh-SEL-sus) scoffed at the notion that ancient authorities were the final word on the workings of nature. Paracelsus offered an alternative to accepted medical theory, put forth by the ancient physician Galen (ca. 131–201), who was as revered as Aristotle. Galen (GAY-len) believed that an imbalance of bodily "humors" caused illness. Paracelsus substituted a theory of chemical imbalance that anticipated our modern understanding of pathology. He was wildly popular wherever he taught because he successfully treated many illnesses and lectured openly to laymen.

Neo-Platonism, another school of thought, had a more systematic and far-reaching impact. Neo-Platonism was a revival, primarily in Italian humanist circles, of certain aspects of Plato's thought. It contributed directly to innovation in science because it emphasized the abstract nature of true knowledge and thus encouraged mathematical investigation. This provided a spur to astronomical studies, which, since ancient times, had been concerned more with mathematical analysis of heavenly movements than with physical explanations for them. Also, like Hermeticism and Paracelsianism, Neo-Platonism had a mystical dimension that encouraged creative speculation about the nature of matter and the organization of the universe. Neo-Platonists were particularly fascinated by the sun as a symbol of the one divine mind or soul at the heart of all creation.

**The Traditional Universe** In this print from around 1600, heavenly bodies are depicted orbiting the earth in perfectly circular paths. Notice the horse-drawn chariot near the top of the image, which represents the Greek god of the sun circling the earth.

Bettmann/Corbis

## The Challenge by Copernicus

**Nicholas Copernicus** (1473–1543), son of a German merchant family in Poland, pursued wide-ranging university studies in philosophy, law, astronomy, mathematics, and medicine—first in Cracow in Poland and then in Bologna and Padua in Italy. In Italy, he was exposed to Neo-Platonic ideas. Copernicus (kuh-PURR-nih-kus) took a degree in canon (church) law in 1503 and became a cathedral canon (a member of the cathedral staff) in the city of Frauenburg (modern Poland), where he pursued his own interests in astronomy, while carrying out administrative duties. When the pope asked Copernicus to assist with the reform of the Julian calendar, he replied that reform of the calendar required reform in astronomy. His major work, *De Revolutionibus Orbium Caelestium (On the Revolution of Heavenly Bodies*, 1543), was dedicated to the pope in the hopes that it would help with the task of calendar reform—as indeed it did. The Gregorian calendar, issued in 1582 during the pontificate of Gregory XIII (r. 1572–1585), was based on Copernicus's calculations.

Copernicus postulated that the earth and all the other planets orbit the sun. He did not assert that the earth does in fact move around the sun but offered the heliocentric system as a mathematical construct, useful for predicting the movements of planets, stars, and the sun. However, he walked a thin line between making claims for a mathematical construct, on the one hand, and physical reality, on the other. Scholars now believe that Copernicus was himself persuaded that the **heliocentric theory** was correct. He had searched in ancient sources for thinkers who believed the earth moved. Other astronomers, familiar with his work and reputation, urged him to publish the results of his calculations. But not until 1542, twelve years after finishing the work, did he send *De Revolutionibus* to be published. He received a copy just before his death the next year.

By affirming the earth's movement around the sun, while also salvaging features of the old system, Copernicus faced burdens of explanation not faced by Ptolemy. For example, Copernicus still assumed that the planets traveled in circular orbits, so he was forced to retain some epicycles in his schema to account for the circular motion. In general, however, the Copernican account of planetary motion was simpler than the Ptolemaic account. But his work only slowly led to conceptual revolution, as scientists worked with his calculations and assembled other evidence to support the heliocentric theory.

The most important reason that fundamental conceptual change followed Copernican theory so gradually was that Copernicus did not resolve the physical problems his ideas raised. If Copernicus were right, the earth would have to be made of the same material as other planets. How, then, would Copernicus explain the motion of objects on earth—the fact that they fall to earth—if it was not in their nature to fall toward the heavy, stationary earth? In Copernicus's system, the movement of the earth caused the *apparent* motion of the stars. But if the stars did not rotate in their crystalline sphere, what made all other heavenly bodies move?

Copernicus was not as troubled by these questions as we might expect him to have been. Since ancient times, mathematical astronomy—the science of measuring and predicting the movements of heavenly bodies—had been far more important than, and had proceeded independently of, physical explanations of observed motion. Nevertheless, as Copernicus's own efforts to support his hypothesis reveal, his theories directly contradicted many of the supposed laws of motion. The usefulness of his theories to other astronomers meant that the contradictions between mathematical and physical models for the universe would have to be resolved. Copernicus himself might be best understood as the last Ptolemaic astronomer, working within inherited questions and with known tools. His work itself did not constitute a revolution, but it did start one.

## The First Copernican Astronomers

In the first generation of astronomers after the publication of *De Revolutionibus* in 1543, we can see the effects of Copernicus's work. His impressive computations rapidly won converts among fellow astronomers who continued to develop Copernican theories. By the second quarter of the seventeenth century, they and many others accepted the heliocentric theory as a reality and not just as a useful mathematical fiction. The three most important astronomers

**Nicholas Copernicus**
Polish astronomer who initiated the Scientific Revolution by proposing that the earth and other planets orbit the sun.

**heliocentric theory**
Means "sun-centered." Theory of Nicholas Copernicus that the earth and other planets orbit the sun.

to build on Copernican assumptions, and on the work of one another, were the Dane Tycho Brahe (1546–1601), the German Johannes Kepler (1571–1630), and the Italian Galileo Galilei (1564–1642).

## Tycho Brahe

**Tycho Brahe** Danish astronomer and first European to collect new astronomical data by using instruments to observe the celestial bodies.

Like generations of observers before him, **Tycho Brahe** (BRAH) had been stirred by the majesty of the regular movements of heavenly bodies. After witnessing a partial eclipse of the sun, he abandoned a career in government, befitting his noble status, and became an astronomer. Brahe was the first truly post-Ptolemaic astronomer because he was the first to improve on the data that the ancients and all subsequent astronomers had used. Ironically, no theory of planetary motion could have reconciled the data that Copernicus had used: They were simply too inaccurate, based, as they were, on naked-eye observations, even when errors of translation and copying, accumulated over centuries, had been corrected.

In 1576, the king of Denmark showered Brahe with properties and pensions enabling him to build an observatory, Uraniborg, on an island near the capital, Copenhagen. At Uraniborg, Brahe improved on ancient observations with large and very finely calibrated instruments that permitted precise measurements of celestial movements by the naked eye. His attention to precision and frequency of observation produced results that were twice as accurate as any previous data had been.

As a result of his observations, Brahe agreed with Copernicus that the various planets did rotate around the sun, not around the earth. He still could not be persuaded that the earth itself moved, for none of his data supported such a notion. Brahe's lasting and crucial contribution was his astronomical data. They would become obsolete as soon as observations from telescopes were accumulated about a century later. But in the meantime, they were used by **Johannes Kepler** to further develop Copernicus's model and arrive at a more accurate heliocentric theory.

## Johannes Kepler

**Johannes Kepler** German astronomer who developed three laws of planetary motion, known as Kepler's laws, which mathematically confirmed the Copernican heliocentric theory.

Kepler was young enough to be exposed to Copernican ideas from the outset of his training, and he quickly recognized in Brahe's data the means of resolving the problems in Copernican analysis. Though trained in his native Germany, Kepler went to Prague, where Brahe spent the last years of his life at the court of the Holy Roman emperor after a quarrel with the Danish king. There, Kepler became something of an apprentice to Brahe. After Brahe's death in 1601, Kepler kept his mentor's records of astronomical observations and continued to work at the imperial court as Rudolf II's court mathematician.

Kepler's contribution to the new astronomy, like that of Copernicus, was fundamentally mathematical. In it, we can see the stamp of the Neo-Platonic conviction about the purity of mathematical explanation. Kepler spent ten years working to apply Brahe's data to the most intricate of all the celestial movements—the motion of the planet Mars—as a key to explaining all planetary motion. Mars is close to the earth, but its orbital path is farther from the sun. This combination produces dramatic and puzzling variations in the apparent movement of Mars to an earthly observer.

The result of Kepler's work was laws of planetary motion that, in the main, are still in use. First, Kepler eliminated the need for epicycles by correctly asserting that planets follow elliptical, and not circular, orbits. Elliptical orbits could account, both mathematically and visually, for the motion of the planets when combined with Kepler's second law, which describes the *rate* of a planet's motion around its orbital path. Kepler noted that the speed of a planet in its orbit slows proportionally as the planet's distance from the sun increases. A third law demonstrates that the distance of each planet from the sun and the time it takes each planet to orbit the sun are in a constant ratio.

Kepler's work was a breakthrough because it mathematically confirmed the Copernican heliocentric hypothesis. In so doing, the work directly challenged the ancient worldview, in which heavenly bodies constantly moved in circular orbits around a stationary earth. Kepler's laws invited speculation about the properties of heavenly and terrestrial bodies alike. In fact, a new physics would be required to explain the novel motion that Kepler had posited. Kepler

STELLÆBURGUM five OBSERVATORIUM SUBTERRANEVM, A TYCHONE BRAHE Nobili Dano. IN INSULA HVÆNA, EXTRA ARCEM URANIAM, EXTRVCTVM CIRCA ANNVM M D LXXXIIII.

Private Collection/Archives Charmet/The Bridgeman Art Library

**Tycho Brahe's Observatory** Brahe gathered the best talent, including German instrument makers and Italian architects, to build his state-of-the-art observatory near Copenhagen. Brahe named the complex Uraniborg, for Urania, the muse of astronomy.

himself, in Neo-Platonic fashion, attributed planetary motion to the sun: "[The sun] is a fountain of light, rich in fruitful heat, most fair, limpid and pure . . .called king of the planets for his motion, heart of the world for his power . . .Who would hesitate to confer the votes of the celestial motions on him who has been administering all other movements and changes by the benefit of the light which is entirely his possession?"*

## Galileo and the Triumph of Copernicanism

Galileo Galilei holds a preeminent position in the development of astronomy because, first, he provided compelling new evidence to support Copernican theory and, second, he contributed to the development of a new physics—or, more precisely, mechanics—that could account for the movements of bodies in new terms. In short, he began to close the gap between the new astronomy and new explanations for the behavior of matter. Just as important, his efforts to publicize his findings and his condemnation by the church spurred popular debate about Copernican ideas in literate society and helped to determine the course science would take.

Galileo's career also illustrates, in dramatic fashion, the dependence of scientists on and their vulnerability to patronage relationships. Born to a minor Florentine noble family, Galileo began studying medicine at the nearby University of Pisa at the age of 17 but became intrigued by problems of mechanics and mathematics. He began studying those disciplines at Pisa under the tutelage of a Florentine court mathematician and became a lecturer in mathematics there in 1589, at age 25, after publishing promising work in mechanics. Three years later, well-connected fellow mathematicians helped him secure a more prestigious professorship at the University of Padua, where Copernicus had once studied. Galileo skillfully cultivated the learned Venetian aristocrats (Venice ruled Padua at this time) who controlled academic appointments and secured renewals and salary raises over the next eighteen years.

During his years at Pisa and Padua, Galileo pursued his revolutionary work in mechanics, although he did not publish the results of his experiments until much later. Galileo's

**Galileo Galilei** Italian physicist and astronomer who provided evidence supporting the heliocentric theory and helped develop the science of mechanics.

*Quoted in Thomas S. Kuhn, *The Copernican Revolution* (Cambridge, Mass.: Harvard University Press, 1985), p. 131.

principal contribution to mechanics lay in his working out of an early theory of inertia. As a result of a number of experiments with falling bodies (balls rolling on carefully constructed inclines—not free-falling objects that, according to myth, he dropped from the Leaning Tower of Pisa), Galileo ventured a new view of what is "natural" to objects. Galileo's view was that uniform motion is as natural as a state of rest. In the ancient and medieval universe, all motion needed a cause, and all motion could be explained in terms of purpose. "I hold," Galileo countered, "that there exists nothing in external bodies . . . but size, shape, quantity and motion."* Galileo retained the old assumption that motion was somehow naturally circular. Nevertheless, his theory was a crucial step in explaining motion according to new principles and in fashioning a worldview that accepted a mechanical universe devoid of metaphysical purpose.

The results of this work were, for the most part, not published until the end of his life. In the meantime, Galileo became famous for his astronomical observations, which he began in 1609 and which he parlayed into a position back at the Florentine court. Early that year, Galileo learned of the invention of a primitive telescope (which could magnify distant objects only three times) and quickly improved on it to make the first astronomically useful instrument. In *Sidereus Nuncius (The Starry Messenger,* 1610), he described his scrutiny of the heavens with his telescope in lay language. He documented sighting previously undetectable stars, as well as moons orbiting the planet Jupiter. In another blow to ancient descriptions of the universe, he noted craters and other "imperfections" on the surface of the moon. Three years later, he published his solar observations in *Letters on Sunspots.* Sunspots are regions of relatively cool gaseous material that appear as dark spots on the sun's surface. For Galileo, sunspots and craters on the moon proved that the heavens are not perfect and changeless but rather are like the supposedly "corrupt" and changeable earth. His telescopic observations also provided further support for Copernican heliocentrism. Indeed, Galileo's own acceptance of Copernicanism can be dated to this point because magnification revealed that each heavenly body rotates on its axis: Sunspots, for example, can be tracked across the visible surface of the sun as the sun rotates.

Galileo had already been approached by various Italian princes and in turn sought to woo their support with gifts of some of his earlier inventions, such as a military compass. He aimed his *Starry Messenger* at the Medici dukes of Florence, naming Jupiter's moons the "Medicean Stars" and publishing the work to coincide with the accession of the young Cosimo II, whom he had tutored as a youth. In 1610, he returned in triumph to his native Tuscany as court philosopher to the grand duke. Soon, however, his own fame and the increasing acceptance of Copernicanism aroused opposition. In 1615, Galileo was denounced to the Inquisition by a Florentine friar. Galileo defended himself to his patrons and to the wider scientific community by arguing, in print, that the new science did not challenge religion. (See the feature, "The Written Record: Galileo Asserts Science and Religion Are Compatible" on page 493.) After an investigation, the geokinetic theory (that the earth moves) was declared heretical, but Galileo himself was allowed to continue to use Copernican theory, but only as a theory. Indeed, a number of the most fervent practitioners of the new science continued to be clergymen who followed Galileo's work with interest. A new pope, elected in 1623, was a Tuscan aristocrat and an old friend of Galileo. Galileo dedicated his work on comets, *The Assayer* (1624), to Urban VIII in honor of his election.

Now in his 60s, Galileo began to work on a book that summarized his life's work—*Dialogue on the Two Chief Systems of the World* (1632), structured as a conversation among three characters debating the merits of Copernican theory. Given the work's sensitive subject matter, Galileo obtained explicit permission from the pope to write it and cleared some portions with censors before publication. The work was the most important single source in its day for

## SECTION SUMMARY

- The Scientific Revolution began in 1543 with the publication of Copernicus's mathematical calculations supporting the heliocentric theory.

- Tycho Brahe and Johannes Kepler confirmed Copernicus's hypothesis with new data and more thorough mathematical explanations of the motions of planets.

- Galileo's observations with his telescope provided new evidence to support Copernican theory; his experiments in mechanics contributed to new explanations for the behavior of matter.

- Galileo's advocacy of Copernicanism led to his condemnation by the church.

*Quoted in Margaret C. Jacob, *The Cultural Meaning of the Scientific Revolution* (Philadelphia: Temple University Press, 1988), p. 18.

## Galileo Asserts Science and Religion Are Compatible

*After Galileo Galilei's work on sunspots was released, many learned followers grew anxious about the implications of the new science. In the letter excerpted here, published in 1615 and widely circulated, Galileo reassures the mother of Cosimo II, the dowager grand duchess of Tuscany, that the new science does not contradict Christianity.*

Some years ago, as Your Serene Highness well knows, I discovered in the heavens many things that had not been seen there before our own age. The novelty of these things, as well as some consequences which followed from them ... stirred up against me no small number of professors—as if I had placed these things in the sky with my own hands in order to upset nature and overturn the sciences ... [These professors] go about invoking the Bible, which they would have minister to their deceitful purposes. Contrary to the sense of the Bible and the intention of the holy Fathers, if I am not mistaken, they would extend such authorities until even in purely physical matters—where faith is not involved—they would have us altogether abandon reason and the evidence of our own senses in favor of some biblical passage, though under the surface meaning of its words this passage may contain a different sense. ...

I think that in discussions of physical problems we ought to begin not from the authority of scriptural passages, but from sense experience and necessary demonstrations. ... I should judge that the authority of the Bible was designed to persuade men of those articles and propositions which, surpassing all human reasoning, could not be made credible by science, or by any means other than through the very mouth of the Holy Spirit. ...

But I do not feel obliged to believe that the same God who has endowed us with senses, reason and intellect has intended to forgo their use and by some other means to give us knowledge which we can attain by them. He would not require us to deny sense and reason in physical matters which are set before our eyes and minds by direct experience or necessary demonstrations. This must be especially true in those sciences of which but the faintest trace ... is to be found in the Bible. Of astronomy, for instance, so little is found that none of the planets except Venus are so much as mentioned. ...

Now, if the Holy Spirit has purposely neglected to teach us propositions of this sort as irrelevant to the highest goal (that is, to our salvation), how can anyone affirm that it is obligatory to take sides on them, and that one belief is required by faith, while another side is erroneous? ... I would assert here something that was heard from [a respected cleric]: ... "the intention of the Holy Ghost is to teach us how to go to heaven, not how heaven goes." ... [And] in St. Augustine we read: "If anyone shall set the authority of Holy Writ against clear and manifest reason, ... he opposes to the truth not the meaning of the Bible, which is beyond his comprehension, but rather his own interpretation. ..."

Moreover, we are unable to affirm that all interpreters of the Bible speak with divine inspiration, for if that were so there would exist no differences between them about the sense of a given passage. Hence [it would be wise] not to permit anyone to usurp scriptural texts and force them in some way to maintain any physical conclusion to be true, when at some future time the senses ... may show the contrary. Who indeed will set bounds to human ingenuity? Who will assert that everything in the universe capable of being perceived is already discovered and known?

### Questions

1. *How does Galileo justify pursuing scientific investigation against certain claims of faith?*

2. *Do you think that Galileo's arguments would have been reassuring to the grand duchess? Why or why not?*

3. *Why might the arguments have further angered those church officials already hostile toward Galileo's work?*

Source: *Discoveries and Opinions of Galileo*, by Galileo Galilei, translated by Stillman Drake, copyright © 1957 by Stillman Drake. Used by permission of Doubleday, a division of Random House, Inc.

the popularization of Copernican theory, but it led to renewed concerns in Rome. Galileo had clearly overstepped the bounds of discussing Copernicanism in theory only and appeared to advocate it. Simplicio, the character representing the old worldview, was, as his name suggests, an example of ignorance, not wisdom.

Moreover, the larger political context affecting Galileo's patrons and friends had changed. The pope was being threatened by the Spanish and Austrian Habsburg rulers for his tepid support in the Thirty Years' War, in which Catholic forces were now losing to Protestant armies (see page 438). He could no longer be indulgent towards his friend, Galileo. Galileo was forced to stand trial for heresy in Rome in 1633. When, in a kind of plea-bargain arrangement, he pled guilty to a lesser charge of inadvertently advocating Copernicanism, Pope Urban intervened to insist on a weightier penalty. Galileo's book was banned, he was forced to formally renounce his "error," and he was sentenced to house arrest. Galileo lived confined, though comfortably at home and continuing his investigations of mechanics, until his death eight years later.

# The Scientific Revolution Expands, ca. 1600–1700

> *How and why did new theories about astronomy lead to a broader Scientific Revolution?*

Galileo's work found such a willing audience in part because Galileo, like Kepler and Brahe, was not working alone. Dozens of other scientists were examining old problems from the fresh perspective offered by the breakthroughs in astronomy. Some analyzed the nature of matter, now that it appeared that all matter in the universe was somehow the same, despite its varying appearances. Many of these thinkers addressed the metaphysical issues that their investigations inevitably raised. They began the complex intellectual and psychological journey toward a new worldview, one that accepted the existence of an infinitely large universe of undifferentiated matter with no obvious place in it for humans.

## The Uses of the New Science

**Francis Bacon** England's lord chancellor during the reign of James I and author of influential works encouraging the empirical scientific method and inductive reasoning.

No less a man than **Francis Bacon** (1561–1626), lord chancellor of England during the reign of James I, wrote a utopian essay extolling the benefits of science for a peaceful society and for human happiness. In *New Atlantis*, published one year after his death, Bacon argued that science would produce "things of use and practice for man's life."* In *New Atlantis* and *Novum Organum* (1620), Bacon reveals his faith in science by advocating patient, systematic observation and experimentation to accumulate knowledge about the world. He argues that the proper method of investigation "derives axioms from . . . particulars, rising by gradual and unbroken ascent, so that it arrives at the most general axioms of all. This is the true way but untried."**

**empirical method** Philosophical view developed by Bacon and Locke, which holds that all knowledge is based on observation and experimentation and that general principles should be derived from particular facts.

Bacon did not undertake experiments himself, although his widely read works were influential in encouraging both the **empirical method** (relying on observation and experimentation) and inductive reasoning (deriving general principles from particular facts). Given the early date of his writings, it might seem difficult to account for his confidence in the benefits of science. Bacon was a visionary, but his writings reflect the widespread interest in science within his elite milieu, an interest actively encouraged by the state. In another of his writings, he argues that a successful state should concentrate on effective "rule in religion *and nature*, as well as civil administration."†

Bacon's pronouncements reflect the fact that an interest in exploring nature's secrets and exercising "dominion over nature" had become an indispensable part of princely rule. Princely courts were the main sources of financial support for science and the primary sites of scientific work during Bacon's lifetime. Part of the impetus for this development had come from the civic humanism of the Italian Renaissance, which had celebrated the state and service to it and had provided models both for educated rulers and for cultivated courtiers. Attention to science and to its benefits for the state also reflects the scope, and pragmatism, of princely resources and ambitions: the desire of rulers for technical expertise in armaments, fortification, construction, navigation, and mapmaking. (See the feature, "The Visual Record: Modern Maps" on pages 498–499.)

The lure of the New World and the drive for overseas trade and exploration especially encouraged princely support of scientific investigation. A renowned patron of geographic investigation, from mapmaking to navigation, was Henry, prince of Wales (d. 1612), eldest son of James I. Prince Henry patronized technical experts such as gunners and seamen, as well as those with broader and more theoretical expertise. One geographer at his court worked on the vital problem of calculating longitude, sketched the moon after reading and emulating Galileo's work with the telescope, and, in the spirit of empiricism associated with

---

*Quoted in Margaret C. Jacob, *The Cultural Meaning of the Scientific Revolution* (Philadelphia: Temple University Press, 1988), p. 33.
**Quoted in Alan G. R. Smith, *Science and Society in the Sixteenth and Seventeenth Centuries* (New York: Science History Publications, 1972), p. 72.
†Quoted in Margaret C. Jacob, *The Cultural Meaning of the Scientific Revolution* (Philadelphia: Temple University Press, 1988), p. 32 (emphasis added).

Bacon, compiled information about the new territory Virginia, including the first dictionary of any Native American language.

Science was an ideological, as well as a practical, tool for power. Most courts housed collections of marvels, specimens of exotic plants and animals, and mechanical contrivances. These collections demonstrated the ruler's interest in investigation of the world—in other words, his or her status as an educated individual. Collections and the work of court experts also enhanced the ruler's reputation as a patron and person of power. Galileo was playing off such expectations when he named his newly discovered moons of Jupiter "Medicean Stars." Like all patronage relationships, the status was shared by both partners; indeed, the attention of a patron was a guarantee of the researcher's scientific credibility.

By the beginning of the seventeenth century, private salons and academies where investigators might meet on their own were another significant milieu of scientific investigation. These, too, had their roots in the humanist culture of Italy, where circles of scholars without university affiliations had formed. Though also dependent on private resources, these associations were an important alternative to princely patronage, since a ruler's funds might wax and wane according to his or her other commitments. Private organizations could avoid the stark distinctions of rank that were inevitable at courts, yet mimicked courts in the blend of scholars and educated courtiers they included. This more collegial, but still privileged, environment also fostered a sense of legitimacy for the science pursued there: Legitimacy came from the recognition of fellow members and, in many cases, from publication of work by the society itself.

The earliest academy dedicated to scientific study was the *Accademia Segreta* (Secret Academy), founded in Naples in the 1540s. The members pursued experiments together in order, in the words of one member, "to make a true anatomy of the things and operations of nature itself."* During the remainder of the sixteenth century and on into the seventeenth, such academies sprang up in many cities. The most celebrated was the *Accademia dei Lincei* (ack-uh-DAY-mee-uh day-ee lin-CHAY-ee), founded in Rome by an aristocrat in 1603. Its most famous member, Galileo, joined in 1611. The name "Lincei," from *lynx*, was chosen because of the legendary keen sight of that animal, an appropriate mascot for "searchers of secrets." Galileo's fame and the importance of his discoveries forced all such learned societies to take a stand for or against Copernicanism. Throughout the seventeenth century, the investigation of nature would continue in increasingly sophisticated institutional settings.

## Scientific Thought in France

Philosophers, mathematicians, and educated elites thus engaged in lively debate and practical investigation throughout Europe in the first half of the seventeenth century. In France, the great questions about cosmic order were being posed, ironically, at a time of political disorder. The years following the religious wars saw the murder of Henry IV, another regency, and further civil war in the 1620s (see pages 428–429). In this environment, questions about order in the universe and the possibilities of human knowledge took on particular urgency. It is not surprising that a Frenchman, **René Descartes** (1596–1650), created the first fully articulated alternative worldview.

## Descartes and a New Worldview

Descartes (day-KART) developed and refined his thinking in dialogue with a circle of other French thinkers. His work became more influential among philosophers and laypeople than the work of some of his equally talented contemporaries because of its thoroughness and rigor, grounded in Descartes's mathematical expertise, and because of his graceful, readable French. His system was fully presented in his *Discours de la méthode* (*Discourse on Method*, 1637). Descartes described some of his intellectual crises in his later work, *Meditations* (1641).

**René Descartes**
French philosopher and mathematician who emphasized skepticism and deductive reasoning in his most influential treatise, *Discourse on Method*. He offered the first alternative physical explanation of matter after the Copernican revolution.

*Quoted in Bruce T. Moran, ed., *Patronage and Institutions: Science, Technology and Medicine at the European Court* (Rochester, N.Y.: Boyden Press, 1991), p. 43.

Descartes accepted Galileo's conclusion that the heavens and the earth are made of the same elements. He drew on ancient atomic models (that had not, then, been generally accepted) to create a new theory about the nature of matter. His theory that all matter is made up of identical bits, which he named "corpuscles," is a forerunner of modern atomic and quantum theories. Descartes believed that all the different appearances and behaviors of matter (for example, why stone is always hard and water is always wet) could be explained solely by the size, shape, and motion of these "corpuscles." Descartes's was an extremely mechanistic explanation of the universe. It nevertheless permitted new, more specific observations and hypotheses and greater understanding of inertia. For example, because he reimagined the universe as being filled with "corpuscles" free to move in any direction, "natural" motion no longer seemed either circular (Galileo's idea) or toward the center of the earth (Aristotle's idea). The new understanding of motion would be crucial to Isaac Newton's work later in the century.

In his works, Descartes tries to resolve the crisis of confidence that the new discoveries about the universe had produced. The collapse of the old explanations about the world made Descartes and other investigators doubt not only what they knew but also their capacity to know anything at all. Their physical senses—which denied that the earth moved, for example—had been proved untrustworthy. Descartes's solution was to reenvision the human rational capacity, the mind, as completely distinct from the world—that is, as distinct from the human body and its unreliable sense perceptions. In a leap of faith, Descartes presumed that God would not have given humans a mind if that mind consistently misled them. For Descartes, God became the guarantor of human reasoning capacity, and humans were distinguished by that capacity. This is the significance of his famous claim "I think, therefore I am."

Descartes thus achieved a resolution of the terrifying doubt about the world—a resolution that exalted the role of the human knower. The Cartesian universe was one of mechanical motion, not purpose or mystical meaning, and the Cartesian human being was preeminently a mind that could apprehend that universe. In what came to be known as "Cartesian dualism," Descartes proposed that the human mind is detached from the world and yet, at the same time, can objectively analyze the world.

**A Collection of Naturalia**    Collections of exotic specimens, such as this display in Naples, symbolized the ruler's authority by suggesting his or her power over nature. f Typ 620.73.451, Houghton Library, Harvard Library

Descartes's ambitious view of human reason emphasizes deductive reasoning (a process of reasoning in which the conclusion follows necessarily from the stated premises), a natural consequence of his philosophical rejection of sense data. The limits of deductive reasoning for scientific investigation would be realized and much of Cartesian physics rejected by the end of the century. Nevertheless, Descartes's assumption about the objectivity of the observer would become an enduring part of scientific practice. In Descartes's day, the most radical aspect of his thought was the reduction of God to the role of guarantor of knowledge. Many fellow scientists and interested laypeople were fearful of Descartes's system because it seemed to encourage "atheism." In fact, Descartes's faith had been necessary for the construction of his new world system—but the system did work without God.

Descartes would have been surprised and offended by charges of atheism, but he knew that his work would antagonize the church. He moved to the Netherlands to study in 1628, and his *Discourse* was first published there. His long residence in the Netherlands led him to advocate religious toleration late in his life. In 1649, at the urging of an influential friend with contacts at the Swedish court, Descartes accepted the invitation of Queen Christina to visit there. Christina was an eager but demanding patron, who required Descartes to lecture on scientific topics at 5:00 a.m. each day. The long hours of work and harsh winter weather took their toll on his health, and Descartes died of pneumonia after only a few months in Sweden.

## Pascal and the Limits of Scientific Knowledge

A contemporary of Descartes, fellow Frenchman Blaise Pascal (1623–1662), drew attention in his writings and in his life to the limits of scientific knowledge. The son of a royal official, Pascal (pahss-KAHL) was perhaps the most brilliant mind of his generation. A mathematician like Descartes, he stressed the importance of mathematical representations of phenomena, built one of the first calculating machines, and invented probability theory. He also carried out experiments to investigate air pressure, the behavior of liquids, and the existence of vacuums.

Pascal's career alternated between periods of intense scientific work and religious retreat. Today, he is well known for his writings justifying the austere Catholicism known as Jansenism (see page 456) and for his explorations of the human soul and psyche. His *Pensées* (*Thoughts*, 1657) consists of the published fragments of his defense of Christian faith, which remained unfinished at the time of his death. Pascal's appeal for generations after him may lie in his attention to matters of faith and of feeling. His most famous statement, "The heart has its reasons which reason knows not," can be read as a declaration of the limits of the Cartesian worldview.

## *Science and Revolution in England*

The new science had adherents and practitioners throughout Europe by 1650. Dutch scientists in the commercial milieu of the Netherlands, for example, had the freedom to pursue practical and experimental interests. The Dutch investigator Christiaan Huygens (HI-ghenz) (1629–1695) worked on a variety of problems, including air pressure and optics. In 1657, he invented and patented the pendulum clock, the first device to measure accurately small units of time, essential for a variety of measurements.

England proved a unique environment for the development of science in the middle of the century. In a society torn by civil war, differing positions on science became part and parcel of disputes over Puritanism, church hierarchy, and royal power. Scientific, along with political and religious, debate was generally encouraged by the collapse of censorship, beginning in the 1640s.

During the 1640s, natural philosophers with Puritan leanings were encouraged in their investigations by dreams that science, of the practical Baconian sort, could be the means by which the perfection of life on earth could be brought about and the end of history—the reign of the saints preceding the return of Christ—could be accelerated. Their concerns ranged from improved production of gunpowder (for the armies fighting against Charles I) to surveying and mapmaking. Perhaps the best-known member of this group was Robert Boyle

## Modern Maps

Modern mapping was developed during the Scientific Revolution. Like most of the changes associated with the Scientific Revolution, changes in mapping were the result of several influences: innovations in Renaissance art, knowledge gleaned from voyages of exploration, the impact of new astronomical discoveries, the interest and support of princely patrons, and the spread of new ideas by means of print. All of these factors enabled Europeans of this era to have a literally new view of their world. Yet, as in the work of Copernicus, developments in mapping also depended on the continued use of data accumulated in previous centuries. In the examples shown here, we can see the dramatic progress in mapmaking over the course of the sixteenth and seventeenth centuries.

Consider the brightly colored map of western Europe and North Africa reproduced here. It is a reproduction from a 1584 atlas of printed sea charts made by a Dutchman, Lucas Waghenauer. To our eye, the map may look decorative, even quaint. Sailing ships and sea monsters, not drawn to scale, populate the oceans. Most of the major states, such as England and France, are adorned with a crest identifying their ruling dynasties.

Because some of its features appear decorative to us, we may not realize the considerable innovation that the map represented in its day. First, it is an example of the revolutionary method of depicting space achieved in the Renaissance. The discovery of linear perspective by Renaissance artists enabled them to create the illusion of three-dimensional space in their paintings and to likewise depict territory, on a map, as imagined from the perspective of a distanced observer. In addition, the landforms appear in relatively accurate relationship to one another because mapmakers, following the newly recovered *Geography* by Ptolemy, used increasingly accurate projections of the globe to represent landforms on a two-dimensional map.*

The projection used for this map was particularly useful because compass bearings could be represented as straight lines. The many straight lines that crisscross this map are called "rhumb" lines; they represent compass headings that could be used to navigate between two points. Compass bearings between points on coastlines appeared on hand-drawn medieval sea charts (after the invention of the compass in about 1250). So, this sixteenth-century map combines medieval knowledge with new knowledge

**Europe and North Africa, 1584** John Webb/The Art Archive at Art Resource, NY

of geography and of how to depict landforms accurately. In addition, the information in this map was all the more useful because it was published, along with many other sea charts, in book form.

Now, let us look at the apparently simpler map of the coastline of France, made about one hundred years later, in 1693. We immediately note that virtually all the decorative elements are gone. There are no sea monsters and no ships to sail the abundant seas. The map is a line drawing; it is not even colored. The simplified style of the map by itself testifies to further progress in mapmaking, and to the ability of users to absorb information from maps. To make sense of this map, the viewer would need to be familiar with the representation of France from other maps since, for example, the land borders are not sketched in.

Indeed, the map conveys abundant information, all of which reflects scientific advancement over the intervening

---

*This discussion of the evolution of mapmaking and of these examples draws on the work of Norman J. W. Thrower, *Maps and Civilization* (Chicago: University of Chicago Press, 1996), chaps. 5 and 6.

**The French Coastline, 1693**

100 years. The figure of a compass marks the Paris meridian, advertising that the site of the city has been precisely determined by means of its longitude. A horizontal line marks its latitude. More accurate calculation of longitude had been made possible by the work of Johannes Kepler and Galileo Galilei, whose mapping of heavenly bodies provided known points in the night sky from which to calculate the longitude of the observer's position on earth. Calculation of latitude had always been easier, since it involved only determining the angle of the sun above the horizon, but it also became more precise by use of better instrumentation in the seventeenth century. (Note: Above and to the right of the compass symbol are modern circular and oval stamps identifying the archive where the map is housed; these marks would not have appeared when the map was originally published.)

After 1650, French cartographers, among others, systematically collected astronomical observations from around the world so they could map all known lands more precisely. In addition to claiming the correct coordinates for Paris, this map also dramatically corrects earlier maps of the coastline of France. The map superimposes a corrected view (the darker line) of the coastline over an older rendering (the fainter line, mostly outside of the darker line). Thus, this map not only provides information, but also boldly demonstrates the progress of mapmaking itself.

The legend of the map calls attention to this progress. It reads, "Map of France, corrected by order of the King by the observations of Messieurs of the Academy of Sciences." The map thus also documented royal patronage of scientific work. It is interesting, however, that the king is mentioned discreetly, in what is coming to be a standardized label on the map. The information in the map stands alone, without royal crests or decorations, because the public that viewed the map by now accepted and expected updated knowledge about the world.

## Questions

1. *What different types of information does the first map supply? Identify as many as you can.*

2. *What would have appeared most impressive about the second map, to a contemporary?*

(1627–1691). In his career, we can trace the evolution of English science through the second half of the seventeenth century.

Boyle and his colleagues were theoretically eclectic, drawing on Cartesian mechanics and even Paracelsian chemical theories. They attacked the English university system, still under the sway of Aristotelianism, and proposed widespread reform of education. They were forced to moderate many of their positions, however, as the English civil wars proceeded. Radical groups, such as the Levellers, used Hermeticism and the related Paracelsianism as part of their political and religious tenets. The Levellers and other radical groups drew on the Hermetic notion that matter is imbued with divine spirit; they believed that each person was capable of divine knowledge and a godly life without the coercive hierarchy of church and royal officials.

Boyle and his colleagues responded to these challenges. They gained institutional power when they accepted positions at Oxford and Cambridge. They formed the core of the Royal Society of London, which they persuaded Charles II to recognize and charter on his accession to the throne in 1660. They worked out a theoretical position that combined the orderliness of mechanism, a continued divine presence in the world, and a Baconian belief in scientific progress. This unwieldy set of notions was attractive to the educated elite of the day, who wanted the certainties of science but did not want to give up certain authoritarian aspects of the old Christian worldview.

Their most creative contribution, both to their own cause and to the advancement of science, was their refinement of experimental philosophy and practice. In 1660, Boyle published *New Experiments Physico-Mechanical*. The work describes the results of his experiments with an air pump he had designed, and it lays out general rules for experimental procedure. Descartes had accounted for motion by postulating that "corpuscles" of matter interact, thereby eliminating the possibility of a vacuum in nature. Recent experiments on air pressure suggested otherwise, however, and Boyle tried to confirm their findings with his air pump.

Boyle's efforts to demonstrate that a vacuum could exist—by evacuating a sealed chamber with his pump—were not successes by modern standards because his experiments could not readily be duplicated. Boyle tied the validity of experimental results to the agreement of witnesses to the experiment—a problematic solution, since only investigators sympathetic to his hypothesis and convinced of his credibility usually witnessed the results. In response to a Cambridge scholar who criticized his interpretation of one experiment, Boyle replied that he could not understand his critic's objections, "the experiment having been tried both before our whole society [the Royal Society of London], and very critically, by its royal founder, his majesty himself."* In other words, rather than debate differing interpretations, Boyle appealed to the authority and prestige of the participants. In English science of the mid-seventeenth century, therefore, we have a further example of the fact that new truths, new procedures for determining truth, and new criteria for practitioners were all being established simultaneously.

## The Achievement of Isaac Newton

The Copernican revolution reached its high point with the work of the Englishman **Isaac Newton** (1643–1727), born one year almost to the day after Galileo died. Newton completed the new explanation for motion in the heavens and on earth that Copernicus's work had required and that Kepler, Galileo, and others had sought.

After a difficult childhood and an indifferent education, Newton entered Cambridge University as a student in 1661. Copernicanism and Cartesianism were being hotly debated, though not yet officially studied. Newton made use of Descartes's work in mathematics to develop his skill on his own, and by 1669 he had invented calculus. (He did not publish his work at the time, and another mathematician, Gottfried von Leibniz [LIBE-nits], later independently developed calculus and vied with Newton for credit.)

Newton won a fellowship at Cambridge in 1667 and became a professor of mathematics in 1669, at the recommendation of a retiring professor with whom he had shared his work

**Isaac Newton** English physicist, mathematician, and natural philosopher. His mathematical computation of the laws of gravity and planetary motion, which he combined with a fully developed theory of inertia, completed the explanation for motion initiated by Nicholas Copernicus.

*Quoted in Steven Shapin, *A Social History of Truth* (Chicago: University of Chicago Press, 1994), p. 298.

on calculus. With less demanding teaching assignments, he was able to devote much of the next decade to work on optics—an important area of study for testing Descartes's corpuscular theory of matter.

In the 1680s, Newton experienced a period of self-imposed isolation from other scientists after a particularly heated exchange with one colleague, provoked by Newton's difficult temperament. During this decade, he returned to the study of alternative theories about matter. As a student at Cambridge, he had been strongly influenced by the work of a group of Neo-Platonists who were critical of Cartesian theory that posited God as a cause of all matter and motion but removed God, or any other unknown or unknowable force, as an explanation for the behavior of matter. The Neo-Platonists' concerns were both religious and scientific. As Newton says in some of his early writing, while a student, "However we cast about we find almost no other reason for atheism than this [Cartesian] notion of bodies having . . . a complete, absolute and independent reality."*

Newton now read treatises in alchemy and Hermetic tracts and began to imagine explanations for the behavior of matter (such as for bits of cloth fluttered from a distance by static electricity) that Cartesian corpuscular theory could not readily explain. Precisely what the forces were that caused such behavior, he was not sure, but his eclectic mind and his religious convictions enabled him to accept their existence.

It was this leap that allowed him to propose the existence of gravity—a mysterious force that accounts for the movements of heavenly bodies in the vacuum of space. Others had speculated about the existence of gravity; indeed, the concept of inertia worked out by Galileo, Descartes, and others suggested the need for the concept of gravity. Otherwise, if a planet were "pushed" (say, in Kepler's view, by the "motive force" of the sun), it would continue along that course forever unless "pulled back" by something else.

Newton's extraordinary contribution to a new mechanistic understanding of the universe was the mathematical computation of the laws of gravity and planetary motion, which he combined with a fully developed concept of inertia. In 1687, Newton published *Philosophia Naturalis Principia Mathematica* (*Mathematical Principles of Natural Philosophy*; usually called *Principia*). In this mathematical treatise—so intricate that it was baffling to laypeople, even those able to read Latin—Newton laid out his **laws of motion** and expressed them as mathematical theorems that can be used to test future observations of moving bodies. Then he demonstrated that these laws also apply to the solar system, confirming the data already gathered about the planets and even predicting the existence of an, as yet, unseen planet. His supreme achievement was his law of gravitation, with which he could predict the discovery of the invisible planet. This law states that every body, indeed every bit of matter, in the universe exerts over every other body an attractive force proportional to the product of their masses and inversely proportional to the square of the distance between them. Newton not only accounted for motion but definitively united heaven and earth in a single scheme and created a convincing picture of an orderly nature.

**PHILOSOPHICAL TRANSACTIONS.**

*February 19. 16 71/72.*

**Isaac Newton Publishes a Paper**   This table of contents from the publication of the Royal Society of London reveals that the issue contains one of Isaac Newton's papers on optics. Notice that this issue's contents also include a review of a book about a sea voyage and an essay on music.
© The Royal Society

**laws of motion** The laws of gravity, planetary motion, and inertia first laid out in the seventeenth century by Isaac Newton.

---

*Quoted in Margaret C. Jacob, *The Cultural Meaning of the Scientific Revolution* (Philadelphia: Temple University Press, 1988), p. 89.

Neither Newton nor anyone else claimed that his theorems resolved all questions about motion and matter. Exactly what gravity is and how it operates were not clear, as they still are not. Newton's laws of motion are taught today because they still adequately account for most problems of motion. The fact that so fundamental a principle as gravity remains unexplained in no way diminishes Newton's achievement but is clear evidence of the nature of scientific understanding: Science provides explanatory schemas that account for many—but not all—observed phenomena. No schema explains everything, and each schema contains open doorways that lead both to further discoveries and to blind alleys. Newton, for example, assumed that the forces that accounted for gravity would mysteriously work on metals so that, as alchemists predicted, they might "quickly pass into gold."*

After the publication of *Principia*, Newton was more of a celebrated public figure than a practicing scientist. He helped lead resistance to James II's Catholicizing policies in the university, and he became the familiar of many other leading minds of his day, such as John Locke (see page 509). He also, later in his life, was one of the developers of calculus. Reflecting on the cumbersome mathematics he still used when writing *Principia*, one scholar has wondered, "what manner of man he was who could use as a weapon what we can scarcely lift as a burden."**

Newton became the president of the Royal Academy of Sciences in 1703 and was knighted in 1705, the first scientist to be so distinguished. By the end of his life, universities in England were dominated by men who acclaimed and built on his work. The transformation of the institutional structure of science in England was complete.

## Developments in Chemistry, Biology, and Medicine

The innovations in astronomy that led to the new mechanistic view of the behavior of matter did not automatically spill over to other branches of science. In astronomy, innovation came after the ancient and medieval inheritance had been fully assimilated and its errors disclosed. Other branches of science followed their own paths, though all were strongly influenced by the **mechanistic worldview**.

**mechanistic worldview**
Seventeenth-century philosophical view that saw the world as a machine that functions in strict obedience to physical laws, without purpose or will.

In chemistry, the mechanistic assumption that all matter was composed of small, equivalent parts was crucial to understanding the properties and behaviors of compounds (combinations of elements). But knowledge of these small units of matter was not yet precise enough to be of much use in advancing chemistry conceptually. Nevertheless, the flawed conceptual schema did not hold back all chemical discovery and development. Lack of understanding of gases, and of the specific elements in their makeup, for example, did not prevent the improvement of gunpowder. Indeed, unlike the innovations in astronomy, conceptual breakthroughs in chemistry and biology owed a great deal to the results of plodding experiment and the slow accumulation of data.

A conceptual leap forward was made in biology in the sixteenth and seventeenth centuries as a result of practical knowledge because biological knowledge was mostly a byproduct of the practice of medicine. The recent discovery of *On Anatomical Procedures*, a treatise by the ancient physician Galen, encouraged dissection and other research. Andreas Vesalius (1514–1564), in particular, made important advances by following Galen's example. Born in Brussels, Vesalius (vuh-SAY-lee-us) studied at the nearby University of Louvain and then at Padua, where he was appointed professor of surgery. He ended his career as physician to Emperor Charles V and his son, Philip II of Spain. In his teaching at Padua, Vesalius acted on the newly recovered Galenic teachings by doing dissections himself rather than giving the work to technicians. In 1543, he published versions of his lectures as an illustrated compendium of anatomy, *De Humani Corporis Fabrica* (*On the Fabric of the Human Body*).

The results of his dissections of human corpses, revealed in this work, demonstrated a number of errors in Galen's knowledge of human anatomy, much of which had been derived from dissection of animals. Neither Vesalius nor his immediate successors, however, questioned overall Galenic theory about the functioning of the human body, any more than Copernicus had utterly rejected Aristotelian physics.

---

*Quoted in Margaret C. Jacob, *The Cultural Meaning of the Scientific Revolution* (Philadelphia: Temple University Press, 1988), p. 25.
**Quoted in Alan G. R. Smith, *Science and Society in the Sixteenth and Seventeenth Centuries* (New York: Science History Publications, 1972), p. 130.

The slow movement from new observation to changed explanation is clearly illustrated in the career of the Englishman William Harvey (1578–1657). Much like Vesalius, Harvey was educated first in his own land and then at Padua, where he benefited from the tradition of anatomical research. Also like Vesalius, he had a career as a physician, first in London and later at the courts of James I and Charles I.

Harvey postulated the circulation of the blood—postulated rather than discovered because, owing to the technology of the day, he could not observe the tiny capillaries where the movement of arterial blood into the veins occurs. After conducting vivisectional experiments on animals that revealed the actual functioning of the heart and lungs, he reasoned that circulation of the blood must occur. He carefully described his experiments and his conclusions in *Exercitatio Anatomica de Motu Cordis et Sanguinis in Animalibus* (1628), usually shortened to *De Motu Cordis* (*On the Motion of the Heart*).

Harvey's work challenged Galenic anatomy and, like Copernicus's discoveries, created new burdens of explanation. According to Galenic theory, the heart and lungs helped each other to function. The heart sent nourishment to the lungs through the pulmonary artery, and the lungs provided raw material for the "vital spirit," which the heart gave to the blood to sustain life. The lungs also helped the heart sustain its "heat." This heat was understood to be an innate property of organs, just as "heaviness," in traditional physics, had been considered an innate property of earthbound objects.

From his observations, Harvey came to think of the heart in mechanistic terms: as a pump to circulate the blood. But he adjusted, rather than abandoned, Galenic theories concerning "heat" and "vital spirit." The lungs had been thought to "ventilate" the heart by providing air to maintain "heat," just as a bellows blows air on a fire. In light of his discovery of the pulmonary transit (that all of the blood is pumped through the lungs and back through the heart), Harvey suggested instead that the lungs carried out some of these functions for the blood, helping it to concoct the "vital spirit." Only in this sense did he think of the heart as a machine, circulating this life-giving material throughout the body.

Harvey's explanation of bodily functions, in light of his new knowledge, did not constitute a rupture with Galenic tradition. But by the end of his life, Harvey's own adjustments of Galenic theory were suggesting new conceptual possibilities. His work inspired additional research in physiology, chemistry, and physics. Robert Boyle's efforts to understand vacuums can be traced in part to questions Harvey raised about the function of the lungs and the properties of air.

Courtesy, Dover Publications

**Vesalius on Human Anatomy** The meticulous illustrations in Vesalius's work helped ensure its success. The medium of print was essential for accurate reproduction of scientific drawings. Note also the way the human body, in this drawing of musculature, is depicted as dominating the landscape.

## SECTION SUMMARY

- Interest in the new science spread in the seventeenth century as many scholars accepted Copernican theory and as rulers realized the possible advantages of scientific advances.
- René Descartes built on the work of Galileo to formulate a new theory about the nature of matter.
- Descartes believed that humans could understand nature by using reason, not by trusting sensory data.
- English scientists, such as Robert Boyle, began to use experimental methods.
- Isaac Newton developed new laws of motion, still in use today, that explain the behavior of matter on earth and in space with a single set of mathematical principles.
- Advances in the life sciences included new anatomical discoveries by Andreas Vesalius and work by William Harvey on the circulation of the blood.

# The New Science in Context: Society, Politics, and Religion

*How did the new scientific worldview lead people to challenge traditional notions of society, the state, and religion?*

Scientists wrestled with questions about God and human capacity every bit as intently as they attempted to find new explanations for the behavior of matter and the motion of the heavens. Eventually, the profound implications of the new scientific worldview would affect thought and behavior throughout society. Once people no longer thought of the universe in hierarchical terms, they could question the hierarchical organization of society. Once people questioned the authority of traditional knowledge about the universe, the way was clear for them to begin to question traditional views of the state, the social order, and even the divine order. Such profound changes of perspective took hold very gradually, however. The advances in science did lead to revolutionary cultural change, but until the end of the seventeenth century, traditional institutions and ideologies limited its extent.

## The Beginnings of Scientific Professionalism

Institutions both old and new supported the new science developing in the sixteenth and seventeenth centuries. Some universities were the setting for scientific breakthroughs, but court patronage, a well-established institution, also sponsored scientific activity. The development of the Accademia dei Lincei, to which Galileo belonged, and of other academies was a step toward modern professional societies of scholars, although these new organizations depended on patronage.

In England and France, royally sponsored scientific societies were founded in the third quarter of the century, reflecting rulers' keen interest in science. The Royal Society of London, though charted by the king in 1660, received no money. It remained an informal institution sponsoring amateur scientific interests, as well as specialized independent research. (See the image "Isaac Newton Publishes a Paper," on page 501, for an example of the mixed interests of members of the society.) The Académie Royale des Sciences in France, established in 1666 by Jean-Baptiste Colbert, Louis XIV's minister of finance (see page 455), sponsored research but also supported chosen scientists with pensions. These associations were extensions to science of traditional kinds of royal recognition and patronage. Thus, the French Académie was well funded but tightly controlled by the government of Louis XIV, while the Royal Society of London received little of Charles II's scarce resources or precious political capital. Like the earlier academies, these royally sponsored societies published their fellows' work; in England, publication of the *Philosophical Transactions of the Royal Society* began in 1665.

The practice of seventeenth-century science took place in so many diverse institutions—academies, universities, royal courts—that neither *science* nor *scientist* was rigorously defined. Science, as a discipline, was not yet detached from broad metaphysical questions. Boyle, Newton, Pascal, and Descartes all concerned themselves with questions of religion, and all thought of themselves not as scientists but, like their medieval forebears, as natural philosophers. These natural philosophers were still members of an elite who met in aristocratic salons to discuss literature, politics, or science with equal ease and interest. Nevertheless, the beginnings of a narrowing of the practice of science to a tightly defined, truly professional community are evident in these institutions.

## Women Scientists and Institutional Constraints

The importance of court life and patronage to the new science had, at first, enabled women to be actively involved in the development of science. Women ran important salons in France; aristocratic women everywhere were indispensable sources of patronage for scientists; and women themselves were scientists, combining, as did men, science with other pursuits. Noblewomen and daughters of gentry families had access to education in their homes, and a number of such women were active scientists—astronomers, mathematicians, and botanists. The astronomer Maria Cunitz (KOO-nits) (1610–1664), from Silesia (a Habsburg-controlled province, now in modern Poland), learned six languages with the encouragement of her father, a physician. Later, she published a useful simplification of some of Kepler's mathematical calculations. Women from some artisanal families also received useful training at home. Such was the case of the German entomologist Maria Sibylla Merian (1647–1717). Merian learned the techniques of illustration in the workshop of her father, an artist in Frankfurt. She later used her artistic training and her refined powers of observation to study and record the features and behaviors of insects and plants in the New World.

Margaret Cavendish, duchess of Newcastle (1623–1673), wrote several major philosophical works, including *Grounds of Natural Philosophy* (1668). She was a Cartesian but was influenced by Neo-Platonism. She believed matter to have "intelligence" and thus disagreed with Descartes's views on matter, but she criticized fellow English philosophers on the grounds that, like Descartes, she distrusted sensory knowledge as a guide to philosophy.

Margaret Cavendish was aware of the degree to which her participation in scientific life depended on informal networks and on the resources available to her because of her aristocratic status. Women scientists from more modest backgrounds, without Cavendish's resources, had to fight for the right to employment, as public institutions gained importance as settings for the pursuit of science. The German astronomer Maria Winkelman (VINK-el-mahn) (1670–1720), for example, tried to succeed her late husband in an official position in the Berlin Academy of Sciences in 1710, after working as his unofficial partner during his tenure as astronomer to the academy. The academy withheld an official position from Winkelman after her husband's death, however, despite her experience and accomplishments (she had discovered a new comet, for example, in 1702). The secretary of the academy stated: "That she be kept on in an official capacity to work on the calendar or to continue with observations simply will not do. Already during her husband's lifetime the society was burdened with ridicule because its calendar was prepared by a woman. If she were now to be kept on in such a capacity, mouths would gape even wider."* Winkelman worked in private observatories but was able to return to the Berlin Academy only as the unofficial assistant to her own son, whose training she herself had supervised.

As the new science gained in prestige, women scientists often found themselves marginalized. While women were routinely accepted as members of Italian academies, they were excluded from formal membership in the academies in London and Paris, although they could use the academies' facilities and received prizes from the societies for their work. In addition, scientific rhetoric made it difficult to imagine women as scientists. Works by seventeenth-century scientists are filled with references to nature as a woman who must be "conquered," "subdued," or "penetrated."

**Astronomers Elisabetha and Johannes Hevelius**  The Heveliuses were one of many collaborating couples among the scientists of the seventeenth century. Women were usually denied pensions and support for their research when they worked alone, however. Private Collection/Joerg Hejkal/The Bridgeman Art Library

## The New Science, the State, and the Church

The new natural philosophy had implications for traditional notions about the state. The new worldview that all matter, whether in the heavens or on earth, was identical and answerable to discernible natural laws gradually undermined political systems resting on a belief in the inherent inequality of persons and on royal prerogative. By the middle of the eighteenth century, a fully formed alternative political philosophy would argue for more "rational" government in keeping with the rational, natural order of things. But the change came slowly, and while it was coming, traditional rulers found much to admire and utilize in the new science.

Technological possibilities of the new science were very attractive to governments. Experiments with vacuum pumps had important applications in the mining industry, for

---

*Quoted in Londa Schiebinger, *The Mind Has No Sex?* (Cambridge, Mass.: Harvard University Press, 1989), p. 92.

example. Governments also sponsored pure, and not only applied, scientific research. A French naval expedition to Cayenne, in French Guiana, led to refinements of the pendulum clock but had, as its main purpose, progressive observations of the sun to permit the calculation of the earth's distance from the sun. (See the feature, "The Global Record: Voyages for Scientific Observation" on page 507.) Members of the elite saw the opportunity not only for practical advances but also for prestige and, most important, confirmation of the orderliness of nature. It is hard to overestimate the psychological impact and intellectual power of this fundamental tenet of the new science—namely, that nature is an inanimate machine that reflects God's design not through its purposes but simply by its orderliness. Thus, in the short run, the new science supported a vision of order that was very pleasing even to an absolute monarch, such as Louis XIV.

As we have seen, scientists themselves flourished in close relationships with princes and actively sought their patronage. Christiaan Huygens left the Netherlands to accept the patronage of Louis XIV and produced, in France, some of his most important work in optics and mechanics. Huygens had learned from his father, secretary to the princes of Orange in the Netherlands, that a princely court not only offered steady support but also opened doors to other royal academies and salons. Huygens published some of his early research through the Royal Society in London, thanks to contacts his father had established. When Galileo left his position at Padua for the Medici court in Florence, he wrote to a friend, "It is not possible to receive a salary from a Republic [Venice] . . . without serving the public, because to get something from the public one must satisfy it and not just one particular person; . . . no one can exempt me from the burden while leaving me the income; and in sum I cannot hope for such a benefit from anyone but an absolute prince."*

Scientists and scientific thought also remained closely tied to religion in both practical and institutional ways during the seventeenth century. Both religion and the Catholic Church, as an institution, were involved with scientific advancement from the time of Copernicus. Copernicus himself was a cleric, as were many philosophers and scientists after him. This is not surprising, for most research in the sciences to this point had occurred within universities sponsored and staffed by members of religious orders, who had the education, time, and resources necessary for scientific investigation. Some of Descartes's closest collaborators were clerics, as were certain of Galileo's aristocratic patrons and his own protégés. Moreover, religious and metaphysical concerns were central to the work of virtually every scientist. The entire Cartesian process of reasoning about the world, for example, was grounded in Descartes's certainty about God. Copernicus, Kepler, Newton, and others believed they perceived God's purpose in the mathematical regularity of nature.

The notion that religion was the opponent of science in this era is a result of Galileo's trial and represents a distortion even of that event. It is true that the new astronomy and mechanics challenged traditional interpretations of Scripture, as well as the fundamentals of physics and metaphysics that were taught in universities. Thus, in its sponsorship of universities, the church was literally invested in the old view, even though individual churchmen investigated and taught Copernican ideas. The rigid response of the church hierarchy to Galileo is partially explained by the aftermath of the Protestant Reformation, which, in the minds of many churchmen—including Galileo's accusers and some of his judges—had demonstrated the need for a firm response to any challenge to the church's authority. Galileo seemed particularly threatening because he was well known, wrote for a wide audience, and, like the Protestants, presumed to interpret the Scriptures. Galileo may well have escaped punishment entirely had it not been for the political predicament faced by the pope at the time of his trial, however.

The condemnation of Galileo shocked many clerics, including the three who had voted for leniency at his trial. Clerics who were also scientists continued to study and teach the new science where and when they could. Copernicanism was taught by Catholic missionaries abroad. To be sure, Galileo's trial did have a chilling effect on scientific investigation in many Catholic regions of Europe. Investigators could and did continue their research, but many could publish results only by smuggling manuscripts to Protestant lands. After the middle of the seventeenth century, many of the most important empirical and theoretical innovations in

*Quoted in Richard S. Westfall, "Science and Patronage," *ISIS* 76 (1985): 16.

## Voyages for Scientific Observation

*In this excerpt from his 74-page publication, royal astronomer and geographer Giovanni Cassini, who worked for Louis XIV of France, describes the necessity of sending trained astronomical observers to Cayenne (now the capital of French Guiana in South America) in order to gather accurate data about the sun. Two expeditions were sent, in 1672–1673 and 1681–1682, and Cassini's book is a compilation of all the data collected. Note Cassini's praise for the king and his reference to Cayenne as "subject to His Majesty." In fact, the French had struggled to keep control of Cayenne after its founding in 1643 – disease, attacks by Native Americans and competition from the Spanish and English kept the French colony there very insecure.*

A very considerable error in the tables of the movement of the sun affects also the table of the movement of the planets, whose movements appear to be composed both of their own movement and of the movement of the sun since, as the Copernicans say, the earth also moves and all the movements of the other bodies appear to relate to it. . . .

One of the principle causes of these errors in the movement of the sun is the effect of the refraction of the sun's rays in the atmosphere, which was not properly understood by earlier astronomers.

And because in all observations of the sun that had commonly been used to establish the tables had been made [in the northern hemisphere] with reference to the distance of the pole and the obliquity of the ecliptic, it is a given that they were wrongly calculated because the effect of the refraction of light was not understood. Thus the tables of the movement of the sun had errors which could nevertheless be corrected by making new observations [without relying on these calculations]. . .

Twenty years ago, an effort to arrive at the corrections in the following table was undertaken. By the refractions in this table, we have corrected the observations of the sun on which the tables of its movements had been established.

Such important observations could only be accomplished in the torrid zones close to the equator, where the sun passes through its zenith at noon twice a year. It was thus necessary to undertake a difficult voyage and plan a long stay in a climate with insufferable heat. But what is not possible for the French nation in the service of so great a king?

The Academy (of Sciences), having considered the importance of this expedition and the means to execute it, judged that there was no location more appropriate and convenient for these observations than the island of Cayenne which is five degrees' distance north of the equator and is subject to His Majesty and is frequently visited by naval vessels.

### Questions

1. *Why might Cassini have felt the explanations about the need for more observations of the sun were necessary, especially in a work devoted to publishing the data?*

2. *What is the significance of the way Cassini describes conditions in Cayenne, and why it was chosen as the best location for the observations?*

---

Giovanni Domenico Cassini, *Les élémens de l'astronomie verifiez par monsieur Cassini par le rapport de ses tables aux observations de M. Richer faites en l'isle de Caïenne* (Paris, 1684), trans. Kristen B. Neuschel, pp. 4–6.

---

science occurred in Protestant regions. However, Protestant leaders had also not been receptive to Copernican ideas at first because the ideas seemed to defy scriptural authority as well as common sense. In 1549, one of Martin Luther's associates wrote: "The eyes are witnesses that the heavens revolve in the space of twenty four hours. But certain men, either from love of novelty or to make a display of ingenuity, have concluded that the earth moves. . . . Now it is want of honesty and decency to assert such notions. . . . It is part of a good mind to accept the truth as revealed by God and to acquiesce in it."*

Protestant thinkers were also as troubled as Catholics by the metaphysical dilemmas that the new theories seemed to raise. In 1611, one year after Galileo's *Starry Messenger* appeared, the English poet John Donne (1573–1631) reflected on the confusion that now reigned in human affairs, with the heavenly hierarchy dismantled:

> *[The] new Philosophy calls all in doubt,*
> *The Element of fire is quite put out,*
> *The Sun is lost, and th'earth, and no man's wit*
> *Can well direct him where to look for it*
>
> *. . . . . . . . . . .*
>
> *Tis all in pieces, all coherence gone;*
> *All just supply, and all Relation:*

---

*Quoted in Thomas S. Kuhn, *The Copernican Revolution* (Cambridge, Mass.: Harvard University Press, 1985), p. 191.

**Science and Royal Power** This painting memorializes the founding of the French Académie des Sciences and the building of the royal observatory in Paris. Louis himself is at the center of the painting, reflecting the symbolic importance of royal power in the sponsorship of science.

Erich Lessing/Art Resource, NY

*Prince, Subject, Father, Son, are things forgot,*
*For every man alone thinks he hath got*
*To be a Phoenix, and that then can be*
*None of that kinde, of which he is, but he.*

The challenge of accounting, in religious terms, for the ideas of Copernicus and Descartes became more urgent for Protestants as the ideas acquired an anti-Catholic status after the trial of Galileo in 1633 and as they became common scientific currency by about 1640. As we have seen, Newton was able to develop his theories on motion and gravity in part because of a religious certainty about divine force that could account for the motion of bodies in a vacuum. In short, religion did not merely remain in the scientists' toolbox of explanations; it remained a fundamental building block of scientific thought and central to most scientists' lives, whether they were Catholic or Protestant.

## The New Science and Political Thought at the End of the Seventeenth Century

Traditional institutions and ideologies checked the potential effects of the new science for a time, but by the middle of the seventeenth century, political theory was beginning to reflect the impact of the mechanistic worldview. Political philosophers began to doubt that either the world or human society was an organic whole in which each part was distinguished in nature and function from the rest. Thomas Hobbes, John Locke, and others reimagined the bonds that link citizens to one another and to their rulers.

### Thomas Hobbes

**Thomas Hobbes** English philosopher who argued in *Leviathan* that people are made up of mechanistic appetites and so need a strong ruler to govern them. However, he also envisioned citizens as potentially equal and constrained neither by morality nor by natural obedience to authority.

Because of the political turmoil in England, **Thomas Hobbes** (1588–1679) spent much of his productive life on the Continent. After the beginnings of the parliamentary rebellion, he joined a group of royalist émigrés in France. He met Galileo and lived for extended periods

---

*Complete Poetry and Selected Prose of John Donne*, ed. John Hayward (Bloomsbury, England: Nonesuch Press, 1929), p. 365, quoted in Kuhn, p. 194.

in Paris, in contact with the circle of French thinkers that included Descartes. Like Descartes, he theorized about the nature and behavior of matter and published a treatise on his views in 1655.

Hobbes is best known today for *Leviathan* (1651), his treatise on political philosophy. In *Leviathan*, Hobbes applies to the world of human beings his largely Cartesian view of nature as composed of "self-motivated," atom-like bits of matter. Hobbes viewed people as mechanistically as he viewed the rest of nature. In his view, people are made up of appetites of various sorts—the same kind of innate forces that drive all matter. The ideal political system, he concluded, is one in which a strong ruler controls the disorder that inevitably arises from the clash of people's desires. Unlike medieval philosophers, Hobbes did not draw analogies between the state and the human body (the king as head, judges and magistrates as arms, and so forth). Instead, he compared the state to a machine that "ran" by means of laws and was kept in good working order by a skilled technician—the ruler.

Hobbes's pessimism about human behavior and his insistence on the need for restraint imposed from above reflect, as does the work of Descartes, a concern for order in the wake of upheaval—in Hobbes's case, civil war in his native England. This concern was one reason he was welcomed into the community of French philosophers, who were naturally comfortable with royalty as a powerful guarantor of order. But Hobbes's work, like theirs, was a radical departure because it envisioned citizens as potentially equal and constrained neither by morality nor by natural obedience to authority.

## John Locke

Another Englishman, **John Locke** (1632–1704), offered an entirely different vision of natural equality among people and, consequently, of social order. Locke's major works, *Essay on Human Understanding* (1690) and *Two Treatises of Government* (1690), reflect the experimentalism of Robert Boyle, the systematizing rationality of Descartes, and other strands of the new scientific thought. In his *Essay*, Locke provides a view of human knowledge more pragmatic and utilitarian than the rigorous mathematical model of certainty used by many other philosophers. He argues that human knowledge is largely the product of experience. He agrees with Descartes that reason orders and explains human experience, but unlike Descartes, he doubts that human reason has unlimited potential to comprehend the universe. Locke, however, offered a more optimistic vision of the possible uses of reason. Whereas Descartes was interested in mentally ordering and understanding the world, Locke was interested in actually functioning *in* the world.

Locke's treatises on government reflect his notion of knowledge based on experience, as well as his particular experiences as a member of elite circles following the Restoration in England. Trained in medicine, he served as personal physician and general political assistant to one of the members of Parliament most opposed to Charles II's pretensions to absolutist government. When James II acceded to the throne in 1685, Locke remained in the Netherlands, where he had fled to avoid prosecution for treason. He became an adviser to William of Orange and returned to England with William and Mary in 1688. Locke's view of the principles of good government came to reflect the pro-parliamentary stance of his political milieu.

Unlike Hobbes, Locke argued that people are capable of self-restraint and mutual respect in their pursuit of self-interest. The state arises, he believed, from a contract that individuals freely enter into to protect themselves, their property, and their happiness from possible aggression by others. They can invest the executive and legislative authority to carry out this protection in monarchy or any other governing institution, though Locke believed that the English Parliament was the best available model. Because sovereignty resides with the people who enter into the contract, rebellion against the abuse of power is justified. At the core of Locke's schema is thus a revolutionary vision of political society based on human rights.

Locke's experience as an English gentleman is apparent in his emphasis on private property, which he considered a fundamental human right. Nature, he believed, cannot benefit humankind unless it is worked by human hands, as on a farm, for example. Private ownership of property guarantees its productivity and entitles the owner to participate in Locke's imagined contract. Indeed, Locke's political vision is unequivocal, and unbending, on the nature

**John Locke** English philosopher who asserted that the state arises from a contract that individuals freely endorse. Therefore, because sovereignty resides with the people, rebellion against abuse of power is justified—a revolutionary vision of a political society based on human rights.

of property. Locke even found a justification for slavery. He also did not consider women to be independent beings in the same way as men, deserving of the same rights. The family, he felt, is a separate domain from the state, not bound by the same contractual obligations. Locke and many other seventeenth-century thinkers were unable to imagine a new physical or political reality without invoking a notion of gender as a "natural" principle of order and hierarchy. Margaret Cavendish, among others, disputed the validity of such arbitrary distinctions in capacities and rights between men and women. Another Englishwoman, Mary Astell (1666–1731), explicitly challenged Locke's views of women, and his objectivity on the question, in a treatise written in 1700. She wrote, "If absolute sovereignty be not necessary in a state, how comes it to be so in a family? . . . . Is it not then partial in men to the last degree to contend for and practice that arbitrary domination in their families which they abhor and exclaim against in the state?"* Nevertheless, Locke's use of gender as an arbitrary organizing principle gave his bold new vision of rights for certain men a claim to being "natural."

## Skepticism and the Spread of Scientific Rationality

Although traditional gender distinctions limited and reinforced most facets of political thought, in other areas, the fact of uncertainty and the need for tolerance were embraced. In another of Locke's influential works, the impassioned *Letter on Toleration* (1689), he argues that religious belief is fundamentally private and that only the most basic Christian principles need be accepted by everyone. Others went further than Locke by entirely removing traditional religion as necessary to morality and public order. Fostering this climate of religious skepticism were religious pluralism in England and the self-defeating religious intolerance of Louis XIV's persecution of Protestants.

Pierre Bayle (1647–1706), a Frenchman of Protestant origins, argued that morality can be wholly detached from traditional religion. Indeed, Bayle concluded, one need not be a Christian at all to be a moral being. Bayle cited as an example of morality the philosopher Baruch Spinoza (1632–1677), a Dutch Jew who had been cast out of his local synagogue for supposed atheism. Even so, Spinoza believed the state to have a moral purpose and human happiness to have spiritual roots.

Bayle's skepticism toward traditional knowledge was more wide-ranging than his views on religion. His best-known work, *Dictionnaire historique et critique* (*Historical and Critical Dictionary*, 1702), was a compendium of observations about and criticisms of virtually every thinker whose works were known at the time, including such recent and lionized figures as Descartes and Newton. Bayle was the first systematic skeptic, and he relentlessly exposed errors and shortcomings in all received knowledge. His works were very popular with elite lay readers. Bayle's countryman Bernard de Fontenelle (fon-tuh-NEL) (1657–1757), secretary to the Académie des Sciences from 1699 to 1741, was the greatest popularizer of the new science of his time. His *Entretiens sur la Pluralité des Mondes* (*Conversations on the Plurality of Worlds*, 1686) went through numerous editions and translations. It was, as the title implies, an informally presented description of the infinite universe of matter. He also helped spread the new science by publishing descriptions of the work of the Académie's scientists. Fontenelle is a fitting figure with whom to end a discussion of the Scientific Revolution because he represents, and worked to accomplish, the transfer of the new science into political and social philosophy—a movement we know as the "Enlightenment." A fully developed secular worldview, with revolutionary implications for human affairs, would be the product of the Enlightenment in the next century.

### SECTION SUMMARY

- New institutions, such as academies, supported scientific work and were forerunners of modern scientific associations.

- European rulers were eager to sponsor scientific work both for its practical benefits and for its symbolic importance for their power.

- Scientific work remained closely tied to religion in both intellectual and institutional ways. Political thought in the seventeenth century, as represented by Locke and Bayle, began to reflect the new science's confidence in human reason.

- Women scientists were disadvantaged by the institutional settings for the new science and by the way notions about gender were used in the new science and political philosophy.

---

*Moira Ferguson, ed., *First Feminists: British Women Writers, 1578–1799* (Bloomington: Indiana University Press, 1985), p. 193.

# Chapter Summary

◆ *How did the Copernican theory challenge traditional views of the universe?*

The Scientific Revolution began with developments in astronomy. Because of astronomy's role in explanations of the world and human life that prevailed in the Middle Ages, changes in astronomical theory were bound to have widespread effects on other knowledge and beliefs. Copernicus's heliocentric theory led to wider scientific and philosophical innovation also because of the context in which it was received. Recent recoveries of new ancient texts in the Renaissance and the discovery of previously unknown lands in the New World made it possible to imagine challenging ancient scientific authority. The interest of princes in both the prestige and the practical use of science helped support the work of scientists. Other scientists, following Copernicus, built on his theories, culminating in the work of Galileo, who supported Copernican theory with additional data and widely published his findings.

◆ *How and why did new theories about astronomy lead to a broader Scientific Revolution?*

The Frenchman Descartes was the first to fashion a systematic explanation for the operations of all matter to replace the medieval view. The political and intellectual climate in England, meanwhile, encouraged the development of experimental science and inductive reasoning. Isaac Newton provided new theories to explain the behavior of matter and expressed them in mathematical terms that could apply to either the earth or the cosmos. With his work, traditional astronomy and physics were overturned, replaced by a vision of a universe of matter that behaves not according to a higher purpose but rather as a machine.

◆ *How did the new scientific worldview lead people to challenge traditional notions of society, the state, and religion?*

New institutions in the form of private, as well as officially sponsored, scientific societies rose up to support scientists' research and the publication of their work. These societies were particularly important before the new science became accepted in universities, although they excluded some practitioners of the new science, particularly women. Rulers made use of the new science for the practical results it offered, despite the ideological challenge scientific thinking presented to their arbitrary power. The relationship of religion to the new science was equally complex and contrary. Some religious leaders scorned the new science; most scientists, whether Catholic or Protestant, worked to accommodate both the new science and their religious beliefs. By the end of the seventeenth century, however, the hierarchical Christian worldview, grounded in the old science, was being challenged on many fronts, most notably in the work of the political philosophers Hobbes and Locke, who both challenged traditional justifications for royal authority on the grounds of natural law. Locke's work was particularly important for the future because he argued that governments can exist only with the consent of the governed.

# Key Terms

**Nicholas Copernicus** (p. 489)
**heliocentric theory** (p. 489)
**Tycho Brahe** (p. 490)
**Johannes Kepler** (p. 490)
**Galileo Galilei** (p. 491)
**Francis Bacon** (p. 494)
**empirical method** (p. 494)

**René Descartes** (p. 495)
**Isaac Newton** (p. 500)
**laws of motion** (p. 501)
**mechanistic worldview** (p. 502)
**Thomas Hobbes** (p. 508)
**John Locke** (p. 509)

CourseMate

Go to the CourseMate website at **www.cengagebrain.com** for additional study tools and review materials—including audio and video clips—for this chapter.

# Index